SPSS® UPDATE 7-9

New Procedures and Facilities for Releases 7-9

Series Editors:

C. Hadlai Hull

Norman H. Nie

New York St. Louis San Francisco Auckland Bogotá Hamburg
Johannesburg London Madrid Mexico Montreal New Delhi
Panama Paris São Paulo Singapore Sydney Tokyo Toronto

SPSS UPDATE 7-9
Copyright © 1981 by Norman H. Nie and C. Hadlai Hull.
All rights reserved.
Printed in the United States of America.
No part of this publication may be reproduced, stored in a retrieval system, or transmitted, in any form or by any means, electronic, mechanical, photocopying, recording, or otherwise, without the prior written permission of the publisher.

   67890SMSM 8976543

This book was set in Times Roman by SPSS Inc. with the cooperation of Black Dot, Inc.

The editor was Charles Stewart.

Library of Congress Cataloging in Publication Data

Main entry under title:

SPSS update 7-9   :   new procedures and
facilities for releases 7-9.

    Includes index.
    1. SPSS (Electronic computer system)   I. Hull,
C. Hadlai.   II. Nie, Norman H.
HA32.S18   001.64'2   80-27630
ISBN 0-07-046542-8

Preface

The SPSS® Batch System has been substantially extended and refined since Release 6, the version documented in *SPSS*, Second Edition (McGraw-Hill, 1975). In Releases 7 and 8 four new statistical procedures and a report generator were added, and full communication was established between the batch system and the SCSS™ Conversational System. Release 9 contains three new statistical procedures and an option for device-independent graphics.

Several exisiting facilities have been substantially or completely rewritten, and most have been modified to offer new options, improved accuracy, or improved performance. A few such changes will affect control decks set up under Release 6: see Appendix A.

NEW FACILITIES

The following procedures were added in Release 7 or 8:

- REPORT: Flexible formatting and labeling for case listings and aggregate statistics.
- SURVIVAL: Life tables, graphs of survival functions, and comparisons of survival functions between groups.
- NPAR TESTS: Fourteen nonparametric tests.
- MULT RESPONSE: Frequency distributions and crosstabulations of multiple-response variables.
- RELIABILITY: Analysis of additive scales plus repeated measures and two-way factorial ANOVA.
- GET SCSS/SAVE SCSS: Facilities for using or creating SCSS Conversational System masterfiles.

New procedures in Release 9:

- MANOVA: A general linear models procedure.
- BOX JENKINS: Identification, estimation, and forecasting for univariate time series.
- NEW REGRESSION: Multiple regression analysis with extensive facilities for residual analysis.
- SPSS® GRAPHICS: Procedures for generating pie charts, bar graphs, and line plots.

MAJOR REVISIONS

The following are some of the more significant changes made to facilities documented in *SPSS*, Second Edition:

- DATA SELECTION AND MODIFICATION: New capabilities include production of exact-size and reproducible random samples, normal or uniform distributions of random numbers, a date function, handling of constants in DO REPEAT, and a lag facility.
- SORT CASES: Entirely rewritten for Release 8, SORT CASES can group cases and define subfiles automatically and can be used before any procedure.
- DISCRIMINANT: Release 8 DISCRIMINANT is an entirely new subprogram. The specifications in SPSS, Second Edition, are fully implemented, with several additions.
- EXTENDED INPUT FORMAT FACILITY: Additional format items beyond those included in standard FORTRAN formats permit reading files which contain binary, packed decimal, zoned decimal, or floating point data.

Many of those changes were made in Release 7; all are available in both Release 8 and Release 9.

The following people contributed to the programs
described in this manual or to this manual itself:

Tony Babinec
ViAnn Beadle
Philip Burns
Elaine Chow
Roger Deschner
Steve Drach
Susan Flynn
Jonathan Fry
Robert Gruen
Jean Jenkins
Florence Landrum
Nancy Morrison
Marija Norušis
Mindaugus Pleskys
Amy Reuss
Sue Schott
Keith Sours
Sydney Springer
C. Ming Wang

Other SPSS Inc. Titles from McGraw-Hill Book Company:

SPSS, Second Edition
SPSS Primer
SPSS Pocket Guide, Release 9

SPSS-11: The SPSS® Batch System for the DEC PDP-11®

SCSS: A Guide to the SCSS™ Conversational System

User's Manual for IDA
Conversational Statistics

Please contact the Marketing Department of SPSS Inc. for information about the SPSS Batch
System, the SPSS-11 System, the SCSS Conversational System, and the IDA Interactive Data
Analysis and Forecasting System.

SPSS Inc.
Suite 3300
444 North Michigan Avenue
Chicago, Illinois 60611
(312) 329-2400

CONTENTS

Chapter 5 REPORT: Flexible Format Report Generator 166

Chapter 1

MANOVA:
Multivariate Analysis of Variance

SPSS MANOVA is a generalized multivariate analysis of variance and covariance program which will perform univariate and multivariate linear estimation and tests of hypotheses for any crossed and/or nested design with or without covariates. The user has complete control of the model specification. For example, several effects can be lumped together into a single term. Also, interaction between factors and covariates is allowed.

The sections beginning with 1.2 present univariate analysis of variance models, which include balanced incomplete block designs, confounding designs, nested designs, and split-plot designs. Special features such as collapsing error terms, specifying multiple error terms, partitioning degrees of freedom, contrasts, orthogonal polynomials and analysis of covariance are also discussed.

Tests of significance for a multivariate analysis of variance model include hypotheses and error matrices, four multivariate test criteria, dimension reduction analysis, univariate F tests, and step-down analysis. In addition, principal components analysis and discriminant analysis can be requested. They are documented beginning in Section 1.31.

The sections beginning with 1.38 present multivariate multiple linear regression analysis, which can be considered a special case of multivariate analysis of covariance in which all the independent variables are covariates. Canonical correlation analysis is also discussed.

MANOVA enables the user to analyze a large class of repeated measures designs. The observation can be either single-valued or vector-valued. Covariates, varying or constant across the repeated measures, can also appear in the model. These facilities are described beginning in Section 1.43.

Section 1.51 describes the graphics features available in MANOVA.

MANOVA may require an additional scratch file for which provision must be made in the job setup. See Appendix L for information for the IBM/OS version.

1.1 OVERVIEW

MANOVA specifications are entered via the MANOVA command itself and a number of optional subcommands that fall into the three categories outlined below. For more detail on these, see Section 1.52.

The MANOVA command has the following general format:

```
MANOVA          <dependent variable list> BY <factor list> WITH
                <covariate list>/
```

The MANOVA command, with no subcommands, is the only required specification. A dependent variable list of one variable activates univariate analysis; more than one dependent variable activates multivariate analysis of variance.

Subcommands in the first category specify the factor and data structures of the design. WSFACTOR provides the within-subjects factors for a repeated measures design.

```
WSFACTOR = <factor list>/
```

1

TRANSFORM requests a linear transformation of the dependent variables and covariates.

```
TRANSFORM (variable listl/variable list2/...) =

    [ORTHONORM]    { DEVIATIONS (refcat)   }
                   { DIFFERENCE            }
    [BASIS]        { HELMERT               }
    [CONTRAST]     { SIMPLE (refcat)       }    /
                   { REPEATED              }
                   { POLYNOMIAL [(metric)] }
                   { SPECIAL (matrix)      }
                   { WSDESIGN <effect list> }
```

WSDESIGN specifies the model for the within-subjects factors and RENAME can be used to rename the transformed variables.

```
WSDESIGN = < effect list > /

RENAME = newnamel, newname2,../
```

The second category contains subcommands PRINT, PLOT, and PUNCH, which control the amount of optional output produced by MANOVA.

```
PRINT    =   CELLINFO( [MEANS] [SSCP] [COV] [COR] )
  or
NOPRINT      HOMOGENEITY( [BARTLETT] [COCHRAN] [BOXM] )

             DESIGN( [ONEWAY] [OVERALL] [BIAS] [DECOMP]
                     [SOLUTION]                          )

             PRINCOMPS( [COR] [COV] [MINEIGEN(eigcut)]
                        [NCOMP(n)] [ROTATE(rottyp)] )

             ERROR( [SSCP] [COV] [COR] [STDV] )

             SIGNIF( [HYPOTH] [MULTIV] [EIGEN]
                     [DIMENR] [UNIV] [STEPDOWN]
                     [AVERF] [BRIEF] [SINGLEDF] )

             DISCRIM( [RAW] [STAN] [ESTIM] [COR]
                      [ROTATE(rottyp)] [ALPHA(alpha)] )

             PARAMETERS( [ESTIM] [COR] [ORTHO] [NEGSUM] )

             OMEANS[ ( VARIABLES(var list)
                       TABLES( table requests ) ) ]

             PMEANS[ ( VARIABLES(var list)
                       TABLES( table requests )
                       ERROR( errorn ) ) ]

             POBS [ ERROR( errorn ) ]

             FORMAT( [WIDE]   )    /
                     [NARROW]

PLOT     =   [CELLPLOTS] [NORMAL] [BOXPLOTS]
             [STEMLEAF]  [ZCORR]  [PMEANS]
             [POBS]
             [ SIZE( nhor , nvert ) ]            /

PUNCH    =   CELLINFO( [MEAN] [SSCP] [COR] [COV] [STDV] )

             ERROR( [SSCP] [COR] [COV] [STDV] )

             PMEANS [ ( ERROR( errorn ) ) ]

             POBS [ ( ERROR( errorn ) ) ]            /
```

The last category consists of the subcommands that indicate the computational options and model specifications. METHOD provides several options for parameter estimation.

```
METHOD = MODELTYPE( [MEANS]        )
                    [OBSERVATIONS]

                      [CHOLESKY]
         ESTIMATION( [QR]          [LASTRES]   [CONSTANT]  )
                     [BALANCED] [NOLASTRES] [NOCONST]
                     [NOBALANCED]

         SSTYPE( [SEQUENTIAL] )           /
                 [UNIQUE]
```

ANALYSIS subsets and/or reorders the variables.

```
ANALYSIS = <dep var list> WITH <covar list>/
                    - or -
ANALYSIS[((CONDITIONAL)  ]     =      (<dep list 1> WITH <covar list 1>/
         [(UNCONDITIONAL)]               <dep list 2> WITH <covar list 2>/ ...)
                         WITH <covar list> /
```

```
                                 - or -
         ANALYSIS( REPEATED  [CONDITIONAL]      )      /
                             [UNCONDITIONAL]
```

PARTITION subdivides the degrees of freedom of a factor.

```
         PARTITION(factorname) [= (dfl, df2,..)]  /
```

CONTRAST indicates the type of contrast desired for a factor.

```
                                { DEVIATION [(refcat)]  }
                                { DIFFERENCE             }
                                { HELMERT                }
         CONTRAST(factorname) =  { SIMPLE [(refcat)]     }   /
                                { REPEATED               }
                                { POLYNOMIAL [(metric)]  }
                                { SPECIAL (matrix)       }
```

ERROR specifies the error term to be used in the model.

```
                { WITHIN or W              }
                { RESIDUAL or R            }
         ERROR = { WITHIN + RESIDUAL or WR }   /
                { n                        }
```

DESIGN specifies the design model to be analyzed.

```
         DESIGN = effectl, effect2,../
```

The DESIGN specification should be the last subcommand of a complete MANOVA run. All the computational and output options are applied to the subsequent DESIGN models unless overridden.

As an example of specifications for MANOVA, consider the following:

```
MANOVA      Y BY A(1,3) B(1,4) WITH X/
            PRINT=CELLINFO(MEANS)/
            METHOD=ESTIMATION(BALANCED)/
            DESIGN=A,B/
            METHOD=ESTIMATION(QR)/
            DESIGN=A,B,A BY B/
```

An analysis of covariance model is specified with Y as the dependent variable, X as the covariate, and A and B as factor variables with three and four levels respectively. The PRINT subcommand requests cell information. The METHOD subcommand indicates that a special balanced processing method be used for parameter estimation. These two options apply to the first DESIGN specification, which requests a main effects model. The second METHOD subcommand requests the (default) QR method for estimating the parameters in the second DESIGN specification (a full model). The PRINT subcommand applied to the first DESIGN will also apply to the second DESIGN.

Note that if the last command is not a DESIGN specification, MANOVA will generate a full model design specification for the problem.

1.2   UNIVARIATE ANALYSIS OF VARIANCE

The basic features of MANOVA useful for univariate analysis of variance are illustrated in the following example taken from Winer (1971, p. 436). An experiment was conducted to evaluate the relative effectiveness of three drugs (Factor DRUG) in bringing about behavioral changes in two categories of patients (Factor CAT). Three patients of each category were assigned at random to one of three drugs, and criterion ratings (Y) were made for each patient. The data are given in Table 1.2.

Table 1.2

CAT		DRUG		
		1	2	3
	1	8	10	8
		4	8	6
		0	6	4
	2	14	4	15
		10	2	12
		6	0	9

Figure 1.2 shows SPSS commands to accomplish the analysis of variance of the data. The MANOVA specification defines Y to be the dependent variable and CAT and DRUG the factor variables with two and three levels respectively. Since only one dependent variable (Y) is indicated, a univariate analysis of variance is requested.

Figure 1.2

```
RUN NAME          A UNIVARIATE 2*3 EXAMPLE.
COMMENT           THE DATA ARE TAKEN FROM WINER(1971) PAGE 436.
                  Y    : THE DEPENDENT VARIABLE.
                  CAT  : FACTOR WITH 2 LEVELS.
                  DRUG : FACTOR WITH 3 LEVELS.
VARIABLE LIST     CAT DRUG Y
INPUT FORMAT      FREEFIELD
INPUT MEDIUM      CARD
MANOVA            Y BY CAT(1,2) DRUG(1,3)/
READ INPUT DATA
1 1  8
1 1  4
1 1  0
1 2 10
1 2  8
1 2  6
1 3  8
1 3  6
1 3  4
2 1 14
2 1 10
2 1  6
2 2  4
2 2  2
2 2  0
2 3 15
2 3 12
2 3  9
END INPUT DATA
FINISH
```

The default model generated from the MANOVA specifications is a full factorial. For this example the model is

$$Y_{ijk} = \mu + \alpha_i + \beta_j + (\alpha\beta)_{ij} + \epsilon_{ijk}$$

where α_i is the main effect of category i, β_j is the main effect of drug j, and $(\alpha\beta)_{ij}$ is the interaction of patient category i and drug j. For the various tests, it is necessary to assume that the error terms, ϵ_{ijk}, are independently identically distributed as normal with mean 0 and variance σ^2.

1.3 Default Output

The default output (without any PRINT subcommand) from a MANOVA run includes

1 An analysis of variance (ANOVA) table. As shown in Figure 1.3a, it gives the sum of squares, degrees of freedom, mean square, *F* value, and the probabilities of each *F* value. The within-cells error term (default error-term if it exists) is used to obtain all the *F* values.

Figure 1.3a

TESTS OF SIGNIFICANCE FOR Y USING SEQUENTIAL SUMS OF SQUARES

SOURCE OF VARIATION	SUM OF SQUARES	DF	MEAN SQUARE	F	SIG. OF F
WITHIN CELLS	106.00000	12	8.83333		
CONSTANT	882.00000	1	882.00000	99.84906	0.0
CAT	18.00000	1	18.00000	2.03774	.179
DRUG	48.00000	2	24.00000	2.71698	.106
CAT BY DRUG	144.00000	2	72.00000	8.15094	.006

2 Statistics for parameter estimation (Figure 1.3b). These consist of estimates of the parameters (COEFF), the standard errors of the estimates (STD. ERR.), the t-value for testing that the parameter is zero, the two-tailed significance of the test, and 95% confidence intervals for the parameters. (Note that the parameters estimated here are not the original α_i, β_j, or $(\alpha\beta)_{ij}$; instead, contrasts of the parameters are estimated. See Section 1.52 for detailed information.)

Figure 1.3b

```
ESTIMATES FOR Y

CONSTANT

  PARAMETER          COEFF.        STD. ERR.       T-VALUE       SIG. OF T     LOWER .95 CL     UPPER .95 CL
       1        7.0000000000        .70053         9.99245          .000         5.47368          8.52632
CAT

  PARAMETER          COEFF.        STD. ERR.       T-VALUE       SIG. OF T     LOWER .95 CL     UPPER .95 CL
       2       -1.0000000000        .70053        -1.42749          .179        -2.52632           .52632
DRUG

  PARAMETER          COEFF.        STD. ERR.       T-VALUE       SIG. OF T     LOWER .95 CL     UPPER .95 CL
       3        0.0                 .99070         0.0             1.000        -2.15854          2.15854
       4       -2.0000000000        .99070        -2.01878          .066        -4.15854           .15854
CAT BY DRUG

  PARAMETER          COEFF.        STD. ERR.       T-VALUE       SIG. OF T     LOWER .95 CL     UPPER .95 CL
       5       -2.0000000000        .99070        -2.01878          .066        -4.15854           .15854
       6        4.0000000000        .99070         4.03756          .002         1.84146          6.15854
```

1.4   Use of the PRINT Subcommand

Additional printed output can be obtained by using the PRINT subcommand. For instance, tests of homogeneity of within-cells variance are produced by specifying

```
MANOVA          Y BY CAT(1,2) DRUG(1,3)/
                PRINT=HOMOGENEITY(BARTLETT,COCHRAN)/
```

The output (Figure 1.4a) includes Bartlett's test and Cochran's test. The significance (P) of both tests is also given.

Figure 1.4a

```
UNIVARIATE HOMOGENEITY OF VARIANCE TESTS

VARIABLE .. Y

        COCHRANS C(2,6) =                        .30189, P =   .829 (APPROX.)
        BARTLETT-BOX F(5,185) =                  .38601, P =   .858
```

The cell statistics, including the mean, standard deviation, number of observations, and the 95% confidence intervals for the population means can be obtained using

```
MANOVA          Y BY CAT(1,2) DRUG(1,3)/
                PRINT=CELLINFO(MEANS)/
```

The output from the above PRINT subcommand is given in Figure 1.4b.

Figure 1.4b

```
CELL MEANS AND STANDARD DEVIATIONS

VARIABLE .. Y

       FACTOR           CODE              MEAN       STD. DEV.       N     95 PERCENT CONF. INTERVAL

CAT                      1
   DRUG                  1             4.00000       4.00000         3        -5.93666       13.93666
   DRUG                  2             8.00000       2.00000         3         3.03167       12.96833
   DRUG                  3             6.00000       2.00000         3         1.03167       10.96833

CAT                      2
   DRUG                  1            10.00000       4.00000         3          .06334       19.93666
   DRUG                  2             2.00000       2.00000         3        -2.96833        6.96833
   DRUG                  3            12.00000       3.00000         3         4.54751       19.45249

FOR ENTIRE SAMPLE                      7.00000       4.31141        18         4.85599        9.14401
```

1.5 Specifying a Model with the DESIGN Subcommand

If the desired model is not the default full factorial, the model must be specified using the DESIGN subcommand. To specify a model that includes only the main effect terms, use

```
MANOVA       Y BY CAT(1,2) DRUG(1,3)/
             DESIGN= CAT,DRUG/
```

If there are three factors, (A, B, and C) with three levels each, the model containing only main effects and the A BY B and B BY C interactions is specified by

```
MANOVA       Y BY A B C (1,3)/
             DESIGN= A, B, C, A BY B, B BY C/
```

The keyword BY in the DESIGN subcommand indicates an interaction term. Thus a three-way interaction is written as A BY B BY C.

1.6 Specifying the ERROR Term

Unless otherwise requested, the within-cells mean square is used as the denominator for all the F values. If there is no within-cells error, the residual error is used. The residual mean square is the mean square for all terms not specified in the DESIGN subcommand. For example, if the model containing only main effects for DRUG and CAT is requested using

```
                DESIGN= CAT,DRUG/
```

the residual error term is the mean square for the CAT BY DRUG interaction. For the three-factor design specification developed previously, the residual error corresponds to the sum of squares for the pooled A BY C and A BY B BY C interactions since they are not included in the DESIGN specification.

The ERROR subcommand designates the error term to be used for the analysis. See Section 1.91 for rules governing the use of the ERROR subcommand. If different error terms are to be used for the various terms in the design specification, this is indicated in the DESIGN subcommand. See Section 1.92 for further details.

1.7 An Example Using DESIGN and ERROR

The following commands request a main effects model for the data of Figure 1.2. The pooled interaction term (denoted as R for residual) and within-cells error (denoted as W) are used as the error.

```
MANOVA       Y BY CAT(1,2) DRUG(1,3)/
             ERROR=W+R/
             DESIGN=CAT,DRUG/
```

The error subcommand must precede the design specification to which it applies. The analysis of variance table from the preceding commands is given in Figure 1.7.

Figure 1.7

```
TESTS OF SIGNIFICANCE FOR Y USING SEQUENTIAL SUMS OF SQUARES

SOURCE OF VARIATION              SUM OF SQUARES      DF    MEAN SQUARE           F      SIG. OF F

WITHIN+RESIDUAL                      250.00000       14      17.85714
CONSTANT                             882.00000        1     882.00000     49.39200        0.0
CAT                                   18.00000        1      18.00000      1.00800        .332
DRUG                                  48.00000        2      24.00000      1.34400        .292
```

The result in Figure 1.7 can also be obtained by specifying

```
MANOVA       Y BY CAT(1,2) DRUG(1,3)/
             DESIGN = CAT VS W+R, DRUG VS W+R/
```

1.8 Partitioning the Sum of Squares

Often it is desirable to partition the sum of squares associated with the various effects into a number of components that are more relevant to the individual questions of interest. See Cochran and Cox (1957).

In procedure MANOVA partitions are controlled by the keyword PARTITION followed by the name of the factor and the degrees of freedom associated with each component.

To partition the sum of squares for factor DRUG into two components with one degree of freedom each, the following commands can be used.

```
MANOVA          Y BY CAT(1,2) DRUG(1,3)/
                PARTITION(DRUG)=(1,1)/
                DESIGN=CAT,DRUG(1),DRUG(2),CAT BY DRUG/
```

The first component is denoted by DRUG(1), and the second by DRUG(2). The output is given in Figure 1.8.

Figure 1.8

TESTS OF SIGNIFICANCE FOR Y USING SEQUENTIAL SUMS OF SQUARES

SOURCE OF VARIATION	SUM OF SQUARES	DF	MEAN SQUARE	F	SIG. OF F
WITHIN CELLS	106.00000	12	8.83333		
CONSTANT	882.00000	1	882.00000	99.84906	0.0
CAT	18.00000	1	18.00000	2.03774	.179
DRUG(1)	12.00000	1	12.00000	1.35849	.266
DRUG(2)	36.00000	1	36.00000	4.07547	.066
CAT BY DRUG	144.00000	2	72.00000	8.15094	.006

- -

ESTIMATES FOR Y

CONSTANT

PARAMETER	COEFF.	STD. ERR.	T-VALUE	SIG. OF T	LOWER .95 CL	UPPER .95 CL
1	7.0000000000	.70053	9.99245	.000	5.47368	8.52632

CAT

PARAMETER	COEFF.	STD. ERR.	T-VALUE	SIG. OF T	LOWER .95 CL	UPPER .95 CL
2	-1.0000000000	.70053	-1.42749	.179	-2.52632	.52632

DRUG(1)

PARAMETER	COEFF.	STD. ERR.	T-VALUE	SIG. OF T	LOWER .95 CL	UPPER .95 CL
3	0.0	.99070	0.0	1.000	-2.15854	2.15854

DRUG(2)

PARAMETER	COEFF.	STD. ERR.	T-VALUE	SIG. OF T	LOWER .95 CL	UPPER .95 CL
4	-2.0000000000	.99070	-2.01878	.066	-4.15854	.15854

CAT BY DRUG

PARAMETER	COEFF.	STD. ERR.	T-VALUE	SIG. OF T	LOWER .95 CL	UPPER .95 CL
5	-2.0000000000	.99070	-2.01878	.066	-4.15854	.15854
6	4.0000000000	.99070	4.03756	.002	1.84146	6.15854

The default contrasts used for partitioning are deviation contrasts (see Section 1.89). The deviation contrasts are not orthogonal, so the two contrasts for DRUG(1) and DRUG(2) are not independent.

1.9 Types of Contrasts

The MANOVA procedure allows specification of six different contrast types: deviation, difference, Helmert, simple, repeated, and polynomial. The user can also input any other contrast matrix via the SPECIAL keyword.

For example, to specify user-supplied orthogonal contrasts for the DRUG factor, the following commands can be used:

```
MANOVA          Y BY CAT(1,2) DRUG(1,3)/
                CONTRAST(DRUG)=SPECIAL(1 1 1 -1 2 -1 1 0 -1)/
                PARTITION(DRUG)=(1,1)/
                DESIGN=CAT,DRUG(1),DRUG(2),CAT BY DRUG(1),
                    CAT BY DRUG(2)/
```

The first set of coefficients (1 1 1) is always the weights for obtaining the constant term. Following the weights vector are the contrasts. The number of contrasts should be equal to the degrees of freedom for the factor. The first contrast (-1 2 -1) defines a contrast between level 2 and the combination of levels 1 and 3 for factor DRUG. The second contrast (1 0 -1) requests a comparison between levels 1 and 3 of DRUG. For most applications, the user shoud be sure that each set of contrast coefficients sum to zero.

Since the inner product of the two contrasts is 0 and the sample sizes in all cells are equal, i.e., $(-1)(1) + 2(0) + (-1)(-1) = 0$, the two contrasts are independent. In this example, the DRUG(1) partition can be used to test the hypothesis $\beta_2 = (\beta_1 + \beta_3)/2$ while the second contrast tests $\beta_1 = \beta_3$. The ANOVA table is given in Figure 1.9.

Figure 1.9

```
TESTS OF SIGNIFICANCE FOR Y USING SEQUENTIAL SUMS OF SQUARES

SOURCE OF VARIATION              SUM OF SQUARES    DF    MEAN SQUARE         F      SIG. OF F

WITHIN CELLS                         106.00000     12       8.83333
CONSTANT                             882.00000      1     882.00000   99.84906       0.0
CAT                                   18.00000      1      18.00000    2.03774        .179
DRUG(1)                               36.00000      1      36.00000    4.07547        .066
DRUG(2)                               12.00000      1      12.00000    1.35849        .266
CAT BY DRUG(1)                       144.00000      1     144.00000   16.30189        .002
CAT BY DRUG(2)                         0.0          1       0.0        0.0           1.000
```

The above discussion of orthogonal contrasts assumes that the cell frequencies are equal. For the use of the orthogonal contrasts in unbalanced designs, see Section 1.16.

1.10 Designs with Unequal Cell Frequencies

In many experiments, it may not be possible to have equal numbers of observations for each cell. Such designs are termed *unbalanced* or *nonorthogonal*. In nonorthogonal designs the effects are correlated with each other and cannot be estimated independently of one another. That is, the component sum of squares will not add up to the total sum of squares because the main effects will usually not be independent of each other and the interaction effects will not be independent of the main effects. Different ANOVA solutions can be obtained for the same design depending on the "type" of sum of squares calculated. For example, in an unbalanced design with two factors A and B, the sum of squares for main effect A differs depending on whether effect A is the only one in the model or whether it is added to a model already containing effect B.

1.11 Sequential Sums of Squares (Fitting Constants)

Sequential sums of squares are the default type calculated by MANOVA. The sums of squares for each effect are "adjusted" for all effects previously entered into the model. That is, the sum of squares for an effect is adjusted only for all terms to the left of it in the DESIGN subcommand. All terms to the right are ignored. Therefore the order in which terms are specified on the DESIGN subcommand, or the MANOVA command if a DESIGN subcommand is not present, is important. Different orders may produce different results. For the two-factor design specified using

        DESIGN=A,B/

the B main effect is adjusted for A and the overall mean, while A is adjusted only for the mean. If the model is specified as

        DESIGN=B,A/

the A main effect is adjusted for B and the mean, while the B effect is adjusted only for the mean.

Since several DESIGN subcommands can be used in one invocation of the MANOVA procedure, it is possible to obtain easily various sums of squares. For example, in a two-factor model, to obtain the main effect sum of squares adjusted for other main effects and the interaction effect adjusted for main effects, specify both

        DESIGN=A,B,A BY B/
        DESIGN=B,A, A BY B/

The first ANOVA table will contain B adjusted for A, and A BY B adjusted for both main effects. The second ANOVA table will contain A adjusted for B and the interaction adjusted for both main effects.

1.12 Regression Model Sum of Squares (Weighted Squares of Means)

It is possible to obtain sums of squares adjusted for all effects listed on the DESIGN subcommand, by specifying

        METHOD=SSTYPE(UNIQUE)/

For the two-factor model this results in main effect A being adjusted for both B and the A BY B interaction. Similarly B is adjusted for A and the interaction, while the interaction is adjusted for main effects A and B.

1.13 Decomposition and Bias Matrices

If the design is unbalanced and the default sequential sums of squares are used, the decomposition and bias matrices may be of interest. They are obtained by specifying

        PRINT=DESIGN(DECOMP,BIAS)/

The elements in the upper triangle of the decomposition matrix are used to obtain the sum of squares for each effect in the model. Consider a 2×3 factorial design, where T is the upper triangle of the decomposition matrix.

$$T = \begin{pmatrix} t_{11} & t_{12} & t_{13} & t_{14} & t_{15} & t_{16} \\ 0 & t_{22} & t_{23} & t_{24} & t_{25} & t_{26} \\ 0 & 0 & t_{33} & t_{34} & t_{35} & t_{36} \\ 0 & 0 & 0 & t_{44} & t_{45} & t_{46} \\ 0 & 0 & 0 & 0 & t_{55} & t_{56} \\ 0 & 0 & 0 & 0 & 0 & t_{66} \end{pmatrix}$$

The first row of T represents the CONSTANT effect, the second row represents the effect of A, the third and fourth rows are the effects of B, and the last two rows are the effects of AB. If $\mathbf{h'} = (h_1 \ h_2 \ h_3 \ h_4 \ h_5 \ h_6)$ is the least-squares estimate of the contrasts of effects, then the sequential sums of squares for the effects are as shown in Table 1.13.

Table 1.13

Source	Sum of Squares
CONSTANT	$(t_{11}h_1+t_{12}h_2+t_{13}h_3+t_{14}h_4+t_{15}h_5+t_{16}h_6)^2$
A	$(t_{22}h_2+t_{23}h_3+t_{24}h_4+t_{25}h_5+t_{26}h_6)^2$
B adjusted A	$(t_{33}h_3+t_{34}h_4+t_{35}h_5+t_{36}h_6)^2+(t_{44}h_4+t_{45}h_5+t_{46}h_6)^2$
AB adjusted A,B	$(t_{55}h_5+t_{56}h_6)^2+(t_{66}h_6)^2$

If the DESIGN specification for this example is

```
DESIGN=A,B,A BY B/
```

then the bias matrix is a 4×4 upper triangular matrix, since the order of the bias matrix is the number of effects in the model (in this case, CONSTANT, A, B, and A BY B). The (i,j)th element of this matrix is obtained by summing the squared elements of the T matrix, which are in the rows of effect i and the columns of effect j. The bias matrix for this example is

$$\begin{pmatrix} t_{11}^2 & t_{12}^2 & t_{13}^2 + t_{14}^2 & t_{15}^2 + t_{16}^2 \\ 0 & t_{22}^2 & t_{23}^2 + t_{24}^2 & t_{25}^2 + t_{26}^2 \\ 0 & 0 & t_{33}^2 + t_{34}^2 + t_{44}^2 & t_{35}^2 + t_{36}^2 + t_{45}^2 + t_{46}^2 \\ 0 & 0 & 0 & t_{55}^2 + t_{56}^2 + t_{66}^2 \end{pmatrix}$$

The bias matrix can be used as a measure of the degree of the confounding among effects. For example, the coefficients corresponding to h_3 and h_4 (factor B) in the calculation of sum of squares of A are t_{23} and t_{24}; thus $t_{23}^2 + t_{24}^2$ (squaring is to avoid the sign) can be used as a confounding index between A and B.

1.14 Redundant Effects

If there are empty cells in the design, some effects in the model may not be estimable. MANOVA determines the redundant effects by orthonormalization of the design matrix and prints the information. Figure 1.14 indicates that the interaction effects in columns 10 and 12 in the design matrix are not estimable because of empty cells.

Figure 1.14

```
REDUNDANCIES IN DESIGN MATRIX

   COLUMN     EFFECT

      10      A BY B
      12      (SAME)
```

1.15 Solution Matrices

For any connected design, the hypotheses associated with the sequential sums of squares are weighted functions of the population cell means with weights depending on the cell frequencies (e.g. see Searle(1971), pp. 306-313). For designs with every cell filled, it can be shown that the hypotheses corresponding to the regression model sums of squares are the unweighted hypotheses about the cell means. With empty cells the hypotheses will depend on the pattern of the missingness. In such cases, one can request that the solution matrix, which contains the coefficients of the linear combinations of the cell means being tested, be printed by specifying

```
PRINT=DESIGN(SOLUTION)/
```

For example, in a 2 × 3 (factors A, B) design with one empty cell. The solution matrix P of this design would be

$$P = \begin{pmatrix} p_{11} & p_{21} & p_{31} & p_{41} & p_{51} & 0 \\ p_{12} & p_{22} & p_{32} & p_{42} & p_{52} & 0 \\ p_{13} & p_{23} & p_{33} & p_{43} & p_{53} & 0 \\ p_{14} & p_{24} & p_{34} & p_{44} & p_{54} & 0 \\ p_{15} & p_{25} & p_{35} & p_{45} & p_{55} & 0 \\ p_{16} & p_{26} & p_{36} & p_{46} & p_{56} & 0 \end{pmatrix}$$

The first column of P indicates that the hypothesis corresponding to the sum of squares of CONSTANT is

$$p_{11}\mu_{11} + p_{12}\mu_{12} + p_{13}\mu_{13} + p_{14}\mu_{21} + p_{15}\mu_{22} + p_{16}\mu_{23} = 0$$

where μ_{ij} is the population mean of cell (i,j).

Similarly, column 2 of P represents the coefficients of the linear combinations of cell means being tested for the sum of squares of A, columns 3 and 4 are for the sum of squares of B, and the last two columns are for the sum of squares of AB.

An Example.   The following example is taken from Bancroft (1968, p. 20). Quantitative chemical experiments were run to determine the reacting weights of silver (SILVER) and iodine (IODINE) in silver iodine. Five different batches of silver and two different batches of iodine were used in the experiment. These were treated, and then a determination of the reacting weights was made. The coded data are given in Table 1.15. Note that there are two empty cells in the experiment.

Table 1.15

			Silver			
		1	2	3	4	5
Iodine	1	22 25	41 41	29 20 37	49 50	55
	2	-1 40 18	23 13	–	61	–

The MANOVA commands illustrated in Figure 1.15a produce the analysis shown in Figures 1.15b-1.15d.

Figure 1.15a

```
RUN NAME         A 5*2 DESIGN WITH EMPTY CELLS.
COMMENT          DATA ARE TAKEN FROM BANCROFT(1968) PAGE 20.
VARIABLE LIST    SILVER IODINE RESP
INPUT FORMAT     FREEFIELD
INPUT MEDIUM     CARD
MANOVA           RESP BY SILVER(1,5) IODINE(1,2)/
                 PRINT=DESIGN(DECOMP,BIAS)/
                 DESIGN=SILVER,IODINE,SILVER BY IODINE/
                 DESIGN=IODINE,SILVER,SILVER BY IODINE/
READ INPUT DATA
1 1 22
1 1 25
1 2 -1
1 2 40
1 2 18
2 1 41
2 1 41
2 2 23
2 2 13
3 1 29
3 1 20
3 1 37
4 1 49
4 1 50
4 2 61
5 1 55
END INPUT DATA
FINISH
```

The two DESIGN subcommands are used to obtain the sum of squares for IODINE adjusted for SILVER and vice versa. The decomposition and bias matrices are also requested.

The output (Figure 1.15b) indicates that two degrees of freedom for the SILVER BY IODINE interaction effects are lost because of the empty cells. Therefore, instead of four degrees of freedom, it has only two.

Figure 1.15b

```
REDUNDANCIES IN DESIGN MATRIX

     COLUMN      EFFECT

         9      SILVER BY IODINE
        10        (SAME)
```

The decomposition and bias matrices and ANOVA table for the first DESIGN subcommand are given in Figure 1.15c.

Figure 1.15c

```
TRIANGULAR DECOMPOSITION OF DESIGN
          PARAMETER

PARAMETER          1            2            3            4            5            6

         1     -4.00000     -1.00000      -.75000      -.50000      -.50000     -1.00000
         2      1.73205     -2.23607      -.11180      -.22361      -.22361      1.34164
         3      1.41421      -.63060     -2.10357      -.28523      -.28523       .76061
         4      1.41421      -.63060      1.19303      1.90227       .32521      1.06028
         5      1.73205      -.77233      -.27090      1.60122      1.87427      -.17493
         6      1.41421      -.63060      -.22119      -.10682      1.33325      3.38625
         7      1.00000      -.44590      -.15640      -.07554       .94275     -2.92061
         8      1.00000     -1.44590     -1.19649     -1.00287      -.76008      1.11430

          PARAMETER

PARAMETER          7            8

         1       .50000       .25000
         2      -.22361      -.55902
         3      -.64177      -.53481
         4       .53460       .44550
         5       .44982       .37485
         6      1.41750      1.18125
         7     -1.67054      1.00232
         8     -1.49674     -1.26491

- - - - - - - - - - - - - - - - - - - - - - - - - - - - - - - - - - - - - - - -
BIAS COEFFICIENTS FOR SEQUENTIAL ORDERING

          EFFECT

EFFECT             1            2            3            4

         1     16.00000      2.06250      1.00000       .31250
         2      0.0         16.93750      3.53333      1.88750
         3      0.0          0.0         11.46667      3.40465
         4      0.0          0.0          0.0          5.39535

- - - - - - - - - - - - - - - - - - - - - - - - - - - - - - - - - - - - - - - -
TESTS OF SIGNIFICANCE FOR RESP USING SEQUENTIAL SUMS OF SQUARES

SOURCE OF VARIATION          SUM OF SQUARES     DF    MEAN SQUARE          F      SIG. OF F

WITHIN CELLS                    1041.66667       8     130.20833
CONSTANT                       17095.56250       1   17095.56250    131.29392        0.0
SILVER                          2572.30417       4     643.07604      4.93882        .027
IODINE                           149.95504       1     149.95504      1.15165        .315
SILVER BY IODINE                 491.51163       2     245.75581      1.88740        .213
```

The PRINT subcommand applies to both DESIGN specifications. Figure 1.15d presents only the analysis of variance table for the second design specification.

Figure 1.15d

```
TESTS OF SIGNIFICANCE FOR RESP USING SEQUENTIAL SUMS OF SQUARES

SOURCE OF VARIATION          SUM OF SQUARES     DF    MEAN SQUARE          F      SIG. OF F

WITHIN CELLS                    1041.66667       8     130.20833
CONSTANT                       17095.56250       1   17095.56250    131.29392        0.0
IODINE                           473.20417       1     473.20417      3.63421        .093
SILVER                          2249.05504       4     562.26376      4.31819        .037
SILVER BY IODINE                 491.51163       2     245.75581      1.88740        .213
```

1.16 Orthogonal Contrasts for Unequal Numbers of Replicates

For balanced designs, two treatment contrasts are orthogonal if the cross products of the contrast coefficients sum to zero. When treatments have unequal numbers of replicates, for contrasts to be orthogonal the weighted sum of cross products, where the weights are the reciprocals of the numbers of replicates, must be zero. For example, suppose the numbers of replicates for five treatments are 4, 2, 1, 5, and 1 respectively; then contrasts (4,2,-6, 0, 0) and (4, 2, 1, 5, -12) are orthogonal, since $4 \times 4/4 + 2 \times 2/2 + (-6)(1)/1 = 0$.

Figure 1.16a illustrates the use of the orthogonal contrasts in a one-way unbalanced design in which the numbers of observations for treatments are 4, 4, 1, and 1, respectively. Note that specification of the PARTITION command without degrees of freedom results in single-degree-of-freedom partitions.

Figure 1.16a

```
RUN NAME          ORTHOGONAL CONTRASTS FOR UNBALANCED DESIGN.
VARIABLE LIST     TREATMNT,Y
N OF CASES        10
INPUT MEDIUM      CARD
INPUT FORMAT      FIXED(F1.0,F2.0)
MANOVA            Y BY TREATMNT(1,4)/
                  PRINT=DESIGN(BIAS)/
                  CONTRAST(TREATMNT)=SPECIAL(1 1 1 1
                                             1 -1 0 0
                                             4 4 -8 0
                                             4 4 1 -9)/
                  PARTITION(TREATMNT)/
                  DESIGN=TREATMNT(1),TREATMNT(2),TREATMNT(3)/
READ INPUT DATA
1 8
1 7
2 8
2 9
310
1 6
1 7
2 8
2 6
4 9
FINISH
```

In this example, TREATMNT(1) defines a comparison between treatments 1 and 2; TREATMNT(2) is the contrast between treatment 3 and the combination of treatments 1 and 2; and TREATMNT(3) can be used to test the hypothesis that the average of the first three treatment effects is equal to the last treatment effect. All pairs of contrasts are orthogonal since $(1)(4)/4 + (-1)(4)/4 = 0$, $(1)(4)/4 + (-1)(4)/4 = 0$, and $(4)(4)/4 + (4)(4)/4 + (-8)(1)/1 = 0$. The F tests are therefore independent. The bias matrix and the ANOVA table corresponding to Figure 1.16a are given in Figure 1.16b.

Figure 1.16b

BIAS COEFFICIENTS FOR SEQUENTIAL ORDERING

EFFECT	1	2	3	4
1	10.00000	0.0	.00434	.00278
2	0.0	2.00000	0.0	0.0
3	0.0	0.0	.01389	0.0
4	0.0	0.0	0.0	.01111

TESTS OF SIGNIFICANCE FOR Y USING SEQUENTIAL SUMS OF SQUARES

SOURCE OF VARIATION	SUM OF SQUARES	DF	MEAN SQUARE	F	SIG. OF F
WITHIN CELLS	6.75000	6	1.12500		
CONSTANT	608.40000	1	608.40000	540.80000	0.0
TREATMNT(1)	1.12500	1	1.12500	1.00000	.356
TREATMNT(2)	6.12500	1	6.12500	5.44444	.058
TREATMNT(3)	1.60000	1	1.60000	1.42222	.278

The second example is adapted from Cochran and Cox (1957, p. 46). The experiment was conducted to compare the effectiveness of four soil fumigants in keeping down the number of eelworms in the soil. The fumigants were CN, CS, CM, and CK. Each fumigant was tested both in a single and double dose. The control was used as another treatment. The nine treatments are denoted as C00 (control), CN1 (CN with single dose), CS1, CM1, CK1, CN2 (CN with double dose), CS2, CM2, and CK2. There were four replications for each dose of each fumigant and 16 replications of the control. The desired subdivisions of the treatment sum of squares are as follows:

1 If the effect of the fumigants is proportional to the dose, then both CN1 and CN2/2 are the estimate of the effect of CN per unit dose. The pooled estimate of this effect is (CN1 + 2(CN2))/5. The differences in the linear responses to the four fumigants can be measured by the following three contrasts:

```
(0   1  -1   0   0   2  -2   0   0)
(0   1   1  -2   0   2   2  -4   0)
(0   1   1   1  -3   2   2   2  -6)
```

2 The curvature of the treatment CN is measured by C00 − (2CN1) + CN2. The differences in curvature are compared by the quantities CN2 -2(CN1), (the C00 term cancelled out in the comparison) or by the following three contrasts:

```
(0   2  -2   0   0  -1   1   0   0)
(0   2   2  -4   0  -1  -1   2   0)
(0   2   2   2  -6  -1  -1  -1   3)
```

3 The sum of squares between levels (control: 0 level; treatments with single dose: level 1; treatments with double level: level 2) can be partitioned into a component due to the linearity between levels and one representing the curvature between levels. The former is given by the comparison of −1(level 0) +0(level 1) +1(level 2), or the contrast (−4 0 0 0 0 1 1 1 1). The curvature between levels is measured by 1(level 0) −2(level 1) +1(level 2), or the contrast (−4 −2 −2 −2 −2 1 1 1 1).

The above partitions can be summarized by the following MANOVA CONTRAST subcommand:

```
CONTRAST(TREATMNT)=SPECIAL(1   1   1   1   1   1   1   1   1
                           0   1  -1   0   0   2  -2   0   0
                           0   1   1  -2   0   2   2  -4   0
                           0   1   1   1  -3   2   2   2  -6
                           0   2  -2   0   0  -1   1   0   0
                           0   2   2  -4   0  -1  -1   2   0
                           0   2   2   2  -6  -1  -1  -1   3
                          -4   0   0   0   0   1   1   1   1
                           4  -2  -2  -2  -2   1   1   1   1)/
      PARTITION(TREATMNT)=(3 3 1 1)/
      DESIGN=BLOCK TREATMNT(1)  TREATMNT(2)
             TREATMNT(3)  TREATMNT(4)/
```

Note that TREATMNT(1), TREATMNT(2), TREATMNT(3), and TREATMNT(4) are the effects of the differences in linear response, in curvature, linear response between levels, and curvature between levels, respectively. Also, it can be verified that the effects are orthogonal.

1.17 Analysis of Covariance

SPSS MANOVA can perform an analysis of covariance in which interval-scaled independent variables (covariates) are used in conjunction with categorical variables (factors). Analysis of covariance is a technique that combines the features of analysis of variance and regression. A two-way analysis of covariance model with two covariates can be described as follows:

$$Y_{ijk} = \mu + \alpha_i + \gamma_j + (\alpha\gamma)_{ij} + \beta_1(X_{1ijk} - \overline{X}_1) + \beta_2(X_{2ijk} - \overline{X}_2) + \epsilon_{ijk}$$

where Y_{ijk} is the dependent variable, α_i, γ_j are the main effects, and $(\alpha\gamma)_{ij}$ is the interaction effect. X_1, X_2 are the covariates, and $\overline{X}_1$, $\overline{X}_2$ are the means for the two covariates.

In the covariance model, Y has a (multiple) linear regression (see Section 1.38) on X_1 and X_2 with regression coefficients β_1 and β_2. The regression procedure is used to remove the variation in the dependent variable due to covariates.

From the standpoint of the analysis of variance model, the covariate model is essentially an analysis of variance model on the corrected scores or

$$Y_{ijk} - \beta_1(X_{1ijk} - \overline{X}_1) - \beta_2(X_{2ijk} - \overline{X}_2) = \mu + \alpha_i + \gamma_j + (\alpha\gamma)_{ij} + \epsilon_{ijk}$$

which is the analysis of variance model for Y adjusted for the two covariates.

The following illustrative example is taken from Snedecor and Cochran (1967, p. 422). The model is a one-way analysis of covariance with one covariate. The experiment was conducted to evaluate the effect of three drugs on the treatment of leprosy. For each patient, six sites were selected. The variate X, based on laboratory tests, is a score representing the abundance of leprosy bacilli at these sites before the experiment began. Variate Y is a similar score after several months of treatment. Drugs 1 and 2 are antibiotics, while drug 3 is an inert drug included as a control. Ten patients were selected for each treatment. The MANOVA commands are as follows:

```
MANOVA        Y BY DRUG(1,3) WITH X/
              PRINT= PMEANS/
```

Inclusion of covariates in a model is indicated by the keyword WITH on the MANOVA command. The PRINT = PMEANS (see Section 1.50) specification requests the predicted and adjusted (for covariate) means of treatments.

The output includes the analysis of covariance summary table shown in Figure 1.17a, which gives the sum of squares due to regression (adjusted for the factor DRUG), and the sum of squares due to DRUG adjusted for regression.

Figure 1.17a

```
TESTS OF SIGNIFICANCE FOR Y USING SEQUENTIAL SUMS OF SQUARES

SOURCE OF VARIATION              SUM OF SQUARES     DF    MEAN SQUARE          F     SIG. OF F

WITHIN CELLS                         417.20260      26      16.04625
REGRESSION                           577.89740       1     577.89740    36.01447        0.0
CONSTANT                              31.92864       1      31.92864     1.98979        .170
DRUG                                  68.55371       2      34.27686     2.13613        .138
```

In addition, the estimated regression coefficient (B), the standardized regression coefficient (BETA), the standard error of the regression coefficient and the t-value of the test that $\beta = 0$ are also given (Figure 1.17b). Note that $(6.00121)^2 = 36.014$, which is the F value for the regression in the ANOVA table.

Figure 1.17b

```
REGRESSION ANALYSIS FOR WITHIN CELLS ERROR TERM

DEPENDENT VARIABLE ..Y

COVARIATE         B         BETA      STD. ERR.    T-VALUE    SIG. OF T  LOWER .95 CL  UPPER .95 CL

X          .9871838111  .7620649867    .16450      6.00121       .000       .64905        1.32531
```

The adjusted and predicted means for the factor DRUG are shown in Figure 1.17c.

Figure 1.17c

```
ADJUSTED AND ESTIMATED MEANS

VARIABLE .. Y

     FACTOR        CODE      OBS. MEAN    ADJ. MEAN    EST. MEAN    RAW RESID.   STD. RESID.

DRUG               1          5.30000      6.71496      5.30000       0.0          0.0
DRUG               2          6.10000      6.82393      6.10000       0.0          0.0
DRUG               3         12.30000     10.16110     12.30000       0.0          0.0
```

Since MANOVA allows the inclusion of interval-scaled variables in the DESIGN specification, the analysis of covariance can also be obtained using the following MANOVA commands:

```
MANOVA        Y,X, BY DRUG(1,3)/
              ANALYSIS = Y/
              DESIGN = X, DRUG/
              DESIGN = DRUG,X/
```

The ANALYSIS subcommand is used to select Y as the dependent variable. The first DESIGN subcommand produces the DRUG effects adjusted for the covariate (X). The output is given in Figure 1.17d.

Figure 1.17d

```
TESTS OF SIGNIFICANCE FOR Y USING SEQUENTIAL SUMS OF SQUARES

SOURCE OF VARIATION              SUM OF SQUARES     DF    MEAN SQUARE          F     SIG. OF F

WITHIN+RESIDUAL                      417.20260      26      16.04625
CONSTANT                            1872.30000       1    1872.30000   116.68144        0.0
X                                    802.94369       1     802.94369    50.03932        0.0
DRUG                                  68.55371       2      34.27686     2.13613        .138
```

The second DESIGN specification requests the regression effect (X) adjusted for the factor DRUG (Figure 1.17e).

Figure 1.17e

```
TESTS OF SIGNIFICANCE FOR Y USING SEQUENTIAL SUMS OF SQUARES

SOURCE OF VARIATION          SUM OF SQUARES    DF    MEAN SQUARE         F    SIG. OF F

WITHIN+RESIDUAL                   417.20260    26      16.04625
CONSTANT                         1872.30000     1    1872.30000   116.68144       0.0
DRUG                              293.60000     2     146.80000     9.14855       .001
X                                 577.89740     1     577.89740    36.01447       0.0
```

The regression coefficient can be obtained from the estimate of the parameters for factor X (Figure 1.17f).

Figure 1.17f

```
ESTIMATES FOR Y

CONSTANT

PARAMETER        COEFF.      STD. ERR.     T-VALUE    SIG. OF T    LOWER .95 CL    UPPER .95 CL

    1       -2.6957729061     1.91108     -1.41060       .170        -6.62406         1.23252

DRUG

PARAMETER        COEFF.      STD. ERR.     T-VALUE    SIG. OF T    LOWER .95 CL    UPPER .95 CL

    2       -1.1850365374     1.06082     -1.11709       .274        -3.36559          .99551
    3       -1.0760652052     1.04130     -1.03339       .311        -3.21648         1.06435

X

PARAMETER        COEFF.      STD. ERR.     T-VALUE    SIG. OF T    LOWER .95 CL    UPPER .95 CL

    4         .9871838111      .16450      6.00121       .000          .64905         1.32531
```

From the covariance model given above, it follows that there is a common regression coefficient for the given X. This implies that the within-treatment regression coefficients are homogeneous. The assumption of homogeneity of regression coefficients in the analysis of covariance can be assessed by introducing a treatment by covariate interaction term in the model.

A test for no interaction between DRUG effects and covariate is equivalent to testing the hypothesis that the pooled within-treatment regression coefficient is appropriate. The test for treatment by covariate interaction, which is referred to as the test for regression parallelism, can be obtained in MANOVA as follows:

```
MANOVA       Y, X BY DRUG(1,3)/
             ANALYSIS = Y/
             DESIGN = X, DRUG, X BY DRUG/
```

The analysis of variance table for this DESIGN specification is given in Figure 1.17g.

Since X BY DRUG is not significant, the hypothesis of the homogeneity of the within-treatment regression is not rejected.

Figure 1.17g

```
TESTS OF SIGNIFICANCE FOR Y USING SEQUENTIAL SUMS OF SQUARES

SOURCE OF VARIATION          SUM OF SQUARES    DF    MEAN SQUARE         F    SIG. OF F

WITHIN+RESIDUAL                   397.55795    24      16.56491
CONSTANT                         1872.30000     1    1872.30000   113.02805       0.0
X                                 802.94369     1     802.94369    48.47255       0.0
DRUG                               68.55371     2      34.27686     2.06924       .148
X BY DRUG                          19.64465     2       9.82232      .59296       .561
```

1.18 Analysis of Covariance with Separate Regression Estimates

Consider a 2 × 2 (Factors A, B) design with covariate X. The model (using dummy variables) can be written as

$$Y_{ijk} = \mu + \beta(X_{ijk} - \bar{X}) + \alpha_1 Z_{ijk} + \alpha_2 U_{ijk} + \alpha_3 Z_{ijk} U_{ijk} + \epsilon_{ijk}$$

where

$Z_{ijk} = 1$ if i = 2 (level 2 of A is applied)
        0   otherwise

$U_{ijk} = 1$ if j = 2 (level 2 of B is applied)
        0   otherwise

If the interaction terms between the covariate and factor variables are added to the model, then

$$Y_{ijk} = \mu + \beta(X_{ijk} - \overline{X}) + \alpha_1 Z_{ijk} + \alpha_2 U_{ijk} + \alpha_3 Z_{ijk} U_{ijk}$$
$$+ (\alpha\beta)_1(X_{ijk} - \overline{X})Z_{ijk} + (\alpha\beta)_2(X_{ijk} - \overline{X})U_{ijk} + (\alpha\beta)_3(X_{ijk} - \overline{X})Z_{ijk}U_{ijk} + \epsilon_{ijk}$$

A test of H_0: $(\alpha\beta)_1 = (\alpha\beta)_2 = (\alpha\beta)_3 = 0$ is equivalent to testing the hypothesis that the regression slopes are the same for all cells. This test can be performed by specifying the following MANOVA commands:

```
MANOVA          Y X BY A(1,2),B(1,2)/
                ANALYSIS=Y/
                DESIGN=X,A,B,A BY B,
                   X BY A + X BY B + X BY A BY B/
```

The effects X BY A, X BY B, and X BY A BY B are lumped together to provide the test of the parallelism hypothesis. If the test is not significant, the usual analysis of covariance model can be used to perform the analysis.

If the assumption of the homogeneity of the slope is violated, one of the following three models might be used:

1   The model of different slopes for each level of factor A. This model can be justified by testing $(\alpha\beta)_2 = (\alpha\beta)_3 = 0$. The MANOVA specification for the test is

```
                DESIGN=X,A,B,A BY B,
                   X BY B + X BY A BY B/
```

If the test is not significant, the following DESIGN specifications can be used for the analysis of covariance of this model:

```
                DESIGN=X WITHIN A, A, B, A BY B/
                DESIGN=A, B, A BY B, X WITHIN A/
```

The X WITHIN A term represents the regression effects that are separately estimated within each level of A. The first DESIGN specification requests the main effects and interaction adjusted for the covariate effects. The second DESIGN specification gives the regression effect (last term) adjusted for A, B and AB.

2   The model of different slopes for each level of factor B. The appropriate test for this model is $(\alpha\beta)_1 = (\alpha\beta)_3 = 0$ and is obtained by specifying

```
                DESIGN= X, A, B, A BY B, X BY A + X BY A BY B/
```

The analysis of covariance is obtained by using

```
                DESIGN=X WITHIN B, A, B, A BY B/
                DESIGN=A, B, A BY B, X WITHIN B/
```

3   The model of different slopes for each cell. The MANOVA specifications for this model are

```
                DESIGN=X WITHIN A BY B, A, B, A BY B/
                DESIGN=A, B, A BY B, X WITHIN A BY B/
```

The X WITHIN A BY B term represents the regression slopes, which are different for each cell.

The same procedure can be simply extended to multiple covariates. For a 2×2 design with covariates Z1 and Z2, the X term is replaced by CONTIN(Z1,Z2) throughout the DESIGN specification discussed above. The keyword CONTIN incorporates Z1 and Z2 into a single effect. Thus the following specfications may be used for the analysis of covariance for model 1 with covariates Z1 and Z2.

```
MANOVA          Y Z1 Z2 BY A(1,2) B(1,2)/
                ANALYSIS=Y/
                DESIGN=Z1, Z2, A, B, A BY B,
                   CONTIN(Z1,Z2) BY B + CONTIN(Z1,Z2)BY A BY B/
                DESIGN=CONTIN(Z1,Z2) WITHIN A, A, B, A BY B/
                DESIGN=A, B, A BY B, CONTIN(Z1,Z2) WITHIN A/
```

The first DESIGN specification is used to test the model, while the second and third models are for the analysis of covariance.

6

An Example.

The following example is taken from Searle (1971, pp. 287,375). An experiment was conducted to compare the effects of three different types of fertilizer and four varieties of grain on the weight of grain (WEIGHT). The milligrams of seed planted (MSEED) for each plot were also recorded and used as the covariate. The SPSS commands and data for model 3 are presented in Figure 1.18a, and the analysis of variance tables in Figure 1.18b.

Figure 1.18a

```
RUN NAME        EMPTY CELLS EXAMPLE FROM SEARLE(1971).
COMMENT         DATA ARE TAKEN FROM P. 287 AND P. 375.
VARIABLE LIST   TREATMNT, VARIETY, WEIGHT, MSEED
N OF CASES      18
INPUT FORMAT    FREEFIELD
INPUT MEDIUM    CARD
MANOVA          WEIGHT MSEED BY TREATMNT(1,3), VARIETY(1,4)/
                ANALYSIS=WEIGHT/
                DESIGN = MSEED WITHIN VARIETY BY TREATMNT ,
                   VARIETY, TREATMNT, VARIETY BY TREATMNT/
                DESIGN = TREATMNT, VARIETY, VARIETY BY TREATMNT,
                   MSEED WITHIN VARIETY BY TREATMNT/
READ INPUT DATA
1  1  8   2
1  1 13   4
1  1  9   3
1  3 12   7
1  4  7   3
1  4 11   5
2  1  6   5
2  1 12   3
2  2 12   6
2  2 14   4
3  2  9   6
3  2  7   2
3  3 14   6
3  3 16   8
3  4 10   4
3  4 14   6
3  4 11   5
3  4 13   7
FINISH
```

Figure 1.18b

TESTS OF SIGNIFICANCE FOR WEIGHT USING SEQUENTIAL SUMS OF SQUARES

SOURCE OF VARIATION	SUM OF SQUARES	DF	MEAN SQUARE	F	SIG. OF F
WITHIN+RESIDUAL	4.30000	3	1.43333		
CONSTANT	2178.00000	1	2178.00000	1519.53488	.000
MSEED WITHIN VARIETY BY TREATMNT	92.11472	8	11.51434	8.03326	.057
VARIETY	5.31810	3	1.77270	1.23677	.433
TREATMNT	36.16611	2	18.08306	12.61609	.035
VARIETY BY TREATMNT	.10107	1	.10107	.07051	.808

TESTS OF SIGNIFICANCE FOR WEIGHT USING SEQUENTIAL SUMS OF SQUARES

SOURCE OF VARIATION	SUM OF SQUARES	DF	MEAN SQUARE	F	SIG. OF F
WITHIN+RESIDUAL	4.30000	3	1.43333		
CONSTANT	2178.00000	1	2178.00000	1519.53488	.000
TREATMNT	10.50000	2	5.25000	3.66279	.157
VARIETY	36.78571	3	12.26190	8.55482	.056
VARIETY BY TREATMNT	34.71429	2	17.35714	12.10963	.037
MSEED WITHIN VARIETY BY TREATMNT	51.70000	7	7.38571	5.15282	.103

1.19 Randomized Block Designs

In this design the experimental unit is divided into groups (blocks). The main object of this is to keep the experimental errors within each group as small as possible. The accuracy of the experiment is increased by making comparisons within the resulting relatively homogeneous experimental units. The model for this design is

$$Y_{ij} = \mu + \beta_i + \tau_j + \epsilon_{ij}$$

where β_i is the block effect and τ_j is the treatment effect.

1.20   Complete Randomized Block Designs

A randomized block design is called complete if each block contains every level of the treatment. Table 1.20 is an example of a complete randomized block design with four treatments, A, B, C, and D, and three blocks.

Table 1.20

Block

1	2	3
A	D	A
B	B	C
C	A	B
D	C	D

Let Y, TRT, and BLK be the response, treatment, and block variables respectively. The MANOVA commands needed to perform the analysis of this design are

```
MANOVA        Y BY BLK(1,3) TRT(1,4)/
              DESIGN=BLK,TRT/
```

In most applications the significance of the block differences is assumed, and treatment effects are corrected for the block effects. (Although it does not make any difference here since the design is balanced and complete, in general the treatment effects should be adjusted.)

1.21   Balanced Incomplete (Randomized) Block Designs (BIB)

In some randomized block designs it may not be possible to apply all treatments in every block. If the block size is less than the number of treatments, the design is called incomplete. An incomplete block design is called balanced if

- Each block contains exactly k treatments
- Each treatment appears in r blocks
- Any pair of treatments appears together λ times

Thus a BIB can be described in terms of the parameters t (number of treatments), b (number of blocks), k, r, and λ.

Table 1.21 is an example of a BIB design with t = 4, b = 4, k = 3, r = 3, and λ = 2.

Table 1.21

Block

1	2	3	4
A	D	A	B
B	B	D	C
C	A	C	D

The following example is taken from Cochran and Cox (1957, p. 443). It is a BIB design with t = 6, b = 15, k = 2, r = 5, and λ = 1. The blocks are grouped into 5 replications.

The SPSS commands for this analysis are given in Figure 1.21a. The first design model specification requests the blocks within replications adjusted for treatment effects. The second model asks for the treatment effects adjusted for the blocks.

Figure 1.21a

```
RUN NAME         TYPE 1 BALANCED INCOMPLETE BLOCK DESIGN.
COMMENT          DATA ARE TAKEN FROM COCHRAN & COX(1957).
VARIABLE LIST    REPLICS, TREATMNT, BLOCKS, DEP
INPUT MEDIUM     CARD
INPUT FORMAT     FIXED(3F1.0,F2.0)
N OF CASES       UNKNOWN
MANOVA           DEP BY REPLICS(1,5), TREATMNT(1,6), BLOCKS(1,3)/
                 DESIGN = REPLICS, TREATMNT, BLOCKS W REPLICS/
                 DESIGN = REPLICS, BLOCKS W REPLICS, TREATMNT/
READ INPUT DATA
111 7
12117
13226
14225
....
....
54326
55332
56127
END INPUT DATA
FINISH
```

The ANOVA tables from the output for Figure 1.21a are given in Figure 1.21b.

Figure 1.21b

TESTS OF SIGNIFICANCE FOR DEP USING SEQUENTIAL SUMS OF SQUARES

SOURCE OF VARIATION	SUM OF SQUARES	DF	MEAN SQUARE	F	SIG. OF F
RESIDUAL	77.33333	10	7.73333		
CONSTANT	19712.03333	1	19712.03333	2548.96983	0.0
REPLICS	298.46667	4	74.61667	9.64871	.002
TREATMNT	1059.76667	5	211.95333	27.40776	.000
BLOCKS W REPLICS	213.40000	10	21.34000	2.75948	.062

- -

TESTS OF SIGNIFICANCE FOR DEP USING SEQUENTIAL SUMS OF SQUARES

SOURCE OF VARIATION	SUM OF SQUARES	DF	MEAN SQUARE	F	SIG. OF F
RESIDUAL	77.33333	10	7.73333		
CONSTANT	19712.03333	1	19712.03333	2548.96983	0.0
REPLICS	298.46667	4	74.61667	9.64871	.002
BLOCKS W REPLICS	753.00000	10	75.30000	9.73707	.001
TREATMNT	520.16667	5	104.03333	13.45259	.000

1.22 Partially Balanced Incomplete Block Designs (PBIB)

Because balanced incomplete block designs often require a large number of blocks, it may not be possible to find a design that fits the size of the experiment. A general class of BIB designs that do not have the uniform variances for treatment contrasts but still permit the estimation of treatment differences are the partially balanced incomplete block designs.

Consider the design in Table 1.22, with $t = 20$, $k = 4$, $r = 2$ and $b = 10$. Recall that for a BIB design any pair of treatments must appear together λ times. In this design, some treatments occur together in the same blocks and some do not. This is the main difference between BIB and PBIB designs.

Table 1.22

Blocks

1	2	3	4	5	6	7	8	9	10
A	M	E	Q	I	A	B	C	D	E
B	N	F	R	J	K	L	M	N	O
C	O	G	S	K	F	G	H	I	J
D	P	H	T	L	P	Q	R	S	T

PBIB designs represent a large class of designs, many of which can be found in Cochran and Cox (1957). An example with t = 15, b = 15, k = 4, and r = 4 is given on p. 456 of that text. The MANOVA commands and the output ANOVA table are given in Figure 1.22a and Figure 1.22b.

Figure 1.22a

```
RUN NAME          15 X 15 PARTIALLY BAL. INC. BLOCK DESIGN.
COMMENT           DATA ARE TAKEN FROM COCHRAN & COX(1957) P.456.
VARIABLE LIST     BLOCKS, TREATMNT, DEP
INPUT MEDIUM      CARD
N OF CASES        UNKNOWN
INPUT FORMAT      FIXED(2F2.0,8X,F3.0)
MANOVA            DEP BY BLOCKS(1,15), TREATMNT(1,15)/
                  DESIGN = BLOCKS, TREATMNT/
READ INPUT DATA
  1  1           2.6
  1  9           2.5
 113             2.0
 115             2.4
  2  1           2.7
  ..              .
  ..              .
  ..              .
 15  4           2.5
 15  8           3.2
 1510            2.4
 1511            3.1
END INPUT DATA
FINISH
```

Figure 1.22b

TESTS OF SIGNIFICANCE FOR DEP USING SEQUENTIAL SUMS OF SQUARES

SOURCE OF VARIATION	SUM OF SQUARES	DF	MEAN SQUARE	F	SIG. OF F
RESIDUAL	2.68589	31	.08664		
CONSTANT	448.26654	1	448.26654	5173.80518	0.0
BLOCKS	4.92333	14	.35167	4.05887	.001
TREATMNT	1.56411	14	.11172	1.28948	.268

1.23   Latin and Other Squares

A Latin square is a design in which each treatment appears exactly once in each row and column. The main interest is still on the estimation of treatment differences, but two restrictions are put on the randomization of the treatment assignment. The model of this design is

$$Y_{ijk} = \mu + \alpha_i + \beta_j + \gamma_k + \epsilon_{ijk}$$

where α_i, β_j and γ_k are the row, column and treatment effects respectively. An example of a 4 × 4 Latin square is shown in Table 1.23a.

Table 1.23a

		Column			
		1	2	3	4
	1	A	C	D	B
	2	D	B	C	A
Row	3	C	A	B	D
	4	B	D	A	C

The following MANOVA specifications may be used to analyze a 4 × 4 Latin square.

```
MANOVA      Y BY ROW(1,4),COL(1,4),TRT(1,4)/
            DESIGN=ROW,COL,TRT/
```

If another restriction on the randomization is placed on a Latin square, we have a Graeco-Latin square. Table 1.23b exhibits a 4 × 4 Graeco-Latin square.

Table 1.23b

Column

		1	2	3	4
	1	A δ	B α	D β	C γ
	2	B γ	A β	C α	D δ
Row	3	C β	D γ	B δ	A α
	4	D α	C δ	A γ	B β

In this design the third restriction has levels α, β, γ, δ. Note that α, β, γ and δ not only each appear exactly once within each row and column, but they also appear exactly once with each level of treatments A, B, C, D. The Graeco-Latin square can be constructed by superimposing an orthogonal (same size) Latin square on the original Latin square. In other words, the third restriction factor along with column and row is also a 4 × 4 Latin square. It has treatments α, β, γ, δ and is orthogonal to the original Latin square with treatments A, B, C, and D. Here orthogonality means each letter in one Latin square appears exactly once in the same position as each letter of the other square.

The analysis of variance for a Graeco-Latin square is very similar to that for a Latin square. Let GREEK denote the third restriction factor on a 4 × 4 Graeco-Latin square. The MANOVA specifications would be

```
MANOVA          Y BY ROW(1,4), COL(1,4), GREEK(1,4), TRT(1,4)/
                DESIGN=ROW,COL,GREEK,TRT/
```

Note that a small Graeco-Latin square design may not be very practical, since very few degrees of freedom are left for the residual.

1.24 Factorial Designs

In a factorial design, the effects of several different factors are investigated simultaneously. Suppose we wish to study the effects of two factors on the yield of a chemical. The first factor is temperature at 100°F, 200°F, and 300°F. The other factor is pressure at 20 psi and 40 psi. This experiment is a two-factor factorial design with three levels for the first factor and two levels for the second. The treatments for this experiment are the 6 combinations of the levels of the factors. The model for the 3 × 2 factorial design is

$$Y_{ijk} = \mu + \alpha_i + \beta_j + (\alpha\beta)_{ij} + \epsilon_{ijk}$$

where α_i is the temperature effect, β_j is the pressure effect, and $(\alpha\beta)_{ij}$ is the temperature-pressure interaction.

A factorial experiment containing one observation per cell (treatment) constitutes one replicate of the design. The design may be replicated k times in two possible ways. If each observation has different experimental conditions for replications within cells (e.g., each replicate is a block), the design is crossed by another factor within k levels (i.e., block effect). If the experimental condition is the same for the replications within cells, the number of factors remains unchanged, and the variation within cells is attributed to the error.

The following example illustrates the use of MANOVA to perform the analysis of a 4 × 4 × 3 factorial in randomized blocks (two blocks) with a covariate. The data are taken from Cochran and Cox (1957, p. 176).

The model contains the main effects (NTREAT, LENPER, CURRENT), all two-way interactions (NTREAT BY LENPER,...,LENPER BY CURRENT), and the three-way interaction (NTREAT BY LENPER BY CURRENT). The SPSS commands for this analysis are shown in Figure 1.24a and the analysis of variance table in Figure 1.24b.

Figure 1.24a

```
RUN NAME        4*4*3 FACTORIAL IN RANDOMIZED BLOCKS.
COMMENT         4*4*3 FACTORIAL IN RANDOMIZED BLOCKS WITH
                COVARIATE. FROM COCHRAN AND COX(1957)  PAGE 176.
VARIABLE LIST   REPLIC,LENPER,CURRENT,NTREAT,Y,X
INPUT MEDIUM    CARD
INPUT FORMAT    FIXED(4F1.0,F2.0,F3.0)
N OF CASES      96
IF              (LENPER EQ 5) LENPER = 4
IF              (NTREAT EQ 3) NTREAT = 2
IF              (NTREAT EQ 6) NTREAT = 3
MANOVA          Y BY REPLIC(1,2), LENPER(1,4), CURRENT(1,4),
                   NTREAT(1,3) WITH X/
                DESIGN = REPLIC,NTREAT,LENPER,CURRENT,NTREAT BY LENPER,
                         NTREAT BY CURRENT, LENPER BY CURRENT,
                         NTREAT BY LENPER BY CURRENT/
READ INPUT DATA
111172152
111374131
111669131
112161130
112361129
112665126
113162141
113365112
113670111
114185147
114376125
114661130
121167136
121352110
121662122
122160111
  .   .   .   .   .
  .   .   .   .   .
  .   .   .   .   .
254159102
254358 98
254688135
FINISH
```

Figure 1.24b

TESTS OF SIGNIFICANCE FOR Y USING SEQUENTIAL SUMS OF SQUARES

SOURCE OF VARIATION	SUM OF SQUARES	DF	MEAN SQUARE	F	SIG. OF F
RESIDUAL	2211.96526	46	48.08620		
REGRESSION	987.52432	1	987.52432	20.53654	.000
CONSTANT	1316.19933	1	1316.19933	27.37166	0.0
REPLIC	.27456	1	.27456	.00571	.940
NTREAT	441.20522	2	220.60261	4.58765	.015
LENPER	180.52285	3	60.17428	1.25138	.302
CURRENT	2111.03300	3	703.67767	14.63367	0.0
NTREAT BY LENPER	211.79056	6	35.29843	.73407	.625
NTREAT BY CURRENT	467.84848	6	77.97475	1.62156	.163
LENPER BY CURRENT	404.37365	9	44.93041	.93437	.505
NTREAT BY LENPER BY CURRENT	1021.61800	18	56.75656	1.18031	.315

1.25 Nested Designs

A nested design arranges the experimental units hierarchically. For example, consider an experiment to compare the yield of wheat per acre for different areas in a given state. Five counties are selected at random, then three townships are randomly selected from each county. From each township two farms are selected and the yield of wheat per acre is obtained. The resulting experiment produces $5 \times 3 \times 2 = 30$ experimental units. The factors of this experiment are county and township, and the township effects are *nested* under the county factor, since a given township appears only under one of the five counties. In other words, the county factor is not *crossed* with township factor and so the interaction between county and township is not estimable.

The model for this two-factor nested design is

$$Y_{ijk} = \mu + \alpha_i + \beta_{j(i)} + \epsilon_{ijk}$$

where α_i is the county effect and $\beta_{j(i)}$ is the township effect nested under the county effect.

Since α_i should be tested against variation within α_i, i.e., $\beta_{j(i)}$, the following MANOVA specfications can be used:

```
MANOVA          Y BY COUNTY(1,5),TOWN(1,3)/
                DESIGN=COUNTY VS 1, TOWN WITHIN COUNTY=1 VS WITHIN/
```

Note that the first keyword WITHIN (or just W) indicates nesting. The DESIGN specification requests that COUNTY be tested against the error 1 term, which is the effect of TOWN (nested within COUNTY), and that the within-cells error term (second WITHIN) be used for testing the TOWN effect.

When crossing and nesting are both used in the design, attention must be paid to the choice of appropriate error terms for testing the various effects. Consider a three-factor example, with factors A, B, and C. If

1 C is nested within B, and B is nested within A, the model is

$$Y_{ijk} = \mu + \alpha_i + \beta_{j(i)} + \gamma_{k(ij)} + \epsilon_{ijk}$$

The DESIGN specification should be

```
DESIGN=A VS 1, B W A=1 VS 2, C W B W A=2 VS WITHIN/
```

2 C is nested within B, and B is crossed with A, the model is

$$Y_{ijk} = \mu + \alpha_i + \beta_j + (\alpha\beta)_{ij} + \gamma_{k(j)} + (\alpha\gamma)_{ik(j)} + \epsilon_{ijk}$$

The rule for writing down the model is that no interaction in which the subscript j appears twice is in the model. For example, interactions $(\beta\gamma)_{jk(j)}$ and $(\alpha\beta\gamma)_{ijk(j)}$ do not exist.

Since C is nested within B, β_j is tested against $\gamma_{k(j)}$. The appropriate error term for α_i and $(\alpha\beta)_{ij}$ is the residual of the A-B two-way table, $(\alpha\gamma)_{ik(j)}$, which is the interaction effect of α_i and $\gamma_{k(j)}$. If the number of observations per cell is greater than one, then $(\alpha\gamma)_{ik(j)}$ and $\gamma_{k(j)}$ can be tested against the within-cells error term. The DESIGN specification for this model is

```
DESIGN=A VS 2, B VS 1, C W B=1 VS WITHIN,
       A BY B VS 2, A BY C W B=2 VS WITHIN/
```

3 C is crossed with B, and B is nested within A. The model and the DESIGN specification are the same as those in (2) except for the names of the effects.

An experiment (Hicks, 1973, p. 195) was conducted to compare a new gun-loading method with the existing one (factor METHOD). Three teams were chosen randomly from each of three groups. Each team used the two methods of gun loading in random order. The data and SPSS commands for the analysis are as given in Figure 1.25a, and the ANOVA table is presented in Figure 1.25b.

Figure 1.25a

```
RUN NAME        NESTED DESIGN.
COMMENT         DATA ARE TAKEN FROM HICKS(1973) P. 194.
COMMENT         METHOD : 2 LEVELS CROSSED WITH GROUP.
COMMENT         GROUP  : 3 LEVELS.
COMMENT         TEAM   : 3 LEVELS NESTED WITHIN GROUP.
COMMENT         NUMBER OF OBSERVATIONS PER CELL = 2.
VARIABLE LIST   GROUP,TEAM,METHOD,RESP
N OF CASES      UNKNOWN
INPUT FORMAT    FREEFIELD
INPUT MEDIUM    CARD
MANOVA          RESP BY METHOD(1,2),GROUP,TEAM(1,3)/
                DESIGN=METHOD VS 1,GROUP VS 2,
                METHOD BY GROUP VS 1,TEAM W GROUP=2,
                METHOD BY TEAM W GROUP=1/
READ INPUT DATA
1 1 1 20.2
1 1 1 24.1
1 1 2 14.2
1 1 2 16.2
1 2 1 26.2
1 2 1 26.9
  .  .   .
  .  .   .
  .  .   .
3 3 1 21.8
3 3 1 23.5
3 3 2 12.7
3 3 2 15.1
END INPUT DATA
FINISH
```

Figure 1.25b

```
TESTS OF SIGNIFICANCE FOR RESP USING SEQUENTIAL SUMS OF SQUARES

SOURCE OF VARIATION                  SUM OF SQUARES      DF    MEAN SQUARE            F      SIG. OF F

WITHIN CELLS                            41.58993         18       2.31055
CONSTANT                             13455.99443          1    13455.99443    5823.71557        0.0

ERROR 1                                 10.72164          6       1.78694
METHOD                                 651.95062          1     651.95062      364.84200        0.0
METHOD BY GROUP                          1.18721          2        .59361         .33219        .730

ERROR 2                                 39.25829          6       6.54305
GROUP                                   16.05166          2       8.02583       1.22662         .358
```

1.26   Confounding Designs

In some factorial designs it may not be possible to apply all factor combinations in every block. Two methods can be used to handle this problem. The first one is the BIB designs discussed in Section 1.21. Another method for circumventing this difficulty is to reduce the size of a block by sacrificing the estimation of certain higher-order interactions. Consider a $2 \times 2 \times 2$ factorial experiment, with factors A, B, and C. Let abc denote the experimental unit with all three factors at the high level (since each factor has two levels, one is low and one is high), ab denote the unit where A and B are at the high level and c is at the low level. Thus if a letter appears, that factor is at the high level; otherwise, it is at the low level. When all factors appear at the low level it is designated by (1). Suppose we arrange the $2 \times 2 \times 2$ factorial in two blocks as in Table 1.26a.

Table 1.26a

Block	
1	**2**
abc	ab
a	ac
b	bc
c	(1)

The effect of A is estimated by comparing the observations receiving high and low levels of A, i.e.,

$$abc + a + ab + ac - b - c - bc - (1)$$

and so on.

Note that the ABC interaction is estimated from the comparison

$$abc + a + b + c - ab - ac - bc - (1)$$

which is the same as the difference between blocks 1 and 2. Hence we cannot distinguish between the block effects and the ABC interaction. The ABC interaction is said to be *confounded* with the block effect.

If this experiment were replicated four times, the layout might be as shown in Table 1.26b.

Table 1.26b

Replication 1 Block		Replication 2 Block		Replication 3 Block		Replication 4 Block	
1	**2**	**1**	**2**	**1**	**2**	**1**	**2**
abc	ab	abc	(1)	bc	b	c	ab
a	ac	b	bc	ac	a	b	ac
b	bc	a	ac	ab	c	abc	(1)
c	(1)	c	ab	(1)	abc	a	bc

Since the confounded effect (ABC) is the same for all four replications, ABC is *completely* confounded with blocks. The MANOVA specifications needed for this example are

```
MANOVA          Y BY REPLIC(1,4), BLOCK(1,2), A, B, C(1,2)/
                DESIGN=REPLIC,BLOCK W REPLIC, A, B, C, A BY B, A BY C, B BY C/
```

Note that the model does not include A BY B BY C, which is confounded with BLOCK W REPLIC.

It is possible to test the ABC interaction if some interaction other than ABC is confounded in some of the replications. One possible layout would be that given in Table 1.26c.

Table 1.26c

Replication 1 Block		Replication 2 Block		Replication 3 Block		Replication 4 Block	
1	2	1	2	1	2	1	2
abc	ab	b	ab	ac	ab	ac	a
a	ac	a	c	(1)	bc	ab	bc
b	bc	ac	(1)	abc	a	b	abc
c	(1)	bc	abc	b	c	c	(1)

In replication 1, ABC is confounded with blocks. In replication 2, the AB interaction is confounded with blocks. For replications 3 and 4, AC and BC are confounded.

For this example, A, B, and C are free of the block effects and three-fourths information for AB, AC, BC, and ABC can be obtained, since the unconfounded interactions can be estimated in three out of four of the replications. Hence we say AB, AC, BC, and ABC are *partially* confounded with blocks. The MANOVA specifications for this $2 \times 2 \times 2$ factorial with partial confounding are

```
MANOVA          Y BY REPLIC(1,4), BLOCK(1,2),A, B, C(1,2)/
                DESIGN=REPLIC,BLOCK W REPLIC, A, B, C, A BY B, A BY C,
                   B BY C, A BY B BY C/
```

More complex confounding designs can be found in Davies (1954) and Cochran and Cox (1957).

Another Example   The following example is taken from Cochran and Cox (1957, p. 205). The data are a $3 \times 3 \times 2$ factorial in blocks of six units with three blocks in each of four replications. Interactions AB and ABC are partially confounded with blocks. The SPSS commands for this analysis are given in Figure 1.26a.

Figure 1.26a

```
RUN NAME        CONFOUNDING IN MIXED SERIES.
COMMENT         CONFOUNDING IN MIXED SERIES. 3*3*2 FACTORIAL
COMMENT         FROM COCHRAN AND COX(1957)  P. 205
COMMENT         SECOND ANALYSIS GIVES AB TWO-WAY TABLE ADJUSTED FOR BLOCK
COMMENT         THIRD ANALYSIS GIVES AC TWO-WAY TABLE ADJUSTED FOR BLOCKS
COMMENT
COMMENT         FACTOR A : 8-8-6 FERTILIZER APPLIED IN THE ROW,
COMMENT                      3 LEVELS -- 0 (NONE), 1 (200 LB.), 2 (400 LB.)
COMMENT         FACTOR B : MEALS, 3 LEVELS -- 0 (NONE), 1 (TUNG MEAL),
COMMENT                                       2 (COTTONSEED MEAL).
COMMENT         FACTOR C : 8-8-6 FERTILIZER APPLIED AS SIDE-DRESSING,
COMMENT                      2 LEVELS -- 0 (NONE), 1 (200 LB.).
VARIABLE LIST   REPLICS,BLOCKS,A,B,C,DEP
INPUT MEDIUM    CARD
INPUT FORMAT    FIXED(2X,5F1.0,8X,F3.0)
N OF CASES      72
MANOVA          DEP BY REPLICS(1,4),BLOCKS(1,3),A(0,2),B(0,2),C(0,1)/
                DESIGN = REPLICS,BLOCKS WITHIN REPLICS,A,B,C,
                      A BY B,A BY C, B BY C, A BY B BY C/
                DESIGN = REPLICS,BLOCKS W REPLICS,CONSPLUS A AND B/
                DESIGN = REPLICS,BLOCKS W REPLICS,CONSPLUS A AND C/
READ INPUT DATA
      11011     82
      11020     70
      11100     80
      11121     86
      11201     74
      11210     86
      12001     67
      12010     55
      ....       .
      ....       .
      ....       .
      42210     66
      43001     90
      43010     58
      43100     81
      43121     67
      43211     68
      43220     56
FINISH
```

The first DESIGN specification requests an analysis of variance for this experiment (Figure 1.26b).

Figure 1.26b

TESTS OF SIGNIFICANCE FOR DEP USING SEQUENTIAL SUMS OF SQUARES

SOURCE OF VARIATION	SUM OF SQUARES	DF	MEAN SQUARE	F	SIG. OF F
RESIDUAL	8909.36190	43	207.19446		
CONSTANT	461120.05556	1	461120.05556	2225.54237	0.0
REPLICS	3836.61111	3	1278.87037	6.17232	.001
BLOCKS WITHIN REPLICS	2836.33333	8	354.54167	1.71115	.123
A	1116.02778	2	558.01389	2.69319	.079
B	253.69444	2	126.84722	.61221	.547
C	868.05556	1	868.05556	4.18957	.047
A BY B	1129.34921	4	282.33730	1.36267	.263
A BY C	2995.02778	2	1497.51389	7.22758	.002
B BY C	423.52778	2	211.76389	1.02205	.368
A BY B BY C	1015.95556	4	253.98889	1.22585	.314

The second and third analyses give the AB and AC two-way means adjusted for the block effects (Figure 1.26c). For more information about the use of CONSPLUS to obtain marginal means and summary tables, see Section 1.50.

Figure 1.26c

CONSPLUS A AND B

PARAMETER	COEFF.	STD. ERR.	T-VALUE	SIG. OF T	LOWER .95 CL	UPPER .95 CL
12	72.1964285714	6.02764	11.97757	0.0	60.10109	84.29176
13	73.2261904762	6.02764	12.14841	0.0	61.13086	85.32152
14	79.7023809524	6.02764	13.22283	0.0	67.60705	91.79771
15	86.7738095238	6.02764	14.39600	0.0	74.67848	98.86914
16	87.8035714286	6.02764	14.56684	0.0	75.70824	99.89891
17	79.4226190476	6.02764	13.17641	0.0	67.32729	91.51795
18	89.0297619048	6.02764	14.77026	0.0	76.93443	101.12510
19	74.3452380952	6.02764	12.33406	0.0	62.24990	86.44057
20	77.7500000000	6.02764	12.89892	0.0	65.65467	89.84533

CONSPLUS A AND C

PARAMETER	COEFF.	STD. ERR.	T-VALUE	SIG. OF T	LOWER .95 CL	UPPER .95 CL
12	62.5833333333	4.21611	14.84385	0.0	54.13406	71.03261
13	87.5000000000	4.21611	20.75372	0.0	79.05073	95.94927
14	84.3333333333	4.21611	20.00264	0.0	75.88406	92.78261
15	85.0000000000	4.21611	20.16076	0.0	76.55073	93.44927
16	82.7500000000	4.21611	19.62709	0.0	74.30073	91.19927
17	78.0000000000	4.21611	18.50046	0.0	69.55073	86.44927

1.27 Split-plot Designs

In many factorial designs, it may not be possible to completely randomize the assignment of treatments to the experimental unit. Consider, for example, an experiment to compare three varieties of wheat (factor A) and two different types of fertilizer (factor B). Three locations are selected as blocks. Three levels of A are randomly assigned to plots of equal area within each block. After A is assigned, each plot is "split" into halves (called subplots) to receive the random assignment of B. What is the difference between a complete 3×2 factorial and the 3×2 split-plot design? In a 3×2 factorial, each block is divided into six subplots to receive the random assignment of treatment combinations of A and B. In the split-plot design, two treatment combinations that have the same level of A are always in the same plot. If the subplot is considered the experimental unit, the plot is a "small" block of size 2. The differences among these "small" blocks are the differences between levels of A, since the main effects of A are confounded. A split-plot design is a design in which certain main effects are confounded.

Intuitively, the variation of plots within A should be used as the error term to test for the main effects of A. The effects of plot within A can be partitioned into two parts. One is the block effects and another is the block and A interaction. Thus the model for a split-plot design is

$$Y_{ijk} = \mu + \alpha_i + \beta_k + (\alpha\beta)_{ik} + \gamma_j + (\alpha\gamma)_{ij} + \epsilon_{ijk}$$

where α_i is the A effect, β_k is the block effect, $(\alpha\beta)_{ik}$ is the interaction of A and block and is the error term for testing A, γ_j is the B effect, $(\alpha\gamma)_{ij}$ is the AB interaction, and ϵ_{ijk} is the residual used as the error term for testing B and AB.

Another model is

$$Y_{ijk} = \mu + \alpha_i + \beta_k + (\alpha\beta)_{ik} + \gamma_j + (\alpha\gamma)_{ij} + (\beta\gamma)_{jk} + (\alpha\beta\gamma)_{ijk} + \epsilon_{ijk}$$

$(\beta\gamma)_{jk}$ is the error term for γ_j, $(\alpha\beta\gamma)_{ijk}$ is the error term for $(\alpha\gamma)_{ij}$, and if the number of observations per cell is greater than 1, then $(\alpha\beta)_{ik}$, $(\beta\gamma)_{jk}$ and $(\alpha\beta\gamma)_{ijk}$ can be tested against the within-cells error.

The following MANOVA specifications may be used to perform an analysis of variance of a 3 × 2 split-plot design:

```
MANOVA          Y BY BLOCK(1,3), A(1,3), B(1,2)/
                DESIGN=BLOCK, A VS 1, A BY BLOCK=1, B, A BY B/
```

In the above DESIGN specification, effect A is tested against the error 1 term which is the interaction of A and BLOCK. Effects B and AB are tested against the residual, since there is no within-cells error in this example.

This type of design can be extended by subdividing each subplot into sub-subplots, etc. The model for a split-split-plot design would be

$$Y_{ijkl} = \mu + \alpha_i + \beta_l + (\alpha\beta)_{il} + \gamma_j + (\alpha\gamma)_{ij} + \pi_{ijl} + \delta_k + (\alpha\delta)_{ik} + (\gamma\delta)_{jk} + (\alpha\gamma\delta)_{ijk} + \epsilon_{ijkl}$$

where δ_k is the effect for the sub-subplot factor, π_{ijl} = subplot residual = $(\gamma\beta)_{jl} + (\alpha\gamma\beta)_{ijl}$, ϵ_{ijkl} is the residual, and $(\alpha\beta)_{il}$, π_{ijl}, and ϵ_{ijkl} are the appropriate error terms for plot, subplot, and sub-subplot factors, respectively.

An example of a split-split-plot design is taken from Hicks (1973, p. 223). The SPSS commands are given in Figure 1.27a.

Figure 1.27a

```
RUN NAME        SPLIT-SPLIT-PLOT DESIGN.
COMMENT         DATA ARE TAKEN FROM HICKS(1973) PAGE 223.
COMMENT         LAB : THREE DIFFERENT LABORATORIES--PLOT FACTOR.
COMMENT         TEM : THREE LEVELS OF TEMPERATURE--SUB-PLOT FACTOR.
COMMENT         MIX : THREE TYPES OF MIX--SUB-SUB-PLOT FACTOR.
COMMENT         FOUR REPLICATES (BLOCK).
VARIABLE LIST   BLOCK LAB TEM MIX RESP
N OF CASES      UNKNOWN
INPUT FORMAT    FIXED(4F1.0,1X,F4.1)
INPUT MEDIUM    CARD
MANOVA          RESP BY BLOCK(1,4),LAB,TEM,MIX(1,3)/
                DESIGN=BLOCK,LAB VS 1,LAB BY BLOCK=1,
                       TEM VS 2,LAB BY TEM VS 2,TEM BY BLOCK+
                       LAB BY TEM BY BLOCK=2,
                       MIX,LAB BY MIX,TEM BY MIX,LAB BY TEM BY MIX/
READ INPUT DATA
1111 18.6
1112 14.5
1113 21.1
1121  9.5
1122  7.8
1123 11.2
1131  5.4
1132  5.2
1133  6.3
1211 20.0
1212 18.4
1213 22.5
     .
     .
     .
4321  9.5
4322  9.0
4323 11.4
4331  4.8
4332  5.4
4333  5.8
END INPUT DATA
FINISH
```

As can be seen from the DESIGN specification, the interaction of LAB and BLOCK is the error term for the plot factor LAB, the interaction of TEM and BLOCK and the interaction of LAB, TEM, and BLOCK are pooled together as the error term for the subplot factors. The sub-subplot factors are to be tested against the residual. The analysis of variance from the output for this run is shown in Figure 1.27b.

Figure 1.27b

```
TESTS OF SIGNIFICANCE FOR RESP USING SEQUENTIAL SUMS OF SQUARES

SOURCE OF VARIATION             SUM OF SQUARES      DF    MEAN SQUARE            F    SIG. OF F

RESIDUAL                             13.40499       54        .24824
CONSTANT                          14697.66168        1   14697.66168   59207.32736         0.0
BLOCK                                 9.41435        3       3.13812      12.64143         0.0
MIX                                 145.71785        2      72.85893     293.50127         0.0
LAB BY MIX                             .33926        4        .08482        .34167        .849
TEM BY MIX                           43.68696        4      10.92174      43.99659         0.0
LAB BY TEM BY MIX                     1.07740        8        .13467        .54252        .819

ERROR 1                              16.10982        6       2.68497
LAB                                  40.66356        2      20.33178       7.57244        .023

ERROR 2                               9.88335       18        .54907
TEM                                3119.50650        2    1559.75325    2840.69330         0.0
LAB BY TEM                            4.93650        4       1.23412       2.24764        .104
```

1.28 Analysis of Carry-over Effects

If different treatments are applied in sequence to the same unit, residual or carry-over effects may be present in the experiment. By including dummy factors, MANOVA enables the user to perform an analysis of variance with residual effects.

The following example is taken from Cochran and Cox (1957, p. 133). The experiment compares three feeding methods (A, B, and C) on the milk yield of dairy cows. The experiment consists of two 3×3 Latin squares. The rows of the squares represent the successive periods of application, while the columns represent the cows. The data are as follows:

	Square 1			Square 2		
	Cow 1	Cow 2	Cow 3	Cow 4	Cow 5	Cow 6
Period 1	A(38)	B(109)	C(124)	A(86)	B(75)	C(101)
Period 2	B(25)	C(86)	A(72)	C(76)	A(35)	B(63)
Period 3	C(15)	A(39)	B(27)	B(46)	C(34)	A(1)

In addition to the direct (treatment) effects τ_a, τ_b and τ_c, the treatments also contain the residual effects r_a, r_b, and r_c for the period immediately following the one in which they are applied. Thus for cow 2 in the third period, the expected total treatment effect is $\tau_a + r_c$, since A is applied in this period and C in the preceding period. Similarly, the expected total treatment effect is $\tau_a + r_b$ for cow 2 in the second period.

If we let CEFFECT be the (dummy) factor of residual effects and assign

CEFFECT = 1 if no residual effects
2 if r_a is the residual effect
3 if r_b is the residual effect
4 if r_c is the residual effect

then the values of CEFFECT in this example would be

	Square 1			Square 2		
	Cow 1	Cow 2	Cow 3	Cow 4	Cow 5	Cow 6
Period 1	1	1	1	1	1	1
Period 2	2	3	4	2	3	4
Period 3	3	4	2	4	2	3

If the effects of CEFFECT are divided into groups using the following contrasts:

(1   1   1   1)
(3 −1 −1 −1)
(0   2 −1 −1)
(0   0   1 −1)

and the pooled effect of second and third contrasts is CEFFECT(2), then CEFFECT(2) can be used to obtain a test of $r_a = r_b = r_c$. Since the second contrast (0, 2, -1, -1) specifies a test on $r_a = (r_b + r_c)/2$, and the third contrast (0, 0, 1, -1) a test of $r_b = r_c$, jointly they test the hypothesis $r_a = r_b = r_c$.

The above can be done by using the following MANOVA specifications.

```
CONTRAST(CEFFECT)=SPECIAL(1 1 1 1, 3 −1 −1 −1,
                  0 2 −1 −1,0 0 1 −1)/
PARTITION (CEFFECT)=(1,2)/
```

The CONTRAST subcommand indicates the contrast coefficients for factor CEFFECT. The PARTITION subcommand divides the CEFFECT factor into 2 groups for the contrasts. The first group has one degree of freedom with the contrast (3, -1, -1, -1). The second group (CEFFECT(2)) corresponds to the second and third contrasts lumped together and has two degrees of freedom.
The complete MANOVA command file is given in Figure 1.28a.

Figure 1.28a

```
RUN NAME        ANALYSIS OF VARIANCE WITH CARRY-OVER EFFECTS.
COMMENT         DATA IS TAKEN FROM COCHRAN AND COX(1957) PAGE 135.
                CEFFECT REPRESENTS THE CARRY-OVER EFFECTS.
                    CEFFECT=1 IF NO RESIDUAL EFFECTS.
                          2 IF RESIDUAL EFFECT A.
                          3 IF RESIDUAL EFFECT B.
                          4 IF RESIDUAL EFFECT C.
VARIABLE LIST   PERIOD,COW,SQUARE,TREATMNT,CEFFECT,DEP
INPUT MEDIUM    CARD
INPUT FORMAT    FIXED(2X,5F1.0,F10.0)
N OF CASES      18
MANOVA          DEP BY PERIOD(1,3),COW(1,6),SQUARE(1,2),
                    TREATMNT(1,3), CEFFECT(1,4)/

                CONTRAST(CEFFECT) = SPECIAL(1 1 1 1, 3 -1 -1 -1,
                                            0 2 -1 -1, 0 0 1 -1  )/

                PARTITION(CEFFECT) = (1,2)/

                DESIGN = COW, PERIOD WITHIN SQUARE,
                        CEFFECT(2), TREATMNT/
                DESIGN = COW, PERIOD WITHIN SQUARE,
                        TREATMNT, CEFFECT(2)/
READ INPUT DATA
   11111    38.
   12121   109.
   13131   124.
   14211    86.
   15221    75.
   16231   101.
   21122    25.
   22133    86.
   23114    72.
   24232    76.
   25213    35.
   26224    63.
   31133    15.
   32114    39.
   33122    27.
   34224    46.
   35232    34.
   36213     1.
FINISH
```

In the first DESIGN specification, treatment effects are adjusted for the residual effects, and the converse holds in the second DESIGN specification. The ANOVA summary tables for both models are given in Figure 1.28b.

Figure 1.28b

TESTS OF SIGNIFICANCE FOR DEP USING SEQUENTIAL SUMS OF SQUARES

SOURCE OF VARIATION	SUM OF SQUARES	DF	MEAN SQUARE	F	SIG. OF F
RESIDUAL	199.25000	4	49.81250		
CONSTANT	61483.55556	1	61483.55556	1234.29974	0.0
COW	5781.11111	5	1156.22222	23.21149	.005
PERIOD WITHIN SQUARE	11489.11111	4	2872.27778	57.66179	.001
CEFFECT(2)	38.42222	2	19.21111	.38567	.703
TREATMNT	2854.55000	2	1427.27500	28.65295	.004

TESTS OF SIGNIFICANCE FOR DEP USING SEQUENTIAL SUMS OF SQUARES

SOURCE OF VARIATION	SUM OF SQUARES	DF	MEAN SQUARE	F	SIG. OF F
RESIDUAL	199.25000	4	49.81250		
CONSTANT	61483.55556	1	61483.55556	1234.29974	0.0
COW	5781.11111	5	1156.22222	23.21149	.005
PERIOD WITHIN SQUARE	11489.11111	4	2872.27778	57.66179	.001
TREATMNT	2276.77778	2	1138.38889	22.85348	.006
CEFFECT(2)	616.19444	2	308.09722	6.18514	.060

Note that in this example, the number of observations receiving r_a, r_b, and r_c are equal (4). If the design is not balanced with respect to residual effects, contrast coefficients for unequal numbers of replicates must be used to create the desired residual effects.

1.29 Tukey's Test for Nonadditivity

In factorial designs with only one observation per cell there is no within-cell error and thus no direct estimate of the experimental error. Frequently, the highest-order interaction is assumed to be part of the experimental error and its mean square is used to provide a denominator for F tests on the remaining model terms. One method of checking the tenability of this no-interaction assumption is provided by Tukey's test for nonadditivity (Tukey(1949)).

SPSS-MANOVA can perform Tukey's test by using the fact that Tukey's sum of squares for nonadditivity is the linear × linear component of interaction in the metric of the estimates of the main effects (see Winer(1971) page 395). Tukey's test requires two separate runs:

1 The first run obtains main effect parameter estimates using an additive main effects model.

2 The second run uses the parameter estimates from the first run as the metric in polynomial contrasts for the factors; the design specifies a linear × linear single-degree-of-freedom interaction term which actually provides the sum of squares for Tukey's test.

To illustrate this procedure consider the data in Table 1.29 taken from Winer(1971), page 474. These data comprise a 3 × 4 factorial with one observation per cell.

Table 1.29

		B			
		1	2	3	4
	1	8	12	16	20
A	2	2	2	14	18
	3	5	4	9	22

First, estimates of main effects are computed by using the following MANOVA specifications.

```
MANOVA          Y BY A(1,3) B(1,4)/
                PRINT=PARAMETERS(NEGSUM)/
                DESIGN= A, B/
```

The PRINT=PARAMETERS(NEGSUM) results in the printing of the estimate of the last main effect as the negative sum of the previous estimates. The default deviation contrast must be used to get these estimates. Figure 1.29a displays the estimates.

Figure 1.29a

```
ESTIMATES FOR Y

CONSTANT

PARAMETER         COEFF.        STD. ERR.       T-VALUE       SIG. OF T     LOWER .95 CL     UPPER .95 CL

     1        11.0000000000       .84984        12.94366         .000         8.92054         13.07946

A

PARAMETER         COEFF.        STD. ERR.       T-VALUE       SIG. OF T     LOWER .95 CL     UPPER .95 CL

     2         3.0000000000      1.20185         2.49615         .047          .05919          5.94081
     3        -2.0000000000      1.20185        -1.66410         .147        -4.94081           .94081
     4        -1.0000000000         .              .              .              .                .

B

PARAMETER         COEFF.        STD. ERR.       T-VALUE       SIG. OF T     LOWER .95 CL     UPPER .95 CL

     4        -6.0000000000      1.47196        -4.07620         .007        -9.60174        -2.39826
     5        -5.0000000000      1.47196        -3.39683         .015        -8.60174        -1.39826
     6         2.0000000000      1.47196         1.35873         .223        -1.60174         5.60174
     7         9.0000000000         .              .              .              .                .
```

In the second run, orthogonal polynomial contrasts for each factor are requested. The metric for each factor consists of the parameter estimates for that factor's categories produced by the initial run:

```
CONTRAST(A)=POLYNOMIAL(3 -2 -1)/
CONTRAST(B)=POLYNOMIAL(-6 -5 2 9)/
```

Each factor is then partitioned so that the first partition contains the linear component of the orthogonal polynomial contrast:

```
PARTITION(A)/
PARTITION(B)/
```

Lastly, the design specifies a main effects model along with the linear × linear component of the interaction:

```
DESIGN=A, B, A(1) BY B(1)/
```

The resulting ANOVA table appears in Figure 1.29b.

Figure 1.29b

TESTS OF SIGNIFICANCE FOR Y USING SEQUENTIAL SUMS OF SQUARES

SOURCE OF VARIATION	SUM OF SQUARES	DF	MEAN SQUARE	F	SIG. OF F
RESIDUAL	34.33855	5	6.86771		
CONSTANT	1452.00000	1	1452.00000	211.42418	.000
A	56.00000	2	28.00000	4.07705	.089
B	438.00000	3	146.00000	21.25890	.003
A(1) BY B(1)	17.66145	1	17.66145	2.57166	.170

The F test for the A(1) BY B(1) interaction is Tukey's test for nonadditivity.

Note that Tukey's test for nonadditivity can be extended to higher-order factorial experiments.

1.30 Simple Effects

The presence of a significant interaction in a two-way design precludes the testing of the main effects. Instead, the effect of one factor differs at each level of the other factor. Frequently one may wish to test the significance of these differential effects. Such tests are generally called tests of simple effects.

Simple effects can be tested in SPSS-MANOVA by using the nesting facility of the DESIGN subcommand. As an example, consider the data presented in Figure 1.2 for which the ANOVA table appears in Figure 1.3a. Here the interaction is significant at the 0.006 level. Simple effects tests are desired to examine the category differences for each of the drugs. The following DESIGN subcommand accomplishes this:

```
DESIGN=DRUG, CAT WITHIN DRUG(1), CAT WITHIN DRUG(2),
       CAT WITHIN DRUG(3)/
```

Here CAT WITHIN DRUG(1) tests the difference in means between category 1 and category 2 for the first level of drug. Similarly, the two successive effects test for category differences for the second and third drugs, respectively. Note that DRUG appears first in the design. This eliminates any confounding effects of CAT. Figure 1.30a presents the output of this design.

Figure 1.30a

TESTS OF SIGNIFICANCE FOR Y USING SEQUENTIAL SUMS OF SQUARES

SOURCE OF VARIATION	SUM OF SQUARES	DF	MEAN SQUARE	F	SIG. OF F
WITHIN CELLS	106.00000	12	8.83333		
CONSTANT	882.00000	1	882.00000	99.84906	0.0
DRUG	48.00000	2	24.00000	2.71698	.106
CAT WITHIN DRUG(1)	54.00000	1	54.00000	6.11321	.029
CAT WITHIN DRUG(2)	54.00000	1	54.00000	6.11321	.029
CAT WITHIN DRUG(3)	54.00000	1	54.00000	6.11321	.029

The simple effects of the three drugs within each category of patients can be tested in the same manner.

In higher-order designs one may want tests of simple effects for both interactions and main effects. For example, consider a three-way factorial design with factors A, B, and C, each with two levels. Should the three-way interaction appear significant then an examination of the second-order interaction terms at various levels of the third factor would be in order. To accomplish this, the following DESIGN subcommands would be used:

```
DESIGN=A, B, C, A BY B, A BY C, B BY C,
       B BY C WITHIN A(1), B BY C WITHIN A(2)/

DESIGN=A, B, C, A BY B, A BY C, B BY C,
       A BY B WITHIN C(1), A BY B WITHIN C(2)/

DESIGN=A, B, C, A BY B, A BY C, B BY C,
       A BY C WITHIN B(1), A BY C WITHIN B(2)/
```

Test of simple main effects can be requested as well. To test factor A within the B BY C treatment combinations the following DESIGN subcommand is used:

```
DESIGN=B, C, B BY C, A WITHIN B(1) BY C(1),
       A WITHIN B(1) BY C(2), A WITHIN B(2) BY C(1),
       A WITHIN B(2) BY C(2)/
```

It may also be desirable to compare two or more means at particular levels of another factor or treatment combinations. For example, it may be interesting to compare the effectiveness of drug 1 with drug 2 within each patient category. Such comparisons can be performed by extending the methods used for ordinary simple effects. The procedure is as follows:

1 Define a contrast incorporating the comparisons of interest such as

```
CONTRAST(DRUG)=SPECIAL(1 1 1 -1 0 2 -1 -1)/
```

2 Partition the factor into the desired components by specifying

```
PARTITION(DRUG)/
```

In subsequent designs, DRUG(1) will refer to the drug 1 versus drug 2 comparison. DRUG(2) will refer to the drug 1 versus drugs 2 and 3 combined comparison.

3 Request regression-approach sums of squares by using

```
METHOD=SSTYPE(UNIQUE)/
```

This is mandatory even for orthogonal designs, because DRUG(1) and DRUG(2) are not independent.

4 Specify the designs as for ordinary simple effects, but expand the simple effects terms according to the CONTRAST/PARTITION specification:

```
DESIGN=CAT, DRUG(1) WITHIN CAT(1),
            DRUG(1) WITHIN CAT(2),
            DRUG(2) WITHIN CAT(1),
            DRUG(2) WITHIN CAT(2)/
```

Figure 1.30b presents the output for this design.

Figure 1.30b

```
TESTS OF SIGNIFICANCE FOR Y USING UNIQUE SUMS OF SQUARES
```

SOURCE OF VARIATION	SUM OF SQUARES	DF	MEAN SQUARE	F	SIG. OF F
WITHIN CELLS	106.00000	12	8.83333		
CONSTANT	882.00000	1	882.00000	99.84906	0.0
CAT	18.00000	1	18.00000	2.03774	.179
DRUG(1) WITHIN CAT(1)	24.00000	1	24.00000	2.71698	.125
DRUG(2) WITHIN CAT(2)	18.00000	1	18.00000	2.03774	.179
DRUG(1) WITHIN CAT(2)	96.00000	1	96.00000	10.86792	.006
DRUG(2) WITHIN CAT(1)	18.00000	1	18.00000	2.03774	.179

1.31 MULTIVARIATE TESTS OF SIGNIFICANCE

1.32 Standard MANOVA Output

In the univariate F test, the F value is a function of the ratio (SSH)/(SSE), where SSH is the sum of squares due to the hypothesis and SSE the sum of squares due to error. Significance tests in multivariate analysis of variance models are based on functions of the eigenvalues of the matrix $S_h S_e^{-1}$, where S_h is the matrix of the sums of squares and cross products (SSCP) for the hypothesis and S_e is the SSCP matrix for the error. The MANOVA procedure computes four statistics used for significance tests: Roy's largest root, Wilks' lambda, Hotelling's trace, and Pillai's criterion. (All of these are functions of the eigenvalues.)

The MANOVA commands for the multivariate analysis are exactly the same as in the univariate case, except that two or more response variables are specified instead of one. Figure 1.32a, given below, illustrates the use of MANOVA to analyze the dental calculus reduction data in Finn (1974). The response variables in this example are RCAN, RLI, and RCI.

Figure 1.32a

```
RUN NAME        DENTAL CALULUS DATA FROM FINN(1974) PAGE C-56
FILE NAME       DATA FOR ANTI-CALCULUS AGENT
VARIABLE LIST   YEAR,TR,RCAN,RLI,RCI,LCI,LLI,LCAN
INPUT FORMAT    FIXED(2F1.0,6F2.0)
N OF CASES      107
MISSING VALUES  YEAR TO LCAN(BLANK)
MANOVA          RCAN,RLI,RCI BY YEAR(1,2),TR(1,5)/
READ INPUT DATA
11 2 2 1 2 2 1
11 0 0 0 2 1 0
11 0 0 4 4 0 0
11 2 2 2 3 2 2
 . . . . . . .
 . . . . . . .
23 0 1 3 4 3 0
23 1 0 1 0 1 0
23 0 1 0 0 0 0
23 0 1 6 4 1 0
FINISH
```

Since no DESIGN specifications are given in Figure 1.32a, a full factorial model is assumed. The standard output (without the PRINT subcommand) includes

1 General information about the design. This includes the number of observations, the number of levels of each effect, and the redundant effects (if any) in the model. This output is given in Figure 1.32b for the dental calculus data. (Three degrees of freedom are lost in the interaction effect because of empty cells.)

Figure 1.32b

```
107 CASES ACCEPTED.
  0 CASES REJECTED BECAUSE OF OUT-OF-RANGE FACTOR VALUES.
  0 CASES REJECTED BECAUSE OF MISSING DATA.
  7 NON-EMPTY CELLS.
- - - - - - - - - - - - - - - - - - - - - - - - - - - - - - - - - - - -
CORRESPONDENCE BETWEEN EFFECTS AND COLUMNS OF BETWEEN-SUBJECTS DESIGN

STARTING  ENDING
COLUMN    COLUMN   EFFECT NAME

   1        1      CONSTANT
   2        2      YEAR
   3        6      TR
   7       10      YEAR BY TR
- - - - - - - - - - - - - - - - - - - - - - - - - - - - - - - - - - - -
REDUNDANCIES IN DESIGN MATRIX

   COLUMN    EFFECT

      8      YEAR BY TR
      9      (SAME)
     10      (SAME)
```

2 Multivariate tests of the significance of each effect in the model. The four test statistics previously mentioned are given. Each of these statistics is a function of the nonzero eigenvalues λ_i of the matrix $S_hS_e^{-1}$. The number of nonzero eigenvalues, s, is equal to the minimum of the number of dependent variables, q, and the degrees of freedom for the tested effect, n_h. The distributions of these statistics, under the null hypothesis, depend on q, n_h, and n_e (the error degrees of freedom).

Pillai's criterion. This test statistic, sum of $\lambda_i/(1+\lambda_i)$, can be approximated by an F variate (see Pillai, 1960). (The degrees of freedom are a function of q, n_h, and n_e.)

Hotelling's trace. This is the statistic T = sum of λ_i, which is equal to the trace of $S_hS_e^{-1}$. The critical points of the distribution of T have been tabulated by Pillai (1960) and depend on S = min(p,q), M = $(|n_h - q| - 1)/2$, and N = $(n_e - q - 1)/2$. (The values of S, M, and N for each effect are printed by MANOVA.) MANOVA also gives an approximate F statistic based on T, where the degrees of freedom depend on q, n_h and n_e.

Wilks' lambda. This test statistic, product of $1/(1+\lambda_i)$, can be transformed, using Rao's formula (Rao, 1973), into an approximate F statistic with degrees of freedom determined by q, n_h, and n_e.

Roy's largest root criterion. Upper percentage points of the distribution of this test statistic, $\lambda_l/(1+\lambda_l)$, where λ_l is the largest eigenvalue of $S_hS_e^{-1}$, can be found in Heck (1960), Pillai (1967), and Morrison (1976). This distribution, like that of Hotelling's trace, depends on S, M, and N.

For the dental calculus data, the multivariate tests of the hypothesis that there is no TR effect (adjusted for the YEAR effect) are presented in Figure 1.32c.

Figure 1.32c

```
EFFECT .. TR

MULTIVARIATE TESTS OF SIGNIFICANCE (S = 3, M = 0, N = 48)

TEST NAME          VALUE        APPROX. F      HYPOTH. DF      ERROR DF      SIG. OF F

PILLAIS           .20122        1.79739          12.00         300.00          .048
HOTELLINGS        .22813        1.83769          12.00         290.00          .042
WILKS             .80733        1.82255          12.00         259.58          .045
ROYS              .14402
```

The name of the test statistic is given under TEST NAME and its value listed under VALUE. For Pillai's criterion, Hotelling's trace, and Wilks lambda, approximate F statistics are given, with the degrees of freedom under HYPOTH. DF and ERROR DF and the p-values under SIG. OF F. A comparison (with references) of the powers of these four tests can be found in Morrison (1976).

3 Eigenvalues and canonical correlations. The nonzero eigenvalues of $S_h S_e^{-1}$ and the corresponding canonical correlations for each effect in the model are given. For example, the results for the effect TR are shown in Figure 1.32d.

Figure 1.32d

```
EIGENVALUES AND CANONICAL CORRELATIONS

ROOT NO.      EIGENVALUE          PCT.        CUM. PCT.      CANON. COR.

   1            .16825         73.75366       73.75366        .37950
   2            .05253         23.02709       96.78075        .22340
   3            .00734          3.21925      100.00000        .08538
```

The canonical correlation coefficients ρ_i are calculated as $\rho_i^2 = \lambda_i/(1 + \lambda_i)$; they are the canonical correlations between the response variables and the effect. ρ_i also measures the correlation between the ith canonical variate of the response variables and the tested effect (in certain linear combinations). The canonical correlations in this example can also be obtained by using the following dummy variables to represent the YEAR and TR effects.

X_1 = 1 if YEAR = 2
    0 otherwise

Y_1 = 1 if TR = 2
    0 otherwise

.
.

Y_4 = 1 if TR = 5
    0 otherwise

If X_1 is already in the regression equation (since TR is adjusted for YEAR) and the within-cells SSCP matrix is used as the error matrix, then the ρ_i's above are the canonical correlations between RCAN, RLI and RCI, and Y_1, Y_2, Y_3, and Y_4.

4 Dimension reduction analysis. Dimension reduction analysis, based on Wilks' lambda, is used to assess the dimensionality of a significant relationship between the response variables and the tested effect. The first test is based on all the eigenvalues and is equivalent to the overall Wilks' lambda test; the second test is performed on all the eigenvalues except the largest, and so on. Hence the value of Wilks' lambda for testing roots n_1 to n_2 is found by calculating the product from $i = n_1$ to $i = n_2$ of $1/(1+\lambda_i)$.

MANOVA also prints the approximate F statistic for each of these Wilks' lambda statistics. For the effect TR, the output in Figure 1.32e is obtained.

Figure 1.32e

```
DIMENSION REDUCTION ANALYSIS

ROOTS          WILKS LAMBDA             F        HYPOTH. DF      ERROR DF       SIG. OF F

1 TO 3            .80733          1.82255        12.00          259.58          .045
2 TO 3            .94316           .97402         6.00          240.16          .443
3 TO 3            .99271           .36286         2.00          198.00          .696
```

Dimension reduction analysis can be interpreted as follows: If the roots from n_o to s are not significant (in other words, if the s - n_o + 1 smallest canonical correlations are not significantly different from zero), we may say that the data do not provide evidence of association in more than n_o − 1 dimensions (only n_o − 1 discriminant functions are significant). In the dental calculus example, only one canonical correlation is significant at the 0.05 level for the TR effect.

5 Univariate analysis of variance results for each of the q response variables. In our example, Figure 1.32f gives the results obtained for the effect TR.

Figure 1.32f

UNIVARIATE F-TESTS WITH (4,100) D. F.

VARIABLE	HYPOTH. SS	ERROR SS	HYPOTH. MS	ERROR MS	F	SIG. OF F
RCAN	6.18306	137.89515	1.54577	1.37895	1.12097	.351
RLI	28.07315	261.87433	7.01829	2.61874	2.68002	.036
RCI	69.55358	423.98046	17.38839	4.23980	4.10123	.004

The sum of squares for the tested effect (HYPOTH. SS) and for the error (ERROR SS) of each response variable are the appropriate diagonal elements of S_h and S_e respectively.
Output for the YEAR effect and the YEAR BY TR interaction is given in Figure 1.32g.

Figure 1.32g

EFFECT .. YEAR BY TR
MULTIVARIATE TESTS OF SIGNIFICANCE (S = 1, M = 1/2, N = 48)

TEST NAME	VALUE	APPROX. F	HYPOTH. DF	ERROR DF	SIG. OF F
PILLAIS	.02445	.81881	3.00	98.00	.487
HOTELLINGS	.02507	.81881	3.00	98.00	.487
WILKS	.97555	.81881	3.00	98.00	.487
ROYS	.02445				

- -

EIGENVALUES AND CANONICAL CORRELATIONS

ROOT NO.	EIGENVALUE	PCT.	CUM. PCT.	CANON. COR.
1	.02507	100.00000	100.00000	.15637

- -

DIMENSION REDUCTION ANALYSIS

ROOTS	WILKS LAMBDA	F	HYPOTH. DF	ERROR DF	SIG. OF F
1 TO 1	.97555	.81881	3.00	98.00	.487

- -

UNIVARIATE F-TESTS WITH (1,100) D. F.

VARIABLE	HYPOTH. SS	ERROR SS	HYPOTH. MS	ERROR MS	F	SIG. OF F
RCAN	.09862	137.89515	.09862	1.37895	.07152	.790
RLI	1.08877	261.87433	1.08877	2.61874	.41576	.521
RCI	9.73563	423.98046	9.73563	4.23980	2.29625	.133

- -

EFFECT .. YEAR

MULTIVARIATE TESTS OF SIGNIFICANCE (S = 1, M = 1/2, N = 48)

TEST NAME	VALUE	APPROX. F	HYPOTH. DF	ERROR DF	SIG. OF F
PILLAIS	.04077	1.38843	3.00	98.00	.251
HOTELLINGS	.04250	1.38843	3.00	98.00	.251
WILKS	.95923	1.38843	3.00	98.00	.251
ROYS	.04077				

- -

EIGENVALUES AND CANONICAL CORRELATIONS

ROOT NO.	EIGENVALUE	PCT.	CUM. PCT.	CANON. COR.
1	.04250	100.00000	100.00000	.20192

- -

DIMENSION REDUCTION ANALYSIS

ROOTS	WILKS LAMBDA	F	HYPOTH. DF	ERROR DF	SIG. OF F
1 TO 1	.95923	1.38843	3.00	98.00	.251

- -

UNIVARIATE F-TESTS WITH (1,100) D. F.

VARIABLE	HYPOTH. SS	ERROR SS	HYPOTH. MS	ERROR MS	F	SIG. OF F
RCAN	3.54279	137.89515	3.54279	1.37895	2.56919	.112
RLI	6.83291	261.87433	6.83291	2.61874	2.60923	.109
RCI	12.97332	423.98046	12.97332	4.23980	3.05989	.083

Remember, the (default) sequential approach is used to obtain the S_h matrix for each effect. Thus YEAR BY TR is adjusted for TR and YEAR, and TR is adjusted for YEAR.

6 Parameter estimates and related statistics for each response variable. These consist of the standard errors of the parameter estimates, t-values and their significance levels (two-tailed), and 95% confidence intervals for the parameters. The parameters estimated depend on the contrasts chosen for the reparameterization. The output shown in Figure 1.32h describes the parameters for the dental calculus example.

Figure 1.32h

```
ESTIMATES FOR RCAN

CONSTANT

    PARAMETER         COEFF.        STD. ERR.       T-VALUE       SIG. OF T      LOWER .95 CL      UPPER .95 CL

        1           .7455586081       .15426        4.83313         .000           .43951           1.05161

YEAR

    PARAMETER         COEFF.        STD. ERR.       T-VALUE       SIG. OF T      LOWER .95 CL      UPPER .95 CL

        2          -.0565476190       .25221        -.22420         .823          -.55693            .44384

TR
    PARAMETER         COEFF.        STD. ERR.       T-VALUE       SIG. OF T      LOWER .95 CL      UPPER .95 CL

        3          -.0312728938       .26335        -.11875         .906          -.55374            .49120
        4           .6443223443       .43965        1.46553         .146          -.22793           1.51658
        5          -.2604395604       .24892       -1.04626         .298          -.75430            .23342
        6           .3109890110       .51656         .60204         .549          -.71386           1.33583

YEAR BY TR

    PARAMETER         COEFF.        STD. ERR.       T-VALUE       SIG. OF T      LOWER .95 CL      UPPER .95 CL

        7           .0922619048       .34499         .26744         .790          -.59218            .77671
        8           0.0              .              .               .              .                 .
        9           0.0              .              .               .              .                 .
       10           0.0              .              .               .              .                 .

- - - - - - - - - - - - - - - - - - - - - - - - - - - - - - - - - - - - - - - - - - - - - - - - - - - - - - - -

ESTIMATES FOR RLI

CONSTANT

    PARAMETER         COEFF.        STD. ERR.       T-VALUE       SIG. OF T      LOWER .95 CL      UPPER .95 CL

        1          1.0793376068       .21258        5.07729         .000           .65758           1.50109

YEAR

    PARAMETER         COEFF.        STD. ERR.       T-VALUE       SIG. OF T      LOWER .95 CL      UPPER .95 CL

        2           .0327380952       .34757         .09419         .925          -.65683            .72231

TR

    PARAMETER         COEFF.        STD. ERR.       T-VALUE       SIG. OF T      LOWER .95 CL      UPPER .95 CL

        3           .8313766789       .36291        2.29087         .024           .11138           1.55138
        4           .6657020757       .60587        1.09875         .275          -.53633           1.86773
        5          -.2549328449       .34304        -.74317         .459          -.93551            .42564
        6          -.3120757021       .71186        -.43839         .662         -1.72439           1.10023

YEAR BY TR

    PARAMETER         COEFF.        STD. ERR.       T-VALUE       SIG. OF T      LOWER .95 CL      UPPER .95 CL

        7           .3065476190       .47542         .64480         .521          -.63667           1.24976
        8           0.0              .              .               .              .                 .
        9           0.0              .              .               .              .                 .
       10           0.0              .              .               .              .                 .

- - - - - - - - - - - - - - - - - - - - - - - - - - - - - - - - - - - - - - - - - - - - - - - - - - - - - - - -

ESTIMATES FOR RCI

CONSTANT

    PARAMETER         COEFF.        STD. ERR.       T-VALUE       SIG. OF T      LOWER .95 CL      UPPER .95 CL

        1          2.0558302808       .27049        7.60038         0.0          1.51918           2.59248

YEAR

    PARAMETER         COEFF.        STD. ERR.       T-VALUE       SIG. OF T      LOWER .95 CL      UPPER .95 CL

        2          -.3988095238       .44225        -.90177         .369         -1.27622            .47860

TR

    PARAMETER         COEFF.        STD. ERR.       T-VALUE       SIG. OF T      LOWER .95 CL      UPPER .95 CL

        3          1.1763125763       .46177        2.54741         .012           .26018           2.09245
        4          1.4540903541       .77091        1.88619         .062          -.07538           2.98356
        5          -.3713064713       .43648        -.85068         .397         -1.23727            .49466
        6           .3429792430       .90578         .37866         .706         -1.45405           2.14001

YEAR BY TR

    PARAMETER         COEFF.        STD. ERR.       T-VALUE       SIG. OF T      LOWER .95 CL      UPPER .95 CL

        7           .9166666667       .60493        1.51534         .133          -.28349           2.11682
        8           0.0              .              .               .              .                 .
        9           0.0              .              .               .              .                 .
       10           0.0              .              .               .              .                 .
```

1.33 Optional MANOVA Output

Other output related to multivariate significance tests can be obtained by using the PRINT subcommand. Such optional output includes

1 The error matrix. For every error matrix used in the model,

                PRINT=ERROR(SSCP)/

can be used to obtain the error SSCP matrix, S_e. Although only one error matrix, the within-cells error matrix, was used in Figure 1.32a, more than one error matrix is sometimes used (e.g., in multivariate nested designs). The error matrix for Figure 1.32a is given in Figure 1.33a.

Figure 1.33a

```
WITHIN CELLS SUM-OF-SQUARES AND CROSS-PRODUCTS

                    RCAN           RLI           RCI

RCAN            137.89515
RLI             101.90797     261.87433
RCI              81.03938     217.53449     423.98046
```

The error variance-covariance and error correlation matrices can also be obtained, by specifying

                PRINT=ERROR(COV,COR)/

2 The hypothesis SSCP matrix. The matrix S_h for each effect can be obtained by specifying

                PRINT=SIGNIF(HYPOTH)/

This matrix is adjusted for the covariates (if any). The hypothesis SSCP matrix for the TR effect in Figure 1.32a is given in Figure 1.33b.

Figure 1.33b

```
EFFECT .. TR
ADJUSTED HYPOTHESIS SUM-OF-SQUARES AND CROSS-PRODUCTS

                    RCAN           RLI           RCI

RCAN              6.18306
RLI               8.26479      28.07315
RCI              15.81805      41.86935      69.55358
```

3 Roy-Bargmann step-down analysis (Roy and Bargmann, 1958). For each effect, step-down tests (which depend on the ordering of the response variables) can be performed by specifying

                PRINT=SIGNIF(STEPDOWN)/

The number of tests for effects in a step-down analysis is equal to the number of response variables in the model. For the first response variable, the test statistic is the same as the univariate F statistic. The test statistic for the second response variable is identical to the univariate test statistic that would result if the first response variable were treated as a covariate. The test statistic for the third response variable is adjusted for the first two variables, and so on. A significant test statistic for the kth response variable indicates that this variable is important for testing the hypothesis that the effect is zero and cannot be accounted for by a linear combination of the preceding $k-1$ variables. Since testing begins with the last variable and proceeds backwards until a significant result is obtained, the variables assumed to be important in testing an effect should appear early in the step-down ordering. MANOVA uses the ordering of the response variables given in the MANOVA variable list. The step-down analysis for the TR effect in Figure 1.32a is given in Figure 1.33c.

Figure 1.33c

```
ROY-BARGMAN STEPDOWN F - TESTS

VARIABLE    HYPOTH. MS    ERROR MS    STEP-DOWN F    HYPOTH. DF    ERROR DF    SIG. OF F

RCAN           1.54577     1.37895       1.12097          4           100         .351
RLI            4.78488     1.88446       2.53912          4            99         .045
RCI            4.57059     2.48108       1.84218          4            98         .127
```

4 The average F test. If

```
PRINT=SIGNIF(AVERF)/
```

is specified, MANOVA outputs an averaged F test for each tested effect. This is particularly useful for repeated measures designs (see Section 1.44). The sum of squares for the effect and the sum of squares for the error in the averaged F test are obtained by summing over the hypothesis sum of squares and the error sum of squares, respectively, for each variable. The averaged F test for the TR effect in the dental calculus example is given in Figure 1.33d.

Figure 1.33d

```
AVERAGED F-TEST WITH (12,300) D. F.

           HYPOTH. SS      ERROR SS    HYPOTH. MS    ERROR MS        F       SIG. OF F

 (AVER.)   103.80979      823.74994     8.65082      2.74583     3.15052       .000
```

5 A brief table of multivariate significance tests. A summary table, similar to the univariate ANOVA table, (with Wilks' lambda and the corresponding approximate F statistic replacing the univariate F) can be obtained by specifying

```
PRINT=SIGNIF(BRIEF)/
```

Note that the BRIEF specification overrides requests for the standard multivariate significance tests, the hypothesis SSCP matrix, and step-down analysis. The BRIEF output for Figure 1.32a is given in Figure 1.33e.

Figure 1.33e

```
TESTS OF SIGNIFICANCE FOR WITHIN CELLS USING SEQUENTIAL SUMS OF SQUARES

SOURCE OF VARIATION          WILKS LAMBDA  APPROX MULT F   SIG. OF F   AVERAGED F   SIG. OF F

CONSTANT                        .46843       37.07044        0.0       76.86413       0.0
YEAR                            .95923        1.38843        .251       2.83448       .038
TR                              .80733        1.82255        .045       3.15052       .000
YEAR BY TR                      .97555         .81881        .487       1.32601       .266
```

1.34 Principal Components Analysis

Principal components analysis (which is performed on each error matrix used in the model) can be requested via the PRINT subcommand. If

```
PRINT=PRINCOMPS(COR)/
```

is specified, the principal components of the error correlation matrix are printed, while

```
PRINT=PRINCOMPS(COV)/
```

produces the principal components of the error-covariance matrix.

The output for a principal components analysis includes

1 A table listing the eigenvalues of the error matrix (COR or COV) and the proportion and cumulative proportion of the total variance accounted for by each component.

2 The principal components of the error matrix.

3 The determinant of the error matrix, the Bartlett test of sphericity, and F max tests. The Bartlett test statistic, which has an approximate chi-square distribution with $q(q-1)/2$ degrees of freedom, is used to test the hypothesis that the population error correlation matrix is an identity matrix (or, equivalently, that the population error variance-covariance matrix is a diagonal matrix). The F max statistic (the ratio of the largest to the smallest diagonal element of the error variance-covariance matrix) is used to test the hypothesis that the variances of the q response variables are equal. The critical points of the distribution of F max under the null hypothesis can be found in Winer (1971) and depend on q and n_e. Both the Bartlett test and F max test can be obtained simply by requesting the error correlation matrix; i.e., by specifying

```
PRINT=ERROR(COR)/
```

in a MANOVA run. It is not necessary to perform a principal components analysis in order to obtain these statistics.

The output from a principal components analysis performed on the dental calculus data is given in Figure 1.34.

Figure 1.34

```
EIGENVALUES OF WITHIN CELLS CORRELATION MATRIX

              EIGENVALUE      PCT OF VAR       CUM PCT

        1       2.02696        67.56528        67.56528
        2        .67398        22.46611        90.03139
        3        .29906         9.96861       100.00000

- - - - - - - - - - - - - - - - - - - - - - - - - - - - - - - - - - - - - -

NORMALIZED PRINCIPAL COMPONENTS

          COMPONENTS

VARIABLES         1               2               3

RCAN          -.73816         -.65197         -.17338
RLI           -.90389          .08961          .41827
RCI           -.81551          .49081         -.30667

- - - - - - - - - - - - - - - - - - - - - - - - - - - - - - - - - - - - - -

DETERMINANT =                    .40855
BARTLETT TEST OF SPHERICITY =  87.87194 WITH 3 D. F.
SIGNIFICANCE =                   .000


F(MAX) CRITERION =              3.07466 WITH (3,100) D. F.
```

MANOVA also enables the user to rotate the principal components loadings. The keywords for specifying the type of rotation are VARIMAX, QUARTIMAX, and EQUIMAX (see *SPSS, Second Edition*, pp. 484-485, for a description of these three rotations). NOROTATE inhibits rotation. For example, if

```
PRINT=PRINCOMPS(COR,ROTATE(VARIMAX))/
```

is specified, a principal components analysis is performed on each error correlation matrix and the varimax method is used to rotate the component loadings. By default, all components are rotated. Fewer components may be rotated by specifying the number of components to be rotated, in parentheses, after the NCOMP keyword or by specifying a cutoff value for the eigenvalues, in parentheses, after the MINEIGEN keyword. For example, specifying

```
PRINT=PRINCOMPS(COR,ROTATE(VARIMAX),NCOMP(2))/
```

causes only the first two components to be rotated. If

```
PRINT=PRINCOMPS(COR,ROTATE(VARIMAX),MINEIGEN(1.5))/
```

is specified, only those components associated with eigenvalues greater than 1.5 will be rotated.

1.35 Discriminant Analysis

MANOVA can be used to perform discriminant analysis for each effect in the model. The PRINT subcommand requesting discriminant analysis has the format

```
PRINT=DISCRIM(output list)/
```

The output list may include requests for

1 The raw discriminant function coefficients. These are obtained for each tested effect by specifying

```
PRINT=DISCRIM(RAW)/
```

2 The standardized discriminant function coefficients. If

```
PRINT=DISCRIM(STAN)/
```

is specified, the standardized discriminant function coefficients (obtained by multiplying each raw coefficient by the corresponding standard deviation of the variable) will be printed.

3 The effect estimates in the discriminant function space. To obtain the estimates of each effect for the canonical variables, specify

```
PRINT=DISCRIM(ESTIM)/
```

The canonical variables are defined here as the canonical variates associated with the response variables.

4 The correlations between response variables and canonical variables. These are obtained by specifying

```
PRINT=DISCRIM(COR)/
```

As an indication of how much each response variable contributes to the canonical variate, these correlations aid in the interpretation of the canonical variables.

For the dental calculus data, a discriminant analysis for the effect TR is requested by specifying

```
PRINT=DISCRIM(RAW,STAN,ESTIM,COR)/
```

The resulting output is given in Figure 1.35.

Figure 1.35

```
RAW DISCRIMINANT FUNCTION COEFFICIENTS
            FUNCTION NO.
VARIABLE               1

RCAN            .02507
RLI            -.14814
RCI            -.40728

- - - - - - - - - - - - - - - - - - - - - - - - - - - - - - - - - - - - - - - -

STANDARDIZED DISCRIMINANT FUNCTION COEFFICIENTS
            FUNCTION NO.
VARIABLE               1

RCAN            .02944
RLI            -.23973
RCI            -.83862

- - - - - - - - - - - - - - - - - - - - - - - - - - - - - - - - - - - - - - - -

ESTIMATES OF EFFECTS FOR CANONICAL VARIABLES
            CANONICAL VARIABLE
PARAMETER              1

    3           -.60303
    4           -.67469
    5            .18246
    6           -.08566

- - - - - - - - - - - - - - - - - - - - - - - - - - - - - - - - - - - - - - - -

CORRELATIONS BETWEEN DEPENDENT AND CANONICAL VARIABLES
            CANONICAL VARIABLE
VARIABLE               1

RCAN           -.38019
RLI            -.77143
RCI            -.98526
```

Discriminant analysis results are reported only for those functions (or corresponding canonical correlations; see Section 1.32) that are significant at level α. The default value of α is 0.15. In Figure 1.32a, the dimension reduction analysis for the TR effect indicates that only the first canonical correlation is significant (the observed significance level is 0.045); hence only one discriminant function is reported in the output displayed above. The value of α can be set by specifying a number between 0 and 1, in parentheses, after the keyword ALPHA. Thus,

```
PRINT=DISCRIM(RAW,COR,ALPHA(0.5))/
```

produces discriminant function coefficients and the correlations between response variables and canonical variables that correspond to discriminant functions with significance levels than 0.5. If $\alpha = 1.0$ is specified, MANOVA reports all the discriminant functions.

The correlations between the response variables and the canonical variables can be rotated by adding the ROTATE keyword to the PRINT subcommand. (The types of rotation available are described in 1.34.) For example,

```
PRINT=DISCRIM(COR,ROTATE(VARIMAX),ALPHA(1.0))/
```

produces the correlations between the response variables and all the canonical variables and rotates the canonical variables (using the varimax method).

1.36 Box's M Test

The assumption of homogeneous within-cells variance-covariance matrices can be assessed by Box's M test, a multivariate analog of Bartlett's test. If

```
PRINT=HOMOGENEITY(BOXM)/
```

is specified, MANOVA will print Box's M statistic and an approximate F statistic with its p- value. The results of Box's M test for the dental calculus data are given in Figure 1.36.

Figure 1.36

```
MULTIVARIATE TEST FOR HOMOGENEITY OF DISPERSION MATRICES


BOXS M =                      114.53559
F WITH (36,2404) DF =           2.67721, P =    .000 (APPROX.)
CHI-SQUARE WITH 36 DF =        98.09416, P =    .000 (APPROX.)
```

1.37 Multivariate Analysis of Covariance

MANOVA will also perform a multivariate analysis of covariance. Figure 1.37a illustrates this use of MANOVA.

Figure 1.37a

```
    RUN NAME        DENTAL CALCULUS DATA FROM FINN(1974) PAGE C-56
    FILE NAME       DATA FOR ANTI-CALCULUS AGENT
    VARIABLE LIST   YEAR,TR,RCAN,RLI,RCI,LCI,LLI,LCAN
    INPUT FORMAT    FIXED(2F1.0,6F2.0)
    N OF CASES      107
    MISSING VALUES  YEAR TO LCAN(BLANK)
    MANOVA          RCAN,RLI,RCI BY YEAR(1,2),TR(1,5) WITH LCI/
    READ INPUT DATA
    11 2 2 1 2 2 1
    11 0 0 0 2 1 0
    11 0 0 4 4 0 0
    11 2 2 2 3 2 2
    .  . . . . . .
    .  . . . . . .
    .  . . . . . .
    23 0 1 3 4 3 0
    23 1 0 1 0 1 0
    23 0 1 0 0 0 0
    23 0 1 6 4 1 0
    FINISH
```

RCAN, RLT, and RCI are the response variables and LCI the covariate in this example. The discussion of univariate analysis of covariance in Section 1.17 can be generalized.

When a covariate is specified, multivariate significance testing and parameter estimation are adjusted for the covariate; i.e., both S_h and S_e are adjusted. For the dental calculus data, the multivariate significance tests for the TR effect, adjusted for the covariate LCI, are given in Figure 1.37b.

Figure 1.37b

```
EFFECT .. TR

MULTIVARIATE TESTS OF SIGNIFICANCE (S = 3, M = 0, N = 47 1/2)

TEST NAME          VALUE      APPROX. F     HYPOTH. DF      ERROR DF      SIG. OF F

PILLAIS            .18149      1.59371         12.00         297.00         .092
HOTELLINGS         .20468      1.63178         12.00         287.00         .082
WILKS              .82485      1.61631         12.00         256.93         .087
ROYS               .13641
```

```
EIGENVALUES AND CANONICAL CORRELATIONS

ROOT NO.    EIGENVALUE        PCT.      CUM. PCT.     CANON. COR.

    1          .15796       77.17431     77.17431        .36934
    2          .04095       20.00838     97.18269        .19835
    3          .00577        2.81731    100.00000        .07572
```

```
DIMENSION REDUCTION ANALYSIS

ROOTS       WILKS LAMBDA           F      HYPOTH. DF      ERROR DF      SIG. OF F

1 TO 3         .82485       1.61631        12.00         256.93         .087
2 TO 3         .95515        .75412         6.00         237.72         .607
3 TO 3         .99427        .28215         2.00         196.00         .754
```

```
UNIVARIATE F-TESTS WITH (4,99) D. F.

VARIABLE    HYPOTH. SS     ERROR SS      HYPOTH. MS     ERROR MS           F        SIG. OF F

RCAN          4.20875      119.32324       1.05219      1.20529        .87298         .483
RLI           4.15057      152.39986       1.03764      1.53939        .67406         .612
RCI          18.00210      123.66477       4.50052      1.24914       3.60290         .009
```

MANOVA also prints multivariate significance tests of the hypothesis that the regression coefficients are zero, under the heading EFFECT..WITHIN CELLS REGRESSION. (WITHIN CELLS indicates that the within-cells error matrix was used in the model.) These tests for the dental calculus data of Figure 1.37a are shown in Figure 1.37c. (See Section 1.38 for a more detailed discussion of regression analysis.)

Figure 1.37c

```
EFFECT .. WITHIN CELLS REGRESSION

MULTIVARIATE TESTS OF SIGNIFICANCE (S = 1, M = 1/2, N = 47 1/2)

TEST NAME         VALUE      APPROX. F      HYPOTH. DF      ERROR DF      SIG. OF F

PILLAIS          .72613      85.72625          3.00          97.00          0.0
HOTELLINGS      2.65133      85.72625          3.00          97.00          0.0
WILKS            .27387      85.72625          3.00          97.00          0.0
ROYS             .72613

- - - - - - - - - - - - - - - - - - - - - - - - - - - - - - - - - - - - - - - - - - - - - - - -

EIGENVALUES AND CANONICAL CORRELATIONS

ROOT NO.      EIGENVALUE        PCT.      CUM. PCT.    CANON. COR.   SQUARED COR.

     1          2.65133     100.00000    100.00000      .85213         .72613

- - - - - - - - - - - - - - - - - - - - - - - - - - - - - - - - - - - - - - - - - - - - - - - -

DIMENSION REDUCTION ANALYSIS

ROOTS       WILKS LAMBDA             F      HYPOTH. DF      ERROR DF      SIG. OF F

1 TO 1          .27387        85.72625        3.00          97.00          0.0

- - - - - - - - - - - - - - - - - - - - - - - - - - - - - - - - - - - - - - - - - - - - - - - -

UNIVARIATE F-TESTS WITH (1,99) D. F.

VARIABLE    SQ. MUL. R      MUL. R      ADJ. R-SQ.    HYPOTH MS      ERROR MS          F      SIG. OF F

RCAN          .13468        .36699        .07350       18.57190      1.20529     15.40872     .000
RLI           .41804        .64656        .37689      109.47447      1.53939     71.11537     .000
RCI           .70832        .84162        .68770      300.31570      1.24914    240.41814     0.0
```

The estimated parameters for the regression of each response variable on the covariate are also listed, together with standard errors, t-values, and confidence intervals. For Figure 1.37a, the results in Figure 1.37d were obtained.

Figure 1.37d

```
REGRESSION ANALYSIS FOR WITHIN CELLS ERROR TERM

DEPENDENT VARIABLE ..RCAN

COVARIATE           B           BETA      STD. ERR.     T-VALUE    SIG. OF T   LOWER .95 CL   UPPER .95 CL

LCI        .1731949251    .3669895761      .04412      3.92539       .000         .08565         .26074

DEPENDENT VARIABLE ..RLI

COVARIATE           B           BETA      STD. ERR.     T-VALUE    SIG. OF T   LOWER .95 CL   UPPER .95 CL

LCI        .4204974555    .6465616861      .04986      8.43299       0.0          .32156         .51944

DEPENDENT VARIABLE ..RCI

COVARIATE           B           BETA      STD. ERR.     T-VALUE    SIG. OF T   LOWER .95 CL   UPPER .95 CL

LCI        .6964596479    .8416200881      .04492     15.50542       0.0          .60733         .78559
```

1.38 MULTIVARIATE MULTIPLE LINEAR REGRESSION

1.39 The Multivariate Linear Regression Model

The univariate regression model

$$Y_i = \beta_0 + \beta_1 X_{i1} + \dots + \beta_p X_{ip} + \epsilon_i$$

expresses the ith observation of the dependent variable Y as a linear function of p independent variables X_i and the error term ϵ_i.

The ϵ_i are assumed to be independent and normally distributed with mean 0 and variance σ^2, and the β_i's are the unknown parameters to be estimated. The multivariate extension of this model is

$$\mathbf{Y}_i = \mathbf{B}_0 + \mathbf{B}_1 X_{i1} + \ldots + \mathbf{B}_p X_{ip} + \boldsymbol{\epsilon}_i \ = \mathbf{B}_0 + \mathbf{B'X}_i + \boldsymbol{\epsilon}_i$$

where $\mathbf{Y}_i = (Y_{i1}\ Y_{i2} \ldots Y_{iq})'$ is a vector of q response variables for observation i, the X_j are independent variables, the $\mathbf{B}_j$ are q × 1 vectors containing the regression parameters, and the $\boldsymbol{\epsilon}_i$ vectors are the errors (assumed to be independent and to have a q-variate normal distribution with mean **0** and covariance matrix Σ).

1.40   MANOVA Multivariate Regression Analysis

MANOVA provides estimates of $\mathbf{B}_0$, **B**, and Σ and tests the hypothesis that B = 0. The constant vector $\mathbf{B}_0$ is included in the model unless the subcommand

```
METHOD=ESTIMATION(NOCONSTANT)/
```

is included in the MANOVA run. When NOCONSTANT is specified, the regression line or plane is forced to pass through the origin (i.e., $\mathbf{B}_0$ is assumed to be **0** in the equation). Four test statistics (described in Section 1.32) are given for testing the hypothesis that B = 0: Pillai's criterion, Hotelling's trace, Wilks' lambda, and Roy's largest root. All of these are functions of the nonzero eigenvalues of $S_h S_e^{-1}$, where S_h is the regression SSCP matrix and S_e is the error SSCP matrix.

In Figure 1.40a (taken from Finn, 1974), the dependent variable consists of two divergent measures of achievement, synthesis (SYNTH) and evaluation (EVAL), and the independent variables are a general intelligence index (INTEL) and three measures of creativity (CONOBV, CONRMT, and JOB). Three cross products between the creativity measures and INTEL are formed to represent the interaction terms of the model. Figure 1.40a shows the standard SPSS command file for this problem. COMPUTE statements are used to create the interaction terms.

Figure 1.40a

```
RUN NAME        MULTIVARIATE MULTIPLE REGRESSION
COMMENT         DATA ARE TAKEN FROM FINN(1974)   C-3
VARIABLE LIST   SYNTH EVAL CONOBV CONRMT JOB INTEL
INPUT MEDIUM    CARD
INPUT FORMAT    FREEFIELD
MISSING VALUES  SYNTH TO INTEL(9.9)
N OF CASES      UNKNOWN
COMPUTE         CI1=CONOBV*INTEL
COMPUTE         CI2=CONRMT*INTEL
COMPUTE         CI3=JOB*INTEL
MANOVA          SYNTH EVAL WITH INTEL CONOBV CONRMT JOB CI1 CI2 CI3/
                PRINT=DISCRIM(RAW,STAN,ESTIM,COR)/
READ INPUT DATA
5 1 20.0 5.0 13.0 106.0
0 0 13.0 3.0 10.0  97.0
6 2  9.9 4.0  5.0  90.0
4 2 10.0 3.0 15.0 121.0
1 2 12.0 2.0  4.0  99.0
7 1 25.0 5.0 23.0 120.0
1 2 21.0 3.0 11.0  91.0
   .    .    .    .     .
   .    .    .    .     .
   .    .    .    .     .
3 2 15.0 4.0 12.0 107.0
6 6 22.0 10.0 23.0 143.0
0 0 12.0 2.0 13.0 101.0
4 1 12.0 6.0 10.0 115.0
3 0 10.0 5.0 10.0  97.0
3 1 21.0 3.0 20.0  92.0
END INPUT DATA
```

Note that no factor variables are specified in the MANOVA procedure card and the keyword WITH is used to separate the response and independent variables.

The standard output includes multivariate significance tests and the statistics for parameter estimation described in Section 1.32. The following tests and statistics are of particular interest:

1 Tests of H_0:B=**0** and H_0:$\mathbf{B}_0$=**0**. These are automatically printed, along with the multiple R^2 and adjusted R^2 for each response variable regressed on the independent variables. This portion of the output for Figure 1.40a is given in Figure 1.40b.

Figure 1.40b

```
EFFECT .. WITHIN CELLS REGRESSION

MULTIVARIATE TESTS OF SIGNIFICANCE (S = 2, M = 2, N = 24 1/2)

TEST NAME        VALUE       APPROX. F     HYPOTH. DF      ERROR DF      SIG. OF F

PILLAIS          .55946       2.88501        14.00         104.00         .001
HOTELLINGS      1.05995       3.78553        14.00         100.00         .000
WILKS            .47077       3.33286        14.00         102.00         .000
ROYS             .49886

- - - - - - - - - - - - - - - - - - - - - - - - - - - - - - - - - - - - - - - - -

EIGENVALUES AND CANONICAL CORRELATIONS
ROOT NO.      EIGENVALUE        PCT.       CUM. PCT.   CANON. COR.  SQUARED COR.

      1          .99544       93.91374     93.91374      .70630       .49886
      2          .06451        6.08626    100.00000      .24617       .06060

- - - - - - - - - - - - - - - - - - - - - - - - - - - - - - - - - - - - - - - - -

DIMENSION REDUCTION ANALYSIS

ROOTS        WILKS LAMBDA          F       HYPOTH. DF      ERROR DF      SIG. OF F

1 TO 2          .47077       3.33286        14.00         102.00         .000
2 TO 2          .93940        .55565         6.00         105.00         .765

- - - - - - - - - - - - - - - - - - - - - - - - - - - - - - - - - - - - - - - - -

UNIVARIATE F-TESTS WITH (7,52) D. F.

VARIABLE    SQ. MUL. R     MUL. R    ADJ. R-SQ.    HYPOTH MS     ERROR MS         F     SIG. OF F

SYNTH         .45390       .67372      .38039      11.59727      1.87825     6.17450      .000
EVAL          .36102       .60085      .27500       9.60230      2.28783     4.19712      .001

- - - - - - - - - - - - - - - - - - - - - - - - - - - - - - - - - - - - - - - - -

EFFECT .. CONSTANT

MULTIVARIATE TESTS OF SIGNIFICANCE (S = 1, M = 0, N = 24 1/2)

TEST NAME        VALUE       APPROX. F     HYPOTH. DF      ERROR DF      SIG. OF F

PILLAIS          .01764        .45782         2.00          51.00         .635
HOTELLINGS       .01795        .45782         2.00          51.00         .635
WILKS            .98236        .45782         2.00          51.00         .635
ROYS             .01764

- - - - - - - - - - - - - - - - - - - - - - - - - - - - - - - - - - - - - - - - -

EIGENVALUES AND CANONICAL CORRELATIONS

ROOT NO.      EIGENVALUE        PCT.       CUM. PCT.   CANON. COR.

      1          .01795      100.00000    100.00000      .13281

- - - - - - - - - - - - - - - - - - - - - - - - - - - - - - - - - - - - - - - - -

DIMENSION REDUCTION ANALYSIS

ROOTS        WILKS LAMBDA          F       HYPOTH. DF      ERROR DF      SIG. OF F

1 TO 1          .98236        .45782         2.00          51.00         .635

- - - - - - - - - - - - - - - - - - - - - - - - - - - - - - - - - - - - - - - - -

UNIVARIATE F-TESTS WITH (1,52) D. F.

VARIABLE     HYPOTH. SS     ERROR SS     HYPOTH. MS      ERROR MS          F      SIG. OF F

SYNTH         1.13385       97.66914      1.13385        1.87825      .60367        .441
EVAL           .12773      118.96726       .12773        2.28783      .05583        .814
```

2 Estimates of the regression coefficients B and B_0 with their standard errors, t values for testing $H_0: \beta_i = 0$, and 95% confidence intervals for each β_i. The output in Figure 1.40c was obtained for Figure 1.40a.

Figure 1.40c

```
REGRESSION ANALYSIS FOR WITHIN CELLS ERROR TERM

DEPENDENT VARIABLE ..SYNTH

COVARIATE          B           BETA       STD. ERR.    T-VALUE    SIG. OF T   LOWER .95 CL   UPPER .95 CL

INTEL       .0555153073    .4727752433     .05165      1.07475      .287       -.04814        .15917
CONOBV      .2008178054    .7838261472     .24128       .83231      .409       -.28334        .68498
CONRMT      .1410916362    .2648440705     .47795       .29520      .769       -.81799       1.10018
JOB        -.3208770046   -.9994055945     .33236      -.96544      .339       -.98781        .34606
CI1        -.0015680423   -.6955227162     .00234      -.66986      .506       -.00627        .00313
CI2        -.0009030738   -.2073789045     .00443      -.20380      .839       -.00979        .00799
CI3         .0030798107   1.2548388165     .00314       .98169      .331       -.00322        .00938

DEPENDENT VARIABLE ..EVAL

COVARIATE          B           BETA       STD. ERR.    T-VALUE    SIG. OF T   LOWER .95 CL   UPPER .95 CL

INTEL      -.0094648415   -.0790004191     .05701      -.16602      .869       -.12386        .10493
CONOBV     -.1937798157   -.7413104806     .26629      -.72770      .470       -.72813        .34057
CONRMT      .4295086197    .7901962055     .52750       .81424      .419       -.62900       1.48801
JOB        -.2833034910   -.8648268789     .36682      -.77233      .443      -1.01937        .45277
CI1         .0023782808   1.0339290659     .00258       .92057      .362       -.00281        .00756
CI2        -.0032614042   -.7340404855     .00489      -.66690      .508       -.01307        .00655
CI3         .0025330022   1.0115178798     .00346       .73156      .468       -.00441        .00948

- - - - - - - - - - - - - - - - - - - - - - - - - - - - - - - - - - - - - - - - - - - -

ESTIMATES FOR SYNTH ADJUSTED FOR 7 COVARIATES

CONSTANT

PARAMETER       COEFF.       STD. ERR.    T-VALUE    SIG. OF T   LOWER .95 CL   UPPER .95 CL
    1      -4.0520586339     5.21524      -.77696      .441       -14.51720       6.41309

- - - - - - - - - - - - - - - - - - - - - - - - - - - - - - - - - - - - - - - - - - - -

ESTIMATES FOR EVAL ADJUSTED FOR 7 COVARIATES

CONSTANT

PARAMETER       COEFF.       STD. ERR.    T-VALUE    SIG. OF T   LOWER .95 CL   UPPER .95 CL
    1       1.3600318232     5.75585       .23629      .814       -10.18992      12.90999
```

All of the output related to multivariate significance tests that can be obtained by using the PRINT phrase as described in Section 1.33 is also available in the multivariate regression analysis.

1.41 Canonical Analysis

MANOVA can also be used to obtain the canonical correlation between the dependent and independent variables entered into the multivariate regression model. Canonical correlation analysis obtains the linear combinations $u_i=\mathbf{a}_i'\mathbf{Y}$ and $v_i=\mathbf{b}_i'\mathbf{X}$ $(i=1,2,..min(p,q))$ such that the sample correlation between u_1 and v_1, is maximized. The sample correlation between u_2 and v_2 is greatest among all linear combinations uncorrelated with u_1 and v_1, and so on. The $\mathbf{a}_i$ and $\mathbf{b}_i$ are the canonical coefficients for the dependent and independent variables, respectively, and the pairs of linear combinations u_i and v_i are called the canonical variates.

The format of the PRINT subcommand requesting canonical analysis is

        PRINT=DISCRIM(output list)/

The output list may include requests for

1 The raw canonical coefficients. If

        PRINT=DISCRIM(RAW)/

is specified, the raw canonical coefficients for the dependent variables and the independent variables are produced. For Figure 1.40a, the output in Figure 1.41a is obtained.

Figure 1.41a

```
RAW CANONICAL COEFFICIENTS FOR DEPENDENT VARIABLES

          FUNCTION NO.

VARIABLE            1

SYNTH            .40444
EVAL             .22637

- - - - - - - - - - - - - - - - - - - - - - - - - - - - - - - - - - - - - - - - - - - -
```

```
RAW CANONICAL COEFFICIENTS FOR COVARIATES

           FUNCTION NO.

COVARIATE              1

INTEL              .02876
CONOBV             .05288
CONRMT             .21845
JOB               -.27454
CI1               -.00014
CI2               -.00156
CI3                .00258
```

2 The standardized canonical coefficients. If

```
        PRINT=DISCRIM(STAN)/
```

is specified, the standardized canonical coefficients (obtained by multiplying each raw coefficient by the corresponding standard deviation of the variable) are printed. The standardized canonical coefficients for Figure 1.40a are given in Figure 1.41b.

Figure 1.41b

```
STANDARDIZED CANONICAL COEFFICIENTS FOR DEPENDENT VARIABLES

          FUNCTION NO.

VARIABLE             1

SYNTH             .70415
EVAL              .40212

- - - - - - - - - - - - - - - - - - - - - - - - - - - - - - - - - - - - - - -

STANDARDIZED CANONICAL COEFFICIENTS FOR COVARIATES

          CAN. VAR.

COVARIATE            1

INTEL             .42636
CONOBV            .35939
CONRMT            .71393
JOB             -1.48875
CI1              -.10475
CI2              -.62467
CI3              1.82693
```

3 The correlations between the variables and each canonical variate. These correlations are obtained by specifying

```
        PRINT=DISCRIM(COR)/
```

and indicate the contribution of each variable to the canonical variate. The percentage and cumulative percentage of the total variation accounted for by each canonical variate are printed as well. The percentage of variation in the dependent variable accounted for by the ith canonical variate is calculated as (the sum of squares of correlations between dependent variable and the ith canonical variable) $\times$ 100/ (number of response variables). The percentage of variation in the independent variable accounted for by the ith canonical variate is obtained similarly. Finally, MANOVA prints the redundancy of the dependent variable given the availability of the independent variables (Cooley and Lohnes, 1971), under the heading PCT VAR COV. This is calculated as the proportion of variance accounted for by the ith canonical variate multiplied by the corresponding squared canonical coefficient. The redundancy of the independent variables given the availability of the dependent variable appears in the printed output under PCT VAR DEP and is obtained in a similar way. For Figure 1.40a, the output in Figure 1.41c was obtained.

Figure 1.41c

```
CORRELATIONS BETWEEN DEPENDENT AND CANONICAL VARIABLES

          FUNCTION NO.

VARIABLE             1

SYNTH             .94733
EVAL              .82794

- - - - - - - - - - - - - - - - - - - - - - - - - - - - - - - - - - - - - - -
```

VARIANCE EXPLAINED BY CANONICAL VARIABLES OF DEPENDENT VARIABLES

CAN. VAR.	PCT VAR DEP	CUM PCT DEP	PCT VAR COV	CUM PCT COV
1	79.14597	79.14597	39.48249	39.48249

- -

CORRELATIONS BETWEEN COVARIATES AND CANONICAL VARIABLES

CAN. VAR.

COVARIATE	1
INTEL	.94646
CONOBV	.30260
CONRMT	.56188
JOB	.57787
CI1	.62672
CI2	.69288
CI3	.79114

- -

VARIANCE EXPLAINED BY CANONICAL VARIABLES OF THE COVARIATES

CAN. VAR.	PCT VAR DEP	CUM PCT DEP	PCT VAR COV	CUM PCT COV
1	22.34706	22.34706	44.79657	44.79657

Note that although the number of canonical variates is equal to $s = \min(p,q)$, MANOVA prints only those variates that have a significant canonical correlation. The default significance level is 0.15 and can be changed by using the ALPHA specification, as described in Section 1.35.

1.42 Residuals

MANOVA will calculate and print predicted values and residuals for each response variable if

```
PRINT=POBS/
```

is specified in a MANOVA run (POBS stands for predicted observation). The output also includes the case numbers, observed values, and standardized residuals (obtained by dividing the residuals by the error standard deviation).

If multiple error terms are specified in an analysis of covariance model and the residuals for each case are needed, the ERROR subphrase should be used to designate which error term's regression coefficients are to be used in calculating the predicted values. Any error term defined in the design can be used. Consider, for example, a 3×2 factorial design with repeated measures on factor B, a SUBJECT factor nested within factor A, and a covariate X. (See Section 1.44 for a discussion of the repeated measures design.) The following MANOVA cards may be used to obtain residuals and significance tests for the model.

```
MANOVA          Y BY A(1,3) SUBJECT(1,3) B(1,2) WITH X/
                PRINT=POBS(ERROR(2))/
                DESIGN=A VS 1, B VS 2, A BY B VS 2,
                   SUBJECT W A = 1, B BY SUBJECT W A = 2/
```

ERROR(2) within the POBS phrase indicates that the regression coefficients associated with error term 2 are to be used to calculate the predicted values for the model (error term 2 is defined in the DESIGN specification as the interaction between B and SUBJECT (within A)).

Various residual plots (observed versus predicted values, observed values versus standardized residuals, predicted values versus standardized residuals, and case number versus standardized residuals) are also available. For a discussion of the graphic features of MANOVA see Section 1.51.

1.43 SPECIAL TOPICS

1.44 Repeated Measures Designs

1.45 Introduction

Designs in which multiple observations are made on a single experimental unit are called repeated measures designs. For example, if a patient's blood pressure is recorded daily for five days after administration of antihypertensive are medication, five repeated observations are obtained for the same case. If only one variable is being measured, say systolic blood pressure, the design is termed singly multivariate. If several variables, such as standing and recumbent systolic and diastolic blood pressures are recorded, the design is doubly multivariate. Since multiple observations are made on the same experimental unit, they are not independent. Special procedures must therefore be used for analysis of repeated measures data.

There are several possible strategies for analysis of repeated measures designs. Both univariate and multivariate solutions can be obtained. Selection of a strategy should be based on the appropriateness of the necessary assumptions as well as power considerations.

1.46   An Example

Data from a repeated measures design found in Winer (1971, p. 546) are shown in Table 1.46. They consist of accuracy scores obtained by adjusting three dials (DIAL) under two levels of background noise (NOISE) during three consecutive ten-minute periods (PERIOD). Each subject is observed nine times, once at each combination of period and dial type. PERIOD and DIAL are called within- subjects factors, while NOISE is called a between-subjects factor. If subject is considered a factor, then the subject factor is crossed with PERIOD and DIAL but nested under NOISE level.

Table 1.46

Noise	Subject	Periods:	1			2			3		
		Dials:	1	2	3	1	2	3	1	2	3
1	1		45	53	60	40	52	57	28	37	46
	2		35	41	50	30	37	47	25	32	41
	3		60	65	75	58	54	70	40	47	50
2	4		50	48	61	25	34	51	16	23	35
	5		42	45	55	30	37	43	22	27	37
	6		56	60	77	40	39	57	31	29	46

1.47   Obtaining a Univariate Analysis the Hard Way

The univariate analysis of the repeated measures design displayed in Table 1.46 is obtained by treating subject as a random effect nested under the NOISE factor. The model is called a mixed-effects model, and the resulting analysis is a mixed-model analysis of the repeated measures design.

The technique described in Section 1.25 can be used to determine the appropriate error terms for testing the various effects. Table 1.47 summarizes the effects and corresponding error terms for this example.

Table 1.47

Effect	Error Term
NOISE	Subject within NOISE
PERIOD NOISE × PERIOD	PERIOD × Subject within NOISE
DIAL NOISE × DIAL	DIAL × Subject within NOISE
PERIOD × DIAL NOISE × PERIOD × DIAL	PERIOD × DIAL × SUBJECT within NOISE

Figure 1.47a shows an SPSS command file that can be used to perform a univariate analysis of the repeated measures design for the data in Table 1.46. The resulting ANOVA table is presented in Figure 1.47b. A somewhat complicated DESIGN specification is needed because of the multiple error terms in the model. In the next section, a much easier approach to the same problem is given.

Figure 1.47a

```
RUN NAME        UNIVARIATE ANALYSIS OF REPEATED MEASURES DESIGN.
COMMENT         DATA ARE TAKEN FROM WINER(1971) PAGE 546.
VARIABLE LIST   NOISE SUBJECT PERIOD DIAL Y
INPUT FORMAT    FIXED(4F1.0,1X,F2.0)
N OF CASES      54
INPUT MEDIUM    CARD
MANOVA          Y BY NOISE(1,2) SUBJECT(1,3) PERIOD DIAL(1,3)/
                DESIGN=NOISE VS 1, SUBJECT W NOISE=1, PERIOD VS 2,
                       DIAL VS 3, PERIOD BY SUBJECT W NOISE=2,
                       DIAL BY SUBJECT W NOISE=3, NOISE BY PERIOD VS 2,
                       NOISE BY DIAL VS 3, PERIOD BY DIAL VS 4,
                       PERIOD BY DIAL BY SUBJECT W NOISE=4,
                       NOISE BY PERIOD BY DIAL VS 4/
READ INPUT DATA
1111 45
1112 53
1113 60
1121 40
1122 52
 ...  .
 ...  .
 ...  .
2322 39
2323 57
2331 31
2332 29
2333 46
FINISH
```

Figure 1.47b

TESTS OF SIGNIFICANCE FOR Y USING SEQUENTIAL SUMS OF SQUARES

SOURCE OF VARIATION	SUM OF SQUARES	DF	MEAN SQUARE	F	SIG. OF F
RESIDUAL	0.0	0			
CONSTANT	105868.16667	1	105868.16667	.	.
ERROR 1	2491.11111	4	622.77778		
NOISE	468.16667	1	468.16667	.75174	.435
ERROR 2	234.88889	8	29.36111		
PERIOD	3722.33333	2	1861.16667	63.38884	.000
NOISE BY PERIOD	333.00000	2	166.50000	5.67077	.029
ERROR 3	105.55556	8	13.19444		
DIAL	2370.33333	2	1185.16667	89.82316	0.0
NOISE BY DIAL	50.33333	2	25.16667	1.90737	.210
ERROR 4	127.11111	16	7.94444		
PERIOD BY DIAL	10.66667	4	2.66667	.33566	.850
NOISE BY PERIOD BY DIAL	11.33333	4	2.83333	.35664	.836

The mixed-model analysis requires that the variances of the dependent variable be equal for all factor combinations, and that the correlations of the dependent variable at different combinations of within-subjects factors be equal. The MANOVA procedure provides a test, discussed in the next section, for this assumption of compound symmetry.

If compound symmetry appears to be violated, the multivariate approach can be used. In general, the univariate approach is somewhat more powerful, especially for small sample sizes. Note that in the MANOVA procedure, the univariate results can be obtained from the multivariate analysis output. This is important since the multivariate specifications are much simpler than the univariate mixed- model approach just outlined.

1.48 Trend Analysis

Since both PERIOD and DIAL are statistically significant, one may wish to investigate the growth trends for PERIOD and DIAL. If a trend analysis for PERIOD is desired, this effect can be partitioned into a linear effect, PERIOD(1), and a quadratic effect, PERIOD(2), by using the following specifications.

```
CONTRAST(PERIOD)=POLYNOMIAL/
PARTITION(PERIOD)/
```

Equally spaced PERIOD levels are assumed here; for the use of CONTRAST and PARTITION subcommands when levels are unequally spaced, see Sections 1.88 and 1.89.

As shown in Table 1.47, the test for a PERIOD effect used the PERIOD × (subject within NOISE) error term. For the orthogonal polynomial components of PERIOD, we can either use this error term to test for PERIOD(1) and PERIOD(2) effects or decompose PERIOD × (subject within NOISE) into PERIOD(1) × (subject within NOISE) and PERIOD(2) × (subject within NOISE) and use these as the error terms for PERIOD(1) and PERIOD(2), respectively. The choice of procedure depends in part on the assumptions of the model (see Bock, 1975, p. 460). Unless PERIOD(1) × (subject within NOISE) and PERIOD(2) × (subject within NOISE) both have a fairly large number of degrees of freedom, the single error term PERIOD × (subject within NOISE) is generally used because this test is more powerful.

All interaction terms containing PERIOD can also be partitioned; for example, NOISE × PERIOD has two components, NOISE × PERIOD(1) and NOISE × PERIOD(2), and the pooled and separated error terms described above may be used to test for these two effects. The MANOVA specifications for trend analyses of PERIOD and DIAL are presented in Figure 1.48a, and the resulting ANOVA table is displayed in Figure 1.48b.

Figure 1.48a

```
MANOVA          Y BY NOISE(1,2) SUBJECT(1,3) PERIOD DIAL(1,3)/
                CONTRAST(PERIOD)=POLYNOMIAL/
                CONTRAST(DIAL)=POLYNOMIAL/
                PARTITION(PERIOD)/
                PARTITION(DIAL)/
                DESIGN=NOISE VS 1, SUBJECT W NOISE=1, PERIOD(1) VS 2,
                      PERIOD(2) VS 2, DIAL(1) VS 3,
                      DIAL(2) VS 3, PERIOD BY SUBJECT W NOISE=2,
                      DIAL BY SUBJECT W NOISE=3, NOISE BY PERIOD VS 2,
                      NOISE BY DIAL VS 3, PERIOD BY DIAL VS 4,
                      PERIOD BY DIAL BY SUBJECT W NOISE=4,
                      NOISE BY PERIOD BY DIAL VS 4/
```

Figure 1.48b

TESTS OF SIGNIFICANCE FOR Y USING SEQUENTIAL SUMS OF SQUARES

SOURCE OF VARIATION	SUM OF SQUARES	DF	MEAN SQUARE	F	SIG. OF F
RESIDUAL	0.0	0	.		
CONSTANT	105868.16667	1	105868.16667	.	.
ERROR 1	2491.11111	4	622.77778		
NOISE	468.16667	1	468.16667	.75174	.435
ERROR 2	234.88889	8	29.36111		
PERIOD(1)	3721.00000	1	3721.00000	126.73226	0.0
PERIOD(2)	1.33333	1	1.33333	.04541	.837
NOISE BY PERIOD	333.00000	2	166.50000	5.67077	.029
ERROR 3	105.55556	8	13.19444		
DIAL(1)	2256.25000	1	2256.25000	171.00000	0.0
DIAL(2)	114.08333	1	114.08333	8.64632	.019
NOISE BY DIAL	50.33333	2	25.16667	1.90737	.210
ERROR 4	127.11111	16	7.94444		
PERIOD BY DIAL	10.66667	4	2.66667	.33566	.850
NOISE BY PERIOD BY DIAL	11.33333	4	2.83333	.35664	.836

1.49 The Multivariate Approach

In the multivariate analysis of repeated measures designs, the responses of a case are treated as an h-dimensional response vector. In the current example each subject responds to nine variables, each variable representing a unique DIAL and PERIOD combination. Thus the design for Table 1.46 can be treated as a multivariate one-way design with NOISE as the grouping variable. The model can be written as

$$\mathbf{Y}_{ij} = \mathbf{\mu} + \alpha_i + \epsilon_{ij}$$

where $\mathbf{Y}_{ij} = (Y_{ij1} \dots Y_{ijh})'$, α_i is the treatment effect and the ϵ_{ij} are the errors (assumed to be independent with an h-variate normal distribution having mean $\mathbf{0}$ and a covariance matrix Σ). As long as Σ is positive definite, the covariance structure of the Y_{ijk} can have any pattern. This assumption is of course much less restrictive than the mixed-model assumption of compound symmetry.

The following SPSS MANOVA commands can be used to perform a multivariate analysis of the repeated measures data in Table 1.46.

```
MANOVA          Y1 TO Y9 BY NOISE(1,2)/
                WSFACTORS = PERIOD(3), DIAL(3)/
                WSDESIGN = PERIOD DIAL PERIOD BY DIAL/
                PRINT = SIGNIF(BRIEF)/
                ANALYSIS(REPEATED)/
                DESIGN = NOISE
```

Variables Y1 to Y9 are the nine response variables. The WSFACTORS subcommand indicates that
there are two within-subjects factors, each having three levels. The order in which the variables are
specified in the WSFACTORS list is very important since it indicates the levels of PERIOD and
DIAL corresponding to Y1 to Y9. The following table gives the correspondence between the
variables:

Variable	PERIOD	DIAL
Y_1	1	1
Y_2	1	2
Y_3	1	3
Y_4	2	1
Y_5	2	2
Y_6	2	3
Y_7	3	1
Y_8	3	2
Y_9	3	3

If the order of the two within-subjects factors is reversed in the WSFACTORS subcommand, the
PERIOD and DIAL headings must be interchanged in the above table. For example, Y_7 would
correspond to DIAL level 3 and PERIOD 1.

The WSDESIGN subcommand specifies the model for the within-subjects factors. The model
fit need not be saturated. To specify an additive model, use

```
WSDESIGN = PERIOD DIAL/
```

The subcommand ANALYSIS(REPEATED) indicates that a repeated measures analysis is
desired. The model for the between-subjects factors is specified, as always, by the DESIGN
subcommand. Since there is only one between-subjects factor in this experiment, the command is
DESIGN = NOISE.

The subcommand PRINT = SIGNIF(BRIEF) requests printing of brief multivariate output.
Excerpts from this output are shown in Figure 1.49.

Figure 1.49

```
TESTS OF SIGNIFICANCE FOR Y1 USING SEQUENTIAL SUMS OF SQUARES

SOURCE OF VARIATION          SUM OF SQUARES      DF    MEAN SQUARE         F      SIG. OF F

WITHIN CELLS                    2491.11111        4     622.77778
CONSTANT                      105868.16667        1  105868.16667    169.99349       .000
NOISE                            468.16667        1     468.16667       .75174       .435

- - - - - - - - - - - - - - - - - - - - - - - - - - - - - - - - - - - - - - - - - - - - - - -

TESTS OF SIGNIFICANCE FOR WITHIN CELLS USING SEQUENTIAL SUMS OF SQUARES

SOURCE OF VARIATION      WILKS LAMBDA APPROX MULT F   SIG. OF F   AVERAGED F   SIG. OF F

PERIOD                       .05060      28.14526       .011      63.38884       .000
NOISE AND PERIOD             .15607       8.11102       .062       5.67077       .029

- - - - - - - - - - - - - - - - - - - - - - - - - - - - - - - - - - - - - - - - - - - - - - -

TESTS OF SIGNIFICANCE FOR WITHIN CELLS USING SEQUENTIAL SUMS OF SQUARES

SOURCE OF VARIATION      WILKS LAMBDA APPROX MULT F   SIG. OF F   AVERAGED F   SIG. OF F

DIAL                         .01614      91.45623       .002      89.82316        0.0
NOISE AND DIAL               .56498       1.15495       .425       1.90737       .210

- - - - - - - - - - - - - - - - - - - - - - - - - - - - - - - - - - - - - - - - - - - - - - -

TESTS OF SIGNIFICANCE FOR WITHIN CELLS USING SEQUENTIAL SUMS OF SQUARES

SOURCE OF VARIATION      WILKS LAMBDA APPROX MULT F   SIG. OF F   AVERAGED F   SIG. OF F

PERIOD BY DIAL               .00075     331.44500       .041       .33566       .850
NOISE AND PERIOD BY DIAL     .00043     581.87500       .031       .35664       .836
```

Wilks' lambda (with the corresponding approximate F) can be used to test for within- subjects
factor effects, if the compound symmetry assumption appears to be violated. The averaged F
statistics in the output are identical to the univariate mixed-model results displayed in Figure 1.47b.

Testing the hypothesis of compound symmetry is equivalent to testing the hypothesis that the
covariance matrix of the transformed variables is a diagonal matrix (Bock, 1975, p. 459). Thus, the
Bartlett test for sphericity can be used. MANOVA performs this Bartlett test for the transformed
variables if the TRANSFORM or WSDESIGN subcommand is present.

MANOVA also performs the analysis of covariance on repeated measures data. If the
covariates are constant over the repeated measures, only between-subject factors are adjusted; and
if the covariates vary across the repeated measures, both between- and within-subjects factors are
adjusted.

1.50 Tables of Means

MANOVA prints marginal and n-way table means for the response variables and covariates. Both weighted and unweighted observed means are reported, and adjusted means and adjusted predicted means can be requested. Consider, for example, a two-way analysis of covariance for the data displayed in Table 1.50, with Y as the response variable and X as the covariate.

Table 1.50

		A 1		A 2		A 3		A 4	
		Y	X	Y	X	Y	X	Y	X
B	1	8	2	8	7	10	5	6	3
		7	5	9	9			4	5
	2	6	4	8	3	6	2	9	3
		7	5	6	2				

The weighted mean for a particular treatment is obtained by summing the scores of all subjects receiving that treatment and dividing by the total number of subjects included in the summation. For example, the weighted mean of Y for the first level of factor B (B_1) is

$(8+7+8+9+10+6+4)/7 = 7.429$

The unweighted treatment mean is obtained by averaging the cell means receiving that treatment. Thus the unweighted mean of Y for B_1 is

$(7.5+8.5+10+5)/4 = 7.75$

Tables of combined observed means (OMEANS) are requested by a PRINT subcommand of the form

```
PRINT=OMEANS(VARIABLE(varlist),TABLES(factor list))/
```

The varlist within the VARIABLE specification contains the names of the variables (response variables and/or covariates) for which observed means are to be calculated. If no list is given, the observed means for all variables are reported. The factor list within the TABLES specification specifies the desired combinations of means. For the above example,

```
PRINT=OMEANS(TABLES(A,A BY B))/
```

produces the treatment means (weighted and unweighted) of Y and X for factors A and AB; and

```
PRINT=OMEANS(VARIABLE(Y),TABLES(A,B))/
```

requests the treatment means of Y for factors A and B. The combined observed means obtained using the second PRINT subcommand are given in Figure 1.50a.

Figure 1.50a

```
COMBINED OBSERVED MEANS FOR A
VARIABLE .. Y

          A
          1       WGT.      7.00000
                  UNWGT.    7.00000

          2       WGT.      7.75000
                  UNWGT.    7.75000

          3       WGT.      8.00000
                  UNWGT.    8.50000

          4       WGT.      6.33333
                  UNWGT.    7.00000
```

```
COMBINED OBSERVED MEANS FOR B
VARIABLE .. Y


     B

     1       WGT.      7.42857
             UNWGT.    7.75000

     2       WGT.      7.14286
             UNWGT.    7.37500
```

A similar PRINT subcommand can be used to obtain the means adjusted for covariates and the adjusted predicted means (PMEANS). If no covariates are present in the model, the adjusted mean (labeled ADJ. MEAN in the output) and the adjusted predicted mean (labeled EST. MEAN) are the same and are equal to the predicted cell mean (Finn, 1974, p. 376).

To obtain tables of combined (adjusted) predicted means, the user should specify

```
PRINT=PMEANS(VARIABLE(varlist),TABLES(factor list))/
```

Note that varlist may contain only response variables here. The PMEANS output always includes the adjusted means and adjusted predicted means of each cell for those response variables specified in the VARIABLE specification. Thus, for the above example,

```
PRINT=PMEANS(TABLES(A,B))/
```

produces a table of the adjusted means and adjusted predicted means of Y for each cell and the marginal adjusted predicted means for factors A and B (see the output in Figures 1.50b and 1.50c). Note that if varlist and factor list are not both given in the PMEANS subcommand, only the output shown in Figure 1.50c is printed.

Figure 1.50b

```
COMBINED ESTIMATED MEANS FOR A
VARIABLE .. Y

     A

     1     UNWGT.    7.01630

     2     UNWGT.    7.65761

     3     UNWGT.    8.51630

     4     UNWGT.    7.05978
- - - - - - - - - - - - - - - - - - - - - - - - - - - - - - - -
COMBINED ESTIMATED MEANS FOR B
VARIABLE .. Y

     B

     1     UNWGT.    7.66848

     2     UNWGT.    7.45652
```

Figure 1.50c

```
ADJUSTED AND ESTIMATED MEANS

VARIABLE .. Y
     FACTOR       CODE      OBS. MEAN   ADJ. MEAN   EST. MEAN   RAW RESID.  STD. RESID.

A                  1
  B                1        7.50000     7.55978     7.49767     .00233      .00191
  B                2        6.50000     6.47283     6.49767     .00233      .00191

A                  2
  B                1        8.50000     8.16848     8.49767     .00233      .00191
  B                2        7.00000     7.14674     6.99767     .00233      .00191

A                  3
  B                1       10.00000     9.92935     9.99767     .00233      .00191
  B                2        7.00000     7.10326     6.99767     .00233      .00191

A                  4
  B                1        5.00000     5.01630     4.99767     .00233      .00191
  B                2        9.00000     9.10326     8.99767     .00233      .00191
```

If multiple error terms are used in an analysis of covariance model, an additional ERROR specification should be used in the PMEANS subcommand to indicate which error term's regression coefficients are to be used to calculate the predicted means. The general format of the PMEANS subcommand is therefore

```
PRINT=PMEANS(VARIABLE(varlist),TABLES(factor list),
    ERROR(error term))/
```

For the plots associated with PMEANS, see Section 1.51.

Note the difference between PMEANS and POBS: PMEANS requests the adjusted means and adjusted predicted means for each cell, while POBS prints the predicted value for each case.

MANOVA also computes the standard errors of the weighted and unweighted means, although these cannot be obtained by using the OMEANS command. Tables of means adjusted for the factors (not the covariates), which are frequently desired for confounded designs, are also available. To obtain these statistics, the keyword CONSPLUS must be used in the DESIGN specification. CONSPLUS always appears with a factor list, which can consist of a single factor name (as in CONSPLUS A) or several factor names connected by the keyword BY or AND (as in CONSPLUS A BY B). When CONSPLUS and a factor name appear in the DESIGN specification, a contrast matrix is formed so that the parameters associated with the term CONSPLUS factor name consist, after reparameterization, of the population cell means. For example, if CONSPLUS A is specified in the above example, a contrast matrix for A is formed so that the parameter associated with CONSPLUS A would be

$$\begin{pmatrix} \mu + \alpha_1 \\ \mu + \alpha_2 \\ \mu + \alpha_3 \\ \mu + \alpha_4 \end{pmatrix}$$

These consist of the constant (μ) plus the effects of A (hence the name CONSPLUS). For CONSPLUS A BY B, the parameters to be estimated would be

$$\begin{pmatrix} \mu + \alpha_1 + \beta_1 + (\alpha\beta)_{11} \\ \mu + \alpha_1 + \beta_2 + (\alpha\beta)_{12} \\ \vdots \\ \mu + \alpha_4 + \beta_2 + (\alpha\beta)_{42} \end{pmatrix}$$

the population cell means associated with A and B.

It can be shown that the weighted means are the estimates that result when only the factor of interest appears with CONSPLUS, while the unweighted means result when all factors in the full model appear with CONSPLUS. For example,

```
DESIGN=CONSPLUS A/
```

produces the weighted means of factor A, while

```
DESIGN=CONSPLUS A,B,A BY B/
```

produces the unweighted means of factor A. These means are adjusted for any covariates present in the model.

For the above example, the following specifications may be used to obtain the unweighted means of Y for factor B, the adjusted cell means, and the standard errors of these means.

```
MANOVA          Y,X BY A(1,4),B(1,2)/
                ANALYSIS=Y/
                DESIGN=A,CONSPLUS B, A BY B/
                ANALYSIS=Y WITH X/
                DESIGN=CONSPLUS A BY B/
```

The first ANALYSIS subcommand defines Y as the response variable and the first DESIGN specification requests the unweighted means for factor B. The relevant output is shown in Figure 1.50d. (When only means and their standard errors are desired, the ANOVA table is irrelevant and can be ignored.)

Figure 1.50d

```
CONSPLUS B
```

PARAMETER	COEFF.	STD. ERR.	T-VALUE	SIG. OF T	LOWER .95 CL	UPPER .95 CL
4	7.7500000000	.44194	17.53625	.000	6.66861	8.83139
5	7.3750000000	.44194	16.68772	.000	6.29361	8.45639

The unweighted means for B are printed under COEFF and the standard errors given under STD. ERR. Figure 1.50e shows the output corresponding to the second ANALYSIS and DESIGN specifications (these define X as the covariate and request the A × B two-way table means adjusted for X).

Figure 1.50e

```
CONSPLUS A BY B

 PARAMETER        COEFF.       STD. ERR.      T-VALUE       SIG. OF T     LOWER .95 CL     UPPER .95 CL
     1          7.5621118012     .89838        8.41753         .000          5.25280          9.87143
     2          6.4751552795     .86708        7.46777         .001          4.24629          8.70402
     3          8.1708074534    1.60903        5.07810         .004          4.03473         12.30688
     4          7.1490683230    1.05838        6.75470         .001          4.42845          9.86969
     5          9.9316770186    1.24988        7.94611         .001          6.71881         13.14455
     6          7.1055900621     .96509        7.36262         .001          4.62478          9.58640
     7          5.0186335404     .86442        5.80577         .002          2.79660          7.24067
     8          9.1055900621    1.29333        7.04042         .001          5.78103         12.43015
```

Several comments about the use of CONSPLUS are in order. First, which error mean square is used to calculate the standard errors of the weighted and unweighted means depends on the factors listed after CONSPLUS. Consider, for example, the 3 × 4 factorial design (with factors A and B and randomized blocks) specified by the following MANOVA command.

```
MANOVA          Y BY A(1,3),B(1,4) BLOCK(1,3)/
                DESIGN=CONSPLUS B/
                DESIGN=BLOCK,A,CONSPLUS B, A BY B/
```

The first DESIGN subcommand produces the weighted means for the four levels of B. If the number of observations per cell is at most one, the default error term, in this case, would be the residual corresponding to the lumped effect of BLOCK, A, A × B, A × BLOCK, B × BLOCK and A × B × BLOCK. The second DESIGN subcommand produces the unweighted means for B, and the error term is the residual corresponding to the lumped effect of A × BLOCK, B × BLOCK, and A × B × BLOCK. If there is at least one cell with more than one observation, however, the error term is the within-cells error when either of the above DESIGN specifications is used.

Second, in a two-way ANOVA model, the estimates associated with the CONSPLUS B term obtained by specifying

```
DESIGN=A,CONSPLUS B,A BY B/
```

are, in general, different from those obtained by specifying

```
DESIGN=A,CONSPLUS B/
```

This is the case for any n-way design unless the design is balanced and complete. The estimates of CONSPLUS B obtained by using the first DESIGN specification are the unweighted means for B, while the estimates of CONSPLUS B obtained by using the second DESIGN specification can be interpreted as the weighted means of B adjusted for factor A (assuming the default sequential decomposition of sums of squares). Thus, the weighted means adjusted for the factors can be obtained by specifying

```
DESIGN=factors to be adjusted for, CONSPLUS factor list/
```

One might, for example, wish to adjust for the block effects. In Figure 1.26a, the interaction A × B is partially confounded with blocks, so that the A × B two-way table means must be adjusted for block effects. This can be done by specifying

```
DESIGN=REPLICS,BLOCK WITH REPLICS, CONSPLUS A BY B/
```

The estimates associated with CONSPLUS A BY B are the weighted A × B means (see Figure 1.26c). Note that the standard errors of these means, shown in Figure 1.26c, are based on the residual error for this particular DESIGN model. The user should be aware of this before attempting to make inferences based on these standard errors.

1.51   Plots

Graphical analysis is an important part of data analysis, and many plots useful for assessing the validity of the MANOVA model's assumptions can be obtained by using the PLOT subcommand. This subcommand has the following format:

```
PLOT=keyword(s)/
```

Any of the following keyword specifications can be used:

CELLPLOTS Plots of cell statistics, including a plot of cell means versus cell variances, a plot of cell means versus cell standard deviations, and a histogram of cell means, are reported for each interval variable (response variables and covariates) defined in the MANOVA specification card. The first two plots aid in detecting heteroscedasticity (nonhomogeneous variances) and in determining an appropriate transformation of the data (if one is needed). The third plot gives distributional information for the cell means. These are illustrated in Figure 1.51a.

Figure 1.51a

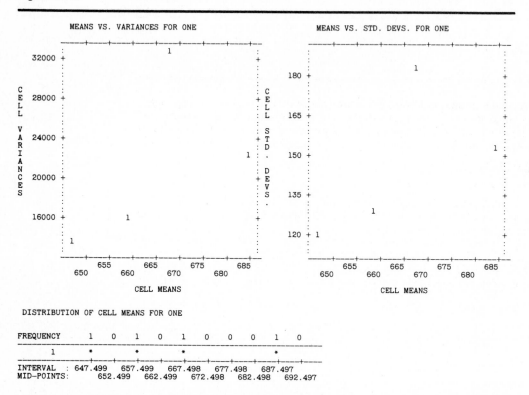

BOXPLOTS Boxplots (Tukey, 1977) for each interval variable can be requested. These plots can be used to compare the centers and spreads of the cell distributions and to detect outliers. An example of boxplots produced by MANOVA is shown in Figure 1.51b.

Figure 1.51b

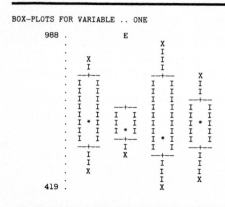

STEMLEAF   A stem-and-leaf plot (Tukey, 1977) for each interval variable can be obtained. (The units used in the stem are determined by the programs.) This plot contains more detailed information about the distribution of a variable than that contained in a histogram. Figure 1.51c gives examples of stem-and-leaf plots produced by MANOVA.

Figure 1.51c

```
STEM-AND-LEAF DISPLAY FOR VARIABLE .. ONE
    4 . 257
    5 . 02345667889999
    6 . 01445567
    7 . 0011568
    8 . 4555
    9 . 1359
```

NORMAL   This keyword produces a normal probability plot and a detrended normal probability plot for each interval variable. If a variable is normally distributed, the points of its normal probability plot will tend to form a straight line. The detrended normal probability plot displays the deviations of each ranked point from normal expected values. For a normally distributed random variable, the points of this plot should be clustered about 0. The detrended plot can also give information about the shape of the distribution (skewness and kurtosis). Both plots can be used to assess the marginal normality of each variable. A sample output showing these plots is given in Figure 1.51d.

Figure 1.51d

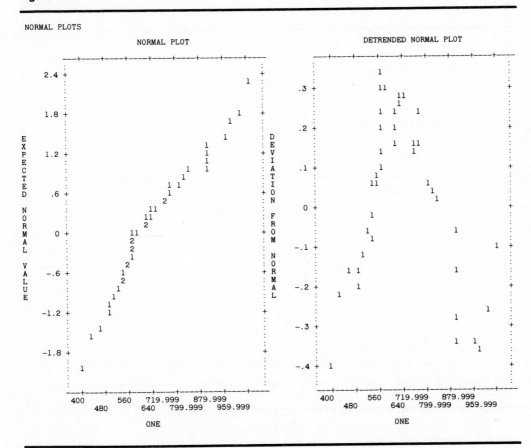

ZCORR For each (adjusted) error correlation matrix, a half-normal plot for the absolute values of Fisher's z-transformation of the correlation coefficient is produced. If the population error correlation matrix is an identity matrix, the plot should show a reasonably straight line (Everitt, 1978). A sample output with p = 6 (where p is the number of response variables) is given in Figure 1.51e.

Figure 1.51e

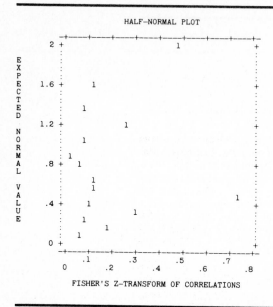

PMEAN This keyword requests, for each response variable, plots of the observed, adjusted, and estimated means and a plot of the standardized residuals for each cell. Note that

```
PRINT=PMEANS/
```

must also be specified for these plots to be produced. A sample output is shown in Figure 1.51f.

Figure 1.51f

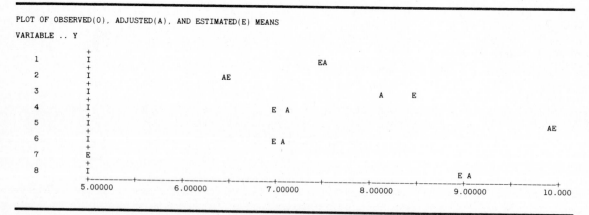

POBS This keyword produces six plots, all but one of which are residual plots. They are

A plot of observed versus predicted values. This plot can be used to examine the model's goodness of fit for each individual response variable.

A plot of observed values versus standardized residuals.

A plot of predicted values versus standardized residuals and a plot of case number versus standardized residuals. If the model is adequate, both plots should show a horizontal band of residuals centered at 0.

A normal probability plot and a detrended normal probability plot for the standardized residuals. These two plots are used to examine the marginal distributions of the residuals.

Note that

```
PRINT=POBS/
```

must be specified for these plots to be produced.

1.52   MANOVA COMMANDS

The following sections elaborate upon the MANOVA subcommands and specifications outlined in Section 1.1.

1.53   Dependent Variable List

The *dependent variable list* specifies those variables to be used as dependent variables in the analyses. The TO convention may be used. The role of a variable, whether it is a dependent variable or a covariate, may be changed later via the ANALYSIS specification.

1.54   Factor List

The *factor list* specifies those SPSS variables to be used as factors in the forthcoming analyses. These variables should be nominal or ordinal in scale. Each factor is followed by a pair of parentheses enclosing two integers: the first denotes the lowest value for a factor, the second denotes the highest value for a factor.

Cases with values of the factor outside these bounds are excluded from the analysis. The difference between the bounds gives the number of levels for the factor. If several factors have the same value range, a list of factors followed by a single value range in parentheses may be specified.

For example, suppose there are three factors, FACTOR1, FACTOR2, FACTOR3, each of which takes on values from 3 to 5. The following are then equivalent:

```
FACTOR1(3,5), FACTOR2(3,5), FACTOR3(3,5)
FACTOR1, FACTOR2, FACTOR3(3,5)
```

This implies that all cases wherein the values of FACTOR1, FACTOR2, or FACTOR3 lie outside the range 3 through 5 will be excluded from the analysis. Also note that each of the factors has three levels:

FACTOR1 = 3 — 1st level
FACTOR1 = 4 — 2nd level
FACTOR1 = 5 — 3rd level

Since MANOVA assumes integer values for factor levels, non-integer valued factors should be recoded to have consecutive integer values. For example, the alphanumeric variable RELIGION which has 6 values—'CATH', 'PROT', 'JEW ', 'NONE', 'OTHE', ' '—could be converted to a factor with integer values as follows:

```
RECODE      RELIGION('CATH'=1)('PROT'=2)('JEW '=3)('NONE'=4)
                     ('OTHE'=5)('     '=99)
MISSING VALUES RELIGION(99)
```

Probably the missing category should not be included in the analysis; hence the MISSING VALUES specification. This leaves RELIGION as a factor with five categories or levels which would be indicated by writing

```
RELIGION(1,5)
```

on the MANOVA command. Certain "one-cell" designs, such as univariate and multivariate regression analysis, canonical correlation, and one-sample Hotelling T^2, do not require a factor. To facilitate these analyses, the factor list, including the keyword BY, may be omitted.

1.55   Covariate List

The *covariate list* following the keyword WITH specifies those interval-valued (continuous) variables to be used as covariates in the analysis. Omit the keyword WITH and the covariate list if no covariates are used. A covariate may later be used as a dependent variable by using the ANALYSIS specification.

1.56 WSFACTORS

The WSFACTORS specification provides the names and number of levels for within-subjects factors. The syntax is

```
WSFACTORS = name1(11), name2(12).../
```

Each name(i) cannot be the same as that of any grouping (between-subjects) factor, dependent variable, or covariate in the current MANOVA run. The l(i) are the levels for each factor.

Only one WSFACTORS specification may appear in a given MANOVA command. When used it must be the first subcommand after the initial variable definition. There may be no more than 10 within- subjects and grouping factors together.

Here are some examples:

1 A single within-subject factor with three levels:

```
WSFACTORS = PERIOD(3)/
```

2 Two within-subjects factors, each with three levels:

```
WSFACTORS = PERIOD, DIAL(3)/
```

(The same propagation of level numbers is done here as for between-subjects factors in the initial variable list.)

3 Three within-subjects factors:

```
WSFACTORS = PERIOD(3), DIAL(3), TIME(6)/
```

The order in which variables are presented on the dependent variables list defines the values of those variables at the various combinations of levels of each of the within-subjects factors. The number of dependent variables must be an integral multiple of the product of the levels of the within-subject factors. For example, suppose that temperature and weight have been measured at two different times (AM and PM) on three successive days in four groups of animals. The following MANOVA specifications may be used to indicate this experimental structure:

```
MANOVA      TEMP1 TO TEMP6,
            WEIGHT1 TO WEIGHT6 BY GROUP(1,4)/
            WSFACTOR = AMPM(2), DAY(3)/
                    .
                    .
```

There are six variables representing the values of each of the dependent variables temperature and weight. The order in which the variables are presented is important: They must be specified in the order corresponding to the matching levels of the within-subjects factors. For the above example,

Variable	AMPM	DAY
TEMP1, WEIGHT1	1	1
TEMP2, WEIGHT2	1	2
TEMP3, WEIGHT3	1	3
TEMP4, WEIGHT4	2	1
TEMP5, WEIGHT5	2	2
TEMP6, WEIGHT6	2	3

The index value of the rightmost within-subjects factor in the WSFACTOR list increments most rapidly.

Note that the above example is incomplete; generally, the analysis of a design incorporating within- subject factors requires either a pre-analysis transformation of the data or the use of the SPSS MANOVA TRANSFORM or WSDESIGN specifications. See the TRANSFORM and WSDESIGN sections for more information.

1.57 TRANSFORM

The TRANSFORM specification provides for linear transformation of all (or selected subsets of) the dependent variables and covariates. There may be any number of such transformations in a MANOVA run. The general form is

```
TRANSFORM (variable list1/variable list2/...) =
         [ORTHONORM]   { DEVIATIONS (refcat)    }
                       { DIFFERENCE             }
         [BASIS]       { HELMERT                }
         [CONTRAST]    { SIMPLE (refcat)        }
                       { REPEATED               }
                       { POLYNOMIAL [(metric)]  }
                       { SPECIAL (matrix)       }
                       { WSDESIGN <effect list> }
```

The *varlists* specify those variables to be transformed. Each of these lists must contain the same number of variables. The transformation is applied to each list. All dependent variables and covariates are transformed if no lists appear. Variables not included in one of the lists are left untouched.

Available transformations include all those available as factor contrasts. CONTRAST requests that the specific transformation be generated from the contrast matrix of the given type, while BASIS requests generation from the corresponding one-way basis. See the CONTRAST subcommand for the details of the different matrices. However, CONTRAST is ignored if WSDESIGN is the transformation type chosen; contrasts for within-subjects factors may be supplied via the CONTRAST= subcommand (see below).

ORTHONORM requests that the transformation matrix be orthonormalized by rows before use. Redundant rows are zeroed.

Alternatively, the transformation may be generated from a set of effects written in terms of the within-subjects factors using WSDESIGN. This approach eases the specification of within-subject design matrices for repeated-measures problems.

There may be any number of TRANSFORM specifications. The effect of each lasts until the next is encountered.

Some examples of the use of TRANSFORM follow.

1.58   REPEATED—repeated differences

Schematically, this transformation is

$$
\begin{array}{lll}
(\text{VAR1}) & (1/p\ 1/p\ 1/p\ \ldots\ 1/p\ 1/p) & (\text{VAR1}) \\
(\text{VAR2}) & (\ 1\ \ -1\ \ \ 0\ \ \ldots\ \ 0\ \ \ 0\ ) & (\text{VAR2}) \\
(\text{VAR3}) & (\ 0\ \ \ \ 1\ \ -1\ \ \ldots\ \ 0\ \ \ 0\ ) & (\text{VAR3}) \\
. \quad = & (\qquad\quad \ldots \quad\quad) & . \\
. & (\qquad\quad \ldots \quad\quad) & . \\
. & (\qquad\quad \ldots \quad\quad) & . \\
(\text{VARp}) & (\ 0\ \ \ \ 0\ \ \ \ 0\ \ \ldots\ \ 1\ \ -1\ ) & (\text{VARp}) \\
(\text{new variables}) & (p{\times}p\ \text{transformation matrix}) & (\text{old variables})
\end{array}
$$

where p is the number of variables being transformed. For example, the specification TRANS-FORM(A,B,C) = REPEATED/ results in the following for each case:

- A is replaced by (A+B+C)/3
- B is replaced by (A-B)
- C is replaced by (B-C)

This transformation is useful in profile analysis and repeated measures designs where difference scores are needed.

1.59   POLYNOMIAL (metric) — orthogonal polynomial transformation

The variables in the transformation list are fitted by orthogonal polynomials. The first variable is replaced by the mean, the second by the linear component, the third by the quadratic component, and so on.

The metric for the transformation may follow the keyword POLYNOMIAL in parentheses. The metric is the set of coefficients for the linear polynomial and indicates the spacing between the points represented by the values of the variables. For equal spacing, a metric consisting of the integers 1 to p, where p is the number of variables transformed, suffices:

```
TRANSFORM(A,B,C,D) = POLYNOMIAL(1,2,3,4)/
```

The above can also be written as POLYNOMIAL/ without specifying the metric. When not specified, the metric defaults to successive integers. However, unequal spacing may also be presumed. For example, consider the case of fitting a set of five variables representing five successive measurements of body weight. To explore the significance of any curvilinear trend in the change in body weight with respect to time the various polynomial components must be extracted.

Assume a scheme like the following:

Variable	Contents
WT1	Body weight on 1st day
WT2	Body weight on 3rd day
WT3	Body weight on 7th day
WT4	Body weight on 12th day
WT5	Body weight on 20th day

The required polynomial components will be obtained by stating

```
TRANSFORM(WT1,WT2,WT3,WT4,WT5)=POLYNOMIAL(1,3,7,12,20)/
```

The transformation in matrix terms is

(WT1)	mean		(		)	(WT1)
(WT2)	linear comp.		(	orthogonal polynomial	)	(WT2)
(WT3)	quadratic comp.	=	(	coeficients generated	)	(WT3)
(WT4)	cubic comp.		(	from metric	)	(WT4)
(WT5)	quartic comp.		(		)	(WT5)
(new variables)			(	transformation matrix	)	(old variables)

The results of the transformation are

New Variable	Original contents for each case replaced by
WT1	(WT1+WT2+WT3+WT4+WT5) / 5
WT2	linear component of polynomial
WT3	quadratic component of polynomial
WT4	cubic component of polynomial
WT5	quartic component of polynomial

1.60 SPECIAL (matrix) — any user-specified linear transformation

The arbitrary transformation matrix is entered rowwise within the pair of parentheses following the keyword SPECIAL. The matrix must be square with the number of rows and columns equal to the number of variables being transformed. For example, the transformation

```
(1  1  -1)
(2  0   1)
(1  0  -1)
```

appears as

```
TRANSFORM(VAR1,VAR2,VAR3)=SPECIAL( 1  1  -1,
                                   2  0   1,
                                   1  0  -1 )/
```

on the MANOVA command.

1.61 Multiple variable lists

The transformation of above example is to be applied to two sets of variables, VAR1 to VAR3 and VAR4 to VAR6. In matrix terms we write

(VAR1)		(1	1	-1	0	0	0)	(VAR1)
(VAR2)		(2	0	1	0	0	0)	(VAR2)
(VAR3)	=	(1	0	-1	0	0	0)	(VAR3)
(VAR4)		(0	0	0	1	1	-1)	(VAR4)
(VAR5)		(0	0	0	2	0	1)	(VAR5)
(VAR6)		(0	0	0	1	0	-1)	(VAR6)

We could write the TRANSFORM specification for this as follows:

```
TRANSFORM(VAR1 TO VAR3, VAR4 TO VAR6) =
         SPECIAL(1 1 -1 0 0  0,
                 2 0  1 0 0  0,
                 1 0 -1 0 0  0,
                 0 0  0 1 1 -1,
                 0 0  0 2 0  1,
                 0 0  0 1 0 -1 ) /
```

However, we can abbreviate this using multiple variable lists:

```
TRANSFORM(VAR1 TO VAR3/VAR4 TO VAR6) =
         SPECIAL( 1  1  -1
                  2  0   1
                  1  0  -1 ) /
```

1.62 WSDESIGN—specification of a within-subjects design

The WSDESIGN specification creates a within-subjects transformation matrix based upon the current ordering of the interval variables in the transformation lists and the product of the levels of the within-subjects factors. The transformation matrix is generated from the basis matrices corresponding to the contrast matrices specified in any preceding CONTRAST subcommands for the within-subjects factors. Generally, the transformation matrix should be orthonormalized by requesting ORTHONORM on the TRANSFORM as well, since this allows recovery of the mixed-model results from the multivariate analysis. Effects using the within-subjects factors may be specified as in the DESIGN= subcommand (see below) with these restrictions:

- Error term references/definitions are not allowed.
- CONSPLUS may not appear.
- CONSTANT may not appear.
- Interval variables may not appear.
- Between-subjects factors may not appear.

The first row of the transformation matrix generated from this design is always a row of ones (for the constant term). Successive rows are generated from the given effects in left-to-right order.

Consider the example presented under the WSFACTORS subcommand wherein the weight and temperature have been measured at two different times (AM and PM) on three successive days in four groups of animals. Assume we want a simple comparison of the two levels of the AMPM factor and comparisons of adjacent days in the DAY factor. Then we could write the following transformation to handle this design:

```
MANOVA        TEMP1 TO TEMP6,
              WEIGHT1 TO WEIGHT6 BY GROUP(1,4)/
              WSFACTOR = AMPM(2), DAYS(3)/
              CONTRAST(DAY) = REPEATED/
              TRANSFORM = WSDESIGN AMPM, DAYS, AMPM BY DAYS/
```

Note that the WSDESIGN subcommand may also be used separately from the TRANSFORM specification. See the next section for further details.

1.63 WSDESIGN

The WSDESIGN subcommand specifies a within-subjects model. Actually, the WSDESIGN subcommand is a short-cut form of the TRANSFORM specification. The description of WSDESIGN under TRANSFORM also applies to the syntax of the free-standing WSDESIGN subcommand. The following are actually equivalent:

```
WSDESIGN  =   <effects> /
```

```
TRANSFORM = ORTHO WSDESIGN  <effects> /
```

See the WSDESIGN specification under the TRANSFORM specification for more details.

1.64 RENAME

Sometimes it is desirable to rename the dependent variables and covariates of an analysis within an SPSS MANOVA procedure run, particularly if those variables have been transformed using TRANSFORM. The RENAME specification provides this temporary renaming capability. The format is

```
RENAME = newname1, newname2,..., newnamep/
```

where each newnamei is the new name for the ith interval variable as specified previously in the MANOVA command. All dependent variables and covariates must be accounted for in the RENAME specification. However, a variable may be "renamed" to itself, or the new name may be '*'—in which case the original name is retained.

For example, suppose the following MANOVA procedure defines an analysis of interest:

```
MANOVA        A,B,C,V4,V5 BY TREATMNT(1,3)/
              TRANSFORM(A,B,C)=REPEATED/
```

The TRANSFORM results in the following new meanings for the variables:

Variable	New Meaning
A	(A+B+C)/3
B	A-B
C	B-C
V4	V4 (unchanged)
V5	V5 (unchanged)

The following RENAME specification could be used to clarify the new meanings of the variables:

```
RENAME = MEANABC, AMINUSB, BMINUSC, *, */
```

Successive output from this MANOVA run will print MEANABC instead of the variable name A; likewise, AMINUSB will be printed instead of B, and BMINUSC will be printed instead of C. V4 and V5 are unchanged.

Following is another example of renaming:

```
MANOVA        WT1,WT2,WT3,WT4,WT5 BY TREATMNT(1,3)/
              TRANSFORM = POLYNOMIAL (1,2,3,4,5)/
              RENAME = MEAN,LINEAR, QUAD,CUBIC,QUARTIC/
```

NOTE: References to the dependent variables or covariates in specifications following the RENAME must use the new names. The old names are completely forgotten.

1.65 METHOD

The METHOD subcommand provides for specifying a number of computational options. The syntax of this subcommand is

```
METHOD = MODELTYPE(  [MEANS]          )
                     [OBSERVATIONS]

         ESTIMATION( [QR]        [BALANCED]   [LASTRES]    [CONSTANT]    )
                     [CHOLESKY]  [NOBALANCED] [NOLASTRES]  [NOCONSTANT]

         SSTYPE( [SEQUENTIAL] )             /
                 [UNIQUE]
```

1.66 MODELTYPE

The MODELTYPE keyword specifies the type of model to be used in parameter estimation. MEANS requests that the model written in terms of cell means be used (the default) while OBSERVATIONS requests that the model written in terms of observations be used. The observations model is always used when interval variables have been specified in the DESIGN subcommand. Note that computing parameter estimates using the observations model is much costlier than obtaining the same estimates using the means model. Thus, use of the observations model is not suggested unless it is needed.

1.67 ESTIMATION

The ESTIMATION keyword specifies how the estimation of parameters—the fundamental numerical process in MANOVA—is to be accomplished. The default is to estimate parameters using Householder transformations to effect a QR (orthogonal) decomposition of the design matrix. This method bypasses forming the normal equations (and the inaccuracies which can result from creating the cross-product matrix) and generally results in extremely accurate estimates of the parameters. This processing is also selected by requesting the QR keyword. A less expensive—and sometimes less accurate procedure —is to solve the normal equations using the Cholesky method. This processing is selected by specifying the CHOLESKY keyword. Lastly, for balanced and orthogonal problems, a special balanced processing may be requested by specifying BALANCED. SPSS MANOVA will use this special processing if possible. The requirements are

• All cells must be filled.
• The cell-means model must apply.
• The cell sizes for all cells must be equal.
• The contrast type for each factor must be orthogonal.

Note that if the special balanced processing is requested, but the design does not conform to the requirements for that processing, then the regular method (full least-squares using QR or Cholesky) will be used. To suppress the balanced processing in cases where it would normally be used, the NOBALANCED keyword may appear. Estimation then proceeds using the QR or Cholesky methods, whichever is in force.

Factorial designs involving many factors frequently include a highest-order interaction term corresponding to a large number of columns in the reduced model-matrix and thus a large number of estimated parameters. The computational labor involved can be significantly reduced if parameter estimates for the interaction are not required even though the significance test for the interaction is desired. This is because the sum of squares attributable to this effect may be obtained by subtraction if this interaction is ordered last in the model. LASTRES causes MANOVA to compute the last effect in the design by subtracting the among-groups sum of squares and cross-products from the total sum of squares and cross-products. LASTRES may also be valuable in cases involving missing cells—the labor of determining the confounded effects is saved. NOLASTRES reverses the effect of LASTRES. NOTE: The last effect with LASTRES specified may not contain any interval variables. Also, LASTRES may not be used if UNIQUE (see SSTYPE below) is used. This is because the sum of squares will not add up to the total sum of squares, except for balanced designs. Thus the sum of squares for the last effect cannot be computed by subtraction.

CONSTANT requests that a constant (intercept) term be included in the model even if one is not explicitly specified in the DESIGN subcommand. NOCONSTANT requests that the constant term not be included unless explicitly specified in the DESIGN subcommand.

1.68 SSTYPE

By default, SPSS MANOVA partitions the sums of squares attributable to terms in the model in a hierarchical fashion. A term is corrected for all terms to its left in a given design specification, and is confounded with all terms to its right. This sequential decomposition results in an orthogonal decomposition of the sums of squares—the sums of squares for model terms do not overlap. These sums of squares are also produced when the keyword SEQUENTIAL appears.

For unbalanced designs, however, the sums of squares for any one ordering of effects may not be sufficient. Further, the hypotheses corresponding to those sums of squares for any but the last term in the ordering can be difficult to interpret since in parametric terms they represent combinations of means weighted by the observed cell frequencies. An alternate set of sums of squares which may be of greater interest is that which results from ordering each term last in the design—i.e., each term is corrected for every other term in the model. Such sums of squares correspond to unweighted combinations of means. These sums of squares may be obtained by specifying UNIQUE.

Note that the sums of squares produced by UNIQUE are not orthogonal except for balanced designs. Thus, they will not add up to the total sum of squares for the model.

1.69 PRINT/NOPRINT

The PRINT and NOPRINT subcommands control the amount of printed output produced by SPSS MANOVA. The syntax for both subcommands is identical; PRINT requests that specified output be produced while NOPRINT suppresses it. The syntax is

```
PRINT     =    CELLINFO( [MEANS] [SSCP] [COV] [COR] )
  or
NOPRINT        HOMOGENEITY( [BARTLETT] [COCHRAN] [BOXM] )
               DESIGN( [ONEWAY] [OVERALL] [BIAS] [DECOMP]
                       [SOLUTION]        )
               PRINCOMPS( [COR] [COV] [MINEIGEN(eigcut)]
                          [NCOMP(n)] [ROTATE(rottyp)] )
               ERROR( [SSCP] [COV] [COR] [STDV] )
               SIGNIF( [HYPOTH] [MULTIV] [EIGEN]
                       [DIMENR] [UNIV] [STEPDOWN]
                       [AVERF] [BRIEF]        )
               DISCRIM( [RAW] [STAN] [ESTIM] [COR]
                        [ROTATE(rottyp)] [ALPHA(alpha)] )
               PARAMETERS( [ESTIM] [COR] [ORTHO] [NEGSUM] )
               OMEANS[ ( VARIABLES(var list)
                         TABLES( table requests ) ) ]
               PMEANS[ ( VARIABLES(var list)
                         TABLES( table requests )
                         ERROR( errorn ) ) ]
               POBS [ ERROR( errorn ) ]
               FORMAT( [WIDE]     )    /
                       [NARROW]
```

In the following, a * following a keyword designates the default output produced by SPSS MANOVA if no PRINT or NOPRINT subcommand appears.

1.70 CELLINFO

CELLINFO may be used to request the following statistics:

MEANS Cell means, standard deviations, and counts
SSCP   Cell sums of squares and cross-products
COV   Cell variance/covariance matrices
COR   Cell correlation matrices

1.71 HOMOGENEITY

HOMOGENEITY may be used to request the following statistics which test for homogeneity of variance:

BARTLETT Bartlett-Box F test
COCHRAN   Cochran's C
BOXM   Box's M (multivariate case only)

Note that computation of Box's M requires the variance-covariance matrices for each cell, and is thus a very expensive statistic in terms of both time and memory.

1.72 DESIGN

DESIGN may be used to request the following:

ONEWAY The one-way bases for each factor
OVERALL The overall reduced-model basis
DECOMP The QR/CHOLESKY decomposition of the design
BIAS Contamination coefficients displaying the bias present in the design
SOLUTION Coefficients of the linear combinations of the cell means being tested

The decomposition of the design (DECOMP) and the bias (BIAS) computed from the decomposition can provide valuable information on the confounding of the effects and the estimability of the chosen contrasts. This is particularly useful in designs with unpatterned empty cells.

1.73 PRINCOMPS

PRINCOMPS requests a principal-components analysis of each error SSCP in the multivariate case. Principal components of the error correlation matrix are produced by specifying COR; principal components of the error variance-covariance matrix are produced by specifying COV. Factors extracted from these matrices are corrected for group differences and covariates. Such factors tend to be more useful than factors extracted from an uncorrected matrix when significant group differences are present or a significant amount of error variance is accounted for by the covariates.

(Note that a principal components analysis requires the extraction of eigenvalues and eigenvectors, an expensive process if many dependent variables are specified.)

The ROTATE(rottyp) keyword provides for rotating the principal component loadings. Descriptions of the three rotations, VARIMAX, EQUAMAX and QUARTIMAX, may be found in section 24.3 of the SPSS manual. The NOROTATE specification inhibits rotation. If the ROTATE keyword does not appear, no rotations are performed.

All components are rotated by default. A lesser number may be rotated by specifying that number in parentheses after the NCOMP keyword, i.e., NCOMP(n), or by specifying the cutoff value for eigenvalues as MINEIGEN(eigcut) . For example,

```
PRINT = PRINCOMPS( COR ROTATE(VARIMAX) NCOMP(3) )/
```

would rotate the first three components, while

```
PRINT = PRINCOMPS( COR ROTATE(VARIMAX) MINEIGEN(1.5) )/
```

would rotate those components associated with eigenvalues greater than 1.5.

Specification of n greater than the number of components results in rotation of all the components; specification of n less than two results in rotation of at least two components. However, if fewer than two eigenvalues are greater than eigcut, no rotation is performed.

1.74 ERROR

ERROR may be used to request

SSCP Error sums of squares and cross-products matrix
COV Error variance-covariance matrix
COR Error correlation matrix and standard deviations
STDV Error standard deviations (univariate case)

SPSS MANOVA routinely prints the determinant and a test of no-association for each error matrix in the multivariate case. The test of no-association is a test of sphericity, and is most useful when the dependent variables are transformed variables in a repeated-measures analysis.

1.75 SIGNIF

SIGNIF may be used to request

HYPOTH The hypothesis SSCP matrix
MULTIV* Multivariate F tests for group differences
EIGEN* Eigenvalues of $S_h S_e^{-1}$
DIMENR* A dimension-reduction analysis
UNIV* Univariate F tests
STEPDOWN Roy-Bargmann stepdown F tests
AVERF An averaged F test (for repeated measures)
BRIEF A shortened multivariate output; overrides all the above if requested

NOTE: The output with BRIEF specified consists of a table similar in appearance to a univariate ANOVA table but with the generalized F and Wilks' lambda replacing the univariate F. This feature is useful in the analysis of repeated-measures designs.

1.76   DISCRIM
DISCRIM requests that a discriminant analysis be performed for each effect in a multivariate analysis. Specific output which may be requested is

RAW   Raw discriminant function coefficients
STAN   Standardized discriminant function coefficients
ESTIM   Effect estimates in discriminant function space
COR   Correlations between the dependent and canonical variables defined by the discriminant functions.

The ROTATE(rottyp) keyword provides for rotation of the correlations between the dependent and canonical variates obtained for each effect. (This does not include the multivariate test of regression; rotation is not performed in this case.) The available rotation types are the same as for the ROTATE keyword of the PRINCOMPS specification.

No rotation is performed unless there are at least two significant canonical variates. The number of significant canonical variates depends upon the rank of $S_h S_e^{-1}$ for a given effect, and also upon the significance level chosen. This significance level is 0.15 by default, but it may be changed by using the ALPHA(alpha) keyword. The alpha value specified with ALPHA(alpha) indicates the cutoff value for the significance of the discriminant functions in multivariate analysis; alpha must be a decimal number from zero to one (0.0 to 1.0). Discriminant analysis results are reported only for those functions with a significance less than alpha. The default value of alpha is 0.15. Setting alpha=1.0 results in the printing of all discriminant functions. Specifying alpha to be negative or greater than one results in alpha being set to the default of 0.15.

Examples:

```
PRINT = DISCRIM( RAW ALPHA(0.0) ) /    reports no functions
PRINT = DISCRIM( RAW ALPHA(1.0) ) /    reports all functions
PRINT = DISCRIM( RAW ALPHA(.05) ) /    reports functions signibcant
                                           at .05 level or better
```

In the case of a multivariate regression term, special extra output is produced automatically if DISCRIM appears. This includes a comprehensive canonical correlation analysis.

1.77   PARAMETERS
PARAMETERS requests output relating to the estimated parameters. This includes

ESTIM*   The estimates themselves, along with their standard errors, t-tests, and confidence intervals.
ORTHO   The orthogonal estimates of parameters used to produce the sums of squares
COR   Correlations among the parameters
NEGSUM   For main-effects, the negative sum of the other parameters (representing the parameter for the omitted category)

1.78   OMEANS
The OMEANS specification requests tables of combined observed means. The general format is

```
OMEANS( VARIABLES(varlist) TABLES(table-requests) )
```

Varlist contains the names of those variables for which combined observed means are to be calculated. This list may contain the name of any dependent variable or covariate. Should no list be given, combined means for all variables will be reported. Both weighted and unweighted means are reported.

Table-requests may be one of the following:

• A single grouping factor name yielding a marginal table
• Several grouping factor names connected by the keyword BY yielding summary tables
• The keyword CONSTANT yielding the grand mean

As an example, suppose the following MANOVA specification appears:

```
MANOVA        V1 TO V10 BY A(1,2), B(1,3) WITH V11 TO V15/
              PRINT = OMEANS( TABLES( A, B, A BY B ) )/
```

This requests the following tables of weighted and unweighted means on variables V1 to V10 and V11 to V15:

```
      A   (collapsing over B)
      B   (collapsing over A)
  A BY B  (the observed cell means themselves)
```

However,

```
PRINT = OMEANS( VARIABLES( V1, V11 ) TABLES( A ) )/
```

requests only the A table for variables V1 and V11.

Entering
```
PRINT = OMEANS( VARIABLES( V1, V11 ) TABLES(CONSTANT) )/
```

produces only the grand means for variables V1 and V11.

1.79 PMEANS

PMEANS requests computation of predicted and adjusted (for covariates) means. These are produced for each design for each error term in the design. Note that this is an expensive set of statistics to produce.

Predicted/adjusted means combined across subclasses may be obtained by use of the VARIABLES, TABLES, and ERROR specifications. The general format is

```
PMEANS( VARIABLES(varlist) TABLES(table-requests)
        ERROR(error) ) /
```

Only dependent variables may appear in the varlist. The format of the varlist and the table-requests is the same as for OMEANS.

The PMEANS specification should precede the DESIGN specifications to which it applies. A given PMEANS remains in effect for all subsequent designs until another PMEANS subcommand appears.

In designs with covariates and multiple error terms the ERROR(error) specification should be used to designate which error term's regression coefficients are to be used in calculating the predicted means. The format for specifying an error term with ERROR follows that of the ERROR= subcommand. Should no ERROR(error) appear when it is needed then no predicted means output will appear. Predicted means are also suppressed if the last term is being calculated by subtraction (METHOD = ESTIM(LASTRES)) or the design contains the CONSPLUS keyword (see DESIGN= below).

1.80 POBS

POBS requests printing of predicted values and residuals for each case used in the analysis. The output includes

• The observed value of each dependent variable
• The predicted value of each dependent variable
• The raw residual (observed − predicted)
• The standardized residual (raw residual divided by the error standard deviation)

As with PMEANS, the ERROR specification should appear for designs with covariates and multiple error terms. No output results if the error term is not specified when needed. Predicted observations are also suppressed if the last term is being calculated by subtraction (METHOD = ESTIM(LASTRES)) or the design contains the CONSPLUS keyword (see DESIGN= below).

Note that the PUNCH subcommand also provides a POBS ERROR specification. The error terms requested should be the same. If they differ then the last appearing is used.

If the designated error term does not exist for a given design then no predicted values or residuals are calculated. This is an expensive set of statistics to compute.

1.81 PLOT

The PLOT subcommand requests that plots be produced by SPSS MANOVA. The general syntax of this subcommand is

```
PLOT    =    [CELLPLOTS] [NORMAL] [BOXPLOTS]
             [STEMLEAF]  [ZCORR]  [PMEANS] [POBS]
             [ SIZE( nhor , nvert ) ]              /
```

CELLPLOTS   CELLPLOTS produces the following plots for each interval variable:

        Cell means versus cell variances

        Cell means versus cell standard deviations

        Histogram of cell means

        The first two plots above aid in detecting heteroscedasticity in the input data. The third aids in identifying outlying means.

NORMAL   NORMAL produces a normal plot and a detrended normal plot for each interval variable. The data for each variable are ranked and these ranks are plotted against the expected normal deviate or detrended expected normal deviate for that rank. These plots aid in detecting non-normality and outlying observations.

Note that these plots are expensive in terms of memory, as all of the input data must be stored in order to compute ranks. Should there not be enough memory to store the data, SPSS MANOVA will print a warning and skip these plots.

BOXPLOTS   BOXPLOTS requests Tukey's boxplots for each interval variable. Boxplots provide a simple graphic means of comparing the cells in terms of mean location and spread. Note that the data must be stored in memory for these plots as well. Again, if the data will not fit, then boxplots are not produced.

STEMLEAF   STEMLEAF requests a stem-and-leaf display for each interval variable. This display details the distribution of each interval variable as a whole. Again, these plots require storage of the data in memory and will not be produced if the data do not fit.

ZCORR   ZCORR requests a half-normal plot of the partial correlations among the dependent varibles in a multivariate analysis. The correlations are first transformed using Fisher's Z. A straight line indicates that no significant correlations exist among the dependent variables.

PMEANS   PMEANS requests the following plots:

A group-order plot of the estimated, adjusted, and observed means for each dependent variable

A group-order plot of the mean residuals for each dependent variable

Note that PRINT = PMEANS must be specified or this plot will not be produced.

POBS   POBS requests the following plots:

A plot of observed values versus standardized residuals

A plot of predicted values versus standardized residuals

A plot of case number versus standardized residuals

A normal probability plot and a detrended normal probability plot for the standardized residuals

Note that PRINT=POBS must be specified or this plot will not be produced.

SIZE   By default, all plots are printed so that the plot area occupies 40 horizontal spaces and 25 vertical spaces. This allows two plots to be printed side-by-side and four plots to be printed on a printer page in standard batch-size output. However, the size for the plots may be changed using the SIZE keyword:

```
SIZE( nhor , nvert )
```

where nhor gives the number of horizontal characters in the plot image and nvert the number of vertical lines in the plot image.

User-specified plot sizes will be adjusted should they fall outside the range of the specific device on which the plot is to be printed.

1.82 PUNCH

The PUNCH subcommand is used to request that certain output be routed to the current alternate output file. (This does not necessarily mean that this output will be punched on cards.) The general form of this subcommand is

```
PUNCH  =    CELLINFO( [MEANS]  [SSCP]
                      [COR] [COV] [STDV] )
           ERROR   ( [SSCP] [COR] [COV] [STDV] )
           PMEANS( ERROR( error ) )
           POBS  ( ERROR( error ) )            /
```

1.83 CELLINFO

CELLINFO may be used to request the following matrix materials:

MEANS   Cell means
SSCP   Sum of squares and cross-products matrix
COR   Correlation matrix
COV   Variance/covariance matrix
STDV   Vector of standard deviations

If COR is requested and STDV appears, then the correlation matrix will have ones along the main diagonal. If COR appears but STDV does not then the standard deviations appear along the main diagonal.

1.84 ERROR

ERROR requests output of each error matrix for each design in each analysis. The allowed forms are

SSCP   The sums of squares and cross-products matrix
COV   The variance/covariance matrix
COR   The correlation matrix with standard deviations along the diagonal

All three forms may be requested simultaneously; they will appear on the output file in the same order as the keywords are listed above.

Note that this option can be prolix; care should be taken in its use.

1.85 PMEANS

PMEANS requests estimated and adjusted means. The ERROR(error) keyword indicates which error term's regression coefficients are to be used in computing the predicted means. Any conflict between the error term specified here and that in the PRINT subcommand is resolved by using whichever appears last.

1.86 POBS

POBS requests output of predicted values and residuals for each case. One output record appears for each dependent variable for each design. The format is

Columns	Contents	Format
1 – 8	SEQNUM	F8.0
9 – 16	SUBFILE	A8
17 – 26	CASWGT	F10.4
27 – 44	observed	G18.7
45 – 62	predicted	G18.7
63 – 77	residual	G15.7

The ERROR(error) specification may be used to select the error term whose regression coefficients are to be used in calculating the predicted values. See the POBS specification of the PRINT= specification for a discussion of how conflicts between the subcommands are resolved.

1.87 ANALYSIS

The ANALYSIS specification provides for subsetting and/or reordering of the variables. Variables may be dropped from a given analysis, dependent variables may be made covariates, or covariates may be made dependent variables. There are three formats for this subcommand:

```
ANALYSIS = <dep var list> WITH <covar list>/
                     - or -
ANALYSIS[((CONDITIONAL)  ]    =
        [(UNCONDITIONAL)]
          (<dep list 1> WITH <covar list 1>/
           <dep list 2> WITH <covar list 2>/ ...)
          WITH <covar list> /
                     - or -
ANALYSIS( REPEATED  [CONDITIONAL]    )    /
                    [UNCONDITIONAL]
```

In the first form, the <dep var list> is the new list of dependent variables and <covar list> is the new list of covariates. All variables in both lists must have already appeared in the original variable list of the current MANOVA command. The list of covariates (and thus WITH) need not appear if there are no covariates.

In the second form, each <dep var list> and corresponding <covar list> requests a separate analysis. No overlap is allowed in any of the lists. CONDITIONAL requests that, when more than one analysis list appears, subsequent lists include as covariates all previously listed variables in the previous lists. UNCONDITIONAL requests that each list be used "as is" independent of the others. Also note that a final covariate list may appear outside the parentheses. These covariates apply to every list contained within the parentheses, regardless of whether CONDITIONAL or UNCONDITIONAL appears. The variables in this global covariate list must not duplicate any variables in the individual lists.

The third form of the ANALYSIS subcommand requests an automatic repeated measures analysis. Both CONDITIONAL and UNCONDITIONAL analyses may be selected.

The ANALYSIS specification completely overrides the dependent variables list and covariates list in the MANOVA command. However, the factor list is not affected by the ANALYSIS specification.

Here are some examples illustrating the uses of ANALYSIS.

1 Changing dependent variable C to a covariate:
```
MANOVA        A,B,C BY FAC(1,4)/
              .
              ANALYSIS=A,B WITH C/
```

2 Changing covariate D to a dependent variable:
```
MANOVA        A,B,C BY FAC(1,4) WITH D,E/
              .
              ANALYSIS=A,B,C,D WITH E/
```

3 Deleting variables B,C,D and E from the analysis
```
MANOVA        A,B,C BY FAC(1,4) WITH D,E/
              .
              ANALYSIS=A/
```

4 Multiple variable lists:
```
MANOVA        A,B,C BY FAC(1,4) WITH D,E/
              .
              ANALYSIS = (A,B/ C/ D WITH E)/
```

Here three separate analyses are requested: One with A and B as dependent variables, the second with C dependent, and the third with D dependent and E a covariate. Note that the same effect could ostensibly be obtained by writing three separate ANALYSIS subcommands, but the single subcommand above is much cheaper to use. This is because separate ANALYSIS subcommands require complete reestimation for all subsequent designs, whereas the compound ANALYSIS only requires reordering already-computed estimates.

5 Global covariate list:
```
MANOVA        A, B, C, D, E, F BY FAC(1,4)/
              .
              ANALYSIS = ( A, B/ C/ D WITH E ) WITH F /
```

Here the same three separate analyses are requested as in 4 above but in addition variable *F* is to be used as a covariate in each list. This example is equivalent to writing
```
MANOVA        A, B, C, D, E, F BY FAC(1,4)/
              .
              ANALYSIS = ( A, B WITH F/ C WITH F/ D WITH E,F ) /
```

Variables not included in the ANALYSIS subcommand may be incorporated into the analysis via the DESIGN subcommand. A full discussion appears in that section.

The third form of the ANALYSIS subcommand requests an automatic cycling through the within-subjects effects defined by a previously-appearing TRANSFORM WSDESIGN or WSDESIGN subcommand. Should neither of these subcommands have appeared, then the ANALYSIS(REPEATED) subcommand is ignored. Otherwise, the effect is as if an ANALYSIS subcommand of type two above had been entered with variable lists defined by the within-subjects factors. However, the labeling of effects will be improved if the ANALYSIS(REPEATED) feature is used.

For example, consider the example previously discussed under WSFACTORS and WSDESIGN:
```
MANOVA        TEMP1 TO TEMP6 BY GROUP(1,4)
                  WITH WEIGHT1 TO WEIGHT6/
              WSFACTORS = AMPM(2), DAY(3) /
              WSDESIGN  = AMPM, DAY, AMPM BY DAY /
              ANALYSIS(REPEATED)/
```

In this case ANALYSIS(REPEATED) produces the same results as specifying
```
              ANALYSIS = ( TEMP1 WITH WEIGHT1 /
                           TEMP2 WITH WEIGHT2 /
                           TEMP3, TEMP4 WITH WEIGHT3, WEIGHT4/
                           TEMP5, TEMP6 WITH WEIGHT5, WEIGHT6 ) /
```

1.88 PARTITION

The PARTITION specification provides for subdividing the degrees of freedom of a factor. The general format is
```
              PARTITION(factorname) = (ndf1,ndf2,...,ndfn)/
```

where factorname is the name of the factor, and the parenthesized list of integer values ndf1, ndf2, ... indicates the number of degrees of freedom for each partition. Each value in the list must be greater than zero and less than or equal to the total number of degrees of freedom for the factor (=one less than the number of levels for the factor). Further, the sum of the partition degrees of freedom must be less than or equal to the total number of degrees of freedom for the factor. The maximum number of partitions allowed for a factor (achieved by specifying each $ndf_i = 1$) is likewise the total number of degrees of freedom for the factor. If the sum of the ndf_i totals less than the degrees of freedom for the factor, then a final partition category containing the left-over degrees of freedom is automatically generated.

For example, consider the factor TREATMNT, which has twelve levels, or eleven degrees of freedom. To partition TREATMNT into single degrees of freedom, write

```
PARTITION(TREATMNT) = (1,1,1,1,1,1,1,1,1,1,1)/
```

or, using a repeat factor,

```
PARTITION(TREATMNT) = (11*1)/
```

Another way to request a single-degree-of-freedom breakdown is

```
PARTITION(TREATMNT)/
```

i.e., the default degrees of freedom vector consists of all ones. This is also the initial partition ascribed to any factor.

To partition TREATMNT into three subdivisions, the first containing three degrees of freedom, the second two degrees of freedom, the third six degrees of freedom, write

```
PARTITION(TREATMNT) = (3,2,6)/
```

This could also have been written

```
PARTITION(TREATMNT) = (3,2)/
```

SPSS MANOVA will automatically generate a third partition with (11 - 3 - 2) or 6 degrees of freedom in this case.

1.89 CONTRAST

The CONTRAST specification indicates the type of contrast desired for a factor. The general format for this specification is

```
                        { DEVIATION [(refcat)]   }
                        { DIFFERENCE             }
                        { HELMERT                }
CONTRAST(factorname) =  { SIMPLE [(refcat)]      }   /
                        { REPEATED               }
                        { POLYNOMIAL [(metric)]  }
                        { SPECIAL (matrix)       }
```

where factorname is the factor whose contrast is being selected.

DEVIATION   Chosen by default: the usual deviations from the grand means of the dependent variable. In matrix terms, these contrasts have the form:

mean	(	1/k	1/k	. . .	1/k	1/k	)
df(1)	(	1-1/k	-1/k	. . .	-1/k	-1/k	)
df(2)	(	-1/k	1-1/k	. . .	-1/k	-1/k	)

where k is the number of levels for the factor.

For example, the deviation contrasts for a factor with three levels are

```
(  1/3   1/3   1/3 )
(  2/3  -1/3  -1/3 )
( -1/3   2/3  -1/3 )
```

The deviation for the last category is omitted. However, it is the negative sum of the deviation for the other categories (since the deviations must sum to zero).

It may be of interest to omit another category other than the last. This may be done by specifying the number of the omitted category in parentheses after DEVIATION. For example, the request

```
CONTRAST(FACTOR) = DEVIATION(2) /
```

where FACTOR has three levels results in a contrast matrix of the form

```
(   1/3    1/3    1/3  )
(   2/3   -1/3   -1/3  )
(  -1/3   -1/3    2/3  )
```

where the deviations for the first and third categories are obtained and the second is omitted.

DIFFERENCE   Difference or Reverse Helmert contrasts: compare levels of a factor with the mean of the previous levels of the factor. The general matrix form is

mean	(	1/k	1/k	1/k	...	1/k	)
df(1)	(	-1	1	0	...	0	)
df(2)	(	-1/2	-1/2	1	...	0	)
.				.		
.				.		
df(k-1)	(	-1/(k-1)	-1/(k-1)	-1/(k-1)	...	1	)

where k is the number of levels of the factor.

    For example, a factor with four levels would have a difference contrast matrix of the following form:

```
(  1/4    1/4    1/4   1/4)
( -1      1      0     0  )
( -1/2   -1/2    1     0  )
( -1/3   -1/3   -1/3   1  )
```

SIMPLE   Simple contrasts: compare each level of a factor to the last. The general matrix form is

mean	(	1/k	1/k	...	1/k	1/k	)
df(1)	(	1	0	...	0	-1	)
df(2)	(	0	1	...	0	-1	)
.				.		
.				.		
df(k-1)	(	0	0	...	1	-1	)

where k is the number of levels of the factor.

    For example, a factor with four levels would have a simple contrast matrix of the following form:

```
( 1/4   1/4   1/4    1/4)
( 1     0     0     -1  )
( 0     1     0     -1  )
( 0     0     1     -1  )
```

Sometimes it is useful to use another category besides the last as a reference category. This may be done by specifying the level of the reference category in parentheses after SIMPLE. For example, the request

```
        CONTRAST(FACTOR) = SIMPLE(2)/
```

where FACTOR has four levels results in a contrast matrix of the form

```
( 1/4   1/4   1/4   1/4)
( 1    -1     0     0  )
( 0    -1     1     0  )
( 0    -1     0     1  )
```

HELMERT   Helmert contrasts. The general matrix form is

mean	(	1/k	1/k	...	1/k	1/k	)
df(1)	(	1	-1/(k-1)	...	-1/(k-1)	-1/(k-1)	)
df(2)	(	0	1	...	-1/(k-2)	-1/(k-2)	)
.	(		.		.		)
.	(		.		.		)
.	(		.		.		)
df(k-2)	(	0	0	1	-1/2	-1/2	)
df(k-1)	(	0	0	...	1	-1	)

where k is the number of levels of the factor.

For example, a factor with four levels would have a Helmert contrast matrix of the following form:

```
( 1/4    1/4    1/4    1/4)
( 1     -1/3   -1/3   -1/3)
( 0      1     -1/2   -1/2)
( 0      0      1     -1  )
```

POLYNOMIAL   Orthogonal polynomial contrasts. The keyword POLYNOMIAL may be followed in parentheses by the coefficients of the linear polynomial (metric) indicating the spacing between levels of the treatment measured by the given factor. For equal spacing, specification of the integers from 1 to k (k being the number of levels of the factor) suffices. Equal spacing is not necessary, however, and thus the metric need not be successive integers.

For example, suppose factor DRUG represents different dosages of a drug given to three groups. If the dosage administered to the second group is twice that of the first group, and that of the third group three times that of the first group, then the treatment levels are equally spaced and an appropriate metric for this situation would consist of consecutive integers:

```
CONTRAST(DRUG)=POLYNOMIAL(1,2,3)/
```

If, however, the second group is given four times the dosage level of the first group, and the third group is given seven times that of the first, then an appropriate metric would be

```
CONTRAST(DRUG)=POLYNOMIAL (1,4,7)/
```

In either case the result of the contrast specification is that the first degree of freedom for DRUG will contain the linear effect of the dosage levels and the second degrees of freedom will contain the quadratic effect. In general, the first degree of freedom receives the linear effect, the second degree of freedom the quadratic effect, the third degree of freedom the cubic, and so on for the higher-order effects. Polynomial contrasts are especially useful in tests of trends and for investigating the nature of response surfaces. Polynomial contrasts may also be used to perform non-linear curve-fitting, such as curvilinear regression.

If not specified, the metric defaults to consecutive integers. For example,

```
CONTRAST(DRUG) = POLYNOMIAL/
```

is the same as

```
CONTRAST(DRUG) = POLYNOMIAL (1,2,3)/
```

REPEATED   Compare adjacent levels of a factor. The general matrix form is

```
mean      (   1/k    1/k    1/k    . . .    1/k    1/k    )
df(1)     (   1     -1      0      . . .    0      0      )
df(2)     (   0      1     -1      . . .    0      0      )
  .                          .                     .
  .                          .                     .
  .                          .                     .
df(k-1)   (   0      0      0      . . .    1     -1      )
```

where k is the number of levels for the factors.

For example, the repeated contrasts for a factor with four levels are

```
( 1/4    1/4    1/4    1/4)
( 1     -1      0      0  )
( 0      1     -1      0  )
( 0      0      1     -1  )
```

These contrasts are useful in profile analysis and wherever difference scores are needed.

SPECIAL   A user-defined contrast. This specification allows entry of special contrasts in the form of square matrices with as many rows and columns as there are levels of the factor. The first row entered is always that for the mean (constant term), and represents the set of weights indicating how other factors (if any) are to be averaged over the given factor. Generally these are all one.

The remaining rows of the matrix contain the special contrasts indicating the desired comparisons between levels of the factor. Most frequently, orthogonal contrasts are used. Orthogonal contrasts are statistically independent and nonredundant. Contrasts are orthogonal if (a) for each row, contrast coefficients sum to zero, and (b) the products of corresponding coefficients for all pairs of disjoint rows also sum to zero.

For example, suppose TREATMNT has four levels and we are interested in comparing the various levels of treatment with each other. An appropriate special contrast would be

```
(1    1    1    1)    weights for mean calculation
(3   -1   -1   -1)    compare 1st with 2nd through 4th
(0    2   -1   -1)    compare 2nd with 3rd and 4th
(0    0    1   -1)    compare 3rd with 4th
```

which would be specified in the MANOVA command as follows:

```
CONTRAST(TREATMNT) = SPECIAL(  1    1    1    1
                               3   -1   -1   -1
                               0    2   -1   -1
                               0    0    1   -1  )/
```

Note that this is an orthogonal contrast:

Each row except the means row sums to zero:

```
ROW 2   3 + (-1) + (-1) + (-1) = 3 - 3 = 0
ROW 3   2 + (-1) + (-1)        = 2 - 2 = 0
ROW 4   1 + (-1)               = 1 - 1 = 0
```

Products of each pair of disjoint rows sum to zero:

```
ROWS 2 and 3   3(0) + (-1)(2) + ( -1)(-1) + (-1)(-1) = 0
ROWS 2 and 4   3(0) + (-1)(0) + (-1)(1) + (-1)(-1)   = 0
ROWS 3 and 4   0(0) + 2(0) + (-1)1 + (-1)(-1)        = 0
```

The special contrasts need not be orthogonal. However, they must not be a linear combination of each other. If they are, subprogram MANOVA will report that and processing will cease. Difference, Helmert, and polynomial contrasts are orthogonal contrasts.

1.90   SETCONST

The SETCONST subcommand provides for setting important constants used throughout the MANOVA procedure. The format of this subcommand is

```
SETCONST = [ZETA(zeta)] [EPS(eps)]   /
```

ZETA sets the absolute value of zero used for printing purposes and when constructing basis matrices for estimation. The default value of ZETA is 10^{-8}.

EPS sets the relative value of zero used in checking the diagonal elements of matrices when performing the QR reduction or Cholesky decompositions. The default value of EPS is 10^{-8}.

1.91   ERROR

The ERROR= subcommand specifies the default error term to be used for each between-subjects effect in subsequent designs. The syntax is

```
          { WITHIN or W                }
          { RESIDUAL or R              }
ERROR =   { WITHIN + RESIDUAL or WR    }   /
          { n                          }
```

WITHIN or W is the within-cells error term. RESIDUAL or R is the residual error term. WR or RW is the pooled within-cells and residual error term. These three are the standard default error terms. The choice of which to use is made as follows:

1 The within-cells error term is used if it exists.

2 If there is no within-cells error, the residual error is used.

3 For designs processed using the observations model, the pooled within-cells and residual error term is the default.

If the pooled within-cells and residual error is requested, and one of these does not exist, then the other error term alone is used.

A model term may also be specified as the default error by giving its error-term number. The error- term numbers must be explicitly defined in the DESIGN subcommand. Should the specified error-term number not be defined for a particular design, then the significance tests using that error term are not carried out (although the parameter estimates and hypothesis sums of squares are presented).

For example,

```
MANOVA          DEP BY A(1,2), B(1,4)/
                ERROR = 1/
                DESIGN = A, B, A BY B = 1/
                DESIGN = A, B/
```

The default error is to be the error 1 term. This applies to the first design since the A BY B term is present in the model and is defined as error term 1. However, the A BY B term is not present in interaction, and no other term has been defined as error 1 instead. Thus, no significance tests for A and B are printed, although the hypothesis sums of squares are reported.

1.92 DESIGN

The DESIGN subcommand specifies the between-subjects model to be analyzed. The default model, initiated when no DESIGN specification is present (or just the word DESIGN appears) is a full factorial. If the model is actually specified, the keyword DESIGN is followed by an equals sign and a list of effects to be included in the model. Each effect is separated from its neighboring effects by blanks or commas. A slash terminates the design specification.

Following is a summary of the formats for effects:

1 A simple factor name:

```
DESIGN = AGE, TREATMNT /
```

2 CONTIN enclosing a list of interval variable names:

```
DESIGN = CONTIN(COVARI)
```

Interval variable names included in the design can only be those not mentioned in the previous ANALYSIS subcommand, i.e., those variables otherwise not specified as either dependent variables or covariates in the previous ANALYSIS subcommand. The order of variables excluded from an analysis is the same relative order as originally defined by the original MANOVA variable list. For example, in

```
MANOVA          A, B, C BY F(1,2) WITH D, E/
                ANALYSIS = B WITH D /
```

the order of the interval variables excluded from the analysis is A, C, E.

For example,

```
DESIGN = CONTIN(A TO E)/
```

incorporates all interval variables from A to E into a single effect with as many degrees of freedom as variables in the list.

Some other legal examples are

```
DESIGN = CONTIN(A,B,C TO E,F)/
DESIGN = CONTIN(A)/
DESIGN = A, CONTIN(B), CONTIN(C TO E)/
```

Note that B and CONTIN(B) are identical. Also note that the TO convention may not be used outside of parentheses, i.e.,

```
DESIGN = A TO E/
```

is not correct.

This usage of interval variables allows for unusual covariate analyses. For example, consider

```
MANOVA          A,B,C,D BY F1,F2 (1,2)/
                ANALYSIS = A /
                DESIGN = CONTIN(B, C), F1, D, F2 /
```

Here covariates B and C are to be eliminated from both factors F1 and F2 but covariate D is to be eliminated only from factor F2.

The above example, without parentheses in the DESIGN specification, generates covariate analysis with covariates B and C not lumped together, with covariate B unadjusted and covariate C adjusted for B. The rest of the covariate analysis is the same as the previous one. (This example assumes that hierarchical sums of squares are being used—the default.)

3 BY indicates an interaction:

```
DESIGN = AGE BY TREATMNT /
```

Interactions are allowed between factors and interval variables (excluded via an ANALYSIS subcommand as in 2 above) but not between interval variables. For example, suppose FAC1 is a factor and COV1, COV2 are interval variables. Then some valid interactions are

```
COV1 BY FAC1
CONTIN(COV1, COV2) BY FAC1
FAC1 BY COV2
```

Invalid interactions would be

```
COV1 BY COV2, COV1 BY COV1, COV1 BY COV2 BY COV1
```

COMPUTE statements may be used to create interval variable by interval variable interactions. For example, consider

```
*COMPUTE     XX = X * X
*COMPUTE     XY = X * Y
MANOVA       X, Y, XX, XY BY FAC(1,4)/
             ANALYSIS = Y/
             DESIGN = X, XX, XY, FAC/
```

An important use of factor-by-variable interactions is to produce an effect which may be used to test the homogeneity of regression hypothesis fundamental to covariate analysis. For example, assume an analysis with one dependent variable Y and two covariates, Z1 and Z2, with two factors AGE and TREATMNT. To test the hypothesis of parallel (homogeneous) covariates, one could use:

```
MANOVA       Y, Z1,Z2 BY AGE(1,5),TREATMNT(1,3) /
             ANALYSIS = Y /
             DESIGN = CONTIN( Z1 Z2 ),AGE,TREATMNT, AGE BY TREATMNT,
                      CONTIN(Z1,Z2) BY AGE +
                      CONTIN(Z1,Z2) BY TREATMNT +
                      CONTIN(Z1,Z2) BY AGE BY TREATMNT/
```

The last effect, a lumped continuous-variable-by-factor effect, tests the parallelism hypothesis. It is important that the effects of the common regression CONTIN(Z1,Z2) and group mean differences (AGE, TREATMNT, AGE BY TREATMNT) be removed before testing the effect of separate regressions provided by CONTIN(Z1, Z2) BY AGE + ...

4 WITHIN or W indicates nesting:

```
             DESIGN = AGE WITHIN TREATMNT /
             DESIGN = TREATMNT, COV1 WITHIN TREATMNT /
```

The second design asks that the regression coefficients of the continuous variable COV1 within each cell of the factor TREATMNT be calculated.

```
             DESIGN = A WITHIN B BY C BY D /
```

This design states that factor A is nested within B BY C BY D. This example indicates that the term to the left of WITHIN is nested in the term to the right of WITHIN, up to the end of the term or a +.

5 + lumps effects together:
   In

```
             AGE + AGE BY TREATMNT
```

the terms AGE and AGE BY TREATMNT are to be lumped together into a single term. Note that BY has a higher priority than +.

6 A factor name followed by an integer in parentheses can have one of two different meanings, depending on the context.
   In

```
             DESIGN = AGE(2) BY TREATMNT
```

'AGE(2)' refers to the second partition of AGE as previously defined in a PARTITION specification. In general, to refer to a given subdivision of a factor in the DESIGN, follow the factor name by the number, in parentheses, of the subdivision. Thus, if AGE has eleven levels and appears in a partition subcommand like

```
             PARTITION(AGE) = (6,3,2)
```

AGE(2) refers to the second partition containing three degrees of freedom.
   However, in

```
             DESIGN = TREATMNT WITHIN AGE(2)
```

factor TREATMNT is nested within the second level of factor AGE, not the second partition. The rule is that subscripts on factors appearing after a WITHIN (or W) refer to levels of the factor. Otherwise, subscripts refer to partitions.

7 CONSPLUS can be used to obtain estimates which consist of the sums of the parameter values and the grand means of the dependent variables. Thus,

```
             DESIGN = CONSPLUS AGE /
```

results in the means for each dependent variable being added to the parameters for each level of AGE. This process produces weighted marginals for each of the dependent variables by AGE. Since these means are adjusted for any covariates present, they are also the customary adjusted means when covariates are used.

Unweighted means may be obtained by specifying the saturated model, less those terms "contained" by an effect, and prefixing the effect whose means are to be found by CONSPLUS. For example, to find the unweighted marginal means for AGE in a two-factor design, write

```
DESIGN = CONSPLUS AGE, TREATMNT, AGE BY TREATMNT/
```

Of course, the OMEANS and PMEANS subcommands may also be used to find such marginal and adjusted means. However, only by using the CONSPLUS approach can the standard errors of the marginal means be obtained.

Note that only one CONSPLUS should appear in a given design.

8 Error terms

(a) Referring to common error terms   Three of the most frequently used error terms are (1) within-cells, (2) residual, (3) combined within-cells and residual. These error terms are represented symbolically in the DESIGN specification as follows:

(1) WITHIN or W—within-cells error terms (2) RESIDUAL or R—residual error term (3) WR or RW—combined within-cells and residual error terms

The general format to indicate that a term is to be tested against one of these error terms is

```
terms-to-be-tested  (AGAINST)   error term
                    ( VS  )
```

For example, to specify that the term AGE BY SEX is to be tested against the residual error term, write

```
AGE BY SEX AGAINST RESIDUAL
              or
AGE BY SEX VS R
```

(b) Creating special error terms   For many designs the common error terms above are not sufficient (as with components of variance models). MANOVA provides for the creation of up to ten user-defined error terms. Any term in the design may be declared to be an error term.

To create an error term, write

```
term = n
```

where n is an integer from 1 to 10. For example,

```
AGE BY TREATMNT = 1
```

designates the term AGE BY TREATMNT to be error term 1.

To use such a special error term in a test of significance write

```
         (AGAINST)
term     ( VS  ) n
```

For example, to declare that AGE BY TREATMNT is to be special error-term number 2, and also that it is to be tested against the residual error term, write

```
AGE BY TREATMNT = 2 VS RESIDUAL
```

NOTE: Any term present in the design but not given in the DESIGN specification is lumped into the residual error term.

9 CONSTANT to include the constant term in a model. Generally, the constant (correction to mean) term is automatically included in the model. However, if NOCONSTANT is specified in the METHOD subcommand, the constant is not included unless it is specifically indicated in the DESIGN by using the keyword CONSTANT:

```
DESIGN = CONSTANT, AGE /
```

An error term may be specified for the constant just as for any other effect.

For example,

```
DESIGN = CONSTANT VS 1 ......../
```

NOTE: This use of the keyword CONSTANT obviates its use as a factor name.

1.93 OPTIONS and STATISTICS available

There is no STATISTICS command needed with MANOVA; if one is specified, it is ignored. All optional statistics are requested with MANOVA control subcommands like PRINT and PLOT.

The following option, specified in the OPTIONS command, is available.

1 Inclusion of missing data. With this option, all missing-value declarations are ignored, and all cases are included in the computation. The default is to delete cases listwise. There is no pairwise deletion option in SPSS MANOVA. NOTE: OPTION 1 is automatically invoked if no variable or factor mentioned in the initial MANOVA command has missing values declared.

1.94 REFERENCES

Bancroft, T.A. *Topics in Intermediate Statistical Methods.* Ames, Iowa: The Iowa State University Press, 1968.

Bock, R.D. *Multivariate Statistical Methods in Behavioral Research.* New York: McGraw-Hill, 1975.

Cochran, W.G., and G.M. Cox. *Experimental Design.* 2nd Edition. New York: Wiley, 1957.

Cooley, W.W., and P.R. Lohnes. *Multivariate Data Analysis.* New York: Wiley, 1971.

Davies, O.L. *Design and Analysis of Industrial Experiments.* New York: Hafner, 1954.

Everitt, B.S. *Graphical Techniques for Multivariate Data.* New York: North-Holland, 1978.

Finn, J.D. *A General Model for Multivariate Analysis.* New York: Holt, Rinehart and Winston, 1974.

Heck, D.L. Charts of some upper percentage points of the distribution of the largest characteristic root. *Annals of Math. Stat.,* 31: pp. 625-642.

Hicks, C.R. *Fundamental Concepts in the Design of Experiments.* 2nd Edition. New York: Holt, Rinehart and Winston, 1973.

Morrison, D.F. *Multivariate Statistical Methods.* 2nd Edition. New York: McGraw-Hill, 1976.

Pillai, K.C.S. Upper percentage points of the largest root of a matrix in multivariate analysis. *Biometrika,* 54: pp. 189-193, 1967.

Rao, C.R. *Linear Statistical Inference and its Applications.* 2nd Edition. New York: Wiley, 1973.

Roy, J., and R.E. Bargmann. Tests of multiple independence and the associated confidence bounds. *Annals of Math. Stat.,* 29: pp. 491-503, 1958.

Searle, S.R. *Linear Models.* New York: Wiley, 1971.

Snedecor, G.W., and W.G. Cochran. *Statistical Methods.* 6th Edition. Ames, Iowa: The Iowa State University Press, 1967.

Tukey, J.W. *Exploratory Data Analysis.* Addison-Wesley, 1977.

Winer, B.J. *Statistical Principles in Experimental Design.* New York: McGraw-Hill, 1971.

MANOVA was designed and programmed by Philip Burns of Northwestern University and documented by C. Ming Wang and Philip Burns.

Chapter 2

BOX-JENKINS:
Analysis of Time Series

The SPSS BOX-JENKINS procedure may be used to fit and forecast time series data by means of a general class of statistical models. The current version of the routine can analyze univariate time series.

SPSS BOX-JENKINS will model a variable with equally spaced observations in time and no missing values. In its most general form, the model is as follows:

$$\phi(B) \, \Phi(B^s) \, (1 - B)^d \, (1 - B^s)^D \, (Z_t)^\lambda = \theta(B) \, \Theta(B^s) \, a_t$$

That is, an observation at a given time is modelled as a function of its past values and/or current and past values of the random shocks, both at nonseasonal and seasonal lags. Sometimes, it may be necessary to transform the data in one or more of the following ways:

- Log or power transform—to induce constant amplitude in the series over time so that residuals from the fitted model will have a constant variance
- Nonseasonal differencing—to convert a nonstationary series containing stationary changes in level or slope into a stationary series with a constant mean and variance
- Seasonal differencing—to model systematic, periodic variation (another form of nonstationarity) in the data

The modelling of time series data is usually done in three steps. First, a tentative model for a series is identified. Second, estimates of parameters are obtained, and a set of diagnostic statistics and plots are examined. If the model is deemed acceptable, the third step, generation of forecasts, can then be done. If the model is inadequate, then other models may be entertained until an acceptable fit is obtained, at which time forecasts can be computed. Thus, fitting and forecasting of a given time series typically entails several computer runs in batch mode. For this reason, SPSS BOX-JENKINS syntax is flexibly designed so that sufficient information can be requested easily and efficiently.

2.1 USE OF SPSS BOX-JENKINS:
AN EXAMPLE OF IDENTIFICATION, FITTING,
AND FORECASTING

In the following example, SPSS BOX-JENKINS is used to model and forecast Series G from Box and Jenkins, *Time Series Analysis: Forecasting and Control*. This series consists of monthly totals, in thousands, of international airline passengers from January 1949 to December 1960.

A good way to begin is to obtain a plot of the time series and a plot of the autocorrelation function of the series. In SPSS BOX-JENKINS, this is accomplished by the command

```
BOX-JENKINS    VARIABLE=Y/PLOT=SERIES/IDENTIFY
```

The above syntax tells SPSS that variable Y contains the time series of interest. A plot of the series is also requested. By default, the autocorrelation function is plotted and summary statistics for the series are printed when IDENTIFY is invoked. The default number of lags for which autocorrelations are plotted is 25. In general, BOX-JENKINS syntax has unique initial three letters; thus

```
    BOX-JENKINS    VARIABLE=Y/PLOT=SERIES/IDENTIFY
```

and

```
    BOX-JENKINS    VAR=Y/PLO=SER/IDE
```

are equivalent specifications.

The output from the above command consists of the series plot and summary statistics on the series (Figure 2.1a) and a plot of the autocorrelation function (Figure 2.1b).

Figure 2.1a   Run 1—Series Plot and Summary Statistics

```
GRAPHIC DISPLAY OF SERIES FOR VARIABLE Y
DATA - *
MEAN - .

  OBS     DATA        80.00    280.00    480.00    680.00    880.00
                     :---------:---------:---------:---------:
    1    112.000     :         *         .
    2    118.000     :         *         .
    3    132.000     :          *        .
    4    129.000     :         *         .
    5    121.000     :         *         .
    6    135.000     :          *        .
    7    148.000     :          *        .
    8    148.000     :          *        .
    9    136.000     :          *        .
   10    119.000     -        *          .
   11    104.000     :       *           .
   12    118.000     :         *         .
   13    115.000     :         *         .
   14    126.000     :         *         .
   15    141.000     :          *        .
   16    135.000     :          *        .
   17    125.000     :        *          .
   18    149.000     :          *        .
   19    170.000     :           *       .
   20    170.000     -           *       .
   21    158.000     :           *       .
   22    133.000     :         *         .
   23    114.000     :       *           .
   24    140.000     :         *         .
```

```
  120    337.000     -              .  *
  121    360.000     :              .   *
  122    342.000     :              . *
  123    406.000     :              .    *
  124    396.000     :              .   *
  125    420.000     :              .    *
  126    472.000     :              .      *
  127    548.000     :              .         *
  128    559.000     :              .          *
  129    463.000     :              .     *
  130    407.000     -              .   *
  131    362.000     :              . *
  132    405.000     :              .   *
  133    417.000     :              .    *
  134    391.000     :              .   *
  135    419.000     :              .    *
  136    461.000     :              .     *
  137    472.000     :              .      *
  138    535.000     :              .         *
  139    622.000     :              .            *
  140    606.000     -              .           *
  141    508.000     :              .       *
  142    461.000     :              .     *
  143    390.000     :           *  .
  144    432.000     :              .    *
```

```
MEAN VALUE OF THE PROCESS
  0.28030E 03

STANDARD DEVIATION OF THE PROCESS
  0.11955E 03
```

The plot of Series G exhibits three noteworthy attributes. There is an upward tendency in series values from 1949 to 1960, and the series exhibits a periodic component consisting of a regular seasonal pattern with peaks occurring in late summer months of each year. Finally, the series values show greater amplitude in recent years than in earlier ones. Thus, the series is nonstationary and heteroscedastic, and both of these characteristics ought to be taken into account in fitting a model to the series.

Figure 2.1b   Run 1—Autocorrelation Function Plot

```
AUTOCORRELATION FUNCTION FOR VARIABLE Y
AUTOCORRELATIONS *
TWO STANDARD ERROR LIMITS .
      AUTO. STAND.
LAG   CORR.  ERR.  -1  -.75  -.5 -.25   0   .25  .5   .75   1
                   :----:----:----:----:----:----:----:----:
  1   0.948  0.082                      .  :  .                  *
  2   0.876  0.082                      .  :  .               *
  3   0.807  0.081                      .  :  .             *
  4   0.753  0.081                      .  :  .           *
  5   0.714  0.081                      .  :  .          *
  6   0.682  0.080                      .  :  .         *
  7   0.663  0.080                      .  :  .        *
  8   0.656  0.080                      .  :  .        *
  9   0.671  0.080                      .  :  .        *
 10   0.703  0.079                      .  :  .         *
 11   0.743  0.079                      .  :  .          *
 12   0.760  0.079                      .  :  .          *
 13   0.713  0.078                      .  :  .         *
 14   0.646  0.078                      .  :  .        *
 15   0.586  0.078                      .  :  .      *
 16   0.538  0.077                      .  :  .     *
 17   0.500  0.077                      .  :  .    *
 18   0.469  0.077                      .  : *.
 19   0.450  0.076                      .  : *.
 20   0.442  0.076                      .  : *.
 21   0.457  0.076                      .  : *.
 22   0.482  0.076                      .  :  *
 23   0.517  0.075                      .  :  .*
 24   0.532  0.075                      .  :  .*
 25   0.494  0.075                      .  : *.
```

Nonstationarity of the series is also suggested by the autocorrelation function since the early autocorrelations remain large rather than dying out quickly. A periodicity of 12 is suggested by the value of 0.760 at the twelfth lag, which is larger than autocorrelations at neighboring lags.

The varying amplitude of a series can often be removed by use of a log or power transform. Since elements of demographic and economic systems often grow over time, we might suspect that a logarithmic transformation is appropriate. We shall employ the log transform and plot the transformed series to see whether or not the transform works. The periodicity in the data will be handled by differencing the data at the seasonal lag and seeing if fitting a seasonal parameter is also required. The upward tendency in the data will be taken into account by application of nonseasonal differencing. All of the above, and more, is accomplished by the following command specification:

```
BOX-JENKINS    VARIABLE=Y/LOG/DIFFERENCE=0 THRU 2/PERIOD=12/
               SDIFFERENCE=0 THRU 2/LAG=49/PLOT=TSERIES/IDENTIFY
```

The specification field on the BOX-JENKINS command requests the following:

- Analysis of variable Y
- A logarithmic (natural) transformation of the series
- Nonseasonal differencing of the series of degrees 0,1,2 (to be explained below)
- Seasonal differencing of degrees 0,1,2, with a period of 12 months indicated (to be explained below)
- Setting of the lag parameter in the program to 49
- A plot of the transformed series
- Plots of autocorrelation functions (by default)

Use of the THRU convention in the DIF and SDIF subcommands implies that three times three, or nine, combinations of seasonal and nonseasonal differencing are being considered. This, in effect, implements what has been termed the "variate difference" method (O. D. Anderson, 1976). In general, data should be differenced to that degree, or combination of degrees, that is just sufficient to induce stationarity. For a given series with a large enough sample size, the variance of the series decreases as a consequence of differencing until stationarity is achieved, and then increases rapidly with subsequent differencing steps. For Series G, we suspect from general experience that differencing of degree one at both seasonal and nonseasonal lags will suffice; the specification of combinations of degrees of differencing will give information that will strengthen or weaken that suspicion. The variate difference method, when used in conjunction with series plots and plots of the autocorrelation function, will often prove to be useful and is easily accomplished in SPSS BOX-JENKINS.

Partial output from the second BOX-JENKINS command is shown in Figures 2.1c and 2.1d. The plot of the transformed series with no differencing appears in Figure 2.1c.

Figure 2.1c   Run 2—Plot of Log Transformed Series

```
GRAPHIC DISPLAY OF LOG TRANSFORMED SERIES FOR VARIABLE Y
DATA - *
MEAN - .

 OBS    DATA         4.80      5.30      5.80      6.30      6.80
                 :---------:---------:---------:---------:---------:
   1   4.71850    :       *            .
   2   4.77068    :        *           .
   3   4.88280    :          *         .
   4   4.85981    :         *          .
   5   4.79579    :        *           .
   6   4.90527    :          *         .
   7   4.99721    :           *        .
   8   4.99721    :           *        .
   9   4.91265    :          *         .
  10   4.77912    -        *           .
  11   4.64439    :      *             .
  12   4.77068    :        *           .
  13   4.74493    :       *            .
  14   4.83628    :         *          .
  15   4.94876    :          *         .
  16   4.90527    :          *         .
  17   4.82831    :         *          .
  18   5.00395    :           *        .
  19   5.13580    :            *       .
  20   5.13580    -            *       .
  21   5.06259    :           *        .
  22   4.89035    :         *          .
  23   4.73620    :      *             .
  24   4.94164    :          *         .
```

```
 120   5.82008    -            .      *
 121   5.88610    :            .       *
 122   5.83481    :            .      *
 123   6.00635    :            .        *
 124   5.98141    :            .       *
 125   6.04025    :            .        *
 126   6.15698    :            .         *
 127   6.30627    :            .          *
 128   6.32615    :            .           *
 129   6.13773    :            .         *
 130   6.00881    -            .        *
 131   5.89164    :            .       *
 132   6.00389    :            .        *
 133   6.03309    :            .        *
 134   5.96871    :            .       *
 135   6.03787    :            .        *
 136   6.13340    :            .         *
 137   6.15698    :            .         *
 138   6.28227    :            .          *
 139   6.43294    :            .            *
 140   6.40688    -            .           *
 141   6.23048    :            .        *
 142   6.13340    :            .       *
 143   5.96615    :            .      *
 144   6.06843    :            .       *
```

```
VARIABLE - Y        SERIES LENGTH - 144
DEGREE OF NONSEASONAL DIFFERENCING - 0 DEGREE OF SEASONAL DIFFERENCING - 0

MEAN VALUE OF THE PROCESS
 0.55421E 01

STANDARD DEVIATION OF THE PROCESS
 0.43992E 00
```

Note that the amplitude of the series is now roughly constant over time. However, the transformed Series G still shows nonstationarity in the form of seasonality and changes in level. The mean of the transformed series is 5.542 and the standard deviation is 0.4399; since the transformed series is not stationary, the standard deviation will serve as a benchmark against which the combinations of seasonal and nonseasonal differencing can be evaluated.

Following the series plot, there appear nine sets of autocorrelation function plots and summary statistics corresponding to the indicated combinations of degrees of differencing. For the sake of example, only one of these autocorrelation function plots is shown in Figure 2.1d. Autocorrelation plots in BOX-JENKINS consist of autocorrelations up to the specified number of lags along with 2 standard error limits, the latter computed on the assumption that the time series is white noise, that is, random. Standard errors are calculated using the method documented in Ling and Roberts, 1980, which differs from the method documented in Box and Jenkins, 1976.

Figure 2.1d   Run 2—Autocorrelation of Series Differenced at Degree 1 Seasonal and Nonseasonal

```
VARIABLE - Y       SERIES LENGTH - 131
DEGREE OF NONSEASONAL DIFFERENCING -  1 DEGREE OF SEASONAL  DIFFERENCING -  1

MEAN VALUE OF THE PROCESS
 0.29089E-03

STANDARD DEVIATION OF THE PROCESS
 0.45673E-01


AUTOCORRELATION FUNCTION FOR VARIABLE Y
AUTOCORRELATIONS *
TWO STANDARD ERROR LIMITS .

      AUTO. STAND.
LAG   CORR.  ERR.  -1  -.75  -.5 -.25   0  .25  .5  .75   1
                   :----:----:----:----:----:----:----:----:
  1  -0.341  0.086            *     .   :   .
  2   0.105  0.085            .     .   :*  .
  3  -0.202  0.085            *.    .   :   .
  4   0.021  0.085            .     .   *   .
  5   0.056  0.084            .     .   :*  .
  6   0.031  0.084            .     .   :*  .
  7  -0.056  0.084            .     .  *:  .
  8  -0.001  0.083            .     .   *   .
  9   0.176  0.083            .     .   : *.
 10  -0.076  0.083            .    *.   :   .
 11   0.064  0.082            .     .   :*  .
 12  -0.387  0.082            *     .   :   .
 13   0.152  0.082            .     .   : * .
 14  -0.058  0.081            .    *:   .
 15   0.150  0.081            .     .   : * .
 16  -0.139  0.081            .   *  .   :   .
 17   0.070  0.080            .     .   :*  .
 18   0.016  0.080            .     .   *   .
 19  -0.011  0.079            .     .  *:  .
 20  -0.117  0.079            .    *:   .
 21   0.039  0.079            .     .   :*  .
 22  -0.091  0.078            .    *:   .
 23   0.223  0.078            .     .   :  *.
 24  -0.018  0.078            .     .  *:  .
 25  -0.100  0.077            .    *:   .
 26   0.049  0.077            .     .   :*  .
 27  -0.030  0.077            .     .  *:  .
 28   0.047  0.076            .     .   :*  .
 29  -0.018  0.076            .     .   *   .
 30  -0.051  0.075            .    *:   .
 31  -0.054  0.075            .    *:   .
 32   0.196  0.075            .     .   : *.
 33  -0.122  0.074            .    *  :   .
 34   0.078  0.074            .     .  :*  .
 35  -0.152  0.073            .   *  .   :   .
 36  -0.010  0.073            .     .   *   .
 37   0.047  0.073            .     .   :*  .
 38   0.031  0.072            .     .   :*  .
 39  -0.015  0.072            .     .   *   .
 40  -0.034  0.071            .     *:   .
 41  -0.066  0.071            .     *:   .
 42   0.095  0.071            .     .  :*. .
 43  -0.090  0.070            .    *.   :   .
 44   0.029  0.070            .     .  :*  .
 45  -0.037  0.069            .     *:   .
 46  -0.042  0.069            .     *:   .
 47   0.108  0.069            .     .   :*. .
 48  -0.050  0.068            .     *:   .
 49   0.105  0.068            .     .   :*. .
```

As shown in Figure 2.1d, the smallest standard deviation is associated with the series for which DIF equals 1 and SDIF equals 1. The autocorrelation function of this differenced series has significant autocorrelations at lags one and twelve, which suggests that the doubly differenced series is not random and can be modelled. By comparison, other combinations of differencing are not as good.

Next, we might like to see a plot of the differenced series for some visual indication of stationarity, and we might also wish to see a plot of the partial autocorrelation function as an aid in model identification. To obtain these, an SPSS run using the following BOX-JENKINS command would suffice:

```
BOX-JENKINS    VARIABLE=Y/LOG/DIFFERENCE=1/SDIFFERENCE=1/
               PERIOD=12/LAG=49/PLOT=PAC,DSE/IDENTIFY
```

The first line is the same as before except differencing of the series is specified for only degree 1. Note that a plot of the partial autocorrelation function and a plot of the differenced series are requested in the PLOT= subcommand. Since a log transformation is invoked, differencing is done on the log-transformed data.

Results from the third BOX-JENKINS run are shown in Figures 2.1e and 2.1f.

Figure 2.1e   Run 3—Plot of the Differenced Series

```
GRAPHIC DISPLAY OF DIFFERENCED SERIES FOR VARIABLE Y
DEGREE OF NONSEASONAL DIFFERENCING - 1 DEGREE OF  SEASONAL DIFFERENCING  1
DATA - *
MEAN - .

 OBS    DATA           -0.15    -0.05     0.05     0.15     0.25
                       :--------:--------:--------:--------:--------:
    1  0.391645E-01    :                     . *
    2  0.360489E-03    :                     *.
    3 -0.204954E-01    :                   * .
    4 -0.129395E-01    :                   *..
    5  0.661488E-01    :                     .   *
    6  0.399141E-01    :                     . *
    7  0.0             :                     *.
    8  0.113535E-01    :                     .*
    9 -0.387144E-01    :                 * .
   10 -0.194168E-01    -                   *.
   11  0.791492E-01    :                     .    *
   12  0.608444E-01    :                     .   *
   13 -0.574493E-01    :                * .
   14  0.586710E-01    :                     .   *
   15 -0.445480E-01    :                 *.
   16  0.130706        :                     .      *
   17 -0.141345        :            *        .
   18 -0.203295E-01    :                  * .
   19  0.0             :                     *.
   20 -0.516605E-02    -                    *.
   21  0.449066E-01    :                     .  *
   22  0.501604E-01    :                     .  *
   23 -0.770626E-01    :              *  .
   24 -0.541496E-02    :                    *.

  120 -0.368214E-01    -                * .*
  121 -0.130854E-01    :                    .*.
  122 -0.102379        :              *      .
  123  0.120465        :                     .     *
  124 -0.352592E-01    :                 * .
  125  0.856400E-02    :                     *.
  126  0.137711E-02    :                     *.
  127 -0.459347E-01    :                *.
  128  0.120239E-01    :                     .*
  129  0.318298E-01    :                     . *
  130 -0.500813E-01    -               * .
  131 -0.996399E-02    :                    *.

MEAN VALUE OF THE PROCESS
  0.29089E-03

STANDARD DEVIATION OF THE PROCESS
  0.45673E-01
```

Figure 2.1f   Run 3—Plot of Partial Autocorrelation Function

```
PARTIAL AUTOCORRELATIONS *
TWO STANDARD ERROR LIMITS .

      PR-AUT STAND.
 LAG  CORR.  ERR.  -1  -.75  -.5 -.25   0   .25  .5   .75   1
                    :----:----:----:----:----:----:----:----:
  1  -0.341  0.087              *        . .
  2  -0.013  0.087                       .*.
  3  -0.193  0.087            *.          .
  4  -0.125  0.087              *         .
  5   0.033  0.087                       . *.
  6   0.035  0.087                     . *.
  7  -0.060  0.087                      .*.
  8  -0.020  0.087                       .* .
  9   0.226  0.087                       . * .
 10   0.043  0.087                       . *.
 11   0.047  0.087                       . *.
 12  -0.339  0.087            *           .
 13  -0.109  0.087                    .* .
 14  -0.077  0.087                    .* .
 15  -0.022  0.087                   *.
 16  -0.140  0.087              *      .
 17   0.026  0.087                     .* .
 18   0.115  0.087                     .* .
 19  -0.013  0.087                    .* .
 20  -0.167  0.087             *       .
 21   0.132  0.087                     . * .
 22  -0.072  0.087                    .* .
 23   0.143  0.087                     . * .
```

The plot of the differenced series (Figure 2.1e) shows that stationarity has been obtained. The autocorrelation function and partial autocorrelation function plots (Figures 2.1d and 2.1f) together suggest fitting a model with one moving average parameter and one seasonal moving average parameter. This is, of course, an example in which the message of the autocorrelation and partial autocorrelation plots is easily deciphered. The autocorrelation function plot is produced as part of the results of the BOX-JENKINS request. However, the plot is the same as shown in Figure 2.1d.

The above three runs constitute model identification. Having tentatively identified a model, we next estimate the parameters of the model. This can be accomplished by

```
BOX-JENKINS     VARIABLE=Y/LOG/DIFFERENCE=1/SDIFFERENCE=1/
                PERIOD=12/LAG=49/Q=1/SQ=1/NCONSTANT/ITERATE=100/
                BFR=13/PLOT=RAC,RES/IDENTIFY/ESTIMATE
```

Note that specifications for transformations, differencing, and autoregressive and moving average terms at consecutive and seasonal lags are indicated first. In more detail, the syntax is as follows:

• The specifications through LAG=49 are as before.
• Q=1/SQ=1/—This is the first model explicitly specified. Q refers to nonseasonal moving average parameters, while SQ refers to seasonal moving average parameters. In both instances, one parameter is being specified.
• NCONSTANT/—We want to constrain the constant term (analogous to the intercept term in ordinary least squares regression contexts) to be equal to zero. In general, when degrees of differencing are invoked, the level of the series will be approximately zero, and the constant can be constrained to equal zero.
• ITERATE=100/—The estimation routine is an iterative search algorithm; therefore, 100 iterations are specified. It is unlikely that 100 iterations will be required. The default of 40 iterations will usually suffice, but there will be instances where the search algorithm will fail to converge. Failure to converge may indicate model misspecification, and you will have to investigate this possibility. In general, if you want to avoid failures to converge, specify a relatively large number of iterations; if you want to avoid paying for a lot of iterations for what may be a misspecified model, then accept the default.
• BFR=13/—13 backforecasts are to be used in estimation. In general, a nonzero backforecast specification will be slightly more expensive than omission of the specification, but it will often lead to a final model with a smaller residual variance.
• PLOT=RAC,RES/—A plot of the residual series values and a plot of the residual autocorrelation function are requested. Of these two plots, the residual autocorrelation plot is probably the more useful. If the specified model is "good," the residual series should be white noise (random) and therefore uncorrelated for all lags. This should be reflected in the residual autocorrelation plot. Except for sampling variation, values of the autocorrelations should not be statistically significantly different from zero. The residual autocorrelation function plot is shown in Figure 2.1h.
• IDENTIFY/ESTIMATE/—Identification is invoked by using the keyword IDENTIFY so that initial parameter estimates are obtained. These are printed and are also used by the estimation algorithm. Final parameter estimates are produced by the ESTIMATE keyword. The IDENTIFY keyword may be omitted in the above command, in which case initial parameter estimates are all zero.

Estimation results are shown in Figure 2.1g.

Figure 2.1g   Run 4—Initial Values for Parameters and Final Estimated Values

```
INITIAL ESTIMATE OF PARAMETERS

OVERALL CONSTANT
 0.29089E-03

MOVING AVERAGE PARAMETER AT LAG      1
 0.0

RESIDUAL VARIANCE=  0.20860E-02


INITIAL VALUES OF PARAMETERS

MOVING AVERAGE PARM AT LAG      1
 0.0

PERTURBATION INCREMENTS
 0.10000E 00

CONVERGENCE TOLERANCES
 0.10000E-02

SEASONAL MOVING AVERAGE PARM AT LAG     12
 0.0

PERTURBATION INCREMENTS
 0.10000E 00

CONVERGENCE TOLERANCES
 0.10000E-02

INITIAL FUNCTION VALUE  0.27328E 00
```

```
NONLINEAR ESTIMATION RESULTS

PAR  LAG    ESTIMATE     STD ERROR     T RATIO

MA    1     0.39531      0.80474E-01   4.9123
SMA  12     0.61406      0.69522E-01   8.8327

VARIANCE OF RESIDUALS   0.13423E-02

COVARIANCE MATRIX OF THE ESTIMATES

PAR  LAG
 MA    1   0.64760E-02 -0.32702E-03
SMA   12  -0.32702E-03  0.48333E-02

CORRELATION MATRIX OF THE ESTIMATES

PAR  LAG
 MA    1   1.00000 -0.05845
SMA   12  -0.05845  1.00000

MEAN VALUE OF RESIDUAL SERIES
  0.34489E-03

STANDARD DEVIATION OF RESIDUAL SERIES
  0.36227E-01

VARIANCE OF RESIDUAL SERIES
  0.13124E-02

DIAGNOSTIC CHI-SQUARE STATISTICS FOR RESIDUAL SERIES  1

LAG  CHI-SQ.  D.F.  PROB.
  6    5.90      4   0.2064
 12    9.36     10   0.4984
 18   13.92     16   0.6050
 24   25.52     22   0.2727
 30   28.74     28   0.4260
 36   35.63     34   0.3916
 42   41.39     40   0.4099
 48   44.33     46   0.5424
 49   48.64     47   0.4067
```

Figure 2.1h   Run 4—Residual Autocorrelation Function Plot

```
RESIDUAL AUTOCORRELATION FUNCTION FOR VARIABLE Y
AUTOCORRELATIONS *
TWO STANDARD ERROR LIMITS .

     AUTO. STAND.
LAG  CORR.  ERR.  -1 -.75  -.5 -.25   0  .25  .5  .75   1
                  :----:----:----:----:----:----:----:----:
  1  0.017  0.086                     . * .
  2  0.019  0.085                     . * .
  3 -0.126  0.085                   * . .
  4 -0.142  0.085                   * .: .
  5  0.050  0.084                     .:* .
  6  0.062  0.084                     . *.
  7 -0.073  0.084                    .* : .
  8 -0.038  0.083                    . *: .
  9  0.103  0.083                     . :* .
 10 -0.078  0.083                    . * : .
 11  0.025  0.082                     . * .
 12 -0.010  0.082                     .* .
 13  0.032  0.082                     . :* .
 14  0.043  0.081                     . :* .
 15  0.048  0.081                     . :* .
 16 -0.156  0.081                   * . : .
 17  0.025  0.080                     . *.
 18 -0.001  0.080                     . * .
 19 -0.106  0.079                   .* : .
 20 -0.102  0.079                   .* : .
 21 -0.032  0.079                    . *: .
 22 -0.027  0.078                    . *: .  .*.
 23  0.220  0.078                     . :* .
 24  0.032  0.078                     . :* .
```

Note that the initial estimate of the nonseasonal moving average parameter is zero. Initial estimates of seasonal parameters will always be zero, so in this particular case, the IDENTIFY keyword could have been omitted with no loss. Default values of certain tuning parameters are used in estimation. The "Function value" that prints as part of the intermediate iteration results is the sum of squares function S, described in Box and Jenkins, 1976. For Series G, convergence criteria are met after 19 iterations and results are printed, along with related statistics. Output includes

- Estimated final parameter values and their standard errors
- Residual variance, equal to the mean squared error
- Variance-covariance matrix of estimated parameters

- Correlation matrix of estimated parameters. High correlations may indicate model inadequacies such as over parameterization or insufficient differencing.
- Mean, standard deviation, and variance of the residual series; chi-square statistic associated with the residual autocorrelation function.

For Series G, the final model is

$$(\text{dif}^1)(\text{DIF}_{12}{}^1)(\ln Z_t) = (1 - .395B)(1 - .614B^{12})a_t$$

In light of the encouraging diagnostics, especially the residual autocorrelation function and the correlation matrix of estimated parameters, the model is deemed adequate. SPSS BOX-JENKINS can now be used to forecast the series.

Forecasts are obtained by using the following BOX-JENKINS command:

```
BOX-JENKINS    VARIABLE=Y/LOG/DIFFERENCE=1/SDIFFERENCE=1/PERIOD=12/
               Q=1/SQ=1/FQ=(.39531)/FSQ=(.61406)/
               ORIGIN=-24/PLOT=FCF,FLF,CIN/FORECAST
```

The command syntax through the SQ keyword is familiar. Final values for the nonseasonal and seasonal moving average parameters, that were obtained in the previous run, are input here by means of the FQ and FSQ subcommands. ORIGIN=-24 requests that the forecast origin be the observation in the data 24 back from the last series observation. Finally, a plot of the forecast function, fixed lead forecasts, and associated confidence intervals is requested.

BOX-JENKINS first prints the parameter estimates that it is using. The augmented autoregressive matrix contains information on both differencing and autoregressive parameters, if any, used in the model. In our example, the augmented autoregressive matrix contains information solely on differencing. The forecast error summary table gives the forecast variance and forecast standard error for increasing leads, as well as the impulse response function, which corresponds to Box and Jenkins' psi weights.

The forecast function is summarized in a table that can be read: (1) horizontally, to compare forecasts from past observations with a given series observation; (2) diagonally, to obtain increasing lead forecasts from a given origin; and (3) vertically, to obtain fixed lead forecasts from consecutive observations. The table of forecast functions is displayed in Figure 2.1i.

Figure 2.1i   Run 5—Summary Table of Forecast Functions

```
FORECASTS AT INCREASING LEAD FOR VARIABLE Y
STARTING ORIGIN AT   120
```

LEAD TIME OBS DATA	1	2	3	4	5	6	7	8	9	10	11	12
120 337.000												
121 360.000	350.025											
122 342.000	340.275	334.543										
123 406.000	394.962	393.756	387.123									
124 396.000	390.939	384.477	383.304	376.846								
125 420.000	403.543	400.416	393.798	392.596	385.982							
126 472.000	486.893	475.265	471.583	463.788	462.373	454.583						
127 548.000	534.437	544.571	531.566	527.448	518.729	517.146	508.434					
128 559.000	545.396	537.193	547.380	534.308	530.168	521.405	519.813	511.056				
129 463.000	468.815	461.883	454.936	454.563	452.493	448.987	441.565	440.218	432.801			
130 407.000	407.755	410.844	404.769	398.681	406.241	396.539	393.467	386.963	385.782	379.283		
131 362.000	355.442	355.840	358.536	353.234	347.922	354.519	346.053	343.372	337.696	336.665	330.994	
132 405.000	399.073	394.686	395.128	398.122	392.235	386.335	393.661	384.260	381.283	374.981	373.836	367.538
133 417.000	418.444	414.730	410.171	410.631	413.741	407.624	401.493	409.106	399.336	396.242	389.693	388.503
134 391.000	398.169	399.002	395.461	391.114	391.552	394.518	388.685	382.839	390.098	380.782	377.832	371.587
135 419.000	460.233	465.317	466.291	462.153	457.072	457.585	461.051	454.234	447.402	455.886	444.999	441.551
136 461.000	423.617	448.356	453.309	454.258	450.226	445.277	445.776	449.153	442.511	435.856	444.121	433.515
137 472.000	462.841	439.768	465.450	470.593	471.577	467.392	462.254	462.772	466.278	459.383	452.474	461.054
138 535.000	541.713	535.332	508.645	538.350	544.297	545.436	540.596	534.652	535.252	539.307	531.332	523.341
139 622.000	610.063	614.680	607.440	577.158	610.864	617.613	618.905	613.413	606.668	607.349	611.950	602.901
140 606.000	623.974	616.705	621.372	614.053	583.442	617.515	624.337	625.643	620.091	613.274	613.961	618.613
141 508.000	514.737	523.916	517.813	521.732	515.586	489.884	518.493	524.221	525.318	520.656	514.932	515.509
142 461.000	448.040	451.624	459.677	454.322	457.760	452.369	429.818	454.919	459.945	460.907	456.817	451.795
143 390.000	400.727	393.877	397.027	404.107	399.399	402.422	397.682	377.857	399.924	404.342	405.188	401.592
144 432.000	439.001	446.263	438.635	442.143	450.027	444.785	448.151	442.872	420.794	445.369	450.289	451.231
145	450.195	454.592	462.113	454.213	457.846	466.010	460.582	464.067	458.601	435.739	461.186	466.281
146		426.503	430.669	437.794	430.310	433.752	441.486	436.343	439.646	434.467	412.808	436.916
147			482.031	486.740	494.792	486.334	490.224	498.965	493.153	496.885	491.032	466.554
148				492.168	496.976	505.198	496.562	500.533	509.458	503.524	507.334	501.359
149					508.212	513.176	521.666	512.748	516.850	526.066	519.938	523.873
150						583.240	588.938	598.681	588.447	593.153	603.730	596.697
151							668.039	674.565	685.724	674.002	679.393	691.508
152								665.766	672.269	683.391	671.708	677.082
153									558.657	564.114	573.446	563.644
154										496.579	501.430	509.725
155											430.125	434.326
156												478.014

The final printed table consists of forecasted values from the end of the series along with 95% confidence limits for the forecasts. Note that, unlike some other forecast routines, SPSS BOX-JENKINS, when possible, prints forecasts in the original scale of the series, instead of in transformed units, because internal transformation was used. The plot of the forecast function shows

- Series values (data)
- One-step-ahead forecasts for series values along with confidence bounds on the forecast values
- Forecasts from the end of the series along with their confidence bounds

The table of forecasted values and the plot of forecasts for Series G is shown in Figure 2.1j.

Figure 2.1j   Run 5—Forecasted Values and Plot

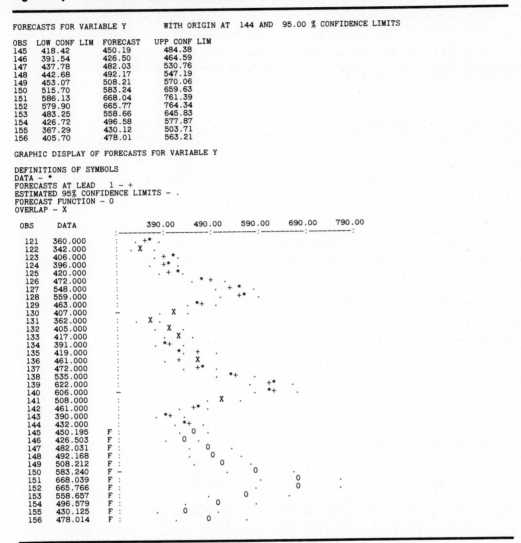

```
FORECASTS FOR VARIABLE Y          WITH ORIGIN AT   144 AND  95.00 % CONFIDENCE LIMITS

OBS   LOW CONF LIM   FORECAST    UPP CONF LIM
145     418.42        450.19        484.38
146     391.54        426.50        464.59
147     437.78        482.03        530.76
148     442.68        492.17        547.19
149     453.07        508.21        570.06
150     515.70        583.24        659.63
151     586.13        668.04        761.39
152     579.90        665.77        764.34
153     483.25        558.66        645.83
154     426.72        496.58        577.87
155     367.29        430.12        503.71
156     405.70        478.01        563.21

GRAPHIC DISPLAY OF FORECASTS FOR VARIABLE Y

DEFINITIONS OF SYMBOLS
DATA - *
FORECASTS AT LEAD   1 - +
ESTIMATED 95% CONFIDENCE LIMITS - .
FORECAST FUNCTION - 0
OVERLAP - X

OBS      DATA        390.00    490.00    590.00    690.00    790.00
                      :---------:---------:---------:---------:---------:
 121    360.000      :    . +* .
 122    342.000      :  . X  .
 123    406.000      :    .  + *.
 124    396.000      :    . +* .
 125    420.000      :    . +  *.
 126    472.000      :        . * + .
 127    548.000      :         .   + *  .
 128    559.000      :          .  +*  .
 129    463.000      :      . *+  .
 130    407.000      -       .  X  .
 131    362.000      :   . X  .
 132    405.000      :     . X  .
 133    417.000      :     . X  .
 134    391.000      :    .*+  .
 135    419.000      :     .*.  +
 136    461.000      :    . + X .
 137    472.000      :      . +* .
 138    535.000      :       .  *+  .
 139    622.000      :            . +*
 140    606.000      -            .*+ .
 141    508.000      :      . X  .
 142    461.000      :     .+*  .
 143    390.000      :   . *+  .
 144    432.000      :     .*+  .
 145    450.195    F :      .  0 .
 146    426.503    F :     .  0 .
 147    482.031    F :      .  0  .
 148    492.168    F :      .  0  .
 149    508.212    F :       .  0  .
 150    583.240    F -          .   0        .
 151    668.039    F :               . 0        .
 152    665.766    F :               . 0      .
 153    558.657    F :          . 0      .
 154    496.579    F :      .   0    .
 155    430.125    F :     .  0   .
 156    478.014    F :      .  0   .
```

2.2   BOX-JENKINS SYNTAX

2.3   Level of Analysis Specification

The three steps in the analysis of a time series model are specified by three keywords in BOX-JENKINS.

IDENTIFY   Produces statistics used for model identification

ESTIMATE   Produces parameter estimates

FORECAST   Produces forecast functions

At least one of these keywords is required on a BOX-JENKINS command. They must be the last specification on the command following all other possible keywords.

2.4   Variable Specification

```
VARIABLE=varname or varlist/
```

The varname following the VARIABLE= keyword is the name of a variable representing time series data measured at equally-spaced intervals. Missing values in the series are not allowed. A list of variables can be specified following the VARIABLE= keyword. Univariate time series analysis is performed for each variable listed.

2.5 Transformations of the Series

The variable under consideration can be log-transformed within the BOX-JENKINS procedure by using the LOG= subcommand.

```
LOG=(constant)
```

When transformation is called for, it is more conveniently done here than in the data transformation language outside the procedure, since results will be internally back-transformed and expressed in the original units whenever feasible. The log transform calculates

newvar=ln(oldvar+constant)

where ln indicates that the base e is being used, and constant is a value added to the series values prior to taking logs. This is useful to prevent taking logs of negative numbers. The constant can be omitted from the specification.

The power transform

```
POWER=(power,constant)
```

calculates

newvar=(oldvar+constant)**power

The power transform or log transform is often useful when the series exhibits heteroscedasticity. One or the other transformation can be used in a given analysis, but not both. The constant can be omitted from the specification.

Nonseasonal differencing of the series is indicated by using the DIFFERENCE keyword.

```
DIFFERENCE=number THRU number BY number
```

The first number is the lowest desired degree of differencing (greater than or equal to zero), the second number is the highest desired degree of differencing, and the third number is the increment (default=1). Ordinarily, no more than two or three degrees of differencing will be required to achieve stationarity and to overdifference, if variate differencing is being done. DIF= number will result in the specified degree of differencing. In the absence of a DIF= specification, differencing will not be done.

The keyword for seasonal differencing works analogously to the DIFFERENCE keyword.

```
SDIFFERENCE=number THRU number BY number
```

If seasonal differencing is requested, be sure to include a specified period.

NOTE: Difference ranges, using the keyword THRU on the DIFFERENCE or SDIFFE-RENCE subcommand, can be specified with the ESTIMATE or FORECAST keywords. However, this results in the calculation of several different models, and can lead to extra expense and voluminous output.

The PERIOD subcommand specifies the number of observations that comprise a period.

```
PERIOD=number
```

This, of course, is a function of both the time interval between consecutive observations and the manifest seasonal periodicity in the data. The default value of PERIOD is 1.

The LAG= keyword specifies the highest lag to be considered in computing the autocovariance function, the autocorrelation function, the partial autocorrelation function, and the residual autocorrelation function.

```
LAG=number
```

The default value is 25.

2.6 Model Specifications

The number of autoregressive parameters to be fit.

```
P=number THRU number
```

The number of moving average parameters to be fit.

```
Q=number THRU number
```

The number of seasonal autoregressive parameters to be fit.

```
SP=number THRU number
```

The number of seasonal moving average parameters to be fit.

    SQ=number THRU number

The THRU keyword is optional. One number representing the total number of parameters to be fit can follow the keyword. The default number for all of these specifications is zero.
    NOTE: Use of the THRU keyword on one or more of the above specifications will give rise to many separate model invocations. This could lead to voluminous output and some expense if you go straight into ESTIMATE or FORECAST after such a specification. If you simply invoke IDENTIFY, you will obtain initial parameter estimates for nonseasonal parameters, along with the usual identification output.
    When you wish to fit either single or nonsequential moving average terms, they may be specified by means of the MALAG subcommand.

    MALAG=number,number,...,number

Simply specify numbers corresponding to the order or lag that you want fit. Thus, Q=3 and MALAG=1,2,3 are equivalent specifications; SQ=1/PER=12 and MALAG=12 are equivalent; but Q=3 and MALAG=1,3 specify different models. The latter specification fits no moving average parameter at lag 2, whereas the former does.
    The ARLAG specification is analogous to the MALAG specification.

    ARLAG=number,number,...,number

The difference is that ARLAG specifies single or nonsequential fitting of autoregressive terms, thus facilitating fitting more generalized models than those implied by P= requests.
    The MALAG and ARLAG specifications are alternatives to the Q= and P= subcommands, respectively. Although it is not required, the program will accept both P and ARLAG or Q and MALAG specifications in the same run. If both P= and ARLAG= are specified, the same number of autoregressive terms as specified by the P= subcommand must be given in the ARLAG list. Similarly, the MALAG list must contain the same number of terms as specified in the Q= subcommand.
    The above model specification keywords can be used with the IDENTIFY keyword or the ESTIMATE keyword when final estimates and model diagnostics are desired. The following parameters can be used only with the ESTIMATE keyword.

    CONSTANT or NCONSTANT

One of these can be used to indicate whether or not a constant parameter is to be fit. The default is CONSTANT.
    The keyword CENTER is used to center values around their mean before estimation is done.

    NCENTER or CENTER

Ordinarily, if CENTER is chosen, the implication is that you do not wish to search on the overall constant during final parameter estimation. The default is NCENTER.

2.7 Estimation Algorithm Specifications

The ITERATE subcommand indicates the maximum number of iterations the estimation routine is to use in parameter estimation.

    ITERATE=number

The default is 40.
    The number of backforecasts to be generated for use in estimation is indicated by

    BFR=number

The default number is 0. There is no inherent program limit as to the maximum allowable number of backforecasts that can be specified. As a rule of thumb, a larger number should be specified when modelling seasonal autoregressive series, and smaller numbers can be specified for seasonal moving average, autoregressive, and moving average series.
    Box and Jenkins discuss a set of simultaneous inequalities that constitute invertibility conditions for models with up to three moving average parameters.

    NTEST or TEST

Specifying TEST instructs BOX-JENKINS to check the estimated parameters at each iteration against these invertibility conditions. The default is NTEST.
    The FPR keyword specifies the interval at the end of which current estimated values from iterative estimation are to be printed.

    FPR=number

The default is 5, which implies that you will get printed results at every fifth iteration.

The following subcommands can be used to specify perturbation increments that are used by the estimation routine in final parameter estimation:

```
PCON=(number)
PP=(number,number,....,number)
PQ=(number,number,....,number)
PSP=(number,number,....,number)
PSQ=(number,number,....,number)
```

Perturbation increments need not be specified by you, as they have default values of 0.1 which will usually suffice. These specifications will prove especially useful if you do not want a particular parameter to be searched on because it has some known a priori value. Declare its value using the relevant initial parameter keyword and set its perturbation increment to zero.

These specifications must have matching P, Q, SP, and SQ specifications. Perturbation increments cannot be specified if "number THRU number" has been indicated on matching P, Q, SP, or SQ specifications.

Default convergence tolerances are equal to 0.001. This means that when estimated parameters in two consecutive iterations differ by no more than 0.001, the search algorithm will stop. If you prefer that some other value, more or less stringent, be used, then you can supply your own value by means of the convergence specifications.

```
TCON=(number)
TP=(number,number,....,number)
TQ=(number,number,....,number)
TSP=(number,number,....,number)
TSQ=(number,number,....,number)
```

These keywords must also have matching P, Q, SP, and SQ specifications.

2.8 Specifying Initial Estimates of Parameters

The following subcommands are used to input initial parameter estimates into SPSS BOX-JENKINS.

```
ICON=(number)
IP=(number,number,....,number)
IQ=(number,number,....,number)
ISP=(number,number,....,number)
ISQ=(number,number,....,number)
```

The initial estimates may have been obtained from a previous IDENTIFY run, or you may have some initial value to input that has been otherwise obtained. These keywords must have matching P, Q, SP, and SQ specifications. Initial parameter estimates cannot be specified if "number THRU number" has been indicated on matching P, Q, SP, or SQ specifications.

2.9 Forecast Specifications

The two numbers in the ORIGIN subcommand give the range of series values that are to be considered forecast origins.

```
ORIGIN=number THRU number
```

You can supply two positive numbers that correspond to sequential case numbers. Negative numbers can also be used, in which case the implication is that you wish to count back from the end of the series. Use of the THRU keyword is optional. You can specify one forecast origin by using the form ORIGIN=number. The default forecast origin is the last case in the file.

The LEAD keyword is used to specify the highest lead desired.

```
LEAD=number
```

The default lead is 12.

The CIN keyword specifies the desired forecast confidence level expressed as a percentage.

```
CIN=number
```

The default level is 95.

The following keywords are used to input final parameter estimates into BOX-JENKINS for the purpose of generating forecasts.

```
FCON=(number)
FP=(number,number,....,number)
FQ=(number,number,....,number)
FSP=(number,number,....,number)
FSQ=(number,number,....,number)
```

These keywords must also have matching P, Q, SP, and SQ specifications.

2.10   The PRINT= Subcommand

The following keywords are used on the PRINT= subcommand to request printed values for various functions and series:

ACF   Autocorrelation function
PACF   Partial autocorrelation function
ACVF   Autocovariance function
SER   Time series
TSER   Log- or power-transformed series
DSER   Differenced series
RESID Values of the residual series, when a model has been estimated
RACF   Residual autocorrelation function

Invocation of FORECAST will result in forecast results being printed without an explicit request. Thus, no forecast keywords need be named on the PRINT= subcommand.

2.11   The PLOT= Subcommand

All keywords that appear above under PRINT= can also be specified under PLOT=, with the exception of ACV, the autocovariance function. If you are interested in plots, the PLOT= subcommand should suffice, as PRINT= requests for the same series or functions would produce redundant information. This is because printed values are either in the plot or contiguous to it. Three additional PLOT= keywords can be used with the FORECAST specification.

FCF   Forecast function
FLF   Fixed lead forecasts
CIN   Confidence intervals

If the forecast origin is other than the end of the series, then one-step-ahead forecasts are plotted for all series values starting with the forecast origin, and increasing lead forecasts are plotted from the end of the series. If the origin is not specified, one-step-ahead forecasts are plotted from the beginning of the series.

2.12   REFERENCES

Anderson, O.D. *Time Series Analysis and Forecasting—The Box-Jenkins Approach.* Boston: Butterworth, 1976.

Box, G.E.P., and G.M. Jenkins. *Time Series Analysis: Forecasting and Control.* San Francisco: Holden-Day, 1976.

Fuller, Wayne A. *Introduction to Statistical Time Series.* New York: Wiley, 1976.

Ling, Robert F., and Harry V. Roberts. *User's Manual for IDA.* Palo Alto: Scientific Press, 1980.

Nelson, Charles R. *Applied Time Series Analysis for Managerial Forecasting.* San Francisco: Holden-Day, 1973.

BOX-JENKINS was designed and programmed by Mindaugas Pleskys and documented by Tony Babinec and Nancy Morrison.

Chapter 3

NEW REGRESSION

The NEW REGRESSION procedure incorporates recent methodological developments. There are five equation-building methods: forward entry, backward elimination, stepwise selection, forced entry, and forced removal. These methods can be used together to explore several models for a set of variables or to obtain the desired final model. The missing-value treatments available are listwise deletion, pairwise deletion, mean substitution, and inclusion of missing values. Descriptive statistics include univariate summary statistics, such as the mean and standard deviation, and such bivariate statistics as correlations and the variance-covariance matrix. Variable selection criteria, such as p values for the entry and removal of variables, have default values that can be overridden. A statistics profile governs the display of statistical results (for both the regression equation as a whole and for its component variables). The residuals branch of the procedure produces casewise plots, normal probability plots, histograms, and scatterplots—all useful in detecting violations of the regression model assumptions. Residual output has been enhanced by adding statistics that aid in detecting influential data points, outliers, and violations of model assumptions. These statistics include the Studentized residual, the Studentized deleted residual, Cook's D, and the Mahalanobis distance. Other facilities include generation and saving of regression-related variables, matrix input, internal selection for cross-validation, and regression through the origin.

The syntax for procedure NEW REGRESSION is flexible without being verbose. The procedure is driven by a series of subcommands. Each subcommand groups together a logically related set of operations or definitions and is relatively independent of the specifications used on another subcommand. One set of subcommands is related to the variables and the cases being analyzed. These subcommands specify descriptive statistics to be displayed, variables to be used, missing-value treatment to be used, whether matrix input is to be used in place of cases, whether matrix output is to be written to the raw output file, whether cases are to be selected for computing regression statistics, and the printing width to be used in displays. Most of these subcommands have default options and are not required. A second set of subcommands control the regression model. They specify the dependent variable, statistical criteria to be used in developing the model, methods of entering and removing variables from the model, whether the constant is to be suppressed, and the display of statistics for the model. As with the first group of subcommands, most of these subcommands also have default options and are required only if non-default options are desired. The final set of subcommands control residuals processing including plotting and saving of several different types of residuals. All of these subcommands are optional.

One NEW REGRESSION command can contain multiple sets of subcommands to examine several different models using the same or different sets of variables, different dependent variables, different methods, different missing-value treatments, different statistical criteria, etc. You are not locked into one set of options or statistics that remain in effect for the entire procedure. If on the other hand, you want to develop parallel models using the same options and statistics available, you need not respecify complete sets of subcommands for each model—only those you want to change.

Since NEW REGRESSION is somewhat unique in its syntactical structure and because it offers such a large number of options, this chapter is organized into four sections. The first section, beginning with Section 3.2, provides an overview of the subcommands and how they are related by moving from a relatively simple example to more complex examples. The second section, beginning with Section 3.9, describes each subcommand in detail and includes display examples. The third section, beginning with Section 3.34, is a substantive example of the use of NEW

REGRESSION. The final section, provided for users of the REGRESSION procedure, compares the two procedures and illustrates the syntax for NEW REGRESSION compared to REGRESSION.

Finally a brief note on terminology. "Model" and "design" are used interchangeably in this chapter to refer to an equation or set of equations specified by a dependent variable, set of independent variables, and method or set of combined methods. A design can imply several steps in which variables are entered and/or removed from the current equation. When several variables are simultaneously entered or removed, each variable is noted as a step in displays, but statistics are computed only for the "block" of steps. A "final equation" is the equation obtained after the last step in a design has been executed.

3.1 OPERATION OF THE NEW REGRESSION PROCEDURE

NEW REGRESSION syntax is organized into subcommands. A subcommand is composed of a subcommand keyword identifying it, an equals sign, and an optional set of keyword specifications. Each subcommand is terminated by a slash (/). All keywords including the subcommand keyword can be abbreviated to the first three characters. The equals sign following the subcommand keyword is optional. The subcommands constitute the specification field of NEW REGRESSION and must begin in column 16 or beyond of the command. Subcommands can span continuation lines, and additional blanks or commas can be used to improve readability.

3.2 AN OVERVIEW OF NEW REGRESSION SUBCOMMANDS

This section describes the logic of NEW REGRESSION subcommands and how they are related and briefly summarizes what each subcommand does. Beginning with Section 3.9 a complete description of specifications for each subcommand is presented. This section begins with a simple one-design example using the three required subcommands and proceeds to more complex one- and multiple-design command specifications.

A file containing information on 34 passenger automobiles is used in the following sections to illustrate the operation of NEW REGRESSION. These data are obtained from *Motor Trend* magazine. In addition, one deliberately contrived case has been added to the file as an outlier. The dependent variable is MPG (miles per gallon) and the independent variables are various characteristics of automobiles including curb weight, engine displacement, and other variables hypothesized to be good predictors of fuel efficiency.

3.3 Minimum Specifications Required for a Single Regression Design

To build a simple regression model, you must specify three subcommands, a VARIABLES= subcommand listing the variables to be analyzed, a DEPENDENT= subcommand specifying the dependent variable, and a subcommand specifying the method to be used. For example,

```
NEW REGRESSION VARIABLES=DISP TO MPG/
               DEPENDENT=MPG/
               STEPWISE/
```

produces a stepwise regression for the variables DISP through MPG, with MPG treated as the dependent variable and the other variables in the list treated as independent variables. In addition to accepting a variable list following SPSS conventions, the VARIABLES= subcommand has additional keywords that automatically build the list from subsequent specifications or use a previous list; see Section 3.11. The DEPENDENT= subcommand can contain one or more variables (see Section 3.12). NEW REGRESSION provides a separate subcommand corresponding to each of the five equation- building methods noted above. In the above example, the STEPWISE subcommand produces stepwise regression. (The method subcommands are discussed in Section 3.13). Since keywords can be abbreviated to the first three characters and equals signs are optional, the example shown above could be abbreviated to

```
NEW REGRESSION VAR DISP TO MPG/ DEP MPG/ STE/
```

3.4 Combining Methods

After a method has been executed, the equation obtained as the last step for that method can be further modified by another method. For example, the following command enters variables DISP and WEIGHT as a block, then enters CARB and TIRES as a block.

```
NEW REGRESSION VARIABLES=DISP WEIGHT CARB TIRES MPG/DEPENDENT=MPG/
               ENTER=DISP WEIGHT/ENTER=CARB TIRES
```

When methods are stacked in this manner, the current equation is not cleared between methods.

3.5 Minimum Specifications for Several Regression Designs

There are three basic ways to specify more than one design on one procedure command. First, you can use a new VARIABLES= and its associated DEPENDENT= subcommand to signal a new design.

```
NEW REGRESSION VARIABLES=DISP TO MPG/DEPENDENT=MPG/STEPWISE/
                VARIABLES=LOCATION TO EPA/DEPENDENT=EPA/
                STEPWISE
```

In this example, a different set of variables is being used for each regression model.

Second, you can specify multiple variables in one DEPENDENT= subcommand, as in

```
NEW REGRESSION VARIABLES=DISP TO MPG EPA/DEPENDENT=MPG EPA/STEPWISE
```

In this example NEW REGRESSION first uses MPG as the dependent variable, then EPA as the dependent variable in a new regression design. MPG is not used as an independent variable when EPA is the dependent variable, nor is EPA used as an independent variable when MPG is dependent.

Third, you can use multiple DEPENDENT= subcommands, as in

```
NEW REGRESSION VARIABLES=DISP TO MPG EPA/DEPENDENT=MPG/STEPWISE/
                DEPENDENT=EPA/STEPWISE
```

This example does not produce exactly the same analysis as the previous example. Here, EPA is considered an independent variable in the first design, and MPG is considered an independent variable in the second design. Multiple DEPENDENT= subcommands are useful when you wish to specify different criteria, statistics, or options associated with the regression design through the use of optional subcommands discussed in Section 3.7.

When you wish to specify different descriptive statistics, missing data treatment, and so on using optional subcommands for the variable list (Section 3.6), you have to enter another VARIABLES= subcommand listing the same set of variables used previously. In this instance, you can use a special keyword phrase, (PREVIOUS), in subsequent VARIABLES= subcommands to indicate the previous variable list (see Section 3.11). When the special keyword (COLLECT) is used with the VARIABLES= subcommand, the list of variables is assembled from the DEPENDENT= subcommands and the methods subcommands. See Sections 3.7 and 3.8 for examples of the use of the (COLLECT) keyword.

Each VARIABLES= subcommand indicates that a new regression analysis is to be initiated with a new set of variables and forces SPSS to calculate another set of correlation coefficients for the new set of variables. Multiple DEPENDENT= subcommands associated with one variable list do not force SPSS to calculate new correlation coefficients.

3.6 Optional Subcommands for the Variable List

Six optional subcommands concerning the variable list are available. When used, they must precede a VARIABLES= subcommand, and they remain in effect for subsequent VARIABLES= subcommands until overridden.

The DESCRIPTIVES= subcommand is used to select descriptive statistics for the variables named in the VARIABLES= subcommand. By default, no descriptive statistics are displayed. The DESCRIPTIVES= subcommand used without any keyword specifications produces means, standard deviations, and correlations. Additional keyword specifications are available to obtain variances, the covariance matrix and other statistics. See Section 3.17 for keyword specifications.

The following example demonstrates the use of multiple DESCRIPTIVES= subcommands:

```
NEW REGRESSION DESCRIPTIVES/
                VARIABLES=DISP TO MPG/ DEPENDENT=MPG/
                    STEPWISE/
                DESCRIPTIVES=NONE/
                VARIABLES=LOCATION TO EPA/ DEPENDENT=EPA/
                    STEPWISE/
```

The default descriptive statistics are printed for the first design and no descriptive statistics are printed for the second. If the second DESCRIPTIVES= subcommand were omitted, default descriptive statistics would be printed for both designs.

The MISSING= subcommand specifies the missing-value treatment for each VARIABLES= subcommand. The default is to delete cases listwise. Other methods are available. A missing-value treatment remains in effect for subsequent variable lists until overridden. For example,

```
NEW REGRESSION DESCRIPTIVES/
                VARIABLES=DISP TO TIRES MPG/
                    DEPENDENT=MPG/
                    STEPWISE/
                MISSING=PAIRWISE/
                VARIABLES=(PREVIOUS)/
                    DEPENDENT=MPG/
                    STEPWISE/
```

accepts the default listwise missing-value treatment for the first design and then changes it to pairwise for the second. The VARIABLES= subcommand specification is required since the the correlation coefficients must be recalculated when the missing-value treatment is changed.

NEW REGRESSION accepts matrix input in lieu of raw data and also writes out matrix materials for use with SPSS and other programs. The READ= subcommand specifies the type of matrix input being read and the WRITE= subcommand specifies the type of matrix output being written to the raw output unit. Only one READ= subcommand can be used in a single NEW REGRESSION command, but the procedure can read in multiple matrices corresponding to multiple VARIABLES= subcommands. When used, the READ= subcommand *must be the first subcommand* specified. The following example demonstrates the use of the READ= subcommand:

```
NEW REGRESSION READ/VARIABLES=DISP WEIGHT HP CARBS TIRES/
               DEPENDENT=WEIGHT/ENTER
```

The WRITE= subcommand writes out matrix materials including means, standard deviations, and correlation or covariance matrices. Unlike the READ= subcommand, multiple WRITE= subcommands can be used. The keyword NONE is available to turn off the writing of matrix materials for subsequent VARIABLES= subcommands.

The SELECT= subcommand selects a subset of cases for analysis. Only selected cases contribute to the regression equation but residuals and predicted values for nonselected cases can be calculated and reported separately. The SELECT= subcommand specification is a simple logical relation. Multiple SELECT= subcommands can be used with multiple VARIABLES= subcommands, as in

```
NEW REGRESSION SELECT=LOCATION EQ 1/
               DESCRIPTIVES/
               VARIABLES=DISP TO MPG/
                  DEPENDENT=MPG/
                  STEPWISE/
               SELECT=LOCATION EQ 2/
               VARIABLES=DISP TO MPG/
                  DEPENDENT=MPG/
                  STEPWISE/
               SELECT=(ALL)/
               VARIABLES=DISP TO MPG/
                  DEPENDENT=MPG/
                  STEPWISE/
```

This command produces three stepwise analyses; the first on cases corresponding to LOCATION equal to 1, the second on cases with LOCATION equal to 2, and the third on all cases. All three VARIABLES= subcommands are necessary since the correlation coefficients must be recalculated for each design that uses different data selection criteria.

The WIDTH= subcommand overrides the default width of 132 characters within which SPSS displays output. Unlike other NEW REGRESSION subcommands, the WIDTH= subcommand can appear anywhere within the command. If you use multiple WIDTH= subcommands, the last specified width controls the display of all printed output produced by NEW REGRESSION. Section 3.23 summarizes specifications for the WIDTH= subcommand. The following example demonstrates the use and placement of the WIDTH= subcommand:

```
NEW REGRESSION DESCRIPTIVES/
               WIDTH 80/
               VARIABLES=DISP TO MPG/
                  DEPENDENT=MPG/
                  STEPWISE
```

In summary, the subcommands concerning the variable list must precede the VARIABLES= subcommand to which they apply and remain in effect until overridden. In general, they can be used in any order prior to the VARIABLES= subcommand. There are two exceptions to these rules. First, the WIDTH= subcommand can be used anywhere and is set once for all display. Second, the READ= subcommand is used only once and must be the first subcommand when used.

3.7 Optional Subcommands for the Equation

Three optional subcommands concerning the regression equation are available. These subcommands must precede the DEPENDENT= subcommand to which they apply and remain in effect for subsequent DEPENDENT= subcommands until overridden.

The CRITERIA= subcommand is used to override tolerance criteria for all methods and to override probability of F to enter and remove for the forward, backward, and stepwise methods. NEW REGRESSION provides defaults for these criteria; thus the CRITERIA= subcommand is normally used to change the defaults. Subsequent CRITERIA= subcommands can be used to change the criteria currently in effect, as in

```
NEW REGRESSION VARIABLES=DISP TO MPG/
               CRITERIA=FIN,FOUT/
               DEPENDENT=MPG/
               STEPWISE/
               CRITERIA=DEFAULTS/DEPENDENT=MPG/
               STEPWISE
```

In this example, the first CRITERIA= subcommand specifies that *F*-to-enter and *F*-to- remove criteria be used. The second CRITERIA= subcommand returns to the default criteria, *probabilities of F-to-enter* and *F-to-remove*. See Section 3.25 for a full discussion of the CRITERIA= subcommand.

The STATISTICS= subcommand is used to display a number of statistics for each regression equation. By default, NEW REGRESSION prints R^2 and related statistics, regression coefficients and related statistics, and statistics for variables not currently in the equation. The STATISTICS= subcommand overrides this default list and remains in effect for subsequent designs until overridden by another STATISTICS= subcommand, as in

```
NEW REGRESSION DESCRIPTIVES/
               VARIABLES=(COLLECT)/
                    STATISTICS=DEFAULTS,HISTORY,LABEL/
                    DEPENDENT=MPG/
                    STEPWISE DISP TO TIRES/
                    STATISTICS=DEFAULTS,CI/
                    DEPENDENT=MPG/
                    BACKWARD DISP TO TIRES/
```

This example requests the default statistics for both designs, a step history and variable labels for the first, and 95% confidence intervals for the regression parameters for the second. The keyword specifications for the STATISTICS= subcommand are discussed in Section 3.26.

The ORIGIN subcommand is used to force regression through the origin. Once specified it remains in effect for all subsequent designs until turned off with subcommand NOORIGIN. For example,

```
NEW REGRESSION VARIABLES=DISP TO MPG/
               ORIGIN/
               DEPENDENT=MPG/
               STEPWISE/
```

All of these subcommands must precede the DEPENDENT= subcommand to which they apply and can be entered in any order. They are usually placed immediately prior to the DEPENDENT= command but can also precede the VARIABLES= subcommand.

3.8 Optional Subcommands for Residuals Analysis

Four subcommands are available for producing and analyzing residuals following the last step in a regression design. Any one of these subcommands directs NEW REGRESSION to calculate residuals. However, more than one may be required to obtain the desired printed and written output. Unlike other subcommands discussed previously, residuals subcommands must be specified for each equation to be analyzed—they do *not* remain in effect for subsequent designs. The data are reread for each equation for which residual analysis is requested.

The RESIDUALS= subcommand directs SPSS to calculate and display histograms, probability plots, and outlier plots of any of a number of residuals and related statistics. It must immediately follow the last method subcommand, as in

```
NEW REGRESSION VARIABLES=(COLLECT)/
               DEPENDENT=MPG/
               BACKWARD DISP TO TIRES/
               RESIDUALS
```

which requests all the default RESIDUALS= specifications. The keyword specifications for the RESIDUALS= subcommand are discussed in Section 3.30.

The CASEWISE= subcommand directs SPSS to print casewise plots of outliers or of all cases. Any of the calculated standardized residuals can be sequentially plotted, and observed values as well as predicted values of the dependent variable can be listed. The following example demonstrates the use of the CASEWISE= subcommand:

```
NEW REGRESSION VARIABLES=(COLLECT)/
               DEPENDENT=MPG/
               BACKWARD DISP TO TIRES/
               RESIDUALS/
               CASEWISE=PLOT,DEPENDENT,PRED/
```

In this example, the CASEWISE= subcommand prints an outlier casewise plot of the standardized residual, and the values of MPG and predicted MPG. The keyword specifications for the CASEWISE= subcommand are discussed in Section 3.31.

The SCATTERPLOT= subcommand prints scatterplots of any of the variables in the design as well as various residuals and predictors. For example,

```
NEW REGRESSION VARIABLES=(COLLECT)/
               DEPENDENT=MPG/
               BACKWARD DISP TO TIRES/
               SCATTERPLOT= (*PRED,DISP) (*PRED,*RESID)
```

plots the predicted values against variable DISP, and the predicted values against the residuals. The SCATTERPLOT= subcommand is discussed in Section 3.32.

The SAVE= subcommand saves predicted variables and residuals on a raw output file for use in subsequent analysis. For example,

```
NEW REGRESSION VARIABLES=(COLLECT)/
                DEPENDENT=MPG/
                BACKWARD DISP TO TIRES/
                RESIDUALS/
                CASEWISE=PLOT,DEPENDENT,PRED,RESID,DRESID/
                SCATTERPLOT(*PRED,DISP),(*PRED,*RESID)/
                SAVE= PRED SEPRED RESID SRESID SDRESID/
```

saves the predicted values, standard error of the predicted values, residuals, Studentized residuals, and Studentized deleted residuals on the raw output file. The SAVE= subcommand is discussed in Section 3.33.

The residuals subcommands can be used in any order following the method subcommand to which they apply. Although you can combine methods subcommands, you can use residuals subcommands only after the last method subcommand for a given DEPENDENT= subcommand.

3.9 SPECIFICATIONS FOR NEW REGRESSION SUBCOMMANDS

The following sections describe in detail the subcommand specifications used to operate NEW REGRESSION. Keywords marked with double asterisks are the defaults you get if you do not enter the subcommand at all. Keywords marked with a single asterisk are the defaults you get if you enter the subcommand alone with no specifications.

3.10 Basic Subcommands

Three basic subcommands are required to operate NEW REGRESSION: VARIABLES=, DEPENDENT=, and one of the five method subcommands.

3.11 Naming the Variables: The VARIABLES= Subcommand

Specification of a design begins with a list of the variables to be used. Since more than one design can be developed in a single invocation of NEW REGRESSION, there can be more than one VARIABLES= subcommand. The possible specifications are

varlist   *All dependent and independent variables to be used in regression designs.*

(COLLECT)   *Assemble the list of variables from the DEPENDENT= subcommands and from each of the regression method subcommands.*

(PREVIOUS) *Use the variable list named in the previous VARIABLES= specification. Used primarily if you are selecting different cases or altering the missing-value treatment in a second or subsequent design.*

3.12 Naming the Dependent Variables: The DEPENDENT= Subcommand

You name the dependent variable or variables in the DEPENDENT= subcommand. The dependent variable or variables must have been named in the VARIABLES= subcommand unless you are using VARIABLES=(COLLECT). If you name more than one dependent variable, NEW REGRESSION develops an equation (or set of equations) according to your method specifications for each dependent variable named. All methods are executed for the first dependent variable, then the second, etc. None of the variables named in the DEPENDENT= subcommand is treated as an independent variable in any design associated with that DEPENDENT= subcommand.

Each DEPENDENT= subcommand initiates a new regression design and more than one DEPENDENT= subcommand can be specified for the same VARIABLES= subcommand when the same variables are involved.

3.13 Specifying the Method

The actual method or combination of methods used in developing a multiple regression equation is specified by one or more method keywords optionally followed by a list of variables. The keywords are

STEPWISE   *Stepwise regression.* Variables are examined at each step for entry or removal.

FORWARD   *Forward inclusion.* Variables are entered one at a time based on entry criteria.

BACKWARD   *Backward elimination.* All variables are entered and then removed one at a time based on removal criteria.

ENTER   *Forced entry.* The variables named are entered. The default variable list is all independent variables.

REMOVE varlist   *Forced removal.* The variables named are removed.

The *varlist* following the method keyword is required for REMOVE. It is optional for all other keywords unless VARIABLES=(COLLECT) is in force (see Section 3.11), in which case the variable list is required.

With the STEPWISE method, if there are independent variables already in the equation, the variable with the smallest *F* value is examined for deletion. If the probability of that *F* is larger than the removal criterion POUT (see Section 3.25), the variable is removed. The equation is then recomputed without the removed variable and the rest of the variables are examined for removal.

Once no more independent variables need to be removed, all independent variables not in the equation are examined for entry. The variable with the largest *F* value is entered if the probability of that *F* is smaller than the entry criterion PIN and the variable passes the tolerance tests governed by the tolerance criterion, TOLERANCE (see Section 3.25). Once a variable has been entered, all variables in the equation are again examined for removal.

This process continues until no variables in the equation need to be removed and no variables not in the equation are eligible for entry, or until the maximum number of steps has been performed.

With the FORWARD method, variables are entered into the equation one at a time. At each step, the independent variables not yet in the equation are examined for entry. The variable with the largest *F* value is entered if the probability of that *F* is smaller than the entry criterion PIN and the variable passes the tolerance tests governed by the tolerance criterion, TOLERANCE.

With the BACKWARD method, variables that pass the tolerance tests are entered as a group and are then removed from the equation one at a time. At each step, the independent variables already in the equation are examined for removal. The variable with the smallest *F* value is removed if the probability of that *F* is larger than the removal criterion POUT.

All variables referenced with the ENTER keyword that satisfy tolerance levels are entered. Variables are entered one at a time in order of decreasing tolerance but are treated as a block for statistics computed for changes in the equation.

3.14   A Basic Regression Example
The following command produces the default NEW REGRESSION display shown in Figure 3.14.

```
NEW REGRESSION VARIABLES=DISP TO MPG/
               DEPENDENT=MPG/STEPWISE
```

Figure 3.14   Default Display for A Basic Regression Example

```
                    * * * *   M U L T I P L E   R E G R E S S I O N   * * * *

VARIABLE LIST NUMBER  1.  LISTWISE DELETION OF MISSING DATA.

EQUATION NUMBER  1.

DEPENDENT VARIABLE..  MPG        MOTOR TREND MILEAGE


BEGINNING BLOCK NUMBER  1.  METHOD:  STEPWISE


VARIABLE(S) ENTERED ON STEP NUMBER  1..    DISP        ENGINE DISPLACEMENT


MULTIPLE R          0.78047     ANALYSIS OF VARIANCE
R SQUARE            0.60913                     DF     SUM OF SQUARES    MEAN SQUARE
ADJUSTED R SQUARE   0.59729     REGRESSION       1        1170.44377     1170.44377
STANDARD ERROR      4.77062     RESIDUAL        33         751.04154       22.75883

                                F =     51.42811    SIGNIF F = 0.0000
```

```
-------------------- VARIABLES=IN THE EQUATION --------------------        -------------- VARIABLES=NOT IN THE EQUATION --------------

VARIABLE        B         SE B       BETA       T SIG T         VARIABLE    BETA IN  PARTIAL  MIN TOLER      T SIG T

DISP        -0.05100    0.00711   -0.78047    -7.171 0.0000     WEIGHT     -0.30495 -0.20765   0.18124   -1.201 0.2386
(CONSTANT)  33.78269    1.76260               19.166 0.0        HP         -0.13746 -0.08966   0.16627   -0.509 0.6141
                                                                CARBS       0.25338  0.31000   0.58509    1.844 0.0744
                                                                CYLS       -0.01343 -0.00664   0.09556   -0.038 0.9703
                                                                TIRES       0.45154  0.61837   0.73304    4.451 0.0001
```

```
            * * * * * * * * * * * * * * * * * * * * * * * * * * * *
```

```
VARIABLE(S) ENTERED ON STEP NUMBER  2..    TIRES      TYPE OF TIRE


MULTIPLE R           0.87097    ANALYSIS OF VARIANCE
R SQUARE             0.75859                        DF      SUM OF SQUARES     MEAN SQUARE
ADJUSTED R SQUARE    0.74351    REGRESSION           2         1457.62550       728.81275
STANDARD ERROR       3.80731    RESIDUAL            32          463.85981        14.49562

                               F =      50.27814    SIGNIF F = 0.0000



----------------- VARIABLES IN THE EQUATION -----------------        ------------- VARIABLES NOT IN THE EQUATION -------------

VARIABLE          B         SE B      BETA        T SIG T        VARIABLE    BETA IN  PARTIAL  MIN TOLER      T SIG T

DISP         -0.03576    0.00663   -0.54717    -5.394 0.0000     WEIGHT     -0.11888 -0.10069   0.17319   -0.564 0.5771
TIRES         7.96751    1.79004    0.45154     4.451 0.0001     HP         -0.07766 -0.06432   0.16056   -0.359 0.7221
(CONSTANT)   28.60165    1.82584               15.665 0.0        CARBS       0.16505  0.25246   0.43333    1.453 0.1564
                                                                 CYLS        0.09394  0.05889   0.09451    0.328 0.7448

FOR BLOCK NUMBER  1   PIN = 0.050 LIMITS REACHED.
```

The method is STEPWISE, and this design results in two steps (see Figure 3.14). DISP is entered first, then TIRES. None of the remaining variables satisfies the criterion for entry. Note that NEW REGRESSION prints the t value for each coefficient by default, but F can be specified with the STATISTICS= subcommand described in Section 3.26.

3.15 Testing Sets of Predictor Variables: The TEST= Subcommand

The TEST= subcommand offers an easy way to test a variety of models using R-squared change and its test of significance as the criterion for the "best" model. Suppose that you have specified five independent or predictor variables in the VARIABLES= subcommand and your theory leads you to believe that one of four alternative equations is the best predictor of the dependent variable. You could specify four separate sets of subcommands to perform four separate designs, or you can use the TEST= subcommand to do all four tests at one time. And, since the intent of the test is to examine R^2, the printed output is considerably condensed from the usual regression display.

The TEST= subcommand first builds a full model and then removes different subsets of variables from the full model. All the variables named in the subsets constitute the full model. Test subsets are specified in parentheses. A variable can be used in more than one subset and any number of variables can be used in a subset. All variables used in the subsets must have been previously named in the VARIABLES= subcommand.

Figure 3.15a uses the TEST= subcommand to test four sets of predictors.

Figure 3.15a   The TEST= Subcommand

```
NEW REGRESSION VARIABLES=DISP TO MPG/DEPENDENT=MPG/
               TEST=(HP TIRES)(WEIGHT CARBS)(DISP CYLS)
               (CYLS CARBS)
```

Figure 3.15b   TEST= Display

```
                    * * * *   M U L T I P L E   R E G R E S S I O N   * * * *

VARIABLE LIST NUMBER  1.  LISTWISE DELETION OF MISSING DATA.
EQUATION NUMBER  1.

DEPENDENT VARIABLE..   MPG       MOTOR TREND MILEAGE


BEGINNING BLOCK NUMBER  1.  METHOD:  TEST      HP     TIRES    WEIGHT   CARBS    DISP    CYLS


VARIABLE(S) ENTERED ON STEP NUMBER  1..     TIRES     TYPE OF TIRE
                                    2..     CARBS     NUMBER OF CARBURETORS
                                    3..     CYLS      NUMBER OF CYLINDERS
                                    4..     WEIGHT    CURB WEIGHT IN HUNDREDS OF POUNDS
                                    5..     HP        HORSEPOWER
                                    6..     DISP      ENGINE DISPLACEMENT
```

```
HYPOTHESIS TESTS

             SUM OF
    DF       SQUARES  RSQ CHG          F    SIG F    SOURCE

     2     251.47275  0.13087    9.06996   0.0009    HP      TIRES
     2      72.02379  0.03748    2.59771   0.0923    WEIGHT  CARBS
     2      16.18198  0.00842    0.58364   0.5645    DISP    CYLS
     2      69.66586  0.03626    2.51266   0.0992    CYLS    CARBS

     6    1533.32268            18.43430   0.0000    REGRESSION
    28     388.16263                                 RESIDUAL
    34    1921.48531                                 TOTAL
```
_____

```
MULTIPLE R           0.89330      ANALYSIS OF VARIANCE
R SQUARE             0.79799                           DF    SUM OF SQUARES   MEAN SQUARE
ADJUSTED R SQUARE    0.75470      REGRESSION            6       1533.32268     255.55378
STANDARD ERROR       3.72330      RESIDUAL             28        388.16263      13.86295

                                  F  =     18.43430     SIGNIF F = 0.0000
```

```
------------------ VARIABLES IN THE EQUATION ------------------

VARIABLE            B         SE B       BETA         T   SIG T

TIRES          6.59686     1.87925    0.37386     3.510  0.0015
CARBS          2.23131     1.00413    0.32469     2.222  0.0345
CYLS           0.38790     1.16786    0.09228     0.332  0.7423
WEIGHT        -0.11822     0.19578   -0.12493    -0.604  0.5508
HP            -0.06971     0.04228   -0.44569    -1.649  0.1104
DISP          -0.02380     0.02479   -0.36421    -0.960  0.3451
(CONSTANT)    30.09789     5.24468                5.739  0.0000

FOR BLOCK NUMBER  1   ALL REQUESTED VARIABLES ENTERED.
```

Figure 3.15b is the display produced by the TEST= subcommand. Since six different variables are specified in the various subsets for TEST, they constitute the full model against which each of the subsets is tested. The sum of squares for each subset is the change in sum of squares with that subset removed from the full model. The R^2 change for each subset is the change in R^2 with that subset removed from the full model.

3.16   Subcommands for the Variable List

Five commands that precede the VARIABLES= subcommand and are logically connected to it are: DESCRIPTIVES, MISSING, READ, WRITE, and SELECT. In addition, the WIDTH= subcommand which has a unique status as a procedure wide specification is arbitrarily included with these subcommands.

3.17   Descriptive Statistics: The DESCRIPTIVES= Subcommand

You can use the following keyword specifications for the DESCRIPTIVES= subcommand to display statistics for all variables in the VARIABLES= list:

NONE**   *Turn off all descriptive statistics.* If you do not specify any descriptive statistics, none are displayed. If you have requested them for a variable list, use the keyword NONE to turn them off for subsequent variable lists.

DEFAULTS*   *Specifies keywords MEAN, STDDEV, CORR.* If you specify DESCRIPTIVES= with no specifications, these are the defaults.

MEAN   *Variable means.*

STDDEV   *Variable standard deviations.*

VARIANCE   *Variable variances.*

CORR   *Correlation matrix.*

SIG   *One-tailed significance levels of the correlation coefficients.*

BADCORR   *Display the correlation matrix only if some coefficients cannot be computed.* Correlations cannot be computed if one variable is a constant or if there are too few cases because of missing data or case selection.

COV   *Covariance matrix.*

XPROD   *Cross-product deviations from the mean.*

N   *Numbers of cases used to compute correlation coefficients.* Used with pairwise missing- value treatment or mean substitution.

A DESCRIPTIVES= subcommand must appear before the VARIABLES= subcommand to which it applies and it remains in effect until overridden by a new list of descriptive statistics or by specifying DESCRIPTIVES=NONE. Descriptive statistics are displayed only once for each variable list, regardless of the number of models you develop from that variable list. If you use DESCRIPTIVES= more than once, each must be accompanied by a new VARIABLES= subcommand.

3.18 Example Descriptive Statistics

Figure 3.18a shows the use of the DESCRIPTIVES= subcommand to print the default statistics; univariate means, standard deviations, and the correlation matrix. Figure 3.18b shows the display produced by the default DESCRIPTIVES= subcommand.

Figure 3.18a   The DESCRIPTIVES= Subcommand

```
NEW REGRESSION DESCRIPTIVES/VARIABLES=DISP TO MPG/
               DEPENDENT=MPG/STEPWISE
```

Figure 3.18b   Default DESCRIPTIVES= Display

```
                  * * * *   M U L T I P L E   R E G R E S S I O N   * * * *

VARIABLE LIST NUMBER  1.  LISTWISE DELETION OF MISSING DATA.

            MEAN    STD DEV   LABEL

DISP      220.371   115.035   ENGINE DISPLACEMENT
WEIGHT     29.831     7.945   CURB WEIGHT IN HUNDREDS OF POUNDS
HP        118.486    48.065   HORSEPOWER
CARBS       2.543     1.094   NUMBER OF CARBURETORS
CYLS        5.914     1.788   NUMBER OF CYLINDERS
TIRES       0.229     0.426   TYPE OF TIRE
MPG        22.543     7.518   MOTOR TREND MILEAGE

N OF CASES =       35

CORRELATION

            DISP     WEIGHT       HP     CARBS      CYLS     TIRES       MPG

DISP       1.000     0.905     0.913     0.644     0.951    -0.517    -0.780
WEIGHT     0.905     1.000     0.847     0.603     0.849    -0.544    -0.761
HP         0.913     0.847     1.000     0.778     0.874    -0.494    -0.735
CARBS      0.644     0.603     0.778     1.000     0.611    -0.211    -0.354
CYLS       0.951     0.849     0.874     0.611     1.000    -0.514    -0.744
TIRES     -0.517    -0.544    -0.494    -0.211    -0.514     1.000     0.734
MPG       -0.780    -0.761    -0.735    -0.354    -0.744     0.734     1.000
```

3.19 Specifying the Treatment of Missing Values: The MISSING= Subcommand

To select the missing-value treatment, specify one of the following keywords in the MISSING= subcommand:

LISTWISE**   *Listwise deletion of cases with missing values.* If you specify no MISSING= subcommand, by default analyses are performed using only cases with nonmissing values on all variables in the VARIABLES= subcommand.

PAIRWISE   *Pairwise deletion of cases with missing values.* Each correlation coefficient is computed using cases with complete data on the pair of variables correlated, regardless of whether the cases have missing values on any other variables in the VARIABLES= list.

MEANSUBSTITUTION   *Replacement of missing values with the variable mean.* All cases are used in the analyses with the substitutions treated as valid observations.

INCLUDE   *Inclusion of cases with missing values.* All cases are used in the analyses with the missing values considered valid observations.

Specify the missing-value treatment before the VARIABLES= subcommand to which it applies. When listwise deletion of missing values is in effect, only the variables in the current VARIABLES= list are examined. Variables specified in previous VARIABLES= subcommands are not examined unless they are also included in the current variable list.

Since the missing-value treatment specified applies only to the current variable list, within one NEW REGRESSION procedure you can experiment with several different types of missing-value treatment applied to the same design. See the example in Section 3.6.

3.20 Matrix Input: The READ= Subcommand

If you have one or more correlation or covariance matrices to read in instead of raw data, use the READ= subcommand. READ= must be the first subcommand specified. Only one READ= subcommand can be specified in a NEW REGRESSION command. The following specifications are accepted:

DEFAULTS*   *Specifies keywords MEAN, STDDEV, CORR.* If you specify subcommand READ= with no specifications, these are the defaults.

MEAN   *The matrix is preceded by variable means.*

STDDEV   *The matrix is preceded by variable standard deviations.*

VARIANCE   *The matrix is preceded by variable variances.*

CORR   *Correlation matrix.* Alternative to keyword COV.

COV   *Covariance matrix.* Alternative to keyword CORR. You cannot read a covariance matrix with pairwise missing-value treatment.

N   *The matrix is followed by the number or numbers of cases used to compute correlation coefficients.* Overrides an N OF CASES specification.

INDEX   *Index the matrix by the number and order of variables on the VARIABLE LIST command.* Only a single matrix is read.

The input matrix materials must be arranged in the order as given above. Only one of CORR and COV can be specified. Given the defaults for the READ= subcommand, the following three specifications are equivalent.

```
READ= MEAN STDDEV COR/

READ= DEFAULTS/

READ/
```

Keyword DEFAULTS can also be used in conjunction with other keywords to reduce the length of the command, as in

```
READ=DEFAULTS N INDEX/
```

Keyword N following either CORR or COV indicates that the number or numbers of cases on which the correlation coefficients are based follow the matrix. When pairwise missing-value treatment (for keyword CORR only) or mean substitution is used (see Section 3.19), an entire symmetric matrix of *N*s should accompany the matrix; if not, you are warned. If inclusion or listwise missing-value treatment is used, the *N* is the same for each coefficient. In this case, supply a single value in the first 10 columns of the data record following the matrix. Alternatively, it is easier to supply an N OF CASES command and not specify the keyword N on the READ= subcommand in NEW REGRESSION.

    Matrices written by other procedures in SPSS such as PEARSON CORR and REGRESSION can be read by NEW REGRESSION provided that the appropriate READ= subcommand specifications are used. See pp. 308-310 of *SPSS*, Second Edition, for a more complete discussion of the use of matrices within SPSS.

    For a large number of variables and for a NEW REGRESSION command in which several VARIABLES= subcommands refer to some of the same variables, it is convenient to read in a single matrix and use subsets of variables from the matrix in various equations. You can do this by using keyword INDEX to define the structure of the single matrix by the variable names provided on your VARIABLE LIST command. In this case, only one set of matrix materials need be included for several sets of design specifications.

    If you read in more than one matrix, the first matrix is automatically indexed by the number and order of variables in the first VARIABLES= subcommand, the second matrix is indexed by the second VARIABLES= list, and so on. A separate set of data (means, standard deviations, matrix, etc.) must be read in for every VARIABLES= subcommand. You cannot use the (COLLECT) keyword in the VARIABLES= subcommand if the READ= subcommand is used.

    The means, matrices, etc., you wish to read in must be immediately preceded by the READ MATRIX command, which takes the place of the READ INPUT DATA command. Each row of a matrix must be recorded on a separate data line or record and each list of means, standard deviations, or variances must also be on a separate data record. Ten columns are allowed for each entry, and the decimal point must be included. When READ MATRIX is used, an INPUT FORMAT command is not necessary and is overridden if included.

    Figure 3.20 is a complete job setup using matrix input. This example uses two VARIABLES= subcommands. The first set of matrix materials correspond to the first variable list of five variables, the second to the second variable list of four variables.

Figure 3.20   Matrix Input

```
VARIABLE LIST   DISP,WEIGHT,HP,CARBS,CYLS,TIRES,MPG
NEW REGRESSION  READ= DEFAULTS N/
                VARIABLES=DISP,WEIGHT,HP,CARBS,TIRES/
                    DEPENDENT= WEIGHT/
                    STEPWISE/
                VARIABLES=WEIGHT,HP,TIRES,MPG/
                    DEPENDENT= MPG/
                    STEPWISE/
READ  MATRIX
   220.3710    29.8310   118.4860     2.5430     0.2290
   115.0350     7.9450    48.0650     1.0940     0.4270
 1.0000000 0.9050000 0.9130000 0.6440000-0.5170000
 0.9050000 1.0000000 0.8470000 0.6030000-0.5440000
 0.9130000 0.8470000 1.0000000 0.7780000-0.4940000
 0.6440000 0.6030000 0.7780000 1.0000000-0.2110000
-0.5170000-0.5440000-0.4940000-0.2110000 1.0000000
          35
    29.8310   118.4860     0.2290    22.5430
     7.9450    48.0650     0.4270     7.5180
 1.0000000 0.8470000-0.5440000-0.7610000
 0.8470000 1.0000000-0.4940000-0.7350000
-0.5440000-0.4940000 1.0000000 0.7340000
-0.7610000-0.7350000 0.7340000 1.0000000
          35
FINISH
```

3.21 Regression Output Files: The WRITE= Subcommand

The univariate descriptive statistics, correlation and covariance matrices, and Ns can be written to a raw output file using the following keyword specifications for the WRITE= subcommand.

DEFAULTS*   *Specifies keywords MEAN STDDEV CORR.*

MEAN   *Variable means.*

STDDEV   *Variable standard deviations.*

VARIANCE   *Variable variances.*

CORR   *Correlation matrix.*

COV   *Covariance matrix.*

N   *The number or numbers of cases used to compute correlation coefficients.* Used with pairwise missing-value treatment or mean substitution (see Section 3.19).

NONE   *Turn off previous WRITE= specifications.*

A WRITE= subcommand must precede the first VARIABLES= subcommand to which it applies and remains in effect for all subsequent VARIABLES= subcommands until overridden by a new WRITE= specification or turned off by specifying WRITE=NONE.

Given the defaults for the WRITE= subcommand, the following three specifications are equivalent.

```
WRITE= MEAN STDDEV COR/

WRITE= DEFAULTS/

WRITE/
```

Keyword DEFAULTS can also be used in conjunction with other keywords to reduce the length of the command, as in

```
WRITE=DEFAULTS N/
```

The format of the data file\is the same as that expected by SPSS when the READ= subcommand is used (Section 3.20). NEW REGRESSION displays a table describing the exact format of the output file when you write it.

3.22 Selecting Cases: The SELECT= Subcommand

Within the NEW REGRESSION command, you can select a subset of your cases for computing coefficients. Only selected cases contribute to the correlation coefficients and, therefore, to the regression equation. Residuals and predicted values for nonselected cases, however, are calculated, reported separately, and saved (see Section 3.29). To select cases within the NEW REGRESSION command, use the following format:

```
SELECT= varname relation value/
```

The *relation* can be EQ, NE, LT, LE, GT, or GE.

A SELECT= subcommand must appear before the VARIABLES= subcommand to which it applies. Once specified, selection remains in effect until overridden. Selection is cancelled by specifying SELECT=(ALL). For example,

```
NEW REGRESSION SELECT=LOCATION EQ 1/
                  DESCRIPTIVES/
                  VARIABLES=DISP TO MPG/
                      DEPENDENT=MPG/
                      STEPWISE/
                  SELECT=LOCATION EQ 2/
                  VARIABLES=DISP TO MPG/
                      DEPENDENT=MPG/
                      STEPWISE/
                  SELECT=(ALL)/
                  VARIABLES=DISP TO MPG/
                      DEPENDENT=MPG/
                      STEPWISE/
```

produces three stepwise analyses; the first only on cases corresponding to LOCATION equal to 1, the second on cases with LOCATION equal to 2, and the third on all cases. All three VARIABLES= subcommands are necessary since the correlation coefficients must be recalculated for each equation that uses different data selection criteria.

NOTE: If you use a selection variable that has been created with either the UNIFORM or NORMAL function; do *not* use a temporary transformation statement to create the variable. If the variable is created using a temporary transformation, when the file is reread for residual processing, the value of the variable changes and a different set of cases will be selected.

SELECT IF and SAMPLE command specifications in effect outside NEW REGRESSION are honored and the nonselected cases eliminated from computations. That is, no residuals or predictors are generated for cases eliminated with SELECT IF or SAMPLE commands.

3.23 Display Width: The WIDTH= Subcommand

You can control the width within which SPSS displays output from NEW REGRESSION. The default width is 132 characters, but you can specify any width from 60 to 132, as in

```
NEW REGRESSION WIDTH=120/
                  VARIABLES=DISP TO MPG/
                      DEPENDENT=MPG/
                      STEPWISE/
```

The width you choose affects the default regression statistics displayed and the amount of information displayed in a casewise residuals plot; See Sections 3.26 and 3.31 for details.

The WIDTH= subcommand has a special status in NEW REGRESSION. First, it can appear anywhere within the command. Its position does not determine when it is in effect for displayed output—all regression displays are controlled by it. Second, although it can be used more than once in the same NEW REGRESSION command, the last specified width is the only one used.

3.24 Subcommands for the Equation

There are three optional subcommands that concern the regression equation and, therefore, must precede the DEPENDENT= subcommand that initiates the analysis. CRITERIA= is used to change the entry criteria SPSS uses in developing the equation, STATISTICS= is used to control the results displayed as the equation develops, and ORIGIN is used to request an equation with zero constant (regression through the origin).

3.25 Setting Statistical Criteria: The CRITERIA= Subcommand

To avoid numerical difficulties, all variables are tested for *tolerance* prior to entry into an equation. A variable's tolerance is the proportion of variance remaining after the effects of the independent variables already in the equation have been partitioned out. That is, it is one minus the squared multiple correlation of that independent variable with the independent variables already in the equation.

Minimum tolerance is defined as the minimum of the recomputed tolerances of the variables in the equation when a variable is entered at the next step.

A variable must pass both tolerance and minimum tolerance tests in order to enter a regression equation. That is, a variable does not enter an equation if its squared multiple correlation with all the independent variables in the equation is greater than one minus the TOLERANCE value set with the CRITERIA= subcommand; nor does it enter if it would cause the squared multiple correlation for any variable already in the equation to exceed one minus the value of TOLERANCE.

For methods STEPWISE, ENTER, and REMOVE, NEW REGRESSION selects variables according to the *probabilities* of *F-to-enter* and *F-to-remove* (keywords PIN and POUT). These probabilities are functions of the magnitude of the Fs and the degrees of freedom. You can override these default criteria and specify that *F*-to-enter and *F*-to-remove (keywords FIN and FOUT) be used instead to control entry and removal.

Since the probability of F is a function of both the magnitude of the value of F and the degrees of freedom, the probability of a given F changes as the degrees of freedom change. In large samples, the change in the degrees of freedom as variables are entered and removed is small compared to the total number of degrees of freedom, and the relationship between F and the probability of F is rather stable.

If the criterion for entry (PIN or FIN) is less stringent than the criterion for removal (POUT or FOUT), the STEPWISE method can cause the same variable to cycle in and out, over and over until the maximum number of steps is reached (twice the number of independent variables). If you specify a PIN value that is larger than POUT, or a FIN value that is smaller than FOUT, SPSS issues a warning message and adjusts the POUT or FOUT values as the message states.

The criteria under user control are

DEFAULTS**	*Specifies keywords PIN(0.05), POUT(0.1), TOLERANCE(0.01).* For the first equation, if you do not specify any CRITERIA= keywords, these are the defaults. If you have changed the criteria for an equation, use the keyword DEFAULTS to restore these defaults.
PIN(value)	*Probability of F-to-enter.* The default value is 0.05.
POUT(value)	*Probability of F-to-remove.* The default value is 0.1.
FIN(value)	*F-to-enter.* If no value is specified, the default is 3.84.
FOUT(value)	*F-to-remove.* If no value is specified, the default is 2.71.
TOLERANCE(value)	*Tolerance.* The default value is 0.01.
MAXSTEPS(n)	*Maximum number of steps.* For the STEPWISE method, the default is twice the number of independent variables. For the FORWARD and BACKWARD methods, the default maximum is the number of variables meeting the FIN and FOUT or PIN and POUT criteria.

A CRITERIA= subcommand must appear before the DEPENDENT= subcommand that initiates the equation and after the VARIABLES= subcommand. The criteria remain in effect for all subsequent regression analyses until modified. For example,

```
NEW REGRESSION VARIABLES=DISP TO MPG/
               CRITERIA=FIN,FOUT/
               DEPENDENT=MPG/
               STEPWISE/
```

changes the stepwise entry and removal criteria to FIN and FOUT and accepts the default values of 3.84 and 2.71 respectively. Tolerance and the maximum number of steps are unaltered.

Keyword specifications are processed left-to-right. Thus, a keyword is overridden by a contradictory keyword to the right. For example,

```
CRITERIA=PIN(.03) FIN(2.0)/
```

first selects the probability of F-to-enter tests and sets the value to 0.03, then selects F tests and changes the value of FIN, thus negating the first operation.

3.26 Regression Statistics: The STATISTICS= Subcommand

The STATISTICS= subcommand is used to display a number of statistics for the regression equation. The keywords are

DEFAULTS**	*Specifies keywords R, ANOVA, COEFF, OUTS.* In the absence of any STATISTICS= subcommand, these are the default statistics displayed.
R	*Multiple R.* Produces the multiple R, R^2, adjusted R^2, and standard error.
ANOVA	*Analysis of variance table.* Produces the analysis of variance table for the design, F value for multiple R, and significance level of F.
COEFF	*Regression coefficients.* For each variable in the equation, produces the unstandardized regression coefficient (B), the standard error of B, standardized regression coefficient (BETA), t value for B, and two-tailed significance level of t.
OUTS	*Coefficients and statistics for variables not yet in the equation.* Produces the standardized regression coefficient (BETA) if the variable were to enter the equation at the next step, t value for BETA, significance level of t, partial correlation with the dependent variable controlled for all variables in the equation, and minimum tolerance (see Section 3.25).
CHA	*Change in R^2.* Produces the change in R^2 between steps, F value for change in R^2, and significance level of F.
BCOV	*Variance-covariance matrix for unstandardized regression coefficients.* Produces a matrix with the diagonal consisting of variances and with the correlations above the diagonal and covariances below.
XTX	*Sweep matrix.* Produces the current status of the sweep matrix.
COND	*Condition number bounds.* Produces the lower and upper bounds for the condition number of the sweep matrix (Berk, 1978).

ZPP	*Correlation, part and partial correlation.* Produces the zero-order correlation of each independent variable in the equation with the dependent variable and the part and partial correlations with the dependent variable controlled for other independent variables in the equation.
CI	95% confidence interval for β.
SES	*Approximate standard error of BETA.* See Meyer and Younger, 1976.
LABEL	*Variable labels.*
F	*F value for B and significance level of F.* Displayed instead of t and significance of t.
HISTORY	*Step history.* Produces one line of information for each step: the step or block number, multiple R, R^2, significance, change in R^2, significance of the change, and the variable name. If the width (see Section 3.23) is at least 62, F is displayed; if at least 70, adjusted R^2; and if at least 80, the F value for change in R^2.
END	*Step history plus default and requested statistics at the end of the analysis.* Produces one line of information after each stepwise, forward, or backward step, and after each entry or removal block. The default and requested statistics are printed only for the final regression equation developed by the specified methods.
ALL	*All regression equation statistics.*

The STATISTICS= subcommand must appear before the DEPENDENT= subcommand that initiates the equation. It remains in effect for all new equations until overridden by specifying a new list of statistics. For example,

```
NEW REGRESSION DESCRIPTIVES/
               VARIABLES=(COLLECT)/
                    STATISTICS=DEFAULTS,HISTORY,LABEL/
                    DEPENDENT=MPG/
                    STEPWISE DISP TO TIRES/
                    STATISTICS=DEFAULTS,CI/
                    DEPENDENT=MPG/
                    BACKWARD DISP TO TIRES/
```

requests the default statistics for both equations, a step history and variable labels for the first, and 95% confidence intervals for the βs for the second.

3.27 An Example Requesting Nondefault Statistics

In Figure 3.27a the default statistics as well as the sweep matrix (XTX), history of each step, and variance-covariance matrix are printed.

Figure 3.27a   The STATISTICS= Subcommand

```
NEW REGRESSION VARIABLES=(COLLECT)/
               STATISTICS=DEFAULTS XTX HISTORY BCOV/
               DEPENDENT=MPG/
               BACKWARD=DISP TO TIRES
```

Figure 3.27b   Statistics Display Produced by Figure 3.27a

```
                    * * * *   M U L T I P L E   R E G R E S S I O N   * * * *

VARIABLE LIST NUMBER  1.  LISTWISE DELETION OF MISSING DATA.

EQUATION NUMBER  1.

DEPENDENT VARIABLE..  MPG        MOTOR TREND MILEAGE


BEGINNING BLOCK NUMBER  1.  METHOD:  ENTER


VARIABLE(S) ENTERED ON STEP NUMBER  1..    TIRES        TYPE OF TIRE
                                    2..    CARBS        NUMBER OF CARBURETORS
                                    3..    CYLS         NUMBER OF CYLINDERS
                                    4..    WEIGHT       CURB WEIGHT IN HUNDREDS OF POUNDS
                                    5..    HP           HORSEPOWER
                                    6..    DISP         ENGINE DISPLACEMENT


MULTIPLE R          0.89330     ANALYSIS OF VARIANCE
R SQUARE            0.79799                    DF      SUM OF SQUARES      MEAN SQUARE
ADJUSTED R SQUARE   0.75470     REGRESSION      6          1533.32268       255.55378
STANDARD ERROR      3.72330     RESIDUAL       28           388.16263        13.86295

                    F =     18.43430       SIGNIF F = 0.0000
```

```
VAR-COVAR MATRIX OF REGRESSION COEFFICIENTS (B)
BELOW DIAGONAL:  COVARIANCE    ABOVE:  CORRELATION
              TIRES       CARBS       CYLS      WEIGHT        HP         DISP

TIRES        3.53157    -0.28377     0.09566     0.21774     0.20309    -0.09079
CARBS       -0.53547     1.00828     0.01640    -0.04357    -0.62830     0.12966
CYLS         0.20994     0.01924     1.36390     0.11284    -0.05110    -0.70929
WEIGHT       0.08011    -0.00856     0.02580     0.03833    -0.06261    -0.48909
HP           0.01614    -0.02667    -0.00252  -0.518D-03     0.00179    -0.39893
DISP        -0.00423     0.00323    -0.02053    -0.00237  -0.418D-03   0.614D-03


XTX MATRIX

              TIRES       CARBS       CYLS      WEIGHT        HP         DISP    :      MPG

TIRES        1.57216    -0.61206     0.39231     0.66502     0.81043    -0.50828 :    -0.37386
CARBS       -0.61206     2.95915     0.09230    -0.18255    -3.43979     0.99589 :    -0.32469
CYLS         0.39231     0.09230    10.69861     0.89900    -0.53193   -10.35909 :    -0.09228
WEIGHT       0.66502    -0.18255     0.89900     5.93340    -0.48535    -5.31948 :     0.12493
HP           0.81043    -3.43979    -0.53193    -0.48535    10.12886    -5.66906 :     0.44569
DISP        -0.50828     0.99589   -10.35909    -5.31948    -5.66906    19.93729 :     0.36421
            -----------------------------------------------------------------------
MPG          0.37386     0.32469     0.09228    -0.12493    -0.44569    -0.36421 :     0.20201


----------------- VARIABLES IN THE EQUATION -----------------

VARIABLE          B          SE B        BETA          T    SIG T

TIRES          6.59686     1.87925     0.37386      3.510  0.0015
CARBS          2.23131     1.00413     0.32469      2.222  0.0345
CYLS           0.38790     1.16786     0.09228      0.332  0.7423
WEIGHT        -0.11822     0.19578    -0.12493     -0.604  0.5508
HP            -0.06971     0.04228    -0.44569     -1.649  0.1104
DISP          -0.02380     0.02479    -0.36421     -0.960  0.3451
(CONSTANT)    30.09789     5.24468                  5.739  0.0000


FOR BLOCK NUMBER  1   ALL REQUESTED VARIABLES ENTERED.


        * * * * * * * * * * * * * * * * * * * * * * * * * * *

               [Display for Block 2 deleted]

        * * * * * * * * * * * * * * * * * * * * * * * * * * *


                        SUMMARY TABLE
                        -------------

STEP  MULTR   RSQ   ADJRSQ  F(EQU)  SIGF  RSQCH    FCH  SIGCH      VARIABLE  BETAIN CORREL  LABEL
 1                                                          IN:  TIRES     0.7343  0.7343  TYPE OF TIRE
 2                                                          IN:  CARBS    -0.2089 -0.3545  NUMBER OF CARBURETORS
 3                                                          IN:  CYLS     -0.5538 -0.7435  NUMBER OF CYLINDERS
 4                                                          IN:  WEIGHT   -0.3509 -0.7615  CURB WEIGHT IN HUNDREDS OF P
 5                                                          IN:  HP       -0.5492 -0.7355  HORSEPOWER
 6   0.8933 0.7980 0.7547  18.434 0.000  0.7980  18.434 0.000 IN:  DISP     -0.3642 -0.7805  ENGINE DISPLACEMENT
 7   0.8929 0.7972 0.7622  22.799 0.000 -0.0008   0.110 0.742 OUT: CYLS            -0.7435  NUMBER OF CYLINDERS
 8   0.8912 0.7942 0.7667  28.941 0.000 -0.0030   0.430 0.517 OUT: WEIGHT          -0.7615  CURB WEIGHT IN HUNDREDS OF P
```

In Figure 3.27b, Block 2 has been deleted. When the backward command is specified, all variables are first entered as illustrated. Then variables satisfying removal criteria are removed. As noted in the summary table, first CYLS, then WEIGHT are removed from the equation. The summary table itself is specified with the HISTORY keyword.

3.28 Regression through the Origin: The ORIGIN Subcommand
To indicate regression through the origin, simply enter subcommand ORIGIN before the first DEPENDENT= subcommand to which it applies, and after the VARIABLES= subcommand. Once specified, it remains in effect for all subsequent equations until you specify the keyword NOORIGIN.

For example,

```
NEW REGRESSION VARIABLES=DISP TO MPG/
               ORIGIN/
               DEPENDENT=MPG/
               ENTER DISP HP TIRES CARBS
```

Output produced using regression through the origin is so identified.

3.29 Analysis of Residuals
The following subcommands are related to the analysis of residuals: RESIDUALS, CASEWISE, SCATTERPLOT, and SAVE. For each regression design you specify, SPSS can calculate any of eleven temporary variables containing several types of residuals, predicted values, and related measures for analysis within NEW REGRESSION. These temporary variables are referred to by keywords in any of the residuals-related commands. The following keyword variable names are used:

PRED   *Unstandardized predicted values.*
RESID   *Unstandardized residuals.*
DRESID   *Deleted residuals.*
ADJPRED   *Adjusted predicted values.*
ZPRED   *Standardized predicted values.*
ZRESID   *Standardized residuals.*
SRESID   *Studentized residuals.*
SDRESID   *Studentized deleted residuals.*
SEPRED   *Standard error of the predicted values.*
MAHAL   *Mahalanobis' distance.*
COOK   *Cook's distance.* See Cook, 1977.

Any of these temporary variables can be written to an output file for addition to a system file and further analysis using any other SPSS procedure. See Section 3.33.

3.30 Analyzing Residuals: The RESIDUALS= Subcommand
Several measures and plots based on the residuals and predicted values for the regression equation can be displayed. Specifications for the RESIDUALS= subcommand are

DEFAULTS*   *Specifies keywords LARGE, NORMPROB(ZRESID), HISTO-GRAM(ZRESID), OUTLIERS(ZRESID), DURBIN.*

SMALL   *Use small plot sizes.* The default is LARGE if the display width is at least 120 (see Section 3.23) and the PAGESIZE at least 55.

HISTOGRAM(varlist) *A histogram of the temporary variable or variables named.* The default variable is ZRESID. Not available for MAHAL, COOK, or SEPRED.

NORMPROB(varlist)   *A normal probability (P-P) plot of standardized values.* The default variable is ZRESID. Not available for MAHAL, COOK, or SEPRED.

OUTLIERS(varlist)   *The ten worst outliers based on values of the variables specified.* The default variable is ZRESID. Permissible variables are RESID, DRESID, SRESID, SDRESID, MAHAL, and COOK.

DURBIN   *Durbin-Watson test.* See Neter and Wasserman, 1974.

ID(varname)   *Use the values from this variable to label casewise or outlier plots.* Any variable in your file can be named. If ID(varname) is not specified cases are identifed by sequence number and subfile name. ID also labels the sequence plot of cases obtained from the CASEWISE= subcommand. (See Section 3.31.)

The RESIDUALS= subcommand must follow the last method keyword. All calculations and plots requested on the RESIDUALS= subcommand are based on the regression equation produced as a result of the last method specified.

Figure 3.30a   The RESIDUALS= Subcommand

```
NEW REGRESSION VARIABLES=(COLLECT)/
               DEPENDENT=MPG/
               BACKWARD DISP TO TIRES/
               RESIDUALS= DEFAULTS ID(AUTO1) SMALL/
```

Thus Figure 3.30a requests all the default RESIDUALS= displays, a small probability plot and histogram, and an identifier on the outliers plot. These items are not printed until the backward elimination phase of the analysis is completed.

Figure 3.30b is the display produced with the RESIDUALS= subcommand in Figure 3.30a.

Figure 3.30b   Residuals Display Produced by Figure 3.30a

```
RESIDUALS STATISTICS:

          MIN       MAX      MEAN    STD DEV   N                    MIN       MAX      MEAN    STD DEV   N
*PRED    12.3524   35.8995   22.5429  6.6995   35       *RESID    -12.4996   5.3494   0.0000   3.4105   35
*ZPRED   -1.5211    1.9937   -0.0000  1.0000   35       *ZRESID    -3.4427   1.4734   0.0000   0.9393   35
*SEPRED   0.9494    2.2117    1.3407  0.2972   35       *SRESID    -3.8255   1.5561   0.0014   1.0282   35
*ADJPRED 12.1930   36.7261   22.5286  6.8219   35       *DRESID   -15.4335   6.0155   0.0143   4.0976   35
*MAHAL    1.3535   11.6454    3.8857  2.3604   35       *SDRESID   -5.2554   1.5957  -0.0379   1.2029   35
*COOK D   0.0000    0.6870    0.0421  0.1161   35

TOTAL CASES =     35


DURBIN-WATSON TEST =   1.46253
```

```
OUTLIERS - STANDARDIZED RESIDUAL

  SEQNUM  SUBFILE        AUTO1      *ZRESID

      20  MOTREND        FUCC      -3.44272
       8  MOTREND        LEMA       1.47335
      10  MOTREND        SUBU      -1.43977
      27  MOTREND        MAZW       1.41276
       4  MOTREND        TOY4      -1.26030
       5  MOTREND        MAZG       1.18848
      13  MOTREND        RIVI       0.98118
      35  MOTREND        MERC       0.89605
       7  MOTREND        COLT       0.89429
      24  MOTREND        CIVI      -0.79861
```

```
           * * * * * * * * * * * * * * * * * * * * * * * * * * *

HISTOGRAM
STANDARDIZED RESIDUAL
  N EXP N    ( * = 1 CASES,    . : = NORMAL CURVE)
  0  0.03    OUT
  0  0.05   3.00
  0  0.14   2.66
  0  0.31   2.33
  0  0.64   2.00  .
  0  1.17   1.66  .
  3  1.92   1.33  *:*
  3  2.82   1.00  **:
  7  3.72   0.66  ***:***
  3  4.38   0.33  ***.
  5  4.63   0.00  ****:
  6  4.38  -0.33  ***:**
  5  3.72  -0.66  ***:*
  0  2.82  -1.00        .
  2  1.92  -1.33  *:
  0  1.17  -1.66  .
  0  0.64  -2.00  .
  0  0.31  -2.33
  0  0.14  -2.66
  0  0.05  -3.00
  1  0.03    OUT  *
```

```
           * * * * * * * * * * * * * * * * * * * * * * * * * * *
```

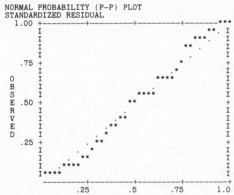

In Figure 3.30b the ten largest outliers are listed. A normal curve is superimposed on the histogram. The colon is used when the normal curve falls on a plotted position. Although the Durbin-Watson test is inappropriate for this analysis, it is displayed because the keyword DEFAULTS was used to simplify the subcommand specification.

3.31 Specifying a Casewise Plot: The CASEWISE= Subcommand

You can display a casewise plot of one of the temporary residuals variables accompanied by a listing of the values of the dependent variable and the values of as many of the other temporary variables as can be displayed in the available page width (Section 3.23). You can label the cases using the values of any variable in your file. The CASEWISE= subcommand has the following specifications:

DEFAULTS*   *Specifies keywords OUTLIERS(3), PLOT(ZRESID), DEPENDENT, PRED, RESID.*

OUTLIERS(value)   *Limit plot to outliers defined by this value.* The plot contains those cases whose absolute value is as large or larger than the value you specify. The default value is 3 for standardized residuals (ZRESID).

PLOT(varname)   *Plot the values of this temporary variable in the casewise plot.* The default variable is ZRESID. Permissible keywords are RESID, DRESID, SRESID, and SDRESID. Since the casewise plot is a standardized plot, unstandardized residuals are plotted as their standardized equivalents.

varlist   *Display the values of these variables.* Any or all of the eleven temporary variables can be specified. The defaults are DEPENDENT (for the dependent variable), PRED, and RESID.

ALL   *Plot all cases.* The casewise plot is of all cases, not just outliers.

For example,

```
NEW REGRESSION VARIABLES=(COLLECT)/
                DEPENDENT=MPG/
                BACKWARD DISP TO TIRES/
                RESIDUALS ID(AUTO1)/
                CASEWISE=ALL,DEPENDENT,PRED,RESID,DRESID/
```

asks for the default casewise plot of the values of the temporary variable ZRESID and a display of the values of the dependent variable and three of the temporary variables for all cases. See Figure 3.31 for the display produced by the example CASEWISE= subcommand.

Figure 3.31   A Casewise Plot

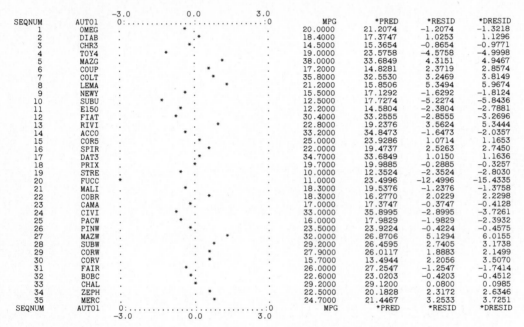

```
DEPENDENT VARIABLE.. MPG        MOTOR TREND MILEAGE

CASEWISE PLOT OF STANDARDIZED RESIDUAL

                      -3.0        0.0        3.0
     SEQNUM   AUTO1   0:..........:..........:0         MPG      *PRED     *RESID    *DRESID
          1    OMEG   .          * .          .      20.0000   21.2074    -1.2074    -1.3218
          2    DIAB   .          . *          .      18.4000   17.3747     1.0253     1.1296
          3    CHR3   .          *.           .      14.5000   15.3654    -0.8654    -0.9771
          4    TOY4   .       *   .           .      19.0000   23.5758    -4.5758    -4.9998
          5    MAZG   .          .     *       .      38.0000   33.6849     4.3151     4.9467
          6    COUP   .          .  *          .      17.2000   14.8281     2.3719     2.8574
          7    COLT   .          .   *         .      35.8000   32.5530     3.2469     3.8149
          8    LEMA   .          .     *       .      21.2000   15.8506     5.3494     5.9674
          9    NEWY   .         *.            .      15.5000   17.1292    -1.6292    -1.8124
         10    SUBU   .      *    .            .      12.5000   17.7274    -5.2274    -5.8436
         11    E150   .        *  .            .      12.2000   14.5804    -2.3804    -2.7881
         12    FIAT   .        *  .            .      30.4000   33.2555    -2.8555    -3.2696
         13    RIVI   .          .   *         .      22.8000   19.2376     3.5624     5.3444
         14    ACCO   .         *.             .      33.2000   34.8473    -1.6473    -2.0357
         15    COR5   .          .*            .      25.0000   23.9286     1.0714     1.1653
         16    SPIR   .          . *           .      22.0000   19.4737     2.5263     2.7450
         17    DAT3   .          .*            .      34.7000   33.6849     1.0150     1.1636
         18    PRIX   .          *             .      19.7000   19.9885    -0.2885    -0.3257
         19    STRE   .         * .            .      10.0000   12.3524    -2.3524    -2.8030
         20    FUCC   *          .             .      11.0000   23.4996   -12.4996   -15.4335
         21    MALI   .         *.             .      18.3000   19.5376    -1.2376    -1.3758
         22    COBR   .          . *           .      18.3000   16.2770     2.0229     2.2298
         23    CAMA   .         *.             .      17.0000   17.3747    -0.3747    -0.4128
         24    CIVI   .       *   .            .      33.0000   35.8995    -2.8995    -3.7261
         25    PACW   .         * .            .      16.0000   17.9829    -1.9829    -2.3932
         26    PINW   .          *.            .      23.5000   23.9224    -0.4224    -0.4575
         27    MAZW   .          .   *         .      32.0000   26.8706     5.1294     6.0155
         28    SUBW   .          . *           .      29.2000   26.4595     2.7405     3.1738
         29    CORW   .          . *           .      27.9000   26.0117     1.8883     2.1499
         30    CORV   .          . *           .      15.7000   13.4944     2.2056     3.5070
         31    FAIR   .         * .            .      26.0000   27.2547    -1.2547    -1.7414
         32    BOBC   .          *.            .      22.6000   23.0203    -0.4203    -0.4512
         33    CHAL   .          *             .      29.2000   29.1200     0.0800     0.0985
         34    ZEPH   .          . *           .      22.5000   20.1828     2.3172     2.6346
         35    MERC   .          .  *          .      24.7000   21.4467     3.2533     3.7251
     SEQNUM   AUTO1   0:..........:..........:0         MPG      *PRED     *RESID    *DRESID
                      -3.0        0.0        3.0
```

3.32   Specifying Scatterplots: The SCATTERPLOT= Subcommand

A series of scatterplots of the temporary variables and the variables in the regression equation can be displayed with the SCATTERPLOT= subcommand. Whenever you specify a temporary variable in a scatterplot, you must precede the keyword with an asterisk to distinguish the temporary variable keyword from a valid variable name. Specifications are

LARGE   *Use large plot sizes.* The default is SMALL for scatterplots. Keyword LARGE requires substantially more computer memory and should be used only when detail is required.

(varname,varname)   *Plot the variables specified.* If the variable is one of the temporary variables, precede the keyword with an asterisk. You cannot name *MAHAL, *COOK, or *SEPRED. However, these variables can be written out and later plotted using the SCATTERGRAM procedure. Otherwise, the name can be any variable used in the regression equation. Specify as many pairs in parentheses as you want plots.

The first variable named in each set of parentheses becomes the vertical-axis variable; the second is the horizontal-axis variable.

Note that *all* scatterplots are standardized in NEW REGRESSION; that is, specifying *RESID is the same as specifying *ZRESID, and *PRED is the same as *ZPRED. To obtain unstandardized scatterplots, save residuals output for processing with procedure SCATTERGRAM in a subsequent step.

The SCATTERPLOT= subcommand must follow the last regression method keyword for the equation you wish to analyze. Figure 3.32a requests two small scatterplots, one of predicted MPG against DISP, the other of predicted MPG against the residual. Both scatterplots use the standardized values of the requested variables.

Figure 3.32a   Residuals Scatterplots—SCATTERPLOT= Subcommand

```
NEW REGRESSION VARIABLES=(COLLECT)/
               DEPENDENT=MPG/
               BACKWARD DISP TO TIRES/
               SCATTERPLOT (*PRED,DISP),(*PRED,*RESID)/
```

Figure 3.32b   Scatterplot Display from Figure 3.32a

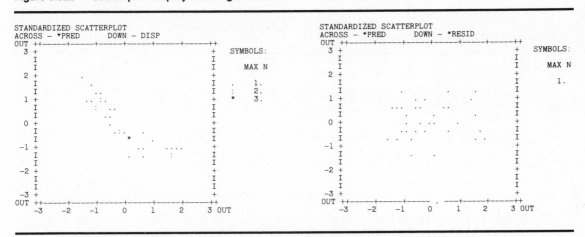

Small scatterplots are printed two-up as in Figure 3.32b Different plotting symbols are used to represent multiple points occurring at the same print position.

3.33   Writing Out Temporary Variables: The SAVE= Subcommand

To write out any or all of the eleven temporary variables calculated by SPSS for residuals analysis, use the SAVE= subcommand with the keywords corresponding to the temporary variables you want to save, as in

```
NEW REGRESSION VARIABLES=(COLLECT)/
               DEPENDENT=MPG/
               BACKWARD DISP TO TIRES/
               RESIDUALS/
               CASEWISE=PLOT,DEPENDENT,PRED,RESID,DRESID/
               SCATTERPLOT(*PRED,DISP),(*PRED,*RESID)/
               SAVE= PRED SEPRED RESID SRESID SDRESID/
```

The format of the file written to the RAW OUTPUT UNIT is a sequence number in columns 1 to 20 followed by each variable written in F10.*n* format. Consult the table displayed by NEW REGRESSION describing the format of the output file.

3.34   AN EXAMPLE

The operation of the NEW REGRESSION procedure is illustrated with data obtained from Mosteller and Tukey's *Data Analysis and Regression* (Data Exhibit 7 from page 566). The data consist of a random sample of 20 schools from *The Coleman Report* for Mid-Atlantic and New England states. The variables are

Y   Verbal mean test score for all sixth graders

X1   Staff salaries per pupil

X2   Percent white-collar fathers of sixth graders

X3   Socioeconomic status composite deviation: sixth-grade means for family size, family intactness, father's education, mother's education, percent white-collar fathers, and home items

X4   Teacher's mean verbal test score

X5   Mother's mean educational level for sixth graders

The dependent variable is mean verbal test score for all sixth graders, measured for 20 schools. The general research problem for this set of data might be to come up with an explanation for the variation between schools in mean verbal test scores.

Assume that two sets of influences are thought to be important: home or family factors and school factors. Measures corresponding to these two sets of influences can be used in a multiple regression to explain variation in mean verbal test score and to study the relative impact of each of the sets of influences on mean verbal test score. Note that variables X1 and X4 can be thought of as school influence variables, while X2, X3, and X5 can be thought of as home influence variables. Moreover, variables in the second set overlap to some extent. As indicated above, X3 is a composite variable that incorporates information from many separate variables, two of which are mother's education and percent white-collar father. X2 and X5 are each a part of X3, and so one would expect that X2 and X5 would be correlated with X3. All three variables in this set are used in the following example because they illustrate well the consequences of using highly correlated, or collinear, data in regression modelling.

3.35 The NEW REGRESSION Command

Figure 3.35 is the command used to explore the model.

Figure 3.35   Complete NEW REGRESSION Command

```
NEW REGRESSION DESCRIPTIVES/
            VARIABLES=X1 TO Y/
               CRITERIA= PIN(1)/
               STATISTICS= DEFAULTS CHANGE BCOV HISTORY/
               DEPENDENT= Y/
               FORWARD/
               CRITERIA= PIN(.1) POUT(.15)/
               DEPENDENT= Y/
               STEPWISE/
               RESIDUALS SMALL NORMPROB(SRESID)/
               CASEWISE ALL DEFAULTS SRESID SDRESID MAHAL COOK/
               SCATTERPLOT(*PRED,*RESID)/
```

Figure 3.35 produces two regression models. For the first model, initiated by the first DEPENDENT= subcommand, PIN is set to 1, so that any variable whose tolerance exceeds 0.01, enters the regression equation. For the equation initiated by the second DEPENDENT= subcommand, PIN and POUT have been set to 0.10 and 0.15 respectively, so that only variables that contribute significantly in a statistical sense to the regression equation are entered and retained. The criteria have been set a bit less stringently than is customary because it is sometimes useful to move tentatively toward the final model by means of progressively stricter criteria. Finally, residual analysis is invoked for the second equation.

3.36 The Results

The first page of display from the regression run appears in Figure 3.36. The first display page contains univariate and bivariate summary information—means, standard deviations, and correlations. The sample size of 20 is small if one were really interested in statistical inference, but nonetheless works well for demonstration purposes. Histograms of the separate variables (run with FREQUENCIES, but not shown) show relatively flat distributions for a few of the variables, but are free of dramatic anomalies. Therefore, the variables are analyzed in their given scales rather than in some transformed scale.

Figure 3.36   Descriptive Statistics

```
                        * * * *  M U L T I P L E   R E G R E S S I O N  * * * *     PAGE   2
      VARIABLE LIST NUMBER  1.  LISTWISE DELETION OF MISSING DATA.

              MEAN     STD DEV    LABEL

      X1      2.731     0.454    STAFF SALARIES PER PUPIL/
      X2     40.906    25.899    6TH GRADE % WHITE COLLAR FATHERS/
      X3      3.141     9.625    SES COMPOSITE DEVIATE/
      X4     25.069     1.314    MEAN TEACHER'S VERBAL TEST SCORE/
      X5      6.255     0.654    6TH GRADE MEAN MOTHER'S EDUC LEVEL/
      Y      35.083     5.817    VERBAL MEAN TEST SCORE--ALL 6TH GRADERS

      N OF CASES =        20

      CORRELATION

                 X1        X2        X3        X4        X5        Y

      X1      1.000     0.181     0.230     0.503     0.197     0.192
      X2      0.181     1.000     0.827     0.051     0.927     0.753
      X3      0.230     0.827     1.000     0.183     0.819     0.927
      X4      0.503     0.051     0.183     1.000     0.124     0.334
      X5      0.197     0.927     0.819     0.124     1.000     0.733
      Y       0.192     0.753     0.927     0.334     0.733     1.000
```

Correlations among the variables are revealing in several respects. First, all correlation coefficients are positive, which indicates that, as scaled, higher scores on a given variable are associated with higher scores on another variable. In particular, higher scores on any independent variable are associated with higher scores on the dependent variable. Second, of all of the independent variables, X3 correlates most highly with the dependent variable, so socioeconomic status may be thought of as the single most important explanatory variable. Third, the independent variables correlate more highly within sets than between sets. For example, X2, X3, and X5 correlate among each other at better than 0.8, and X1 and X4 correlate at 0.5, while the highest correlation between sets is that of X1 and X3, which correlate at 0.23.

3.37 The Forward Inclusion Equation

Consider the first regression equation (Figures 3.37a through 3.37e). The independent variables are entered in the equation in the following order: X3, X4, X1, X5, and X2. As each additional variable is entered, the multiple R and the multiple R^2 increase, though by diminishing amounts. For example, with only X3 in the equation the R^2 value is 0.8596, while with all independent variables in the equation the multiple R^2 is 0.9063.

Figure 3.37a   Forward Inclusion Step 1 Output

```
EQUATION NUMBER  1.

DEPENDENT VARIABLE.. Y          VERBAL MEAN TEST SCORE--ALL 6TH GRADERS

BEGINNING BLOCK NUMBER  1.  METHOD:  FORWARD

VARIABLE(S) ENTERED ON STEP NUMBER  1..    X3         SES COMPOSITE DEVIATE/

MULTIPLE R          0.92716                                    ANALYSIS OF VARIANCE
R SQUARE            0.85963      R SQUARE CHANGE   0.85963                       DF    SUM OF SQUARES    MEAN SQUARE
ADJUSTED R SQUARE   0.85183      F CHANGE        110.23044      REGRESSION        1        552.67562      552.67562
STANDARD ERROR      2.23916      SIGNIF F CHANGE   0.0000       RESIDUAL         18         90.24876        5.01382

                                                               F  =      110.23044    SIGNIF F = 0.0000


------------------------------ VARIABLES IN THE EQUATION ------------------------------

VARIABLE          B          SE B      BETA    CORREL PART COR  PARTIAL      T  SIG T

X3            0.56033      0.05337   0.92716   0.92716  0.92716  0.92716   10.499 0.0000
(CONSTANT)   33.32280      0.52800                                        63.112 .0000
-------------- VARIABLES NOT IN THE EQUATION --------------

VARIABLE    BETA IN  PARTIAL  MIN TOLER        T  SIG T

X1         -0.02176 -0.05652   0.94727    -0.233  .8182
X2         -0.04285 -0.06427   0.31577    -0.266  .7938
X4          0.16937  0.44439   0.96639     2.045  .0566
X5         -0.08026 -0.12290   0.32914    -0.511  .6162
```

Figure 3.37b   Forward Inclusion Step 2 Output

```
DEPENDENT VARIABLE.. Y          VERBAL MEAN TEST SCORE--ALL 6TH GRADERS

VARIABLE(S) ENTERED ON STEP NUMBER  2..    X4        MEAN TEACHER'S VERBAL TEST SCORE/

MULTIPLE R          0.94199                                    ANALYSIS OF VARIANCE
R SQUARE            0.88735      R SQUARE CHANGE   0.02772                       DF    SUM OF SQUARES    MEAN SQUARE
ADJUSTED R SQUARE   0.87410      F CHANGE          4.18329      REGRESSION        2        570.49798      285.24899
STANDARD ERROR      2.06407      SIGNIF F CHANGE   0.0566       RESIDUAL         17         72.42639        4.26038
                                                               F  =       66.95395    SIGNIF F = 0.0000

------------------------------ VARIABLES IN THE EQUATION ------------------------------

VARIABLE          B          SE B      BETA    CORREL PART COR  PARTIAL      T  SIG T

X3            0.54156      0.05004   0.89611   0.92716  0.88092  0.93447   10.822 0.0000
X4            0.74989      0.36664   0.16937   0.33365  0.16650  0.44439    2.045 .0566
(CONSTANT)   14.58268      9.17541                                         1.589 .1304

-------------- VARIABLES NOT IN THE EQUATION --------------

VARIABLE    BETA IN  PARTIAL  MIN TOLER        T  SIG T

X1         -0.13550 -0.34441   0.72777    -1.467  .1616
X2          0.01148  0.01890   0.29581     0.076  .9407
X5         -0.06685 -0.11414   0.32232    -0.460  .6520

          * * * * * * * * * * * * * * * * * * * * * * * * *
```

Figure 3.37c   Forward Inclusion Step 3 Output

```
VARIABLE(S) ENTERED ON STEP NUMBER  3..  X1        STAFF SALARIES PER PUPIL/

MULTIPLE R          0.94906                                ANALYSIS OF VARIANCE
R SQUARE            0.90071    R SQUARE CHANGE   0.01336                 DF   SUM OF SQUARES   MEAN SQUARE
ADJUSTED R SQUARE   0.88209    F CHANGE          2.15331    REGRESSION    3      579.08907     193.02969
STANDARD ERROR      1.99743    SIGNIF F CHANGE   0.1616     RESIDUAL     16       63.83531       3.98971

                                                           F =     48.38192    SIGNIF F = 0.0000

DEPENDENT VARIABLE..  Y       VERBAL MEAN TEST SCORE--ALL 6TH GRADERS

------------------------------- VARIABLES IN THE EQUATION -------------------------------

VARIABLE         B         SE B       BETA    CORREL  PART COR  PARTIAL        T    SIG T

X3            0.55321    0.04907    0.91539  0.92716  0.88802   0.94243    11.273  0.0000
X4            1.03582    0.40479    0.23394  0.33365  0.20158   0.53889     2.559  .0210
X1           -1.73581    1.18290   -0.13550  0.19229 -0.11560  -0.34441    -1.467  .1616
(CONSTANT)   12.11951    9.03643                                            1.341  .1986

-------------- VARIABLES NOT IN THE EQUATION --------------

VARIABLE    BETA IN   PARTIAL   MIN TOLER        T   SIG T

X2          0.02905   0.05077   0.29567      0.197   .8466
X5         -0.05819  -0.10574   0.32119     -0.412   .6863

            * * * * * * * * * * * * * * * * * * * * * * * * * * * *
```

Figure 3.37d   Forward Inclusion Step 4 Output

```
VARIABLE(S) ENTERED ON STEP NUMBER  4..  X5        6TH GRADE MEAN MOTHER'S EDUC LEVEL/

MULTIPLE R          0.94964                                ANALYSIS OF VARIANCE
R SQUARE            0.90182    R SQUARE CHANGE   0.00111                 DF   SUM OF SQUARES   MEAN SQUARE
ADJUSTED R SQUARE   0.87564    F CHANGE          0.16960    REGRESSION    4      579.80275     144.95069
STANDARD ERROR      2.05137    SIGNIF F CHANGE   0.6863     RESIDUAL     15       63.12163       4.20811

                                                           F =     34.44557    SIGNIF F = 0.0000

------------------------------- VARIABLES IN THE EQUATION -------------------------------

VARIABLE         B         SE B       BETA    CORREL  PART COR  PARTIAL        T    SIG T

X3            0.58205    0.08627    0.96310  0.92716  0.54583   0.86726     6.747  0.0000
X4            1.02521    0.41652    0.23155  0.33365  0.19913   0.53637     2.461  .0264
X1           -1.71404    1.21600   -0.13380  0.19229 -0.11404  -0.34200    -1.410  .1791
X5           -0.51735    1.25625   -0.05819  0.73299 -0.03332  -0.10574    -0.412  .6863
(CONSTANT)   15.47153   12.34417                                            1.253  .2293

-------------- VARIABLES NOT IN THE EQUATION --------------

VARIABLE    BETA IN   PARTIAL   MIN TOLER        T   SIG T

X2          0.19412   0.21374   0.11903      0.819   .4267
```

Figure 3.37e   Forward Inclusion Step 5 Output

```
VARIABLE(S) ENTERED ON STEP NUMBER  5..  X2        6TH GRADE % WHITE COLLAR FATHERS/

MULTIPLE R          0.95200                                ANALYSIS OF VARIANCE
R SQUARE            0.90631    R SQUARE CHANGE   0.00449                 DF   SUM OF SQUARES   MEAN SQUARE
ADJUSTED R SQUARE   0.87284    F CHANGE          0.67022    REGRESSION    5      582.68653     116.53731
STANDARD ERROR      2.07430    SIGNIF F CHANGE   0.4267     RESIDUAL     14       60.23785       4.30270

                                                           F =     27.08467    SIGNIF F = 0.0000

------------------------------- VARIABLES IN THE EQUATION -------------------------------

VARIABLE         B         SE B       BETA    CORREL  PART COR  PARTIAL        T    SIG T

X3            0.55576    0.09296    0.91961  0.92716  0.48910   0.84768     5.979  0.0000
X4            1.11017    0.43377    0.25074  0.33365  0.20937   0.56458     2.559  .0227
X1           -1.79333    1.23340   -0.13999  0.19229 -0.11895  -0.36221    -1.454  .1680
X5           -1.81092    2.02739   -0.20370  0.73299 -0.07307  -0.23220    -0.893  .3868
X2            0.04360    0.05326    0.19412  0.75340  0.06697   0.21374     0.819  .4267
(CONSTANT)   19.94857   13.62755                                            1.464  .1653

FOR BLOCK NUMBER  1   ALL REQUESTED VARIABLES ENTERED.
```

Figure 3.37f   HISTORY Output

```
DEPENDENT VARIABLE..  Y        VERBAL MEAN TEST SCORE--ALL 6TH GRADERS

                                    SUMMARY TABLE
                                    -------------

STEP   MULTR    RSQ    ADJRSQ    F(EQU)   SIGF   RSQCH     FCH  SIGCH        VARIABLE  BETAIN  CORREL   LABEL
  1   0.9272  0.8596  0.8518   110.230  0.000  0.8596  110.230  0.000  IN:  X3        0.9272  0.9272   SES COMPOSITE DEVIATE/
  2   0.9420  0.8873  0.8741    66.954  0.000  0.0277    4.183  .057   IN:  X4        0.1694  0.3336   MEAN TEACHER'S VERBAL TEST S
  3   0.9491  0.9007  0.8821    48.382  0.000  0.0134    2.153  .162   IN:  X1       -0.1355  0.1923   STAFF SALARIES PER PUPIL/
  4   0.9496  0.9018  0.8756    34.446  0.000  0.0011    0.170  .686   IN:  X5       -0.0582  0.7330   6TH GRADE MEAN MOTHER'S EDUC
  5   0.9520  0.9063  0.8728    27.085  0.000  0.0045    0.670  .427   IN:  X2        0.1941  0.7534   6TH GRADE % WHITE COLLAR FAT
```

In contrast, the adjusted R^2 does not increase beyond a point as variables are entered. The pattern of the adjusted R^2 is 0.8518, 0.8741, 0.8821, 0.8756, and 0.8728. In general, the adjusted R^2 is sensitive to a small sample size or a relatively large number of predictor variables. The fact that it declines in magnitude after a point means that the five-variable model is worse than some other ones. By "worse" is meant that the obtained fit may perform well for the given set of data but is unlikely to do nearly as well for a new set of data.

The standard error of the estimate behaves in opposite fashion from the adjusted R^2, but works to the same effect. The values of the standard error of the estimate as variables enter are as follows: 2.23916, 2.06407, 1.99743, 2.05137, and 2.07430. The pattern is that of a decrease in value followed by an increase, and the message is the same as that given by the adjusted R^2. It would seem so far that a two- or three-variable model is likely to suffice.

The F CHANGE and its associated significance level provide a formal test of whether bringing in an additional variable results in an improved fit. The pattern of significance levels, 0.0000, 0.0566, 0.1616, 0.6863, 0.4267, shows that at most two independent variables have a statistically significant impact on the dependent variable.

3.38 Collinearity

One of the reasons a two-variable model might be the most appropriate one is that there are two sets of independent variables, each of which correlate highly within. Several statistics in the display from NEW REGRESSION illustrate this fact quite clearly.

An indication of collinearity is found in the correlations of the estimates. When two independent variables are highly correlated, the estimates of their respective regression coefficients are highly negatively correlated. For example, the original correlation of X2 and X5 is 0.927. In the regression equation with all five independent variables in, the correlation of the estimates of the coefficients for X2 and X5 is -0.7794. This means that a range of almost equally good regression fits exists for which the regression coefficient for X2 is larger (smaller) and the regression coefficient for X5 is smaller (larger). It is in this sense that fits of collinear variables are imprecise.

A second indicator of collinearity is the standard error of a regression coefficient. Compare steps two and three of the regression fit to the Coleman data. At step two, the regression coefficient for X4 is 0.7499 with a standard error of 0.3666. At step three, with X1 in the equation, the regression coefficient for X4 is 1.0358 and the standard error of the coefficient has increased to 0.4048.

Thus, there are many indicators of inadequate fit in the statistical portion of NEW REGRESSION. It is important to remember that all of the statistical display should be interpreted in the light of what you know theoretically or what your best guess or expectation is, for there are judgmental elements of analyses that cannot be resolved by a statistic.

3.39 The Stepwise Equation

The second fit to the data is done with the PIN and POUT criteria set more stringently, and this results in a model in which X3 and X4 are retained (Figures 3.39a and 3.39b). The model developed is

$$\widehat{Y}=14.583 + 0.542\times X3 + 0.75\times X4$$
$$(9.18)\quad (0.05)\quad\quad (0.37)$$
$$R^2=0.887$$

Figure 3.39a   Stepwise Elimination Output—Step 1

```
EQUATION NUMBER  2.

DEPENDENT VARIABLE.. Y          VERBAL MEAN TEST SCORE--ALL 6TH GRADERS

BEGINNING BLOCK NUMBER  1.  METHOD:  STEPWISE

VARIABLE(S) ENTERED ON STEP NUMBER  1..   X3        SES COMPOSITE DEVIATE/

MULTIPLE R           0.92716                              ANALYSIS OF VARIANCE
R SQUARE             0.85963      R SQUARE CHANGE  0.85963                    DF   SUM OF SQUARES   MEAN SQUARE
ADJUSTED R SQUARE    0.85183      F CHANGE        110.23044   REGRESSION       1       552.67562     552.67562
STANDARD ERROR       2.23916      SIGNIF F CHANGE   0.0000    RESIDUAL        18        90.24876       5.01382

                                                     F =      110.23044    SIGNIF F = 0.0000

------------------------------ VARIABLES IN THE EQUATION ------------------------------

VARIABLE          B         SE B      BETA    CORREL PART COR PARTIAL      T  SIG T

X3           0.56033    0.05337   0.92716   0.92716   0.92716  0.92716   10.499 0.0000
(CONSTANT)  33.32280    0.52800                                         63.112 .0000

-------------- VARIABLES NOT IN THE EQUATION --------------

VARIABLE   BETA IN PARTIAL  MIN TOLER       T SIG T

X1        -0.02176 -0.05652   0.94727    -0.233 .8182
X2        -0.04285 -0.06427   0.31577    -0.266 .7938
X4         0.16937  0.44439   0.96639     2.045 .0566
X5        -0.08026 -0.12290   0.32914    -0.511 .6162
```

Figure 3.39b   Stepwise Elimination Output—Step 2

```
DEPENDENT VARIABLE.. Y          VERBAL MEAN TEST SCORE--ALL 6TH GRADERS

VARIABLE(S) ENTERED ON STEP NUMBER  2..   X4        MEAN TEACHER'S VERBAL TEST SCORE/

MULTIPLE R            0.94199                                  ANALYSIS OF VARIANCE
R SQUARE             0.88735        R SQUARE CHANGE   0.02772                   DF    SUM OF SQUARES   MEAN SQUARE
ADJUSTED R SQUARE    0.87410        F CHANGE          4.18329   REGRESSION       2        570.49798    285.24899
STANDARD ERROR       2.06407        SIGNIF F CHANGE   0.0566    RESIDUAL        17         72.42639      4.26038

                                                   F =    66.95395    SIGNIF F = 0.0000


--------------------------- VARIABLES IN THE EQUATION ---------------------------------

VARIABLE           B         SE B      BETA     CORREL PART COR  PARTIAL        T    SIG T

X3           0.54156     0.05004    0.89611   0.92716  0.88092   0.93447    10.822  0.0000
X4           0.74989     0.36664    0.16937   0.33365  0.16650   0.44439     2.045   .0566
(CONSTANT)  14.58268     9.17541                                            1.589   .1304

------------ VARIABLES NOT IN THE EQUATION -------------

VARIABLE     BETA IN  PARTIAL  MIN TOLER        T   SIG T
X1          -0.13550  -0.34441   0.72777    -1.467  .1616
X2           0.01148   0.01890   0.29581     0.076  .9407
X5          -0.06685  -0.11414   0.32232    -0.460  .6520

FOR BLOCK NUMBER  1   PIN =  .100 LIMITS REACHED.

                * * * * * * * * * * * * * * * * * * * * * * * * * * * * * *

                                     SUMMARY TABLE
                                     -------------

STEP   MULTR    RSQ   ADJRSQ    F(EQU)    SIGF   RSQCH      FCH SIGCH         VARIABLE  BETAIN  CORREL   LABEL
  1   0.9272  0.8596  0.8518  110.230   0.000  0.8596   110.230  0.000   IN:  X3      0.9272  0.9272   SES COMPOSITE DEVIATE/
  2   0.9420  0.8873  0.8741   66.954   0.000  0.0277     4.183   .057   IN:  X4      0.1694  0.3336   MEAN TEACHER'S VERBAL TEST S
```

3.40 Examining Residuals

Having arrived at what seems like an appropriate regression fit, one can then examine the residuals from the fit to check for violations of the regression model assumptions. The first part of the residuals display consists of a casewise plot of the standardized residuals, along with some related statistics (Figure 3.40a). The standardized residuals fall between bounds slightly larger than plus or minus two standard deviations limits, and are positively and negatively signed with equal frequency.

Figure 3.40a   Residuals Output—Casewise Plot

```
DEPENDENT VARIABLE.. Y          VERBAL MEAN TEST SCORE--ALL 6TH GRADERS

CASEWISE= PLOT OF STANDARDIZED RESIDUAL

          -3.0      0.0      3.0
SEQNUM    0:........:........:0          Y      *PRED    *RESID   *SRESID   *SDRESID    *MAHAL    *COOK D
   1      .       *  .       .       37.0100   38.4291   -1.4191   -0.7345   -0.7241    1.4028    0.0254
   2      .        . *       .       26.5100   26.5384   -0.0284   -0.0152   -0.0147    2.4334    0.0000
   3      .     *  .         .       36.5100   40.5269   -4.0169   -2.0548   -2.2993    1.0060    0.1615
   4      .       *. .       .       40.7000   41.5884   -0.8884   -0.4600   -0.4490    1.4137    0.0100
   5      .        *.        .       37.1000   37.0472    0.0528    0.0264    0.0256    0.1464    0.0000
   6      .        *.        .       33.9000   34.1164   -0.2164   -0.1416   -0.1374    7.6304    0.0055
   7      .        . *       .       41.8000   40.1328    1.6672    0.8548    0.8477    1.0863    0.0292
   8      .        *.        .       33.4000   33.2454    0.1546    0.0771    0.0748    1.1186    0.0001
   9      .        . *       .       41.0100   39.8642    1.1458    0.5966    0.5849    1.5998    0.0184
  10      .        . *       .       37.2000   35.5601    1.6399    0.9807    0.9796    5.5805    0.1679
  11      .      * . .       .       23.3000   25.2482   -1.9482   -1.0811   -1.0869    3.5681    0.1215
  12      .        .   *     .       35.2000   32.7784    2.4216    1.2477    1.2700    1.2509    0.0680
  13      .       *. .       .       34.9000   35.5458   -0.6458   -0.3232   -0.3145    0.2443    0.0023
  14      .        *.        .       33.1000   33.4100   -0.3100   -0.1567   -0.1521    0.5981    0.0007
  15      .      * . .       .       22.7000   24.7933   -2.0933   -1.1876   -1.2032    4.1946    0.1746
  16      .        . *       .       39.7000   39.0889    0.6111    0.3093    0.3009    0.6401    0.0029
  17      .     *  . .       .       31.8000   34.7780   -2.9780   -1.4804   -1.5389    0.0038    0.0386
  18      .        .    *    .       31.7000   27.2283    4.4717    2.3690    2.8080    2.1594    0.3661
  19      .        . *       .       43.1000   41.8521    1.2479    0.6485    0.6371    1.5381    0.0211
  20      .        . *       .       41.0100   39.8783    1.1317    0.5854    0.5738    1.3845    0.0160
SEQNUM    0:........:........:0          Y      *PRED    *RESID   *SRESID   *SDRESID    *MAHAL    *COOK D
          -3.0      0.0      3.0
```

Figure 3.40b   Residuals Output—Normal Probability Plot

```
DEPENDENT VARIABLE.. Y          VERBAL MEAN TEST SCORE--ALL 6TH GRADERS

RESIDUALS STATISTICS:

              MIN       MAX      MEAN    STD DEV    N                      MIN      MAX      MEAN    STD DEV   N

*PRED      24.7933   41.8521   35.0825   5.4796   20       *RESID     -4.0169   4.4717   -0.0000   1.9524   20
*ZPRED     -1.8777    1.2354   -0.0000   1.0000   20       *ZRESID    -1.9461   2.1665   -0.0000   0.9459   20
*SEPRED     0.4625    1.3871    0.7628   0.2452   20       *SRESID    -2.0548   2.3690    0.0030   1.0254   20
*ADJPRED   25.5706   41.7146   35.0696   5.4249   20       *DRESID    -4.4779   5.3468    0.0129   2.3036   20
*MAHAL      0.0038    7.6304    1.9000   1.9669   20       *SDRESID   -2.2993   2.8080    0.0091   1.1121   20
*COOK D     0.0000    0.3661    0.0615   0.0937   20

TOTAL CASES =      20

           * * * * * * * * * * * * * * * * * * * * * * * * * * * * *

NORMAL PROBABILITY (P-P) PLOT
STUDENTIZED RESIDUAL
   1.00 +---------+---------+---------+---------*
        I                                  ****I
        I                               **.   I
        I                             **.      I
        I                            ***       I
    .75 +                          *.          +
        I                         *.           I
  O     I                      ****            I
  B     I                   ***                I
  S     I                  *.                  I
  E .50 +                **                    +
  R     I               **                     I
  V     I             .                        I
  E     I           .  ***                     I
  D     I         ***.**                       I
    .25 +        ***                           +
        I     ****                             I
        I    *.                                I
        I  **                                  I
        I**                                    I
        ----------+---------+---------+---------+
              .25       .5       .75      1.0
```

Figure 3.40c   Residuals Output—Scatterplot

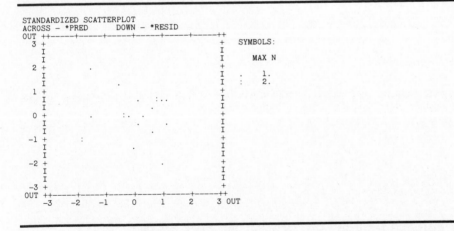

```
STANDARDIZED SCATTERPLOT
ACROSS - *PRED     DOWN - *RESID
OUT ++------+------+------+------+------+------++
  3 +                                    +      SYMBOLS:
    I                                    I
    I                                    I        MAX N
  2 +          .                         +
    I                                    I      :    1.
    I              .                     I      :    2.
  1 +                  .  :...           +
    I                                    I
    I                                    I
  0 +       .         :. .               +
    I                   .     .          I
    I                                    I
 -1 +           :                        +
    I                                    I
    I                                    I
 -2 +                  .                 +
    I                                    I
    I                                    I
 -3 +                                    +
OUT ++------+------+------+------+------+------++
    -3    -2    -1     0     1     2    3 OUT
```

   The most poorly fit cases are numbers 18 and 3, with Studentized residuals of 2.369 and -2.0548 respectively. These two cases also have two of the larger Cook's distances. The normal probability plot of Studentized residuals (Figure 3.40b) shows no dramatic departure from normality, although the plot is not unequivocally normal. The plot of the predicted values versus the residuals (Figure 3.40c) reveals no clear model inadequacies. Case number 18 appears in the upper left as a point with a low predicted value and a large positive residual. That is, given school number 18's values on X3 and X4, the regression fit predicts a lower Y than actually occurs. Case number 3, on the other hand, is overpredicted more than most. It might be interesting to investigate these two schools to see what made them so anomolous. Even given the above points, the obtained fit seems acceptable on the whole.

3.41 HELP FOR OLD FRIENDS

For long-time users of procedure REGRESSION, this section provides comparative commands for both REGRESSION and NEW REGRESSION procedures.

3.42 Some Example Setups

Anything produced by REGRESSION is available in NEW REGRESSION. In the following examples, the NEW REGRESSION setup produces the display available within REGRESSION, as well as additional output.

The commands required to run a path analysis model with four variables, X1, X2, X3, X4 are

```
REGRESSION      VARIABLES=X1 X2 X3 X4/
                REGRESSION=X1 WITH X2 X3 X4(2)/
                REGRESSION=X2 WITH X3 X4(2)/
                REGRESSION=X3 WITH X4
```

or

```
NEW REGRESSION VARIABLES=X1 X2 X3 X4/
               DEPENDENT=X1/ENTER X2 X3 X4/
               DEPENDENT=X2/ENTER X3 X4/
               DEPENDENT=X3/ENTER X4
```

The commands required to run one forward inclusion regression with residuals analysis are

```
REGRESSION      VARIABLES=Y X1 TO X5/
                REGRESSION=Y (5,3.84,.01) WITH X1 TO X5(1)RESID=0/
STATISTICS      4 5 6
```

or

```
NEW REGRESSION VARIABLES=(COLLECT)/DEPENDENT=Y/
               FORWARD=X1 TO X5/RESIDUALS/CASEWISE ALL/
               SCATTERPLOT=(*PRED,*RESID)
```

The commands required to read in a matrix indexed to the VARIABLE LIST are

```
REGRESSION      VARIABLES=Y X1 TO X5/
                REGRESSION=Y WITH X1 TO X5(2)
OPTIONS         4 9
```

or

```
NEW REGRESSION READ= CORR INDEX/
               VARIABLES=(COLLECT)/DEPENDENT=Y/
               ENTER X1 TO X5
```

The commands required to run a forward inclusion, hierarchical model in which several variables are entered together, followed by a another set of variables entered hierarchically are

```
REGRESSION      VARIABLES=Y X1 TO X10/
                REGRESSION=Y WITH X1 TO X5(2) X6 TO X10(1)
```

or

```
NEW REGRESSION VARIABLES=Y X1 TO X10/
               CRITERIA=FIN(.01)MAXSTEPS(80)/
               DEPENDENT=Y/ENTER X1 TO X5/FORWARD X6 TO X10
```

3.43 Differences in Defaults Between REGRESSION and NEW REGRESSION

This section compares defaults for the two procedures by function.

- *Statistical criteria for stepwise entry of variables.* The default criteria for stepwise entry in NEW REGRESSION are *probability of F-to-enter* of 0.05 and tolerance level of 0.01. For REGRESSION, the default criteria are value of *F*-to-enter of 1.0 and tolerance level of 0.001. Default criteria for NEW REGRESSION are much more stringent.

- *Default equation statistics.* The default equation statistics for NEW REGRESSION include the significance of *F* for multiple *R* and *t* values for coefficients. In REGRESSION, the signficance of *F* for multiple *R* is not reported, and *F* values for coefficients are reported.

- *Default method of entry.* NEW REGRESSION has no default method of entry. REGRESSION's default is equivalent to FORWARD.

- *Residuals processing.* The default casewise plot in NEW REGRESSION is a plot of outliers. REGRESSION plots all cases.

3.44 REFERENCES

Berk, K.N. Comparing subset regression procedures. *Technometrics*. 20: pp. 1-6, 1978.

——————. Tolerance and condition in regression computation. *Journal of the American Statistical Association*. 72: pp. 863-866, 1977.

Bliss, C.I. *Statistics in Biology*. New York: McGraw-Hill, 1967.

Cook, R.D. Detection of influential observations in linear regression. *Technometrics*. 19: pp. 15-18, 1977.

Dempster, A.P. *Elements of Continuous Multivariate Analysis*. Reading, Mass.: Addison-Wesley, 1969.

Frane, J.W. A note on checking tolerance in matrix inversion and regression. *Technometrics*. 19: pp. 513-514, 1977.

Gunst, R.F., and R.L. Mason. Advantages of examining *multicollinearities in a regression analysis. Biometrics*. 33: pp. 249-260, 1977.

Hoaglin, D.C., and R.E. Welsch. The hat matrix in regression and ANOVA. *American Statistician*. 32: pp. 17-22, 1978.

Kleinbaum, D.G., and L.L. Kupper. *Applied Regression Analysis and Other Multivariable Methods*. North Scituate, Mass.: Duxbury Press, 1978.

Meyer, L.S., and M.S. Younger. Estimation of standardized coefficients. *Journal of the American Statistical Association*. 71: pp. 154-157, 1976.

Neter, J., and W. Wasserman. *Applied Linear Statistical Models*. Homewood, Ill.: Richard D. Irwin Inc., 1974.

Prescott, P. An approximate test for outliers in linear regression. *Technometrics*. 17: pp. 129-132, 1975.

NEW REGRESSION was designed and programmed by Jean Jenkins and documented by Keith Sours and Tony Babinec.

Chapter 4

SPSS Graphics

The SPSS Graphics Option is a direct link between your familiarity with the SPSS Batch System and the power and versatility of a wide range of graphics hardware. For you, the Graphics Option means that you don't need to learn a new language or transport your data to another system since the Option largely consists of three new procedures—PIECHART, BARCHART, and LINE-CHART—that are fully integrated into the SPSS Batch System. It also means that you don't need access to specific graphics devices since the Option is device-independent and will run on nearly any device currently in the market. Finally, it means that you can take advantage of increased data analysis power with little investment of time and money since you will be able to preview your plots interactively before deciding which are ready for final production.

Pie, bar, and line charts produced by the Graphics Option procedures can be fully labeled, including user-defined upper/lower case titles, footnotes, and comments. They can be produced in two modes, depending on whether you want plots for testing and refining or for final publication and display. You can choose colors and/or patterns according to the type of devices you have available. Multiple pie, bar, or line charts can be plotted on the same page or frame with a common title. The Graphics Option takes advantage of SPSS variable and value labeling facilities and missing- value declarations in setting defaults and providing you with choices. In fact, the full range of SPSS's data definition, manipulation, and transformation facilities are available, as is the convenience of the SPSS system file.

The syntax is simple and familiar to SPSS users. Only the minimum specifications are needed to produce readable and informative plots. However, you have control over a wide range of format choices, labeling, functions, colors and patterns, shading, line markers, axes scaling, interpolation, missing-value treatment choices, etc.—all of which are provided via a familiar set of SPSS command specifications.

SPSS Inc. recognizes the expense of producing high presentation and reproduction quality plots and understands the iterative nature of developing graphic displays. Therefore, the Graphics Option Postprocessor allows you to preview your plots and select those that you want plotted on a final production device. That is, you can sign on to one device—perhaps a black-and-white CRT graphics terminal—and inspect the plots produced by the three procedures, one at a time. As you view the plots, you can direct those that are satisfactory to a final plotting device—perhaps a four-color pen plotter. The Graphics Option also allows you to write out a file that can be accessed by the TELL-A-GRAF software package from ISSCO Inc. if you want to take advantage of its expanded facilities. (Information regarding TELL-A-GRAF can be obtained from ISSCO Inc.)

4.1 OVERVIEW OF THE GRAPHICS OPTION

The SPSS Batch System's Graphics Option procedures are invoked with command keywords PIECHART, BARCHART, and LINECHART. Each procedure operates independently, but with similar syntax. The command keyword begins in column 1 and subcommand specifications begin in column 16 of the command lines. Some Graphics Option subcommands are made up of two keywords. In any case, the subcommand keyword or keywords are optionally followed by an equals sign and one or more specifications. The subcommand specifications must be terminated with a slash. The final slash terminating the entire command is optional.

Several subcommands are common to the three procedures. The only requirement for all three procedures is at least one PLOT subcommand which names the variables and functions to be plotted, as in

```
PIECHART        PLOT=JOBGRADE,DIVISION,STORE,SHIFT/
BARCHART        PLOT=PERCENT WITH JOBGRADE/
LINECHART       PLOT=MEAN(SALARY) WITH TENURE BY JOBGRADE/
```

In addition, each has a series of attribute subcommands that control various display options. The FORMAT, TITLE, FOOTNOTE, COMMENT, COLORS, ORDER, and MISSING subcommands are common to the three procedures. All three procedures feature a SAVE subcommand which allows you to save a file acceptable to the TELL-A-GRAF plotting package (see Section 4.58).

Because the type of plot being generated is different, keyword specifications and defaults for the same subcommand may be different for each procedure. For example, PIECHART's FORMAT specifications include keywords SORT and PERCENT that are not valid for the other two procedures since they describe part of the labeling for the pie chart segments. BARCHART's unique FORMAT specifications include STACKED or CLUSTERED which control how the bar sets are organized, and LINECHART's FORMAT specifications include XGRID, YGRID, and SHADE which request additional display features. On the other hand, all three FORMAT subcommands can specify SIMPLE or FANCY which control the plot quality.

Naturally, each procedure has unique subcommands which allow you to control attributes specific to the type of plot being produced. For example, PIECHART has a SEGMENT LABELS subcommand that is inappropriate for BARCHART and LINECHART which both have LEGEND LABELS subcommands. BARCHART has the BASE AXIS and SIDE AXIS subcommands and LINECHART has similar X AXIS and Y AXIS subcommands.

Since only one PLOT subcommand is required, all other subcommands have defaults. The defaults are appropriate to each procedure and may differ for the same subcommand. For example, the default TITLE is constructed from the PLOT specification and is likely to be different for each procedure since the PLOT specifications differ. Each new PLOT subcommand causes all attributes to return to the defaults. However, the Graphics Option allows you to establish your own defaults by preceding the subcommand keyword or keywords with keyword DEFAULT.

Each procedure produces one or more sections of a file that can either be directly displayed on a plotting device you have selected or, if you have access to more than one device, can be previewed on one device and optionally directed to another for final production. During this preview using SPSSGP, the Graphics Option Postprocessor, you can select which plots you want to be sent to the second device and you can direct multiple plots to appear on the same page.

Although the three procedures operate in a very similar fashion, each is described in this document separately, starting with an overview and an example default plot for each. Details regarding the complete operation of each procedure begins with Section 4.5 for PIECHART, Section 4.20 for BARCHART, and Section 4.37 for LINECHART. Operations of the Graphics Option Postprocessor are described beginning with Section 4.59.

4.2 Overview of the PIECHART Procedure

The Graphics Option PIECHART procedure produces a pie, with each "slice" representing the relative frequency of a category (or cell) of a variable. That is, the circle represents the whole and the segments represent the parts. For example, consider a hypothetical company with a suburban and a downtown store. You want to begin an analysis of the furniture department staff distribution and salaries, trying to track down indications of imbalances between the two stores. To produce a pie chart showing the employee distribution within job categories, the simplest command would be

```
PIECHART        PLOT=JOBGRADE/
```

The plot produced by this command is shown in Figure 4.2. It shows that sales personnel make up over two-thirds of the staff (69.1%), whereas supervisory and managerial personnel account for the other third (22.0% and 8.9% respectively).

Figure 4.2   A Default Pie Chart

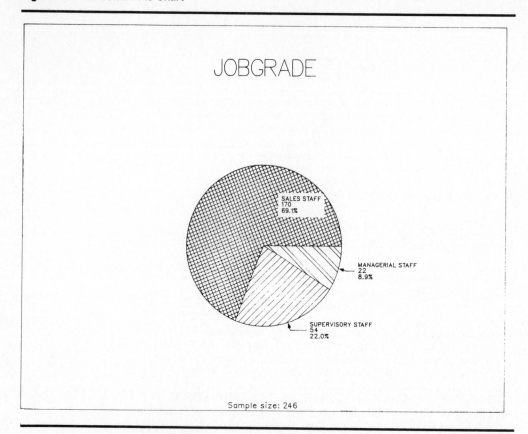

The pie chart in Figure 4.2 uses defaults for all user-controlled attributes such as pie segment order, titles, and labels. The title, for example, is constructed from the PLOT specification, which is simply the name of the variable being plotted in this case. The segment labels are the value labels associated with the variable. The default footnote describes the sample size. Any of these and several other default formatting options can be altered to make the plot exactly what you want. See beginning with Section 4.5 for the complete range of options and how they affect the plot.

4.3   Overview of the BARCHART Procedure

The Graphics Option BARCHART procedure produces a plot with bars whose lengths represent the relative magnitude of each category of a variable. The bar for each category of one variable can be further divided according to the values of a second variable. For example, to produce a bar chart showing the employee distribution within job categories for each shift, the command might be

```
BARCHART        PLOT=PERCENT WITH JOBGRADE BY SHIFT/
```

The plot produced by this command is shown in Figure 4.3. It shows not only that the sales category is by far the largest, but that the percentage of sales personnel is smaller in the second and weekend shifts than in the first shift.

The bar chart in Figure 4.3 uses defaults for all user-controlled attributes such as bar organization, titles, and labels. The default bar organization is to display the bars vertically and to cluster them when there is more than one bar per category. As with the pie chart, the title is constructed from the PLOT specification. Any of these and several other default formatting options can be altered to make the plot display the information in the best possible manner. For instance, you might want to use the BASE AXIS subcommand to relabel the job categories. See beginning with Section 4.20 for the complete range of options and how they affect the plot.

Figure 4.3   A Default Bar Chart

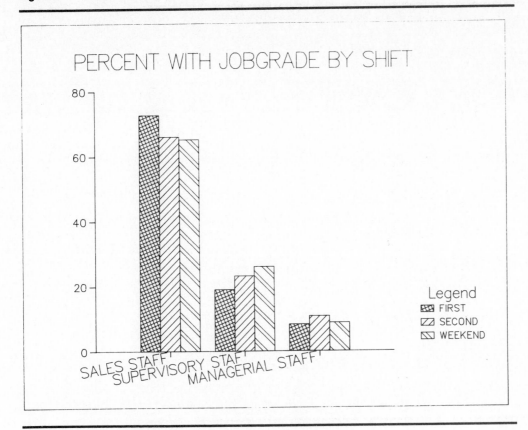

4.4   Overview of the LINECHART Procedure

The Graphics Option LINECHART procedure produces many kinds of plots depending on how you manipulate the functions and formats. However, the basic plot is a scatterplot of observed data points or a curve connecting the observed points (or functions such as the mean of the observed values) of cases on two variables. Also, one curve can be drawn for each value of an additional control variable. For example, to plot the mean salary of employees against time with the company for each job grade, specify

```
LINECHART    PLOT=MEAN(SALARY) WITH TENURE BY JOBGRADE/
```

The plot produced by this command is shown in Figure 4.4. Variable TENURE is the number of months an employee has been with the company. The line chart shows that mean salary levels differ substantially for the three categories and that all have an upward trend the longer one stays in the company.

The line chart in Figure 4.4 uses defaults for all user-controlled attributes such as type of curve, axis measures, line markers, titles, and labels. As with the other procedures, the title is constructed from the PLOT specification. The default scales for the X and Y axis variables are based on the observed values and value ranges for the variables, but are unlabeled. Also by default, each point on the chart is connected with straight lines (of different patterns or colors if there is a control variable) and the points are not marked. The default plot attributes can be altered to enhance or change the plot in a number of ways. For instance, you might want to use the X AXIS and Y AXIS subcommands to describe the units. See beginning Section 4.37 for the complete range of options and how they affect the plot.

Figure 4.4   A Default Line Chart

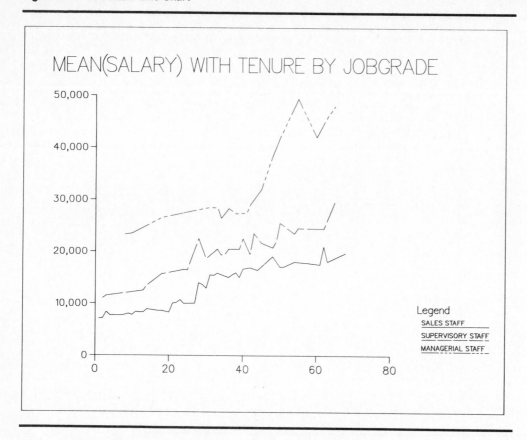

4.5   OPERATION OF PROCEDURE PIECHART

The PIECHART command must include at least one PLOT subcommand to name the variable or variables to be plotted. In addition, PIECHART includes the FORMAT subcommand to control plot quality and contents; TITLE, FOOTNOTE, and COMMENT used for annotation; SEGMENT LABELS used to alter default labels for the pie segments; EXPLODE which names one or more segments for highlighting; COLORS and ORDER used to control colors and patterns; MISSING for selecting the missing value treatment; and SAVE which allows you to save a file for input to the TELL-A-GRAF package. Subcommand keywords are followed in most cases by an optional equals sign and by specifications, and are separated from other subcommands by a slash. Subcommands and their specifications are discussed beginning with the next section.

More than one PLOT subcommand can be specified in a PIECHART command. Unless otherwise altered, all subcommand specifications return to defaults with each new PLOT subcommand. You can establish your own default specifications for subcommands by prefacing the subcommand keyword with DEFAULT, thus eliminating the need for repetitive specifications. Multiple PLOT specifications are discussed in Section 4.16.

4.6   The PLOT Subcommand for PIECHART

The PLOT subcommand for PIECHART names the variables to be plotted, one plot for each variable in a simple variable list. PLOT must be the first subcommand specified. The TO convention for naming a series of variables is not accepted. The variables cannot be alphanumeric; they must be recoded to numeric. Variables need not be integer-valued, but should have a limited number of possible values since PIECHART cannot accommodate more than 15 distinct values.

For example, to see the distribution of employees within job categories, specify

◆ PIECHART   PLOT=JOBGRADE/

The single pie chart produced by this command is shown in Figure 4.2. It accepts the default specifications for all other subcommands.

To display two pie charts, one for job categories and one for shift assignment, specify

PIECHART   PLOT=JOBGRADE,SHIFT/

All changes to default labels, patterns, order, etc., described in the following sections are made subsequent to the PLOT subcommand and apply to both variables. For an alternative allowing you to define each plot separately, see the discussion of multiple PLOT subcommands beginning with Section 4.16.

4.7   Using a Control Variable: Keywords BY and (EACH)

To request that separate pie charts be produced for each value of a control variable, use keyword BY. The BY keyword modifies all variables in the PLOT= list. For example, instead of just showing a pie chart for job categories for the whole company, you can display the number or percentage of employees within job categories for each of two stores.

```
PIECHART      PLOT=JOBGRADE BY STORE/
```

Figure 4.7   Pie Charts from a Control Variable

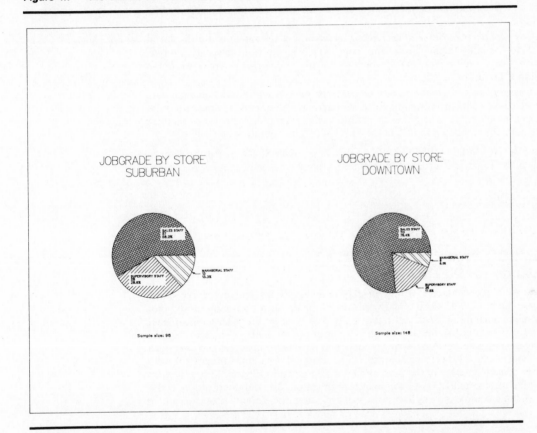

This command produces the two pie charts shown in Figure 4.7, the first for the suburban store (value 1 of STORE) and the second for the downtown store. The difference in the size of the managerial categories between the two stores becomes apparent. See Section 4.18 for a discussion of an alternative method of specifying these two pie charts to take advantage of the postprocessor.

You can manipulate the values of the control variable by specifying keyword EACH and/or a list of values, both within parentheses following the control variable name. By default, a pie chart is produced for each value of the control variable, which is equivalent to following the variable name with (EACH). If you also specify a list of values following keyword EACH, the pie charts produced are limited to one for each of the values in the list. That is,

```
PIECHART      PLOT=JOBGRADE BY DIVISION (EACH 2,3,4)/
```

produces three pie charts, one each for values 2, 3, and 4 of variable DIVISION. If you leave out the keyword EACH, then the values listed within the parentheses are grouped. For example,

```
PIECHART      PLOT=JOBGRADE BY DIVISION (2,3,4)/
```

produces a single pie chart for the subset of cases with values 2, 3, or 4 on variable DIVISION. Only one control variable can be named and only one parenthesized list of values is permitted.

4.8 The FORMAT Subcommand for PIECHART

You can specify the quality and contents of the pie charts using the FORMAT subcommand. Quality refers to the type of characters used, the density of certain lines drawn, and the first pattern used. You can also control the order in which the segments are displayed and whether percentages or counts for each segment are printed. If a keyword is preceded by NO, the opposite effect takes place. Valid keyword specifications (with defaults indicated with asterisks) for the FORMAT subcommand are

SIMPLE*   *Produce a simple plot.* Single stroke characters are drawn and pattern 1 is cross-hatched instead of solid (Section 4.13). This is equivalent to NO FANCY.

FANCY   *Produce a fancy plot.* Double stroke characters are drawn and pattern 1 is solid. This is equivalent to NO SIMPLE.

PERCENT*   *Display the percentage for each segment.* To turn percents off, specify NO PERCENT.

COUNT*   *Display the frequency count for each segment.* To turn counts off, specify NO COUNT.

SORT   *Display the segments in order of increasing frequency.* The segments are displayed smallest to largest starting from the three o'clock position moving counter-clockwise. The default is NO SORT, which means that the segments are displayed in ascending value order.

DUMP   *Dump the data values on the raw output unit.* Each pie is a set of data and each data set is preceded by a record containing PIE *nn* starting in column two, where *nn* is the number of the pie chart. The data set is composed of data pairs of segment number and segment count written in (1X,6G13.6) format. The default is NO DUMP.

Thus, the default pie chart is SIMPLE, PERCENT, COUNT, and NO SORT as can be seen in Figure 4.2. To produce the same plot ordered by frequency count and with increased quality, specify

```
     PIECHART        PLOT=JOBGRADE/
                     FORMAT=FANCY,SORT/
```

The effects of these format changes are shown in Figure 4.15.

4.9 The TITLE, FOOTNOTE, and COMMENT Subcommands for PIECHART

Three subcommands define the character strings displayed as text lines above the pie chart (TITLE), below the pie chart (FOOTNOTE), and vertically along the lower left edge of the plot (COMMENT). Each subcommand can specify strings of up to three lines of fifty characters apiece, specified in one to three strings enclosed in apostrophes (') or quotation marks (''). Apostrophes and quotation marks can be included within a string by being entered twice in succession, but both appear on the plot as apostrophes. Lowercase characters are accepted. One line appears for each string unless strings are concatenated with the plus sign (+). As shown in Figure 4.2, the default title for a pie chart is taken from the PLOT subcommand specification. The default footnote is the sample size and the default comment is null. If you want to alter the default title and add a footnote, specify

```
     PIECHART        PLOT=JOBGRADE/ FORMAT=FANCY,SORT/
                     TITLE='CHICAGO HOME FURNISHING'
                         'Employee Study – Sales Department'/
                     FOOTNOTE='As of December 1980'/
```

The effects of these subcommands are shown in Figure 4.15.

The SPSS Graphics Option chooses the size and positioning of the annotation depending on the number and length of strings. These decisions are made for you so you won't have to repeatedly produce the same plot in order to arrive at an acceptable format. However, you can control the size and positioning by entering blank strings of various lengths before or after the one or two strings you want displayed, as long as you don't exceed three strings. For example, if you want the footnote to appear higher above the plot border than is shown in Figure 4.2, specify

```
          FOOTNOTE='As of December 1980' ' '/
```

If you specify more than one string per subcommand on the same line, they must be separated by one or more blanks or commas. Otherwise, the unseparated apostrophes or quotation marks are interpreted as an apostrophe in a single string. If you continue a string from one line to the next, all blanks at the end of the first line up to column 80 (72 if the NUMBERED command is used) are considered part of the string. Therefore, if you need to continue a long string to the next command line, use the plus sign for concatenation, as in

```
          TITLE='CHICAGO HOME FURNISHING' 'Employee Study '+
          '– Sales Department'/
```

If you intend to place multiple plots on the same page using the postprocessor, see Section 4.18 for a discussion of how to use alternative labels.

4.10 Controlling the Pie Chart Segments

You can control how the pie segments are displayed by altering the default labels, by causing one or more of the segments to be "exploded" out from the center of the pie for emphasis, and by specifying the combination of pattern and color PIECHART uses for each segment.

4.11 Altering Segment Labels:
The SEGMENT LABELS Subcommand

By default, PIECHART labels the pie chart segments with the value labels. If a value label is not available, the segment is labeled with the variable name followed by an equals sign and the value. Override the SEGMENT LABELS subcommand defaults by specifying each value in parentheses followed by a string of up to twenty characters enclosed in apostrophes or quotation marks according to the rules described in Section 4.9, as in

```
PIECHART      PLOT=JOBGRADE/ FORMAT=FANCY,SORT/
              TITLE='CHICAGO HOME FURNISHING'
                    'Employee Study - Sales Department'/
              FOOTNOTE='As of December 1980' ' '/
              SEGMENT LABELS=(1)'Salesclerks' (2)'Supervisors'
                            (3)'Managers'/
```

The effect of altering the default segment labels is shown in Figure 4.15.

Along with the relative size of the segment and whether percents and/or counts are displayed (see Section 4.8), the length of the label affects PIECHART's decision to place annotation inside or outside the segment. The size of the pie drawn varies depending on how many labels must appear outside the segments.

4.12 Emphasizing Segments: The EXPLODE Subcommand

To emphasize one or more of the segments of a pie chart, indicate the category value or values in the EXPLODE subcommand. PIECHART shifts the indicated segments outward along the radius of the pie. For example, to emphasize the relative size of the managerial job grade, specify

```
PIECHART      PLOT=JOBGRADE/ FORMAT=FANCY,SORT/
              TITLE='CHICAGO HOME FURNISHING'
                    'Employee Study - Sales Department'/
              FOOTNOTE='As of December 1980' ' '/
              SEGMENT LABELS=(1)'Salesclerks' (2)'Supervisors'
                            (3)'Managers'/
              EXPLODE=3/
```

See Figure 4.15 for the result of exploding the segment corresponding to value 3 of variable JOBGRADE. By default, no segments are exploded.

4.13 Establishing Patterns:
The ORDER Subcommand in PIECHART

If you do not enter a COLORS subcommand overriding the default of 0 additional colors (Section 4.14), the ORDER and FORMAT subcommands control the order of patterns PIECHART uses for the pie chart segments. The patterns and their corresponding numbers are shown in Figure 4.13. For FORMAT=FANCY, the patterns are the same as for SIMPLE except that pattern 1 is solid instead of cross-hatched. By default patterns are applied in ascending numerical order to the variable values in ascending numerical order. Thus, specifying the SORT keyword in the FORMAT subcommand does not affect which segment gets which pattern, and patterns are consistent across multiple pie charts produced for values of a control variable (Section 4.7).

To choose your own patterns, use the ORDER subcommand to specify the pattern numbers in variable value order. For example, to apply patterns 5, 2, and 1 to the segments corresponding to values 1, 2, and 3 of variable JOBGRADE, specify

```
PIECHART      PLOT=JOBGRADE/ FORMAT=FANCY,SORT/
              TITLE='CHICAGO HOME FURNISHING'
                    'Employee Study - Sales Department'/
              FOOTNOTE='As of December 1980' ' '/
              SEGMENT LABELS=(1)'Salesclerks' (2)'Supervisors'
                            (3)'Managers'/
              EXPLODE=3/
              ORDER=5,2,1/
```

Enter pattern numbers from 1 to 15 for the segments you want to alter, even if you might be respecifying the default value for a particular segment. If you specify fewer pattern numbers than there are segments, the remaining segments have the default patterns in the original sequence. That is, with ORDER=5,2,1, the next pattern numbers are 4,5,6, etc. If you specify more (up to a maximum of 15 with COLORS=0), the remainder are not used. The effect of choosing a different pattern compared to the default patterns shown in Figure 4.2 is shown in Figure 4.15. You can select the same pattern for different segments by repeating its order number.

Figure 4.13   The PIECHART Patterns

SIMPLE PIECHART Patterns

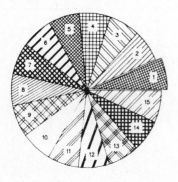

FANCY PIECHART Patterns

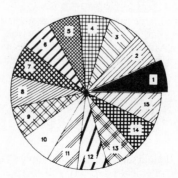

4.14   Establishing Colors:
The COLORS Subcommand in PIECHART

If you intend to produce your plots on a color device, you must know how many colors the device supports in addition to black. A black-and-white device supports 0 additional colors, a four-pen plotter supports 3 additional colors. The default specification for the COLORS subcommand is 0.

If you intend to produce your pie chart on a four-color device, to take advantage of the three additional colors, specify

        COLORS=3 /

Table 4.14   The ORDER/COLORS Interaction

COLORS=2	Pattern 1 2 3 4 5 6 7 8 9 . . .	COLORS=3	Pattern 1 2 3 4 5 6 7 8 9 . . .
Red	1 3 5 7 9 11 13 15 17 . . .	Red	1 4 7 10 13 16 19 22 25 . . .
Green	2 4 6 8 10 12 14 16 18 . . .	Green	2 5 8 11 14 17 20 23 26 . . .
		Blue	3 6 9 12 15 18 21 24 27 . . .

If you specify more than 0 colors, you can use ORDER numbers greater than 15. PIECHART uses the additional colors to draw the segments, generating patterns in an expanded order compared to that documented in Section 4.13. To determine the color/pattern associated with a given ORDER number, generate a matrix of order numbers with colors as the rows and patterns as the columns. For example, if you have COLORS=3 (red, green, blue), your matrix looks like the second matrix in Table 4.14. Note that pattern 1 is solid only for FORMAT=FANCY. Therefore, if you want the segments to begin with solid colors, you must request a FANCY plot (see Section 4.8).

For instance, look at the FANCY order of black and white patterns shown in Figure 4.13. Assume that you have three additional colors that correspond to red, green, and blue and that ORDER is left to the default order. The segment of a pie corresponding to the lowest value of the variable is drawn with the first additional color and the first pattern, thus making it solid red. The second and third segments corresponding to the second and third highest values of the variable are solid green and solid blue respectively. The fourth, fifth, and sixth segments are drawn with red, green, and blue stripes respectively according to pattern 2. However, specifying ORDER= 1,2,3,13,14,15 generates the same first three solid color segments, but selects pattern 5 for the fourth, fifth, and sixth segments (see Table 4.14).. Therefore, on a color device, to predict the display pattern of a segment, you must know the order of the segment, the number and order of the additional colors, and the order of the patterns (and whether the plot is FANCY or SIMPLE).

You can specify the same pattern number in the ORDER subcommand if COLORS is greater than 0, but you must do it from your matrix of order numbers based on color and pattern. For example, with ORDER=1,2,1,2 and COLORS=2 (e.g., red and green), the first four segments are solid red, solid green, solid red, solid green respectively (with FORMAT=FANCY).

4.15 Handling Missing Values:
The MISSING Subcommand in PIECHART

By default, PIECHART does not include a case in calculating the segments of a pie if the case has missing values on either the variable being plotted or the control variable. You can alter the default by using the MISSING subcommand with one of the following keyword specifications.

PIEWISE*   *Omit cases with missing values on the plot or the control variable.* If more than one plot variable is specified in the PLOT subcommand, each is treated separately with regard to missing value treatment. Therefore, each pie chart could be based on a different set of cases.

PLOTWISE   *Omit cases with missing values on any plot variable or on the control variables.* All pie charts produced from the PLOT command are based on the same cases.

NONE   *Include all cases regardless of missing values.*

For example, if you want PIECHART to ignore missing data declarations for all variables specified in the PLOT subcommand, use keyword NONE. Clerical and other staff (JOBGRADE=4) are declared missing to SPSS and therefore were omitted from the pie chart shown in Figure 4.2, perhaps to separate support personnel from the rest of the staff. To include them in the final display, specify

```
PIECHART        PLOT=JOBGRADE/ FORMAT=FANCY,SORT/
                TITLE='CHICAGO HOME FURNISHING'
                  'Employee Study - Sales Department'/
                FOOTNOTE='As of December 1980' ' '/
                SEGMENT LABELS=(1)'Salesclerks' (2)'Supervisors'
                       (3)'Managers' (4)'Support'/
                EXPLODE=3/ ORDER=5,2,1,10/
                MISSING=NONE/
```

The plot produced by this command is shown in Figure 4.15. Note that the additional segment label and the additional pattern were added to account for the inclusion of the missing value. If these additions were not specified, the segment label would have defaulted to the value label, as indicated in Section 4.11, and the pattern would have been pattern 4 from Figure 4.13 instead of the completely blank pattern selected with number 10.

The difference between PIEWISE and PLOTWISE missing value treatments arises only if you specify more than one plot variable on the PLOT subcommand. That is, if you specify

```
PIECHART        PLOT=JOBGRADE,DIVISION,SHIFT/
```

a plot is produced first for JOBGRADE with cases being omitted if they have missing data for job grade, a second plot is produced for DIVISION with cases omitted with missing division information, etc. Instead, if you specify

```
PIECHART        PLOT=JOBGRADE,DIVISION,SHIFT/ MISSING=PLOTWISE
```

the three pie charts are produced, but this time cases are omitted if they are missing data on any of the three variables.

Figure 4.15   An Enhanced Pie Chart

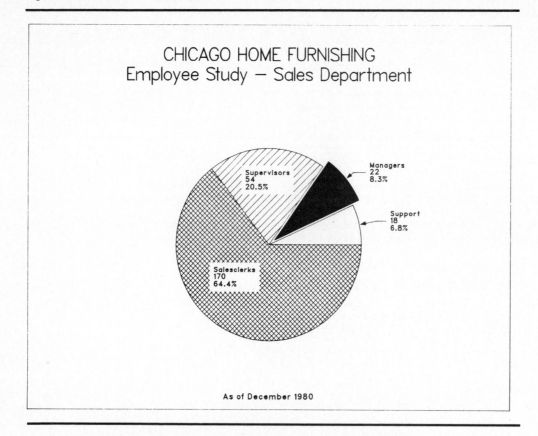

4.16 Multiple PLOT Subcommands for PIECHART

More than one PLOT subcommand can be specified in a PIECHART command. This is helpful particularly when some attributes are common to all plots. However, some attributes may be specific to each plot. Since a second and subsequent PLOT subcommand returns all other subcommands to their defaults, you either have to respecify all attributes following each PLOT subcommand or you can establish your own defaults and respecify only unique attributes. By specifying the keyword DEFAULT before any of the attribute subcommands FORMAT, TITLE, FOOTNOTE, COMMENT, EXPLODE, ORDER, COLORS, or MISSING, you establish what the default specifications are for the duration of the PIECHART command.

In the complete example shown in Section 4.15, you might want to add a PLOT command to generate a pie chart of the division to which each of the employees in the sales department are assigned. If you simply enter a PLOT=DIVISION subcommand following the last subcommand affecting the previous plot, the pie chart for the variable specified will look very much like the plot shown in Figure 4.2 since all other subcommands return to defaults. A better approach is to decide which of the subcommands for the first PLOT subcommand are also applicable to the second, and then make those the defaults. All other subcommands specific to the second plot (shown in Figure 4.16) are then specified.

If you want the plot quality the same and also want the segments sorted, the first subcommand you want to establish as the default is the FORMAT subcommand. Since the company, store, department, and date produced are the same, the TITLE and FOOTNOTE specifications apply to both plots. Finally, since you want the other staff included in both parts, the MISSING=NONE specification should also apply to both plots (see the example command below).

For the second plot, you want to specify different segment labels, and prefer to have no segment exploded and want PIECHART to use the default segment patterns. Therefore, you specify SEGMENT LABELS following the second PLOT subcommand and leave out the EXPLODE and ORDER subcommands so they return to their defaults. Therefore, the complete command that produces both the plot shown in Figure 4.15 and the one shown in Figure 4.16 is

```
PIECHART      PLOT=JOBGRADE/ DEFAULT FORMAT=FANCY,SORT/
              DEFAULT TITLE='CHICAGO HOME FURNISHING'
                    'Employee Study - Sales Department'/
              DEFAULT FOOTNOTE='As of December 1980' ' '/
              SEGMENT LABELS=(1)'Salesclerks' (2)'Supervisors'
                            (3)'Managers' (4)'Support'/
              EXPLODE=3/ ORDER=5,2,1,10/
              DEFAULT MISSING=NONE/
              PLOT=DIVISION/
              SEGMENT LABELS=(1)'Carpeting' (2)'Appliances'
                            (3)'Furniture' (4)'Hardware'/
```

Figure 4.16   The Pie Chart from the Second PLOT Subcommand

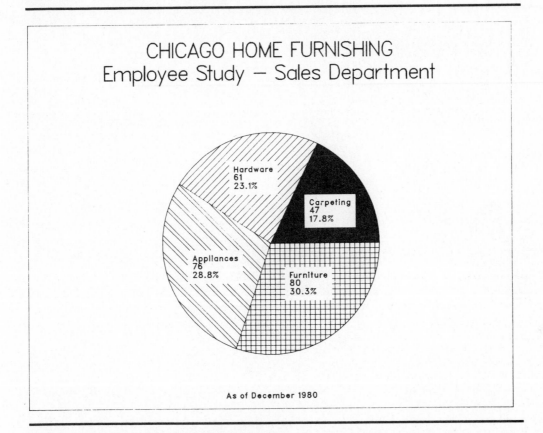

4.17   Special Plotting Applications

There are some general considerations in deciding how to approach your plotting tasks that apply equally to PIECHART, BARCHART, and LINECHART, or to combinations of the three. Two of these considerations—anticipating multiple plots per page and entering aggregate data—are presented in the following sections.

4.18   Anticipating Multiple Plots per Page

If you intend to use the Graphics Option Postprocessor (Section 4.59) to place your plots on the same page, you might consider alternative ways of specifying the individual plots. The most obvious example is to use the TITLE subcommand to describe each plot and use the titling option in the postprocessor to assign the general title. With specific regard to pie charts, you would probably want to run separate PLOT subcommands for each value of the control variable in order to take advantage of TITLE or FOOTNOTE to describe the specific subpopulations. For example, to label the charts shown in Figure 4.7 and to enhance them fully as shown for the single pie chart in 4.15, specify

```
PIECHART          PLOT=JOBGRADE BY STORE(1)/
                  DEFAULT FORMAT=FANCY,SORT/
                  TITLE='Sales Department' 'Suburban Store'/
                  DEFAULT FOOTNOTE='As of December 1980' ' '/
                  DEFAULT SEGMENT LABELS=(1)'Salesclerks'
                         (2)'Supervisors' (3)'Managers' (4)'Support'/
                  DEFAULT EXPLODE=3/
                  DEFAULT ORDER=5,2,1,10/
                  DEFAULT MISSING=NONE/
                  PLOT=JOBGRADE BY STORE(2)/
                  TITLE='Sales Department' 'Downtown Store'/
```

The plots are then put on the same page using the postprocessor, producing Figure 4.18.

Figure 4.18   Multiple Plots on a Page

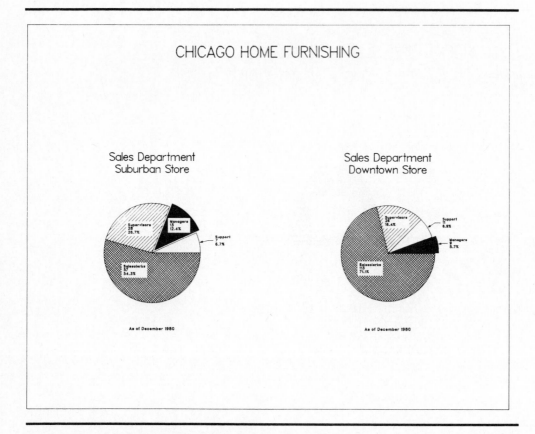

4.19   Entering Aggregate Data for Plots

Sometimes it may be more efficient for you to enter already computed data to produce plots for presentation rather than to go back to the raw data solely for the plots. Entering the computed values and using the WEIGHT command may be cheaper and faster. For example, to reproduce the pie chart shown in Figure 4.15, enter one data line per segment. The complete SPSS command setup with the data would be

```
RUN NAME          ENTERING COMPUTED DATA
DATA LIST         FIXED/1 JOBGRADE 1 JWEIGHT 3-5
INPUT MEDIUM      CARD
N OF CASES        4
WEIGHT            JWEIGHT
PIECHART          PLOT=JOBGRADE/ FORMAT=FANCY,SORT/
                  TITLE='CHICAGO HOME FURNISHING'
                        'Employee Study - Sales Department'/
                  FOOTNOTE='As of December 1980' ' '/
                  SEGMENT LABELS=(1)'Salesclerks' (2)'Supervisors'
                             (3)'Managers' (4)'Support'/
                  EXPLODE=3/ ORDER=5,2,1,10/
READ INPUT DATA
1 170
2  54
3  22
4  18
FINISH
```

4.20   OPERATION OF PROCEDURE BARCHART

The BARCHART command must include at least one PLOT subcommand to identify the function (count, percent, mean, etc.) and to name the variable or variables to be plotted. In addition, BARCHART includes the FORMAT subcommand to control plot quality and contents; TITLE, FOOTNOTE, and COMMENT used for annotation; BASE AXIS and SIDE AXIS used to label and define the axes parameters; LEGEND TITLE and LEGEND LABELS used to provide a title and labels for the bar chart legend; COLORS and ORDER used to control colors and patterns; and MISSING for selecting the missing value treatment. The SAVE subcommand, which allows you to save a file for input to the TELL-A-GRAF package, is documented in Section 4.58. Subcommand keywords are followed in most cases by an optional equals sign and by specifications, and are separated from other subcommands by a slash. Subcommands and their specifications are discussed beginning with the next section.

More than one PLOT subcommand can be specified in a BARCHART command. Unless otherwise altered, all subcommand specifications return to defaults with each new PLOT subcommand. You can establish your own defaults by prefacing the subcommand keyword with DEFAULT, thus eliminating the need for repetitive specifications. Multiple PLOT specifications are discussed beginning with Section 4.36.

4.21   The PLOT Subcommand for BARCHART

The PLOT subcommand for BARCHART defines the function and names the variable or variables for which a bar chart is produced. The PLOT subcommand for BARCHART is divided into three parts:

- The required *function part* names the function (and the variable when appropriate) that determines the length of the bars, thus controlling the *side axis*.
- The required *WITH part* names the variable or variables whose categories determine the number of bars or bar sets, thus controlling the *base axis*.
- The optional *BY part* subdivides each bar into a set of bars according to the categories of a *control variable*.

In the example from Section 4.3,

```
BARCHART      PLOT=PERCENT WITH JOBGRADE BY SHIFT/
```

PERCENT is the function that determines the side axis scale and, therefore, the length of each bar. The actual number of bars is determined by the number of values in both JOBGRADE and SHIFT. JOBGRADE controls the number of sets of bars and its values and labels form the base axis. SHIFT controls the number of bars in each set and its values and labels appear in the legend. As the plot produced by this example shows in Figure 4.3, JOBGRADE is described in three sets of bars and SHIFT is described by three bars in each set.

PLOT must be the first subcommand specified. None of the variables named can be alphanumeric; they must be recoded to numeric. The base axis variable or variables named in the WITH part need not be integer-valued, but should have a limited number of possible cells since each value or combination of values is represented by one bar (or set of bars in a controlled plot). In any case, BARCHART cannot accommodate more than 100 bars or sets of bars. Likewise, the variable or variables named in the BY part need not be integer-valued, but can have no more than 15 possible values.

4.22   The Minimum PLOT Specification: The Function and WITH Parts

The first required part of the PLOT subcommand is the name of a function which establishes the side axis. If the function is a count or a percent, there is no variable named. If the function is a mean or a sum, the name of the variable is enclosed in parentheses following the function keyword. Functions are

COUNT	*Plot cell frequencies.*
CCOUNT	*Plot the cumulative frequency across cells.*
PERCENT	*Plot cell percentages.*
CPERCENT	*Plot the cumulative percentage across cells.*
MEAN(varname)	*Plot cell means of the variable.*
SUM(vaname)	*Plot cell sums of the variable.*
CSUM(varname)	*Plot the cumulative sum of the variable across cells.*

The function part is usually followed immediately by the keyword WITH and the name of the variable whose values form the cells and therefore determine the number of bars on the base axis.

This completes the minimum required syntax of the PLOT subcommand in BARCHART. For example, to compare the mean length of time employees have been with the company, specify

```
BARCHART       PLOT=MEAN(TENURE) WITH JOBGRADE/
```

The function selected is the MEAN and the dependent variable is TENURE, which is the length of time an employee has been with the company measured in months. The WITH part names variable JOBGRADE, which means that one bar is produced for each job grade. The plot produced by this example is developed in the next section by adding a control variable.

4.23 Using a Control Variable: The BY Part

Adding a control variable is simply a matter of specifying the keyword BY followed by the control variable, as in

```
◆ BARCHART       PLOT=MEAN(TENURE) WITH JOBGRADE BY SHIFT/
```

The plot produced by this command is shown in Figure 4.23. It accepts defaults for all other BARCHART subcommands. To see this example fully developed as the discussion of altering the default specifications for the other subcommands progresses, pick up the discussion beginning with Section 4.27. To see the complete syntax possibilities for the PLOT subcommand, see the following sections on qualifying each variable named with a selector, on specifying multiple variables within each part, and on specifying cross-products.

Figure 4.23   A Default Bar Chart with Cell Means

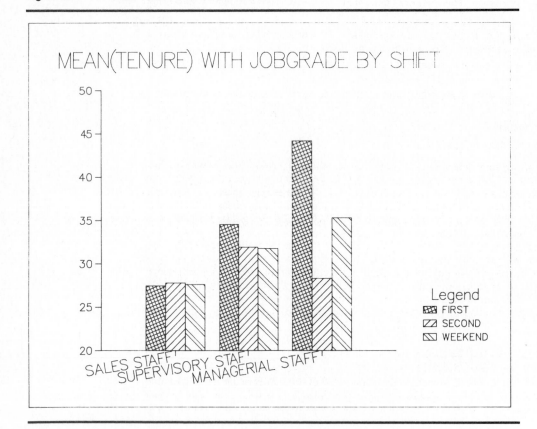

4.24 Specifying Selectors

Each variable named in the function, WITH, and BY parts of the PLOT subcommand can be followed by parentheses enclosing a selector which consists of a logical operator and a value or list of values, as in SHIFT(NE 3). Relational operators are LT, LE, EQ, NE, GE, and GT which mean respectively less than, less than or equal to, equal to, not equal to, greater than or equal to, and greater than. If you omit the logical operator, EQ is assumed. EQ and NE can be followed by a list of numbers where (EQ 1,2,3) means equal to 1, 2, or 3, and (NE 1,2,3) means not equal to 1, 2, and 3. All other operators are followed by a single value. If a case satisfies the condition, it is used in constructing the bar chart specified.

For example, to produce a bar chart of the mean tenure of only the first shift within job categories, specify SHIFT(EQ 1) in the BY part. Or, since the EQ operator is assumed if none is included in the parentheses, specify

```
BARCHART      PLOT=MEAN(TENURE) WITH JOBGRADE BY SHIFT(1)/
```

To limit the same bar chart to include only supervisors and managers (values 2 and 3), specify either JOBGRADE(EQ 2,3) or

```
BARCHART      PLOT=MEAN(TENURE) WITH JOBGRADE(2,3) BY SHIFT(1)/
```

If you want the bar chart to be limited to those who have been with the company at least one year, specify

```
BARCHART      PLOT=MEAN(TENURE(GE 12)) WITH JOBGRADE BY SHIFT/
```

Since the variable named in the function part is already enclosed in parentheses, the selector for that variable must be included within those parentheses as shown in this example.

4.25 Specifying Multiple Variables

The PLOT subcommand for BARCHART produces a single plot regardless of the number of variables named in the PLOT subcommand. That is, while more than one variable can be specified in the function and WITH parts (not the BY part) of the PLOT specification, multiple variables cause changes in the organization of the bars and in the side axis scale in a single plot; they do not produce multiple plots. For instance, the specification

```
BARCHART      PLOT=MEAN(TENURE) WITH JOBGRADE,DIVISION BY SHIFT/
```

produces a bar chart whose base axis is divided into two separated charts, the first chart for job categories and the second for the departmental divisions (see Figure 4.30).

You can use the multiple variable feature to emphasize differences in categories of the base axis variable by introducing the selector. For example, you could cause office staff (value 3 for managers and missing value 4 for support personnel) and floor staff (supervisors and managers) to be plotted in separate charts on the same plot by specifying

```
BARCHART      PLOT=PERCENT WITH JOBGRADE(GE 3) JOBGRADE(LE 2) BY SHIFT/
              MISSING=NONE/
```

(See Section 4.35 on including missing values.) Note that functions (PERCENT in this example) are calculated separately for the multiple variables. That is, the percents will total to 100 for office staff and for floor staff.

You can also name more than one function to be plotted on the same bar chart, as in MEAN(VAR1,VAR2) or PERCENT(VAR1),CPERCENT(VAR1). This provision should be used with caution since the side axis scale must accommodate the minimum and maximum values for each function. That is, you could specify both count and percent for a base axis variable, but while the percent can only go from 0 to a maximum of 100, the count could have a minimum and maximum completely beyond 100, or be very small. Likewise, you can specify that the mean of two dependent variables be plotted in the same bar chart, but unless the scales of the two variables are the same or similar, the scales may be badly matched.

The result of multiple function specifications is represented in bar sets within categories of the base axis variable in the same manner as for a control variable. That is, the specification

```
BARCHART      PLOT=MEAN(TENURE,JTENURE) WITH JOBGRADE/
```

generates two bars for each category of JOBGRADE (see Figure 4.25), the first for the mean company tenure and the second for the mean job tenure. This order is important for specifying your own legend labels (Section 4.32) and patterns (Section 4.33).

Any combination of naming multiple variables in the two parts of the PLOT subcommand can be specified, and more than two variables can be named in each part. However, each additional variable named increases the amount of information contained in a single bar chart and, therefore, increases the detail. Complicated bar charts can become too cluttered to be readable. Consider the alternative of multiple plots discussed in Section 4.36, particularly since you have the possibility of putting them on the same page when you use the postprocessor discussed in Section 4.59.

Figure 4.25   Multiple Functions

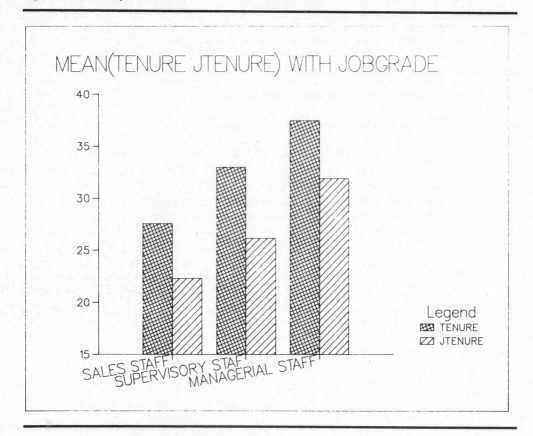

4.26 Specifying Cross-Products

The cross-products of up to three variables can be specified in the WITH and BY parts of the PLOT subcommand for BARCHART. For instance, to combine the two store and the three shift categories into a single six-category BY variable in the same plot, specify

```
BARCHART        PLOT=PERCENT WITH JOBGRADE BY STORE*SHIFT/
```

As can be seen in Figure 4.26, this specification causes the bars describing job grade percents to be plotted left-to-right in a vertical plot for the suburban first shift, the suburban second shift, the suburban weekend shift, the downtown first shift, the downtown second shift, and the downtown weekend shift. That is, the values of the first variable named in a cross-products specification rotate slowest. This order is important for specifying your own legend labels (Section 4.32) and patterns (Section 4.33). If you specify

```
BARCHART        PLOT=MEAN(TENURE) WITH JOBGRADE*STORE BY SHIFT/
```

BARCHART produces a plot of mean tenure for each shift for suburban sales staff, downtown sales staff, suburban supervisors, downtown supervisors, etc. The values of the first cross-products variable rotate slowest, which is important for specifying your own base axis category labels (Section 4.30) and bar patterns (Section 4.33).

You can specify cross-products of up to three variables in either the WITH or BY parts of the PLOT specification, but the cross-products cannot produce more than 15 cells. You cannot specify crossproducts for dependent variables in the function part.

Figure 4.26   A Cross-products Control Variable

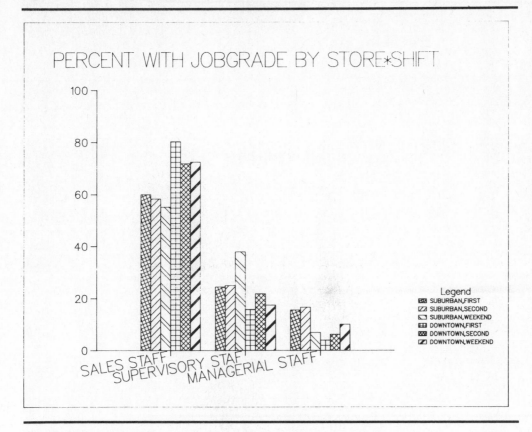

4.27   The FORMAT Subcommand for BARCHART

You specify the display quality and format of the bar charts using the FORMAT subcommand. You can ask that the display format be horizontal rather than vertical and that sets of bars be hidden or stacked rather than clustered. The format keywords are

VERTICAL*   *Plot a vertical bar chart.* This is equivalent to NO HORIZONTAL.

HORIZONTAL   *Plot a horizontal bar chart.* This is equivalent to NO VERTICAL. Overrides the default VERTICAL plot.

CLUSTERED*   *Plot clustered bar sets.*

HIDDEN   *Plot hidden bar sets.* Bars in a set appear as if they are stacked one in front of the other with the smallest in front to the biggest in back. Overrides the default CLUSTERED format.

STACKED   *Plot stacked bar sets. Bars in a set are stacked one on top of* the other. This generally requires a greater range of values along the side axis. Overrides the default CLUSTERED format.

As the previous examples show, the default format is VERTICAL and CLUSTERED when the chart includes bar sets. See the examples of hidden and stacked bar charts (placed on the same plot using the postprocessor) in Figure 4.27. Which of the styles you choose depends mostly on what you want to show. The difference between vertical and horizontal bar charts is probably negligible, except that vertical charts are more traditional. However, base axis labels are probably easier to read in a horizontal plot. The differences among clustered, hidden, and stacked bar sets are more pronounced, but still depend largely on preferences.

Figure 4.27   Hidden and Stacked Bar Charts

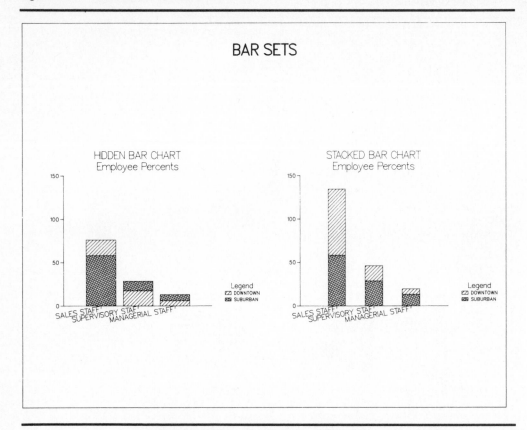

You can also control the plot quality—the the type of characters used, the density of certain lines drawn, and the first shade pattern. For bar charts, format options also allow you to request a frame around the chart, grid lines within the chart, and counts within the bars. If one of the following keywords is preceded by NO, the opposite effect takes place.

SIMPLE* *Produce a simple plot.* Single stroke characters and solid grids are drawn, and pattern 1 is cross-hatched instead of solid (Section 4.33). This is equivalent to NO FANCY.

FANCY *Produce a fancy plot.* Double stroke characters and dashed grid lines are drawn, and pattern 1 is solid. This is equivalent to NO SIMPLE.

COUNT *Display the frequency count for each bar.* The number of cases represented by each bar is displayed within the bar. The default is NO COUNT.

FRAME *Draw a frame around the chart.* The base and side axes lines are completed around the chart. The default is NO FRAME.

GRID *Draw grid lines within the chart.* Grid lines perpendicular to the bars are drawn across the chart. The default is NO GRID.

DUMP *Dump the data values on the raw output unit.* Each legend entry is a set of data and each data set is preceded by a record containing BARSET *nn* starting in column two, where *nn* is the number of the legend entry. The data set is composed of data triples of base axis value, side axis value, and count written in (1X,6G13.6) format. The default is NO DUMP.

Thus, the default bar chart quality is SIMPLE, NO COUNT, NO FRAME, and NO GRID as can be seen in any of the previous examples. For example, if you want to frame the chart started in Section 4.23 and make it horizontal with increased quality, specify

```
BARCHART      PLOT=MEAN(TENURE) WITH JOBGRADE BY SHIFT/
              FORMAT=HORIZONTAL,FRAME,FANCY/
```

The effects of these format changes are shown in Figure 4.35.

4.28   The TITLE, FOOTNOTE, and COMMENT Subcommands for BARCHART

Three subcommands affect the text displayed along with your bar chart. These subcommands define the character strings displayed as lines of text above the chart (TITLE), below the chart (FOOTNOTE), and vertically along the lower left edge of the plot (COMMENT). They are specified according to the rules described in Section 4.9.

As shown in the previous figures, the default title for a bar chart is taken from the PLOT subcommand specification. The default footnote and comment are null. To alter each of these defaults, specify

```
BARCHART      PLOT=MEAN(TENURE) WITH JOBGRADE BY SHIFT/
              FORMAT=HORIZONTAL,FRAME,FANCY/
●             TITLE='CHICAGO HOME FURNISHING'
●                   'Employee Tenure — Sales Department'/
●             FOOTNOTE='As of December 1980'/
●             COMMENT='G.Wong, D.P.'/
```

The effects of these subcommands are shown in Figure 4.35.

4.29   Controlling the Axes and the Bars

You can control how the BARCHART base and side axes are scaled and labeled with the BASE AXIS and SIDE AXIS subcommands. The SIDE AXIS subcommand can also be used to establish a reference line or a root value to either side of which the bars extend. With the LEGEND TITLE and LEGEND LABELS subcommands, you can specify your own title and labels for the control variable or variables. Finally, you can control patterns or colors using the ORDER and COLORS subcommands.

4.30   Specifying the Base Axis: The BASE AXIS Subcommand

By default, BARCHART does not provide a base axis label, but labels the axis divisions (see Figure 4.23), which can become quite complicated with more complex WITH specifications.

You can specify an axis label of up to 40 characters within apostrophes or quotation marks (according to rules described in Section 4.9) as the first specification in the BASE AXIS subcommand or immediately following the NAME keyword. To control the base axis divisions, use one of the following keywords, immediately after the axis label if one is specified.

LABELED*   *Label the base axis divisions.* If no labels are provided, BARCHART labels the base axis divisions with the value labels. If a value label is not available, the division is labeled with the variable name followed by an equals sign and the value (depending on the complexity of the WITH specification). You can provide your own labels as strings of up to 16 characters enclosed in apostrophes or quotation marks following the LABELED keyword.

LINEAR   *Divide the base axis linearly.* BARCHART computes the division marks based on the range of the base axis variable. This keyword can be used only with a single base axis variable.

MONTHLY   *Give the base axis divisions monthly labels.* JAN corresponds to values 1, 13, 25, etc.; FEB corresponds to 2, 14, etc. This keyword can be used only with a single base axis variable.

NAME 'label'   *Assign this label to the base axis.* The base axis label is either the first BASE AXIS= specification or follows the NAME keyword anywhere else in the specification field. This label can be up to 40 characters long and must be enclosed in apostrophes or quotation marks.

For example, to label the base axis and to give the divisions your own labels rather than the value labels, specify

```
BARCHART      PLOT=MEAN(TENURE) WITH JOBGRADE BY SHIFT/
              FORMAT=HORIZONTAL,FRAME,FANCY/
              TITLE='CHICAGO HOME FURNISHING'
                    'Employee Tenure — Sales Department'/
              FOOTNOTE='As of December 1980'/
              COMMENT='G.Wong, D.P.'/
●             BASE AXIS='Job Category' LABELED 'Salesclerks'
●                   'Supervisors' 'Managers'/
```

The effect of altering the default base axis labels is shown in Figure 4.35.

The alternative method of specifying a base axis label would be simply to use the NAME keyword, as in

```
              BASE AXIS=LABELED 'Salesclerks' 'Supervisors' 'Managers'
                  NAME'Job Category'/
```

When you specify your own labels for a complex base axis specification, you must follow the order in which new categories are generated for cross-products and you must account for the space between multiple variables on the base axis. For cross-products, the new categories are generated with the first variable's values rotating slowest. For example, the specification WITH STORE*JOBGRADE generates six categories, STORE=1 and JOBGRADE=1, STORE=1 and JOBGRADE=2, STORE=1 and JOBGRADE=3, STORE=2 and JOBGRADE=1, etc. For multiple variable specifications, you must add a label, usually ' ', for the space between the separate base axis variables. Take, for example, the specification

```
BARCHART        PLOT=MEAN(TENURE) WITH JOBGRADE,DIVISION BY SHIFT/
                BASE AXIS=LABELED 'Salesclerks' 'Supervisors' 'Managers'
                        ' ' 'Carpeting' 'Appliances' 'Furniture' 'Hardware'/
```

The blank label accounts for the blank space on the base axis between JOBGRADE and DIVISION (see Figure 4.30).

Figure 4.30   A Multiple Variable Bar Chart

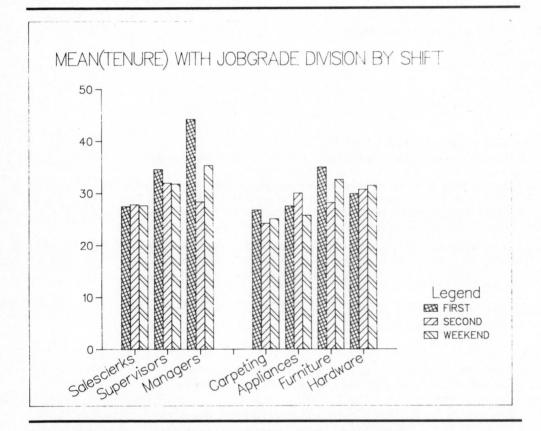

4.31   Specifying the Side Axis: The SIDE AXIS Subcommand

The SIDE AXIS subcommand defines the label and scale of the side axis, which is always parallel to the bars regardless of whether the chart is vertical or horizontal. The first specification can be an optional axis label of up to 40 characters in quotation marks or apostrophes according to the rules described in Section 4.9. This label can be assigned alternatively following the NAME keyword documented below. The remainder of the SIDE AXIS specification defines the scale and the reference according to the following keywords:

LINEAR*	*Divide the side axis on a linear scale.*
LOG	*Divide the side axis on a logarithmic scale.* Overrides LINEAR.
RANGE min,max	*Use these values for the scale.* The minimum and maximum default to the lowest and highest values resulting from the function part of the PLOT subcommand. These values may not be the exact scale limitations, but are used to fit an appropriate scale. RANGE does not limit the bars, so it is possible for a bar to extend beyond the limits of the chart.
ROOT value	*Extend the bars to either side of this value.* This is used to create a "hanging" bar chart. The root value must be within RANGE if specified. The default root value is the same as the minimum. A reference line is drawn through the root value unless REFERENCE specifies a different value.

REFERENCE value   *Draw a line through this value perpendicular to the bars.* The reference value must be within RANGE if specified.

NAME 'label'   *Assign this label to the side axis.* The side axis label is either the first SIDE AXIS= specification or follows the NAME keyword anywhere else in the specification field. This label can be up to 40 characters long and must be enclosed in apostrophes or quotation marks.

For example, to label the side axis, provide your own range, and provide a reference line at the mean value for the data, specify

```
BARCHART      PLOT=MEAN(TENURE) WITH JOBGRADE BY SHIFT/
              FORMAT=HORIZONTAL,FRAME,FANCY/
              TITLE='CHICAGO HOME FURNISHING'
                    'Employee Tenure - Sales Department'/
              FOOTNOTE='As of December 1980'/
              COMMENT='G.Wong, D.P.'/
              BASE AXIS='Job Category' LABELED 'Salesclerks'
                       'Supervisors' 'Managers'/
              SIDE AXIS='Mean Tenure in Months'
                       RANGE 0,50 REFERENCE 29.7/
```

See the plot in Figure 4.35 for the results of this specification.

Hanging bar charts are particularly useful when you want to emphasize differences from some particular value. For example, to show how much on the average people deviated from the mean length of employment for the company, specify

```
BARCHART      PLOT=MEAN(TENURE) WITH JOBGRADE BY SHIFT/
              FORMAT=FRAME/
              BASE AXIS=LABELED 'Salesclerks' 'Supervisors' 'Managers'
                       NAME'Job Category'/
              SIDE AXIS=ROOT 27.9 NAME 'Deviations from mean tenure'/
```

See the plot generated by this command in Figure 4.31.

Figure 4.31   A Hanging Bar Chart

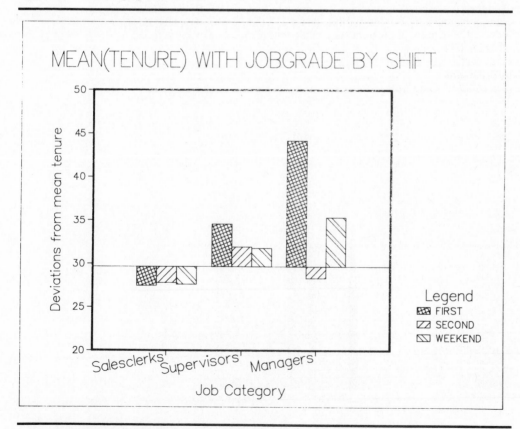

4.32 Specifying Legends:
The LEGEND TITLE and LEGEND LABELS Subcommands

To reformat the legend that appears to the right of the bar chart describing the bar sets, use the LEGEND LABEL subcommand to provide a title of up to 20 characters enclosed in quotation marks or apostrophes according to the rules described in Section 4.9. The default title is

LEGEND. To provide your own labels for the categories of the control variable or variables or multiple functions, use the LEGEND LABELS subcommand. These labels can be up to 20 characters, also enclosed in apostrophes. For a single function and a single BY variable, the control variable's value labels are used by default; and if there are no value labels, the variable name followed by the value is used. For multiple functions and/or multiple control variables, combinations of the function keyword, value labels, and the variable name followed by the value are used. When the PLOT specification is complicated, however, you should probably provide your own labels, according to the order described in Section 4.26 for a cross-products control variable. If you have specified multiple functions, the functions rotate slowest.

If you provide your own legend labels, specify them as BARCHART displays them in the bar sets, left- to-right in a horizontal chart and bottom-to-top in a vertical chart. This order corresponds to ascending value order in the case of simple control variable specifications, or in the order the categories are generated in complex plot specifications. For example, to title the legend box and provide your own labels for the control variable SHIFT, specify

```
BARCHART        PLOT=MEAN(TENURE) WITH JOBGRADE BY SHIFT/
                FORMAT=HORIZONTAL,FRAME,FANCY/
                TITLE='CHICAGO HOME FURNISHING'
                     'Employee Tenure - Sales Department'/
                FOOTNOTE='As of December 1980'/
                COMMENT='G.Wong, D.P.'/
                BASE AXIS='Job Category' LABELED 'Salesclerks'
                     'Supervisors' 'Managers'/
                SIDE AXIS='Mean Tenure in Months'
                     RANGE 0,50 REFERENCE 29.7/
                LEGEND TITLE='Shift'/
                LEGEND LABELS='Day' 'Evening' 'Weekend'/
```

4.33 Establishing Patterns:
The ORDER Subcommand in BARCHART

If you do not enter a COLORS subcommand overriding the default of 0 additional colors (Section 4.34), the ORDER and FORMAT subcommands control the order of patterns BARCHART uses for the bars. The patterns and their corresponding numbers are shown in Figure 4.33. By default, patterns are applied in the ascending numerical order that the bars in a set are drawn. For sets of bars generated by cross-products, the patterns apply to the new categories in the same order as the legend labels discussed in Section 4.32.

Figure 4.33   The BARCHART Patterns

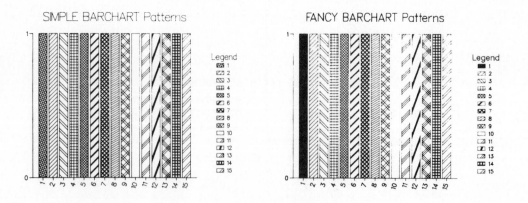

To choose your own patterns, use the ORDER subcommand to specify the corresponding numbers in variable value order for single control variables; or in generated order for complex plot specifications. For example, if you want patterns 1, 5, and 9 applied to the set of bars representing variable SHIFT, specify

```
BARCHART        PLOT=MEAN(TENURE) WITH JOBGRADE BY SHIFT/
                FORMAT=HORIZONTAL,FRAME,FANCY/
                TITLE='CHICAGO HOME FURNISHING'
                     'Employee Tenure - Sales Department'/
                FOOTNOTE='As of December 1980'/
                COMMENT='G.Wong, D.P.'/
                BASE AXIS='Job Category' LABELED 'Salesclerks'
                     'Supervisors' 'Managers'/
                SIDE AXIS='Mean Tenure in Months'
                     RANGE 0,50 REFERENCE 29.7/
                LEGEND TITLE='Shift'/
                LEGEND LABELS='Day' 'Evening' 'Weekend'/
                ORDER=1,5,9/
```

Enter pattern numbers from 1 to 15 for the bars you want to alter, even if you might be respecifying the default value for a particular bar. If you specify fewer pattern numbers than there are bars in each set, the remaining bars have the default patterns in the original sequence. If you specify more, the remainder are not used (up to a maximum of 15). The effect of choosing a different pattern is shown in Figure 4.35. To select the same pattern for different bars in a set, repeat the order number.

4.34 Establishing Colors: The COLORS Subcommand in BARCHART

To produce color plots, you must know how many colors the device supports in addition to black. A black and white device supports 0 additional colors, a four-pen plotter supports 3 additional colors. The default specification for the COLORS subcommand is 0.

If you intend to produce your bar chart on a four-color device, to take advantage of the three additional colors, specify

```
COLORS=3/
```

If you specify more than 0 colors, BARCHART uses the additional colors to draw the bars in a set, generating patterns in an expanded order compared to that documented in Section 4.33. To determine the color/pattern associated with a given ORDER number, generate a matrix of order numbers with colors as the rows and patterns as the columns. For example, if you have COLORS=3, your matrix looks like the second matrix in Table 4.14. Note that pattern 1 is solid only for FORMAT=FANCY. Therefore, if you want the bars to begin with solid colors, you must request a FANCY plot (see Section 4.27).

For instance, look at the FANCY order of black and white patterns shown in Figure 4.33. Assume that you have three additional colors that correspond to red, green, and blue and that ORDER is left to the default order. The first bar in a set is drawn with the first additional color and the first pattern, thus making it solid red. The second and third bars in a set are solid green and solid blue respectively. The fourth, fifth, and sixth bars are drawn with red, green, and blue stripes respectively according to pattern 2. However, specifying ORDER=1,2,3,13,14,15 generates the same first three solid color bars, but selects pattern 5 for the fourth, fifth, and sixth bars (see Table 4.14). Therefore, on a color device, to predict the display pattern of a bar, you must know the order of the bar, the number and order of the additional colors, and the order of the patterns (and whether the plot is FANCY or SIMPLE).

You can specify the same pattern number in the ORDER subcommand if COLORS is greater than 0, but you must do it from your matrix of order numbers based on color and pattern (see Table 4.14). For example, with ORDER=1,2,1,2 and COLORS=2 (e.g., red and green), the first four bars would be solid red, solid green, solid red, solid green respectively (for FORMAT=FANCY).

4.35 Handling Missing Values: The MISSING Subcommand in BARCHART

By default, BARCHART does not include a case in calculating the set of bars within a base variable category if the case has missing values on the variable being plotted, the control variable, or the independent variables. You control missing value treatment by using the MISSING subcommand with one of the following keyword specifications.

BARWISE*   *Omit cases with missing values on the variable used in the bar being produced.* If you specify multiple variables in the function, WITH, or BY parts of the PLOT subcommand, cases are examined for missing values for each variable independently.

PLOTWISE   *Omit cases with missing values on any variable named in the PLOT subcommand.* Bars of the same pattern produced from multiple variable specifications are based on the same cases.

NONE   *Include all cases regardless of missing values.*

If you want BARCHART to ignore missing data declarations for all variables specified in the PLOT subcommand, use keyword NONE. For example, clerical and other staff were omitted from the bar chart shown in Figure 4.3, perhaps to separate support personnel from the rest of the staff. To include them in the final display, specify

```
BARCHART        PLOT=MEAN(TENURE) WITH JOBGRADE BY SHIFT/
                FORMAT=HORIZONTAL,FRAME,FANCY/
                TITLE='CHICAGO HOME FURNISHING'
                     'Employee Tenure - Sales Department'/
                FOOTNOTE='As of December 1980'/
                COMMENT='G.Wong, D.P.'/
                BASE AXIS='Job Category' LABELED 'Salesclerks'
                     'Supervisors' 'Managers' 'Support'/
                SIDE AXIS='Mean Tenure in Months'
                     RANGE 0,50 REFERENCE 29.6/
                LEGEND TITLE='Shift'/
                LEGEND LABELS='Day' 'Evening' 'Weekend'/
                ORDER=1,5,9/
                MISSING=NONE/
```

The plot produced by this command is shown in Figure 4.35. The additional base axis category label and the different reference value were specified to account for the inclusion of the missing value. If these additions were not specified, the base axis category label would have defaulted to the value label and the reference line describing the grand mean would not have been correct for the full set of cases in the chart.

Figure 4.35   An Enhanced Bar Chart

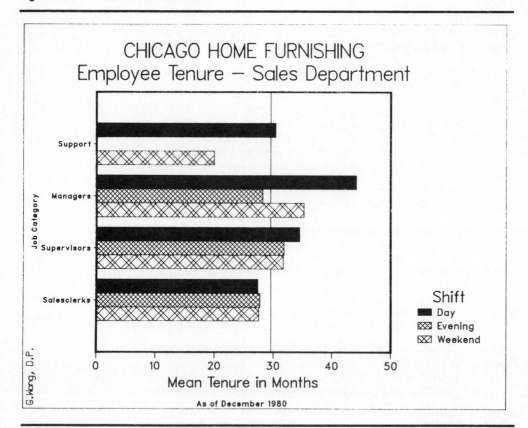

The difference between BARWISE and PLOTWISE missing value treatments arises only if you specify more than one variable in any part of the PLOT subcommand, not if you specify only single variables or cross-products. That is, if you specify

```
BARCHART        PLOT=MEAN(TENURE) WITH JOBGRADE,DIVISION/
```

a chart is produced first for JOBGRADE with cases being omitted if they have missing data for job grade or tenure, a second chart is produced on the same base axis for DIVISION with cases omitted with missing division or tenure information, etc. Instead, if you specify

```
BARCHART        PLOT=MEAN(TENURE) WITH JOBGRADE,DIVISION/
                MISSING=PLOTWISE/
```

the two charts are produced with cases omitted if they are missing data on either of the two WITH variables or TENURE.

4.36 Multiple PLOT Subcommands for BARCHART

More than one PLOT subcommand can be specified in a BARCHART command. This is helpful particularly when some attributes are common to all plots and others are specific to each plot. Since a second and subsequent PLOT subcommand returns all other subcommands to their defaults, you either have to respecify all attributes following each PLOT subcommand or you can establish your own defaults and respecify only unique attributes. By specifying the keyword DEFAULT before any of the attribute subcommands FORMAT, TITLE, FOOTNOTE, COMMENT, X AXIS, Y AXIS, LEGEND TITLE, LEGEND LABELS, ORDER, COLOR, or MISSING, you establish what the default specifications are for the duration of the BARCHART command.

For example, you might want to add a PLOT command to the example shown in Section 4.35 in order to generate a bar chart of mean salaries. If you simply enter a PLOT subcommand substituting SALARY for TENURE following the last subcommand affecting the previous plot, the bar chart for the variable specified will look very much like the plot shown in Figure 4.23 since all other subcommands return to defaults. A better approach is to decide which of the subcommands for the first PLOT are also applicable to the second, and then make those the defaults. All other subcommands specific to the second plot can then be specified. For example, the following command produces both the plot shown in 4.35 and the one shown in 4.36.

```
BARCHART     PLOT=MEAN(TENURE) WITH JOBGRADE BY SHIFT/
             DEFAULT FORMAT=HORIZONTAL,FRAME,FANCY/
             TITLE='CHICAGO HOME FURNISHING'
                    'Employee Tenure — Sales Department'/
             DEFAULT FOOTNOTE='As of December 1980'/
             COMMENT='G.Wong, D.P.'/
             DEFAULT BASE AXIS='Job Category' LABELED 'Salesclerks'
                    'Supervisors' 'Managers' 'Support'/
             SIDE AXIS='Mean Tenure in Months'
                    RANGE 0,50 REFERENCE 29.6/
             DEFAULT LEGEND TITLE='Shift'/
             DEFAULT LEGEND LABELS='Day' 'Evening' 'Weekend'/
             DEFAULT ORDER=1,5,9/
             DEFAULT MISSING=NONE/
             PLOT=MEAN(SALARY) WITH JOBGRADE BY SHIFT/
             TITLE='CHICAGO HOME FURNISHING'
                    'Employee Salaries — Sales Department'/
             SIDE AXIS='Mean Yearly Salary' REFERENCE 15300/
```

Figure 4.36   The Plot from the Second PLOT Subcommand

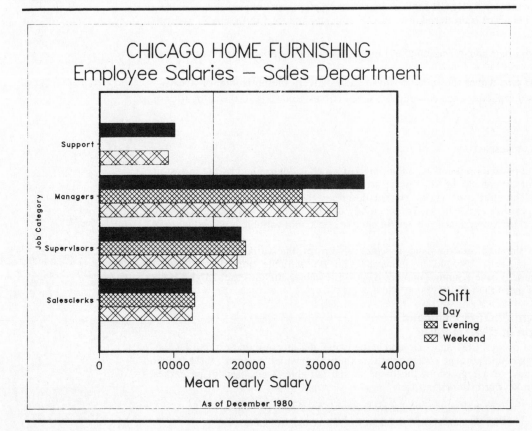

If you want the same plot quality and format for the second PLOT subcommand, the first subcommand you want to establish as the default is FORMAT. Since the date produced, the base variable, and the control variable are the same, the FOOTNOTE, BASE AXIS, LEGEND TITLE, LEGEND LABELS, and ORDER specifications apply to both plots. However the title should change to reflect the change in content. The comment can be allowed to return to the default null string. Finally, since you want the other staff included in both bar charts, the MISSING=NONE specification should also apply to both plots.

Since you want to specify a different side axis label and a different reference line, you specify SIDE AXIS following the second PLOT subcommand. Therefore, the plot produced by the second PLOT subcommand (shown in Figure 4.36) looks very much like the first one (shown in Figure 4.35).

4.37   OPERATION OF PROCEDURE LINECHART

The LINECHART command must include at least one PLOT subcommand to identify the function (count, percent, mean, regression, etc.) and to name the variable or variables to be plotted. In addition, LINECHART includes the FORMAT subcommand to control plot quality and contents; TITLE, FOOTNOTE, and COMMENT used for annotation; X AXIS and Y AXIS used to label and define the axes; the CURVES subcommand used to define the way points are connected with or without markers; LEGEND TITLE and LEGEND LABELS used to provide a title and labels for the line chart legend; COLORS and ORDER used to control colors, line patterns and markers, and shade patterns; and MISSING for selecting the missing value treatment. The SAVE subcommand, which allows you to save a file for input to the TELL-A-GRAF package, is documented in Section 4.58. Subcommand keywords are followed in most cases by an optional equals sign and by specifications, and are separated from other subcommands by a slash. Subcommands and their specifications are discussed beginning with the next section.

More than one PLOT subcommand can be specified in a LINECHART command. Unless otherwise altered, all subcommand specifications return to defaults with each new PLOT subcommand. You can establish your own defaults by prefacing the subcommand keyword with DEFAULT, thus eliminating the need for repetitive specifications. Multiple PLOT specifications are discussed in Section 4.54.

4.38   The PLOT Subcommand for LINECHART

The PLOT subcommand for LINECHART defines the function and names the variable or variables for which a line chart is produced. The PLOT subcommand for LINECHART is divided into three parts:

- The required *function part* names the function (and the dependent variable when appropriate) that determines the vertical or *Y axis*.
- The required *WITH part* names the variable whose values govern the horizontal or *X axis*.
- The optional *BY part* separates each curve into a set of curves according to the categories of a *control variable*.

In the example

```
LINECHART     PLOT=MEAN(ATTEND) WITH AGE BY SEX/
```

MEAN is the function plotted on the Y axis, the range of which is determined by the lowest and highest mean values of variable ATTEND (church attendance). AGE is the variable whose values are on the X axis. Therefore, the curve plotted describes the relationship between church attendance and the person's age. This curve is actually divided into two curves describing the relationship between church attendance and age for each sex since that variable is named in the BY part.

PLOT must be the first subcommand specified. None of the variables named can be alphanumeric; they must be recoded to numeric. The BY variable named need not be integer-valued, but should have a limited number of possible values. In any case, LINECHART cannot accommodate more than 15 curves on a line chart.

4.39   The Minimum PLOT Specification:
The Function and WITH Parts

The first required part of the PLOT subcommand is the name of a function that establishes the Y axis. If the function is a count, percent, or a proportion, there is no variable named. If the function is a mean, sum, values, or a regression, the name of the variable is enclosed in parentheses following the function keyword. Functions are

COUNT	*Plot the frequency of each value of the X axis variable.*
CCOUNT	*Plot the cumulative frequency of the X axis variable.*

PERCENT	*Plot the relative frequency of each value of the X axis variable.*
CPERCENT	*Plot the cumulative relative frequency of the X axis variable.*
PROPORTION	*Plot the proportion of each value of the X axis variable.*
CPROPORTION	*Plot the cumulative proportion of the X axis variable.*
MEAN(varname)	*Plot the means of the Y axis variable for values of the X axis variable.*
SMEAN(varname)	*Plot the standardized means of the Y axis variable.*
MEANSD(varname)	*Plot the mean plus and minus one standard deviation.* Functions MEANSD2 and MEANSD3 request the mean plus and minus two and three standard deviations respectively.
SUM(varname)	*Plot the sums of the Y axis variable for values of the X axis variable.*
CSUM(varname)	*Plot the cumulative sum of the X axis variable.*
VALUES(varname)	*Plot the values of the Y axis variable for values of the X axis variable.* This is a scatterplot, so the default is not to connect the points (see Section 4.49).
REG(varname)	*Plot the regression of Y on X.*
REGM90(varname)	*Plot the regression line and the 90 percent confidence interval for the mean.* Functions REGM95 and REGM99 request the regression line and the 95 and 99 percent confidence intervals for the mean.
REGI90(varname)	*Plot the regression line and the 90 percent confidence interval for an individual observation.* Functions REGI95 and REGI99 request the regression line and the 95 and 99 percent confidence intervals for an individual observation.

The mean and standard deviation plots (MEANSD, MEANSD2, MEANSD3) and the regression line with confidence intervals (REGM90, REGI90, REGM95, etc.) each generate at least three curves. If a control variable is specified, they generate three times the number of values of the control variable. The ORDER subcommand (Section 4.51) default is reset in order to make plus/minus standard deviation lines and upper/lower confidence bounds identical in pattern and color. Override this default with caution.

Note that, if the X axis variable is continuous, there is no grouping for the mean functions (MEAN, SMEAN, MEANSD, etc.). Therefore the curves generated could look like a scatterplot with all points connected since each point is likely to be the mean for individual values of the X axis variable. If you want to group, use the SPSS RECODE command.

The function part is usually followed immediately by the keyword WITH and the name of the variable whose values determine the X axis. This completes the minimum required syntax of the PLOT subcommand in LINECHART. For example, to plot the mean salary with the length of time employees have been with the company, specify

```
LINECHART    PLOT=MEAN(SALARY) WITH TENURE/
```

The function selected is the MEAN and the dependent variable is SALARY. The X axis (independent) variable is TENURE, which is the length of time an employee has been with the company measured in months. The plot produced by this example is developed in the next section by adding a control variable.

4.40   Using a Control Variable: The BY Part
Adding a control variable is simply a matter of specifying the keyword BY followed by the control variable. For example, if you name JOBGRADE in the BY part, the curve describing the mean salary with tenure for the whole company is broken into several curves, one for each job grade.

```
♦ LINECHART    PLOT=MEAN(SALARY) WITH TENURE BY JOBGRADE/
```

The plot produced by this command is shown in Figure 4.4. It accepts defaults for all other LINECHART subcommands. To see this example fully developed as the discussion of altering the default specifications for the other subcommands progresses, pick up the discussion beginning with Section 4.44. To see the complete syntax possibilities for the PLOT subcommand, see the following sections on qualifying each variable named with a selector, on specifying multiple variables within each part, and on superimposing one line chart on top of another.

4.41   Specifying Selectors
Each variable named in the function, WITH, and BY parts of the PLOT subcommand can be followed by parentheses enclosing a selector which consists of a logical operator and a value or list of values, as in SHIFT(NE 3). Relational operators are LT, LE, EQ, NE, GE, and GT which mean respectively less than, less than or equal to, equal to, not equal to, greater than or equal to, and greater than. If you omit the logical operator, EQ is assumed. EQ and NE can be followed by a list of numbers where (EQ 1,2,3) means equal to 1, 2, or 3, and (NE 1,2,3) means not equal to 1, 2, and 3. All other operators are followed by a single value. If a case satisfies the condition, it is used in constructing the line chart specified.

For example, to produce a line chart of the mean salary with tenure for sales staff only, specify JOBGRADE(EQ 1) in the BY part. Or, since the EQ operator is the default, specify

```
LINECHART    PLOT=MEAN(SALARY) WITH TENURE BY JOBGRADE(1)/
```

This example is developed in Section 4.42.

To limit the same line chart to those with at least one year at the company, specify

```
LINECHART    PLOT=MEAN(SALARY) WITH TENURE(GE 12) BY JOBGRADE(1)/
```

If you want the line chart to be limited to those who have a salary of $15,000 or above, specify

```
LINECHART    PLOT=MEAN(SALARY(GE 15000)) WITH TENURE BY JOBGRADE/
```

Since the variable named in the function part is already enclosed in parentheses, the selector for that variable must be included within those parentheses as shown in this example.

4.42 Specifying Multiple Functions

Multiple variable specifications are prohibited in the WITH and BY parts of the PLOT subcommand for LINECHART. For an alternative, see Section 4.43 on superimposing line charts.

More than one function can be specified in the PLOT subcommand and more than one variable can be specified for the same function. For instance, the specification

```
LINECHART    PLOT=MEAN(SALARY) VALUES(SALARY) WITH TENURE BY JOBGRADE(2)/
```

produces one curve for the mean salary superimposed on a scatterplot of the salary values (drawn in that order). The plot is limited to a single category of JOBGRADE. This plot is shown in Figure 4.54.

You can also name more than one variable for the same function. With either multiple functions or multiple variables for the same function, be careful that scales of the variables are comparable and that the ranges produced by the functions are similar. That is, you can specify that the mean of two dependent variables be plotted in the same line chart, but unless the scales of the two variables are the same or similar, the scales may be badly matched.

The result of multiple specifications in the function part is represented in multiple curves in the same way that multiple curves are drawn for values of a control variable. Each additional variable named or function specified increases the amount of information contained in a single line chart and, therefore, increases the detail. In any case, you cannot put more than 15 curves on one chart. Complicated line charts can become too cluttered to be readable. Consider the alternative of multiple plots discussed in Section 4.54, particularly since you have the possibility of putting them on the same page when you use the postprocessor option discussed in Section 4.59.

4.43 Superimposing Line Charts

You can repeat the set of function, WITH, and optional BY parts within a single PLOT subcommand for LINECHART in order to superimpose multiple line charts on the same plot. For example, if you have both measures of employee tenure with the company and tenure in a particular job grade (variable JTENURE), you may want to compare the two measures with salary levels on the same plot.

```
LINECHART    PLOT=MEAN(SALARY) WITH TENURE BY JOBGRADE(2)
             MEAN(SALARY) WITH JTENURE BY JOBGRADE(2)/
```

Note that the scale calculated for both the X and Y axes are based upon the results of both line charts. Therefore, the variables named in both the function and WITH parts of the two specifications must be similar. Note also that the BY variable specification affects only the function and WITH specifications immediately preceding it. That is, if the first BY specification did not appear in the example above, only the plot of mean salary with JTENURE would be limited to cases within the second job category.

4.44 The FORMAT Subcommand for LINECHART

Specify the display quality and format of the line charts using the FORMAT subcommand. Quality refers to the type of characters used, the density of certain lines drawn, and the first shade pattern. For line charts, format options include a frame around the chart, grid lines within the chart, and shading below the curves. If one of the following keywords is preceded by NO, the opposite effect takes place.

SIMPLE*   *Produce a simple plot.* Single stroke characters, single curves, and solid grids are drawn, and shade pattern 1 is cross-hatched instead of solid (Section 4.50). This is equivalent to NO FANCY.

FANCY   *Produce a fancy plot.* Double stroke characters, dense curves, and dashed grid lines are drawn, and pattern 1 is solid. This is equivalent to NO SIMPLE.

FRAME   *Draw a frame around the chart.* The X and Y axes lines are completed around the chart. The default is NO FRAME.

XGRID	*Draw grid lines perpendicular to the X axis.*
YGRID	*Draw grid lines perpendicular to the Y axis.*
GRID	*Draw grid lines in both directions.* The default is NO GRID.
SHADE	*Stack the curves and shade between them.* This is similar to a stacked bar chart. The curves must have identical ranges. The default is NO SHADE. See the example in Section 4.57.
DUMP	*Dump the data values on the raw output unit.* Each curve (or set of scatterplot values) is a set of data and each data set is preceded by a record containing CURVE *nn* starting in column two, where *nn* is the number of the curve. The data set is composed of data pairs of X axis value and Y axis value written in (1X,6G13.6) format. The default is NO DUMP.

Thus, the default line chart quality is SIMPLE, NO FRAME, NO GRID, and NO SHADE as can be seen in any of the previous examples. To frame the chart started in Section 4.40 and produce it with increased quality, specify

```
   LINECHART    PLOT=MEAN(SALARY) WITH TENURE BY JOBGRADE/
 ♦              FORMAT=FRAME,FANCY/
```

The effects of these format changes are shown in Figure 4.53.

4.45 The TITLE, FOOTNOTE, and COMMENT Subcommands for LINECHART

The three subcommands that affect the text displayed along with your line chart are TITLE for putting lines of text above the chart, FOOTNOTE below the chart, and COMMENT vertically along the lower left edge of the plot (COMMENT). They are specified according to the rules describe in Section 4.9.

As shown in the previous figures, the default title for a line chart is taken from the PLOT subcommand. The default footnote and comment are null. For example, if you want a different title and need a footnote, specify

```
   LINECHART    PLOT=MEAN(SALARY) WITH TENURE BY JOBGRADE/
                FORMAT=FRAME,FANCY/
 ♦              TITLE='CHICAGO HOME FURNISHING'
 ♦                    'Employee Salary Analysis – Sales Department'/
 ♦              FOOTNOTE='As of December 1980'/
```

The effects of these subcommands are shown in Figure 4.53.

4.46 Controlling the Axes and the Curves

You can control how the X and Y axes are scaled and labeled with the X AXIS and Y AXIS subcommands. The CURVES subcommand is used to specify how curves are to be connected with or without markers. With the LEGEND TITLE and LEGEND LABELS subcommands, you can specify your own title and labels for the control variable or variables. Finally, you can control the patterns and markers or colors chosen to distinguish the different curves (and shading) using the ORDER and COLORS subcommands.

4.47 Specifying the X Axis: The X AXIS Subcommand

By default, LINECHART does not provide a X axis label and the axis is linear with no division labels (see Figure 4.4 for an example). You can specify an axis label of up to 40 characters within apostrophes or quotation marks (according to rules described in Section 4.45) as the first specification in the X AXIS subcommand or following the keyword NAME documented below. To control the X axis divisions, use one of the following keywords.

LINEAR*	*Divide the X axis linearly.* LINECHART computes the division marks based on the range of the X axis variable.
LOG	*Divide the X axis on a logarithmic scale.* Overrides LINEAR.
RANGE min,max	*Use these values for the scale.* The minimum and maximum default to the lowest and highest values of the X axis variable. These values may not be the exact scale limitations, but are used to fit an appropriate scale. RANGE can be specified only with LINEAR or LOG scales.
LABELED	*Label the X axis.* If no labels are provided, LINECHART labels the X axis divisions with the value labels. If a value label is not available, the division is labeled with the variable name followed by an equals sign and the value. You can provide your own labels as strings of up to 16 characters enclosed in apostrophes or quotation marks following the LABELED keyword. Overrides LINEAR.

MONTHLY	*Give the X axis divisions monthly labels.* JAN corresponds to values 1, 13, 25, etc.; FEB corresponds to 2, 14, etc. Overrides LINEAR.
REFERENCE value	*Draw a vertical reference line through this value.* The value specified must be within the user specified RANGE.
NAME 'label'	*Assign this label to the X axis.* The X axis label is either the first X AXIS= specification or follows the NAME keyword anywhere else in the specification field. This label can be up to 40 characters long and must be enclosed in apostrophes or quotation marks.

For example, to label the X axis and to specify a reference line at the mean value for TENURE, specify

```
LINECHART    PLOT=MEAN(SALARY) WITH TENURE BY JOBGRADE/
             FORMAT=FRAME,FANCY/
             TITLE='CHICAGO HOME FURNISHING'
                  'Employee Salary Analysis - Sales Department'/
             FOOTNOTE='As of December 1980'/
             X AXIS='Employment Tenure in Months' REFERENCE 29.7/
```

The effects of adding a label and a reference line to the X axis is shown in Figure 4.53.

When you request LABELED or MONTHLY for the X axis, LINECHART may not be able to add the labels if the number of values across the axis is too great, otherwise they would be too tiny. In this case, the axis is forced to LINEAR.

4.48 Specifying the Y Axis: The Y AXIS Subcommand

The Y AXIS subcommand defines the label and scale of the Y axis. The first specification can be an optional axis label of up to 40 characters in quotation marks or apostrophes according to the same rule described in Section 4.45. This label can be specified alternatively following the NAME keyword documented below. The remainder of the Y AXIS specification defines the scale and the reference according to the following keywords:

LINEAR*	*Divide the Y axis on a linear scale.*
LOG	*Divide the Y axis on a logarithmic scale.* Overrides LINEAR.
RANGE min,max	*Use these values for the scale.* The minimum and maximum default to the lowest and highest values resulting from the function part of the PLOT subcommand. These values may not be the exact scale limitations, but are used to fit an appropriate scale. RANGE can be specified only with LINEAR or LOG axes.
REFERENCE value	*Draw a line through this value perpendicular to the Y axis.* The reference value must be within RANGE if specified.
NAME 'label'	*Assign this label to the Y axis.* The Y axis label is either the first Y AXIS= specification or follows the NAME keyword anywhere else in the specification field. This label can be up to 40 characters long and must be enclosed in apostrophes or quotation marks.

For example, to label the Y axis and provide a reference line at the mean salary for the whole company, specify

```
LINECHART    PLOT=MEAN(SALARY) WITH TENURE BY JOBGRADE/
             FORMAT=FRAME,FANCY/
             TITLE='CHICAGO HOME FURNISHING'
                  'Employee Salary Analysis - Sales Department'/
             FOOTNOTE='As of December 1980'/
             X AXIS='Employment Tenure in Months' REFERENCE 29.7/
             Y AXIS='Mean Salary' REFERENCE 15600/
```

See the plot in Figure 4.53 for the results of this specification.

4.49 Controlling the Curves: The CURVES Subcommand

Curves are drawn on the plot in a specific order. If they are the result of a BY (control) variable, they are generated in ascending value order for that variable (JOBGRADE=1 first, JOBGRADE =2 second, etc.). If they are the result of multiple functions or multiple variables for the same function, they are created as the functions or variables are specified left-to-right. If there are multiple specifications in the function part and there is a control variable, the function part rotates slowest. For example, in the specification

```
LINECHART    PLOT=MEAN(INCOME1,INCOME2) WITH EDUC BY SEX/
```

four curves are drawn: the first is the mean of INCOME1 for the first value of SEX, the second is the mean of INCOME1 for the second value of SEX, the third and fourth are the mean of INCOME2 for each value of SEX.

If the function is the mean with standard deviations or a regression line with confidence bounds, the mean or regression line is drawn first, then the plus standard deviation or the upper bound, then the minus standard deviation or the lower bound. Note that, in discussions of order, the VALUES function generates a "curve" in the normal order, even though lines are not drawn through the points.

You can follow the general rule that curves are drawn left-to-right as you specify functions and variables left-to-right in the PLOT subcommand. The same rule applies when more than one line chart is superimposed on the same plot.

You must know this order not only to assign patterns (see Section 4.51) or legend labels (Section 4.50) but to distinguish an individual curve or a subset of curves on the CURVES subcommand.

Use the CURVES subcommand to define the type of interpolation and the existence of marker sybols for each curve, for a subset of the curves, or for all curves. The first CURVES specification must be the keyword ALL or a number list indicating the curves you are specifying. The list is composed of integer numbers from 1 to the number of curves. You can use the keyword TO to specify a range, as in 2 TO 5. Any number not mentioned leaves the corresponding curve at its default. You can then control the curves with the following keywords.

STRAIGHT*   *Use a straight line to connect the data points.* This is the default for all functions except VALUES.

SPLINE   *Use a spline interpolation to connect the data points.*

STEP   *Draw the curve in steps centered on the data points.*

POINTS   *Don't connect the data points.* This is the default for the VALUES function.

MARKERS   *Place markers at every point on the curves.* The default specification is NO MARKERS for curves. Also by default, the function VALUES has markers since there is no curve. Keyword NO is used with MARKERS to turn off a user-defined default.

To define groups of curves, you can repeat the entire specification beginning with the number list. For example, if you prefer to have the first three curves connected with spline interpolated lines and the fourth connected in steps (anticipating inclusion of the fourth job grade in the final plot), specify

```
LINECHART      PLOT=MEAN(SALARY) WITH TENURE BY JOBGRADE/
               FORMAT=FRAME,FANCY/
               TITLE='CHICAGO HOME FURNISHING'
                    'Employee Salary Analysis – Sales Department'/
               FOOTNOTE='As of December 1980'/
               X AXIS='Employment Tenure in Months' REFERENCE 29.7/
               Y AXIS='Mean Salary' REFERENCE 15600/
               CURVES=1 TO 3 SPLINE, 4 STEP/
```

The curves drawn in this manner are shown in Figure 4.53.

4.50 Specifying Legends:
The LEGEND TITLE and LEGEND LABELS Subcommands

Use the LEGEND LABEL subcommand to provide a title for the legend box of up to 20 characters enclosed in quotation marks or apostrophes according to the rules described in Section 4.45. The default title is the word Legend. To provide your own labels for the categories of the control variable and/or to the multiple functions, use the LEGEND LABELS subcommand. These labels can be up to 20 characters, also enclosed in apostrophes. For a single function and a BY variable, the control variable's value labels are used by default; and if there are no value labels, the variable name followed by the value is used. For multiple functions and a control variable, combinations of the function keyword, value labels, and the variable name followed by the value are used. When the PLOT specification is complicated, however, you should probably provide your own labels, according to the order described in Section 4.49.

For example, to title the legend box and provide your own labels for the control variable JOBGRADE, specify

```
LINECHART      PLOT=MEAN(SALARY) WITH TENURE BY JOBGRADE/
               FORMAT=FRAME,FANCY/
               TITLE='CHICAGO HOME FURNISHING'
                    'Employee Salary Analysis – Sales Department'/
               FOOTNOTE='As of December 1980'/
               X AXIS='Employment Tenure in Months' REFERENCE 29.7/
               Y AXIS='Mean Salary' REFERENCE 15600/
               CURVES=1 TO 3 SPLINE, 4 STEP/
               LEGEND TITLE='Job Category'/
               LEGEND LABELS='Salesclerks' 'Supervisors'
                    'Managers' 'Support'/
```

The fourth legend label appears in the final plot shown in Figure 4.53 as a result of including the previously missing fourth category.

4.51 Establishing Patterns:
The ORDER Subcommand in LINECHART

If you do not enter a COLORS subcommand overriding the default of 0 additional colors (Section 4.52), the ORDER and FORMAT subcommands control the order of patterns and markers

LINECHART uses for curves or for the shading (see Section 4.44 for the SHADE specification in FORMAT). The default line patterns and the markers associated with them are shown in Figure 4.51a and the shade patterns are shown in Figure 4.51b. By default, curve or shade patterns are applied in the order curves are drawn on each plot, which is the order described in Section 4.49.

Figure 4.51a   The LINECHART Curve Patterns and Markers

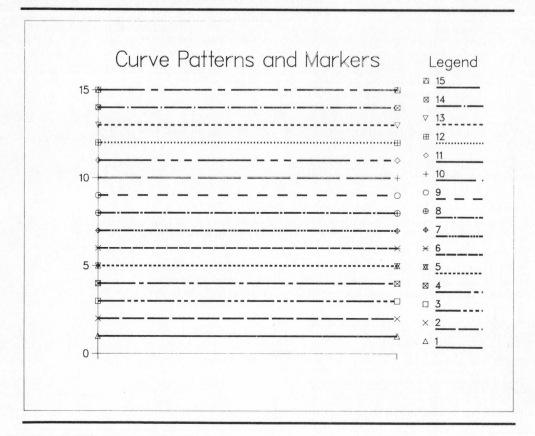

To choose your own curve patterns, use the ORDER subcommand to specify the corresponding pattern numbers in the order the curves are drawn. For example, if you want solid curve pattern 1 applied to the fourth curve representing the support staff for variable JOBGRADE and curve patterns 5, 6, and 7 applied to the first three categories, specify

```
LINECHART     PLOT=MEAN(SALARY) WITH TENURE BY JOBGRADE/
              FORMAT=FRAME,FANCY/
              TITLE='CHICAGO HOME FURNISHING'
                    'Employee Salary Analysis - Sales Department'/
              FOOTNOTE='As of December 1980'/
              X AXIS='Employment Tenure in Months' REFERENCE 29.7/
              Y AXIS='Mean Salary' REFERENCE 15600/
              CURVES=1 TO 3 SPLINE, 4 STEP/
              LEGEND TITLE='Job Category'/
              LEGEND LABELS='Salesclerks' 'Supervisors'
                            'Managers' 'Support'/
              ORDER=5,6,7,1/
```

Enter pattern numbers from 1 to 15 for the curves or shading you want to alter, even if you might be respecifying the default value for a particular curve. If you specify fewer pattern numbers than there are curves, the remaining curves have the default patterns in the original sequence. If you specify more, the remainder are not used (up to a maximum of 15). The effect of choosing a different pattern is shown in Figure 4.53. You can select the same pattern for different curves in a set by repeating its order number.

Use caution in overriding the default patterns when you are using any of the mean functions with standard deviations or the regression functions with confidence limits (Section 4.39). The default patterns are set so that the standard deviation curves and the confidence limits have the same pattern. If you want to override them, they are created following the mean curve or the regression curve, with the plus standard deviation or the upper confidence limit coming next.

You should also know something about the resolution of the final device you intend to use to produce the final plots. If the device has high resolution, you can use any curve pattern you want. If it has relatively low resolution, you may want to stay with the default patterns since they are chosen to be distinguishable on these kinds of devices.

Figure 4.51b   The LINECHART Shade Patterns

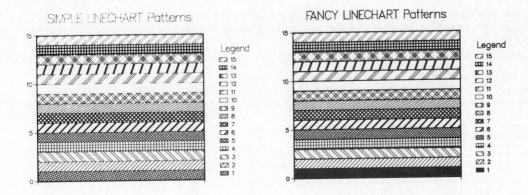

4.52   Establishing Colors:
The COLORS Subcommand in LINECHART

If you intend to produce your plots on a color device, you must know how many colors the device supports in addition to black. A black and white device supports 0 additional colors, a four-pen plotter supports 3 additional colors. The default specification for the COLORS subcommand is 0.

If you intend to produce your line chart on a four-color device, to take advantage of the three additional colors, specify

```
COLORS=3 /
```

If you specify more than 0 colors, LINECHART uses the additional colors to draw the curves and markers, generating patterns in an expanded order compared to that documented in Section 4.51. To determine the color/pattern associated with a given ORDER number, generate a matrix of order numbers with colors as the rows and patterns as the columns. For example, if you have COLORS=3, your matrix looks like the second matrix in Table 4.14.

For instance, look at the order of black and white line patterns and markers shown in Figure 4.33. Assume that you have three additional colors that correspond to red, green, and blue and that ORDER is left to the default order. The first curve is drawn with the first additional color and the first pattern, thus making it solid red with triangle markers if requested. The second and third curves are solid green and solid blue respectively. The fourth, fifth, and sixth curves are drawn with red, green, and blue dashed lines respectively according to pattern 2. However, specifying ORDER=1,2,3,13,14,15 generates the same first three solid color curves, but selects pattern 5 for the fourth, fifth, and sixth curves (see Table 4.14). Therefore, on a color device, to predict the display pattern of a curve, you must know the order of the curve, the number and order of the additional colors, and the order of the patterns and markers.

The same rules apply in the case of shaded line charts, except that you must also know whether the plot is FANCY or SIMPLE since the shade pattern 1 is solid for FANCY plots and cross-hatched for SIMPLE plots. To take full advantage of a color device, you probably want to request a FANCY plot for shaded line charts.

You can specify the same pattern number in the ORDER subcommand if COLORS is greater than 0, but you must do it from your matrix of order numbers based on color and pattern (see Table 4.14). For example, with ORDER=1,2,1,2 and COLORS=2 (e.g., red and green), the first four curves would be solid red, solid green, solid red, solid green respectively. The same would hold true for a FANCY color plot with shading.

4.53 Handling Missing Values: The MISSING Subcommand in LINECHART

By default, LINECHART does not include a case in calculating data points if the case has missing values on the variables involved in the particular curve. You can control missing value treatment by using the MISSING subcommand with one of the following keyword specifications.

LINEWISE* *Omit cases with missing values on the variable used in the curve being produced.* If you specify multiple variables or multiple functions in the function part of the PLOT subcommand, cases are examined for missing values for each variable independently. Also, if you superimpose line charts, cases are examined for each chart separately.

PLOTWISE *Omit cases with missing values on any variable named in the PLOT subcommand.* Line charts produced from multiple variable specifications or from superimposed line charts are based on the same cases.

NONE *Include all cases regardless of missing values.*

To tell LINECHART to ignore missing data declarations for all variables specified in the PLOT subcommand, use keyword NONE. For example, clerical and other staff were omitted from the line chart shown in Figure 4.4 to separate support personnel from the rest of the staff. To include them in the final display, specify

```
LINECHART      PLOT=MEAN(SALARY) WITH TENURE BY JOBGRADE/
               FORMAT=FRAME,FANCY/
               TITLE='CHICAGO HOME FURNISHING'
                 'Employee Salary Analysis - Sales Department'/
               FOOTNOTE='As of December 1980'/
               X AXIS='Employment Tenure in Months' REFERENCE 29.6/
               Y AXIS='Mean Salary' REFERENCE 15300/
               CURVES=1 TO 3 SPLINE, 4 STEP/
               LEGEND TITLE='Job Category'/
               LEGEND LABELS='Salesclerks' 'Supervisors'
                 'Managers' 'Support'/
               ORDER=5,6,7,1/
               MISSING=NONE/
```

Figure 4.53   An Enhanced Line Chart

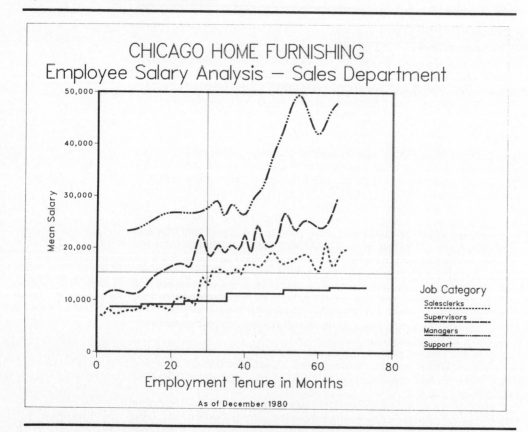

The plot produced by this command is shown in Figure 4.53. Note that the additional curve, the fourth legend category label, the different reference values, and the additional pattern were

specified to account for the inclusion of the missing value. If these additions were not specified, the curve would have been connect with a straight line, the legend category label would have defaulted to the value label, and the pattern would have been pattern 5 from Figure 4.51a instead of the solid pattern selected with number 1. The reference lines describing the means would not have been correct for the full set of cases in the chart.

4.54   Multiple PLOT Subcommands for LINECHART

More than one PLOT subcommand can be specified in a LINECHART command. This is helpful particularly when some attributes are common to all plots. However, some attributes may be specific to each plot. Since a second and subsequent PLOT subcommand returns all other subcommands to their defaults, you either have to respecify all attributes following each PLOT subcommand or you can establish your own defaults and respecify only unique attributes. By specifying the keyword DEFAULT before any of the attribute subcommands FORMAT, TITLE, FOOTNOTE, COMMENT, X AXIS, Y AXIS, CURVE, LEGEND TITLE, LEGEND LABELS, ORDER, COLOR, or MISSING, you establish what the default specifications are for the duration of the LINECHART command.

For example, in the complete example shown in Section 4.53, you might want to add the line chart shown in Section 4.42 showing a multiple function specification. You can decide which of the subcommands for the first PLOT are also applicable to the second, and then make those the defaults. All other subcommands specific to the second plot can then be specified or allowed to return to system defaults. For example, the following command produces both the plot shown in 4.53 and the one shown in 4.54.

```
LINECHART        PLOT=MEAN(SALARY) WITH TENURE BY JOBGRADE/
                 DEFAULT FORMAT=FRAME,FANCY/
                 DEFAULT TITLE='CHICAGO HOME FURNISHING'
                    'Employee Salary Analysis - Sales Department'/
                 DEFAULT FOOTNOTE='As of December 1980'/
                 DEFAULT X AXIS='Employment Tenure in Months' REFERENCE 29.6/
                 DEFAULT Y AXIS='Mean Salary' REFERENCE 15300/
                 CURVES=1 TO 3 SPLINE, 4 STEP/
                 LEGEND TITLE='Job Category'/
                 LEGEND LABELS='Salesclerks' 'Supervisors'
                    'Managers' 'Support'/
                 ORDER=5,6,7,1/
                 MISSING=NONE/
                 PLOT=MEAN(SALARY) VALUES(SALARY) WITH TENURE BY JOBGRADE(2)/
```

Figure 4.54   The Plot from the Second PLOT Subcommand

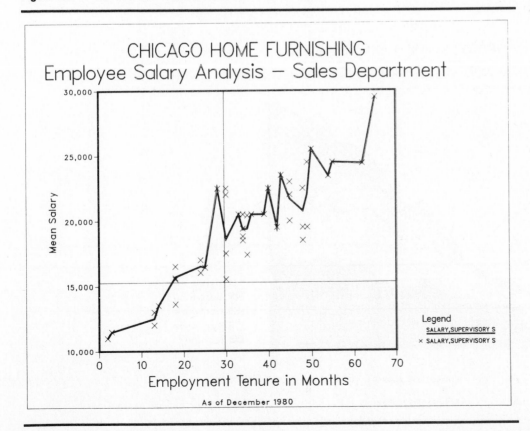

If you want the plot quality and format the same for the second PLOT subcommand, the first subcommand you want to establish as the default is FORMAT. Since the company, the date produced, and the X and Y axes variables are the same, the TITLE, FOOTNOTE, X AXIS, and Y AXIS specifications apply to both plots. However the pattern order and the legend should change to reflect the change in content. In fact, you can simply let them revert to defaults. Finally, since you want only supervisors (JOBGRADE=2) included in the chart, you don't need the MISSING=NONE specification and can let it return to the default LINEWISE.

4.55 LINECHART Applications

LINECHART applications are probably more varied than either PIECHART or BARCHART, particularly because of the additional functions that are available and because you can superimpose many curves on the same chart. Also, a single line chart can vary from a single curve, a scatterplot, and a shaded line chart. While it is impossible to prevent the iteration process necessary to arrive at a readable and informative plot by giving you all possible examples, you may obtain a better idea of what you want and how to get it through the examples that follow.

4.56 Plotting Regression Lines

To produce a regression line and confidence intervals superimposed on a scatterplot, the considerations are the same as for any of the multiple curve functions and for superimposing one plot on another. That is, three curves are produced for the regression function: the regression line, the upper confidence bound, and the lower confidence bound. If you want the regression line superimposed on a scatterplot, you must use the VALUES function. For example, to produce a regression line and confidence bounds for the mean salary of supervisory staff members based on their tenure with the company, superimposed on a scatterplot, specify

```
SELECT IF      (JOBGRADE EQ 2)
LINECHART      PLOT VALUES(SALARY) REGM95(SALARY) WITH TENURE/
               FORMAT FRAME,FANCY/
               TITLE 'CHICAGO HOME FURNISHING'
                     'Employee Salary Analysis - Sales Department'
                     'Supervisory Staff'/
               X AXIS 'Employment Tenure in Months'/
               Y AXIS 'Yearly Salary'/
```

Figure 4.56   A Regression Line with Confidence Bounds

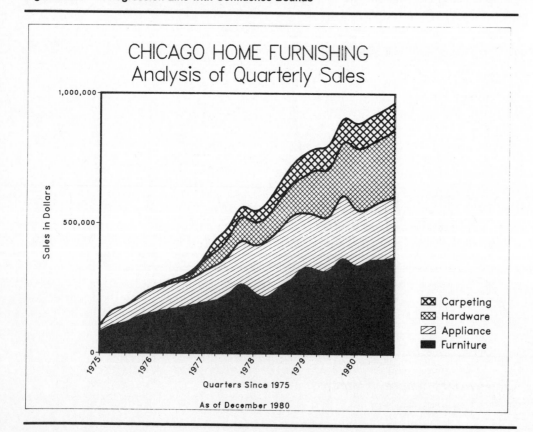

4.57 Shaded Line Charts

To produce a shaded line chart with two or more curves, the X axis ranges and the Y axis scales must be identical. For instance, the plot shown in Figure 4.53 cannot be shaded since the minimum and maximum values of TENURE vary for the four job categories. In addition, it wouldn't make any sense to stack the mean salary values on the Y axis.

A better example is found in another data file for the same company where sales figures are recorded for the four divisions in variables FURN, APPL, HARD, and CARP for each quarter since January, 1975. Since the hardware and carpeting divisions were opened up in 1976, sales values of 0 were entered for previous quarters. To produce a plot of gross receipts across quarters subdivided into the four divisions, specify

```
LINECHART       PLOT SUM(FURN,APPL,HARD,CARP) WITH QUARTER/
                FORMAT FRAME,FANCY,SHADE/
                TITLE 'CHICAGO HOME FURNISHING'
                      'Analysis of Quarterly Sales'/
                FOOTNOTE 'As of December 1980'/
                Y AXIS 'Sales in Dollars'/
                X AXIS 'Quarters Since 1975'
                      LABELED '1975' ' ' ' ' ' ' '1976' ' ' ' ' ' '
                      '1977' ' ' ' ' ' ' '1978' ' ' ' ' ' ' '1979'
                      ' ' ' ' ' ' '1980' ' ' ' ' ' /
                LEGEND TITLE /
                LEGEND LABELS 'Furniture' 'Appliance'
                              'Hardware' 'Carpeting'/
                CURVES ALL SPLINE/
                ORDER 1,8,5,7/
```

Figure 4.57a   A Shaded Line Chart—Sales

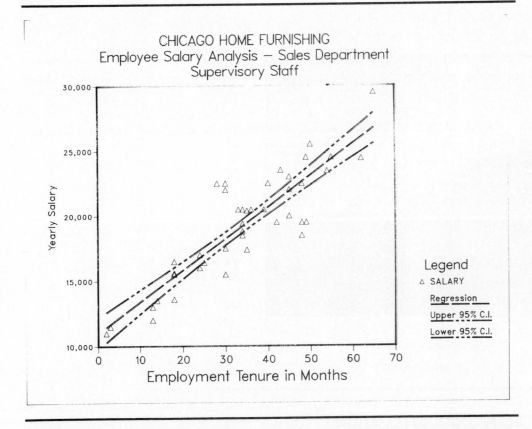

In this example, shown in Figure 4.57a, note how the X axis yearly labels were applied, how the shading patterns were selected from Figure 4.16, and how the legend title was supressed. It makes good sense in this case to stack the curves since the Y axis measures total company sales by quarter.

Sometimes it is also helpful to represent subpopulations as proportions of the whole. In this example, it would be interesting to chart the contribution of each division to the total company sales across time. To do this, four new variables must be computed that measure the percents.

```
COMPUTE         TOTAL=(CARP+FURN+APPL+HARD)
COMPUTE         PCARP=CARP*100/TOTAL
COMPUTE         PFURN=FURN*100/TOTAL
COMPUTE         PAPPL=APPL*100/TOTAL
COMPUTE         PHARD=HARD*100/TOTAL
```

Then, since all the subcommands for the previous example except Y AXIS apply to this plot, the LINECHART command that would produce both the plot shown in Figure 4.57a and the one shown in Figure 4.57b is

```
LINECHART        PLOT SUM(FURN,APPL,HARD,CARP) WITH QUARTER/
                 DEFAULT FORMAT FRAME,FANCY,SHADE/
                 DEFAULT TITLE 'CHICAGO HOME FURNISHING'
                     'Analysis of Quarterly Sales'/
                 DEFAULT FOOTNOTE 'As of December 1980'/
                 Y AXIS 'Sales in Dollars'/
                 DEFAULT X AXIS 'Quarters Since 1975'
                     LABELED '1975' ' ' ' ' ' ' '1976' ' ' ' ' ' '
                         '1977' ' ' ' ' ' ' '1978' ' ' ' ' ' ' '1979'
                         ' ' ' ' ' ' '1980' ' ' ' ' /
                 DEFAULT LEGEND TITLE /
                 DEFAULT LEGEND LABELS 'Furniture' 'Appliance'
                     'Hardware' 'Carpeting'/
                 DEFAULT CURVES ALL SPLINE/
                 DEFAULT ORDER 1,8,5,7/
                 PLOT SUM(PFURN,PAPPL,PHARD,PCARP) WITH QUARTER/
                 Y AXIS 'Percent Total Sales' RANGE 0 100/
```

The RANGE specification on the Y AXIS subcommand for the second plot is necessary in order to force the plot boundary to stop at 100.

Figure 4.57b   A Shaded Line Chart—Percent of Sales

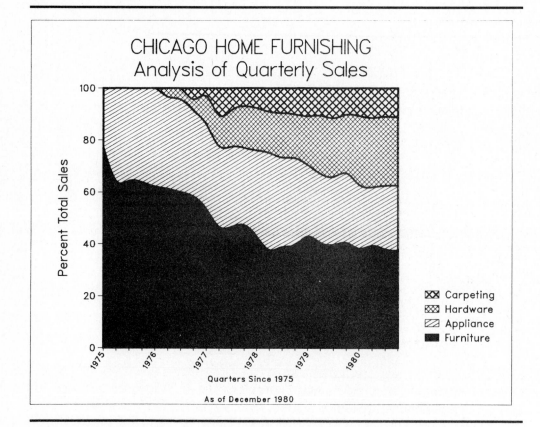

4.58 THE TELL-A-GRAF INTERFACE

The SPSS Batch System's Graphics Option provides all of the basic elements for graphic presentation of pie, bar, and line charts. In addition, many options are provided for enhancing each plot to accommodate various modes of presentation and a number of aesthetic choices. Many of the choices you might have to make through a potentially expensive iteration process are either made for you or are made easier and cheaper via the preview, selection, and combination facilities of the Graphics Option Postprocessor (see Section 4.59).

However, this is not all there is to modification and enhancement of high quality graphics. Each of the three Graphics Option procedures features the SAVE subcommand, which directs a plot to be saved into a permanent file system used by the TELL-A-GRAF graphics system. SPSS-generated plots can be further enhanced with different types and sizes of lettering, extended annotation, layout development, shading, blanking, etc., via the CONTINUE command in TELL-A-GRAF.

TELL-A-GRAF is a convenient, interactive proprietary software product of ISSCO, Integrated Software Systems Corporation, of San Diego, California (4186 Sorrento Valley Boulevard, Suite G, Zip 92121, Telephone 714/452-0170). The documentation for and information about TELL-A-GRAF is available from them. Look especially for discussions of options and annotation in the Reference Manual. Those at installations with TELL-A-GRAF will find the SPSS Graphics Option a bridge between the graphics production they are used to and the data analysis, data archiving, and graphics capabilities of SPSS. Those who do not have TELL-A-GRAF should find this software system a very convenient extension to the SPSS Graphics Option.

The Graphics Option SAVE subcommand can be specified at any point after the PLOT subcommand that initiates the plot you want to save for TELL-A-GRAF. Like the other subcommands for PIECHART, BARCHART, and LINECHART, SAVE is optionally followed by an equals sign, the specification, and a slash. Unlike the attribute subcommands for the three procedures, SAVE cannot be prefaced by DEFAULT.

The specification for SAVE is the name of the plot you will specify on the DRAW or CONTINUE commands in TELL-A-GRAF. The name must begin with an alphabetic character and can be no longer than 12 letters or digits. There is no default.

For example, if you want to save the two pie charts generated in Section 4.16, specify

```
PIECHART       PLOT=JOBGRADE/ DEFAULT FORMAT=FANCY,SORT/
               DEFAULT TITLE='CHICAGO HOME FURNISHING'
                    'Employee Study - Sales Department'/
               DEFAULT FOOTNOTE='As of December 1980'/
               SEGMENT LABELS=(1)'Salesclerks' (2)'Supervisors'
                    (3)'Managers' (4)'Support'/
               EXPLODE=3/ ORDER=5,2,1,10/
               DEFAULT MISSING=NONE/
     ◆         SAVE=CHICAGOPIE1/
               PLOT=DIVISION/
               SEGMENT LABELS=(1)'Carpeting' (2)'Appliances'
                    (3)'Furniture' (4)'Hardware'/
     ◆         SAVE=CHICAGOPIE2/
```

The names CHICAGOPIE1 and CHICAGOPIE2 can then be used with the TELL-A-GRAF CONTINUE command to develop these plots further.

In BARCHART and LINECHART, each SAVE subcommand saves the single plot generated by the preceding PLOT subcommand. In PIECHART, only the last plot generated by a control (BY) variable in a PLOT subcommand is saved.

4.59   THE GRAPHICS OPTION POSTPROCESSOR

The Graphics Option Postprocessor is known as SPSS GP, but it may be available at your installation under another name. It is designed as an interactive system that allows you to preview your plots on one device and send those that you like to a second device for final production. The postprocessor also allows you to combine two or more plots on the same page before sending them to the final plotting device. The interactive version is documented in the next section.

The postprocessor may also be available in batch mode at your installation, usually as a built-in second step to your SPSS Batch System job. See local documentation for a description.

4.60   Using the Postprocessor

With no changes to the software, devices supported by the SPSS Graphics Option include all Tektronix devices, all Calcomp and Calcomp-compatible devices, the Hewlett-Packard 7221, 2648, and 2647 devices, and the Zeta plotters. Additional devices may be available at your installation, so consult local documentation.

To operate the Graphics Option Postprocessor (SPSSGP), you must sign onto your local installations host system and access it under whatever name it has been assigned and according to local documentation. You are immediately prompted for your primary device with the prompt

```
PRIMARY DEVICE?
```

If you don't know the name for your primary device, type HELP. Once you have specified your device, you are prompted with COMMAND?.

You operate the postprocessor with seven commands. They are

HELP   *Give a short explanation of the prompt.* For help regarding any of the commands, enter HELP followed by the command keyword.

PREVIEW   *Display plots in simple format with no colors.* For all subsequent DRAW and SEND commands, your plots are forced to simple format and to black-and-white for preview purposes. This can be overridden at any time by respecifying the default NO PREVIEW, which means that all plots are displayed as created.

ASSIGN *Assign the secondary device.* You are prompted for details. A carriage return to the device prompt assigns the secondary device to the primary device (used to alter your assignment during the postprocessor session).

CONTENTS *Display the plot contents of the file.* The table of contents contains the plot number, plot type, and title text for each plot in the file.

DRAW list *Draw the plots listed on the primary device.* DRAW sets the target pointer to the last plot drawn plus one. If no list is provided, the the target plot is drawn. Keyword ALL is valid.

SEND list *Send the plots listed to the secondary device.* SEND sets the target pointer to the last plot sent. If no number is specified, the last plot drawn is sent. Keyword ALL can be specified.

COMBINE list *Combine and draw the plots listed on the same page.* You are prompted for a title for the combined plots (up to 80 characters). If you issue the SEND command following a COMBINE, the combined page is sent. COMBINE sets the target pointer to the last plot drawn plus one. Keyword ALL is valid.

QUIT *Exit from the postprocessor.*

Any of the number lists following keywords DRAW, SEND, or COMBINE can be a single integer number or a list of numbers corresponding to the plots you want to plot, send, or combine. The list can use the keyword TO to reference a range of plots.

4.61 A Sample Postprocessor Session

To combine the bar charts shown in Figure 4.27, you first sign onto the host system, name your plot file created by SPSS, and invoke the Graphics Option Postprocessor. Instructions must be obtained from your local installation. Once you have successfully signed on and accessed the postprocessor, you are prompted for the graphics device you are using, which is your primary device.

```
SPSS GRAPHICS POSTPROCESSOR
TYPE HELP FOR HELP

PRIMARY DEVICE?
HP2648
```

You name the Hewlett-Packard 2648 device.

```
COMMAND?
CONTENTS

TABLE OF CONTENTS

PLOT
    1  PIE        " JOBGRADE "
    2  PIE        "CHICAGO HOME FURNISHING""Employee Study - Furnitu"
    3  PIE        "CHICAGO HOME FURNISHING""Employee Study - Furnitu"
    4  VC BAR     " MEAN(TENURE) WITH JOBGRADE BY SHIFT "
    5  VH BAR     "HIDDEN BAR CHART""Employee Percents"
    6  VS BAR     "STACKED BAR CHART""Employee Percents"
    7  LINE       " MEAN(SALARY) WITH TENURE BY JOBGRADE "
    8  LINE       "CHICAGO HOME FURNISHING""Employee Salary Analysis"
```

If you don't recall the order in which you created your plots, the CONTENTS command will tell you. In this example, the two plots that you want to combine are 5 and 6.

```
COMMAND?
COMBINE 5 6

TITLE?
BAR SETS
```

It is at this point that the plots are drawn on your HP2648 terminal. Since they appear to be satisfactory, you now want to plot them on your secondary device.

```
COMMAND?
ASSIGN

SECONDARY DEVICE?
HP7221
```

You can name your secondary device at any point and you can change it at any point. In this example, you are naming the HP7221 pen plotter as the secondary device, which must be attached to your HP2648 before you send it plots.

```
COMMAND?
SEND

COMMAND?
```

Once the plot is completed on the secondary device, the postprocessor COMMAND? prompt reappears. You can preview other plots, combine and plot them, change your secondary device, etc. Also, if you don't get rid of your SPSS-created plot file, you can use QUIT to exit from the postprocessor and return to it later to examine the rest of the plots.

4.62 SYNTAX SUMMARIES

The following are modified railroad diagrams for each of the procedures. You can read these diagrams by following the indicated paths left-to-right. When a path moves below the line, it is optional. When a path moves right-to-left above the line, the sequence can be repeated. Whenever a number is encountered in the path within a circle, that is the number of times that path can be taken; otherwise, you take a given path the number of times it takes to specify the plot you want.

Wherever possible, default keywords are indicated in boldface. However, do not take these as absolute, since the absence of a boldface keyword does not mean that there is not a default. For example, there is no default indicated for the TITLE subcommand in any of the procedures, yet all plots have default titles constructed from the PLOT= subcommand.

Use these diagrams as reference only. You must read the text to learn the details.

4.63 PIECHART Syntax

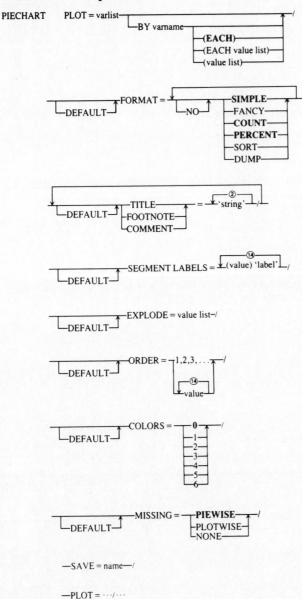

4.64 BARCHART Syntax

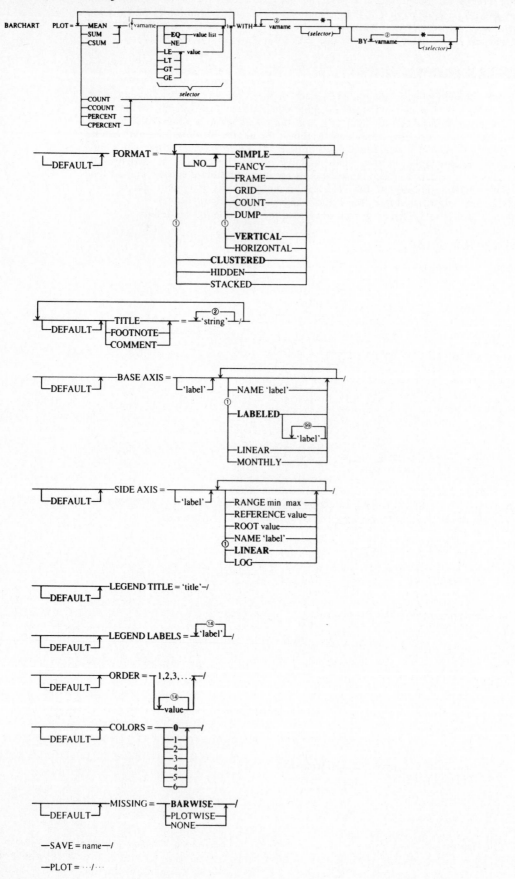

4.65 LINECHART Syntax

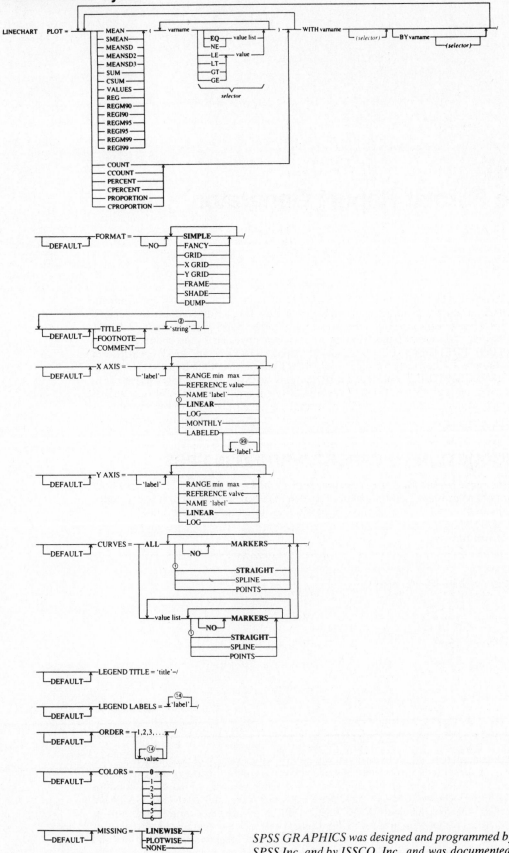

SPSS GRAPHICS *was designed and programmed by Steve Drach at SPSS Inc. and by ISSCO, Inc., and was documented by Keith Sours.*

Chapter 5

REPORT:
Flexible Format Report Generator

Data analysts are often called upon to produce a variety of reports for business, government, schools, hospitals, and other organizations. These reports must frequently conform to specified formats or become parts of carefully formatted presentations. The SPSS Batch System REPORT procedure is a flexible formatter of the types of information provided by procedures such as CONDESCRIPTIVE, FREQUENCIES, CROSSTABS, BREAKDOWN, and LIST CASES, and can be used to generate a wide variety of reports. REPORT calculates all the univariate statistics available in CONDESCRIPTIVE, absolute and relative frequencies available in FREQUENCIES, subpopulation means and statistics available in AGGREGRATE and BREAKDOWN, as well as statistics not directly available in any other SPSS procedure. It can also be used to list the contents of individual cases as in LIST CASES, but with a great deal more control over formatting.

5.1 INTRODUCTION TO REPORT WRITING IN SPSS

An example of a simple report taken from Section 5.28 is shown in Figure 5.1. This fictitious company's personnel records are used throughout this chapter to show how a report is developed from default formatted output through a range of possibilities to a finely tuned display.

Figure 5.1   A Simple Report

```
PERSONNEL REPORT (BASIC)                                            PAGE    1

PRODUCT         AGE    TENURE IN    TENURE IN         ANNUAL
DIVISION               COMPANY      GRADE             SALARY

CARPETING
MEAN             33      2.14         1.47            14221

APPLIANCES
MEAN             34      2.29         1.94            15039

FURNITURE
MEAN             36      2.77         2.22            15894

HARDWARE
MEAN             35      2.54         2.18            15616

TOTAL
MEAN             34      2.47         2.00            15286
```

An SPSS report has a basic structure that you can modify with a variety of subcommands. The body of the report is formatted in rows and columns where the columns correspond to variables and the rows to individual cases or groups of cases. In the report shown in Figure 5.1, columns headed by AGE, TENURE IN COMPANY, TENURE IN GRADE, and ANNUAL SALARY are the variables and the rows labeled CARPETING, APPLIANCES, etc. represent groups of cases based on division within the company. SPSS reports also contain aggregated statistics for groups and subgroups of cases and optional listings of the contents of cases within those groups and subgroups. For example, the report in Figure 5.1 contains the mean for each subgroup, but does not list the contents of each case.

To format the output, REPORT provides full default specifications, but allows you to control

- page lengths, margins, and column widths
- page heads (titles) and running feet (footers)
- labels for variables and statistics

See Figure 5.2 for the page layout of the SPSS report as well as the special subcommand specifications to control its basic structure.

Finally, two special REPORT features are a string function used to concatenate variables and literals for display, and composite functions that allow you to manipulate arithmetically statistics calculated on single variables.

5.2 The General Page Layout of a Report

The complete page layout of the SPSS report and the subcommand specifications used to control the basic structure of the report are shown in Figure 5.2. Use this schematic report for reference as you read through this chapter and as you develop your own reports.

Figure 5.2   The Report Layout

```
----------------------------------<TOP OF PAGE>---------------------------------
                                                              <----- SPACE DEFINED BY LENGTH
                     ************ HEAD ************
                                                              <----- SPACE DEFINED BY HDSPACE

BREAK HEAD          BREAK HEAD          COLUMN   COLUMN   COLUMN   COLUMN
                                        HEAD     HEAD     HEAD     HEAD
                                        [VAR]    [VAR]    [VAR]    [VAR]
                                                              <----- SPACE DEFINED BY CHDSPACE
BREAK A VALUE 1     BREAK B VALUE 1
                                                              <----- SPACE DEFINED BY BRKSPACE
                                        VALUE    VALUE    VALUE    VALUE <----- A CASE
                                        VALUE    VALUE    VALUE    VALUE
                                        VALUE    VALUE    VALUE    VALUE

                    SUMMARY TITLE       AGG.     AGG.     AGG.     AGG.
                                                              <----- SPACE DEFINED BY SKIP
                    BREAK B VALUE 2                                   WITH BREAK= COMMAND
                                                              <----- SPACE DEFINED BY BRKSPACE
                                        VALUE    VALUE    VALUE    VALUE
                                        VALUE    VALUE    VALUE    VALUE
                                        VALUE    VALUE    VALUE    VALUE

                    SUMMARY TITLE       AGG.     AGG.     AGG.     AGG.<----- AGGREGATED STATS FOR CASES
SUMMARY TITLE                           AGG.     AGG.     AGG.     AGG.          BREAK B=2, BREAK A=1
                                                              <----- SPACE DEFINED BY SKIP
BREAK B VALUE 2     BREAK B VALUE 1                                   WITH BREAK= COMMAND
                                                              <----- SPACE DEFINED BY BRKSPACE
                                        VALUE    VALUE    VALUE    VALUE
                                        VALUE    VALUE    VALUE    VALUE
                                        VALUE    VALUE    VALUE    VALUE

                    SUMMARY TITLE       AGG.     AGG.     AGG.     AGG.
                                                              <----- SPACE DEFINED BY SKIP
                    BREAK B VALUE 2                                   WITH BREAK= COMMAND
                                                              <----- SPACE DEFINED BY BRKSPACE
                                        VALUE    VALUE    VALUE    VALUE
                                        VALUE    VALUE    VALUE    VALUE
                                        VALUE    VALUE    VALUE    VALUE

                    SUMMARY TITLE       AGG.     AGG.     AGG.     AGG.
SUMMARY TITLE                           AGG.     AGG.     AGG.     AGG.
                                                              <----- SPACE DEFINED BY FTSPACE
                     ********** RUNNING FOOT **********
                                                              <----- SPACE DEFINED BY LENGTH
---------------------------------<BOTTOM OF PAGE>-------------------------------
|                                                        |
LEFT MARGIN                                          RIGHT MARGIN
```

An SPSS report has page boundaries. The maximum width of the report is 132 print positions, beginning in print position 1 and ending in print position 132. You can decrease the overall width of the report and indent either the left or right margin of the report. For example, the report shown in Figure 5.1 has no left indent and has been assigned a right margin of 80 (the page number is in position 80). The top of the REPORT page begins at line 1 and ends at the bottom of the page whose length is specified by the PAGESIZE command. The report shown in Figure 5.1 begins on the first line of the page with the title (PERSONNEL REPORT etc.), but is less than one page long. You can choose to print the top below the first line of the page and print the last line of the report above the bottom of the page.

Any number of lines of heads and feet can be placed on the page. The example in Figure 5.1, for instance, shows a single-line head. Heads and feet are repeated across pages, and pages can be paginated. The space between the head and the body of the report as well as the space between the body of the report and any running feet can be controlled. In Figure 5.1, the space between the head and the column heads has been limited to one line. In fact, all the spacing indicated by the arrows in Figure 5.2 is subject to your control.

5.3 Columns In a Report:
Break Variables and "Vars" Variables

Columns in a report correspond to two sets of variables: *break* and *"vars"* variables.

Break variables define groups of cases. They are functionally equivalent to procedure BREAKDOWN's BY variables. Columns defined by break variables are placed on the left side of the report (e.g., the column headed PRODUCT DIVISION in Figure 5.1). Multiple break variables can be used to define groups, subgroups within groups, lower-level subgroups within subgroups, etc. Both columns titled BREAK HEAD in Figure 5.2 are break columns: the rightmost break column identifies subgroups within groups defined by the leftmost break column.

"Vars" variables are variables being listed in case listings or summarized with REPORT's set of statistical and arithmetic functions. They are identified in Figure 5.2 by the columns titled COLUMN HEAD. There are three basic types of "vars" variables: actual SPSS variables (e.g., the four variables shown in Figure 5.1), variables created with the REPORT string function, and special placeholders termed *dummy* variables within the REPORT language.

5.4 Rows Within a Report:
Case Listings and Summary Statistics

The rows of a report contain labels for groups or summary statistics in break columns and case listings or summary statistics in "vars" columns. For example, BREAK A VALUE 1 in Figure 5.2 labels the cases for the group with the value 1 on break variable A. The title SUMMARY TITLE labels the statistics being printed for the group. In Figure 5.1, CARPETING is the label for the first subgroup defined by the break variable and MEAN is the summary title.

5.5 Breaks and Break Variables

The concept of a break variable is central to generating a report. REPORT processes cases sequentially and at specified points prints a summary of cases processed since the last set of summary statistics was printed. The point at which it summarizes a set of cases is determined by the change or "break" in the value of the break variable.

Break variables split a file into subpopulations or groups. For example, assume a file containing personnel information on a company organized into sales divisions and each employee works within a specific division. To produce a report that averages salaries by divisions, the file must contain a variable identifing the division. If the file is sorted on this variable so that all employees working in one division are grouped together, REPORT reads through the file storing the information required to compute average salary until the variable identifing the division changes. At this point, REPORT prints the average salary. It then continues to read the file storing the information required for the next set of employees, then prints their average salary, etc. After it reads the last case in the file, it prints average salary for the last division. This is exaclty what is reported in Figure 5.1.

Note that this design implies that a case cannot be in more than one group. A variable defines break groups, and each case has one and only one value for that variable.

REPORT permits breaks within breaks. Using the same example, assume that the file also contains information on which branch store the empoyee works in. Instead of just obtaining average salaries for employees within divisions, REPORT can be used to obtain average salaries for people at each division within each store. The mechanics of a multiple-break-level report are similar to the simple one-break report. Figure 5.5 is a sample data file for such a two-break report.

Figure 5.5   A Sample File Organized for a Two-break Report

```
388551234        1      1
225227242        1      1
455550474        1      1
499662235        1      2
526622535        1      2
270712262        1      2
811123313        1      3
180019205        1      3
424443449        1      3
656788443        1      4
244229262        1      4
377442393        1      4
    .            .
    .            .
577722458        2      1
618822320        2      1
277332292        2      1
791022955        2      2
200225226        2      2
255330272        2      2
299334377        2      2
    .            .
    .            .
```

The first set of columns in Figure 5.5 is a unique employee identification number (i.e., the U.S. social security number). The first single column data item is the store (1 is for suburban, 2 for downtown) and the second single column is the division within which the employee works (1 for carpeting, 2 for appliances, etc.). Other data columns and most of the cases have been removed for demonstration purposes. Note the way in which the file is organized: All employees within a store are grouped together and all employees within each store who work in the same division are grouped together. The file *must* be organized in this manner to insure that the correct set of salaries are being averaged. For example, if not all employees in the same division are together in the file, they will fall into different groups as the value of division changes from case to case and will not be summarized together.

More than one variable can be used to define a break. For example, the file described in Figure 5.5 could be broken down into groups based on both store and division at the same break level. When the file is treated as division within store as first described, summary statistics are printed when the division changes as well as when store changes. However, if they are treated at the same break level, summary statistics are printed only when division changes. See Section 5.29 for this example.

REPORT requires at least one break variable. If the file is not being split into groups for purposes of reporting, REPORT must be given a break variable which is a constant and hence never changes from case to case (see Section 5.24).

5.6 Overview of the REPORT Command

REPORT is an extremely flexible procedure with a large number of options. Flexibility implies some additional complexity in the language. However, the syntax required to produce reports that use the standard format is fairly simple. The REPORT command is divided into major subcommands controlling various parts of the display. Subcommands begin with a keyword that can be abbreviated to the first three letters followed by an equals sign and a set of specifications. Subcommands are separated from each other by slashes. Four are required:

```
REPORT          FORMAT=specifications/
                VARIABLES=specifications/
                BREAK=specifications/
                SUMMARY=specifications
```

The FORMAT= subcommand (Section 5.8) specifies how the report is laid out on a page, whether case listings are to be presented, and whether totals across breaks are to be printed. If the report uses only the default specifications, the FORMAT= subcommand is still required, but has only one specification: DEFAULT.

The VARIABLES= subcommand (Section 5.14) specifies the "vars" variables upon which statistics are computed and for which cases can be listed.

The BREAK= subcommand (Section 5.27) specifies the variables used to define groups. There can be more than one BREAK= subcommand.

The SUMMARY= subcommand (Section 5.31) specifies the statistics to be computed for "vars" variables. It is paired with the BREAK= subcommand. If there is more than one BREAK= subcommand, there can be more than one SUMMARY= subcommand.

REPORT has no separate OPTIONS or STATISTICS. Statistics are specified with keywords, and the handling of missing values is controlled with the optional MISSING= subcommand explained in Section 5.46. With few exceptions, all specifications used in the REPORT command are independent of each other, and defaults can be overridden selectively.

Three special delimiters are used in REPORT subcommand specifications: apostrophes and parentheses (always in pairs) and the slash ending each subcommand. Note that apostrophes always enclose literal strings for heads or titles; parentheses enclose certain keywords and arguments associated with keywords. No space is required around these delimiters, though space can be inserted for clarity.

Only subcommand keywords—those followed by the equals sign—can be abbreviated to the first three characters. Thus FORMAT= can be abbreviated to FOR=, VARIABLES= to VAR=, and so on. Throughout this document and in the error messages for REPORT, the shortened form VARS= is used for the VARIABLES= subcommand.

5.7 A Company Report

Any report requires the four basic subcommands described above. Since defaults are accepted for these subcommands, their specification fields are relatively simple. For a default report, the following specifications are required:

```
REPORT          FORMAT=DEFAULT/
                VARS=varlist/
                BREAK=variable/
                SUMMARY=statistic
```

Figure 5.7   The Default Report

PERSONNEL REPORT (BASIC)   PAGE   1

DIVISION	AGE	TENURE IN COMPANY	TENURE IN GRADE	SALARY--ANNUAL
1				
MEAN	33.15	2.14	1.47	14220.85
2				
MEAN	33.99	2.29	1.94	15039.28
3				
MEAN	35.66	2.77	2.22	15894.06
4				
MEAN	34.54	2.54	2.18	15615.82

Figure 5.7 is a report produced with default specifications. As individual subcommands are described in this chapter, this report will be modified by overriding default subcommand specifications. The complete SPSS command setup to produce the report in Figure 5.7 is

```
RUN NAME          PERSONNEL REPORT (BASIC)
DATA LIST         FIXED/1 S1 1-3 S2 4-5 S3 6-9
                     LNAME1 TO LNAME3 10-21(A) NAME1 TO NAME5 22-41(A)
                     SEX 42 JOBGRADE 43 (A) STORE 44 SALARY 45-49
                     DIVISION 50 SHIFT 51 BDAY BMONTH BYEAR 52-57
                     CMONTH CYEAR JMONTH JYEAR 58-65
INPUT MEDIUM      CARD
COMPUTE           AGE=80-BYEAR
COMPUTE           TENURE=(12-CMONTH +(12*(80-CYEAR)))/12
COMPUTE           JTENURE=(12-JMONTH +(12*(80-JYEAR)))/12
RECODE            JOBGRADE('C'=4)('X'=1)('S'=2)('M'=3)/
VAR LABELS        JOBGRADE JOB GRADE/
                  STORE BRANCH STORE/
                  SALARY SALARY--ANNUAL/
                  TENURE TENURE IN COMPANY/
                  JTENURE TENURE IN GRADE /
VALUE LABELS      JOBGRADE (1) SALES STAFF (2) SUPERVISORY STAFF
                     (3) MANAGERIAL STAFF (4) SUPPORT STAFF/
                  SEX (1) FEMALE (2) MALE/
                  STORE (1) SUBURBAN (2) DOWNTOWN/
                  DIVISION (1)CARPETING (2)APPLIANCES (3)FURNITURE (4)HARDWARE/
                  SHIFT (1) FIRST (2) SECOND (3) WEEKEND/
PRINT FORMATS     LNAME1 TO NAME5(A)
SORT CASES        DIVISION
READ INPUT DATA
388551234FORD         HARIETT L.          1C109200112011530479108O
499662235ZDEB         SUSAN E. A.         1C108700210503600780078O
534007333STANIK       ELIZABETH S.        1C209200311808600679098O
         .
         .
         .
266442692WATSON       CLAUDETTE N.        1M227400431308360378O378
266552702SMITH        LEONARD H.          2M14200033100234107610?6
267562784COOK         MILT E.             2M24600023230333097510?6
END INPUT DATA
REPORT            FORMAT=DEFAULT/
                  VARS=AGE TENURE JTENURE SALARY/
                  BREAK=DIVISION/
                  SUMMARY=MEAN
```

This report uses one break variable, DIVISION, to split a personnel file into separate divisions of a fictitious home furnishings company. Data transformations are used to compute age, years at the company, and years within the job grade. The means for age, salary, tenure within the company and tenure within the job grade are calculated for each division within the company. The file is sorted on DIVISION to insure that cases are appropriately grouped.

5.8   THE FORMAT= SUBCOMMAND

FORMAT= specifications establish the physical dimension of the report and vertical spacing around heads. The FORMAT= subcommand is also used to specify case listings. FORMAT= specifications can be named in any order. The keyword DEFAULT indicates that defaults are acceptable for all FORMAT= specifications.

5.9 Obtaining Case Listings: Keyword LIST

The keyword LIST instructs REPORT to print the contents of cases for variables named on the VARS= subcommand. LIST applies to all variables named on the VARS= subcommand. You cannot selectively specify variables to be listed. If you do not specify LIST, no case listings are printed: the default is NOLIST.

5.10 Obtaining Summary Statistics Across Breaks: Keyword TOTAL

The keyword TOTAL requests that summary statistics be computed and printed across breaks as well as for each break. In a report with one level of break, TOTAL produces for the total number of cases the same summary statistics that are requested for each break within the file. In a report with primary level break STORE and a secondary break level DIVISION within STORE, each time the value of STORE changes, TOTAL produces for all the cases within the STORE-level break the summary statistics requested for the DIVISION-level break. If the summary statistics requested for both break STORE and break DIVISION are identical, TOTAL prints duplicate summary lines. See Section 5.30 for further information. NOTOTAL, the default, requests summaries only for individual breaks.

5.11 Controlling Page Dimensions: Keywords LENGTH and MARGIN

Two keywords are used in the FORMAT= subcommand to control the dimensions and placement of the report within the page:

LENGTH(t,b) The number of lines that the top of the report is to be dropped or the bottom raised within the pagesize (defaults = 0 for both). The default pagesize in SPSS is 54 lines. Longer or shorter pages can be specified with the optional PAGESIZE command (see *SPSS*, Second Edition, p. 74). The LENGTH option within REPORT determines both the maximum length of the report printing area and its vertical position on the page.

MARGINS(l,r) The left and right margins (defaults are 1,132). The columns specified are included in the printing area.

5.12 Controlling Vertical Spacing: Keywords HDSPACE, CHDSPACE, BRKSPACE and FTSPACE

Four keyword specifications are used in the FORMAT= subcommand to control vertical spacing around heads:

HDSPACE(n) The number of lines between the report heading and the column heads (default is 3).

CHDSPACE(n) The lines of space beneath the longest column head (default is 1).

BRKSPACE(n) The lines of space beneath the break head (default is 2).

FTSPACE(n) The minimum number of lines of space between the last listing on the page and the running foot (default is 1).

5.13 Summary of FORMAT= Specifications

The following FORMAT= subcommand contains all specifications and their defaults. It is equivalent to FORMAT=DEFAULT.

```
FORMAT=HDSPACE(3)CHDSPACE(1)BRKSPACE(2)FTSPACE(1)
       LENGTH (0,0)MARGINS(1,132)NOLIST NOTOTAL/
```

Note that no case listings are printed when FORMAT=DEFAULT.

Figure 5.13 illustrates the default report shown in Figure 5.7 modified with FORMAT= specifications. In this report, the space between the header and the column headings is reduced to 1. The space following the break label is deleted. The margins are reduced to 1 and 80 and a totals summary is obtained.

The subcommands required to produce the report in Figure 5.13 are

```
REPORT        FORMAT=MARGINS (1,80) HDSPACE(1) BRKSPACE(0) TOTAL/
              VARS=AGE TENURE JTENURE SALARY/
              BREAK=DIVISION/
              SUMMARY=MEAN
```

Figure 5.13   The Company Report with Formatting Options

```
PERSONNEL REPORT (BASIC)                                             PAGE     1

DIVISION        AGE          TENURE IN     TENURE IN    SALARY——A
                             COMPANY       GRADE        NNUAL
              1
MEAN            33.15         2.14          1.47         14220.85

              2
MEAN            33.99         2.29          1.94         15039.28

              3
MEAN            35.66         2.77          2.22         15894.06

              4
MEAN            34.54         2.54          2.18         15615.82
TOTAL
MEAN            34.47         2.47          2.00         15285.81
```

5.14   THE VARS= SUBCOMMAND

The VARS= subcommand names the variables to be included in the report. It also has optional specifications for column heads and column width and for controlling the contents of "vars" columns. All variables to be listed or for which summary statistics are computed must be named on the VARS= subcommand. Break variables, which are used to split the file into groups, should not be included. The minimum VARS= specification is a list of variables in the order in which they are to appear on the report. The variable list conforms to the conventional variable list in SPSS. It can consist of a list of individual variables separated by common delimiters or an implied list of variables using the TO convention. For example,

```
VARS=A V1 TO V24 B/
```

defines columns for A, V1, all variables located in the file between V1 and V24 (no matter what they are named), V24, and B—in that order.

REPORT also recognizes special placeholder variables and variables constructed within the procedure by the STRING= subcommand. These special dummy variables are discussed in Section 5.15.

The number of variables that can be specified depends upon the width of the report, the width of the variable columns, and the number of BREAK= subcommands.

5.15   Column Contents:
Keywords LABEL, DUMMY, and VALUE

When the LIST option is specified via the FORMAT= subcommand, the contents of "vars" columns are by default the actual values for cases. You can choose to list any defined value labels rather than actual values. The keyword LABEL in parentheses following a variable name lists value labels.

```
VARS=varname(LABEL).../
```

If the variable list contains a set of inclusive variables implied by the keyword TO, (LABEL) applies to the entire set of variables in the list. However, (LABEL) cannot be implied for a set of variables named individually. For example, in

```
VARS=V1 TO V5(LABEL)/
```

(LABEL) applies to all variables implied by V1 TO V5. But, in

```
VARS=V1 V2 V3 V4 V5(LABEL)/
```

(LABEL) applies only to V5. If (LABEL) is specified for a variable and values are encountered for which there are no labels, the value is printed.

Numbers in columns are always right-justified and alphanumerics are always left-justified. Value labels are alphanumeric strings, even though they may contain only numbers. (LABEL) is useful only when LIST is specified on the FORMAT= subcommand. If LIST is not specified, (LABEL) is ignored and does not cause an error.

The keyword (DUMMY) can be used in place of (LABEL) to specify a variable that does not really exist but is used to define a column in the report. Dummy variable columns can be used to control spacing of other columns or to hold statistics computed upon other variables. A dummy variable cannot be an existing SPSS variable. The TO convention cannot be used to generate multiple dummy variables within REPORT.

For completeness, VALUE, which is the default, can be specified in parentheses following a variable name. Thus the complete syntax for specifying column contents is

```
VARS=varname [(VALUE|LABEL|DUMMY)]...varname/
```

5.16 Column Widths

The default column width for SPSS and dummy variables is 9. However, if (LABEL) has been specified for a variable, the default width of its column is 20 since the maximum length of a value label is 20 characters. Default widths can be overridden by a width specified in parentheses following a variable name:

```
VARS=varname [(width)] ... varname [(width)]/
```

For example,

```
SEX(LABEL)(6)
```

is used to list value labels in a column 6 characters wide, rather than one 20 characters wide.

Judicious use of the column width specification produces more compact reports and permits reports containing up to 60 columns. Some care must be taken to insure that the specified column width is sufficient for the contents. In a case listing, asterisks are printed in place of any value that exceeds the column width, but the value is included in any statistics being computed. In summaries, decimal places are dropped to fit statistics within narrow columns, and asterisks are printed if the integer value will not fit. Alphanumeric values and value labels, as well as string variables (Section 5.21), are truncated to fit specified column widths.

5.17 Column Headers

Every column has a column header. By default, REPORT uses the variable label, if one has been defined on the VAR LABELS command. Otherwise, REPORT uses the variable name. You can specify a column head consisting of one or more lines by enclosing a title in apostrophes:

```
VARS=varname ['column head'] ... varname ['column head']/
```

If the column title is more than one line long, each line must be enclosed in apostrophes. For example, DIVISION 'PRODUCT' 'DIVISION' produces a two-line column heading. DIVISION 'PRODUCT DIVISION' would be truncated in a column narrower than 16 characters. Leading blanks can be inserted to center or right-align heads, as in ' PRODUCT' 'DIVISION'.

Column heads cannot be wider than column widths. Specified heads that exceed the column width are truncated. Default heads (variable labels or variable names) will wrap around for as many lines as required to print the entire label. For example, GRADE76(5) prints the following column head:

```
GRADE
IN 19
76
```

while, GRADE76(5)'GRADE' 'IN' '1976' prints the column head:

```
GRADE
IN
1976
```

This wrap-around feature produces vertical heads for columns one character wide. Vertical heads for columns more than one character wide can be specified one character at a time, as in 'A' 'G' 'E' or, to center the head, ' A' ' G' ' E'(3). A null title such as ' ' can be used to completely remove a column header from the report.

Titles such as column headers are permitted in several places within the report. They are always specified within apostrophes and may contain any alphanumeric characters, including special symbols and lower case letters, with one exception: The apostrophe cannot be used within the title since it is used to delimit the string from other specifications.

Column headers are left-justified on a report, but numeric values within the column are right-justified. This tends to produce a report with offset column headers, especially if the column width is considerably wider than the values printed within it. You can insert leading blanks to align the header with the column.

5.18 Intercolumn Spacing

The combination of report width, number of columns, and column widths determines intercolumn spacing. Given *n* columns on a report (including break columns), there are *n-1* intercolumns. REPORT calculates the number of print positions taken by all the columns, and subtracts it from the width of the report. The remaining space is divided into equal inter-columns from 1 to 4 print positions wide. If the report width is wide and the number of print positions required for the columns relatively small, the right side of the report is empty. Dummy variables can be defined to insert extra columns into the report and control spacing between columns. If the dummy variables are given null column headers, REPORT "prints" empty columns, thus producing differential spacing between columns (see Section 5.19).

5.19 Summary of VARS= Specifications

The complete set of specifications for the VARS= subcommand is

```
VARS=varname [(VALUE|LABEL|DUMMY)] ['column head'] [(width)]
     ... varname [(VALUE|LABEL|DUMMY)] ['column head'] [(width)]/
```

The specifications following each variable or variable-TO-variable group apply only to that variable or group. (As noted in above, TO cannot be used with dummy variables.) The specifications are given in any order. If a file contains the variables ID, SEX, JOBGRADE, STORE, SALARY, and DIVISION, and the variable labels EMPLOYEE IDENTIFICATION NUMBER, JOB GRADE, and BRANCH STORE, the following VARS= specifications might be used for a report including a case listing:

```
VARS=ID 'EMPLOYEE''IDENTIFICATION''NUMBER'(14)
     SEX TO STORE (LABEL)(8)
     SALARY
     DIVISION 'PRODUCT''DIVISION'(LABEL)(9)/
```

No column titles are provided for SEX to STORE (implying JOBGRADE) and SALARY so they will have default column titles. No width is specified for SALARY so its width defaults to 9. ID and SALARY are printed as observed values while value labels are printed for SEX to STORE and DIVISION.

Figure 5.19   The Company Report with VARS= Options

```
PERSONNEL REPORT (BASIC)                                     PAGE     1

DIVISION        AGE     TENURE IN     TENURE IN        ANNUAL
                        COMPANY       GRADE            SALARY

             1
MEAN            33       2.14          1.47            14221

             2
MEAN            34       2.29          1.94            15039

             3
MEAN            36       2.77          2.22            15894

             4
MEAN            35       2.54          2.18            15616
TOTAL
MEAN            34       2.47          2.00            15286
```

Figure 5.19 is the company report modified with several VARS= specifications. SALARY is given a new column header and a shorter width and a dummy variable named SPACE is inserted to separate SALARY from the tenure variables.

The subcommands required to produce Figure 5.19 are

```
REPORT      FORMAT=MARGINS (1,80) HDSPACE(1) BRKSPACE(0) TOTAL/
            VARS=AGE(3) TENURE JTENURE
              SPACE(DUMMY)''(4)
              SALARY 'ANNUAL''SALARY'(6)/
            BREAK=DIVISION/
            SUMMARY=MEAN
```

5.20   An Example Report Using VARS= Specifications

Figure 5.20 is a report using several optional VARS= specifications. In this report, made up of data from the October 1980 issue of *Runner's World* magazine, a dummy variable SEP1 is created to provide a slight separation between the column labeled RATING and the more detailed information to the right. Value labels are listed for variables TYPE and STARS, and for LASTYEAR and PREFER simply to blank out zeroes (see Section 5.57 for the interaction of REPORT with VALUE LABELS). Column headers are provided for several variables including a blank one for SEP1. STARS was used as a sort key (descending order) to place each manufacturer's best shoes first.

Figure 5.20   Report with Several VARS= Options

```
                          RATINGS OF TRAINING SHOES
                    RUNNERS WORLD MAGAZINE - OCTOBER, 1980
```

MANUFACTURER	TYPE	SHOE	RATING	REARFOOT IMPACT	FOREFOOT IMPACT	FLEXI-BILITY	SOLE WEAR	REARFOOT CONTROL	SOLE TRACTION	WEIGHT	1979 STARS	READER PREFERENCE
SAUCONY												
	FEMALE	MS TRAINER	******	10.2	13.3	1.58	6.4	22.4	.86	237.7	5	.053
	MALE	TC84	******	9.3	15.1	1.56	6.5	5.2	.85	278.0		.028
	MALE	HORNET 84	******	9.9	13.1	2.65	7.6	3.0	.68	265.0	4	.097

	MALE	JAZZ	*****	8.9	12.7	2.04	7.6	−7.0	.64	270.8		
	MALE	TRAINER 80	*****	10.5	14.5	2.18	4.1	11.5	.82	307.6	5	.232
	FEMALE	TC 84	*****	9.3	14.6	1.46	7.5	1.3	.77	231.1		
	FEMALE	JAZZ	*****	9.0	12.2	1.86	6.1	−7.5	.63	223.0		.013
	FEMALE	MS HORNET	*****	9.8	13.2	2.59	6.4	6.5	.67	224.0	4	.046

```
          COUNT    8
NIKE
          MALE     DAYBREAK        ******   10.8   15.4   2.17  3.7    7.8    .54   304.2   5    .602
          MALE     YANKEE          *****    10.9   13.7   1.93  2.0    9.8    .66   276.6
          FEMALE   LIBERATOR       *****    10.6   14.7   2.20  5.8    6.5    .52   254.2   5    .503
          COUNT    3
ETONIC
          MALE     ECLIPSE TRAINER ******   10.0   12.9   1.65  10.0   −2.6   .51   237.4
          FEMALE   ECLIPSE TRAINER ******   9.6    12.8   1.78  10.0   1.4    .57   204.1
          FEMALE   STABILIZER      *****    10.8   14.4   2.09  2.6    −6.9   .67   235.3   4    .298
          FEMALE   STREETFIGHTER   *****    10.7   15.5   1.66  .7     −7.7   .70   214.1   4    .344
          MALE     STABILIZER      *****    10.3   15.5   2.25  1.2    −.6    .53   283.1   4    .232
          MALE     STREETFIGHTER   *****    10.8   15.5   2.28  1.4    −.4    .61   266.1   4    .222
          COUNT    6
PONY
          MALE     TARGA FLEX      ******   9.6    14.3   1.32  2.5    −22.7  .86   253.0   3
          MALE     SHADOW          *****    9.9    13.8   1.53  2.5    −17.9  .77   270.2
          FEMALE   LADY SHADOW     *****    10.6   17.4   .91   3.0    −7.1   .90   211.8
          COUNT    3
OSAGA
          FEMALE   KT-26           *****    10.7   17.3   1.66  5.5    8.1    .60   223.1   2
          MALE     FAST RIDER      *****    10.5   14.0   2.48  4.9    1.9    .66   296.7   5    .025
          COUNT    2
NEW BALANCE
          MALE     620             *****    12.0   14.6   2.73  1.1    −3.5   .41   242.0   5    .475
          MALE     420             *****    9.8    14.8   2.09  1.8    −17.7  .46   267.9        .516
          FEMALE   420             *****    9.9    13.9   1.94  1.6    −.7    .46   219.3        .411

          COUNT    3


****** HIGHLY RECOMMENDED
*****  RECOMMENDED                                                                PAGE    1
```

The subcommands required to produce the report in Figure 5.20 are

```
SORT CASES    MAKER STARS(D)
*SELECT IF    (STARS GE 5)
REPORT        FORMAT=LIST BRKSPACE(0)/
              STRING=SHOE(NAME1,NAME2,NAME3,NAME4)/
              VARS=TYPE(LABEL)(6)' ''TYPE'
              SHOE(16)' ''SHOE'
              STARS(LABEL)(6)' ''RATING'
              SEP1(DUMMY)(1)' '
              REARIMP(8)'REARFOOT'' IMPACT'
              FOREIMP(8)'FOREFOOT'' IMPACT'
              FLEX(6)'FLEXI-''BILITY'
              SOLEWEAR(4)'SOLE''WEAR'
              REARCONT(8)'REARFOOT'' CONTROL'
              SOLETRAC(8)'    SOLE''TRACTION'
              WEIGHT(6)' ''WEIGHT'
              LASTYEAR(LABEL)(5)' 1979''STARS'
              PREFER(LABEL)(10)'    READER''PREFERENCE'/
              HEAD='RATINGS OF TRAINING SHOES'
                   'RUNNERS WORLD MAGAZINE − OCTOBER, 1980'/
              LFOOT='****** HIGHLY RECOMMENDED'
                    '*****   RECOMMENDED'/
              RFOOT=' ''PAGE )PAGE'/
              BREAK=MAKER(LABEL)'MANUFACTURER'(12)(SKIP(0))/
              SUMMARY=VALIDN '        COUNT'(TYPE)/
```

5.21 THE STRING= SUBCOMMAND

The STRING= subcommand concatenates SPSS variables and literals to create new temporary variables that can be used in a report. It is not one of the four required subcommands. However, it is one of the most useful features of REPORT.

The variables to be listed in a report sometimes exceed the length normally allowed within SPSS. The company report in Figure 5.26, for example, includes names up to twelve characters long. Normally, SPSS alphanumeric variables are limited to four characters and numeric variables to seven digits (depending on the machine implementation). The STRING= subcommand provides a means for overcoming some of the restrictions upon the length of SPSS variables. A name or social security number can be stored as two or more separate variables, and STRING= will concatenate those variables into a single variable that can be included in case listings or used as a break variable.

String variables offer another measure of flexibility: they can include or be composed entirely of 'literals'—characters that remain constant for all cases. The social security number can, as in Figure 5.26, include hyphens as a constant part of the string variable.

5.22 Variables Within Strings

The simplest form of the STRING= subcommand is

```
STRING=stringname (var var var...) stringname.../
```

The name assigned to the string must be unique and must follow SPSS variable naming conventions. Both alphanumeric and numeric variables can be used in strings and can be intermixed. The variables concatenated to form the string are listed in parentheses following the string variable name. If a file contains names stored as four-character alphanumeric variables NAME1 to NAME6, the string NAME can be defined as a single 24-character variable:

```
STRING=NAME(NAME1 NAME2 NAME3 NAME4 NAME5 NAME6)/
```

Note that the keyword TO cannot be used to specify an implied list of variables. There is no fixed limit to the length of a string. However if the string is extremely long, the amount of other information contained in the report is constrained by the limits on the total width of the report.

Each variable in a string can be limited to a character width specified in parentheses immediately following the variable name:

```
STRING=stringname(varname [(width)] ... varname [(width)])/
```

If a width is not specified, the default width is 4 for alphanumeric variables and 10 for numeric variables. The width specified for a variable in a string must be sufficient to contain the largest value for that variable. Asterisks will be printed in place of any numeric value that exceeds the specified width. An alphanumeric value will be truncated. If the specified width exceeds the width of a value, a numeric value will be padded with zeros on the left and an alphanumeric value will be padded with blanks on the right. Thus, if VARA is an alphanumeric variable and VARN is a numeric variable and

```
STRING=STRING1(VARA VARN)/
```

for the case containing VARA=KJ and VARN=241, STRING1 would print as KJ 0000000241, while for

```
STRING=STRING1(VARA(2) VARN(3))/
```

the same values would print as KJ241.

All blanks within an alphanumeric value will be printed in the output. The maximum width that can be specified for any of the variables within a string is 16 characters.

5.23 Literals Within Strings

Strings can be composed entirely of literals, or literals can be intermixed with variables:

```
STRING=stringname('literal')
       stringname('literal' var 'literal').../
```

Literals are stored and printed exactly as spelled and spaced within the apostrophes. For example, assume that a file contains social security numbers stored as three variables, S1, S2, and S3 (see the example command setup in Section 5.7). The social security number can be listed in its usual form, with hyphens, if it is defined by the following STRING= subcommand:

```
STRING= ID(S1(3)'-'S2(2)'-'S3(4))/
```

The width for each of the three variables in the string has been specified because S1, S2, and S3 are numeric variables and the default width would create a string value like

```
0000000111-0000000022-0000003333
```

rather than 111-22-3333.

The report shown in Figure 5.26 is a variation on the company report that uses string variables and literals extensively.

5.24 Use of Strings Within REPORT

String variables can be used in VARS= and BREAK= subcommands. In the VARS= subcommand they are used for case listings. When string variables are used on the VARS= subcommand, the default column width is the width of the string; and the default column title is the string name. In Figure 5.26, four strings are defined to accommodate social security number, surname, and two dates with a slash setting off month/year.

A constant string can be used to separate columns in a report with a column of special characters such as asterisks or vertical bars (if your printer has them). For example,

```
STRING=STAR('*')/
```

defines a string variable STAR equal to the constant "*".

Strings can be used to define breaks. The simplest and cleanest way to write a report that has no real breaks is to define a string variable containing one blank and use it for the break variable, as in

```
STRING=A(' ')/
       .
       .
BREAK=A''/
```

In this example, string variable A is also given a blank break title, and never appears on the report except as an extra intercolumn space.

A string can be used as a real break. For example, a file of insurance policies can contain the agents' names as identifiers. The only way in SPSS to obtain a count of policies by agent is to use the string variable containing the names as a break variable and request the VALIDN for one of the variables in the VARS= list.

The STRING= subcommand can only be used to concatenate variables and literals. It cannot be used to extract substrings from numeric or alphanumeric variables. For instance, if an alphanumeric variable is 4 characters wide, specifying a width of 1 on the STRING= subcommand does not affect the storage of the 4 characters, even though only the first character of the string is printed in the report. The STRING= subcommand never affects storage of variables.

5.25 Summary of STRING= Specifications

The complete syntax for the STRING= subcommand is

```
STRING=  stringname (varname [(width)] ['literal']
         ... varname [(width)] ['literal']) ...
         stringname (varname [(width)] ['literal'])/
```

Default specifications are

- The default width of a numeric variable used in a string is 10.
- The default width of an alphanumeric variable used in a string is 4.

String variables are temporary variables specific to the the given REPORT command and disappear once the command has been executed. A STRING= subcommand must be placed prior to any other subcommand referencing variables created with the STRING= subcommand.

5.26 Example Report Using Strings

Figure 5.26 is a report using four string variables as variables named in the VARS= subcommand.

Figure 5.26   The Company Report Using String Variables

```
PERSONNEL REPORT (BASIC)                                      PAGE    1

PRODUCT     ID NUMBER  SURNAME      BRANCH   COMPANY  JOB       ANNUAL
DIVISION                            STORE    DATE     DATE      SALARY

CARPETING
            688-13-3706  JONES      SUBURBAN  02/79   12/79      10800
            730-26-3520  MCKUEN     DOWNTOWN  06/79   12/79      15530
            725-25-6020  MCANDREWS  DOWNTOWN  06/79   12/79      15520
            244-29-2522  TURNIP     DOWNTOWN  02/78   12/79      26400
            233-00-2352  COOKE      DOWNTOWN  06/79   12/79      15610

   COUNT                                                             5

APPLIANCES
            588-34-3605  HAYES      DOWNTOWN  07/79   12/79       8800

   COUNT                                                             1

FURNITURE
            737-10-0392  HOLCOMB    DOWNTOWN  12/78   12/79      16000

   COUNT                                                             1

HARDWARE
            446-55-4844  CHAFEE     DOWNTOWN  06/79   12/79       9000
            524-35-4695  HARRINGTON DOWNTOWN  07/79   12/79       8800
            623-87-2696  HARRIS     SUBURBAN  02/79   12/79       9800
            655-11-0676  WAYNE      DOWNTOWN  06/79   12/79       9000

   COUNT                                                             4
```

The subcommands used to produce the report in Figure 5.26 are

```
*SELECT IF   (JTENURE EQ 1)
 REPORT      FORMAT=MARGINS (1,80) HDSPACE(1) BRKSPACE(0) LIST/
             STRING=SURNAME(LNAME1 LNAME2 LNAME3)
                    ID(S1(3)'-'S2(2)'-'S3(4))
                    CDATE(CMONTH(2)'/'CYEAR(2))
                    JDATE(JMONTH(2)'/'JYEAR(2))/
             VARS=ID(11)' ID NUMBER ' SURNAME
               STORE (LABEL)(8) ' BRANCH''  STORE'
               CDATE(7)'COMPANY'' DATE'
               JDATE' JOB'' DATE'
               SPACE(DUMMY)''(4)
               SALARY 'ANNUAL''SALARY'(6)/
             BREAK=DIVISION 'PRODUCT''DIVISION' (LABEL)(10)
               (SKIP(1))/
             SUMMARY=VALIDN '  COUNT'(SALARY)
```

This report also uses the (LABEL) option in the VARS= subcommand for variable STORE to list the value labels instead of the values.

Only one STRING= subcommand is permitted per REPORT command, but a maximum of fifty strings can be defined per STRING= subcommand.

5.27 THE BREAK= SUBCOMMAND

BREAK= specifies the variable or set of variables that define a subpopulation within the report (see Section 5.5). BREAK= and the related SUMMARY= (Section 5.31) are the two subcommands that can be issued more than once on the REPORT command. Each BREAK= subcommand defines one break level and the SUMMARY= subcommand immediately following the BREAK= specifications determines the set of statistics to be computed for the cases within that break level.

Since the BREAK= subcommand specifies a column as does the VARS= subcommand, many of its specifications are parallel to the VARS= subcommand.

At least one break must be defined for each REPORT command, and the minimum specification is the name of the break variable or set of break variables:

```
BREAK=varname ... varname/
```

If a change occurs in any one of the set of variables named, the aggregate statistics requested by the SUMMARY= subcommand are calculated and printed.

Missing-value indicators are ignored for variables named on the BREAK= subcommand.

5.28 Specifying Column Heads, Contents, and Width

The BREAK= optional specifications fall into categories: those that override defaults for columns in the same manner as VARS= optional specifications, and an option that controls vertical spacing. The complete syntax for the BREAK= subcommand is

```
BREAK=varname ... varname ['break title'] [(width)]
[(VALUE|LABEL)] [(NOTITLE|TITLE)] [(PAGE|SKIP(n))]/
```

'break title'   A title in apostrophes is used as the heading for the column occupied by the break variable. By default, the variable label, if one has been assigned, or else the name of the break variable is used. (If the break is defined by more than one variable, the label of the first is used.) The break title obeys the same rules as the "vars" column head: multiple lines can be indicated with multiple sets of apostrophes; default heads wrap around within the column width.

(width)   A width in parentheses overrides the default width for the column assigned to the break variable. Default widths are 9 if the value of the break variable is to be printed, 20 if LABEL is specified, or the length of the string if a string variable is specified as a break variable. (See Section 5.21 for a discussion of the STRING= subcommand.) If a break is defined by more than one variable, the value or value label for each variable is printed on a separate line, and the default column width is the longest of the default widths for any of the break variables.

(VALUE|LABEL)   As with other variables, the value or the value label (but not both) can be printed for each value of the break variable. VALUE is the default. Note that the value is printed only once for each break change. It is not repeated at the top of each page for a multiple-page report.

(NOTITLE|TITLE)   TITLE prints the name of the break variable alongside each value or value label. If the variable name is STORE and one of the values is 1, TITLE prints (STORE)   1. TITLE can be used with LABEL. For example, if the variable name is SALARY and one of the value labels is OVER $25,000, TITLE prints (SALARY)OVER $25,000. The TITLE option requires 10 characters of column width (the maximum SPSS variable name plus two parentheses). If a column narrower than 11 characters is specified, TITLE is ignored. If the column is 11 characters or wider but less than 10 plus the width of the value or label, the value or label is replaced by asterisks or truncated. A default column is extended to accommodate TITLE. NOTITLE is the default.

(PAGE|SKIP(n))   By default, the last summary line for a break is followed by two blank lines before the line defining the next break. This vertical spacing can be overridden in one of two ways. If (PAGE) is specified, each break begins on a new page. If (SKIP(n)) is requested, each break begins following a skip of the number of lines specified.

Since only one column is defined per BREAK= subcommand, any optional specifications apply to all variables named on the command. That is, if LABEL is specified, it applies to all break variables. However, if no value labels have been defined for a variable, its values are printed instead.

Figure 5.28   The Company Report with BREAK= Modifications

```
PERSONNEL REPORT (BASIC)                                    PAGE    1

PRODUCT         AGE    TENURE IN    TENURE IN        ANNUAL
DIVISION               COMPANY      GRADE            SALARY

CARPETING
MEAN            33       2.14         1.47            14221

APPLIANCES
MEAN            34       2.29         1.94            15039

FURNITURE
MEAN            36       2.77         2.22            15894

HARDWARE
MEAN            35       2.54         2.18            15616

TOTAL
MEAN            34       2.47         2.00            15286
```

Figure 5.28 is the company report further modified with BREAK= specifications. The value label for DIVISION is printed in a break column 12 spaces wide and the break is given a two line title. In addition, the summary for each break is printed one line below the break title.

The REPORT subcommands required to produce the report in Figure 5.28 are

```
REPORT        FORMAT=MARGINS (1,80) HDSPACE(1) BRKSPACE(0) TOTAL/
              VARS=AGE(3) TENURE JTENURE
               SPACE(DUMMY)''(4)
               SALARY 'ANNUAL''SALARY'(6)/
              BREAK=DIVISION 'PRODUCT''DIVISION' (LABEL)(12)
               (SKIP(1))/
              SUMMARY=MEAN
```

5.29   One- and Two-Break Reports with Two Variables

Figure 5.29a is the company report with two BREAK= subcommands and the same summary request for each break level.

The subcommands required to produce the report in Figure 5.29a are

```
SORT CASES    STORE DIVISION
REPORT        FORMAT=MARGINS (1,80) HDSPACE(1) BRKSPACE(0)/
              VARS=AGE(3) TENURE JTENURE
               SPACE(DUMMY)''(4)
               SALARY 'ANNUAL''SALARY'(6)/
              BREAK=STORE 'BRANCH''STORE' (LABEL)(12) (SKIP(1))/
              SUMMARY=MEAN/
              BREAK=DIVISION 'PRODUCT''DIVISION'(LABEL)(SKIP(0))/
```

Figure 5.29b is a report with one BREAK= subcommand with two variables.

Figure 5.29a   The Company Report Using Multiple Breaks

```
PERSONNEL REPORT (BASIC)                                              PAGE    1

BRANCH       PRODUCT          AGE    TENURE IN   TENURE IN     ANNUAL
STORE        DIVISION                COMPANY     GRADE         SALARY

SUBURBAN     CARPETING
             MEAN            32       2.07        1.52          16004
             APPLIANCES
             MEAN            33       2.21        1.87          16105
             FURNITURE
             MEAN            36       3.03        2.65          18821
             HARDWARE
             MEAN            34       2.59        2.26          16435
MEAN                         34       2.51        2.13          16881

DOWNTOWN     CARPETING
             MEAN            33       2.17        1.45          13465
             APPLIANCES
             MEAN            35       2.37        1.99          14130
             FURNITURE
             MEAN            36       2.64        1.99          14403
             HARDWARE
             MEAN            35       2.49        2.12          14873
MEAN                         35       2.44        1.90          14232
```

The subcommands required to produce the report in Figure 5.29b are

```
SORT CASES    STORE DIVISION
REPORT        FORMAT=MARGINS (1,80) HDSPACE(1) BRKSPACE(0) TOTAL/
              VARS=AGE(3) TENURE JTENURE
               SPACE(DUMMY)''(4)
               SALARY 'ANNUAL''SALARY'(6)/
              BREAK=STORE DIVISION 'STORE/''DIVISION' (LABEL)(12)
               (SKIP(1))/
              SUMMARY=MEAN
```

Figure 5.29b   One Break with Two Variables

```
PERSONNEL REPORT (BASIC)                                    PAGE    1

STORE/          AGE   TENURE IN    TENURE IN        ANNUAL
DIVISION              COMPANY      GRADE            SALARY

SUBURBAN
CARPETING
MEAN            32    2.07         1.52            16004

SUBURBAN
APPLIANCES
MEAN            33    2.21         1.87            16105

SUBURBAN
FURNITURE
MEAN            36    3.03         2.65            18821

SUBURBAN
HARDWARE
MEAN            34    2.59         2.26            16435

DOWNTOWN
CARPETING
MEAN            33    2.17         1.45            13465

DOWNTOWN
APPLIANCES
MEAN            35    2.37         1.99            14130

DOWNTOWN
FURNITURE
MEAN            36    2.64         1.99            14403

DOWNTOWN
HARDWARE
MEAN            35    2.49         2.12            14873

TOTAL
MEAN            34    2.47         2.00            15286
```

5.30   Keyword TOTAL and Multiple Break Reports

TOTAL is a FORMAT= specification that prints summary statistics across breaks. It should be used only in reports requesting only one break level or in reports with multiple break levels that have different summary specifications for each break level. If it is used in multiple-break reports that use the same summary statistics for each break level, it produces redundant summaries. Figure 5.30 is the same report shown in 5.29a illustrating the effect of specifying TOTAL.

Figure 5.30   TOTAL and Multiple Breaks

```
PERSONNEL REPORT (BASIC)                                    PAGE    1

BRANCH      PRODUCT           AGE   TENURE IN    TENURE IN    ANNUAL
STORE       DIVISION                COMPANY      GRADE        SALARY

SUBURBAN    CARPETING
            MEAN              32    2.07         1.52        16004
            APPLIANCES
            MEAN              33    2.21         1.87        16105
            FURNITURE
            MEAN              36    3.03         2.65        18821
            HARDWARE
            MEAN              34    2.59         2.26        16435

            TOTAL
            MEAN              34    2.51         2.13        16881
MEAN                          34    2.51         2.13        16881

DOWNTOWN    CARPETING
            MEAN              33    2.17         1.45        13465
            APPLIANCES
            MEAN              35    2.37         1.99        14130
            FURNITURE
            MEAN              36    2.64         1.99        14403
            HARDWARE
            MEAN              35    2.49         2.12        14873

            TOTAL
            MEAN              35    2.44         1.90        14232
MEAN                          35    2.44         1.90        14232

TOTAL
MEAN                          34    2.47         2.00        15286
```

In Figure 5.30, the summary line following the title 'TOTAL MEAN' is produced by the TOTAL option. However, the same summary is computed automatically as the higher-level break is summarized. If you require statistics for the entire file and your report contains more than one BREAK= subcommand, specify a constant for the highest level break. A variable created with the STRING= subcommand (see Section 5.21) satisfies this requirement.

5.31 THE SUMMARY= SUBCOMMAND

The SUMMARY= subcommand specifies the aggregate statistics to be computed using the variables named on the VARS= subcommand. This subcommand is required. The SUMMARY= subcommand is directly tied to the BREAK= subcommand that specifies the group upon which statistics are to be computed. Every BREAK= subcommand has a SUMMARY= subcommand. However, if the report contains more than one BREAK= subcommand, the SUMMARY= subcommand is required only for the first. If it is omitted for any subsequent BREAK= subcommand, the last previously specified SUMMARY= subcommand is used.

Summary arguments specify the statistics to be computed, the variables for which the statistics are computed, optional summary titles, the number of decimal digits to be printed for summary statistics, and the break column in which the summary title is placed.

5.32 The Basic SUMMARY= Specification

The basic SUMMARY= subcommand includes a set of aggregate statistics and a set of variables on which those statistics are to be computed:

```
SUMMARY=agg ... agg [(varname ... varname)]/
```

The keyword TO cannot be used to imply a set of variables. If the functions are to be performed on all numeric variables included in the VARS= list, the variable list can be omitted:

```
SUMMARY=agg ... agg/
```

Statistics will not be computed for alphanumeric, string, or dummy variables in such a default list; if an alphanumeric, string, or dummy variable is explicitly named for an aggregate function, REPORT will flag it with an error.

The company report in Figure 5.7 has a simple default summary. One aggregate statistic, the mean, is specified without a variable list. Since the variable list is omitted, the mean is computed for all eligible variables named on the VARS= subcommand. The mean for each variable is printed in its corresponding column. The summary title MEAN is printed in the break column.

5.33 Statistics Available Within Report

Aggregate functions are specified by keywords (and, in some instances, arguments within parentheses). The following functions are available:

Keyword	Function
VALIDN	valid number of cases
VARIANCE	variance
SUM	sum of values
MEAN	mean
STDEV	standard deviation
MIN	minimum value encountered
MAX	maximum value encountered
SKEWNESS	skewness
KURTOSIS	kurtosis
PCTGT(n)	percentage of cases with values greater than specified value
PCTLT(n)	percentage of cases with values less than specified value
PCTBTN(n1,n2)	percentage of cases with values between specified values, including those with the specified values
ABFREQ(min,max)	frequency counts for all nonmissing values within range
RELFREQ(min,max)	percentages for all nonmissing values within range
MEDIAN(min,max)	median value for all nonmissing values within range
MODE(min,max)	modal value for all nonmissing values within range

ABFREQ, RELFREQ, MEDIAN, and MODE are computed using the same algorithms used by procedure FREQUENCIES in *integer* mode. Consequently, non-integer values are truncated in computing these statistics.

5.34 Composite Functions

Composite functions are computed upon simple aggregate functions. The following composite functions are available:

Keyword	Function
DIVIDE(agg() agg()[factor])	Divide the first argument by the second and multiply by the optional factor, which can be an integer or decimal number.

PCT(agg() agg())	Give the percentage of the first argument over the second.
SUBTRACT(agg()agg())	Subtract the second argument from the first argument.
ADD(agg() . . . agg())	Add the arguments.
GREAT(agg() . . . agg())	Give the maximum of the arguments.
LEAST(agg() . . . agg())	Give the minimum of the arguments.
AVERAGE(agg() . . . agg())	Give the average of the arguments.

VALIDN, VARIANCE, SUM, MEAN, SD, MIN, MAX, SKEWNESS and KURTOSIS as well as any numerical constants can be used in composite functions. The use of composite functions within reports is described in Section 5.39.

5.35 Multiple Aggregate Functions

More than one aggregate function can be specified for a variable or set of variables within a report. If the same function is applied to several variables, the results are printed on the same line, each under the appropriate column. When two or more functions are requested, the result for each function is printed on a separate line.

Multiple functions for the same set of variables are requested by naming the set of functions followed by the set of variables within parentheses. If the variable list is omitted, the functions are computed for all eligible variables in the VARS= list. For example,

```
SUMMARY=VALIDN SUM MEAN (VARA VARB VARC VARD)/
```

produces the valid number of cases, sum, and mean for variables VARA, VARB, VARC, and VARD.

Figure 5.35 is a report with four aggregate statistics requested: SUM, MEAN, RELFREQ, and MEDIAN.

Figure 5.35   Multiple Summary Simple Report

```
DEMONSTRATE REPORT WITH MULTIPLE SUMMARIES                              PAGE     1


TOTPOP            FOURTH      FIFTH       SIXTH       SEVENTH     EIGHTH
                  VARIABLE    VARIABLE    VARIABLE    VARIABLE    VARIABLE
TOTAL POPULATION
SUM                  477         469         493         491         491
MEAN                4.42        4.34        4.56        4.55        4.55

RELFREQ

TOTAL             100.00      100.00      100.00      100.00      100.00
              0    12.04       13.89       10.19       10.19        8.33
              1    10.19        5.56        7.41        8.33        8.33
              2     9.26       11.11       12.04        8.33       12.96
              3     4.63       14.81       12.04       12.96       11.11
              4    12.04        8.33       11.11       13.89        6.48
              5    12.96        9.26        7.41        9.26       12.96
              6    12.96        7.41        9.26        4.63       10.19
              7     9.26        7.41        9.26       11.11       12.04
              8     6.48       13.89        4.63        8.33        7.41
              9    10.19        8.33       16.67       12.96       10.19

MEDIAN               4.6         4.1         4.3         4.2         4.7
```

The subcommands required to produce the report in Figure 5.35 are

```
REPORT        FORMAT=MARGINS(1,80)BRKSPACE(0)CHDSPACE(0)/
              VARS=
              V4 'FOURTH''VARIABLE'(8)(LABEL)
              V5 'FIFTH''VARIABLE'(8)
              V6 'SIXTH''VARIABLE'(8)
              V7 'SEVENTH''VARIABLE'(8)
              V8 'EIGHTH''VARIABLE'(8)/
              BREAK=TOTPOP(LABEL)(16)(SKIP(1))/
              SUMMARY=SUM MEAN RELFREQ(0,9)MEDIAN(0,9)/
```

5.36 Specifying Summary Titles

Each summary statistic has a title. By default, the keyword used to specify the statistic will be printed in the column corresponding to the level of break being summarized. The default title can be overridden by a summary title defined as a string in apostrophes. For example, the default summary title for VALIDN is VALIDN. To provide a summary title of 'No. of Employees', the following summary specification is used:

```
VALIDN'No. of Employees'(GR78)
```

A summary title wider than the break column will be truncated. Leading blanks can be used to indent summary titles. Unlike other title strings in REPORT, a summary title can be only one line long. If more than one summary statistic is requested, a title can be continued from summary line to summary line to provide more extensive labeling. For example,

```
SUMMARY=SUM'SUMS AND AVERAGES'
        MEAN'BASED ON 1980 5% SAMPLE'
```

produces a two-line summary with a title continuing from the first to the second line. As with other titles in REPORT, a null title can be used.

5.37 Placing Summary Titles in Break Columns

By default, the summary title for a statistic is placed in the break column corresponding to the level of break for the group being summarized. It is possible to place the summary title in a different break column on a report that contains more than one BREAK= subcommand. The column number for the break column placed in parentheses following the aggregate function overrides the default. The following subcommand will place the default title "VALIDN" in the second column regardless of the level of break being summarized:

```
SUMMARY=VALIDN(2)/
```

And the following subcommand specifies a summary title, a column for the title, and the variables to be summarized:

```
SUMMARY=VALIDN'No. of Employees'(2)(GR78 GR77 GR76)/
```

The Report in Figure 5.37 uses summary titles to produce a compact frequencies report.

Figure 5.37   A Multi-titled Summary

```
                      GOVERNMENT POLICY PRIORITIES


REGION            AID TO CONTROL   CIVIL  FOREIGN HIGHER MILITARY INCREASE
                  CITIES INFLATION RIGHTS AID     ED     SPENDING JOBS
EAST

STRONGLY AGREE      7.56   15.00   12.30   15.38   9.17   16.81   12.40
AGREE              31.93   29.17   23.77   18.80  23.33   30.09   18.18
INDIFFERENT        26.89   21.67   21.31   25.64  25.00   22.12   25.62
DISAGREE           19.33   20.00   32.79   28.21  21.67   22.12   31.40
STRONGLY DISAGREE  14.29   14.17    9.84   11.97  20.83    8.85   12.40
  FAVORING         39.50   44.17   36.07   34.19  32.50   46.90   30.58
  OPPOSED          33.61   34.17   42.62   40.17  42.50   30.97   43.80
NO. RESPONDENTS      119     120     122     117    120     113     121

MID

STRONGLY AGREE     11.02   13.79   13.68   10.34  11.21   14.29   14.16
AGREE              28.81   18.10   25.64   25.86  25.00   22.69   23.89
INDIFFERENT        20.34   30.17   23.08   21.55  23.28   24.37   29.20
DISAGREE           24.58   25.00   28.21   21.55  29.31   23.53   21.24
STRONGLY DISAGREE  15.25   12.93    9.40   20.69  11.21   15.13   11.50
  FAVORING         39.83   31.90   39.32   36.21  36.21   36.97   38.05
  OPPOSED          39.83   37.93   37.61   42.24  40.52   38.66   32.74
NO. RESPONDENTS      118     116     117     116    116     119     113

WEST

STRONGLY AGREE     12.82   10.67   12.20   16.44  15.29   16.09   15.85
AGREE              24.36   21.33   28.05   26.03  31.76   28.74   15.85
INDIFFERENT        25.64   25.33   25.61   28.77  22.35   19.54   26.83
DISAGREE           24.36   32.00   20.73   15.07  22.35   28.74   24.39
STRONGLY DISAGREE  12.82   10.67   13.41   13.70   8.24    6.90   17.07
  FAVORING         37.18   32.00   40.24   42.47  47.06   44.83   31.71
  OPPOSED          37.18   42.67   34.15   28.77  30.59   35.63   41.46
NO. RESPONDENTS       78      75      82      73     85      87      82



                      SURVEY CONDUCTED JULY, 1979
```

The subcommands required to produce the report in Figure 5.37 are

```
REPORT       FORMAT=MARGINS(1,80)BRKSPACE(1)CHDSPACE(0)
               LENGTH(1,10)/
             VARS=CITIES'AID TO''CITIES'(6)
             INFLATE'CONTROL''INFLATION'
             CIVIL'CIVIL''RIGHTS'(6)
             AID'FOREIGN''AID'(7)
             HIGHERED'HIGHER''ED'(6)
             MILITARY'MILITARY''SPENDING'(8)
             JOBS'INCREASE''JOBS'(8)
             /
             HEAD='GOVERNMENT POLICY PRIORITIES'/
             FOOT='SURVEY CONDUCTED JULY, 1979'/
             BREAK=SUBFILE'REGION'(18)(SKIP(1))
             /
```

```
SUMMARY=PCTBTN(1,1)'STRONGLY AGREE'
PCTBTN(2,2)'AGREE'
PCTBTN(3,3)'INDIFFERENT'
PCTBTN(4,4)'DISAGREE'
PCTBTN(5,5)'STRONGLY DISAGREE'
PCTBTN(1,2)'   FAVORING'
PCTBTN(4,5)'    OPPOSED'
VALIDN'NO. RESPONDENTS'
```

5.38 Specifying Print Formats for Summaries
Every aggregate function, either simple or composite, has a default print format for the number of decimal digits to be displayed. If the column is not wide enough to print the decimal digits for a given function, REPORT will print fewer. If the column is not wide enough to print the integer portion of the number, asterisks will be printed. The default print formats by function are shown in Table 5.38.

Table 5.38 Default Print Formats for Functions

Function	Print Format
VALIDN	0
VARIANCE	Column width - 1
SUM	Variable's print format
MEAN	Variable's print format + 2
STDEV	Variable's print format + 2
MIN	Variable's print format
MAX	Variable's print format
SKEWNESS	3
KURTOSIS	3
PCTGT	2
PCTLT	2
PCTBTN	2
MEDIAN	1
MODE	0
ABFREQ	0
RELFREQ	2
DIVIDE	Column width - 1
PCT	2
SUBTRACT	Column width - 1
ADD	Column width - 1
GREAT	Column width - 1
LEAST	Column width - 1
AVERAGE	Column width - 1

Other print formats can be specified in parentheses immediately following the variable name. For example,

```
SUM MEAN (A(2) B(3))
```

will print two decimal digits for the sum and mean of variable A and three decimal digits for the sum and mean of variable B. Note that the specification modifies only the variable immediately preceding it and that the parentheses enclosing the print format go within the parentheses for the variable list.

5.39 Using Composite Functions
Section 5.34 describes the types of composite functions available within REPORT. This section describes the syntactical requirements for using composites and the reasons for using them.

Although the syntax for composite functions is similar to the syntax required for simple functions, the specifications are used in different ways. The general syntax for specifying a composite function is

```
agg ['title'][(break col #)] [(varlist[(n)])]
```

where "agg" is the composite function *and* its arguments. For example,

```
PCT(VALIDN(MALE) VALIDN(EMPLOY))
```

is a composite function producing the percentage of employees who are male. Note, however, that this function computes only one result, unlike a simple function which computes results for each variable enclosed in parentheses following it. The purpose of the variable list following a composite function is to inform REPORT in which column(s) to print the result. However, since the default variable list for summary statistics is all numeric variables, if a variable list is not supplied, the same result will be printed in every eligible "vars" column. Thus, it is usually advisable to specify the column in which the result of the composite function is printed. Unlike simple functions, the composite function can be placed in *any* "vars" column, including those defined by dummy variables, string variables, and alphanumeric variables.

Since a composite function includes not only the name of the function but also the arguments to the function, a title specification cannot separate the function name from its arguments but must follow the arguments.

Print formats for composites are specified within parentheses following the name of the variable in whose column the result is to be printed—not within the arguments to the function. Since most composite functions have as a default print format the width of the column−1, it is usually advisable to specify the number of decimal digits to be printed, as in

```
SUMMARY=DIVIDE(MEAN(CRIME)MEAN(POLICE))''(RATIO(3))/
```

There are two basic reasons for using composite functions. First, a composite function can be used to place a summary statistic in a column other than the one for which it is calculated. For example, the sum of VARA is printed in the column corresponding to VARA. It can be placed in any other column with a composite such as

```
ADD(SUM(VARA)) (VARB)
```

Note that this summary adds VARA to nothing. The SUBTRACT, GREAT, LEAST, and AVERAGE composite functions can achieve the same result.

Second, composite functions can be used to manipulate statistics and change the unit of analysis. Certain arithmetic operations between variables produce the same result at either the case level or the subpopulation level. You can subtract the sum of variable A from the sum of variable B and obtain the same answer as subtracting A from B for each case and summing the result. However, dividing the sum of A by the sum of B is not the same as dividing A by B for each case and averaging the results.

5.40   Example Reports Using Composite Functions

Figure 5.40a is a report using the ADD and PCT composite functions.

Figure 5.40a   Composite Functions in Dummy Columns

```
                           REVENUES AND SERVICES
                        ICPR CITY COUNTY DATA FILE
```

STATE	NO. OF CITIES	LOCAL GOV REVENUE PER 1000	RATIO TO NATION	PER CAP. PROPERTY TAX	RATIO TO NATION	HOSPITAL BEDS PER 1000	RATIO TO NATION
ALABAMA AVERAGES	14	1.64	101.25	14.93	22.25	17.79	160.58
ALASKA AVERAGES	1	5.11	315.33	99.00	147.56	19.31	174.29
ARIZONA AVERAGES	8	1.24	76.79	20.00	29.81	5.12	46.23
ARKANSAS AVERAGES	9	.77	47.72	11.89	17.72	10.70	96.57
CALIFORNIA AVERAGES	113	1.26	78.05	33.40	49.78	6.42	57.96
COLORADO AVERAGES	11	1.04	63.89	22.09	32.93	6.80	61.39
CONNECTICUT AVERAGES	17	3.55	218.98	226.35	337.39	12.68	114.45
DELAWARE AVERAGES	1	4.37	269.53	139.00	207.18	23.03	207.82
DISTRICT OF COLUMBIA AVERAGES	1	9.08	560.40	169.00	251.90	17.33	156.39
FLORIDA AVERAGES	28	1.40	86.72	43.86	65.37	10.75	97.03
GEORGIA AVERAGES	12	1.07	66.06	37.33	55.65	11.53	104.07
HAWAII AVERAGES	1	3.84	237.32	199.00	296.62	11.88	107.27
IDAHO AVERAGES	4	.77	47.51	36.25	54.03	7.07	63.77
ILLINOIS AVERAGES	49	1.06	65.32	33.57	50.04	11.07	99.95
INDIANA AVERAGES	20	1.19	73.15	73.25	109.18	12.58	113.56
IOWA AVERAGES	16	1.38	85.07	61.31	91.39	11.56	104.32

The subcommands required to produce Figure 5.40a are

```
REPORT          FORMAT=CHDSPACE(0)BRKSPACE(0)MARGINS(1,100)/
                VARS=D1(DUMMY)'NO.''OF''CITIES'(6)
                    REVENUM
                    D3(DUMMY)'RATIO''TO''NATION'(6)
                    PROPTAX
                    D5(DUMMY)'RATIO''TO''NATION'(6)
                    BED
                    D7(DUMMY)'RATIO''TO''NATION'(6)               /
                HEAD='REVENUES AND SERVICES''ICPR CITY COUNTY DATA FILE'/
                BREAK=T2'STATE'(LABEL)(SKIP(1))/
◆               SUMMARY=ADD(VALIDN(REVENUM) 0)'   AVERAGES'(D1(0))
◆                   MEAN CONTINUE (REVENUM)
◆                   PCT(MEAN(REVENUM) 1.62) CONTINUE(D3)
                    MEAN CONTINUE (PROPTAX)
◆                   PCT(MEAN(PROPTAX) 67.09) CONTINUE (D5)
                    MEAN CONTINUE (BED)
◆                   PCT(MEAN(BED) 11.08) CONTINUE(D7)    /
```

Note that the ADD function is used to move a simple summary function (number of cities) into a dummy variable column. Dummy variables columns are also set up to hold the results of the PCT composite functions. The constants used in the PCT composite functions were obtained from a previous run which provided overall means for REVENUM, PROPTAX, and and BED.

In Figure 5.40b, the DIVIDE composite function is used to compute a grand mean.

Figure 5.40b   Report with Composite Function for Grand Mean

```
CHICAGO TEAMS VERSUS LEAGUE WINNERS, 1979                                    PAGE    1


LEAGUE    TEAM             PLAYER       POSITION  TIMES    RUNS     HITS    RUNS    BATTING
                                                  AT BAT   SCORED           BATTED  AVERAGE
                                                                            IN

NATIONAL  CHICAGO CUBS
                           DEJESUS      SS         636      92      180      52     .283
                           THOMPSON     RF         346      36      100      29     .289
                           BUCKNER      1B         591      72      168      66     .284
                           KINGMAN      LF         532      97      153      15     .288
                           MARTIN       CF         534      74      145      73     .272
                           ONTIVEROS    3B         519      58      148      57     .285
                           FOOTE        C          429      47      109      56     .254
                           DILLARD      2B         166      31       47      24     .283
                           REUSCHEL     P           79       8       13       6     .165

          AVERAGE FOR TEAM                         426      57      118      42     .277


          PITTSBURGH PIRATES
                           MORENO       CF         695      10      196      69     .282
                           FOLI         SS         532      70      153      65     .288
                           PARKER       RF         622       9      193      94     .310
                           STARGELL     1B         424      60      119      82     .281
                           MADLOCK      3B         560      85      167      85     .298
                           MILNER       LF         326      52       90      60     .276
                           GARNER       2B         549      76      161      59     .293
                           OTT          C          403      49      110      51     .273
                           BLYLEVEN     P           70       1        9       3     .129

          AVERAGE FOR TEAM                         465      46      133      63     .287
AVERAGE                                            445      51      126      53     .282
```

The specifications for the report in Figure 5.40b are

```
REPORT          FORMAT=LIST BRKSPACE(0) MARGINS(1,103)/
                STRING=PLAYER (PLAYER1 PLAYER2 PLAYER3)/
                VARS=PLAYER (12)
                    POSITION (8)
                    ATBAT (6) 'TIMES''AT BAT'
                    RUNS (6) ' RUNS''SCORED'
                    HITS (6) ' HITS'
                    RBI (6) ' RUNS''BATTED''  IN'
                    AVERAGE (7) 'BATTING''AVERAGE' /
                BREAK=LEAGUE(LABEL)(8)(PAGE)/
                SUM=MEAN (ATBAT(0) RUNS(0) HITS(0) RBI(0))
                    'AVERAGE FOR TEAM'
◆                   DIVIDE (SUM(HITS)SUM(ATBAT)) CONTINUE (AVERAGE(3))/
                BREAK=TEAM(LABEL)
```

5.41   Multiple Summary Groups

Most of the examples illustrated to this point have specified only one group of aggregate functions and a single set of optional specifications for that group of functions: the variables on which the statistics are to be computed or the print column for a composite function, the print format, the summary title, and the break column for the summary title. In practice, you will often need more than one such combination of functions and optional specifications—for example, the VALIDN for VARA and the MEAN for VARB. SUMMARY= can be followed by any number of "summary groups". Proper handling of summary groups will permit combinations of statistics, variables, and print locations as complex as almost any report might require.

Entering one summary group after another, such as

```
SUMMARY=ABFREQ'FREQUENCIES'(VARA) MEAN(VARB)/
```

comes quite naturally, but understanding how REPORT recognizes and responds to these groups is essential to writing complex summary specifications.

REPORT marks the end of a group of functions when it encounters any of the optional specifications, and it marks the start of the next group when it encounters the next keyword for a function. Any of the optional specifications not explicitly defined within the group (before the next function is named) are supplied by default. Thus the following subcommand contains two summary groups:

```
SUMMARY=VALIDN'NO. OF CASES'MEAN(VARA)/
```

The title for VALIDN signals the end of the summary group, and, by default, VALIDN will be computed for all valid variables in the VARS= subcommand and the summary title "NO. OF CASES" will be printed in the column for the level of break being summarized. MEAN will be computed only for VARA and will have the default title "MEAN" printed in the column for the level of break being summarized.

The following sample subcommands illustrate the operation of summary groups:

```
SUMMARY= SUM MEAN (VARA VARB VARC)/
```

```
SUMMARY= SUM MEAN (VARA) SUM MEAN (VARB) SUM MEAN (VARC)/
```

Either of the above subcommands will produce sums for the three variables, but the first subcommand contains one group and will print the sum for each variable on one line and the mean for each variable on the following line, while the second subcommand contains three groups and will print sum and mean for VARA on the first two lines of the summary, sum and mean for VARB on the next two lines, and so on.

```
SUMMARY= VALIDN'Total Observations' ABFREQ(1,4)
         'Party Preference' (PARTYPR)/
```

The above subcommand contains two summary groups. VALIDN will be computed for all variables, since the first variable group is terminated by the title specification 'Total Observations' and no variable list is specified for that group. Absolute frequencies will be computed only for the variable PARTYPR.

```
SUMMARY= VALIDN (1) ABFREQ(1,4) 'Party Preference' (PARTYPR)/
```

This is the same as the preceding subcommand, except that the default title "VALIDN" will be printed in the first break column regardless of the level of break being summarized. Without the (1), which terminates the first variable group, VALIDN would be computed only for PARTYPR.

The variable list which follows a composite function will apply to all preceding functions in the group. For example,

```
SUMMARY= MEAN SUBTRACT(SUM(SALARY) SUM(TAX))(NET)/
```

If NET is a dummy variable, this subcommand will generate an error, since NET is the variable list for MEAN as well as the column specification for SUBTRACT. A correct subcommand would include a separate variable list for MEAN or, if means are desired for all numeric variables named in the VARS= subcommand, any specification that would set MEAN apart in a separate summary group. The following would calculate the mean for variables SALARY and TAX.

```
SUMMARY= MEAN (SALARY TAX)
         SUBTRACT(SUM(SALARY) SUM(TAX))(NET)/
```

or, to obtain means for all numeric variables:

```
SUMMARY= MEAN 'MEAN' SUBTRACT(SUM(SALARY) SUM(TAX))(NET)/
```

Only one summary title can be specified in each summary group, and it will be used for the first, not the last, summary statistic named in that group. For example,

```
SUMMARY=VALIDN RELFREQ(1,9) MEAN 'N OF RESPONSES' (FAMSIZE)/
```

assigns the title "N OF RESPONSES" to VALIDN. Default titles are used for the other statistics. To assign separate titles to two statistics, two summary groups are required. For example,

```
SUMMARY=VALIDN 'N OF RESPONSES'(FAMSIZE)
        RELFREQ(1,9) MEAN 'PCT OF TOTAL' (FAMSIZE)/
```

5.42 Printing Multiple Summary Groups on the Same Line: Keyword CONTINUE

By default, every summary group begins a new line on the report. If a summary group specifies multiple functions, the results of each function are printed on a separate line. Only one summary statistic can be printed on each line in a single column. The special keyword CONTINUE instructs REPORT to print the current summary group of one aggregate function on the same line as the previous summary group. A summary group containing CONTINUE can include only one function and *must* include a variable list. It cannot be used with either ABFREQ or RELFREQ since these functions themselves print multiple lines. Its format is

```
agg CONTINUE (varname ... varname)
```

Note that CONTINUE comes between the aggregate function and the variable list. It in effect replaces a summary title specification since it places the summary group on the line with the previous summary group which already has been titled. The following example demonstrates the use of CONTINUE with a simple aggregate function:

```
STDEV (A B) MEAN CONTINUE (C D)
```

CONTINUE is useful for printing the results of composite functions. For example, assume a report contains a listing of the batting averages of the Chicago Cubs (see Figure 5.40b). The report contains individual at bats (ATBAT) hits (HITS), strike-outs (SOUTS) and batting averages (AVERAGE). The team batting average is computed using the DIVIDE function and printed in the AVERAGE column with the following arguments:

```
SUM=MEAN (ATBAT(0) RUNS(0) HITS(0) RBI(0))
        'AVERAGE FOR TEAM'
      DIVIDE (SUM(HITS)SUM(ATBAT)) CONTINUE (AVERAGE(3))/
```

If the keyword CONTINUE is not used, the result of the composite function is printed as a separate summary group on the next line.

Figure 5.42 is a report using the CONTINUE function to place means for one set of variables on the same line as the sums.

Figure 5.42   Two Summaries Printed with CONTINUE

```
DIFF SUMS FOR DIFF VARS ON SAME LINE AND SUMTITLE              PAGE    1


TOTPOP                FOURTH      FIFTH       SIXTH       SEVENTH     EIGHTH
                      VARIABLE    VARIABLE    VARIABLE    VARIABLE    VARIABLE
TOTAL POPULATION
SUM:4 5 MEAN:6-8        477         469         4.56        4.55        4.55
```

Since two different statistics are printed on the same line, a special summary title is specified to more clearly identify the numbers. The subcommands required to produce the report in Figure 5.42 are

```
REPORT        FORMAT=MARGINS(1,80)BRKSPACE(0)CHDSPACE(0)/
              STRING=
               TOTPOP('TOTAL POPULATION')/
              VARS=
               V4 'FOURTH''VARIABLE'
               V5 'FIFTH''VARIABLE'
               V6 'SIXTH''VARIABLE'
               V7 'SEVENTH''VARIABLE'
               V8 'EIGHTH''VARIABLE'
               /
              BREAK=TOTPOP /
              SUMMARY=SUM 'SUM:4 5 MEAN:6-8' (V4 V5)MEAN
              CONTINUE (V6 V7 V8)/
```

See the example shown in Section 5.45 for another report that makes extensive use of CONTINUE to place statistics in different columns of the same line.

5.43   Summary of SUMMARY= Specifications

The complete syntax for the SUMMARY= subcommand is

```
SUMMARY= agg agg ... agg
         ['summary title'] [(break column #)]
         [(varname [(decimal digits)] ... )]
         agg [CONTINUE]
         [(varname [(decimal digits)] )]
         ... agg ... /
```

Default specifications are

• If no variable list is specified, all numeric variables on the VARS= subcommand are summarized.
• Default print formats are used for printing summary statistics.
• The name of the summary statistic is used as the summary title.
• The summary title is printed in the break column corresponding to the break summarized.
• Each summary group begins on a new line.

Another summary statistic, a summary title, or a variable list marks the end of a summary group. The CONTINUE can be used in place of a summary title to print the results of the current summary group on the same line as the previous summary group.

Figure 5.43   The Company Report With Summary Specifications

```
PERSONNEL REPORT (BASIC)                                    PAGE    1

PRODUCT        AGE    TENURE IN    TENURE IN        ANNUAL
DIVISION               COMPANY       GRADE          SALARY

CARPETING
   AVERAGE     33        2.1          1.5            14221
   COUNT                                                47

APPLIANCES
   AVERAGE     34        2.3          1.9            15039
   COUNT                                                76

FURNITURE
   AVERAGE     36        2.8          2.2            15894
   COUNT                                                80

HARDWARE
   AVERAGE     35        2.5          2.2            15616
   COUNT                                                61

TOTAL
   AVERAGE     34        2.5          2.0            15286
   COUNT                                               264
```

Figure 5.43 is the updated company report modified with optional summary specifications.

Compare this report to the report in Figure 5.7. What began as a basically readable report has been iteratively transformed into a detailed report suitable for publication or presentation to others. Note that the report has been considerably compressed through the use of formatting options, but at the same time enhanced in its labeling through VARS=, BREAK=, and SUMMARY= options. This report can be further modified with additional titling information.

The subcommands required to produce the report in Figure 5.43 are

```
REPORT        FORMAT=MARGINS (1,80) HDSPACE(1) BRKSPACE(0) TOTAL/
              VARS=AGE(3) TENURE JTENURE
               SPACE(DUMMY)''(4)
               SALARY 'ANNUAL''SALARY'(6)/
              BREAK=DIVISION 'PRODUCT''DIVISION' (LABEL)(12)
               (SKIP(1))/
              SUMMARY=MEAN '  AVERAGE'
               (AGE TENURE(1) JTENURE(1) SALARY)
              VALIDN '   COUNT'(SALARY)
```

5.44   RUNNING HEADS AND FEET

Left, center, and right running heads and feet can be placed on each page of the printed output. Each head or foot can have as many lines as needed with each line specified by a string enclosed in apostrophes:

```
        HEAD='line1' 'line 2' ... 'last line'/
```

Any or all of the following can be specified:

```
        LHEAD='     '/    Left-adjusted head
        RHEAD='     '/    Right-adjusted head
        CHEAD='     '/    Centered head
        LFOOT='     '/    Left-adjusted foot
        RFOOT='     '/    Right-adjusted foot
        CFOOT='     '/    Centered foot
```

HEAD= and FOOT= are equivalent to CHEAD= and CFOOT=, except that HEAD= cannot be used with LHEAD= or RHEAD= and FOOT= cannot be used in combination with LFOOT= or RFOOT=. In addition to these exceptions, only one of each subcommand is permitted per REPORT command, although each subcommand can specify more than one title line. There is no fixed limit to the number of header and running feet lines on a report. These subcommands are optional and can be placed anywhere after the FORMAT= subcommand.

Heads and feet are repeated on each page of a multiple-page report. Centered headers and running feet are placed exactly in the center of the page layout. Note that wide reports with few columns are offset to the left of the center since the maximum intercolumn width is 4 spaces. Centered heads on such reports appear to be offset to the right.

Two special arguments can be used in running heads and feet:

)PAGE   prints the page number right-adjusted in a five character field.

)DATE   prints *mm/dd/yy*.

Typical subcommands using these arguments are

```
LHEAD='PERSONNEL REPORT''PREPARED ON )DATE'/
RHEAD='Page )PAGE'/
```

If neither a running head nor a running foot is specified, a default heading will be generated. If the width of the page is 10 or more characters, "PAGE   n" will appear as a right-adjusted head. If the width is 80 or greater, the RUN NAME will be left-adjusted in the first 64 characters.

A null head can be specified, producing an extra blank line at the top of every page of the report. There is no default foot. Apostrophes cannot be be embedded in titles since they are used in the REPORT syntax to demarcate titles. Specifying a head or foot longer than the report width will generate an error.

Figure 5.44   The Company Report with Titling Information

```
CHICAGO HOME FURNISHINGS                               Page    1
Personnel Report

BRANCH        PRODUCT           AGE TENURE IN TENURE IN    ANNUAL
STORE         DIVISION              COMPANY   GRADE        SALARY

SUBURBAN      CARPETING
                AVERAGE          32    2.1      1.5        16004
                COUNT                                         14
              APPLIANCES
                AVERAGE          33    2.2      1.9        16105
                COUNT                                         35
              FURNITURE
                AVERAGE          36    3.0      2.7        18821
                COUNT                                         27
              HARDWARE
                AVERAGE          34    2.6      2.3        16435
                COUNT                                         29
  AVERAGE                        34    2.5      2.1        16881
  COUNT                                                      105

DOWNTOWN      CARPETING
                AVERAGE          33    2.2      1.4        13465
                COUNT                                         33
              APPLIANCES
                AVERAGE          35    2.4      2.0        14130
                COUNT                                         41
              FURNITURE
                AVERAGE          36    2.6      2.0        14403
                COUNT                                         53
              HARDWARE
                AVERAGE          35    2.5      2.1        14873
                COUNT                                         32
  AVERAGE                        35    2.4      1.9        14232
  COUNT                                                      159

Prepared on  12/31/80
```

Figure 5.44 is a final example of the company report modified through optional subcommand specifications demonstrating the use of headings and a foot to build a final report. The subcommands required to produce the report in Figure 5.44 are

```
REPORT        FORMAT=MARGINS (1,70) HDSPACE(1) BRKSPACE(0) LENGTH(1,17)/
              VARS=AGE(3) TENURE JTENURE
               SPACE(DUMMY)''(4)
               SALARY 'ANNUAL''SALARY'(6)/
              LHEAD='CHICAGO HOME FURNISHINGS''Personnel Report'/
              RHEAD='Page )PAGE'/
              LFOOT='Prepared on )DATE'/
              BREAK=STORE 'BRANCH''STORE' (LABEL)(12)
               (SKIP(1))/
              SUMMARY=MEAN '  AVERAGE'
               (AGE TENURE(1) JTENURE(1) SALARY)
               VALIDN '   COUNT'(SALARY)/
              BREAK=DIVISION 'PRODUCT''DIVISION' (LABEL)(SKIP(0))/
```

Note the use of the LENGTH keyword in the FORMAT= subcommand to force the footer up to the bottom part of the report.

5.45 Manipulating Heads

Figure 5.45 shows a finely formatted table where several iterations were used to develop LHEAD, CHEAD, and RHEAD to encompass several columns of data.

Figure 5.45   An Application with Extensive Titling

```
MONTHLY COMPENSATION BY CATEGORY                                                    PREPARED 10/27/80
CALENDAR YEAR 1979                                                                  PAGE     1
```

									CAUSE OF CLAIM						TOTAL	
	TYPE OF COVERAGE															
	PLAN A		PLAN B		ILLNESS		JOB INJURY		OTHER INJURY		OTHER				TOTAL	
MONTH	NO.	AMOUNT	NO.	AMOUNT	NO.	AMOUNT	NO.	AMOUNT	NO.	AMOUNT	NO.	AMOUNT			NO.	AMOUNT
JANUARY																
TOTAL	4	7940.18	0	M	2	3570.28	2	4369.90	0	M	0	M			4	7940.179
PERCENT		100.00		M		44.96		55.04		M		M				
FEBRUARY																
TOTAL	6	10139.15	0	M	2	5961.55	4	4177.60	0	M	0	M			7	11124.15
PERCENT		91.15		M		53.59		37.55		M		M				
MARCH																
TOTAL	4	13087.70	3	2824.90	1	6985.00	5	8188.90	1	738.70	0	M			7	15912.60
PERCENT		82.25		17.75		43.90		51.46		4.64		M				
APRIL																
TOTAL	5	6006.33	2	912.83	1	535.75	4	5972.91	1	35.00	1	375.50			7	6919.160
PERCENT		86.81		13.19		7.74		86.32		.51		5.43				
MAY																
TOTAL	6	8717.55	1	712.43	3	4674.05	2	3918.50	0	M	2	837.43			7	9429.979
PERCENT		92.45		7.55		49.57		41.55		M		8.88				
JUNE																
TOTAL	6	5138.48	0	M	4	2559.03	2	2579.45	0	M	0	M			6	5138.480
PERCENT		100.00		M		49.80		50.20		M		M				
JULY																
TOTAL	2	2320.00	6	5747.38	6	5747.38	2	2320.00	0	M	0	M			9	8246.319
PERCENT		28.13		69.70		69.70		28.13		M		M				
AUGUST																
TOTAL	3	979.40	4	15567.75	3	5542.20	3	979.40	1	10025.55	0	M			7	16547.15
PERCENT		5.92		94.08		33.49		5.92		60.59		M				
SEPTEMBER																
TOTAL	4	3965.90	5	5371.85	2	3002.50	2	900.00	5	5435.25	0	M			9	9337.750
PERCENT		42.47		57.53		32.15		9.64		58.21		M				

The example report in Figure 5.45 also shows how to use dummy variables and the CONTINUE feature of the SUMMARY= subcommand to put statistics in the correct columns. The symbol "M" indicates that a summary statistic cannot be calculated for that group because all the cases within the group have missing values for that variable. The commands used to produce this report are

```
SORT CASES       MONTH
*IF              (PLAN = 1)EXPA=EXP7
*IF              (PLAN = 2)EXPB=EXP7
*IF              (CAUSE = 1)EXPILL=EXP7
*IF              (CAUSE = 2)EXPJI=EXP7
*IF              (CAUSE = 3)EXPOI=EXP7
*IF              (CAUSE = 4)EXPOTH=EXP7
ASSIGN MISSING EXPA TO EXPOTH (0)
REPORT           FORMAT=HDSPACE(1) BRKSPACE(0) MARGINS(1,123) TOTAL/
                 VARS=EXPA (3) 'NO.'
                     DA (DUMMY)(8) '  AMOUNT'
                     EXPB (3) 'NO.'
                     DB (DUMMY)(8) '  AMOUNT'
                     SPACER1 (DUMMY)(2)' '
                     EXPILL (3) 'NO.'
                     DILL (DUMMY)(8) '  AMOUNT'
                     EXPJI (3) 'NO.'
                     DJI (DUMMY)(8) '  AMOUNT'
                     EXPOI (3) 'NO.'
                     DOI (DUMMY)(8) '  AMOUNT'
                     EXPOTH (3) 'NO.'
                     DOTH (DUMMY)(8) '  AMOUNT'
                     SPACER2 (DUMMY)(2)' '
                     EXP7 (3) 'NO.'
                     D7 (DUMMY)(8) '  AMOUNT'/
                 LHEAD='MONTHLY COMPENSATION BY CATEGORY'
                       'CALENDAR YEAR 1979'''''
                       '        ------TYPE OF COVERAGE------' ' '  /
                       '    ---PLAN A-----  ---PLAN B-----'    /
                 CHEAD='''''''
                       '      ------------------------CAUSE OF CLAIM' ' '
                       '    ---ILLNESS---  -JOB INJURY--  OTHER '   /
```

```
RHEAD='PREPARED )DATE'
      'PAGE )PAGE '''''
       '_____        ____TOTAL____'' '
       'INJURY   ____OTHER____              ' /
BREAK=MONTH (10) (LABEL)/
SUMMARY=VALIDN(EXPA)' TOTAL'
        ADD(SUM(EXPA)) CONTINUE (DA(2))
        VALIDN CONTINUE (EXPB)
        ADD(SUM(EXPB)) CONTINUE (DB(2))
        VALIDN CONTINUE (EXPILL)
        ADD(SUM(EXPILL)) CONTINUE (DILL(2))
        VALIDN CONTINUE (EXPJI)
        ADD(SUM(EXPJI)) CONTINUE (DJI(2))
        VALIDN CONTINUE (EXPOI)
        ADD(SUM(EXPOI)) CONTINUE (DOI(2))
        VALIDN CONTINUE (EXPOTH)
        ADD(SUM(EXPOTH)) CONTINUE (DOTH(2))
        VALIDN CONTINUE (EXP7)
        ADD(SUM(EXP7)) CONTINUE (D7)
        PCT(SUM(EXPA)SUM(EXP7)) (DA) '  PERCENT'
        PCT(SUM(EXPB)SUM(EXP7)) CONTINUE (DB)
        PCT(SUM(EXPILL)SUM(EXP7)) CONTINUE (DILL)
        PCT(SUM(EXPJI)SUM(EXP7)) CONTINUE (DJI)
        PCT(SUM(EXPOI)SUM(EXP7)) CONTINUE (DOI)
        PCT(SUM(EXPOTH)SUM(EXP7)) CONTINUE (DOTH) /
```

5.46 THE MISSING= SUBCOMMAND

The treatment of missing values within REPORT is controlled by the MISSING= subcommand. There are three options:

```
MISSING=VAR|NONE|LIST [(varname varname ... varname [n] )] /
```

VAR (the default) indicates that missing values are treated separately for each variable named on the VARS= subcommand. Missing values are printed in case listings but are not included in summary statistics. NONE specifies that missing value indicators are to be ignored. LIST, on the other hand, eliminates from case listings as well as from summaries any case with a specified number of missing values on a specified list of variables. For example, consider the following subcommand:

```
MISSING= LIST(GRADE74 GRADE75 GRADE76 2)/
```

Any case with missing values on two or more of the variables GRADE74, GRADE75, and GRADE76 will be deleted from case listings and from summaries. If a case is missing for just one or for none of the variables listed, it is not deleted from case listings but is deleted from summaries for those variables for which it is missing. If no variables are specified with LIST, all variables and strings defined by the VARS= subcommand are assumed. If no "n" is specified, the default is 1.

MISSING= specifications apply to strings as well as to other variables. If one variable in a string is missing, the string is missing.

Only variables named on the VARS= subcommand are checked for missing values. A SELECT IF command must be used to eliminate cases missing on break variables.

Only one MISSING= subcommand is permitted for each REPORT command. Since NONE applies to the entire set of variables named in the VARS= subcommand, it cannot be used to selectively ignore missing value indicators for some of the variables. The MISSING VALUES command can be used to turn off previously defined missing values.

The MISSING= subcommand must follow the FORMAT= subcommand and precede the VARS= subcommand. If it references a string created with the STRING= subcommand, it must follow the STRING= subcommand.

5.47 COMMAND ORDER WITHIN REPORT

The order of subcommands (keywords followed by the equals sign) must correspond to the following rules:

- The FORMAT= subcommand must be the first subcommand.
- The VARS= subcommand must precede the BREAK= subcommand.
- The SUMMARY= subcommand must immediately follow the first BREAK= subcommand.
- The STRING= subcommand must precede the VARS= subcommand.
- Running head and feet subcommands can appear anywhere after the FORMAT= subcommand except between the BREAK= and SUMMARY= subcommands.
- The MISSING= subcommand must follow the VARS= subcommand and precede the BREAK= subcommand.

Only the BREAK= and SUMMARY= combination must appear together in REPORT. The SUMMARY= subcommand can be implied for the second and lower level BREAK= subcommands.

5.48   Summary of REPORT Subcommands

All specifications to REPORT are given on one command; there are no separate OPTIONS or STATISTICS. Four subcommands are required on one REPORT command: FORMAT=, VARS= (VARIABLES=), BREAK=, and SUMMARY=. The complete command syntax is

```
1           16
REPORT      FORMAT=   [HDSPACE(n)] [CHDSPACE(n)] [BRKSPACE(n)]
                      [FTSPACE(n)] [LENGTH(t,b)] [MARGINS(l,r)]
                      [LIST|NOLIST] [TOTAL|NOTOTAL] [DEFAULT]/
            [STRING=  stringname (varname [(width)] ['literal']
                      ... varname [(width)] ['literal']) ...
                      stringname (varname [(width)] ['literal'])/]

            VARS=     varname [(VALUE|LABEL|DUMMY)]
                      ['column head'] [(width)]
                      ... varname [(VALUE|LABEL|DUMMY)]
                      ['column head'] [(width)]/

            [MISSING= VAR|NONE|LIST(varname varname ...
                      varname [n])/]

            [HEAD=    'line 1' 'line 2' .../]
            [LHEAD=   'line 1' 'line 2' .../]
            [CHEAD=   'line 1' 'line 2' .../]
            [RHEAD=   'line 1' 'line 2' .../]
            [FOOT=    'line 1' 'line 2' .../]
            [RFOOT=   'line 1' 'line 2' .../]
            [CFOOT=   'line 1' 'line 2' .../]
            [RFOOT=   'line 1' 'line 2' .../]

            BREAK=    varname ... varname ['break title']
                      [(width)] [(VALUE|LABEL)]
                      [(NOTITLE|TITLE)] [(PAGE|SKIP(n))]/

            SUMMARY=  agg agg ... agg
                      ['summary title'] [(summary column number)]
                      [(varname [(decimal digits)] ... )]
                      agg [CONTINUE]
                      [(varname [(decimal digits)] )]
                      ... agg ... /
```

5.49   Limitations for Procedure REPORT

The following formal limitations apply to the REPORT procedure:

- A maximum of 500 variables can be named in the VARS= subcommand.
- A maximum of 10 dummy variables can be defined in the VARS= subcommand.
- A maximum of 50 strings can be defined in the STRING= subcommand.
- The maximum width of a printed report is 132 characters.
-)PAGE can occur only once in either the head or running foot.
- There is a maximum of 20 MODE, MEDIAN, ABFREQ, and RELFREQ requests per summary group.
- There is a maximum of 20 PCTGT, PCTLT, and PCTBTN requests per summary group.
- Workspace is required to store all labeling information, frequency counts if summaries request ABFREQ, RELFREQ, MEDIAN, or MODE, strings and computed summary statistics. 5000 bytes should be sufficient for a report of moderate size with a few strings, heads, and running feet, two break levels, and simple descriptive statistics.

WORKSPACE requirements will significantly increase if ABFREQ, RELFREQ, MEDIAN, or MODE are requested with variables having a wide range of values. The amount of workspace required is

$20 + 4*(max-min+1)$ bytes per variable per function per break

If TOTAL is in effect, workspace requirements are almost doubled. If the same range is used for different statistics for the same variable, only one set of cells is collected. For example,

```
ABFREQ(1,100)(VARA) RELFREQ(1,100)(VARA)
```

will require only 440 bytes.

WORKSPACE requirements will also increase if value labels are printed for variables with many value labels. The amount of workspace required is

$4 + 24*nlabel$ per variable

For example, assume that the case listing contains value labels for the variable STATE and there are 51 value labels corresponding to state names and the District of Columbia, The amount of WORKSPACE required to store the labels is 1228 bytes.

5.50 TRIAL RUNS WITH REPORT

Because REPORT is so flexible and the output has so many components, the first run of a complex report will probably not produce exactly the desired report. For example, the first attempt can reveal awkward column headings, truncated strings, printing overflows, etc. To refine a report with a minimal cost in computer resources, you can run several REPORTs with different specifications using a small file until the intended format is obtained. The data file must be accessed since the EDIT facility only scans the REPORT command for syntax errors and does not display the report format. Obviously, the larger the file, the more important it is to access a small subset of that file in trying out various REPORT specifications. To process a subset of the file as inexpensively as possible, use one of the following techniques:

- The N OF CASES subcommand can be used either when reading raw data or when accessing a system file to limit the number of cases read. SPSS does not attempt to read more cases than the number specified on the N OF CASES command. For example, assume that the file contains 10,000 cases. If the N OF CASES command specifies 10, only the first ten are read.
- If the REPORT contains multiple levels of breaks, and the labeling and spacing of breaks are important considerations, a subset of the entire file containing cases from several breaks can be obtained using the SAMPLE command.

5.51 Subfile Processing

The RUN SUBFILES command can be used with REPORT as with any other statistical procedure. That is, subfiles can be analyzed separately or together. However, the use of RUN SUBFILES with the keyword EACH is equivalent to specifying SUBFILE as the first break level with the BREAK subcommand.

Specifying SUBFILE as a BREAK instead of using RUN SUBFILES EACH has three distinct advantages:

- Less CPU time is required, because various arrays do not have to be re-initialized.
- The TOTAL option in the FORMAT subcommand provides statistics over the total of the subfiles.
- The report can be more compact since new breaks will begin on a new page only if the PAGE option has been selected.

5.52 Sorting Cases for REPORT

Since REPORT processes cases in the file sequentially and reports summary statistics when the break variable(s) change in value, the file must be grouped by break variable(s). The SORT CASES subcommand is the most direct means of reorganizing a file for REPORT. It can be inserted in the command setup prior to the REPORT command and should list the BREAK variables in the order they appear within the REPORT command. For a report with a primary break on variable EDUC and a secondary break on variable SEX, the following sequence of commands is appropriate:

```
   SORT CASES      EDUC SEX
   REPORT          FORMAT= ... /
                   VARS= ... /
                   BREAK=EDUC ... /
                   SUMMARY= ... /
                   BREAK= SEX /
```

Variables can be sorted in descending or ascending order, but they must be grouped together. If a break contains more than one variable, the order in which the variables are named on the SORT CASES subcommand is irrelevant to REPORT and depends solely on the preferred order of the groups for the report.

5.53 REPORT Compared to Other Procedures in SPSS

Many of the features of REPORT can be found in part in other procedures in SPSS, and you may have to decide which is more appropriate for a particular job. Case listings can be obtained using LIST CASES; means, sum, variances, and standard deviations for subpopulations can be obtained using BREAKDOWN; and descriptive statistics can be obtained by FREQUENCIES and CONDESCRIPTIVE. The principal advantage of REPORT over other procedures producing essentially the same types of statistics is the compactness of the output produced and the flexiblity in formatting and labeling that it provides. The example of condensed frequencies (Figure 5.54) provides frequencies and statistics for 20 variables on one page. User control of field width permits the printing of statistics whose magnitude can exceed the printing format within CONDESCRIPTIVE, FREQUENCIES and BREAKDOWN. For example, CONDESCRIPTIVE will not print a statistic whose value is more than 6 digits to the left of the decimal point.

There are some advantages for REPORT that are not so obvious:

- Frequency counts will be printed with decimal digits if the default format is overridden. Therefore, if a file contains non-integer weights, the actual sum of the weights will be printed, and not rounded as in FREQUENCIES.
- Subpopulation medians can be obtained without having to resort to multiple *SELECT IFs, with a considerable savings in both command preparation and computer expenses.
- Composite functions such as the sum of one variable divided by the sum of another variable can be computed and printed in one step. The alternative is to do it manually or to aggregate the cases onto a raw output file and read them back into SPSS or another program.

There are also some REPORT limitations that other procedures producing the same kinds of output do not have:

- Subpopulations can be defined only once via the break variables. In BREAKDOWN they can be defined by several different variables. For example, one BREAKDOWN can define subpopulations first by SEX, then by AGE, etc.
- A limited number of variables can be analyzed on one REPORT command. The number of variables permitted is a function of report width and column widths.
- Frequencies, median, and mode are available only for integer variables.
- The file must be sorted on the break variable(s).

5.54 Using REPORT to Produce Condensed Frequencies and Statistics

Figure 5.54 is a report that prints frequencies and statistics for 20 variables on one page.

Figure 5.54   Condensed Frequencies

CONDENSED FREQUENCIES OUTPUT   PAGE   1

	V1	V2	V3	V4	V5	V6	V7	V8	V9	V10	V11	V12	V13	V14	V15	V16	V17	V18	V19	V20
ABFR																				
TOTA	96	99	97	95	93	97	97	99	94	101	100	95	96	97	101	95	98	99	94	99
1	4	14	13	11	6	8	9	9	10	8	8	12	9	7	13	11	7	12	10	6
2	12	5	12	10	12	13	9	14	11	18	10	10	14	14	7	10	10	7	12	13
3	8	10	8	5	16	13	14	12	9	10	14	11	14	11	9	11	12	15	13	17
4	7	16	12	13	9	12	15	7	13	16	15	12	14	13	14	14	10	9	8	9
5	11	8	8	14	10	8	10	14	11	13	11	10	8	10	9	13	12	17	10	13
6	16	6	8	14	8	10	5	11	10	15	9	11	8	9	11	13	6	11	6	11
7	13	9	11	10	8	10	12	13	8	5	11	13	9	8	17	5	14	11	11	7
8	13	13	13	7	15	5	9	8	11	9	12	10	9	10	14	10	11	10	16	9
9	12	18	12	11	9	18	14	11	11	7	10	6	11	15	7	8	16	7	8	14
RELF																				
TOTA	100.0	100.0	100.0	100.0	100.0	100.0	100.0	100.0	100.0	100.0	100.0	100.0	100.0	100.0	100.0	100.0	100.0	100.0	100.0	100.0
1	4.17	14.14	13.40	11.58	6.45	8.25	9.28	9.09	10.64	7.92	8.00	12.63	9.38	7.22	12.87	11.58	7.14	12.12	10.64	6.06
2	12.50	5.05	12.37	10.53	12.90	13.40	9.28	14.14	11.70	17.82	10.00	10.53	14.58	14.43	6.93	10.53	10.20	7.07	12.77	13.13
3	8.33	10.10	8.25	5.26	17.20	13.40	14.43	12.12	9.57	9.90	14.00	11.58	14.58	11.34	8.91	11.58	12.24	15.15	13.83	17.17
4	7.29	16.16	12.37	13.68	9.68	12.37	15.46	7.07	13.83	15.84	15.00	12.63	14.58	13.40	13.86	14.74	10.20	9.09	8.51	9.09
5	11.46	8.08	8.25	14.74	10.75	8.25	10.31	14.14	11.70	12.87	11.00	10.53	8.33	10.31	8.91	13.68	12.24	17.17	10.64	13.13
6	16.67	6.06	8.25	14.74	8.60	10.31	5.15	11.11	10.64	14.85	9.00	11.58	8.33	9.28	10.89	13.68	6.12	11.11	6.38	11.11
7	13.54	9.09	11.34	10.53	8.60	10.31	12.37	13.13	8.51	4.95	11.00	13.68	9.38	8.25	16.83	5.26	14.29	11.11	11.70	7.07
8	13.54	13.13	13.40	7.37	16.13	5.15	9.28	8.08	11.70	8.91	12.00	10.53	9.38	10.31	13.86	10.53	11.22	10.10	17.02	9.09
9	12.50	18.18	12.37	11.58	9.68	18.56	14.43	11.11	11.70	6.93	10.00	6.32	11.46	15.46	6.93	8.42	16.33	7.07	8.51	14.14
SUM	534	523	486	477	469	493	491	491	469	463	502	454	457	495	515	450	529	478	468	497
MEAN	5.56	5.28	5.01	5.02	5.04	5.08	5.06	4.96	4.99	4.58	5.02	4.78	4.76	5.10	5.10	4.74	5.40	4.83	4.98	5.02
STDE	2.42	2.79	2.74	2.51	2.54	2.68	2.61	2.55	2.59	2.36	2.48	2.49	2.59	2.63	2.52	2.46	2.61	2.43	2.64	2.54
VARI	5.870	7.797	7.510	6.297	6.476	7.201	6.809	6.488	6.720	5.565	6.161	6.195	6.689	6.927	6.370	6.047	6.819	5.899	6.989	6.469
MIN	1	1	1	1	1	1	1	1	1	1	1	1	1	1	1	1	1	1	1	1
MAX	9	9	9	9	9	9	9	9	9	9	9	9	9	9	9	9	9	9	9	9
SKEW	−.280	−.094	−.020	−.053	.088	.125	.103	.035	.046	.275	.078	.013	.252	.099	−.205	.153	−.107	.021	.002	.182
KURT	−1.06	−1.34	−1.38	−1.02	−1.33	−1.30	−1.25	−1.21	−1.21	−.930	−.17	−1.18	−1.21	−1.30	−1.17	−1.00	−1.28	−1.04	−1.39	−1.21
MEDI	5.9	5.1	4.9	5.1	4.8	4.8	4.6	5.0	4.9	4.4	4.8	4.3	4.8	5.3	4.6	5.3	4.9	4.9	4.8	
MODE	6	9	1	5	3	9	4	2	4	2	4	7	2	9	7	4	9	5	8	3

The subcommands required to produce the report in Figure 5.54 are

```
RUN NAME        CONDENSED FREQUENCIES OUTPUT
VARIABLE LIST   V1 TO V20
INPUT FORMAT    FIXED(20F1.0)
INPUT MEDIUM    DISK
N OF CASES      108
MISSING VALUES  ALL(0)
```

```
REPORT              FORMAT= CHDSPACE(0)BRKSPACE(0)/
                    STRING=A('     ')/
                    VARS=V1 TO V20(5)/
                    BREAK=A''/
                    SUMMARY=
                    ABFREQ(0,9)
                    RELFREQ(0,9)
                    SUM MEAN STDEV VARIANCE MIN MAX SKEWNESS KURTOSIS
                    MEDIAN(0,9)MODE(0,9)
```

The STRING= subcommand is used to define a constant break variable. The width of the string defines the column width for the break variable. It is just long enough to print enough characters of the summary titles for identification. The VARS= subcommand specifies a column width of 5, allowing the 20 variables to fit. This width is sufficient to print summaries for descriptive statistics with up to three decimal digits.

5.55 Using REPORT to Produce CROSSBREAK-like Tables

Procedure BREAKDOWN optionally formats statistics for variables broken down by two or more variables into a tabular format when the keyword CROSSBREAK is used. REPORT can also produce such a table. In the CROSSBREAK format some of the columns in the report will correspond to subsets of the file. For example, in Figure 5.45, there are actually two crossbreak tables and a total. The first set of columns corresponds to counts and amounts by type of coverage, and the second set of columns are the counts and amounts by type of claim. If PLAN and CAUSE are the variables determining the categories, and EXP7 is the variable being divided, the following series of IF statements create sets of variables corresponding to the PLAN and CAUSE categories:

```
IF              (PLAN = 1)EXPA=EXP7
IF              (PLAN = 2)EXPB=EXP7
IF              (CAUSE = 1)EXPILL=EXP7
IF              (CAUSE = 2)EXPJI=EXP7
IF              (CAUSE = 3)EXPOI=EXP7
IF              (CAUSE = 4)EXPOTH=EXP7
ASSIGN MISSING EXPA TO EXPOTH (0)
```

Figure 5.55 is a more complicated version of a CROSSBREAK-like report. Variables TIME0, TIME1, TIME2 and TIME3 have been created with IF statements subsetting AMOUNT. The constant used to obtain each cell as a percentage of the total was obtained in a previous run.

Figure 5.55   A CROSSBREAK Application with REPORT

```
                        SUMMARY STATEMENT-ACCOUNTS RECEIVABLE
                                      (AGED)

                              APEX METAL FASTENERS
                                  WAHOO, NE.

    INVOICE TYPE      TOTAL      0-30 DAYS    31-60 DAYS    61-90 DAYS    90+ DAYS

    STOVE BOLTS

    AMOUNT         1793892.12    454246.07    219068.91    257752.65    862824.48
       % OF TYPE       100.00        25.32        12.21        14.37        48.10
       % OF TOTAL       41.02        10.39         5.01         5.89        19.73

    WOOD SCREWS

    AMOUNT         1819160.99    210773.81    675952.69    201093.79    731340.69
       % OF TYPE       100.00        11.59        37.16        11.05        40.20
       % OF TOTAL       41.60         4.82        15.46         4.60        16.72

    METAL SCREWS

    AMOUNT          242695.46      6947.80     60496.29    128750.26     46501.11
       % OF TYPE       100.00         2.86        24.93        53.05        19.16
       % OF TOTAL        5.55          .16         1.38         2.94         1.06

    SPRING WASHERS

    AMOUNT          274648.40    108929.17     49960.95     27329.59     88428.68
       % OF TYPE       100.00        39.66        18.19         9.95        32.20
       % OF TOTAL        6.28         2.49         1.14          .62         2.02

    OTHER

    AMOUNT          242408.61      6083.63     13930.77    106300.07    116094.14
       % OF TYPE       100.00         2.51         5.75        43.85        47.89
       % OF TOTAL        5.54          .14          .32         2.43         2.65

    TOTAL
    AMOUNT         4372805.59    786980.49   1019409.62    721226.37   1845189.11
       % OF TYPE       100.00        18.00        23.31        16.49        42.20
       % OF TOTAL       100.00        18.00        23.31        16.49        42.20


    APEX METAL FASTENERS          CONFIDENTIAL          PREPARED ON  09/26/79
    M.I.S. REPORT 2                                           BY KILGORE TROUT
```

The REPORT subcommands required to produce the report in Figure 5.55 are

```
REPORT          FORMAT=HDSPACE(1)BRKSPACE(1)MARGINS(1,80)
                TOTAL/
                VARS=AMOUNT(10)'   TOTAL'
                TIME0'0-30 DAYS'(10)
                TIME1'31-60 DAYS'(10)
                TIME2'61-90 DAYS'(10)
                TIME3'  90+ DAYS'(10)/
                HEAD='SUMMARY STATEMENT-ACCOUNTS RECEIVABLE''(AGED)'
                '''APEX METAL FASTENERS''WAHOO, NE.'/
                LFOOT='APEX METAL FASTENERS''M.I.S. REPORT 2'/
                RFOOT='PREPARED ON )DATE''BY KILGORE TROUT'/
                CFOOT='CONFIDENTIAL' /
                BREAK=INVTYP(LABEL)(15)(SKIP(1))/
                SUMMARY=SUM'AMOUNT'
                PCT(SUM(AMOUNT)SUM(AMOUNT))'  % OF TYPE'(AMOUNT)
                PCT(SUM(TIME0)SUM(AMOUNT))CONTINUE (TIME0)
                PCT(SUM(TIME1)SUM(AMOUNT))CONTINUE (TIME1)
                PCT(SUM(TIME2)SUM(AMOUNT))CONTINUE (TIME2)
                PCT(SUM(TIME3)SUM(AMOUNT))CONTINUE (TIME3)
                PCT(SUM(AMOUNT)4372805.59)'  % OF TOTAL'(AMOUNT)
                PCT(SUM(TIME0)4372805.59)CONTINUE(TIME0)
                PCT(SUM(TIME1)4372805.59)CONTINUE(TIME1)
                PCT(SUM(TIME2)4372805.59)CONTINUE(TIME2)
                PCT(SUM(TIME3)4372805.59)CONTINUE(TIME3)
```

5.56 Using REPORT to Produce CROSSTABS-like Tables

REPORT can be used to produce CROSSTABS-like tables where columns correspond to the values of one or more variables. Transformations are required to split a variable into several variables, each one corresponding to a category of the original variable. The easiest means of creating such variables is to use the COUNT command:

```
COUNT           MALE=SEX(1)/FEMALE=SEX(2)
```

In this example, all males on the file have a value of 1 for MALE and a value of 0 for FEMALE. Figure 5.56a is one example of such a CROSSTABS-like report.

Figure 5.56a   An Affirmative Action Report

JOB CATEGORIES	TOTAL (1)	MALE (2)	FEMALE (3)	MALE NEGRO (4)	MALE ORIENTAL (5)	MALE INDIAN (6)	MALE SPANISH SURNAME (7)	FEMALE NEGRO (8)	FEMALE ORIENTAL (9)	FEMALE INDIAN (10)	FEMALE SPANISH SURNAME (11)
OFFICIALS & MANAGERS											
COUNTS	48	19	29	7	0	0	0	18	4	0	0
PERCENTAGES		39.58	60.42	14.58	0.0	0.0	0.0	37.50	8.33	0.0	0.0
PROFESSIONALS											
COUNTS	62	29	33	4	3	0	0	6	2	0	0
PERCENTAGES		46.77	53.23	6.45	4.84	0.0	0.0	9.68	3.23	0.0	0.0
TECHNICIANS											
COUNTS	98	17	81	4	1	0	0	33	1	0	0
PERCENTAGES		17.35	82.65	4.08	1.02	0.0	0.0	33.67	1.02	0.0	0.0
OFFICE AND CLERICAL											
COUNTS	67	18	49	3	1	0	0	12	2	0	3
PERCENTAGES		26.87	73.13	4.48	1.49	0.0	0.0	17.91	2.99	0.0	4.48
TOTAL											
COUNTS	275	83	192	18	5	0	0	69	9	0	3
PERCENTAGES		30.18	69.82	6.55	1.82	0.0	0.0	25.09	3.27	0.0	1.09

FORM T

AFFIRMATIVE ACTION PROGRAM

QUARTERLY STATISTICAL REPORT

ORGANIZATIONAL UNIT: ABCD
LOCATION: CHICAGO
TIME PERIOD: 6/78 TO 9/78

DATE OF SURVEY: 02/11/80

PERSON PREPARING REPORT: KARL BILANDIC

The complete set of SPSS commands required to produce the report in Figure 5.56a is

```
GET FILE        PERDATA
COMMENT         GET INTERSECTION OF NONMISSING ETHNIC AND SEX
COMPUTE         SEXRACE=RACE*SEX
ASSIGN MISS     SEXRACE(0)
COMMENT         SET UP VARS COLUMNS
COUNT           MALE=SEX(1)/FEMALE=SEX(2)
MISSING VALUES  MALE FEMALE (0)
DO REPEAT       $OUT=MNEGRO MORIENT MINDIAN MLATINO/
                $VAL=2 TO 5/
IF              (IF SEX EQ 1 AND ETHNIC EQ $VAL)$OUT=1
MISSING VALUES  $OUT(0)
END REPEAT
```

```
DO REPEAT        $OUT=FNEGRO FORIENT FINDIAN FLATINO/
                 $VAL=2 TO 5/
IF               (IF SEX EQ 2 AND ETHNIC EQ $VAL)$OUT=1
MISSING VALUES   $OUT(0)
END REPEAT
SORT CASES       JOBGRADE
REPORT           FORMAT=BRKSPACE(0)CHDSPACE(0)TOTAL/
                 VARS=SEXRACE''''''TOTAL'' (1)'(5)
                 MALE ''''''MALE'' (2)'(5)
                 FEMALE''''''FEMALE''  (3)'(6)
                 MNEGRO'''MALE''NEGRO'.' (4)'(5)
                 MORIENT'''MALE''ORIENTAL''   (5)'(8)
                 MINDIAN'''MALE''INDIAN''   (6)'(6)
                 MLATINO'MALE''SPANISH''SURNAME''  (7)'(7)
                 FNEGRO'''FEMALE''NEGRO'' (8)'(6)
                 FORIENT'''FEMALE''ORIENTAL''   (9)'(8)
                 FINDIAN'''FEMALE''INDIAN'' (10)'(6)
                 FLATINO'FEMALE''SPANISH''SURNAME'' (11)'(7)/
                 LHEAD='FORM T'/
                 CHEAD='AFFIRMATIVE ACTION PROGRAM'''
                 'QUARTERLY STATISTICAL REPORT'/
                 RHEAD='ORGANIZATIONAL UNIT:   ABCD'
                 'LOCATION:   CHICAGO'
                 'TIME PERIOD: 6/78 TO 9/78'/
                 LFOOT='DATE OF SURVEY: )DATE'/
                 RFOOT='PERSON PREPARING REPORT:   KARL BILANDIC'/
                 BREAK=JOBGRADE (SKIP(1))
                 (NOTITLE)(LABEL) /
                 SUMMARY=VALIDN'    COUNTS'
                 PCT(VALIDN(MALE)VALIDN(SEXRACE)) '    PERCENTAGES'
                 (MALE(2))
                 PCT(VALIDN(FEMALE)VALIDN(SEXRACE)) CONTINUE
                 (FEMALE(2))
                 PCT(VALIDN(MNEGRO)VALIDN(SEXRACE)) CONTINUE
                 (MNEGRO(2))
                 PCT(VALIDN(MORIENT)VALIDN(SEXRACE)) CONTINUE
                 (MORIENT(2))
                 PCT(VALIDN(MINDIAN)VALIDN(SEXRACE)) CONTINUE
                 (MINDIAN(2))
                 PCT(VALIDN(MLATINO)VALIDN(SEXRACE)) CONTINUE
                 (MLATINO(2))
                 PCT(VALIDN(FNEGRO)VALIDN(SEXRACE)) CONTINUE
                 (FNEGRO(2))
                 PCT(VALIDN(FORIENT)VALIDN(SEXRACE)) CONTINUE
                 (FORIENT(2))
                 PCT(VALIDN(FINDIAN)VALIDN(SEXRACE)) CONTINUE
                 (FINDIAN(2))
                 PCT(VALIDN(FLATINO)VALIDN(SEXRACE)) CONTINUE
                 (FLATINO(2))
FINISH
```

In this example, the IF commands required to produce the report are placed inside DO REPEAT structures.

The transformation techique used to produce CROSSTABS-like tables can also be used to produce MULT RESPONSE-like tables as in Figure 5.56b.

Figure 5.56b   A MULT RESPONSE Application with REPORT

USING REPORT FOR MULTIPLE RESPONSE APPLICATIONS   PAGE

EDUCATION	TIME	NEWSWEEK	U.S.NEWS & WORLD	ROLLING STONE	NEW REPUBLIC	ROTARY	KIWANIS	MOOSE	ELKS	VFW	TOTAL MAGAZINES READ	NO. OF MSHIPS
GRADE SCH												
COUNT	3	3	0	0	0	6	0	6	3	6	6	21
PCT RESP	50.0	50.0	0.0	0.0	0.0	28.6	0.0	28.6	14.3	28.6		
PCT CASE	16.7	16.7	0.0	0.0	0.0	33.3	0.0	33.3	16.7	33.3		
HIGH SCH												
COUNT	6	6	3	15	3	9	3	3	0	9	33	24
PCT RESP	18.2	18.2	9.1	45.5	9.1	37.5	12.5	12.5	0.0	37.5		
PCT CASE	33.3	33.3	16.7	83.3	16.7	50.0	16.7	16.7	0.0	50.0		
COLLEGE												
COUNT	12	12	15	0	9	9	9	3	3	0	48	24
PCT RESP	25.0	25.0	31.3	0.0	18.8	37.5	37.5	12.5	12.5	0.0		
PCT CASE	57.1	57.1	71.4	0.0	42.9	42.9	42.9	14.3	14.3	0.0		
NO ANSWER												
COUNT	0	0	0	3	0	0	0	0	0	3	3	3
PCT RESP	0.0	0.0	0.0	100.0	0.0	0.0	0.0	0.0	0.0	100.0		
PCT CASE	0.0	0.0	0.0	100.0	0.0	0.0	0.0	0.0	0.0	100.0		
TOTAL												
COUNT	21	21	18	18	12	24	12	12	6	18	90	72
PCT RESP	23.3	23.3	20.0	20.0	13.3	33.3	16.7	16.7	8.3	25.0		
PCT CASE	35.0	35.0	30.0	30.0	20.0	40.0	20.0	20.0	10.0	30.0		

The file producing this report contains two sets of multiple dichotomies (see Chapter 8 in this manual). Variables MAGAZINE and MEMBER are created with COUNT commands. The REPORT commands required to produce the report in Figure 5.56b are

```
REPORT        FORMAT=BRKSPACE(0)CHDSPACE(0)TOTAL MARGINS(1,120)/
              VARS=TIME TO REPUBLIC(8)
                ROTARY TO VFW(7)
              MAGAZINE'TOTAL''MAGAZINES''READ'
              MEMBER'NO. OF''MSHIPS.'(6)
                /
              BREAK=EDUC(LABEL)(10)/
              SUM=VALIDN'COUNT'(TIME NEWSWEEK U.S.NEWS STONE REPUBLIC
              ROTARY KIWANIS MOOSE BPOE VFW)
              SUM CONTINUE(MAGAZINE MEMBER)
              PCT(VALIDN(TIME)SUM(MAGAZINE))'PCT RESP'(TIME(1))
              PCT(VALIDN(NEWSWEEK)SUM(MAGAZINE))CONTINUE(NEWSWEEK(1))
              PCT(VALIDN(U.S.NEWS)SUM(MAGAZINE))CONTINUE(U.S.NEWS(1))
              PCT(VALIDN(STONE)SUM(MAGAZINE))CONTINUE(STONE(1))
              PCT(VALIDN(REPUBLIC)SUM(MAGAZINE))CONTINUE(REPUBLIC(1))
              PCT(VALIDN(ROTARY)SUM(MEMBER))CONTINUE(ROTARY(1))
              PCT(VALIDN(KIWANIS)SUM(MEMBER))CONTINUE(KIWANIS(1))
              PCT(VALIDN(MOOSE)SUM(MEMBER))CONTINUE(MOOSE(1))
              PCT(VALIDN(BPOE)SUM(MEMBER))CONTINUE(BPOE(1))
              PCT(VALIDN(VFW)SUM(MEMBER))CONTINUE(VFW(1))
              PCT(VALIDN(TIME)VALIDN(MAGAZINE))'PCT CASE'(TIME(1))
              PCT(VALIDN(NEWSWEEK)VALIDN(MAGAZINE))CONTINUE(NEWSWEEK(1))
              PCT(VALIDN(U.S.NEWS)VALIDN(MAGAZINE))CONTINUE(U.S.NEWS(1))
              PCT(VALIDN(STONE)VALIDN(MAGAZINE))CONTINUE(STONE(1))
              PCT(VALIDN(REPUBLIC)VALIDN(MAGAZINE))CONTINUE(REPUBLIC(1))
              PCT(VALIDN(ROTARY)VALIDN(MAGAZINE))CONTINUE(ROTARY(1))
              PCT(VALIDN(KIWANIS)VALIDN(MAGAZINE))CONTINUE(KIWANIS(1))
              PCT(VALIDN(MOOSE)VALIDN(MAGAZINE))CONTINUE(MOOSE(1))
              PCT(VALIDN(BPOE)VALIDN(MAGAZINE))CONTINUE(BPOE(1))
              PCT(VALIDN(VFW)VALIDN(MAGAZINE))CONTINUE(VFW(1))
```

5.57   REPORT and Other SPSS Commands

REPORT interacts with other SPSS commands. Data transformations are required for special types of reports described in previous sections. This section describes other commands that affect both the dimensions and contents of reports.

The PRINT FORMATS for a variable instructs SPSS how to print it. If it has a print format of 0, no decimal digits are printed, even though the internal representation is a decimal number. If it has a print format of 0, SPSS tries to print it as an integer, even though it can be an alphanumeric variable. Misspecified print formats produce misleading column contents in REPORT. Default column widths and string widths differ for alphanumeric and numeric variables; thus a misspecified print format for an alphanumeric variable produces an extra-wide string and an extra-wide column.

The MISSING VALUES command is used to define missing values on existing variables and the ASSIGN MISSING command is used to assign missing values to new variables created with transformation statements. REPORT recognizes missing values on variables named on the VARS= subcommand and handles them in accordance with specifications on the MISSING= subcommand. Missing value indicators are ignored for variables named on the BREAK= subcommand.

By default REPORT uses any label assigned using the VAR LABELS command as the column header for "vars" and break columns. To produce a nicely labeled column header, format the variable label to the column width. The VAR LABELS command can also be used to produce empty column heads. SPSS permits a null variable label, as in

```
VAR LABELS      VARX/
```

In this example, VARX is given a null variable label.

The contents of columns can be labels assigned using the VALUE LABELS command in place of values. As with the VAR LABELS command, SPSS permits null value labels as in

```
VALUE LABELS    LASTYEAR(0)/PREFER(0)/
```

This is useful to print blanks for missing data within reports using the LIST option on the FORMAT= subcommand (see Figure 5.20).

The length of a page in a report is determined by the SPSS page size. The PAGESIZE command is used to override the default of 54 lines per page. The NOEJECT option on the PAGESIZE command should not be used.

The number of cases "reported" is controlled by the number of cases being processed in a run. N OF CASES can be used to limit the number of cases processed (see Section 5.50). Whenever, UNKNOWN is specified on the N OF CASES command (the default), SPSS prints the number of cases read as the data are read for the first procedure. This message appears after the last case is read. If REPORT is the first procedure in the run and UNKNOWN is in effect, SPSS prints the message within the REPORT just prior to the last set of summary statistics. The message can be avoided by placing another procedure command before REPORT (such as SORT CASES) or placing a READ INPUT DATA command before REPORT to force an extra pass of the data.

LIST CASES lists the contents of cases as they are being processed by a procedure. It should not be used with REPORT since LIST CASES output interleaves with REPORT output.

The SORT CASES command may be required to organize the file by break variables. See Section 5.52 for a discussion.

5.58 More Sample Reports

Throughout this chapter several reports are presented illustrating topics discussed in individual sections. The following examples demonstrate some of the more complex types of reports possible.

Figure 5.58a   Manipulating Summaries

```
                        ANALYSIS OF SALARIES WITHIN DIVISION AND GROUP


        DIVISION      GROUP           AVG    MEDIAN    MAX      MIN     AVG      AVG
                                    SALARY   SALARY  SALARY   SALARY  SALARY   SALARY
                                                                       MEN     WOMEN

        MARKETING     NEW YORK
                                    24836    24400    35314    10203   25504    24669

                      BOSTON
                                    22101    23457    35387     8632   21797    22442

                      PHILADELPHIA
                                    21526    20578    37967     9590   19250    22950
                      FOR DIVISION  22598    21233    37967     8632   21464    23354

        R & D         NEW YORK
                                    21591    19264    37933     8674   21079    22040

                      BOSTON
                                    22913    21255    35622     9501   24400    22112

                      PHILADELPHIA
                                    20157    19269    36408     9002   19137    21686
                      FOR DIVISION  21434    19270    37933     8674   20876    21956




                                     FISCAL 79 DATA
```

The subcommands required to produce the report in Figure 5.58a are

```
RUN NAME        REPORT EXAMPLE
VARIABLE LIST   DIV,GROUP,SEX,SALARY
INPUT FORMAT    FIXED(3F1.0,F5.0)
INPUT MEDIUM    DISK
VALUE LABELS    DIV(1)MARKETING(2) R & D/
                GROUP(1)NEW YORK(2)BOSTON(3)PHILADELPHIA
IF              (SEX EQ 1)MSALARY=SALARY
IF              (SEX EQ 2)FSALARY=SALARY
MISSING VALUES  MSALARY FSALARY(0)
COMPUTE         MEDIAN=SALARY
SORT CASES      DIV GROUP
REPORT          FORMAT=BRKSPACE(0),MARGINS(10,90)/
                HEAD='ANALYSIS OF SALARIES WITHIN DIVISION AND GROUP'/
                FOOT='FISCAL 79 DATA'/
                VARS=SALARY'  AVG ''SALARY'(6)
                MEDIAN'MEDIAN''SALARY'(6)
                MAX(DUMMY) '  MAX ''SALARY'(6)
                MIN(DUMMY) '  MIN ''SALARY'(6)
                MSALARY'  AVG ''SALARY''  MEN '(6)
                FSALARY'  AVG ''SALARY'' WOMEN'(6)
                /
                BREAK=DIV'DIVISION'(LABEL)(12)(SKIP(2))/
                SUMMARY=MEAN(2)'FOR DIVISION'(SALARY MSALARY FSALARY)
                MEDIAN(8000,38000)CONTINUE(MEDIAN)
                ADD(MAX(SALARY))CONTINUE(MAX(0))
                ADD(MIN(SALARY))CONTINUE(MIN(0))
                /
                BREAK=GROUP'GROUP'(LABEL)(12)(SKIP(1))/
                SUMMARY=MEAN''(SALARY MSALARY FSALARY)
                MEDIAN(8000,38000)CONTINUE(MEDIAN)
                ADD(MAX(SALARY))CONTINUE(MAX(0))
                ADD(MIN(SALARY))CONTINUE(MIN(0))
                /
```

Each "vars" column of this report is used to describe some aspect of the variable SALARY. Composite functions are used to move the minimum and maximum of SALARY into dummy columns. Data transformations are used to split SALARY into two groups (men and women) as described in Section 5.56. Since a composite cannot be used with the median summary statistic, an exact copy of SALARY named MEDIAN is created with a COMPUTE command. The summary title for the higher break level is moved into the lower break column. The report is indented on the left with the MARGINS keyword on the FORMAT= subcommand.

Figure 5.58b   Turning A Report On its Side

```
                     TURNING A REPORT ON ITS SIDE


BREAK                 MEAN    STD DEV       SUM    MINIMUM    MAXIMUM
LOWEST THIRD
   VAR X              61.2      26.7     2629.5        1.0       97.6
   VAR Y              43.7      27.0     1881.2         .9       92.4
   VAR Z              49.2      28.3     2114.6         .5       94.7

MIDDLE THIRD
   VAR X              53.0      28.4     2333.8         .3       93.4
   VAR Y              51.9      27.9     2285.5        2.8       98.3
   VAR Z              54.3      29.8     2387.4        1.2       98.8

HIGHEST THIRD
   VAR X              45.2      32.2      948.3         .3       98.3
   VAR Y              53.4      31.5     1121.6        2.0       98.9
   VAR Z              45.0      31.0      945.9        3.9       97.1
```

The commands required to produce the report in Figure 5.58b are

```
REPORT          FORMAT=CHDSPACE(0)BRKSPACE(0)MARGINS(1,80)/
                HEAD='TURNING A REPORT ON ITS SIDE'/
                VARS=X'    MEAN'(7)
                Y 'STD DEV'(7)
                Z '    SUM'(7)
                MIN'MINIMUM'(DUMMY)(7)
                MAX'MAXIMUM'(DUMMY)(7)/
                BREAK=BREAK (LABEL) (SKIP(1))/
                SUMMARY=ADD(MEAN(X))' VAR X'(X(1))
                ADD(STDEV(X)) CONTINUE (Y(1))
                ADD(SUM(X)) CONTINUE (Z(1))
                ADD(MIN(X)) CONTINUE (MIN(1))
                ADD(MAX(X)) CONTINUE (MAX(1))
                ADD(MEAN(Y))' VAR Y'(X(1))
                ADD(STDEV(Y)) CONTINUE (Y(1))
                ADD(SUM(Y)) CONTINUE (Z(1))
                ADD(MIN(Y)) CONTINUE (MIN(1))
                ADD(MAX(Y)) CONTINUE (MAX(1))
                ADD(MEAN(Z))' VAR Z'(X(1))
                ADD(STDEV(Z)) CONTINUE (Y(1))
                ADD(SUM(Z)) CONTINUE (Z(1))
                ADD(MIN(Z)) CONTINUE (MIN(1))
                ADD(MAX(Z)) CONTINUE (MAX(1))
```

The basic SPSS report contains columns of variables and rows of statistics on the variables. This report is transposed. Rows are variables and columns are statistics. Since this report is considerably different from the basic report, an extensive number of command specifications are required to produce it. Note, this report cannot be written for statistics that themselves have special arguments, nor does it work with case listings.

5.59 Diagnosing Errors in REPORT

Two kinds of errors are possible in using REPORT: errors in syntax or exceeding limitations that REPORT can detect, or errors producing badly formatted reports that REPORT cannot detect. Given the potential complexity of the REPORT command, the number of syntax errors possible approaches infinity. This section describes the most common types of errors made and how they can be resolved.

5.60 Syntax Errors

The following numbered error messages are used by REPORT:

```
1021 =   ERROR ENCOUNTERED WHILE ANALYZING 'FORMAT' SPECS IN REPORT
1022 =   INSUFFICIENT MEMORY, UP WORKSPACE
1023 =   ERROR ENCOUNTERED WHILE ANALYZING 'STRING' SPECS IN REPORT
1024 =   ERROR ENCOUNTERED WHILE ANALYZING 'VARS' SPECS IN REPORT
1025 =   ERROR ENCOUNTERED WHILE ANALYZING 'MISSING' SPECS IN REPORT
1026 =   ERROR ENCOUNTERED WHILE ANALYZING 'HEAD' OR 'FOOT' SPECS IN REPORT
1027 =   ERROR ENCOUNTERED WHILE ANALYZING 'BREAK' SPECS IN REPORT
1028 =   ERROR ENCOUNTERED WHILE ANALYZING 'SUMMARY' SPECS IN REPORT
1029 =   INCONSISTENCIES DISCOVERED IN SPECS OR INSUFFICIENT MEMORY FOR REPORT TASK
1030 =   ERROR ENCOUNTERED WHILE ANALYZING REPORT COMMANDS
```

As elsewhere within SPSS, these messages are printed at the end of the job. In addition, REPORT prints more specific error messages at the point at which they are detected in the input. However, the complexity of the language can often lead to somewhat confusing diagnostics. An error occurring in one part of the command can cause an error to appear in another place. Some of the following common types of syntax errors illustrate this phenomenon.

Figure 5.60a   Missing Slash on a Command

```
            4 REPORT       FORMAT=DEFAULT/
            5              VARS=V1 TO V5
            6              BREAK=BREAK1/
SYMBOL IN 'VARS' LIST WHICH IS NEITHER AN SPSS VARIABLE NOR A STRING

ERROR NUMBER.. 1024. PROCESSING CEASES, ERROR SCAN CONTINUES.

            7              SUM=MEAN
'SUM     ' USED OUT OF SEQUENCE

ERROR CHECK STOPPED

ERROR NUMBER.. 1030. PROCESSING CEASES, ERROR SCAN CONTINUES.
```

All REPORT subcommands must end in a slash. Since the slash is missing from the end of the VARS= subcommand, REPORT assumes that BREAK is a variable name. When REPORT encounters the SUM= subcommand, it has not seen a BREAK= subcommand, having read it as part of an invalid VARS= subcommand; hence the message about the misplaced SUMMARY subcommand.

Figure 5.60b   Unbalanced Apostrophes in Titles

```
            4 REPORT       FORMAT=DEFAULT/
            5              HEAD='THIS HEADER HAS UNBALANCED APOSTROPHES''/
            6              VARS=V1 TO V5/
            7              BREAK=BREAK1/
            8              SUM=MEAN
ERROR ENCOUNTERED WHILE READING LITERAL

ERROR NUMBER.. 1026. PROCESSING CEASES, ERROR SCAN CONTINUES.
```

The HEAD title has unbalanced apostrophes. REPORT continues to read the rest of the command as part of the title until it reaches the end of the REPORT command.

Figure 5.60c   Overlapping Summaries

```
            3 REPORT       FORMAT=DEFAULT/
            4              VARS=V1 TO V5/
            5              BREAK=BREAK1/
            6              SUMMARY=SUM(V1 V2 V3)
            7              MEAN CONTINUE(V1)
OVERLAP OF VARIABLES SPECIFIED IN 'SUMMARY'

ERROR NUMBER.. 1028. PROCESSING CEASES, ERROR SCAN CONTINUES.
```

This report tries to print the mean of variable V1 in the same row and column as the sum of V1.

Figure 5.60d   Insufficient Width

```
            4 REPORT       FORMAT=DEFAULT/
            5              VARS=V1 TO V20/
            6              BREAK=BREAK1/
            7              SUM=MEAN
INSUFFICIENT WIDTH FOR REQUESTED REPORT

ERROR NUMBER.. 1029. PROCESSING CEASES, ERROR SCAN CONTINUES.
```

The default width for a numeric variable is 9, the default width (and maximum width) for a report is 132. This report requires 21*9 (counting the break column) printing positions, plus a minimum of 20 intercolumn spaces.

5.61 Errors REPORT Cannot Detect

REPORT can produce garbled reports because of user errors that do not violate syntactical requirements. The following two examples demonstrate these types of problems.

Figure 5.61a   Wrong Print Format for Variables Used in A String

```
13 REPORT        FORMAT=LIST BRKSPACE(0)HDSPACE(1)/
14               STRING=NAME(NAME1 NAME2 NAME3 NAME4 NAME5)
15               SSN(SS1(3)'-'SS2(2)'-'SS3(4))
16               BIRTH(MOBIRTH(2)'/'DABIRTH(2)'/'YRBIRTH(2))
17               HIRE(MOHIRED(2)'/'YRHIRED(2))/
18               VARS= NAME SEX'SEX'(LABEL)(6) SSN'SOCIAL'
19               'SECURITY''NO.'
20               BIRTH 'DATE''OF''BIRTH' HIRE'DATE''OF''HIRE'
21               GRADE76'GRADE''IN''76'(6)
22               GRADE75'GRADE''IN''75'(6)
23               GRADE74'GRADE''IN''74'(6)/
24               CHEAD='PERSONNEL REPORT''NO. 1'/
25               BREAK=JOBGRADE(LABEL)/
26               SUMMARY=VALIDN''(GRADE76)
```

```
REPORT REQUIRES    2092 BYTES FOR THIS TASK
```

```
                                    PERSONNEL REPORT
                                          NO. 1

JOB CATEGORIES      NAME                              SEX    SOCIAL     DATE   DATE  GRADE GRADE GRADE
                                                             SECURITY   OF     OF    IN    IN    IN
                                                             NO.        BIRTH  HIRE  76    75    74

OFFICIALS & MANAGERS
                    *****************************-2389067040000000000 FEMALE 126-75-4502 06/03/41 12/62    6     5     5
                    *********0000000-14*****************0000000000 MALE   306-45-6264 06/15/44 11/72    0     0    11
                    ***********************0000000000000000000 FEMALE 439-29-3411 01/05/54 06/73    0     0     3
                    000-8674870000000-12***************0000000000 FEMALE 456-85-9603 09/10/47 09/69    5     5     5
                    000-867644*****************0000000000000000000 FEMALE 988-32-9254 09/01/40 11/72    6     5     5
                    *********0000000001000-9267240000000000000000 FEMALE 296-19-7063 07/08/45 10/73    0     0     4
                    ***********************0000000000000000000 FEMALE 807-65-0019 07/06/49 04/73    0     0     5
                    ***********************0000000000000000000 FEMALE 410-21-7117 01/07/52 08/73    0     0     5
                    ***********************0000000000000000000 FEMALE 749-45-3812 07/12/38 09/63   11    11    11
                    *********0000000001*******0000000000000000000 MALE   460-09-5141 12/18/30 05/67    0    14    14
                    *******************0000000000000000000 MALE   590-37-8021 04/02/41 01/74   13    13    13
                    ******************0000000001*********0000000000 MALE   158-34-0628 03/28/44 11/72   11    11    11
                    00000-3212*********000000-212*********0000000000 MALE   601-13-8536 11/02/29 09/71    0    15    15
                    *********000-265837*****************0000000000 MALE   240-57-1268 04/01/28 01/68    9     9     9
                    *********00000000-4*********0000000000000000000 FEMALE 202-59-8145 01/03/42 07/70    8     8     8
                    ***************0000000-1300000000000000000000 FEMALE 322-72-3216 08/17/25 04/63    8     8     8
                    *********0000000001000-8898600000000000000000 FEMALE 614-79-5383 05/07/26 07/65    5     5     5
                    *********************0000000000000000000 MALE   349-36-3224 06/28/45 07/69    3     3     3
                    ***********************0000000000000000000 MALE   145-96-0171 09/05/23 09/70    3     3     3
                    *********000-265838*********0000000000000000000 FEMALE 981-30-6111 01/22/50 04/69    7     7     7
                    *********0000-16582*****************0000000000 MALE   589-47-5641 03/18/19 09/73    3     3     3
                    *********0000000-12*********0000000000000000000 MALE   494-25-4965 06/13/47 06/75    7     7     7
                    ******************0000000-14*********0000000000 MALE   322-74-6991 11/06/23 12/74    7     3     3
                    000000-198*********00000-343700000000000000000 FEMALE 705-96-3014 04/06/47 09/70    5     5     5
```

The string NAME is composed of 5 alphanumeric variables that do not have a print format of A. Thus, REPORT assigns each segment the default width of 10 and attempts to print the internal representation as numbers rather than letters.

Figure 5.61b   Wrong Sort Structure and Too Narrow Columns

```
15 SORT CASES    GROUP DIV
        .
        .
        .

16 REPORT        FORMAT=BRKSPACE(0),MARGINS(10,90)/
17               HEAD='ANALYSIS OF SALARIES WITHIN DIVISION AND GROUP'/
18               FOOT='FISCAL 79 DATA'/
19               VARS=SALARY'  AVG ''SALARY'(4)
20               MEDIAN'MEDIAN''SALARY'(4)
21               MAX(DUMMY) '  MAX ''SALARY'(4)
22               MIN(DUMMY) '  MIN ''SALARY'(4)
23               MSALARY'  AVG ''SALARY''  MEN '(4)
24               FSALARY'  AVG ''SALARY'' WOMEN'(4)
25               /
26               BREAK=DIV'DIVISION'(LABEL)(12)(SKIP(2))/
27               SUMMARY=MEAN(2)'FOR DIVISION'(SALARY MSALARY FSALARY)
28               MEDIAN(8000,38000)CONTINUE(MEDIAN)
29               ADD(MAX(SALARY))CONTINUE(MAX(0))
30               ADD(MIN(SALARY))CONTINUE(MIN(0))
31               /
32               BREAK=GROUP'GROUP'(LABEL)(12)(SKIP(1))/
33               SUMMARY=MEAN''(SALARY MSALARY FSALARY)
34               MEDIAN(8000,38000)CONTINUE(MEDIAN)
35               ADD(MAX(SALARY))CONTINUE(MAX(0))
36               ADD(MIN(SALARY))CONTINUE(MIN(0))
37               /
```

```
REPORT REQUIRES    242520 BYTES FOR THIS TASK
               ANALYSIS OF SALARIES WITHIN DIVISION AND GROUP
```

DIVISION	GROUP	AV SALA	MEDI SALA	MA SALA	MI SALA	AV SALA ME	AV SALA WOM
MARKETING	NEW YORK	****	****	****	8947	****	****
	FOR DIVISION	****	****	****	8947	****	****
R & D	NEW YORK	****	****	****	8199	****	****
	FOR DIVISION	****	****	****	8199	****	****
MARKETING	BOSTON	****	****	****	****	****	****
	FOR DIVISION	****	****	****	****	****	****
R & D	BOSTON	****	****	****	8018	****	M
	FOR DIVISION	****	****	****	8018	****	M
MARKETING	PHILADELPHIA	****	****	****	9518	****	****
	FOR DIVISION	****	****	****	9518	****	****
R & D	PHILADELPHIA	****	****	****	9011	****	****
	FOR DIVISION	****	****	****	9011	****	****

```
                             FISCAL 79 DATA
```

The report is set up to describe groups within division, but the SORT CASES command sorts divisions within groups. In addition, the "vars" columns are restricted to 4 characters in width, which is not wide enough to print the summary statistics.

REPORT was designed and programmed by Harvey Weinstein and was documented by ViAnn Beadle and Robert Gruen.

Chapter 6

SURVIVAL:
Life Table Analysis

SPSS procedure SURVIVAL produces life tables, graphs of survival functions, and comparisons of the survival performance of various subgroups in the sample. SURVIVAL can also write a file which may be used to produce high-quality graphic representation of SURVIVAL output on devices other than line printers. These records can also be used to enter SURVIVAL data into other programs for further analysis.

6.1 INTRODUCTION TO SURVIVAL ANALYSIS

Survival analysis evaluates the time interval between two events, a starting event and a terminal event. It is most commonly used to characterize the survival times of patients with severe illnesses and to study the effects of different treatments on the survival of such patients. It can also be applied to other areas of research where starting and terminal events can be defined and where the interval of time between these events is of interest. In the social sciences, for example, survival analysis can be used to describe and compare the time interval from marriage to divorce for groups of people with different social backgrounds. In economics, survival analysis can be used to study the success rates of different types of businesses.

6.2 Starting and Terminal Events

The choice of starting and terminal events is an important part of survival analysis. In a study of a malevolent illness, the starting point is often the onset of symptoms and, as implied by the term "survival", the terminal event is often death. However, the two events might just as well be defined as the time from first appearance of symptoms to diagnosis, from diagnosis to first disappearance of symptoms, from diagnosis to first recurrence, or from diagnosis to death. In a study of the survival of new businesses, the starting point might be the opening of a new business venture, and the terminal point the failure (closing) of the business or its success (the point at which the business first shows a profit). The only restrictions on the definition of the two events are

• The starting event must occur
• The terminal event must not occur before the starting event
• The terminal event must be defined so that it is impossible for it to occur more than once

It is not necessary that the terminal event happen to every case.

It is important to note that the starting event for an individual is the time of entry into the study, not the time that the study began. For example, suppose that one individual entered during the third month of the study and terminated during the tenth month and another individual entered during the fourth month and terminated during the eleventh month. Both cases would have a survival time of seven months since survival time is measured from an individual's own starting date.

6.3 Censored Observations

If the terminal event for a particular individual has not occurred by the end of the study, the survival time is the interval between the time of entry into the study and the time that the study ended. Such an observation is said to be censored because the survival time is not known exactly, but is known to be of at least a certain duration.

Censored observations arise in two ways. First, an individual may be alive at the time of the completion of the study. If the individual was diagnosed one year before the termination of the study, and is alive when the study ends, all that is known is that the survival time is at least one year. Second, censored observations occur when an investigator loses contact with the subject before the study is completed. The subject may move or refuse to participate further in the study, or may die of causes unrelated to the disease being studied.

Censored observations cannot be treated as missing. The physician would be very unhappy if all of the patients who were still alive were ignored in the analysis of the results, particularly if the results of the treatment were good.

The survival analysis technique does not exclude censored observations. All available data are used; the survival estimates are based on the observed survival times of both censored and uncensored observations.

6.4 Survival Functions

Survival analysis examines the survival experience of a sample at various intervals from the starting event. For example, say that the interval chosen for a study of gravely ill patients is one year and that the starting event is first diagnosis. A number of the patients will survive through the first year following diagnosis and so enter the second interval. A number of those who enter the second interval will survive into the third, and so on.

Within each interval a certain number of cases may withdraw from the study or be lost to follow-up. Instead of dropping those cases from analysis for the interval, it is usually more reasonable to assume that those who withdrew did so, on the average, halfway through the interval. The number exposed to risk during the interval, then, is the number entering the interval minus one half of the number withdrawn. This assumption makes the maximum use of all censored data.

From sample data of this type, a number of functions which characterize the distribution of survival times in the population can be estimated. The three survival functions calculated by procedure SURVIVAL are the cumulative survival rate (the proportion of all cases surviving to the end of each interval), the probability density function (the probability per unit time of dying within a given interval), and the hazard function (the probability per unit time that an individual who has survived to the beginning of an interval will die in that interval). The computation of these functions is based on the actuarial method described by Berkson and Gage (1950). A sample of the tables produced by SURVIVAL and a discussion of the survival functions and other statistics provided is given in the following section. Section 6.6 then discusses the statistics available for comparing the survival experiences of subgroups.

6.5 DATA AND STATISTICS IN THE LIFE TABLE

Figure 6.5 illustrates the statistics provided in the life table produced by SURVIVAL.

Figure 6.5   Sample Life Table

```
    FILE    SAMPLE   (CREATION DATE = 08/17/78)

LIFE TABLE
    SURVIVAL VARIABLE   ONSSURV   MONTHS FROM ONSET TO DEATH
                    FOR   TREATMNT   PATIENT TREATMENT                    =    1  TREATMENT A
```

INTVL START TIME	NUMBER ENTRNG THIS INTVL	NUMBER WDRAWN DURING INTVL	NUMBER EXPOSD TO RISK	NUMBER OF TERMNL EVENTS	PROPN TERMI- NATING	PROPN SURVI- VING	CUMUL PROPN SURV AT END	PROBA- BILITY DENSTY	HAZARD RATE	SE OF CUMUL SURV- IVING	SE OF PROB- ABILTY DENS	SE OF HAZRD RATE
0.0	501.0	0.0	501.0	3.0	0.0060	0.9940	0.9940	0.0012	0.0012	0.003	0.001	0.001
5.0	498.0	1.0	497.5	16.0	0.0322	0.9678	0.9620	0.0064	0.0065	0.009	0.002	0.002
10.0	481.0	1.0	480.5	26.0	0.0541	0.9459	0.9100	0.0104	0.0111	0.013	0.002	0.002
15.0	454.0	0.0	454.0	17.0	0.0374	0.9626	0.8759	0.0068	0.0076	0.015	0.002	0.002
20.0	437.0	0.0	437.0	23.0	0.0526	0.9474	0.8298	0.0092	0.0108	0.017	0.002	0.002
25.0	414.0	1.0	413.5	25.0	0.0605	0.9395	0.7796	0.0100	0.0125	0.019	0.002	0.002
30.0	388.0	1.0	387.5	22.0	0.0568	0.9432	0.7354	0.0089	0.0117	0.020	0.002	0.002
35.0	365.0	1.0	364.5	24.0	0.0658	0.9342	0.6870	0.0097	0.0136	0.021	0.002	0.003
40.0	340.0	0.0	340.0	24.0	0.0706	0.9294	0.6385	0.0097	0.0146	0.022	0.002	0.003
45.0	316.0	1.0	315.5	14.0	0.0444	0.9556	0.6101	0.0057	0.0091	0.022	0.001	0.002
50.0	301.0	1.0	300.5	34.0	0.1131	0.8869	0.5411	0.0069	0.0120	0.022	0.001	0.002
60.0	266.0	0.0	266.0	22.0	0.0827	0.9173	0.4963	0.0045	0.0086	0.022	0.001	0.002
70.0	244.0	2.0	243.0	15.0	0.0617	0.9383	0.4657	0.0031	0.0064	0.022	0.001	0.002
80.0	227.0	3.0	225.5	24.0	0.1064	0.8936	0.4161	0.0050	0.0112	0.022	0.001	0.002
90.0	200.0	2.0	199.0	18.0	0.0905	0.9095	0.3785	0.0038	0.0095	0.022	0.001	0.002
100.0+	180.0	104.0	128.0	76.0	0.5938	0.4063	0.1538	**	**	0.019	**	**

```
**    THESE CALCULATIONS FOR THE LAST INTERVAL ARE MEANINGLESS.

THE MEDIAN SURVIVAL TIME FOR THESE DATA IS  69.18
```

The contents of the thirteen columns of the life table are as follows:

INTERVAL START TIME. The start time of the current interval. Interval width is denoted in the equations below by the symbol (h).

NUMBER ENTERING THIS INTERVAL. The number of cases which have survived to the beginning of the current interval.

NUMBER WITHDRAWN DURING THIS INTERVAL. The number of cases that entered the interval but whose follow-up period ends somewhere in the interval.

NUMBER EXPOSED TO RISK (r). The number exposed to risk in the interval, computed as the number entering the interval minus 1/2 of those withdrawn.

NUMBER OF TERMINAL EVENTS. The number who died in the interval.

PROPORTION OF TERMINAL EVENTS (q). An estimate of the probability of dying in a given interval, computed as the number of terminal events in the interval divided by the number exposed to risk.

PROPORTION SURVIVING (p). The proportion surviving is 1 minus the proportion of terminal events.

CUMULATIVE PROPORTION SURVIVING AT END (S_i). This estimate of the cumulative survival rate at the end of an interval is obtained by multiplying the probabilities of survival up through the present interval. In the sample table (Figure 6.5), the probability of surviving to the 30th month is $.9940 \times .9678 \times .9459 \times .9626 \times .9474 \times .9395 = .7796$. The cumulative survival rate can be plotted with the PLOT(LOGSURV) or PLOT(SURVIVAL) specifications. In those plots, the cumulative proportion surviving at the beginning of each interval is plotted.

PROBABILITY DENSITY (f_i). The estimated probability per unit time of dying in the ith interval. The probability density function for the ith interval is computed as follows:

$$f_i = \frac{S_{i-1}q_i}{h_i}$$

HAZARD RATE (λ_i). The hazard rate is an estimate of the probability per unit time that an individual who has survived to the beginning of a given interval will die within that interval. It is computed as the number of deaths per unit time in the interval, divided by the average number of survivors at the mid-point of the interval:

$$\lambda_i = \frac{2q_i}{h_i(l + p_i)}$$

STANDARD ERROR OF CUMULATIVE PROPORTION SURVIVING. The standard error of the cumulative proportion surviving is

$$SE(S_i) = S_i\sqrt{\sum_{j=1}^{i} \frac{q_i}{r_j p_j}}$$

STANDARD ERROR OF PROBABILITY DENSITY. The standard error of the probability density for interval i is

$$SE(f_i) = \frac{S_{i-1}q_i}{h_i}\sqrt{\sum_{j=1}^{i-1} \frac{q_j}{r_j p_j} + \frac{p_i}{r_i q_i}}$$

STANDARD ERROR OF HAZARD RATE. The standard error of the hazard function for interval i is

$$SE(\lambda_i) = \sqrt{\frac{\lambda_i^2}{r_i q_i}\left\{1 - \left(\frac{\lambda_i h_i}{2}\right)^2\right\}}$$

MEDIAN SURVIVAL TIME. This is the time point at which the value of the cumulative survival function is 0.5. Linear interpolation is used to calculate this value. If the estimated cumulative survival fraction does not go below 0.5, the start time of the last interval is flagged with a "+" to indicate that the median is greater than this.

6.6 DATA AND STATISTICS IN COMPARISONS

Besides displaying survival distributions in the life tables, the user may wish to compare the survival distributions of various subgroups in the sample. Figure 6.6 illustrates the output from a comparison requested by the optional COMPARE specification on the SURVIVAL command (see Section 6.18). Besides information about the number of total, uncensored, and censored cases in each subgroup, the comparison includes a mean survival score for each subgroup and a statistic D describing the probability that the subgroups come from different survival distributions.

SCORE. For each individual a score U is computed by comparing the individual's survival time with that of all other individuals. This score is initially zero and is incremented by one for each case whose survival time is known to be less than the individual's survival time and decremented by one for each case whose survival time is known to surpass that of the individual. If both individuals survive the same length of time but one is censored and the other is not, the censored observation is considered to have the longer survival time. For example, the score of an uncensored observation with a survival time of x will be the number of uncensored observations with survival times less than x minus both the number of observations (censored or uncensored) with survival times greater than x and the number of censored observations with survival times equal to x. The U score for a censored observation will simply be the number of uncensored observations with survival times less than that of the censored observation, since no cases can be known to have survival times greater than that of a censored observation. Where it cannot be determined who survived longer (due to ties or both observations being censored), there is no change in the score.

STATISTIC D. Based on the U, a statistic D is then calculated according to the algorithm of Desu (8). Let

$$W_j = \sum U_i$$

where the sum is taken over all cases in subgroup j, then

$$D = \frac{(N - 1)B}{T}$$

where N is equal to the sum of weights of all cases, and

$$B = \sum^{g} \frac{W_j^2}{N_j}$$

where g is the number of groups and

$$T = \sum U_i^2$$

where the sum is taken over all cases.

D is asymptotically distributed as chi-square with g-1 degrees of freedom under the null hypothesis that the subgroups are samples from the same survival distribution. The larger the D statistic, the more likely that the subgroups come from different survival distributions. The level of significance of D is also given in the output.

Figure 6.6   Sample Survival Comparison

```
   FILE    SAMPLE   (CREATION DATE = 08/17/78)

COMPARISON OF SURVIVAL EXPERIENCE USING THE LEE-DESU STATISTIC
   SURVIVAL VARIABLE  ONSSURV   MONTHS FROM ONSET TO DEATH

         GROUPED BY  TREATMNT  PATIENT TREATMENT

OVERALL COMPARISON    STATISTIC      9.001 D.F.    2   PROB.  0.0111

GROUP  LABEL               TOTAL N   UNCEN    CEN  PCT CEN  MEAN SCORE

    1  TREATMENT A             501     383    118    23.55     20.042
    2  TREATMENT B              97      82     15    15.46    -67.412
    3  TREATMENT C              26      24      2     7.69    -134.69
```

6.7 OPERATION OF PROCEDURE SURVIVAL

The individual case in a survival study will contain a value for one or more survival variables. It might, for example, contain a value for the interval from first diagnosis of serious disease until first recurrence of the disease and another for the interval from first diagnosis until death.

For each survival variable being measured, the case will also have a status. For example, for the time from diagnosis until death, a patient's status might be still living, withdrawn from the study, dead from causes other than the one being studied, or dead from the disease being studied. Each of these possibilities can be assigned a value and the appropriate value recorded for the individual case.

Each case may also have values for control variables such as the patient's age, race, or sex, or the kind of treatment administered. These variables allow the sample to be divided into subgroups for separate table analysis and for comparisons.

The command for SPSS procedure SURVIVAL requires specifications for survival variables, width of intervals to be used, and status. It permits control variables for tables and specifications for graphic output (PLOTS) and comparisons between subgroups defined by the control variables (COMPARE). The general format of SURVIVAL syntax is as follows:

```
SURVIVAL       TABLES=survarlist [BY varlist(lo,hi)... BY

               varlist (lo,hi)...]/

               INTERVALS=THRU n BY a,THRU.../

               STATUS=varname(lo,hi) FOR survarlist.../

               PLOTS[ (ALL)      ]    [=survarlist BY varlist
                      (LOGSURV)
                      (SURVIVAL)
                      (DENSITY)
                      (HAZARD)

               BY varlist...]/

               COMPARE[=survarlist BY varlist BY varlist..] /
```

These specifications are discussed in the following sections. Section 6.24 contains an example of input for a typical SURVIVAL run.

6.8 SPECIFICATIONS FOR SURVIVAL TABLES

Specifications required for output of survival tables are the list of survival variables (with or without control variables) in the TABLES= specification, the width of intervals to be used and time span to be covered in the analysis (INTERVALS=), and the STATUS= specification for each survival variable.

6.9 The TABLES= Specification

The basic configuration of the survival analysis is established in the TABLES= specification which lists dependent (survival) variables and, optionally, first- and second-order control variables. The specification is entered in the following manner:

```
SURVIVAL       TABLES=survarlist [BY varlist(lo,hi) varlist...
               BY varlist(lo,hi) varlist...]/
```

Survival variables are entered first in the TABLES= specification. At least one survival variable must be specified; as many as twenty may be entered. All survival variable values must be positive; negative values are treated as missing data. If one or more negative values are encountered, the warning message AT LEAST ONE NEGATIVE SURVIVAL TIME ENCOUNTERED; TREATED AS MISSING DATA, is issued.

Following the survival variables, one or two groups of control variables may be entered. These variables become the first- and second-order controls, respectively, on the survival analysis. A maximum of two orders of control variables may be entered. A maximum of 100 controls may be specified in the two groups combined.

Survival variables and first- and second-order control variable groups must be separated from each other by the keyword BY.

Each control variable list entered must be accompanied by a parenthesized values range. The first value named represents the low end of the scale, the second, the high. Values must be separated by blanks or commas. The values used to specify the range must be integers. Variable values in the data will be truncated without rounding to integers so that the cases may be assigned to a category.

The specification for a control variable with range 1 through 5 inclusive is entered in the following manner:

```
SURVIVAL       TABLES=survarlist BY varlist(1,5)/
```

To apply one value of a control variable to the analysis, enter a specification of the following form:

```
SURVIVAL       TABLES=survarlist BY varname(1,1).../
```

In this instance, only cases in which the control variable has the value 1 will be processed.

Control variables are optional. If controls are omitted, no comparisons can be done; one survival table will be printed for each survival variable. These tables, and any requested plots, will be based on the entire sample, rather than on a controlled subgroup.

6.10 The INTERVALS= Specification

The INTERVALS= parameter establishes the length of the period under examination and specifies the length of the intervals into which the period is broken. The INTERVALS= parameter has two components: the BY specification sets interval length; the THRU specification names the period to which this interval length is to apply. For example, where a period of ten years (measured in months) is to be broken into four month intervals, the following specification is entered:

```
INTERVALS= THRU 120 BY 4/
```

The first interval is 0-4 months, the second, 4-8 months, the last, 116-120 months. In addition to the specified intervals, a final interval, in this case 120+ months, is automatically created to handle any survival times which exceed the specified range.

The INTERVALS= specifications pertain to the unit of time supplied by the survival variables. In the case of the INTERVALS= statement above, for example, if the survival variables supplied days, the survival tables would supply statistics for 4-day intervals over the first 4 months of the study.

Where possible, it is advisable to enter survival times in the most precise units available. For example, even if SURVIVAL results are to be produced in month-units it is best to enter the data in day-units and then divide by 30 to compute month-units from these, rather than to simply reduce each year-month-day date to a year-month date. Use of the first method retains fractional parts of the month in the SURVIVAL calculations; use of the second does not.

It is possible to designate different INTERVALS= lengths for different portions of the period examined through the use of multiple THRU/BY specifications. This is useful as it may often be desirable to focus closely on certain parts of a treatment period, while taking a more generalized view of the remainder. For example, to request an interval width of two months for the first year of a period, and a width of six months for the remaining nine years, enter:

```
INTERVALS=THRU 12 BY 2,THRU 120 BY 6/
```

When different interval specifications for different portions of the period are being made in this manner, specifications must be made in chronological order, that is, where

```
INTERVALS=THRU n BY a,THRU m BY b/
```

n must always be less than m.

It is not possible to enter different interval specifications for the same or overlapping portions of a period. The specification THRU 120 BY 3,THRU 120 BY 10, for example, is invalid. To examine the ten-year period both every three and every ten months, you must either specify intervals of one month or run two SURVIVAL analyses.

If the specification INTERVALS=THRU n BY a is made in such a way that n/a is not an integer (that is, a does not evenly divide n) n will be increased to the nearest multiple of a. For example, the results of the specification

```
INTERVALS=...THRU 40 BY 3.../
```

is a period of 42 divided into 14 units of 3.

The limit on this method of handling non-integer units of time is reached in such cases as

```
INTERVALS=THRU 49 BY 12 THRU 59 BY 3/
```

When increasing the size of one period to accommodate the specified interval evenly results in so far overstepping the bounds of the next specified period that no intervals of the specified size can be accommodated in that period, processing ceases. In other words, the process of increasing one period is not allowed to completely obliterate the subsequent period.

6.11 The STATUS= Specification

A status variable must be associated with each survival variable included in the analysis. The value of a case on the status variable indicates whether the individual is living, dead, or withdrawn from the study, and thus whether or not the case is censored.

The STATUS= specification is entered in the following manner:

```
STATUS=statusvar(lo,hi) FOR survarlist.../
```

The STATUS= specification associates each survival variable with its status variable through use of the keyword FOR. Each status variable is accompanied by a range specification. The values in the range (including range endpoints) indicate that the event timed by the survival variable—recurrence of disease, death, etc.—has occurred. All other values of the status variable indicate that the event has not occurred. Cases showing values included in the range are uncensored. Other cases are censored. For example, suppose a survival analysis includes the variables ONSSURV, which gives the length of time to death for each subject, and STATUS, which is a status variable with values (1) subject living; (2) subject withdrawn from study; (3) subject dead, cause unrelated to disease; and (4) subject dead, due to disease. To associate the survival variable with the status variable and indicate the range of values for uncensored cases, the following specification is entered:

```
STATUS=STATUS(3,4) FOR ONSSURV/
```

This STATUS specification requests that any death, from whatever cause, be considered a terminal event. If only deaths due to disease were to be considered terminal events (deaths from other causes being treated as withdrawals from the study and therefore as censored observations) the STATUS= specification would be entered as

```
STATUS=CURSTAT(4) FOR TDEATH/
```

A status variable and value must be associated with each survival variable. More than one STATUS= specification may be used and more than one survival variable may be listed in each, but only one status variable and value may be listed.

If FOR and the list of survival variables are omitted, the status variable and value apply to all survival variables not assigned a status variable by some other STATUS= specification.

6.12 Production of Life Tables

On the basis of the TABLES=, INTERVALS=, and STATUS= specifications, procedure SURVIVAL produces one or more life tables. For example, from the specifications

```
SURVIVAL     TABLES=ONSSURV,RECSURV BY TREATMNT (1,3)/
             INTERVALS=THRU 50 BY 5 THRU 100 BY 10/
             STATUS=RECURSIT(1,9) FOR RECSURVE/
             STATUS=STATUS(3,4) FOR ONSSURV/...
```

six life tables are produced, one for each of the survival variables ONSSURV and RECSURV, controlled by each of the three values of TREATMNT. The first of these tables, for the subgroup TREATMENT A (TREATMNT value 1) and the survival variable ONSSURV, is reproduced in Section 6.5, above.

6.13 SPECIFICATIONS FOR SURVIVAL PLOTS

The PLOTS specification requests line printer plots of the survival functions against time. The survival, hazard, and density functions, which are listed in the survival tables, may be plotted. Plots can be produced for the entire sample, if no controls are specified, or for subsets of the sample defined by first- or first- and second-order controls.

The PLOTS specification is entered in the following form:

```
PLOTS[(selection keyword)][=survarlist
BY varlist BY varlist]/
```

6.14 PLOTS Selection Keywords

Selection keywords specify the type of plot to be printed. The five selection keywords are listed below.

PLOTS(ALL)   *Default specification.* As the selection keyword default, entering ALL has the same effect as omitting the selection keyword from the PLOTS specification: all plots will be produced for the specified variables.

PLOTS(LOGSURV)   The keyword *LOGSURV* requests graphs of the cumulative survival distribution, on a logarithmic scale.

PLOTS(SURVIVAL)   *SURVIVAL* requests plots of the cumulative survival distribution on a linear scale.

PLOTS(HAZARD)   *HAZARD* requests graphs of the hazard function.

PLOTS(DENSITY)   *DENSITY* requests graphs of the density function.

More than one type of plot may be requested.

```
PLOTS(HAZARD,DENSITY)
```

requests the hazard and density function plots.

6.15 Specifying Variables for PLOTS

The variables to be used in plotting and their roles are basically defined by the TABLES= specification. The variable lists which follow PLOTS can only eliminate variables from use in plotting. The general form of the PLOTS variable list is

```
[survival variable list
  [BY independent variable list
  [BY control variable list]]]
```

The survival variable list can name all or some of the variables named as survival variables on the TABLES= list. It cannot name any other variables. The keyword TO can be used in its usual sense to name a consecutive list of variables from the TABLES= list. If the TABLES= list reads

```
TABLES= A B D C E F G
```

then B TO E means B D C E. If all the survival variables are to be plotted, the keyword ALL may be used to designate them all. Naming some of the survival variables here will eliminate plots for those not named.

Following the first BY is the list of independent variables. This specification is not allowed unless the TABLES= parameter contains at least one BY. The variables listed here must also appear on the TABLES= list as first-order control variables (that is, they must appear after its first BY). TO and ALL can be used here in the same ways as in the survival variable list. The variables listed here define the groups to be plotted together. That is, if an independent variable defines three groups, a plot using that variable will contain three lines, one for each group defined by that variable.

Control variables (if any) are listed after the second BY following PLOTS. The variables listed here must also be listed as second-order control variables in TABLES= (that is, they must follow its second BY). TO and ALL may be used here as they are used in the survival variable list. The second BY and the list of control variables are invalid if the TABLES= specification does not contain a second BY.

The default PLOTS specification, then, is

```
PLOTS(ALL) = ALL BY ALL BY ALL/
```

or as much of that as has the right number of BY keywords. The user can omit any part of this specification that appears after the last part in which ALL is not desired. The (ALL) after PLOTS can always be omitted. For example, to plot functions computed from some, but not all, of the survival variables, the following will suffice:

```
PLOTS = survival variable list/
```

The program will supply as many BY ALL specifications as needed.

Note that these rules do not allow one to plot functions both with and without control variables and independent variables in one run. To get around this, one can use a constant variable as a control or independent variable or both. For example, if the variable CONST is created with the statement

```
COMPUTE      CONST=1
```

Then all cases are in the "1" group for CONST. The specifications

```
SURVIVAL      TABLES = T1 BY GRP(1,6) CONST(1,1)/
              ...
              PLOTS/
```

give a table for each value of GRP and an overall table plus function plots for the subsamples defined by GRP and plots for the whole sample.

6.16   Production of Plots

If the TABLES= list contains no control variables, a separate plot of each requested function is printed for each survival variable.

If there is one level of control variable, a graph of each survival function requested is printed for each survival variable for each control variable. Each graph contains a line for each group defined by the control variable. For example, if all four types of plots are requested and there are two survival variables and three control variables, $4 \times 2 \times 3 = 24$ graphs will be printed.

If second-order control variables appear on the TABLES= list, a full set of plots for each survival and first-level control variable, as described above, is printed for each value of each second-order control variable. If all four functions are to be plotted and there are three survival variables, two first-order control variables, and two second-order control variables with four and five values respectively, $4 \times 3 \times 2 \times (4+5) = 216$ graphs will be printed.

6.17   Output of PLOTS

On each graph the survival variable (on the vertical axis) is plotted against time (on the horizontal axis) for each first-order control variable's values. The values and value labels of the control variable and the symbol by which each value is represented in the graph are noted below the graph itself. The symbol used to plot a value on the graph is the value itself, for example, for the variable TREATMNT, with values 1, treatment A; 2, treatment B; and 3, treatment C, the symbols "1", "2", and "3" are used to plot the survival function. A graph of the cumulative survival distribution of the values of TREATMNT plotted for the variable ONSSURV is reproduced in Figure 6.17.

Figure 6.17   Sample Graph of Survival Function

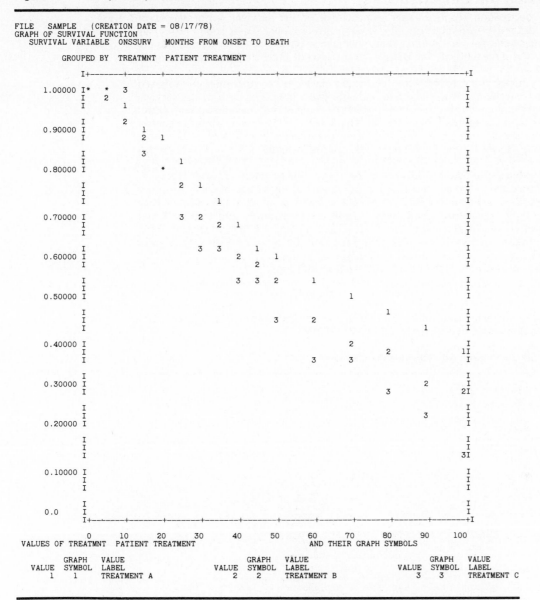

```
FILE   SAMPLE   (CREATION DATE = 08/17/78)
GRAPH OF SURVIVAL FUNCTION
  SURVIVAL VARIABLE  ONSSURV   MONTHS FROM ONSET TO DEATH

        GROUPED BY  TREATMNT  PATIENT TREATMENT

          I+-------+-------+-------+-------+-------+-------+-------+-------+-------+-------+I
  1.00000 I*    *   3                                                                    I
          I    2                                                                         I
          I         1                                                                    I

          I         2                                                                    I
  0.90000 I                 1                                                            I
          I                 2   1                                                        I

          I               3                                                             I
          I                       1                                                      I
  0.80000 I                 *                                                            I

          I                   2   1                                                      I
          I                                                                              I
          I                       1                                                      I

  0.70000 I                   3   2                                                      I
          I                         2   1                                                I
          I                                                                              I

          I                 3   3       1                                                I
  0.60000 I                         2   1                                                I
          I                         2                                                    I

          I                   3   3   2       1                                          I
          I                                                                              I
  0.50000 I                                         1                                    I

          I                                               1                              I
          I                     3       2                                                I
          I                                                   1                          I

  0.40000 I                                             2                                I
          I                                               2                             1I
          I                         3       3                                            I

  0.30000 I                                                   2                          I
          I                                             3                               2I

          I                                                       3                      I
          I                                                                              I
  0.20000 I                                                                              I

          I                                                                              I
          I                                                                              I
          I                                                                             3I

  0.10000 I                                                                              I
          I                                                                              I
          I                                                                              I

          I                                                                              I
  0.0     I                                                                              I
          I+-------+-------+-------+-------+-------+-------+-------+-------+-------+-------+I
           0      10      20      30      40      50      60      70      80      90     100
  VALUES OF TREATMNT  PATIENT TREATMENT                       AND THEIR GRAPH SYMBOLS
```

VALUE	GRAPH SYMBOL	VALUE LABEL		VALUE	GRAPH SYMBOL	VALUE LABEL		VALUE	GRAPH SYMBOL	VALUE LABEL
1	1	TREATMENT A		2	2	TREATMENT B		3	3	TREATMENT C

6.18   SPECIFICATIONS FOR SURVIVAL COMPARISONS

The COMPARE specification requests comparison of the survival of subgroups in the sample defined by control variables' values. The specification is entered in the following form:

```
COMPARE[=survarlist BY varlist BY varlist]
```

6.19   Specifying Variables for COMPARE

The COMPARE variable specifications are made in the same way as are those of PLOTS. The COMPARE variable list specification is optional; if no variable list is entered, the TABLES= list will be used by default. At least one survival variable and one first-order control variable must be specified to make a comparison possible.

Variables not included in the TABLES= list may not be entered under COMPARE. Variables must be entered into COMPARE at the same level as they appear in the TABLES= list, that is, a first- order control may be used only as a first-order control, etc.

Only one SURVIVAL variables list, one first-order controls list, and one second-order controls list may be entered in the COMPARE specification.

6.20 Production of Comparisons

The COMPARE specification requests exact comparisons of the survival performances of subgroups of cases defined by case values on a first-order control variable. These comparisons may be controlled by the addition of second-order control variables. Where second-order controls are included, a comparison of the survival of subgroups of cases is made for each value of each second-order control.

Suppose, for example, that a COMPARE specification includes two first-order controls and two second- order controls, one with three and one with five values. For each of the survival variables, this specification produces one comparison of the categories of each first-order control for each of the values of the second-order controls. Thus, with $3 + 5 = 8$ second-order control variable values, two first-order controls, and two survival variables, $2 \times 2 \times 8 = 32$ overall comparisons will be performed. If no second-order controls are included, $2 \times 2 = 4$ comparisons are performed.

Pairwise comparisons of subgroups' survival performance may be requested with Option 7. When Option 7 is specified, comparisons of each possible pair of the values of each first-order control are performed in addition to the standard overall comparisons of all of the values of each first-order control. In the previous example, supposing first-order controls with three and four values, a total of three sets of pairs exist for the first control, and six for the second. Thus comparing two survival variables in $(6 + 3)$ possible pairs, controlled by the eight second-order control values gives $2 \times 9 \times 8 = 144$ pairwise comparisons.

Figure 6.20 presents the output from the COMPARE specification.

```
                 COMPARE=ONSSURV BY TREATMNT/
     OPTIONS     7
```

In the example, pairwise comparisons of survival, as measured by the variable ONSSURV, are made of the case subgroups defined by the variable TREATMNT.

Figure 6.20   Sample Comparison with Pairwise Comparisons

```
FILE    SAMPLE   (CREATION DATE = 08/17/78)

COMPARISON OF SURVIVAL EXPERIENCE USING THE LEE-DESU STATISTIC

   SURVIVAL VARIABLE  ONSSURV   MONTHS FROM ONSET TO DEATH
          GROUPED BY  TREATMNT  PATIENT TREATMENT

OVERALL COMPARISON    STATISTIC      9.001  D.F.    2   PROB.  0.0111

GROUP  LABEL                TOTAL N   UNCEN    CEN  PCT CEN  MEAN SCORE

    1  TREATMENT A              501     383    118    23.55     20.042
    2  TREATMENT B               97      82     15    15.46    -67.412

    3  TREATMENT C               26      24      2     7.69   -134.69

PAIRWISE COMPARISON   STATISTIC      5.042  D.F.    1   PROB.  0.0247

GROUP  LABEL                TOTAL N   UNCEN    CEN  PCT CEN  MEAN SCORE

    1  TREATMENT A              501     383    118    23.55     13.603
    2  TREATMENT B               97      82     15    15.46    -70.258

PAIRWISE COMPARISON   STATISTIC      4.768  D.F.    1   PROB.  0.0290

GROUP  LABEL                TOTAL N   UNCEN    CEN  PCT CEN  MEAN SCORE

    1  TREATMENT A              501     383    118    23.55      6.4391
    3  TREATMENT C               26      24      2     7.69   -124.08

PAIRWISE COMPARISON   STATISTIC      0.766  D.F.    1   PROB.  0.3814

GROUP  LABEL                TOTAL N   UNCEN    CEN  PCT CEN  MEAN SCORE

    2  TREATMENT B               97      82     15    15.46      2.8454

    3  TREATMENT C               26      24      2     7.69    -10.615
```

COMPARE statistics (survival score and statistic D) are discussed in Section 6.6.

6.21 Approximate Comparisons

Data may be entered into procedure SURVIVAL either as one record per individual or as two records per interval. Whether individual or aggregated records are entered affects the outcome of SURVIVAL comparisons.

When one record per individual is entered, exact comparisons may be done. When the exact comparison method is used, survival scores and statistic D are calculated on the basis of each individual's precise survival experience as it is entered in the data. This method gives obvious benefits in accuracy; its drawback is that processing of exact comparisons requires that all data be held in core simultaneously.

This demand on core may put exact comparisons out of the question for large samples. Furthermore, exact individual-by-individual data may not be available in every survival study: data may have been submitted in the aggregated form on an interval-by-interval basis. In such cases the procedure SURVIVAL options for approximate comparisons may be used.

If aggregated data rather than raw data are entered into procedure SURVIVAL, or if Option 6 is in effect, approximate rather than exact comparisons will be made (see Section 6.23).

If Option 5 is in effect, approximate comparisons will be made if there is not enough room in core to allow for exact comparisons. (see Section 6.25).

Results obtained with approximate comparisons may differ from those obtained using exact comparisons. Under the approximate comparison method, all events—deaths, recurrence, withdrawal, etc.—are assumed to occur at the midpoint of the interval. Under exact comparisons some of these midpoint ties can be resolved. However, if interval widths are not too great, the variation between results from exact comparisons and from approximate comparisons should not be great.

6.22 USE OF THE YRMODA FUNCTION

In order to calculate survival times, SPSS must translate calendar dates into day numbers. SPSS numbers days from October 15, 1582 (the date of the institution of the Gregorian calendar) through the year 47,516. The transformation from date to day number is accomplished through the use of the YRMODA function, available on Release 8 COMPUTE, IF, and SELECT IF commands. For example, the expression

```
COMPUTE        SURVDAY = YRMODA(VARYR,VARMO,VARDA)
```

transforms the year, month, and day of a survival date (where year, month, and day are given by the variables VARYR, VARMO, and VARDA respectively) into a day number. Constants and arithmetic expressions, as well as variable names, may be used as elements in the YRMODA function.

Notice that start times are subtracted from end times. If this relationship is reversed, and end times are subtracted from start times, negative survival times will result. When negative survival times are encountered they are treated as missing data and the warning message, AT LEAST ONE NEGATIVE SURVIVAL TIME ENCOUNTERED, TREATED AS MISSING DATA, is issued.

Survival times may be computed with YRMODA by simple subtractions of the form

```
COMPUTE        SURVAR = YRMODA(ENDYR,ENDMO,ENDDA) -
               YRMODA(ENTERYR,ENTERMO,ENTERDA)
```

where the variables ENTERYR, ENTERMO, and ENTERDA represent the subjects' date of entry into the study, and the variables ENDYR, ENDMO, and ENDDA give the date of death or withdrawal from the study.

Chapter 11 contains information concerning the treatment of invalid or missing data by the YRMODA function and further details.

6.23 ENTERING WEIGHTED DATA

In some cases it may be impossible or inconvenient to enter survival data as one record per individual involved in the study. In some instances, the data may be available only in an aggregated form as records of the number of deaths or withdrawals from the study during each interval. In other cases, where the sample is very large, entering data as one record per individual may make use of COMPARE impossible, as in order to do comparisons all data must be held in core simultaneously.

To provide for such situations, procedure SURVIVAL allows entry of data as records summarizing the survival experience of the group in each interval rather than as one record per individual. When such aggregated data are used, two records are entered for each interval, one for censored and one for uncensored cases. The number of cases included on the record determines its weight.

For example, suppose the interval five to six years shows seven deaths and three withdrawals from the study. Two records are entered for this interval, one for censored, the other for uncensored cases. Each record specifies the interval, the status of the cases, and the number of cases included (which is the weight factor of the record). The two records for the interval five to six years contain the following variables:

	Time	Status	Weight
record 1	5.5	censored	3
record 2	5.5	uncensored	7

Notice that the interval variable TIME has the value 5.5. When weighted data are used, each death or withdrawal is considered to have occurred at the interval midpoint. This use of the approximate time of the survival event will not effect survival tables or plots, which are calculated exactly as if raw data had been used, and (if the same units of time are used) with the same result. Use of weighted data will affect the results of comparisons, although if the intervals are not large, the results obtained from these approximate comparisons should not differ greatly from results obtained using raw data.

6.24 SPECIFICATIONS FOR SURVIVAL: AN EXAMPLE

The following command lines illustrate both the SURVIVAL specifications and the kinds of data definition and data transformation that might be used with raw input data.

```
RUN NAME         SURVIVAL EXAMPLE
DATA LIST        FIXED /1
                 TREATMNT 15
                 ONSETMO 19-20
                 ONSETYR 21-22
                 RECURSIT 48
                 RECURMO 49-50
                 RECURYR 51-52
                 STATUS 56
                 DEATHMO 57-58
                 DEATHYR 59-60
N OF CASES       647
RECODE           ALL (BLANK = -999)
MISSING VALUES   ALL(-999)

COMMENT          TRANSFORM ALL DATES TO RUNNING CALENDAR DAYS
COMPUTE          ONSDATE=YRMODA(ONSETYR,ONSETMO,15)
COMPUTE          RECDATE=YRMODA(RECURYR,RECURMO,15)
COMPUTE          DEATHDT=YRMODA(DEATHYR,DEATHMO,15)

COMMENT          NOW COMPUTE SURVIVAL VARIABLES
COMPUTE          ONSSURV = (DEATHDT-ONSDATE)/30
IF               (RECURSIT EQ 0) RECSURV = ONSSURV
IF               (RECURSIT NE 0) RECSURV = (RECDATE-ONSDATE)/30
ASSIGN MISSING   ONSDATE TO RECSURV(-1)

VAR LABELS       TREATMNT, PATIENT TREATMENT/
                 ONSSURV, MONTHS FROM ONSET TO DEATH/
                 RECSURV, MONTHS FROM ONSET TO RECURRENCE
VALUE LABELS     TREATMNT (1) TREATMENT A (2) TREATMENT B
                 (3) TREATMENT C
SURVIVAL         TABLES=ONSSURV,RECSURV BY TREATMNT(1,3)/
                 STATUS = RECURSIT(1,9) FOR RECSURV/
                 STATUS = STATUS(3,4) FOR ONSSURV/
                 INTERVALS=THRU 50 BY 5 THRU 100 BY 10/PLOTS/COMPARE
OPTIONS          5,7
READ INPUT DATA
                 1   0559                  00000    31162
                 1   0358                  00000    31067
            ...
                 1   0758                  0        41270
FINISH
```

6.25 PROCEDURE SURVIVAL OPTIONS

Procedure SURVIVAL Options on handling missing data, comparisons, and output of records are listed below.

OPTION 1 *Include missing data.* If this option is specified all missing value indicators are ignored and missing data are entered into the calculations exactly as valid data.

OPTION 2 *Casewise deletion of missing data.* Any case which shows a missing value for any of the variables included in the SURVIVAL variable list is excluded from all SURVIVAL calculations.

Missing values default treatment. Procedure SURVIVAL provides groupwise deletion as the missing values default treatment. That is, unless SURVIVAL Option 1 or 2 is specified, a case will be excluded from any calculation involving a variable for which it shows a missing value, but will be included in all other calculations. This approach makes the fullest use of the available valid data. It also makes it likely that the statistics for different groups of variables will be based on different numbers of cases.

OPTION 3 *Compute comparisons only.* If Option 3 is specified survival tables will not be computed from the SURVIVAL TABLES= list and requests for PLOTS, if any, will be ignored. This option allows all available workspace to be reserved for comparisons.

OPTION 4   *Suppress printing of tables.* If Option 4 is specified only the requested plots and comparisons are output.

OPTION 5   *Default to approximate comparisons.* Approximate comparisons will be done if there is not enough core to do exact comparisons. If Option 5 is not set and there is not enough core to do exact comparisons, procedure SURVIVAL will abort.

OPTION 6   *Do approximate comparisons only.* Approximate comparisons are made from interval-grouped data. No attempt is made to compute exact comparisons from the raw data.

OPTION 7   *Perform pairwise comparisons.* In addition to the overall comparison of each first-order control variable's values, a comparison of each possible pair of its values is made. If Option 7 is not set, only the overall comparisons are done.

OPTION 8   *Output survival table data records.* Option 8 requests that all survival table statistics be written in fixed format on BCDOUT for subsequent processing (see Section 6.27).

OPTION 9   *Output survival table data and label records.* Option 9 requests that all survival table labels—including variable names and labels, and value labels—as well as all survival table statistics be written in fixed format on BCDOUT for subsequent processing (see Section 6.27).

6.26   PROCEDURE SURVIVAL LIMITATIONS

- A maximum of 20 survival variables may be specified.
- A maximum of 100 control variables may be specified on the first- and second-order control variable lists combined.
- The INTERVALS= specification may include a maximum of 20 THRU . . . BY . . . clauses.
- A maximum of 35 values may appear on a PLOT. If the control variable for which a PLOT is requested shows more than 35 values, the first 35 will be plotted.
- The number of bytes of workspace required for SURVIVAL is given by

WORKSPACE = $8 \times \max (C + \max (T + P, A), W)$

$C = 2 \times SVAR \times B1 \times B2 \times I$ if tables or plots are to be printed or approximate comparisons are allowed; $C = 0$ otherwise.
SVAR = the number of survival variables named or implied in the TABLES= specification.
B1 = the number of values specified for each first-level control variable, summed over all those variables; B1 = 1 if no first-level control variables are named.
B2 = the number of values specified for each second-level control variable, summed over all those variables; B2 = 1 if no second-level control variables are named.
I = the number of intervals implied by the INTERVALS= specification, including the extra interval for large survival times.

$T = 11 \times I$

$P = 426 \times NPLOTS$
NPLOTS = the number of types of plots requested (0 to 4).

$A = NGC \times (5 + 3 \times I)$ if approximate comparisons are allowed; $A = 0$ otherwise.

NGC = the largest number of groups to be compared (the largest number of values for any first-level control variable involved in comparisons).

$W = \max (5 \times NGC, CSVAR + CB + 1)$ if exact comparisons are to be attempted; $W = 0$ otherwise.

CSVAR = the number of survival variables involved in comparisons.

CB = the number of control variables (at any level) involved in comparisons.

If exact comparisons are requested, the otherwise unused portion of the workspace is used to store cases. Each case requires 4 * (CSVAR + CB + 1) bytes.

6.27   OUTPUT OF RAW DATA

Procedure SURVIVAL outputs raw data records which can be used to produce high quality graphic display of SURVIVAL output on devices other than the line printer or to do further analyses of SURVIVAL data with other programs.

Options 8 and 9 request output of these raw data records. Option 8 requests output of all information on SURVIVAL life tables; this option is used when records for further analysis are desired. Option 9 requests output of both the survival life table information and all table labeling; this option is set when records to be used for production of graphic displays are desired.

6.28   Format of Raw Data Records

Procedure SURVIVAL outputs five types of records. Option 8 requests output of record types 30, its continuation 31, and 40. Option 9 requests output of record types 10, 20, 30, 31, and 40. Each of these record types is described below.

RECORD TYPE 10, output only when Option 9 is set, is formatted as follows:

Columns	Content	Format
1-2	Record type (10)	F2.0
3-7	Table number	F5.0
8-15	Name of survival variable	A8
15-55	Variable label of survival variable	A40
56	Number of BY's (0, 1, or 2)	F1.0
57-60	Number of rows in current survival table	F4.0

The format descriptor A40 is shorthand for a machine dependent format for forty packed contiguous characters. The number (0, 1, or 2) in column 56 specifies the number of orders of control variables (none, first-order, or first- and second-order controls) which have been applied to the life table. The information in columns 57-60 specifies the number of rows in the life table. This number is the number of intervals in the analysis which show subjects entering; intervals in which no subjects enter are not noted in the life tables. One type 10 record is output for each life table.

RECORD TYPE 20, also output only when Option 9 is set, is formatted as follows:

Columns	Content	Format
1-2	Record type (20)	F2.0
3-7	Table number	F5.0
8-15	Name of control variable	A8
16-55	Variable label of control variable	A40
56-60	Value of control variable	F5.0
61-80	Value label for this value	A20

One type 20 record is produced for each control variable on each life table. If only first-order controls have been placed on the survival analysis, one type 20 record will be produced for each table; if second-order controls have also been applied, two type 20 records will be produced per table.

RECORD TYPE 30, and its continuation 31, output both for Options 8 and 9, are formatted as follows:

Columns	Content	Format
1-2	Record type (30)	F2.0
3-7	Table number	F5.0
8-13	Beginning of interval	F6.2
14-21	Number entering interval	F8.2
22-29	Number withdrawn in interval	F8.2
30-37	Number exposed to risk	F8.2
38-45	Number of terminal events	F8.2

Columns	Content	Format
1-2	Record type (31)	F2.0
3-7	Table number	F5.0
8-15	Proportion terminating	F8.6
16-33	Proportion surviving	F8.6
24-31	Cumulative proportion surviving	F8.6
32-38	Probability density	F8.6
40-47	Hazard rate	F8.6
48-54	S.E. of cumulative proportion surviving	F7.4
55-61	S.E. of probability density	F7.4
62-68	S.E. of hazard rate	F7.4

Each type 30 and 31 record pair contains the information from one line of the life table. As many type 30 and 31 record pairs are output for a table as it has lines (this number is noted in columns 56-59 of the type 10 record for the table).

RECORD TYPE 40, produced both under Option 8 and 9, is formatted as follows:

Columns	Content	Format
1-2	Record type (40)	F2.0

Type 40 records indicate the completion of the series of records for one life table.

6.29 Order of Raw Data Record Output

The SURVIVAL record output facility produces records of life table information and labelings for each of the life tables requested by the TABLES= list. All records for a table are output together in sequence.

Records for life tables are output in the same order as the life tables themselves are produced in the printed output. This order is established by the TABLES= list.

All life tables for the first survival variable are output first. The values of the first- and second-order controls rotate, with the values of the first-order controls changing most rapidly. For example, suppose the following table specifications:

```
SURVIVAL      TABLES=A,B BY Q(1,2), R(1,2) BY Y(1,2) Z(1)
```

Life table records, like the life tables themselves, are output from this specification in the following order:

Table No.	Survar	1st Control	Value	2nd Control	Value
1	A	Q	1	Y	1
2			2		
3		R	1		
4			2		
5		Q	1	Y	2
6			2		
7		R	1		
8			2		
9		Q	1	Z	1
10			2		
11		R	1		
12			2		
13	B	Q	1	Y	1
.	.	.	.	.	.
24	B	R	2	Z	1

6.30 REFERENCES

Berkson, J., and R. Gage. Calculation of Survival Rates for Cancer, *Proceedings of the Mayo Clinic,* 25: 1950, p. 270.

Breslow, N. A Generalized Kruskal-Wallis Test for Comparing K Samples Subject to Unequal Patterns of Censorship, *Biometrika,* 57: 1970, pp. 579-594.

Cutler, S. J., and F. Ederer. Maximum Utilization of the Life Table Method in Analyzing Survival, *Journal of Chronic Diseases,* 8: 1958, pp. 699-712.

Gehan, E. Statistical Methods for Survival Time Studies, in *Cancer Therapy: Prognostic Factors and Criteria of Response,* edited by M. J. Staquet, New York: Raven Press, 1975.

Gross, A. J., and V. Clark *Survival Distributions: Reliability Applications in the Biomedical Sciences,* New York: Wiley, 1975.

Kaplan, E., and P. Meier. Nonparametric Estimation from Incomplete Observations, *Journal of the American Statistical Association,* 53: 1958, pp. 457-481.

Lee, E., and M. Desu. A Computer Program for Comparing K Samples with Right-Censored Data, *Computer Programs in Biomedicine,* 2: 1972, pp. 315-321.

Smith, T., and E. Gehan. A Computer Program for Estimating Survival Functions for the Life Table, *Computer Programs in Biomedicine,* 1: 1970, p. 58.

SURVIVAL was originally designed and implemented by Barry Brown, Marcus Schimek, Herman Walker, and Peggy Wright of M. D. Anderson Hospital, the University of Texas at Houston. Their work was supported by the National Cancer Institute grants CA11430 and CA16672. A revised version of this procedure is available in the CDC-6000 version of SPSS distributed by Northwestern University. That version has been extensively revised by Barry Brown and Herman Walker and by SPSS Inc. for inclusion in Release 8.

Chapter 7

NPAR TESTS: Nonparametric Tests

Many statistical procedures require assumptions about the underlying distributions of variables. For example, the t-test, which is used to test whether two samples have the same mean, assumes that both samples are from normally distributed populations which have the same variance. Procedures which make only minimal assumptions about the form of the underlying distributions are called "nonparametric" or "distribution free". For a discussion of nonparametric tests and formulas, see Siegel (1956).

Table 7.1 summarizes the tests available within NPAR TESTS and their applications:

Table 7.1   Nonparametric Tests of Statistical Significance

Data Organization	Nominal Scale	Ordinal Scale
1 Sample	Chi-square Runs	Kolmogorov-Smirnov
2 Related Samples	McNemar	Sign Wilcoxon
k Related Samples	Cochran Q	Friedman Two-way Anova
2 Independent Samples	(Chi-square) (Fisher)	Median Mann-Whitney Kolmogorov-Smirnov Wald-Wolfowitz Moses
k Independent Samples	(Chi-square)	Median Kruskal-Wallis

NOTE: Tests in parentheses are not part of the NPAR TESTS subprogram but are available in other SPSS subprograms.

7.1   NPAR TESTS COMMAND

The NPAR TESTS command contains the control word NPAR TESTS in columns 1 to 15. The specification field contains the test name and associated parameters (if required) followed by an equals sign and a variable list. The variable list for each test specifies one or more variables to be tested. Alphanumeric variables cannot be specified; they must be recoded into numeric form. There may be up to 100 different test requests; each request is separated from the others by a slash (/); the tests may be intermixed in any order. The general format of the NPAR TESTS command is, then

```
NPAR TESTS      test name [(parameters)] = variable list
                [(parameters)]/ test name [(parameters)]
                = variable list [(parameters)]/
                . . .
```

The valid test names are

CHI-SQUARE	Chi-square One-Sample Test
K-S	Kolmogorov-Smirnov One-Sample Test
	Kolmogorov-Smirnov Two-Sample Test
RUNS	One-Sample Runs Test
MCNEMAR	McNemar Test for the Significance of Changes
SIGN	Sign Test
WILCOXON	Wilcoxon Matched-Pairs Signed-Ranks Test
COCHRAN	Cochran Q Test
FRIEDMAN	Friedman Two-Way ANOVA by Ranks
MEDIAN	Median Test
M-W	Mann-Whitney
W-W	Wald-Wolfowitz
MOSES	Moses Test of Extreme Reactions
K-W	Kruskall-Wallis One-Way ANOVA by Ranks

7.2 DATA ORGANIZATION FOR NONPARAMETRIC STATISTICS

Nonparametric statistics available within NPAR TESTS require different types of data organization. Individual tests will require one sample, related samples, or independent samples. Within the context of SPSS data organization, one-sample tests are defined by the entire set of observations for the variable being measured. A one-sample test requires that at least one variable be named following the test name keyword. If more than one variable is named, multiple tests will be run, one per variable.

Related samples are defined by sets or pairs of variables. Tests requiring related samples require that at least two variables be named following the keyword. A special set of conventions applies to the specification of variable lists for paired variable tests that makes it convenient for specifying most testing situations involving large numbers of variables. The format of the variable list is essentially like the variable list for the PEARSON CORR routine. In other words, the list may be of the form

```
VARA,VARB,VARC WITH VARD,VARE,VARF. . .
```

The TO convention may be used to name consecutive variables. A special option, Option 3, determines how the list is interpreted. When Option 3 is in effect, a list of the form VARA,VARB,VARC,.. will be tested sequentially, VARA with VARB, VARB with VARC, etc. If Option 3 is selected for a list containing the keyword WITH, the variables will be handled pairwise. The first variable from the list to the left of the WITH will be paired with the first variable from the list to the right of the WITH. In this case, there should be an equal number of variables on each side of WITH. For example,

```
NPAR TESTS     SIGN=A B C D/
```

will generate tests (A B) (A C) (A D) (B C) (B D) and (C D).

```
NPAR TESTS     SIGN=A B C D/
OPTIONS        3
```

will generate tests (A B) (B C) (C D).

```
NPAR TESTS     SIGN = A B WITH C D
```

will generate tests (A C) (A D) (B C) (B D).

```
NPAR TESTS     SIGN = A B WITH C D
OPTIONS        3
```

will generate tests (A C) (B D).

Independent-sample tests are specified in the form

```
name = dependent varlist BY independent
variable(value, value)/
```

where name is one of the following:

MEDIAN	Median test
M-W	Mann-Whitney U test
K-S	Kolmogorov-Smirnov test
W-W	Wald-Wolfowitz Runs test

MOSES Moses test of extreme reactions
K-W Kruskal-Wallis test

The named test is performed for each variable specified in the dependent variable list. Cases are divided into groups on the basis of each case's value for the independent variable. That is, the independent variable "tags" the case into a particular group.

For the k-independent-sample tests (Median or Kruskal-Wallis), the first value must be less than the second value; each value within the range will define a group.

7.3 NONPARAMETRIC TESTS AVAILABLE IN NPAR TESTS

A summary of each test is presented in this chapter. Users are strongly advised to check one of the references given at the end of this chapter for full details of the nonparametric tests they choose to use.

For each test, the following information is presented:

DATA SCALE: This indicates the minimum scale of data acceptable to the test.

DATA ORGANIZATION: This indicates the data format for the test's model, and the format of the data in SPSS terms.

TYPE OF TEST: This indicates for what type of problem the test is useful.

METHOD: A brief summary of the computations performed for the test is provided.

SPECIFICATIONS: The command specifications required for the test are described.

STATISTICS: Included is a description of the statistics provided.

EXAMPLE: Sample deck setup and output.

7.4 One-Sample Chi-Square Test

DATA SCALE: Nominal

DATA ORGANIZATION: One sample (one variable)

TYPE OF TEST: Goodness of fit. For data that falls into categories, the test is whether a significant difference exists between the observed number of cases in each category and the expected number specified.

METHOD: The observations are tabulated into categories and a chi-square statistic is computed.

SPECIFICATION:

```
CHI-SQUARE= varlist [(lo,hi)]/

           EQUAL
EXPECTED=
           f1, f2,...fn/
```

The notation (lo,hi) may be used if the data are integers, with each value in the range being a distinct category. If this notation is used with non-integer data, a value will be truncated to a whole number and be placed in the appropriate category. Data values outside the range (lo,hi) will be ignored.

If the notation (lo,hi) is not used, each distinct value encountered is defined as a category (e.g., 1.0 would be in a different category from 1.5; whereas if (lo,hi) were used, they would be in the same category).

If the EXPECTED= list is omitted, equal frequencies for all categories are assumed. That is, EXPECTED=EQUAL is the default.

The notation EXPECTED= f1, f2, . . . fn/ is used to specify the distribution against which the sample is tested. SPSS interprets f1 to fn as relative frequencies, so that the user can code the expected frequencies, percentages, or proportions for each category. The frequencies, percentages, or proportions are specified in the ascending numerical order of the number of categories. The notation n*fi means n occurences of value fi.

The number of values specified must match the number of cells specified through (lo,hi), or the number of cells actually encountered in the data if (lo,hi) is not used. For example,

```
CHI-SQUARE= A(1,5)/EXPECTED= 12,3*16,18/
```

would test variable A against the hypothetical distribution of 12 occurrences of 1; 16 occurrences of 2, 3, and 4; and 18 occurrences of 5.

STATISTICS PROVIDED: 1 by n contingency table of cell counts and expected counts; chi-square and degrees of freedom; significance level of chi-square.

EXAMPLE:

```
RUN NAME        CHI-SQUARE TEST, SIEGEL P.45
VARIABLE LIST   POSTPOS, NWINS
INPUT FORMAT    FREEFIELD
N OF CASES      8
VAR LABELS      POSTPOS POST POSITION
WEIGHT          NWINS
NPAR TESTS      CHI-SQUARE= POSTPOS/
                CHI-SQUARE= POSTPOS/ EXPECTED= 22,20,4*18,16,14/
                   CHI-SQUARE= POSTPOS(1,8)/ EXPECTED= EQUAL/
                      CHI-SQUARE= POSTPOS(1,8)/
                EXPECTED= 14 16 4*18 20 22/
OPTIONS         5
READ INPUT DATA
2 19 7 15 4 25 5 17 8 11 3 18 6 10 1 29
FINISH
```

Since the data given in Siegel are number of wins by post position, the data are entered into SPSS in that format. The WEIGHT facility is used to replicate each post position the proper number of times. (The post positions are entered in order 2, 7, 4, 5, etc. for no other reason than to demonstrate the program's flexibility.) Refer to Figure 7.4 for the output of the one-sample chi-square test.

Figure 7.4   One-Sample Chi-Square Test

```
CHI-SQUARE TEST, SIEGEL P.45

FILE   NONAME   (CREATION DATE = 12/01/78)


- - - - - CHI-SQUARE TEST

   POSTPOS   POST POSITION

   VALUE     1.      2.      3.      4.      5.      6.
   COUNT     29.     19.     18.     25.     17.     10.
   EXPECTED  18.00   18.00   18.00   18.00   18.00   18.00

   VALUE     7.      8.
   COUNT     15.     11.
   EXPECTED  18.00   18.00

        CHI-SQUARE            D.F.        SIGNIFICANCE
        16.333                 7              0.022


- - - - - CHI-SQUARE TEST

   POSTPOS   POST POSITION

   VALUE     1.      2.      3.      4.      5.      6.
   COUNT     29.     19.     18.     25.     17.     10.
   EXPECTED  22.00   20.00   18.00   18.00   18.00   18.00

   VALUE     7.      8.
   COUNT     15.     11.
   EXPECTED  16.00   14.00

        CHI-SQUARE            D.F.        SIGNIFICANCE
        9.316                  7              0.231

- - - - - CHI-SQUARE TEST

   POSTPOS   POST POSITION

   VALUE     1.      2.      3.      4.      5.      6.
   COUNT     29.     19.     18.     25.     17.     10.
   EXPECTED  18.00   18.00   18.00   18.00   18.00   18.00

   VALUE     7.      8.
   COUNT     15.     11.
   EXPECTED  18.00   18.00

        CHI-SQUARE            D.F.        SIGNIFICANCE
        16.333                 7              0.022

CHI-SQUARE TEST, SIEGEL P.45

- - - - - CHI-SQUARE TEST

   POSTPOS   POST POSITION

   VALUE     1.      2.      3.      4.      5.      6.
   COUNT     29.     19.     18.     25.     17.     10.
   EXPECTED  14.00   16.00   18.00   18.00   18.00   18.00

   VALUE     7.      8.
   COUNT     15.     11.
   EXPECTED  20.00   22.00

        CHI-SQUARE            D.F.        SIGNIFICANCE
        29.717                 7              0.000
```

7.5   Kolmogorov-Smirnov One-Sample Test

DATA SCALE: Interval (or Ratio)

DATA ORGANIZATION: One sample (one variable)

TYPE OF TEST: Goodness of fit. The routine tests whether the observed data could reasonably have come from a theoretical distribution specified by the user (uniform, normal, or Poisson).

METHOD: The cumulative distribution functions for the observed data and the theoretical distribution are computed, as well as the difference between them. The Kolmogorov-Smirnov Z is determined from the largest difference (positive or negative). The larger the value of Z, the less likely it is that the observed and theoretical distributions are the same.

A word of caution concerning testing against a Poisson distribution: if the mean of the test distribution is large, evaluating the probabilities is a very time-consuming process. If a mean of 100,000 or larger is used, the program will automatically switch to using a normal approximation to the Poisson distribution to avoid excessively long run time. This approximation is not especially accurate (the largest error in a probability is about .003).

If the data do have a Poisson distribution, they cannot be scaled to have a smaller mean and still have a Poisson distribution; the only way to avoid both inaccuracy and expensive runs is to count the phenomena being observed over intervals short enough to give reasonable means.

This test is designed for situations in which the test distribution is entirely specified in advance. When parameters of the test distribution are estimated from the sample, the distribution of the test statistic changes and the test becomes more conservative; that is, the null hypothesis (that the sample is from the specified distribution) will be rejected less often. No correction for this is included in the procedure.

SPECIFICATION:

```
              UNIFORM
    K-S (     NORMAL     [parameters]) = varlist/
              POISSON
```

The specified variables are tested against the named distribution. The parameters for the distribution may be specified by the user, or if omitted, will be calculated from the sample. The parameters for the UNIFORM distribution are the minimum and maximum values (in that order); for the the NORMAL distribution the parameters are the mean and standard deviation (in that order); for the POISSON, the single parameter is the mean.

For example, the tests

```
    K-S (UNIFORM)= A/K-S(NORMAL,0,1)=B/
```

would test variable A against a uniform distribution which has a range the same as the sample for variable A, and would test variable B versus a normally distributed variable with mean 0 and standard deviation 1.

STATISTICS PROVIDED: Number of cases, sample mean, standard deviation, minimum and maximum values as appropriate, the maximum positive, negative, and absolute differences between the theoretical and observed cumulative distribution functions; the Kolmogorov-Smirnov Z; and the 2-tailed probability levels for Z based on the Smirnov (1948) formula using three terms.

EXAMPLE:

```
RUN NAME        KOLMOGOROV-SMIRNOV TEST, CONOVER P.296
VARIABLE LIST   X
INPUT FORMAT    FREEFIELD
N OF CASES      10
NPAR TESTS      K-S (UNIFORM 0,1)= X
READ INPUT DATA
.621 .503 .203 .477 .710 .581 .329 .480 .554 .382
FINISH
```

Figure 7.5 shows the output of the Kolmogorov-Smirnov Test.

Figure 7.5   Kolmogorov-Smirnov Test

```
KOLMOGOROV-SMIRNOV TEST, CONOVER P.296

FILE   NONAME   (CREATION DATE = 12/07/78)

- - - - - KOLMOGOROV - SMIRNOV GOODNESS OF FIT TEST

    X

TEST DIST. - UNIFORM (RANGE =      0.0    TO      1.0000)

        CASES      MAX(ABS DIFF)    MAX(+ DIFF)     MAX(- DIFF)
         10          0.2900           0.2900         -0.2290

        K-S Z        2-TAILED P
        0.917          0.370
```

7.6 Runs Test

DATA SCALE: Dichotomous (2-valued), or data that can be dichotomized (nominal, ordinal, or interval).

DATA ORGANIZATION: One sample (one variable)

TYPE OF TEST: Randomness. This is a test to determine if the order or sequence in which observations are obtained is random.

Given a dichotomous data set, a run is defined as a sequence of one of the values which is preceded and followed by the other data value (or an end of the data set). For example, the following contains seven runs:

```
1 1 0 0 0 1 0 0 0 0 1 0 1
| 1 |  2  |3|   4    |5|6|7|
```

Note that the RUNS= test is only appropriate when the order of cases in the data deck is meaningful. For example, suppose that the order of the data in the deck corresponded to the order in which the data were collected. If there were reason to think that the type of responses varied over the course of the study, then the RUNS= test might be performed to test the randomness of responses over time.

SPECIFICATION:

```
              MEAN
RUNS (  MEDIAN  ) = variable list/
              MODE
              value
```

If one of the keywords MEAN, MEDIAN, or MODE is specified, that sample estimate is computed, values are dichotomized with that parameter as the cutting point, and the RUNS= test is performed. If a value is specified, it is used as the cutting point. Data values below the cutting point are in one category, values greater than or equal to the cutting point are in the other. If the data are already dichotomous (say, 0 and 1), the user can specify the midpoint as (value). For example, a RUNS= test might be performed on coin flips (heads coded 1 and tails coded 0) with the following specification:

```
RUNS (.5)= COIN/
```

STATISTICS PROVIDED: The sample statistics (number of cases, mean, standard deviations, minimum, maximum, median, and mode); the cutting point, the number of runs, the Z; and the two-tailed probability for Z based on a normal approximation. The one-tailed probability is 1/2 the two- tailed probability.

EXAMPLES: The first example specifies two Runs Tests on the variable SCORE; one with the sample median as the cutting point, the other with the value 24.5 as the cutting point. Figure 7.6a shows the input for this run.

Figure 7.6a   Input for Runs Test on SCORE

```
RUN NAME        RUNS TEST, SIEGEL P.55
VARIABLE LIST   SCORE
VAR LABELS      SCORE AGGRESSION SCORE
N OF CASES      24
INPUT FORMAT    FREEFIELD
NPAR TESTS      RUNS(MEDIAN)= SCORE/  RUNS(24.5)= SCORE/
READ INPUT DATA
31 23 36 43 51 44 12 26 43 75 2 3 15 18 78 24 13 27 86 61 13 7 6 8
FINISH
```

Refer to Figure 7.6b for the output of the Runs Test on SCORE.

Figure 7.6b   Output for Runs Test on SCORE

```
RUNS TEST, SIEGEL P.55

FILE   NONAME   (CREATION DATE = 11/29/78)

- - - - - RUNS TEST

     SCORE      AGGRESSION SCORE


        CASES      TEST VALUE      RUNS        LT        GE
         24        25.0000          10         12        12


          Z          2-TAILED P
       -1.0436        0.2967
```

```
- - - - - RUNS TEST

    SCORE      AGGRESSION SCORE


        CASES      TEST VALUE      RUNS        LT          GE
         24         24.5000         10          12          12


          Z        2-TAILED P
       -1.0436       0.2967
```

The second example performs a Runs Test on the variable SEX. The input is shown in Figure 7.6c. and the output in Figure 7.6d.

Figure 7.6c   Input for Runs Test on SEX

```
RUN NAME        RUNS TEST, SIEGEL P.57
VARIABLE LIST   SEX
N OF CASES      50
INPUT FORMAT    FREEFIELD
NPAR TESTS      RUNS (.5)= SEX
READ INPUT DATA
1 0 1 0 1 1 1 0 0 1 0 1 0
1 0 1 1 1 1 0 1 0 1 0 1 1
0 0 0 1 0 1 0 1 0 1 1 0
1 1 0 1 1 1 1 0 1 0 1 1
FINISH
```

Figure 7.6d   Output for Runs Test on SEX

```
RUNS TEST, SIEGEL P.57

FILE    NONAME    (CREATION DATE = 11/29/78)


- - - - - RUNS TEST

    SEX

        CASES      TEST VALUE      RUNS        LT          GE
         50         0.5000          35          20          30


          Z        2-TAILED P
        2.9794       0.0029
```

7.7 McNemar Test

DATA SCALE: Dichotomous (2-value), nominal

DATA ORGANIZATION: Two related samples (paired variables)

TYPE OF TEST: Difference in changes of proportions. The test is most useful in "before and after" experimental designs, to detect any significant changes in proportions of subjects from one category to another. For example, the effect on voter preference of a campaign speech could be tested by analyzing the number of people who switched preference (both to and from the candidate) after hearing the speech.

METHOD: The 2 by 2 contingency table of responses (before vs. after) is formed. From those cases that actually changed value, a chi-square statistic is computed (with Yate's correction for continuity). When the number of changes is less than 10, the binomial distribution is used to compute the significance level.

SPECIFICATION:

```
        MCNEMAR= varlist [WITH varlist]/
```

The specification and interpretation of the variable list are discussed in Section 7.2.

Both variables in a pair should have the same two categories which are determined by the MCNEMAR procedure from the data. Non-dichotomous data should be dichotomized (e.g., with RECODE or *RECODE statements) prior to using the NPAR TEST subprogram. If more than two categories (or only one) are present in the data, a message is printed and the test is not done.

STATISTICS PROVIDED: The 2 by 2 contingency table; the number of cases; for large samples, the chi-square and 2-tailed probability; for small samples, the exact 2-tailed probability from the binomial distribution.

EXAMPLE:

```
RUN NAME        MCNEMAR TEST, SIEGEL P.65
VARIABLE LIST   CONTACT1,CONTACT2,NUMBER
INPUT FORMAT    FREEFIELD
N OF CASES      4
WEIGHT          NUMBER
PRINT FORMATS   CONTACT1,CONTACT2 (0)
NPAR TESTS      MCNEMAR= CONTACT1 CONTACT2
READ INPUT DATA
1 -1 14    1 1 4    -1 -1 3    -1 1 4
FINISH
```

Figure 7.7 shows the output of the McNemar Test.

Figure 7.7   McNemar Test

```
MCNEMAR TEST, SIEGEL P.65

FILE   NONAME   (CREATION DATE = 06/14/76)

- - - - - MCNEMAR TEST


        CONTACT1
WITH CONTACT2
                         CONTACT2
                       1        -1      CASES         25
                   I---------I---------I
CONTACT1      -1 I     4 I      3 I     CHI-SQR     4.500
                   I---------I---------I
               1 I     4 I     14 I     2-TAILED P  0.034
                   I---------I---------I
```

7.8 Sign Test

DATA SCALE: Ordinal

DATA ORGANIZATION: Two related samples (paired variables)

TYPE OF TEST: The signs of the differences between the paired observations are analyzed. If the two variables share a common distribution, the number of positive differences and negative differences should be roughly the same. This is actually a version of the McNemar test applied to ordinal data.

METHOD: The positive and negative differences are counted. Zero differences are ignored. From these counts, a test statistic Z is computed. Under the null hypothesis for large sample sizes, Z is approximately normally distributed with mean 0 and variance 1. If the number of non-zero differences is less than 26, the exact significance level is computed from the binomial distribution.

SPECIFICATION:

```
SIGN= varlist [WITH varlist]/
```

STATISTICS PROVIDED: Number of cases; numbers of positive and negative differences; for large samples, a Z and 2-tailed probability; for small samples, the exact 2-tailed probability from the binomial distribution. (The 1-tailed probability is 1/2 the 2-tailed probability.)

EXAMPLES: The first example shown in Figure 7.8a performs a Signs Test on FATHER with MOTHER. The output is shown in Figure 7.8b.

Figure 7.8a   Input for Signs Test on FATHER with MOTHER

```
RUN NAME        SIGN TEST,  SIEGEL P.70
VARIABLE LIST   MOTHER FATHER
N OF CASES      17
INPUT FORMAT    FREEFIELD
VAR LABELS      MOTHER MOTHER'S INSIGHT RATED/
                FATHER FATHER'S INSIGHT RATED
NPAR TESTS      SIGN= FATHER WITH MOTHER
READ INPUT DATA
4 2 4 3 5 3 5 3 3 3 2 3 5 3 3 3 1 2 5 3 5 2 5 2 4 5 5 2 5 5
5 3 5 1
FINISH
```

Figure 7.8b   Output for Signs Test on FATHER with MOTHER

```
SIGN TEST, SIEGEL P.70

FILE   NONAME   (CREATION DATE = 06/14/76)

- - - - - SIGN TEST


     FATHER      FATHER'S INSIGHT RATED
WITH MOTHER      MOTHER'S INSIGHT RATED

   CASES  -DIFFERENCES  +DIFFERENCES      2-TAILED P (BINOMIAL)
    17          3            11              0.057
```

The second example shows a Sign Test on the two variables BEFORE and AFTER. The input is displayed in Figure 7.8c and the output in Figure 7.8d.

Figure 7.8c   Input for Signs Test on BEFORE with AFTER

```
RUN NAME        SIGN TEST, SIEGEL P.73
VARIABLE LIST   BEFORE, AFTER, COUNT
N OF CASES      4
INPUT FORMAT    FREEFIELD
RECODE          BEFORE, AFTER (0= -1)
WEIGHT          COUNT
NPAR TESTS      SIGN= BEFORE WITH AFTER
READ INPUT DATA
1 0 59
1 1 7
0 0 8
0 1 26
FINISH
```

Figure 7.8d   Output for Signs Test on BEFORE with AFTER

```
SIGN TEST, SIEGEL P.73

FILE   NONAME   (CREATION DATE = 06/14/76)

- - - - - SIGN TEST


   BEFORE
WITH AFTER

   CASES  -DIFFERENCES  +DIFFERENCES      Z       2-TAILED P
    100        59           26          3.471       0.001
```

7.9   Wilcoxon Matched-Pairs Ranked-Signs Test

DATA SCALE: Ordinal

DATA ORGANIZATION: Two related samples (paired variables)

TYPE OF TEST: The differences between the paired observations are analyzed, as in the sign test; however, the magnitude of the difference is also used in the analysis.

METHOD: The differences are ranked, ignoring signs, and the sums of the ranks for positive and negative differences calculated. From the positive and negative rank sums, a test statistic Z is computed. Under the null hypothesis, for large samples sizes, Z is approximately normally distributed with mean 0 and variance 1.

SPECIFICATION:

        WILCOXON = varlist [WITH varlist]/

STATISTICS PROVIDED: The number of cases; number of positive differences and their mean; number of negative differences; Z and its 2-tailed probability.

EXAMPLES: The first example specifies a Wilcoxon Matched Pairs Test for the variables SCHOOL and HOME. The input is shown in Figure 7.9a and the output in Figure 7.9b.

Figure 7.9a   Input for Wilcoxon Matched Pairs Test on SCHOOL with HOME

```
RUN NAME        WILCOXON MATCHED PAIRS TEST, SIEGEL P.79
VARIABLE LIST   SCHOOL, HOME
INPUT FORMAT    FREEFIELD
N OF CASES      8
VAR LABELS      SCHOOL  SOCIAL PERCEPTIVENESS OF SCHOOL TWIN/
                HOME    SOCIAL PERCEPTIVENESS OF HOME TWIN
NPAR TESTS      WILCOXON=ALL
READ INPUT DATA
82 63 69 42 73 74 43 37 58 51 56 43 76 80 85 82
FINISH
```

Figure 7.9b   Output for Wilcoxon Matched Pairs Test on SCHOOL with HOME

```
WILCOXON MATCHED PAIRS TEST, SIEGEL P.79

FILE   NONAME   (CREATION DATE = 06/14/76)

- - - - - WILCOXON MATCHED-PAIRS SIGNED-RANKS TEST

     SCHOOL     SOCIAL PERCEPTIVENESS OF SCHOOL TWIN
WITH HOME       SOCIAL PERCEPTIVENESS OF HOME TWIN

                    6 -RANKS    2 +RANKS
   CASES   TIES   MEAN        MEAN          Z        2-TAILED P
     8      0     5.33        2.00        -1.960      0.050
```

The second example uses the variable D and a computed variable DUM with a constant value of zero for the Wilcoxon Matched Pairs Test. The input is shown in Figure 7.9c and the output in Figure 7.9d.

Figure 7.9c   Input for Wilcoxon Matched Pairs Test on D with DUM

```
RUN NAME        WILCOXON MATCHED PAIRS TEST, SIEGEL P.82
VARIABLE LIST   D
N OF CASES      30
INPUT FORMAT    FREEFIELD
COMPUTE         DUM = 0
VAR LABELS      D DECISION LATENCY TIME
NPAR TESTS      WILCOXON= D WITH DUM/
READ INPUT DATA
-2 0 0 1 0 0 4 4 1 1 5 3 5 3 -1 1 -1 5 8 2 2 2 -3 -2 1 4 8 2 3 -1
FINISH
```

Figure 7.9d   Output for Wilcoxon Matched Pairs Test on D with DUM

```
WILCOXON MATCHED PAIRS TEST, SIEGEL P.82

FILE   NONAME   (CREATION DATE = 06/14/76)

- - - - - WILCOXON MATCHED-PAIRS SIGNED-RANKS TEST

    D          DECISION LATENCY TIME
WITH DUM

                   20 -RANKS    6 +RANKS
   CASES   TIES   MEAN        MEAN          Z        2-TAILED P
    30      4     14.90       8.83        -3.111      0.002
```

7.10   Cochran Q Test

DATA SCALE: Dichotomous (2-valued), nominal

DATA ORGANIZATION: k related samples (k variables)

TYPE OF TEST: Difference in proportions. This is an extension of the McNemar test of significance of changes to the k-sample case. The test is whether the proportions in the categories are the same over all variables.

METHOD: The proportions are computed for each variable, and are used to compute Cochran's Q statistic, which has (approximately) a chi-square distribution.

SPECIFICATION:

```
COCHRAN = varlist/
```

One test is performed using all variables in the variable list.

STATISTICS PROVIDED: The 2 by k contingency table (category vs. variable); the Q value and degrees of freedom; the significance level.

EXAMPLE:

```
RUN NAME        COCHRAN Q TEST, SIEGEL P.164
VARIABLE LIST   R1 TO R3
N OF CASES      18
INPUT FORMAT    FREEFIELD
VAR LABELS      R1 RESPONSE TO NICE INTERVIEW/
                R2 RESPONSE TO RESERVED INTERVIEW/
                R3 RESPONSE TO HARSH INTERVIEW
NPAR TESTS      COCHRAN= R1 TO R3/
READ INPUT DATA
1 1 1   1 1 1   1 1 0   1 1 0   1 1 0   1 1 1   1 1 0   1 1 0 0 0
0   1 1 0   0 1 0   0 0 0   1 0 0   1 1 0   1 1 0   0 1 0   1 0 0
0 0 0
FINISH
```

The output for the Cochran Q Test on R1 to R3 is shown in Figure 7.10.

Figure 7.10   Cochran Q Test

```
COCHRAN Q TEST, SIEGEL P.164

FILE   NONAME   (CREATION DATE = 06/14/76)

- - - - - COCHRAN Q TEST


    R1          RESPONSE TO NICE INTERVIEW
    R2          RESPONSE TO RESERVED INTERVIEW
    R3          RESPONSE TO HARSH INTERVIEW

    VALUE   R1          R2          R3
      1          13.         13.         3.
      0           5.          5.        15.

            CASES    COCHRAN Q      D.F.    SIGNIFICANCE
             18       16.667         2        0.000
```

7.11   Friedman Test

DATA SCALE: Ordinal

DATA ORGANIZATION: k related samples (k variables)

TYPE OF TEST: Tests the null hypothesis that the k samples have been drawn from the same population.

METHOD: For each case, the k variables are ranked from 1 to k. Over all the cases, the mean rank for each variable is computed. From these, a test statistic with (approximately) a chi-square distribution is computed.

SPECIFICATION:

```
FRIEDMAN = varlist/
```

One test is performed using all specified variables.

STATISTICS PROVIDED: The rank sum for each variable; the number of cases; the Friedman chi-square and degrees of freedom; and the significance level.

EXAMPLE: The following example specifies that a Friedman Test be calculated on the three variables RR, RU, and UR. The output from the run is displayed in Figure 7.11.

```
RUN NAME        FRIEDMAN TWO-WAY TEST, SIEGEL P.171
VARIABLE LIST   RR RU UR
N OF CASES      18
INPUT FORMAT    FREEFIELD
VAR LABELS      RR TOTAL REINFORCEMENT/
                RU PARTIAL WITH REINFORCED TRIAL/
                UR PARTIAL WITH UNREINFORCED TRIAL
NPAR TESTS      FRIEDMAN= RR RU UR/
READ INPUT DATA
2 6 4   4 6 2   3 9 6   1 2 3   3 1 2   6 9 3   9 8 7
1 3 2   3 1 2   4 2 3   2 3 1   2 3 1   3 2 1   2 3 1
5 5 2   3 2 1   6 4 2   2 3 1
FINISH
```

Figure 7.11   Friedman Test

```
FRIEDMAN TWO-WAY TEST, SIEGEL P.171

FILE   NONAME   (CREATION DATE = 06/14/76)

- - - - - FRIEDMAN TWO-WAY ANOVA

    RR          TOTAL REINFORCEMENT
    RU          PARTIAL WITH REINFORCED TRIAL
    UR          PARTIAL WITH UNREINFORCED TRIAL

           RR        RU         UR
MEAN RANKS    2.19      2.36       1.44

        CASES    CHI-SQUARE       D.F.   SIGNIFICANCE
         18         8.583           2        0.014
```

7.12   Two-Sample Median Test

DATA SCALE: Ordinal

DATA ORGANIZATION: 2 independent samples (one variable, two groups)

TYPE OF TEST: The test is whether the two groups have been drawn from populations with the same median.

METHOD: The two groups are combined, and the overall median is determined. A 2 by 2 contingency table with counts of the number of cases exceeding and not exceeding the median in the two groups is printed. If the total number of cases is greater than 30, a chi-square statistic is computed; otherwise, Fisher's exact procedure (one-tailed) is used to compute the significance level.

SPECIFICATION:

```
MEDIAN (value) = dependent varlist BY independent
      variable (value1, value2)/
```

The groups are defined by value1 and value2 of the independent variable. If (value) is omitted, the routine computes the sample median and uses it in computing the test statistics. The user may specify the known or theoretical median through the (value) specification. For example,

```
MEDIAN (10.5) = ANXIETY BY EXPLAN (1,2)/
```

See Section 7.2 for more detailed information.

STATISTICS PROVIDED: The 2 by 2 contingency table of the number of cases above and below the median for each group; the total number of cases; for large samples (n > 30), the chi-square and approximate 2-tailed probability; for small samples, Fisher's exact probability.

EXAMPLE: The following example specifies that a Median Test be calculated on the variables ANXIETY by EXPLAN. Two tests are calculated—one with the specified median 10.5 and the second with the sample median. Figure 7.12 shows the output of this example.

```
RUN NAME         MEDIAN TEST, SIEGEL P.114
VARIABLE LIST    EXPLAN, ANXIETY
N OF CASES       39
INPUT FORMAT     FREEFIELD
VAR LABELS       EXPLAN ORAL EXPLANATION OF ILLNESS CODE/
                 ANXIETY ORAL SOCIALIZATION ANXIETY
VALUE LABELS     EXPLAN (1) ABSENT (2) PRESENT
NPAR TESTS       MEDIAN(10.5) = ANXIETY BY EXPLAN(1,2)/
                 MEDIAN = ANXIETY BY EXPLAN(1,2)/
READ INPUT DATA
2 10 2 10 2 10 2 8 2 8 2 6 2 17 2 16 2 15 2 15 2 15 2 14 2 14
2 14 2 13 2 13 2 13 2 12 2 12 2 12 2 12 2 11 2 11 1 13 1 12
1 12 1 10 1 10 1 10 1 10 1 9 1 8 1 8 1 7 1 7 1 7 1 7 1 7 1 6
FINISH
```

Figure 7.12   Median Test

```
MEDIAN TEST, SIEGEL P.114

FILE   NONAME   (CREATION DATE = 06/14/76)

- - - - - MEDIAN TEST

        ANXIETY     ORAL SOCIALIZATION ANXIETY
        BY EXPLAN   ORAL EXPLANATION OF ILLNESS CODE

                        EXPLAN
                         1       2       CASES       39
                    I-------I-------I
MEDIAN        GT I      3 I    17 I    CHI-SQR     9.391
ANXIETY       10.5 I-------I-------I
              LE I     13 I     6 I    2-TAILED P   0.002
                    I-------I-------I
```

```
- - - - - MEDIAN TEST

      ANXIETY    ORAL SOCIALIZATION ANXIETY
   BY EXPLAN     ORAL EXPLANATION OF ILLNESS CODE

                            EXPLAN
                            1         2      CASES        39
                     I---------I---------I
   MEDIAN     GT I        3 I      15 I    CHI-SQR      6.435
   ANXIETY    11 I---------I---------I
              LE I       13 I       8 I    2-TAILED P   0.011
                 I---------I---------I
```

7.13 Mann-Whitney U Test

DATA SCALE: Ordinal

DATA ORGANIZATION: 2 independent samples (one variable, two groups)

TYPE OF TEST: The test can be used to test whether two samples are from the same population. It is more powerful than the Median test, since it uses the rank of each case, not just its location relative to the median.

METHOD: The two groups are combined, and cases are ranked in order of increasing size. The test statistic U is computed as the number of times a score from group 1 precedes a score from group 2. The rationale is that if the samples are from the same population, the distribution of scores from the two groups in the ranked list will be random; a non-random pattern will be indicated by an extreme value of U. For small samples (less than 30 cases), the exact significance level for U is computed using the algorithm of Dineen and Blakesley (1973). For larger samples, U is transformed into a normally distributed statistic, Z.

SPECIFICATION:

```
          M-W = dependent varlist BY independent
                variable (valuel, value2)/
```

STATISTICS PROVIDED: The number of cases and mean rank for each group; the U statistic, corresponding Z (corrected for ties), and its two-tailed probability. In addition, for small samples ($N<30$), the exact two-tailed probability for U (not corrected for ties) is printed.

EXAMPLE: The following example calculates a Mann-Whitney U Test on TRIALS on two samples defined by the variable GROUP, values 0 and 1. The output is displayed in Figure 7.13.

```
RUN NAME         MANN-WHITNEY TEST, SIEGEL P.119
VARIABLE LIST    GROUP, TRIALS
N OF CASES       9
INPUT FORMAT     FREEFIELD
NPAR TESTS       M-W = TRIALS BY GROUP(0,1)
READ INPUT DATA
0 78  0 64  0 75  0 45  0 82    1 110  1 70  1 53  1 51
FINISH
```

Figure 7.13   Mann-Whitney U Test

```
MANN - WHITNEY, SIEGEL, P.119

FILE   NONAME   (CREATION DATE = 12/01/78)

- - - - - MANN-WHITNEY U - WILCOXON RANK SUM W TEST

    TRIALS
  BY GROUP

      GROUP    =        0      GROUP   =        1
     MEAN RANK       NUMBER    MEAN RANK      NUMBER
        5.20            5         4.75           4

                          EXACT           CORRECTED FOR TIES
          U        W     2-TAILED P        Z       2-TAILED P
         9.0     19.0     0.9048         -0.2449     0.8065
```

7.14 Kolmogorov-Smirnov Two-Sample Test

DATA SCALE: Ordinal

DATA ORGANIZATION: 2 independent samples (one variable, two groups)

TYPE OF TEST: Homogeneity (equality) of distribution. This test is sensitive to any type of difference in the two distributions— median, dispersion, skewness, etc. The one-tailed test can be used to determine whether the values of one group are generally larger than the values of the other group.

METHOD: The observed cumulative distributions for both groups are computed; the maximum positive, negative, and absolute differences of these are computed; the Kolmogorov-Smirnov Z is then computed.

SPECIFICATION:

```
K-S = dependent varlist BY independent
      variable (valuel, value2)/
```

STATISTICS PROVIDED: The counts for each group; the maximum positive and negative differences between the cumulative distributions for the two groups; the maximum absolute difference; the Kolmogorov-Smirnov Z statistic and the two-tailed probability level based on the Smirnov (1948) formula using three terms.

EXAMPLES: The first example specifies a Kolmogorov-Smirnov Two-Sample Test on PCTERR for the two samples defined by GRADE, values 7 and 11. The input is shown in Figure 7.14a and the output in Figure 7.14b.

Figure 7.14a   Input for K-S Two-Sample Test on PCTERR by GRADE

```
RUN NAME         K-S TWO-SAMPLE TEST, SIEGEL P.130
VARIABLE LIST    PCTERR, GRADE
N OF CASES       20
INPUT FORMAT     FREEFIELD
VAR LABELS       GRADE GRADE IN SCHOOL/
                 PCTERR PERCENTAGE OF ERRORS
NPAR TESTS       K-S = PCTERR BY GRADE(7,11)
READ INPUT DATA
39.1 7 41.2 7 45.2 7 46.2 7 48.4 7 48.7 7 55.0 7 40.6 7 52.1 7
47.2 7 35.2 11 39.2 11 40.9 11 38.1 11 34.4 11 29.1 11 41.8 11
24.3 11 32.4 11 32.6 11
FINISH
```

Figure 7.14b   Output for K-S Two-Sample Test on PCTERR by GRADE

```
K-S TWO-SAMPLE TEST, SIEGEL P.130

FILE   NONAME   (CREATION DATE = 06/14/76)

- - - - - KOLMOGOROV-SMIRNOV 2-SAMPLE TEST

   PCTERR      PERCENTAGE OF ERRORS
 BY GRADE      GRADE IN SCHOOL

WARNING - DUE TO SMALL SAMPLE SIZE, PROB TABLES SHOULD BE CONSULTED.

    =     7    =    11  MAX(ABS DIFF)   MAX(+ DIFF)   MAX(- DIFF)
         10        10       -0.7000         0.0         -0.7000

        K-S Z      2-TAILED P
        1.565        0.015
```

The second example requests a Kolmogorov-Smirnov Two-Sample Test on IDENTED by GROUP, values 1 and 2. The input for this example is shown in Figure 7.14c and the output in Figure 7.14d.

Figure 7.14c   Input for K-S Two-Sample Test on IDENTED by GROUP

```
RUN NAME         K-S TWO-SAMPLE TEST, SIEGEL P.133
VARIABLE LIST    IDENTED, GROUP, NUMBER
N OF CASES       14
INPUT FORMAT     FREEFIELD
VAR LABELS       IDENTED PHOTOS "IDENTIFIED"
WEIGHT           NUMBER
NPAR TESTS       K-S = IDENTED BY GROUP(1,2)
READ INPUT DATA
1 1 11 1 2 1
4 1 7 4 2 3
7 1 8 7 2 6
10 1 3 10 2 12
13 1 5 13 2 12
16 1 5 16 2 14
19 1 5 19 2 6
FINISH
```

Figure 7.14d   Output for K-S Two-Sample Test on IDENTED by GROUP

```
K-S TWO-SAMPLE TEST, SIEGEL P.133

FILE   NONAME   (CREATION DATE = 06/14/76)

- - - - - KOLMOGOROV-SMIRNOV 2-SAMPLE TEST

    IDENTED      PHOTOS "IDENTIFIED"
  BY GROUP

WARNING - DUE TO SMALL SAMPLE SIZE, PROB TABLES SHOULD BE CONSULTED.

     =     2     =     1   MAX(ABS DIFF)   MAX(+ DIFF)   MAX(- DIFF)
          54          44      -0.4057         0.0025       -0.4057

            K-S Z      2-TAILED P
            1.998        0.001
```

7.15   Wald-Wolfowitz Runs Tests

DATA SCALE: Ordinal

DATA ORGANIZATION: 2 independent samples (one variable, two groups)

TYPE OF TEST: Homogeneity of distribution. This test is applicable for testing whether two populations differ in any respect—median, dispersion, skewness, etc. (It is thus similar to the Kolmogorov-Smirnov test).

METHOD: The observations from both groups are combined and ranked from lowest to highest. Assuming that the samples are from the same population, the two groups should be randomly scattered throughout the ranking. A Runs test is performed using group membership as the criterion. If there are ties involving observations from the two groups, both the minimum and maximum number of runs possible are calculated. If the total sample size is less than 31, the exact one-sided significance level is calculated. Otherwise, the normal approximation is used.

SPECIFICATION:

```
        W-W = dependent varlist BY independent
              variable (valuel, value2)/
```

STATISTICS PROVIDED: The group counts; the number of runs; for large samples, the approximate Z and one-sided significance level.

EXAMPLES: The first example specifies a Wald-Wolfowitz Runs Test on SCORE by the variable SEX. The input is shown in Figure 7.15a and the output in Figure 7.15b.

Figure 7.15a   Input for Wald-Wolfowitz Runs Test on SCORE by SEX

```
RUN NAME        WALD-WOLFOWITZ TEST, SIEGEL P.139
VARIABLE LIST   SCORE
SUBFILE LIST    BOYS(12), GIRLS(12)
INPUT FORMAT    FREEFIELD
COMPUTE         SEX = 2
IF              (SUBFILE EQ 'BOYS') SEX = 1
VAR LABELS      SCORE AGGRESSION SCORE
NPAR TESTS      W-W = SCORE BY SEX(1,2)
READ INPUT DATA
86 69 72 65 113 65 118 45 141 104 41 50
55 40 22 58 16 7 9 16 26 36 20 15
FINISH
```

Figure 7.15b   Output for Wald-Wolfowitz Runs Test on SCORE by SEX

```
WALD-WOLFOWITZ TEST, SIEGEL P.139

FILE   NONAME   (CREATION DATE = 06/14/76)
SUBFILE   BOYS       GIRLS

- - - - - WALD-WOLFOWITZ RUNS TEST

    SCORE        AGGRESSION SCORE
  BY SEX

                                                     EXACT
     =     1     =     2    RUNS       Z        1-TAILED P
          12          12       4    -3.5481      0.0001
```

The second example requests a Wald-Wolfowitz Runs Test on TRIALS for groups defined by values 0 and 1 on TYPE. The input is shown in Figure 7.15c and the output in Figure 7.15d.

Figure 7.15c   Input for Wald-Wolfowitz Runs Test on TRIALS by TYPE

```
RUN NAME        WALD-WOLFOWITZ TEST, SIEGEL P.142
VARIABLE LIST   TYPE, TRIALS
INPUT FORMAT    FREEFIELD
N OF CASES      29
VAR LABELS      TRIALS RELEARNING TRIALS REQUIRED
NPAR TESTS      W-W = TRIALS BY TYPE (0,1)
READ INPUT DATA
0 20   0 55   0 29   0 24   0 75   0 56   0 31   0 45
1 23   1  8   1 24   1 15   1  8   1  6   1 15   1 15
1 21   1 23   1 16   1 15   1 24
1 15   1 21   1 15   1 18   1 14   1 22   1 15   1 14
FINISH
```

Figure 7.15d   Output for Wald-Wolfowitz Runs Test on TRIALS by TYPE

```
WALD-WOLFOWITZ TEST, SIEGEL P.142

FILE   NONAME   (CREATION DATE = 12/01/78)

- - - - - WALD-WOLFOWITZ RUNS TEST

    TRIALS     RELEARNING TRIALS REQUIRED
 BY TYPE

                                                    EXACT
   =       0    =       1    RUNS         Z       1-TAILED P
           8           21       5     -3.3857       0.0005
WARNING -- THERE ARE    1 INTER-GROUP TIES INVOLVING    3 CASES.
ABOVE STATISTICS ARE BASED ON MINIMUM POSSIBLE RUNS.
STATISTICS BELOW ARE BASED ON MAXIMUM POSSIBLE RUNS.

                                                    EXACT
   =       0    =       1    RUNS         Z       1-TAILED P
           8           21       6     -2.9079       0.0023
```

7.16 Moses Test of Extreme Reactions

DATA SCALE: Ordinal

DATA ORGANIZATION: 2 independent samples (one variable, two groups)

TYPE OF TEST: Difference in range. The test is applicable in testing differences in the span of two groups, which makes it useful in situations where it is expected that a condition will affect some subjects in one way and others in the opposite way. For instance, it may be hypothesized that economic recession may tend to radicalize people into left-wing and right-wing groups. This test treats one group as the control group and the other as the experimental.

METHOD: The scores from the two groups are arranged in a single ascending sequence. The span of the control group is computed as the number of cases in the sequence containing the lowest and highest control score. The exact significance level can be computed for the span. The range of span is easily distorted by chance outliers; to minimize this problem, the span is recomputed after the 10% most extreme control scores have been omitted. No adjustments are made for tied observations.

SPECIFICATION:

```
MOSES [(h)] = dependent varlist BY independent
variable (value-control, value-experimental)/
```

The "h" argument may be used to specify the number of observations trimmed from each end for the truncated test. If omitted, 5% from each end are eliminated. The value for the control group must be specified first within the parentheses following the name of the independent variable.

STATISTICS PROVIDED: The number of cases in each group; for the full data set, the span and significance level; for the truncated set, the number deleted from each end (h), the span and significance level.

EXAMPLE: The following example requests two Moses Tests on SCORE by SECTION—using a different group as the control for each test. Figure 7.16 displays the output from this request.

```
RUN NAME        MOSES TEST, EXTREME REACTION, SIEGEL P.149
VARIABLE LIST   SCORE, SECTION
N OF CASES      18
INPUT FORMAT    FREEFIELD
VAR LABELS      SCORE ATTRIBUTION OF AGGRESSION
NPAR TESTS      MOSES = SCORE BY SECTION(1,2)/
                MOSES = SCORE BY SECTION (2,1)
READ INPUT DATA
25  2  5  2  14  2  19  2  0  2  17  2  15  2  8  2  8  2
12  1  16  1  6  1  13  1  13  1  3  1  10  1  10  1  11  1
FINISH
```

Figure 7.16   Moses Test of Extreme Reactions

```
MOSES TEST, EXTREME REACTION, SIEGEL P.149

FILE   NONAME   (CREATION DATE = 06/14/76)

- - - - - MOSES TEST OF EXTREME REACTION

   SCORE      ATTRIBUTION OF AGGRESSION
BY SECTION

    CONTROL  EXPERIMENTAL                        H =   1
  =      1   =           2   SPAN  1-TAILED P  SPAN  1-TAILED P
         9               9     14     0.147      9     0.077

- - - - - MOSES TEST OF EXTREME REACTION

   SCORE      ATTRIBUTION OF AGGRESSION
BY SECTION

    CONTROL  EXPERIMENTAL                        H =   1
  =      2   =           1   SPAN  1-TAILED P  SPAN  1-TAILED P
         9               9     18     1.000     15     0.959
```

7.17   K-Sample Median Test

DATA SCALE: Ordinal

DATA ORGANIZATION: k independent samples (one variable, k groups)

TYPE OF TEST: Difference in central tendency. As the name implies, this is an extension of the two-sample Median test.

METHOD: The common median over all k samples is computed. The 2 by k contingency table of case counts above/not above the median is generated. A chi-square statistic for the table is computed.

SPECIFICATION:

```
MEDIAN (value) = dependent varlist BY independent
        variable (value1, value2)/
```

See Section 7.2 for details. Note that the two-sample and k-sample Median tests are specified in essentially the same format. Which test is performed is actually determined from the (value1, value2) specification. If (value2 − value1 + 1) is greater than 2, the k-sample Median test is performed. For example, in:

```
MEDIAN = A BY B (1,3)/MEDIAN = A BY B(3,1)/
```

the first test would be a k-sample Median test using groups 1, 2 and 3; the second would be a two-sample Median test between groups 1 and 3.

STATISTICS PROVIDED: The 2 by k contingency table of cases above and below the median; the total number of cases and number of groups; the chi-square and significance level.

EXAMPLE: The following example requests a Median Test on VISITS, using EDUC with 6 values (groups) as the independent variable. The output produced by this request is shown in Figure 7.17.

```
RUN NAME        EXTENDED MEDIAN TEST, SIEGEL P.182
VARIABLE LIST   VISITS , EDUC
N OF CASES      44
INPUT FORMAT    FREEFIELD
VAR LABELS      VISITS VISITS TO SCHOOL/
                EDUC LEVEL OF EDUCATION
NPAR TESTS      MEDIAN = VISITS BY EDUC(1,6)/
READ INPUT DATA
4  1  3  1  0  1  7  1  1  1  2  1  0  1  3  1  5  1  1  1  2  2  4  2  1  2  6  2  3  2  2  2  0  2
2  2  5  2  1  2  2  2  1  2  2  3  0  3  4  3  3  3  8  3  0  3  5  3  2  3  1  3  7  3  6  3
5  3  1  3  9  4  4  4  2  4  3  4  2  5  4  5  5  5  2  5  2  6  6  6
*RECODE         EDUC (4 THRU 6 = 4)
NPAR TESTS      MEDIAN = VISITS BY EDUC(1,4)/
FINISH
```

Figure 7.17   K-Sample Median Test

```
EXTENDED MEDIAN TEST, SIEGEL P.182

FILE   NONAME   (CREATION DATE = 06/14/76)

- - - - - MEDIAN TEST

    VISITS     VISITS TO SCHOOL
  BY EDUC      LEVEL OF EDUCATION

      EDUC  1        2        3        4        5        6
  GT MEDIAN  5        4        7        3        2        1
  LE MEDIAN  5        7        6        1        2        1

WARNING - CHI-SQUARE STATISTIC IS QUESTIONABLE HERE.
    6 CELLS HAVE EXPECTED FREQUENCIES LESS THAN 5.
  MINIMUM EXPECTED CELL FREQUENCY IS      1.0

            CASES      MEDIAN    CHI-SQUARE   D.F.  SIGNIFICANCE
             44         2.5       1.895        5       0.863

EXTENDED MEDIAN TEST, SIEGEL P.182

FILE   NONAME   (CREATION DATE = 06/14/76)

- - - - - MEDIAN TEST

    VISITS     VISITS TO SCHOOL
  BY EDUC      LEVEL OF EDUCATION

      EDUC  1        2        3        4
  GT MEDIAN  5        4        7        6
  LE MEDIAN  5        7        6        4

            CASES      MEDIAN    CHI-SQUARE   D.F.  SIGNIFICANCE
             44         2.5       1.295        3       0.730
```

7.18   Kruskal-Wallis One-Way Analysis of Variance

DATA SCALE: Ordinal

DATA ORGANIZATION: k independent samples (one variable, k groups)

TYPE OF TEST: Tests whether all k samples are from the same population.

METHOD: All cases from the k groups are ranked in a single series. The rank sum is computed for each group. From these, the Kruskall-Wallis H statistic is computed, which has approximately a chi-square distribution.

SPECIFICATION:

```
K-W = dependent varlist BY independent
      variable (value1, value2)/
```

STATISTICS PROVIDED: The number of cases and mean rank for each group; H(chi-square) and significance level; H corrected for ties and significance level.

EXAMPLES: The first example requests Kruskal-Wallis analysis on AUTSCORE by GROUP containing 3 groups. The input is shown in Figure 7.18a and the output in Figure 7.18b.

Figure 7.18a   Input for Kruskal-Wallis on AUTSCORE by GROUP

```
RUN NAME       KRUSKAL-WALLIS, SIEGEL P.187
VARIABLE LIST  AUTSCORE, GROUP
INPUT FORMAT   FREEFIELD
N OF CASES     14
VAR LABELS     AUTSCORE AUTHORITARIANISM SCORE
NPAR TESTS     K-W = AUTSCORE BY GROUP(1 3)
READ INPUT DATA
96 1 128 1 83 1 61 1 101 1
82 2 124 2 132 2 135 2 109 2
115 3 149 3 166 3 147 3
FINISH
```

Figure 7.18b   Output for Kruskal-Wallis on AUTSCORE by GROUP

```
KRUSKAL-WALLIS, SIEGEL P.187

FILE    NONAME    (CREATION DATE = 06/14/76)
- - - - - KRUSKAL-WALLIS 1-WAY ANOVA

    AUTSCORE    AUTHORITARIANISM SCORE
  BY GROUP

     GROUP         1       2       3
     NUMBER        5       5       4
  MEAN RANKS     4.40    7.40   11.50
                                        CORRECTED FOR TIES
     CASES    CHI-SQUARE  SIGNIFICANCE  CHI-SQUARE  SIGNIFICANCE
      14        6.406       0.041         6.406       0.041
```

The second example requests a Kruskal-Wallis analysis of variance on WEIGHT using LITTER as the group variable. Figure 7.18c displays the input commands and Figure 7.18d shows the output.

Figure 7.18c   Input for Kruskal-Wallis on WEIGHT by LITTER

```
    RUN NAME        KRUSKAL-WALLIS, SIEGEL P.190
    VARIABLE LIST   WEIGHT
    SUBFILE LIST    L1(10) L2(8) L3(10) L4(8) L5(6) L6(4) L7(6) L8(4)
    INPUT FORMAT    FREEFIELD
    COMPUTE         LITTER = SUBFILE
    RECODE          LITTER ('L1'=1)('L2'=2)('L3'=3)('L4'=4)('L5'=5)
                           ('L6'=6)('L7'=7)('L8'=8)
    VAR LABELS      WEIGHT BIRTH WEIGHT
    NPAR TESTS      K-W = WEIGHT BY LITTER(1 8)
    OPTIONS         5
    READ INPUT DATA
    2.0 2.8 3.3 3.2 4.4 3.6 1.9 3.3 2.8 1.1
    3.5 2.8 3.2 3.5 2.3 2.4 2.0 1.6
    3.3 3.6 2.6 3.1 3.2 3.3 2.9 3.4 3.2 3.2
    3.2 3.3 3.2 2.9 3.3 2.5 2.6 2.8
    2.6 2.6 2.9 2.0 2.0 2.1
    3.1 2.9 3.1 2.5
    2.6 2.2 2.2 2.5 1.2 1.2
    2.5 2.4 3.0 1.5
    FINISH
```

Figure 7.18d   Output for Kruskal-Wallis on WEIGHT by LITTER

```
KRUSKAL-WALLIS, SIEGEL P.190

FILE    NONAME    (CREATION DATE = 12/01/78)
SUBFILE    L1      L2      L3      L4      L5      L6      L7      L8

- - - - - KRUSKAL-WALLIS 1-WAY ANOVA

    WEIGHT      BIRTH WEIGHT
  BY LITTER

     LITTER        1       2       3       4       5       6
     NUMBER       10       8      10       8       6       4
  MEAN RANKS    31.70   27.06   41.40   34.69   17.58   30.50

     LITTER        7       8
     NUMBER        6       4
  MEAN RANKS    11.92   18.00
                                        CORRECTED FOR TIES
         CASES    CHI-SQUARE  SIGNIFICANCE  CHI-SQUARE  SIGNIFICANCE
          56        18.464      0.010        18.565      0.010
```

7.19   OPTIONS AVAILABLE FOR SUBPROGRAM NPAR TESTS

OPTION 1   *Include Missing Data.*

OPTION 2   *Listwise Deletion of Missing Data.* A case is eliminated from all computations if it has a missing value for any of the variables named on the NPAR TEST command.

OPTION 3   *Special Handling of Variable Lists.* In a variable list of the form VARA,VARB,VARC,etc., variables will be tested sequentially: VARA with VARB, VARB with VARC, etc. For a list containing the keyword WITH, the variables will be handled pairwise: The first variable to the left of the WITH will be paired with the first variable to the right of the WITH. In this case, there should be an equal number of variables on each side of WITH.

OPTION 4   *Sample Cases if there are too many.* If too many cases are encountered for a given WORKSPACE, a random sample of the cases will be taken. The sampling algorithm used is described in Chapter 19 on NONPAR CORR (Option 7) in this update manual. Since sampling would invalidate a RUNS= test, this option will be ignored when a RUNS= test is requested.

OPTION 5   *Restrict Output to 75 Printed Columns.*

7.20 STATISTICS AVAILABLE FOR SUBPROGRAM NPAR TESTS

STATISTIC 1   *Basic Statistics.* Mean, maximum, minimum, standard deviation and number of cases will be printed for each variable.

7.21 LIMITATIONS FOR SUBPROGRAM NPAR TESTS

- There is a maximum of 200 test specifications. For tests CHI-SQUARE, K-S (one sample), and RUNS, each variable tested counts as 1; for all other tests, each test is counted as 1, regardless of the number of variables named.
- The amount of SPACE required for execution is determined by

WORKSPACE = NCASES*(NV+3)

where NV is the total number of variables named in the VARIABLES= list of the NPAR command and NCASES is the total number of cases to be processed.

Note that case weighting (WEIGHT or *WEIGHT) affects NCASES in the following way: Each case is replicated the number of times specified by the whole number part of its weight. If there is a fractional part, a random number between zero and one is selected; if this number is less than the fractional part of the weight, the case is replicated an additional time.

    The procedure will terminate with an error message if there is not enough memory available, unless Option 4 is in effect.

7.22 REFERENCES

Conover, W. J. *Practical Nonparametric Statistics*, New York: Wiley, 1971.

Dineen, L. C., and B. C. Blakesley. Algorithm AS 62: A Generator for the Sampling Distribution of the Mann-Whitney U Statistic, *Applied Statistics*, 22: pp. 269-273, 1973.

Hollander, M., and D. A. Wolfe. *Nonparametric Statistical Methods*, New York: Wiley, 1973.

NPAR*   Nonparametric Statistics Package Technical Reports TR42-TR49, Michigan State University.

Siegel, S. *Nonparametric Statistics for the Behavioral Sciences,* New York: McGraw-Hill, 1956.

Smirnov, N. N. Table for Estimating the Goodness of Fit of Emprical Distributions, *Annals of Mathematical Statistics,* 19: pp. 279-281, 1948.

*The Michigan State University NPAR package is the original source of the algorithm for computing the significance level for the Moses Extreme Reaction test.

NPAR TESTS was designed, programmed, and documented by James Tuccy at Northwestern University.

Chapter 8

MULT RESPONSE:
Tabulation of Multiple Response Variables

The MULT RESPONSE procedure provides a mechanism for the analysis of multiple response items. Typically, a multiple response item is a question on a survey to which the respondent might legitimately make more than one reply. Two examples of such items are

• Which news magazines do you read regularly?
• What are the most significant problems facing the U.S.?

Obviously, these questions are phrased to encourage more than a single reply. Such items are not uncommon and are usually coded in one of two forms (ignoring the possibility of multiple punches in a single card column, a practice not supported by SPSS):

• Given a moderate number of possible responses, e.g. 10, one can create an equal number of dichotomous variables with each representing one of the possible answers. For example, on the above magazine readership question, one could utilize five variables corresponding to the five magazines whose names are anticipated as responses. Each of the variables is coded the same, perhaps 1 for "not read", 2 for "read regularly", and 9 for nonreaders.

• If the range of possible responses, as for an open-ended needs and problems item, is large, the use of dichotomies becomes impractical. So one might allocate some number of variables (e.g., 3) to the first n responses given by any respondent. In this case, each variable is coded from 1 to m where m is the number of unique responses. For instance, 1 might be the code for "recession", 2 for "inflation", 3 for "lack of religion", etc. Of course, there will be missing value codes as well, particularly to cover the case of fewer responses than allowed for.

Each of these coding schemes has its values and limitations. The use of dichotomous variables, which we will call "multiple dichotomies", permits their use as crosstabulation control variables and case selection variables. The use of the second coding scheme, which we will call the "multiple response" method for lack of a better term, preserves the order of the responses and permits at least some analysis of the "most important" response as though it were a normal variable. However, conventional techniques do not permit analysis of either coding scheme so as to recognize that any individual respondent may give more than one response to the survey item.

The SPSS MULT RESPONSE procedure provides a mechanism by which items of the types described above may be analyzed. It specifically permits analysis of simple variables, multiple dichotomies, and multiple response items both individually and in conjunction with one another. The procedure provides two types of output: frequency tables similar to those produced by the integer version of FREQUENCIES and n-way tables similar to those produced by the integer version of CROSSTABS.

8.1 Format of the MULT RESPONSE Command

The control field contains the keywords MULT RESPONSE starting in column one, and the specification field contains at least two lists from among the following: GROUPS=, VARIABLES =, FREQUENCIES=, and TABLES=. Specifically, at least one of the first two must be present, and at least one of the last two must be present. The formats of the four lists and their purposes are discussed in the following sections.

8.2 The GROUPS= Specification

```
GROUPS= group name [label] (varlist (value list))
        [group name...]/
```

The GROUPS= list identifies the multiple response items to be analyzed. For convenience, these items are referred to as groups as distinguished from simple variables. They may be either multiple dichotomy groups or multiple response groups. The group name is the name by which the researcher will refer to the group in specifying the desired output and the name by which the group will be identified by SPSS in the output. Each group name must be unique and must not be the same as any variable name which appears on the subsequent VARIABLES= list.

The label is optional and serves the same purpose as a variable label in the output.

The variable list enclosed in the outer set of parentheses is of the general form and identifies the component variables of the group. The inner set of parentheses encloses a value list referring to the variable list. If the variables represent multiple dichotomies, the value list consists of a single integer, the value to be tabulated (normally the "yes" code for the dichotomies). If the variables represent multiple responses, the value list consists of two integers: the lowest and highest codes to be tabulated.

The GROUPS= list must define all the multiple response items to be analyzed and must be terminated by a slash (/).

An example of a GROUPS= list is

```
MULT RESPONSE  GROUPS= MAGAZINE    READERSHIP OF NEWS MAGAZINES
                       (TIME NEWSWEEK USNEWS STONE REPUBLIC(2))
                       PROBLEMS    NATIONAL PROBLEMS MENTIONED
                       (PROB1 TO PROB3(1,34))/
```

8.3 The VARIABLES= Specification

```
VARIABLES= varlist (lo,hi) [varlist...]/
```

The VARIABLES= list follows the GROUPS= list (if present) and identifies all the simple variables to be analyzed. Its format is identical to the VARIABLES= list on the CROSSTABS command. It consists of one or more variable lists of the general form with each variable list followed by a set of two parenthesized values: the lowest and highest values to be tabulated. All the simple variables to be analyzed must be identified on the VARIABLES= list, and the list must be terminated by a slash (/).

An example of a VARIABLES= list is

```
VARIABLES= SEX(1,2) RACE(1,3) EDUC(0,8)/
```

8.4 The FREQUENCIES= Specification

```
FREQUENCIES= item list/
```

The FREQUENCIES= list specifies the simple variables and groups for which frequency tables are desired. The item list may reference groups identified on the GROUPS= list and simple variables identified on the VARIABLES= list. The use of the TO convention in construction of the item list is supported with the following limitations:

- The items preceding and following TO must be of the same type, i.e. either both groups or both simple variables.
- The implied order is that given on the GROUPS= and VARIABLES= lists, not that on the VARIABLE LIST or DATA LIST command (or on the system file).
- The use of the keyword ALL on the FREQUENCIES= list is not supported as it would be ambiguous.

The order in which items are specified on the VARIABLES= list determines the order in which the frequency tables are produced. The FREQUENCIES= list must follow the GROUPS= and VARIABLES= lists and must be terminated by a slash (/).

An example of a FREQUENCIES= list is

```
FREQUENCIES= PROBLEMS SEX TO EDUC/
```

8.5 The TABLES= Specification

```
TABLES= item list BY item list [BY item list...]/
        [item list BY.../]
```

The TABLES= list specifies the n-way tables which are to be produced. It is similar to the

TABLES= list on the CROSSTABS procedure command. It uses the keyword BY to delimit the various dimensions of the n-way tables and uses the slash (/) to delimit the tables themselves. The item lists on the TABLES= list are identical to that contained on the FREQUENCIES= list: each is composed of one or more group names and simple variable names from the GROUPS= and VARIABLES= lists respectively. As with the FREQUENCIES= list, each item list on the TABLES= list can be composed of both types of items and the use of the TO convention is supported subject to the limitations given above.

The first item list for TABLES= defines the groups or simple variables which are to appear on the left side of the tables. Each is a row item and comprises the first dimension of the n-way table. The second item list defines the column variables, those described across the top of the tables, and comprises the second dimension of each table. The third through fifth item lists for TABLES= are optional and are the control variables. Where an item list is composed of more than one item, each item will be used in turn to construct tables. The identity of the items in the leftmost (lowest dimension) list will vary fastest in the construction of tables, as is the case with CROSSTABS.

The TABLES= list must be the last list on the MULT RESPONSE procedure command and should be terminated with a slash (/).

An example of a TABLES= list is

```
TABLES= PROBLEMS BY MAGAZINE EDUC/
MAGAZINE BY EDUC BY SEX RACE/
```

8.6   An Example Run of MULT RESPONSE

The example MULT RESPONSE command shown in Figure 8.6a illustrates all of the elements of the procedure command.

Figure 8.6a   Example of Complete Syntax for MULT RESPONSE

```
MULT RESPONSE   GROUPS= PROBS    NATIONAL PROBLEMS MENTIONED
                          (PROB1 TO PROB3 (0,9))
                        MAGRDR   READERSHIP OF NATIONAL MAGAZINES
                          (TIME REPUBLIC NEWSWEEK STONE (2))/
                VARIABLES= EDUC (1,3)/
                FREQUENCIES= PROBS MAGRDR/
                TABLES= PROBS BY EDUC MAGRDR/
STATISTICS      2
```

This procedure command defines two groups. The first, PROBS, represents a multiple response group composed of three elementary variables coded 0 to 9. The second, MAGRDR, is composed of four dichotomies for which the value 2 is to be tabulated. A simple variable, EDUC, is defined. The FREQUENCIES= list calls for frequency tables on both of the groups, and the TABLES= list requests two tables, PROBS BY EDUC and PROBS BY MAGRDR.

Figure 8.6b   Frequencies of PROBS Multiple Response Group

```
TEST RUN OF MULT RESPONSE

FILE   NONAME   (CREATION DATE = 11/24/76)

GROUP PROBS      NATIONAL PROBLEMS MENTIONED
```

CATEGORY LABEL		CODE	COUNT	PCT OF RESPONSES	PCT OF CASES
RECESSION		1	45	12.2	26.3
INFLATION		2	63	17.1	36.8
LACK OF RELIGION		3	45	12.2	26.3
WATERGATE		4	36	9.8	21.1
RACIAL CONFLICT		5	36	9.8	21.1
UNIONS TOO STRONG		6	9	2.4	5.3
BIG BUSINESS		7	63	17.1	36.8
COMMUNIST AGGRESSION		8	45	12.2	26.3
WEATHER		9	27	7.3	15.8
	TOTAL RESPONSES		369	100.0	215.8
9 MISSING CASES	171 VALID CASES				

The table in Figure 8.6b gives the combined frequencies of the three elementary variables comprising the multiple response group PROBS. The category labels are those of the first elementary variable specified for PROBS in the GROUPS= list.

There are two columns of percentages. The first gives the frequencies as a percent of the total number of responses. The percentages in this column will always sum to 100. The second percentage column gives each frequency as a percent of the total number of valid cases. The percentages in this column may sum to as high as n times 100 where n is the number of elementary variables comprising the group since each case can contribute n to the frequencies. Unless groupwise deletion of missing data is requested, a case is considered missing only when it is missing for all the component variables.

Figure 8.6c   Frequencies of MAGRDR Multiple Dichotomy Group

```
TEST RUN OF MULT RESPONSE

FILE   NONAME   (CREATION DATE = 11/24/76)

GROUP MAGRDR    READERSHIP OF NATIONAL MAGAZINES
     (VALUE TABULATED =     2)

                                         PCT OF  PCT OF
DICHOTOMY LABEL             NAME    COUNT RESPONSES CASES

READS TIME REGULARLY        TIME      63   29.2    50.0

READS REPUBLIC REGULARLY    REPUBLIC  36   16.7    28.6

READS NEWSWEEK REGULARLY    NEWSWEEK  63   29.2    50.0

READS ROLLING STONE REGULARLY STONE  54   25.0    42.9
                                    ----- -----   -----
              TOTAL RESPONSES       216  100.0   171.4

   54 MISSING CASES      126 VALID CASES
```

The table in Figure 8.6c gives the frequencies of the "2" responses to the dichotomies comprising the multiple dichotomy group MAGRDR. The category labels are the variable labels of the component dichotomies. The NAME column gives the names of the dichotomies. The percentage columns are equivalent to those for the preceding table which presented a multiple response group rather than multiple dichotomies. There is a situation unique to dichotomies which may make the associated group missing. In particular, if none of the component dichotomies has a value corresponding to the tabulated value, the group is considered missing on that case.

Figure 8.6d   Crosstabulation of PROBS by EDUC

```
TEST RUN OF MULT RESPONSE
FILE   NONAME   (CREATION DATE = 11/24/76)
* * * * * * * * * *  C R O S S T A B U L A T I O N  * * * * * *
   PROBS    (GROUP) NATIONAL PROBLEMS MENTIONED
 BY EDUC    HIGHEST EDUCATIONAL ATTAINMENT OF RESP * * * * * * *

                 EDUC
           COUNT IGRADE SC HIGH SCH COLLEGE
           COL PCT IHOOL    OOL              ROW
               I                          I TOTAL
               I     1 I    2 I    3 I
PROBS      ----I------I------I------I
          1 I    18 I   18 I    9 I    45
 RECESSION   I  33.3 I 33.3 I 14.3 I  26.3
           I------I------I------I
          2 I     0 I   45 I   18 I    63
 INFLATION   I   0.0 I 83.3 I 28.6 I  36.8
           I------I------I------I
          3 I     9 I    9 I   27 I    45
 LACK OF RELIGION I 16.7 I 16.7 I 42.9 I 26.3
           I------I------I------I
          4 I     0 I    9 I   27 I    36
 WATERGATE   I   0.0 I 16.7 I 42.9 I  21.1
           I------I------I------I
          5 I    27 I    9 I    0 I    36
 RACIAL CONFLICT I 50.0 I 16.7 I  0.0 I 21.1
           I------I------I------I
          6 I     0 I    0 I    9 I     9
 UNIONS TOO STRONG I 0.0 I  0.0 I 14.3 I 5.3
           I------I------I------I
          7 I    18 I   27 I   18 I    63
 BIG BUSINESS I  33.3 I 50.0 I 28.6 I  36.8
           I------I------I------I
          8 I     0 I    9 I   36 I    45
 COMMUNIST AGGRESSION I 0.0 I 16.7 I 57.1 I 26.3
           I------I------I------I
          9 I    18 I    0 I    9 I    27
 WEATHER     I  33.3 I  0.0 I 14.3 I  15.8
           I------I------I------I
      COLUMN      54     54     63    171
      TOTAL      31.6   31.6   36.8  100.0

PERCENTS AND TOTALS BASED ON RESPONDENTS

   171 VALID CASES          9 MISSING CASES
```

Figure 8.6d shows the crosstabulation of a multiple response group, PROBS, by a simple variable, EDUC. The table displays frequencies and column percents (Statistic 2). As noted below the table, percents and totals are based on respondents, not on responses. This explains why the column percents sum to over 100 and why the frequencies in a column sum to more than the column total. The row frequencies sum to the row total since each case may have only one item in each row as long as the column is a simple variable.

Figure 8.6e shows a crosstabulation of a multiple response group, PROBS, by a multiple dichotomy, MAGRDR. The table displays frequencies and column percents. Since both of the table items are groups, both the columns and the rows sum to more than the respective respondent totals given in the table margins. Columns labels are the dichotomous variable names and labels truncated to 20 characters.

Figure 8.6e   Crosstabulation of PROBS by MAGRDR

```
TEST RUN OF MULT RESPONSE
FILE   NONAME   (CREATION DATE = 11/24/76)
* * * * * * * * * * *  C R O S S T A B U L A T I O N  * * * * * *
    PROBS     (GROUP) NATIONAL PROBLEMS MENTIONED
BY MAGRDR    (TABULATING    2) READERSHIP OF NATIONAL MAGAZINES

                   MAGRDR

             COUNT IREADS TI READS RE READS NE READS RO
             COL PCT IME REGUL PUBLIC R WSWEEK R LLING ST   ROW
                   IARLY     EGUL     EGUL     ONE       TOTAL
                   ITIME    IREPUBLICINEWSWEEKISTONE   I
   PROBS     -------I--------I--------I--------I--------I
                 1 I      9 I      0 I      9 I     18 I     27
   RECESSION     I   14.3 I    0.0 I   14.3 I   40.0 I   23.1
                 I--------I--------I--------I--------I
                 2 I     27 I     18 I     18 I     36 I     54
   INFLATION     I   42.9 I   50.0 I   28.6 I   80.0 I   46.2
                 I--------I--------I--------I--------I
                 3 I     18 I      0 I     27 I      9 I     27
   LACK OF RELIGION I 28.6 I   0.0 I   42.9 I   20.0 I   23.1
                 I--------I--------I--------I--------I
                 4 I     27 I     18 I     18 I      0 I     36
   WATERGATE      I   42.9 I   50.0 I   28.6 I    0.0 I   30.8
                 I--------I--------I--------I--------I
                 5 I      0 I      0 I      9 I      9 I      9
   RACIAL CONFLICT I   0.0 I    0.0 I   14.3 I   20.0 I    7.7
                 I--------I--------I--------I--------I
                 6 I      9 I      9 I      9 I      0 I      9
   UNIONS TOO STRONG I 14.3 I  25.0 I   14.3 I    0.0 I    7.7
                 I--------I--------I--------I--------I
                 7 I     18 I      9 I      9 I     27 I     45
   BIG BUSINESS   I   28.6 I   25.0 I   14.3 I   60.0 I   38.5
                 I--------I--------I--------I--------I
                 8 I     27 I     27 I     18 I      0 I     36
   COMMUNIST AGGRESSION I 42.9 I 75.0 I 28.6 I  0.0 I   30.8
                 I--------I--------I--------I--------I
                 9 I      9 I      9 I     18 I      0 I     18
   WEATHER        I   14.3 I   25.0 I   28.6 I    0.0 I   15.4
                 I--------I--------I--------I--------I
           COLUMN       63       36       63       45      117
           TOTAL      53.8     30.8     53.8     38.5    100.0

PERCENTS AND TOTALS BASED ON RESPONDENTS

   117 VALID CASES          63 MISSING CASES
```

8.7   PAIRED Option

By default, when MULT RESPONSE tabulates one multiple response group with another, it tabulates each variable in the first group with each variable in the second group and sums the counts for each cell. Thus, if each of the two groups comprises three variables, a case with valid values for all of those variables contributes nine responses to the table. For example, assume a file containing information on pregnancies where each case is a mother. The file contains information for up to three pregnancies for each observation. Variables for the pregnancies are P1SEX, P2SEX, P3SEX for sex of child and P1AGE, P2AGE, P3AGE for age of mother. Using MULT RESPONSE you define groups PSEX and PAGE:

```
GROUPS=PSEX SEX OF CHILD(P1SEX P2SEX P3SEX(1,2))
       PAGE AGE OF ONSET OF PREGNANCY(P1AGE P2AGE
       P3AGE(1,4))/
```

where age is recoded into four categories.

If you tabulate PSEX with PAGE, a case with information on three pregnancies would define nine responses:

```
P1SEX BY P1AGE
P1SEX BY P2AGE
P1SEX BY P3AGE
      .
      .
P3SEX BY P3AGE
```

If a mother had two boys and two pregnancies between ages 20 and 24, she would appear four times in the summed table. It is quite likely that this is not the information desired. Rather you are interested in the number of male births occurring for pregnancies beginning between ages 20 and 24. In effect, this table is the sum of three tables:

```
PlSEX BY PlAGE
P2SEX BY P2AGE
P3SEX BY P3AGE
```

MULT RESPONSE produces this type of table with a special keyword on table requests: PAIRED.

8.8 Syntax for Paired Multiple Response Tables

Paired tables are requested by ending a table request with the keyword PAIRED enclosed in parentheses following the last variable named on the table request, as in

```
TABLES=PSEX BY PAGE(PAIRED)/
```

A paired table request may also contain simple variables and multiple dichotomies. However, only items part of true multiple response groups are paired. For example,

```
TABLES=PSEX BY PAGE BY EDUC(PAIRED)
```

where EDUC is a simple variable, only pairs PSEX with PAGE. The paired option also applies to a multiple response group used as a controlling variable in a three-way or higher table.

Multiple response groups being paired together must contain the same number of items. Unequal length groups paired together will be flagged as an error.

8.9 Multiple Dichotomies in Paired Tables

Multiple dichotomy groups may be used in paired table requests, but they will not be paired. For example, assume that the file on mothers also includes data on supplements usually taken during pregnancies. You might create a multiple dichotomy group such as

```
GROUPS=SUPP DIET SUPPLEMENTS (IRON A B12(1))
```

The table request

```
TABLES=PSEX BY PAGE BY SUPP(PAIRED)
```

sums together the following 9 three-way tables:

```
PlSEX BY PlAGE BY IRON
PlSEX BY PlAGE BY A
PlSEX BY PlAGE BY B12
P2SEX BY P2AGE BY IRON
           .
           .
           .
P3SEX BY P3AGE BY B12
```

8.10 Output From Paired Tables

Figure 8.10a contains the table produced with the PAIRED option Figure 8.10b, the table produced without the paired option.

Figure 8.10a   Crosstabulation of PSEX by PAGE with PAIRED Option

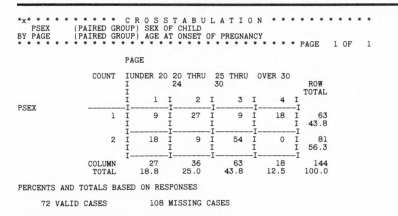

Figure 8.10b   Crosstabulation of PSEX by PAGE without PAIRED Option

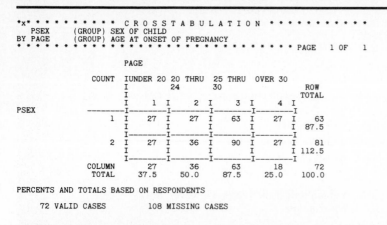

```
*x* * * * * * * * * * C R O S S T A B U L A T I O N * * * * * * * * * * *
  PSEX      (GROUP) SEX OF CHILD
BY PAGE    (GROUP) AGE AT ONSET OF PREGNANCY
* * * * * * * * * * * * * * * * * * * * * * * * * * PAGE   1 OF   1

                          PAGE
                 COUNT  IUNDER 20 20 THRU  25 THRU  OVER 30
                       I             24       30               ROW
                       I                                       TOTAL
                       I     1 I    2 I    3 I    4 I
  PSEX         --------I------I------I------I------I
               1 I    27 I   27 I   63 I   27 I    63
                 I      I      I      I      I   87.5
               I--------I------I------I------I------I
               2 I    27 I   36 I   90 I   27 I    81
                 I      I      I      I      I  112.5
               I--------I------I------I------I------I
              COLUMN    27     36     63     18      72
              TOTAL    37.5   50.0   87.5   25.0   100.0

PERCENTS AND TOTALS BASED ON RESPONDENTS

     72 VALID CASES        108 MISSING CASES
```

A paired table is identified in the output by the adjective PAIRED GROUP in the table header. Note that the number of responses is considerably less for the paired table since only three tables are being summed together. Also note, when a paired table is requested, MULT RESPONSE bases percentages upon responses rather than respondents by default. In non-paired tables, percentages are based on respondents by default (Option 5 may be used to obtain percentages based on responses).

8.11   Options Available for Subprogram MULT RESPONSE

The following options are available for subprogram MULT RESPONSE:

OPTION 1   *Inclusion of Missing Data.* Option 1 causes the missing data indicators to be disregarded and all values to be considered valid.

OPTION 2   *Groupwise Deletion for Multiple Dichotomies.* Causes the "groupwise" deletion of missing values for multiple dichotomies. That is, if one of the dichotomies comprising a group is missing, the case is considered missing for that group.

OPTION 3   *Groupwise Deletion for Multiple Response Groups.* Causes the "groupwise" deletion of missing values for multiple response groups. That is, if one of the elementary variables is missing, the case is considered missing for that multiple response item.

OPTION 4   *Suppress Value Labels.* This option causes the suppression of value labels for other than multiple dichotomies. That is, it affects multiple response groups and simple variables in both frequency and tables.

OPTION 5   *Base Percents on Responses.* Causes the percents and totals in tables to be based on responses rather than on respondents. If this option is specified, the rows and columns in all tables will sum to the row and column totals, and the row and column totals will sum to the table total.

OPTION 6   *Limit Output Width to 75 Characters.* Restricts the number of columns in a table printed on a single page to produce a table which is not more than 75 characters in width, exclusive of carriage control characters. This option is an attempt to produce output which is more compatible with the use of short carriage terminals for remote job entry.

OPTION 11   *Condensed Frequency Table Format.* Forces a "three-up" condensed format for frequency tables involving other than a multiple dichotomy. This format, while conservative of space, necessarily omits some of the information contained in the normal table, such as the category labels. Column headings are necessarily abbreviated.

OPTION 12   *Option 11 Limit to One Full Page.* Causes the condensed format for frequency tables to be used for all items other than multiple dichotomies which have over twenty categories, i.e., those which would require more than one page in the normal format.

8.12   Statistics Available for Subprogram MULT RESPONSE

The statistics available for procedure MULT RESPONSE are

STATISTIC 1   *Include Row Percents in the Tables.*
STATISTIC 2   *Include Column Percents in the Tables.*
STATISTIC 3   *Include 2-way Table Total Percents in the Tables.*

8.13   Limitations to Subprogram MULT RESPONSE

The following limitations apply to procedure MULT RESPONSE:

- The maximum number of symbols which may appear on the MULT RESPONSE command after the GROUPS= list is (SPACE-800)/8. A space allocation of 10,000 would permit 1150 symbols.
- The maximum number of multiple response items which may be defined on the GROUPS= list is 20.
- The maximum number of elementary variables which may be mentioned or implied on the GROUPS= and VARIABLES= lists combined is 100. Each occurence of any variable counts.
- The maximum number of declared categories for a multiple response group or simple variable is 32,767.
- The number of table requests on the TABLES= list may not exceed 10. This does not correspond to the number of resulting tables but to the number of lists delimited by slashes.
- The maximum number of dimensions in a table is five. That is, it is permissible to request a five-way table.
- The maximum number of items (both multiple response and simple) which may be specified or implied on the VARIABLES= and GROUPS= lists combined is 100. Each occurence of any item counts 1.
- The maximum number of non-empty rows in a single table is 200.
- The maximum number of non-empty columns in a single table is 400.

The amount of memory required for MULT RESPONSE is dependent on three quantities which are summed together.

- For each multiple response item defined in the GROUPS= list, 40 bytes are required.
- For each frequency table, $4 \times (NCAT + 1)$ bytes are required where NCAT is the number of categories or dichotomies to be included.
- For each table, you first determine the number of categories (or dichotomies as the case may be) for each dimension. For the first two dimensions, add one to the number of categories. Then multiply the resulting numbers together. That is, for a $2 \times 3 \times 4$ table, you would multiply $(2 + 1) \times (3 + 1) \times 4 = 48$. Then multiply this by four and add four to get the bytes for the entire table. A quick and relatively accurate estimate will be given by adding one to the number of categories in each dimension, multiplying these numbers together and multiplying the result by 4.

The procedure uses whatever space is left over for category labels. For frequency tables, each category label requires 40 bytes, and, for tables, each requires 20 bytes. If there is insufficient space for all the category labels for a given table, some are simply left off the output.

MULT RESPONSE was designed, programmed, and documented by C. Hadlai Hull.

Chapter 9

RELIABILITY:
Analysis of Additive Scales/
Repeated Measures ANOVA

Subprogram RELIABILITY provides a means for evaluating multiple-item additive scales through the computation of widely recognized coefficients of reliability. In addition, RELIABILITY can provide the user with basic summary statistics including item means, standard deviations, inter-item covariance and correlation matrices, scale means, and item-to-scale correlations. Subprogram RELIABILITY can perform a repeated measures design analysis of variance, a two-way factorial ANOVA with one observation per cell, Tukey's test for additivity, Hotelling's T^2 test for equality of means in repeated measures designs, and Friedman's two-way analysis of variance on ranks.

RELIABILITY may use either raw data cases (from a raw input data file or SPSS system file), a correlation matrix, or a covariance matrix. If input consists of raw data cases, any of the SPSS variable transformation features may be used, and statistics can be obtained that are not available with matrix input. On the other hand, savings in computation time may be considerable with matrix input and secondary analysis performed when the raw data is not directly obtainable.

9.1   INTRODUCTION TO RELIABILITY THEORY

Subprogram RELIABILITY provides a large number of reliability coefficients for multiple-item scales, encompassing a large number of differing approaches to reliability definition and estimation. The choice of approach depends upon assumptions.

The assumptions considered in this section are essentially statistical. It makes no difference whether the measurement process involves judges or raters assigning scores to objects, or individuals responding to test questions or sample survey questions. It could also involve measurement of gravitational attraction among subatomic particles using an assortment of instruments. Judges, raters, items, questions or instruments are entered as variables; objects, individuals, and particles are entered as cases into RELIABILITY.

The theoretical or epistemological similarities between these examples are often weak. Further, there are procedural variations within these situations which may make certain coefficients more meaningful than others. In general, the computations performed by the subprogram are designed to be used in those situations where the goal is to assess how reliable a sum or weighted sum across variables is as an estimate of a case's true score.

Suppose that we have a single observation X, which has two components: t the true score and e the error of measurement. Then,

$$X = t + e$$

In general, the concept of reliability refers to how accurate, on the average, the estimate of the true score is in a population of objects to be measured. In this population, let σ_e^2 be the variance of the errors of measurement, σ_t^2 be the variance of the true scores, and σ_o^2 be the variance of the observed scores where, for convenience, the observed score is the sum of the observations for an object. Further, assume that the errors of measurement are independent of the true scores and that the observed score is the sum of the true score and the error. Then the reliability coefficient is defined as

$$\rho_t = \frac{\sigma_t^2}{\sigma_o^2} = \frac{\sigma_o^2 - \sigma_e^2}{\sigma_o^2} = 1 - \frac{\sigma_e^2}{\sigma_o^2}$$

If all of the variation in observed scores is due to errors of measurement, the reliability coefficient will be zero. If there is no error of measurement, the reliability coefficient will be one.

9.2   Assumptions Underlying Reliability Calculations

Estimating reliability requires several assumptions. The minimal set of those assumptions is given by Guttman (1945):

- Reliability is defined as the variation over an indefinitely large number of independent repeated trials of errors of measurement.
- There exists an infinite population of objects for each item being measured.
- The observed values of an individual on an item are experimentally independent of the observed values of any other individual on that or any other item.
- The observed values of an individual on an item are experimentally independent of the observed value for that individual on any other item.
- The variances of the observed scores on each item and the covariances of the observed scores between items exist in the population.

Granted these assumptions, it can be shown that the true reliability has the largest of the six Guttman reliability coefficients as a lower bound.

The first two assumptions define reliability and insure that any conclusions are not bound to a specific population. For those users not interested in generalizing beyond their sample, or beyond a finite population at a specific time, the coefficients computed by RELIABILITY are applicable. However, the rationale for selecting one over another must be based upon other criteria. The reader is referred to discussions of coefficients of stability, equivalence, homogeneity, internal consistency, test-retest, or precision.

The third and fourth assumptions specify that no cheating is going on, that the measurement device is unchanged by the process of measurement, that responses to an item are a function of the content of only that item and are not affected by the content of other items in the scale. In effect, the fourth assumption specifies no interaction between objects and measures.

The fifth assumption is always satisfied in practice, since the scores are finite for all observational techniques which yield finite scores.

One commonly used assumption in reliability theory is missing from Guttman's list. Nowhere in his development does he assume that the items are measuring the same thing. The remainder of the coefficients computed by the subprogram are derived under this type of assumption. Their derivations differ basically in terms of what is meant by measuring "the same thing".

9.3   The Notion of Equivalence

The notion of equivalence has two components, theoretical and statistical. The most restrictive definition of equivalence is called a strictly parallel model. For this model, two items or tests are said to be strictly parallel if they have the same means, the same true score variances over a set of objects being measured, and the same error variance over replications.

When the assumption of equal means is relaxed but the other assumptions are retained, then the model is called a parallel model. If, in addition, the assumption of equal error variances is relaxed, then we have a τ-equivalent model. If we also remove the assumption of equal true score variances, we have a congeneric model.

These various assumptions and models are expressed as follows by classical test theory. For a randomly selected case from a population, the observed score using measurement instrument i is decomposed into a true score t_i and error score ϵ_i, where true and error scores for the same instrument and error scores for different instruments are uncorrelated, that is

$$E[(\text{cov}(t_i,\epsilon_i)] = 0 \text{ and } E[(\text{cov}(\epsilon_i,\epsilon_j)] = 0; i \text{ not equal to } j$$

For simplicity of presentation the mean of the error scores is assumed to be zero, $E(\epsilon_i) = 0$.

If we let τ be a random variable in the population such that the true score on instrument i is

$$t_i = \mu_i + \beta_i\tau$$

then the observed score is given by

$$X_i = \mu_i + \beta_i\tau + \epsilon_i$$

For simplicity, it is assumed that τ has a mean of zero and variance of one in the population. The structure of the observations can be represented by this figure:

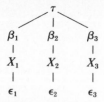

From the assumptions just made, μ_i is the mean of X_i, β_i is the covariance between X_i and τ, and β_i^2 is the true score variance.

The figure above is the underlying model for the congeneric model. The reliability of instrument i is given by

$$\rho_i = \frac{\beta_i^2}{\beta_i^2 + \theta_i^2}$$

where θ_i^2 is the variance of ϵ_i.

In many instances, it is customary to combine the scores for a case into a linear composite to increase reliability. Let α_i be the weight for instrument i such that

$$\gamma = \sum_i \alpha_i(\mu_i + \beta_i\tau + \epsilon_i)$$
$$= \sum_i \alpha_i x_i$$

where y is the scale score or composite score for a given case. The reliability of y is given by

$$\rho = \frac{\sum_i (\alpha_i \beta_i)^2}{\sigma_{\cdot y}^2}$$

This model is referred to as a congeneric model. It is not presently available in RELIABILITY. There are a number of special cases of the congeneric model which are of some interest. The τ-equivalent model hypothesizes that $\beta_1 = \beta_2 = \ldots = \beta_k$, i.e., that the true scores have equal variance. The parallel model hypothesizes that $\beta_1 = \beta_2 = \ldots = \beta_k$ and $\theta_1 = \theta_2 = \ldots = \theta_k$ and the strict parallel model further hypothesizes that $\mu_1 = \mu_2 = \ldots = \mu_k$.

Assuming that τ has a normal distribution in the population of interest and that the error terms are normally distributed, the program calculates maximum likelihood estimates of the parameters, unbiased estimates, and likelihood ratio tests of the model against the general unconstrained model if MODEL=STRICTPARALLEL or MODEL=PARALLEL is specified.

If either the parallel or strict parallel model fits the data, then the optimum weights are equal. Thus, the best linear combination, the composite which maximizes the reliability of the linear combination, is a simple sum of the scores across instruments.

9.4 Discriminant Reliability and Levels of Measurement

Two special topics should be raised: One might be called discriminant reliability; the other is level of measurement.

Discriminant reliability refers to the use of scale scores to distinguish between two or more existing groups in a population. For example, one may be attempting to construct a simple scale measuring psychological stress. Psychiatric observations could be used to divide the subjects into high and low stress groups; and a set of questionnaire items could then be administered which theoretically measure stress. While subprogram RELIABILITY could be used to assess the reliability of the test, it would provide no information on the ability of the scale to distinguish between the two groups. For this type of application, discriminant function analysis is more appropriate. (See the discussion of subprogram DISCRIMINANT in *SPSS*, Second Edition, and in this manual.)

There are three approaches which may be taken to the issue of requisite level of measurement. At the extreme, dichotomous data (0,1) or interval level measurement is demanded. Second, it could be said that ordinal measurement is simply a failure to achieve interval or ratio measurement. This merely inflates the errors of measurement and thus reduces reliability. Third, ordinal level data may be converted to ranks and entered into the program. This would be accomplished by using a matrix of Spearman rank order correlations produced by the nonparametric correlation subprogram in SPSS as input (be sure to use a vector of standard deviations equal to one as well).

9.5 ANALYSIS OF VARIANCE USING SUBPROGRAM RELIABILITY

Subprogram RELIABILITY may be used to perform a single factor repeated measures design analysis of variance, a two-way factorial design with one observation per cell, a complete randomized block design analysis of variance, and Friedman's analysis of variance on ranks. The following table gives the basic relationships between SPSS processing terminology and the terminology usually employed by statistical texts discussing these procedures.

SPSS Processing	Repeated Measures	2-Way Factorial	Randomized Blocks
case(row)	person(object)	treatment A	block
variable(column)	measure(judge)	treatment B	treatment

Subprogram RELIABILITY uses repeated measures design terminology to label its output. An analysis of variance is invoked by Statistic 10.

In the two-way factorial design there are k levels for one experimental factor and n levels for the other factor. Thus there are nk treatment combinations and, with one observation per cell, nk experimental units.

Another related design, for computational purposes, is the complete randomized block design. Rather than randomly assigning the nk experimental units to nk treatment combinations (as in the two-way factorial design with one observation per cell), the experimenter divides the nk experimental units into n matched groups (blocks) each having k members. The k members of each block are randomly assigned to the k treatments. Conceptually, the randomized block design may be approached in two ways. In one sense, the design is merely a two-way factorial design where the blocks are a classification treatment rather than a treatment under direct experimental manipulation. As an alternative, the complete randomized block design may be thought of as a multivariate extension of the matched t test, just as the ordinary one-way analysis of variance is the multiple group extension of the standard t test for a difference between two means. When only two treatments are applied, the F test for differences between treatments is equivalent to the t test described in footnote 1 on page 270 of *SPSS*, Second Edition, since $F=t^2$ in this case. The purpose of matching is to reduce the experimental error by controlling for the effects of one or more nuisance factors. Levels on the matching factor may represent qualitative differences of any kind or combinations of factors. The important point is that the factor or factors underlying the groupings must actually contribute to the variance.

If the factors leading to the matching have nothing to do with the dependent variables, this is an uneconomical way to design an experiment. If, on the other hand, the matching criterion is strongly related to the dependent variable, the design is a highly efficient one. In a sense, the repeated measures design is a special case of the complete randomized block design where each unit is matched with itself. The design is the multivariate extension of the paired or correlated t test described in Chapter 17 of *SPSS*, Second Edition. If only two treatments are used, $F=t^2$. Experiments in which the same elements are used under all k treatments require k observations on each element; hence the term repeated measures. To the extent that the unique characteristics of the subjects remain constant under different treatments, the observations on the same subject will be dependent rather than independent.

In the behavioral sciences, the elements of the population being studied are frequently people. Because of large differences in experience, the response of different people to the same experimental treatment may be highly variable. Much of this variability may be due to preexisting differences. One purpose of a repeated measures design is to provide a control for this difference between experimental subjects.

Repeated measures on the same elements may arise in a number of ways. In studies designed to study learning rates, growth rates, decay rates, and the like, as a function of time or treatment effects, repeated measures on the same experimental unit are an integral part of the design. The order in which the observations are made is dictated by the experimental variables. On the other hand the experimenter may have an option of varying the order of the treatment combinations.

The fact that treatments are applied sequentially to the same experimental unit may introduce major complications. The usefulness of the repeated measures design is limited when carry-over or sequence effects are likely to confound results. If sequence effects are small the repeated measures design may still be used. However, it cannot be overemphasized that this design is to be avoided if sequence effects are likely to be strong and not of primary interest.

9.6   Two-Way Factorial Design With One Observation Per Cell

In the usual two-way factorial design there are m observations per treatment combination. When there is only one observation per treatment combination, no within cells variance estimate is available. The general finite model for the two-way factorial with R levels for the row factor, C levels for the column factor and m observations per combination, is

$$X_{rci} = \mu + \alpha_r + \beta_c + (\alpha\beta)_{rc} + \epsilon_{rci}$$

where μ is the population mean, α_r is the effect of level r of factor A, β_c is the effect of level c of factor B, $(\alpha\beta)_{rc}$ is the interaction effect of treatment combination rc and ϵ_{rci} is the error term. If, for n levels of treatment A (rows), and k levels for treatment B (columns) and m observations per combination, the nkm experimental units are randomly assigned to the nk treatment combinations, then the conditions of the model are met. Then, the sum of the observations squared may be partitioned as in a standard analysis of variance table. In any analysis of variance, the expected values for the mean squares used for computing the F test statistic differ depending upon whether the levels of the treatment variables are fixed or random.

With a single observation per cell, the number of replications per treatment combination (m) is one. Thus, it is impossible to compute a within cells sum of squares and to estimate σ_e^2.

The absence of a direct estimate of the error mean square means that no direct test for interaction between the two factors is possible. Thus the general model contains the assumption of no interaction (see Section 9.10).

9.7 Complete Randomized Block Design

While the experiment is executed differently, the analysis of a complete randomized block design proceeds in the same fashion as a two-way factorial design. As its name implies, the blocking factor is normally considered a random factor (blocks are a random sample of all possible blocks) and the treatment factor is typically (but not always) a fixed factor. No new assumptions are introduced since the variable(s) being used to match experimental units may be considered merely another treatment factor which is classificatory in nature rather than something being manipulated by the experimenter.

As mentioned, however, the efficiency of this design depends upon the assumption that the classification variable(s) affect the dependent (criterion) variable. If this is not the case, then the design is no more efficient than a one-way analysis of variance with n observations per cell; the effort expended to match units is wasted.

9.8 Repeated Measures Design

In a repeated measures design each experimental unit is observed under k treatments (measurements, items). The model for the experiment is

$$X_{ij} = \mu + \pi_i + \gamma_j + \epsilon_{ij}$$

where X_{ij} is the observed response of experimental unit i to treatment j, μ is the mean of all potential observations, and π_i is a constant associated with experimental unit i (but a random variable in the sense that units are usually sampled from a population). The parameter γ_j is the main effect for treatment j, and ϵ_{ij} is, of course, the experimental error associated with X_{ij}.

It is assumed that the parameter associated with experimental unit i, π_i is normally distributed in the population of units with mean zero and variance $\sigma[\pi]^2$. Within the population of observations under treatment 1, the experimental error is assumed to be normally distributed with mean zero and variance σ_1^2. Within the corresponding population under treatment 2, the experimental error is also assumed to be normally distributed with mean zero and variance $\sigma(2)^2$. The experimental errors under the different treatments are assumed independent, and with more than two treatments it is also assumed that the error variances are homogeneous, i.e.,

$$\sigma_{\epsilon_1}^2 = \sigma_{\epsilon_2}^2 = \cdots = \sigma_{\epsilon_k}^2 = \sigma_\epsilon^2$$

At this point, the design resembles the randomized blocks design. This resemblance is specious and misleading. When different experimental units are given different treatments, even though the units are matched, it is reasonable to assume the error portions of their observed scores are independent. However, treating a repeated measures design as a two-way factorial design does not solve the problem even if "subjects" appear as a factor in the analysis. The computations of an analysis of variance for factorial or complete randomized block designs can be applied to this design when a particular form of dependency exists among the observations.

The form of dependency which the assumed model imposes upon the observations can be derived as follows. First assume that the π_i, the effect parameter for unit i, is independent of the error term ϵ_{ij}. Then the variance of the observations under treatment j is the sum of the variances due to experimental error and variance due to differences between the π values. Thus

$$\sigma_{x_1}^2 = \sigma_\epsilon^2 + \sigma_\pi^2$$
$$\sigma_{x_2}^2 = \sigma_\epsilon^2 + \sigma_\pi^2$$

Now the term π_i is common to all measurements on the same unit. Thus the covariance between treatments i and j will not be zero, in general. If this covariance is denoted by $X_i X_j$ then

$$X_i X_j = \sigma_\pi^2$$

Since the above is true for any pair of treatments it is also assumed that the covariances between treatments are homogeneous. Given these additional assumptions, a repeated measures design can be analyzed using the same computational procedures that are used for a two-way factorial with one observation per cell. For historical reasons, and to highlight the fact that additional assumptions are being made, the presentation of the results of an analysis of a repeated measures design differs somewhat from that used for the two-way factorial.

9.9   Effects of Violating Assumptions

It is generally acknowledged that use of the F ratio for hypothesis testing in experimental designs is reasonably robust. That is, the procedure is relatively insensitive to single violations of the underlying assumptions. However, many common violations of assumptions are disastrous in combination. The RELIABILITY procedure provides a test for the additivity assumption and an alternate test which avoids assuming a homogeneous variance-covariance matrix.

9.10   Interaction and Additivity: The Tukey Test

The underlying model for the three analysis of variance designs considered does not contain a term for interaction effects. In effect, it is assumed that no interaction is present. The consequences of violating the assumption of no interaction, or assumption of additivity, depend upon the design, whether the effects are fixed or random, and the tests and comparisons to be made. In all cases, the presence of nonadditivity may mask simple proportional or multiplicative relationships between row and column effects. Further, nonadditivity reduces the precision of the experiments since the estimated error variance is inflated by the component due to nonadditivity. Further, the loss of precision increases as the size of the main effects increases. Violation of the additivity assumption is serious in the two-way factorial fixed effects model. In this case, if interaction is present, then the error sum of squares for the additive model estimate is $\sigma[\epsilon]^2 + \sigma_i^2$ rather than simply the error. Consequently the F ratio used to test for a main effect is an estimate of the ratio

$$\frac{\sigma_\epsilon^2 + k\sigma_A^2}{\sigma_\epsilon^2 + \sigma_i^2}$$

for effect A rather than an estimate of

$$\frac{\sigma_\epsilon^2 + k\sigma_A^2}{\sigma_\epsilon^2}$$

However, since σ_i^2 is nonnegative

$$\frac{\sigma\beta_\epsilon^2 + k\sigma_A^2}{\sigma_\epsilon^2 + \sigma_i^2} < \frac{\sigma_\epsilon^2 + k\sigma_A^2}{\sigma_\epsilon^2}$$

Thus the F ratio in the presence of interaction is a conservative test. A significant result may be interpreted as a rejection of the null hypothesis. A nonsignificant result implies no decision may be made. However, even if significant main effects are found, specific comparisons between treatment means will not usually detect significant differences due to the inflated estimate of the error variance.

If both factors are random, in the presence of interaction the F tests for overall main effects are exact, as are specific comparisons for mixed models, models with one fixed and one random factor. For the usual randomized block design, the F test for main effects of the fixed factor is exact, while the F test for main effects of the random factor is conservative, as in the fully fixed model. For repeated measures designs, the presence of interaction presents certain difficulties. In general, the model is rewritten as

$$X_{ij} = \mu + \pi_i + \tau_j + \pi\tau_{ij} + \epsilon_{ij}$$

and it is assumed that the interaction term $\pi\tau_{ij}$ is a random variable, distributed with a mean of zero under each treatment and homogeneous variances under all treatments. If the error term and interaction term are independent and if π_i and $\pi\tau_{ij}$ have a joint normal distribution then the F ratio testing for no treatment effects remains valid provided the previously stated assumptions of the model are met.

Tukey's test for additivity (Statistic 11) may be used to detect the presence of interaction. The test is most sensitive to a linear × linear or multiplicative form of interaction. Strictly speaking, Tukey's test is valid only for the two-way analysis of variance with both effects fixed. In practice, it may also be used as a guide in the other designs as well.

In situations where Tukey's test is appropriate, interaction may arise because the scale of measurement may have been inappropriately chosen. For example, suppose that for factor A with two levels, the dependent value at the second level is twice that observed at the first level and for factor B with two levels, the dependent value is three times as large at the second level as at the first. The data would then take the form

	b_1	b_2
a_1	1	3
a_2	2	6

Since no random error has been added to these four observations, the error mean square should be zero. If the usual analysis of variance were carried out it would however, suggest the presence of error. The solution for this example is to transform the criterion variable to logs before analysis. Tukey's test provides not only a test to decide if a transformation is necessary but also may suggest a suitable transformation and a test for the success of the transformation.

Tukey's test is related to a transformation of the form $Y=X^p$ in which X is the original scale and a power p is sought such that the effects are additive in the scale Y. Thus, $p=1/2$ represents a square root tranformation, $p=-1$ a reciprocal transformation analyzing $Y=1/X$ instead of X and value of p near 0 may be interpreted as a log transformation since the variable X^p behaves like logX when p is near zero. It is suggested that simple integer powers, log transformations, and simple fractional powers be used for transformations rather than using the five place decimal power computed by RELIABILITY.

If a transformation is theoretically meaningless, but Tukey's test indicates the presence of interaction, then the Tukey test provides a partitioning of the residual sum of squares into interaction and balance components. Assuming that interactions of higher order than linear $\times$ linear are negligible, the balance component may be used as a "purified" estimate of the error sum of squares in a model containing interaction. The F ratios must be recalculated in some instances.

9.11 The Assumption of Homogeneity: Hotellings's T-Squared

In any analysis of variance, the assumption is made that the error terms have homogeneous variance (equal variances) within each treatment combination. In the designs considered in this section there is only one observation per cell so no test of this assumption is possible. It is impossible to obtain separate estimates of this within-cell variation.

Repeated measures designs involving more than two treatments also rest on the assumption that the variance-covariance matrix between treatments (judges, variables, measures) is homogeneous, or that it has the form

$$
\begin{array}{ccc}
v & cv & cv \\
cv & v & cv \\
cv & cv & v
\end{array}
$$

where $v=\sigma^2$, and $cv=\rho\sigma^2$, where treatment variances are equal, error variances are equal, and between treatment covariances are equal.

The F test for equality of treatment means is reasonably robust if the variances are not homogeneous or if the covariances are not homogeneous, but it is not robust if both assumptions are violated. In this case, it gives too many false rejections of the null hypothesis. A conservative test under conditions of heterogeneity due to Box, is given by using one and $n-1$ degrees of freedom to find the probability of the calculated F ratio rather than $k-1$ and $(n-1)(k-1)$ degrees of freedom as are used by RELIABILITY.

Box's conservative test tends to give too many type 1 errors (it fails to reject the null hypothesis) under mild heterogeneity conditions. An exact test of the hypothesis of equal treatment means is provided by Hotellings' T^2 test (Statistic 12). If the homogeneity assumptions are met, then Hotelling's test and the usual F test give identical results.

A large sample likelihood ratio test of the homogenity assumption (sphericity hypothesis) may be generated by specifying MODEL=PARALLEL after the scale list being analyzed (see Section 9.21). The test for goodness of fit of the parallel model is a test for homogeneity of variance.

9.12 Friedman's Analysis of Variance for Ranked Data

Suppose one is interested in determining whether there is any difference between various teachers. Students may be asked to rank the teachers in order of popularity. For example a student may assign a rank of 1 to teacher 3, rank 2 to teacher 1 and rank 1 to teacher 2.

The computational formulas for the repeated measures design may be applied to rank data of this sort. If the experiment is repeated with another sample of the same size, the total sums of squares will be constant if tied ranks are not permitted. Thus, rather than an F statistic, a chi-square statistic is used to test the hypothesis of no difference in mean ranks. Use of the chi-square statistic is called the Friedman test. An index of the extent to which people agree in their rankings is given by Kendall's coefficient of concordance.

Provided that the data are ranks, Option 15 requests the subprogram to calculate Friedman's chi-square statistic for the analysis of variance rather than the usual F statistic and to calculate Kendall's coefficient of concordance.

Note that Friedman's chi-square statistic is also available in the NPAR TEST subprogram. In that subprogram, the data need not be in the form of ranks, but the number of cases is limited by the available workspace.

9.13 Analysis of Variance of Dichotomous Data

In an experiment designed to study the effect of a training program on the success of Federal Disaster Agencies, a sample of agencies was tested before, during, and at intervals after the program in a variety of simulated emergencies. The observations consisted of whether they successfully coped with the emergency or not. Data of this type, where only two outcomes are possible, are referred to as dichotomous data.

To test the hypothesis of no change in the proportion of successful outcomes over time, Cochran's Q statistic is used rather than the usual F statistic, by specifying Option 16.

Cochran's Q statistic is also available in subprogram NPAR TESTS; that subprogram will print an appropriate contingency table for the analysis. The number of cases is, however, limited by the amount of available workspace.

9.14   THE RELIABILITY PROCEDURE CARD

The subprogram is activated by a procedure card containing the control word RELIABILITY beginning in column 1. Each reliability calculation consists of three steps. First, a triangular covariance matrix and vector of means is assembled as directed by a VARIABLES= list. Second, one or more submatrices are selected from the larger matrix as directed by one or more labeled SCALE= lists. Third, the computations are carried out on the appropriate submatrix. The process may be repeated using a second VARIABLES= list and SCALE= lists. The computations actually performed and results printed are controlled by a MODEL= specification and by OPTIONS and STATISTICS cards.

The general format of the RELIABILITY procedure card is

```
RELIABILITY    VARIABLES = varlist/
               SCALE (label) = scale list/ MODEL = model/
               SCALE (label) = scale list/ . . ./
               VARIABLES = varlist/ . . .
```

If the subprogram can infer, from the models specified and the options and statistics selected, that the covariance matrices will not be needed, it will use an alternative computing method which uses less space and time.

9.15   The VARIABLES= List

The variable list following the keyword VARIABLES= must specify all variables to be included in the analysis of subsequent SCALE= lists. Multiple variable lists may be used to reduce space requirements and improve execution speed (see Section 9.31 on limitations).

Variables may be entered onto the RELIABILITY card according to the usual conventions. Lists of variable names may be entered in any order as long as they are separated by common delimiters (commas or blanks). Lists of adjacent variables may be declared by means of the usual TO convention. The two types of lists may be intermixed, producing a variable list of the following type:

```
VARIABLES=VARA,VARD,VARF TO VARN,VARX/
```

All other rules of syntax applying to variable names must be followed, and of course, no variable may be included in the list that has not been previously defined via a VARIABLE LIST or DATA LIST or by a variable transformation.

9.16   Specifying SCALE= Items

The SCALE= specifications allow the user to define all or any subset of the variables in the preceding VARIABLES= list to be a particular scale. For the identification of output, each scale is associated with a label of 1 to 8 alphanumeric characters, consisting of the letters A to Z and digits 0 to 9. For example,

```
SCALE(ATTITUDE)=VAR002 TO VAR004/
```

Scale names may duplicate variable names. Variables may be entered into the scale list according to the usual conventions. However, the keyword TO causes variables to be listed on the output in the order they appear in the preceding variable list of the RELIABILITY card, not as they appear in the file. At least one SCALE= specification must be entered; there is no default.

9.17   Selection of Reliability Analysis: MODEL=

The user selects the desired reliability analysis by inserting the keyword MODEL= directly after the scale list. The keyword is then followed by another keyword specifying the type of analysis to be employed. The keywords are listed below:

ALPHA	Cronbach's α and standardized item α (Default)
SPLIT	Split-half coefficients
GUTTMAN	Guttman's lower bounds for true reliability
STRICTPARALLEL	Maximum likelihood reliability estimate
PARALLEL	Maximum likelihood reliability estimate

The MODEL= specification may be omitted, in which case the ALPHA model is assumed and executed. The MODEL= specifications for the split-half and Guttman coefficients (λ_4) split the items in the scale to create two sets with an equal number of items. In the event the scale contains an odd number of items, the user may override this assignment by specifying the number of items which are contained in the second of the two sets. For example, the following command will result in an analysis with four items in the first half and two items in the second half of the scale.

```
RELIABILITY    VARIABLES=VAR001 TO VAR006/
               SCALE(TEST)=VAR001 TO VAR006/
               MODEL=SPLIT(2)/
```

The actual coefficients computed by RELIABILITY are diverse. Only a few of them were mentioned in the discussion of the assumptions. This section describes these coefficients in computational terms. It discusses only a few of the many possible sets of uses for them and their interpretations.

9.18 The MODEL=ALPHA Specification

This is the default model for the system. Two reliability coefficients are computed by the subprogram: Cronbach's α and a coefficient labeled standardized item α. α is perhaps the most widely used reliability coefficient. If the data are in dichotomous form, α is equivalent to the reliability coefficient KR-20 (Kuder-Richardson-20). If we let S_i^2 be the variance of the measuring instrument item (subtest, variable, column) i, and let S_T^2 be the variance of the sum over the k items, then coefficient α is calculated by the following formula:

$$\alpha = \frac{k}{k-1}\left(1 - \frac{\sum_{i=1}^{k} S_i^2}{S_T^2}\right)$$

Coefficient α is the maximum likelihood estimate of the reliability coefficient if the parallel model is assumed to be true. It is also a member of the Guttman family of coefficients (λ_3) and has been generated under a broad variety of other theoretical assumptions as well. If only two items are used, α is also equal to Guttman's split-half coefficient (λ_4).

The standardized item α is closely related to α. In essence, if the observations on each item are standardized by dividing them by the standard deviation of the item, α would have the value calculated by the subprogram as standardized item α. The computational formula is given by

$$\alpha_s = \frac{k\bar{r}}{1 + (k-1)\bar{r}}$$

where r is the average correlation between items. When there are only two items, the α value is equivalent to the standard Spearman-Brown split-half coefficient.

9.19 The MODEL=SPLIT Specification

Specification of MODEL=SPLIT after a scale list causes four coefficients to be computed. In general, the split model partitions the variables in the scale into two subsets. For each subset or subscale (form) the sum is computed and the reliability calculations make use of only the information contained in the two sums for each case.

The first coefficient calculated is the correlation between forms or between halves. If T_1 and T_2 are the sums of the items in parts 1 and 2, the correlation between halves is the correlation between the sums T_1 and T_2. This correlation measures the extent to which the two halves measure the same thing. It is often used to determine how stable responses to two tests are over time. Another frequent use is when one half is an established test and the other half of the split is a new test being considered for use.

The Spearman-Brown split-half coefficient is given by the following formula:

$$r_{SB} = \frac{2r_{xy}}{1 + r_{xy}}$$

where r_{xy} is the correlation between the two parts. In general, it was designed to answer the question, given two equally reliable parts, how reliable would the whole be if they were combined into one?

The unequal length Spearman-Brown coefficient corrects the Spearman-Brown prophecy formula for unequal reliabilities introduced by having a different number of items in the two parts.

The fourth coefficient, the Guttman split-half, is similar in form to the Spearman-Brown but does not necessarily presume equal reliabilities or equal variances. In fact, when only two items are used, the Guttman split-half is the maximum likelihood estimate of the reliability of the composite under the τ-equivalent model. The computational formula is given by

$$r_G = \frac{2(S_T^2 - S_{T_1}^2 - S_{T_2}^2)}{S_T^2}$$

In words, the Guttman split-half is coefficient α applied to a two-item scale.

Finally, when the split model is requested, coefficient α is computed for each of the two parts.

9.20 The MODEL=GUTTMAN Specification

Guttman (1945) proposed a minimum set of assumptions under which the reliability of a simple sum of scores across items, an equally weighted composite scale, could be estimated. Under these assumptions, all estimates underestimate the true reliability. Strategically, one should pick the largest of the six coefficients computed by the subprogram since one can be sure that the true reliability is higher. Of course, if certain assumptions can be made, then better estimates are possible. The computational formulas used by the subprogram are identical to those given by Guttman.

9.21   The MODEL=PARALLEL Specification

The parallel model has been discussed in some detail. The maximum likelihood estimate of the reliability coefficient in the population is coefficient α. This estimate, like many maximum-likelihood estimates, is biased. A correction for the bias was derived by Kriatoff (1969) and is also computed.

In addition, the subprogram computes the estimated true score variance of an individual item (β^2 in the notation used in this section), the estimated error variance of an individual item (σ^2) and the reliability of an individual item.

9.22   CALCULATING COMPOSITE SCORES

Composite scores or scale scores are not computed by RELIABILITY. However, once a set of items has been analyzed, a composite or set of composites may be constructed using COMPUTE commands. As a general rule of thumb, it is often more useful to compute an average over the variables in the scale for each case rather than a simple sum. This has the advantage of allowing the interpretation of the scale scores in the original metric of the items. For weighted composites this is not as appropriate, of course.

Missing data present special problems in constructing composite scores. Subprogram RELIABILITY options permit either ignoring the search for missing data or listwise deletion of missing data. Two procedures might be considered for handling missing data.

First, one could, before the reliability analysis is carried out, delete any item which has more than 20% of the cases with missing values. Then, replace the remaining missing data on each variable with the mean value of its nonmissing observations. Finally, carry out the reliability analysis. In most instances, this will result in a slight underestimate of the true reliability.

The second alternative uses the same first step but then uses listwise deletion of the missing data to estimate the reliability of a composite. Then to construct a composite score for a case with a missing value, the average value on the non-missing items is used as a scale score provided the case has missing data on fewer than 25% or so of the items. For example, suppose we wish to compute composite scores for a 5 item scale with some missing data. The following SPSS commands would be used if the items had missing data coded as 99.

```
COUNT          NMISS=V1 TO V5(99)
COMPUTE        SCALE=V1+V2+V3+V4+V5
COMPUTE        SCALE=SCALE-99*NMISS
IF             (NMISS GT 1) SCALE=99
IF             (NMISS LE 1) SCALE=SCALE/(5-NMISS)
MISSING VALUES SCALE(99)
```

The COUNT command counts the number of items on which a case has missing data. The first COMPUTE card causes a new variable SCALE to be calculated equal to the sum of the five items in the scale. The second COMPUTE command removes the error in the sum introduced by the missing data. The first IF command assigns a value of 99 to the case if the case has more than one missing value on the items in the scale. The second IF command computes the average score for the case on the items with no missing data. Finally, we inform the system that the newly created variable SCALE has missing data coded as 99.

9.23   SPECIAL CONVENTION
FOR MATRIX INPUT AND OUTPUT

Subprogram RELIABILITY allows the user to enter the data in the usual form as cases or observations (which may be in raw data form or reside in an SPSS system file) or, alternately, to input a correlation matrix or covariance matrix directly to RELIABILITY. This feature enables the user to skip the first and costly step—the computation of a covariance matrix. However, a number of special conventions must be followed.

9.24   Control Cards Required

When either correlation matrices or covariance matrices are being entered, the user must inform the system via the OPTIONS card. In addition, the user must prepare the following SPSS control cards:

- A VARIABLE LIST card is prepared in the usual manner. The list must include all the variables in the matrix. This list serves to name the variables so that they may be appropriately labeled at various points in the output.
- An INPUT MEDIUM card containing one of the following keywords—CARD, TAPE, DISK, OTHER—specifying the location of the matrix must also be prepared. When matrices are located on a medium other than CARD, the JCL cards for a raw data input file must also be prepared.
- An N OF CASES card must also be prepared containing the user's best estimate of the number of cases upon which the matrix was computed. This card is used only for purposes of computing tests of significance and has nothing to do with the number of variables in the matrix or the number of cards to be read.
- A READ MATRIX card must follow the OPTIONS card or the STATISTICS card and must precede the actual matrix if it is entered on cards. The READ MATRIX card serves the same purpose as the READ INPUT DATA card.
- Some data definition cards and data modification cards are not applicable to matrices and therefore may not be entered. For similar reasons, matrices may not be retained as SPSS system files.

9.25 Optional Matrix Forms

Subprogram RELIABILITY accepts either covariance matrices (Option 4) or correlation matrices (Option 5). These matrices may be square (default) or triangular (Option 6). Each row of the matrix is assumed to begin on a new card. Triangular matrices are assumed to be output lower left by rows including the diagonal. If a triangular matrix is formatted as a single vector rather than with each row beginning on a new card, Option 12 must be specified. Correlation matrices must be preceded by the item standard deviations.

9.26 Output of Covariance Matrices and Means

Subprogram RELIABILITY does not have the capability to output correlation matrices for input into other SPSS procedures. It can however, output means and covariance matrices for its own use and for use by other programs. A vector of means and a covariance matrix is output for each VARIABLES= list. Means are normally output with a format of (5E16.7) and triangular covariance matrices are output with a format of (4D20.13). Each row of the matrix begins on a new card unless Option 13 is specified. In this case, each matrix will be output as a single vector. For output of matrices, the user must also prepare the system commands (JCL) for your operating system. See the appropriate operating system appendix in this manual or consult your local SPSS Coordinator.

9.27 Matrix Formats

Correlation matrices are assumed to have the standard SPSS format (8F10.7). Means and standard deviations are assumed to be entered in the form (8F10.4) when correlation matrices are entered. Covariance matrices are assumed to have the format (4D20.13). Vectors of means, if entered (Option 7), are assumed to have the format (5E16.7) when entered with a covariance matrix. If the user wishes to have the subprogram use a different format, the RELIABILITY control card must be modified.

```
RELIABILITY      FORMATS=INPUT(i/j),OUTPUT(k/l),
                 VARIABLES= ...
```

If only the input formats are to be modified, the keyword OUTPUT need not be specified. If only output formats are being modified the keyword INPUT may be deleted. Following the keywords INPUT or OUTPUT, in parentheses separated by a slash are placed the format selection numbers. The first format selection number specifies a format for the means (and standard deviations if a correlation matrix is being entered) and the second format selection number specifies a format for the matrix. If the user wishes to modify one but not both of the default formats, the corresponding number may be deleted but the slash must appear. The valid format selection numbers and the format which will be used are

Selection Number	Format
1	(8F10.0)
2	(8F10.4)
3	(8F10.7)
4	(5D15.7)
5	(4D20.13)

The following example specifies that the means have a format of (8F10.0), the covariance matrix the default format of (4D20.13) for input, the means a format of (8F10.4) for output, and a matrix format of (8F10.4) for output.

```
RELIABILITY     FORMATS=INPUT(1/),OUTPUT(2/2),
                VARIABLES= ...
```

9.28   ALTERNATIVE COMPUTING METHODS

The RELIABILITY procedure employs one of two different computing methods, depending upon the MODEL= specification and upon the options and statistics specified.

Method 1 does not involve computing a covariance matrix. It is faster than method 2 and, for large problems, requires much less workspace. However, it can compute coefficients for only two models (ALPHA and SPLIT), and it does not allow computation of a number of optional statistics, nor does it allow matrix input or output. Subprogram RELIABILITY selects this method whenever it can.

Method 2 does involve computing a covariance matrix for each VARIABLES= list. It is slower than method 1 and requires more space. It allows the procedure to compute all the optional statistics, use any model, and perform any of the optional processing described here.

The two methods differ in one other important respect: Method 1 will continue processing a scale containing variables with zero variance and leave the items in the scale. This treatment is usually preferred. Method 2 will delete the variable (or variables) with zero variance from the scale and continue processing if the deletions leave at least two variables in the scale. If item deletion is required, then method 2 can be forced by using Option 14.

The procedure selects the computing method. Method 1 will be used unless:

- A model other than ALPHA or SPLIT is specified, or
- Any of Options 4 through 14 is specified, or
- Any of Statistics 2, 3, 5, 6, 7, 8, or 12 is specified.

Put another way, if you wish to take advantage of the extra efficiency of method 1, you must:

- Specify only ALPHA or SPLIT models.
- Use only Options 1, 3, 15, and 16.
- Use only Statistics 1, 4, 9, 10 and 11.

9.29   OPTIONS AVAILABLE
FOR SUBPROGRAM RELIABILITY

The default options for subprogram RELIABILITY assume raw data are to be processed using listwise deletion of missing cases and that extended variable labels will be printed. The user will note that the pairwise deletion of missing data option is not available in this subprogram. However, a much greater choice of options for the handling of matrices is available.

Like many SPSS procedures, the options are specified by the insertion of an OPTIONS card in the control-card deck immediately following the procedure card.

OPTION 1   *Inclusion of missing data.* This option causes RELIABILITY to include all cases in the calculations regardless of any missing data values which may be defined. A slight increase in execution speed may result.

Default Option— *Listwise Deletion of Missing Data.* When Option 1 is not specified, cases with missing values are automatically eliminated from all calculations of coefficients within a variable list. Thus, the number of cases will be the same for all scales subsumed under a variable list but may differ between variable lists.

OPTION 2   *Not Used.*

OPTION 3   *Suppression of variable labels.* Selection of this option causes the search for and printing of variable labels to be bypassed. A slight increase in execution speed may result.

OPTION 4   *Input is a covariance matrix.* See Sections 9.23 through 9.27.

OPTION 5   *Input is a vector of standard deviations and a correlation matrix.* See Sections 9.23 through 9.27.

OPTION 6   *Input matrix is triangular.* See Sections 9.23 through 9.27.

OPTION 7   *A vector of means precedes the matrix.* See Sections 9.23 through 9.27.

OPTION 8   *Output covariance matrix.* Specification of Option 8 causes a covariance matrix to be output for each variable list. See Sections 9.23 through 9.27.

OPTION 9   *Index matrices using SPSS VARIABLE LIST.* Option 9 indicates that the user will enter only one large matrix and that subsets of variables from the matrix will be used. The use of this option is convenient when a large number of variables are to be read in and several VARIABLES= lists on the procedure card contain many variables in common. Option 9 cannot be used without Option 4 or 5 and must not be used with Option 6 or 12.

OPTION 10   *Stop after output of matrices and vectors.* Option 10 causes all scale analysis to be bypassed.

OPTION 11   *Output means.* Option 11 causes a vector of means to be produced on the raw output unit for each VARIABLES= list of the RELIABILITY procedure card.

OPTION 12   *Input matrix is formatted as a vector.* Option 12 informs the subprogram that the triangular input matrix is formatted continuously as a single vector rather than having each row of the matrix begin on a new card (record). Matrices in this form occupy many fewer cards. Option 9 must not be used with Option 12 and either Option 4 or 5 must be specified if Option 12 is used.

OPTION 13   *Output matrix as single vector.* RELIABILITY outputs triangular covariance matrices. Option 13 causes this matrix to be output as a single vector rather than having each row begin on a new card (record). A considerable saving in cards may result.

OPTION 14   *Solution method 2.* Specification of Option 14 forces the subprogram to use solution method 2 (using covariance matrices). This option should be selected if you want any of the following:

Deletion of items with zero variance from scales in which they occur. When method 1 is used, these items are left in the scales. The treatment used affects coefficient α, the Tukey estimate (Statistic 11), and the analysis of variance (Statistic 10).

Squared multiple correlations. These are included in the item total statistics (Statistic 9) when method 2 is used, but not when method 1 is used.

Standardized item α. This statistic is not computed using method 1.

Note that specification of a model other than SPLIT or ALPHA, specification of any of Statistics 2, 3, 5, 6, 7, 8, or 12, or any of Options 4 through 13 also force use of method 2. See Section 9.28 for further details.

OPTION 15   *Friedman's chi-square.* Option 15 requests the subprogram to calculate Friedman's two-way analysis of variance by ranks statistic rather than the usual F test for analysis of variance. Option 15 affects only Statistic 10. Kendall's coefficient of concordance is also calculated. Note that the data must be in the form of ranks prior to input.

OPTION 16   *Cochran's Q.* Option 16 is identical in effect to Option 15, but the data are assumed to be dichotomous.

9.30 STATISTICS AVAILABLE
FOR SUBPROGRAM RELIABILITY

The optional statistics which may be obtained from the subprogram are selected by the use of a STATISTICS card. The keyword ALL may be substituted for the numbered list.

STATISTIC 1   *Item means and standard deviations.*

STATISTIC 2   *Inter-item variance-covariance matrix.*

STATISTIC 3   *Inter-item correlations.*

STATISTIC 4   *Scale means and scale variances.*

STATISTIC 5   *Summary statistics for item means.* The average item mean over the number of items, the variance of the item means, the largest item mean, the smallest, the range of the item means, and the ratio of the largest to the smallest.

STATISTIC 6   *Summary statistics for item variances.* The output from Statistic 6 is identical to Statistic 5 but is based upon item variances rather than item means.

STATISTIC 7   *Summary statistics for inter-item covariances.* The output from Statistic 7 is identical to Statistics 5 and 6 but is based upon covariances.

STATISTIC 8   *Summary statistics for inter-item correlations.* The output from Statistic 8 is identical to Statistics 5, 6 and 7 but is based upon correlations.

STATISTIC 9   *Item total statistics.* The output for Statistic 9 includes five statistics dealing with the relationship between the individual items and the items as a set. For each item the following are calculated.

Scale mean if item deleted. This is the mean the scale scores would have if the particular item were deleted from the scale.

Scale variance if item deleted. This is the variance the scale scores would have if the particular item were deleted from the scale.

Corrected item total correlations. For each item, the correlation between that item's score and the scale scores computed from the other items in the set.

Squared multiple correlations. For each item, the item is regressed upon the remaining items in the set making up the scale and the squared multiple correlation coefficient computed. (Not computed if Method 1 is used. See Section 9.28).

Alpha if item deleted. For each item, the reliability coefficient, Cronbach's α, is computed from the other items in the scale.

STATISTIC 10   *Analysis of variance table.*

STATISTIC 11   *Tukey test for additivity.*

STATISTIC 12   *Hotelling's T^2.* This statistic requires considerable extra time to compute. It requires inversion of a matrix of order $k-1$, where k is the number of variables in the scale. Hotelling's T^2 is computed as follows:

Let C be a $k-1$ by k matrix consisting of a $k-1$ by $k-1$ identity matrix with a column of -1's appended on the right. Let X be the column vector of variable means (a k by 1 matrix).

Let X be the vector of item means.

Let $Y = CX$ (a $k-1$ by 1 matrix).

Let S be the covariance matrix of the items (a k by k matrix).

Let n be the sum of weights of the cases.

Let V = the inverse of CSC'.

then $T^2 = n\,Y'V\,Y$

9.31 LIMITATIONS FOR SUBPROGRAM RELIABILITY

- No more than 10 VARIABLES= lists may appear on a given RELIABILITY procedure card.
- No more than 50 SCALE(name)= lists may be defined on a given RELIABILITY procedure card.
- The maximum number of variables that may be specified (including duplicates) on the combined VARIABLES= lists is limited to 500.
- The maximum number of variables that may be specified on any given SCALE(name)= list is limited to 500.
- The maximum number of variables referenced in the combined SCALE(name)= lists (including variables duplicated in 2 or more lists) under a given RELIABILITY procedure is limited to 1000.
- The amount of space required for the execution of subprogram RELIABILITY is determined by

WORKSPACE = 8(NVAR + TRIANGLE + MATRIX)

$$NVAR = \sum_I N_I$$

where N(I) is the number of variables on the Ith VARIABLES= list.

$$TRIANGLE = \sum_I \frac{N_I(N_I + 1)}{2}$$

MATRIX = MAX(MAX + 3)

where MAX is the number of variables in the longest scale list.

The following exceptions apply to the calculation of WORKSPACE:

- If only one scale list is specified TRIANGLE = 0.
- If insufficient core is requested, the subprogram will delete variable lists in the reverse order they were entered until the allocated core is sufficient.

- If calculation method 1 is used, the space is calculated according to the formula:

WORKSPACE = 24(NV + NSV + NS)

where

NV is the number of variables in the combined variable lists.
NSV is the number of variables in the combined scale lists.
NS is the number of scales.

9.32   A NOTE FOR USERS OF PREVIOUS VERSIONS OF RELIABILITY

SPSS RELIABILITY is essentially the same as the version distributed for SPSS Release 6 by Iowa State University with modifications. If you have used that version, please note these changes:

- Option 14 still deals with selection of a computing method, but its sense has been reversed and the subprogram will select a computing method if you let it.
- Options 15 and 16 (dealing with the handling of zero variance items) have been dropped. The treatments they specified are now always used.
- Options 17 and 18 (Friedman's chi-square test and Cochran's Q test) are now Options 15 and 16.
- The limitations on the number of variables in the combined VARIABLES= lists, in each SCALES= list, and in the combined SCALES= lists have been increased to 500, 500, and 1000 respectively.
- The WORKSPACE required when Option 3 is not used has been reduced.
- Hotelling's T^2 (Statistic 12) has been rewritten to give correct results. It now requires considerably more computation time.

9.33   EXAMPLES

The following four examples combine most of the major facilities provided by RELIABILITY. They are not exaustive of the applications, but they are representative and should be helpful.

9.34   Alpha Model, All Statistics, and Calculation Method 2

The first example uses the default model, ALPHA. Since all statistics are requested, method 2 is used in calculating the reliabiility coefficients.

```
TASK NAME       DEFAULT MODEL USING METHOD 2 AND ALL STATISTICS
RELIABILITY     VARIABLES=VAR003 TO VAR010/
                SCALE(NOSPLIT) = VAR003 TO VAR010/
OPTIONS         1 3
STATISTICS      ALL
```

Figure 9.34   Default ALPHA Model—Method 2 and All Statistics

```
RELIABILITY ANALYSIS
DEFAULT MODEL USING METHOD 2 AND ALL STATISTICS          11/21/76      PAGE    3
FILE   NONAME   (CREATION DATE = 11/21/76)

* * * * * * * * * R E L I A B I L I T Y   A N A L Y S I S   F O R   S C A L E   ( N O S P L I T  ) * * * * *
```

		MEANS	STD DEV	CASES
1.	VAR003	2.82222	1.69610	45.0
2.	VAR004	-3.46667	1.82906	45.0
3.	VAR005	2.68889	2.40097	45.0
4.	VAR006	0.73333	3.14354	45.0
5.	VAR007	-0.42222	3.26475	45.0
6.	VAR008	-3.28889	1.35885	45.0
7.	VAR009	1.95556	2.53122	45.0
8.	VAR010	2.57778	1.99418	45.0

```
            COVARIANCE MATRIX

            VAR003    VAR004    VAR005    VAR006    VAR007    VAR008    VAR009    VAR010

VAR003      2.8768

VAR004     -0.3348    3.3455

VAR005      1.1025   -0.0121    5.7646

VAR006      1.2470    0.3500    2.1879    9.8818

VAR007      0.9232    0.0030   -0.2025    1.3167   10.6586

VAR008     -0.6207    0.6803    0.1581    0.1712   -1.0566    1.8465

VAR009      1.1283   -1.4758    0.8949   -0.7167    0.4581   -1.9449    6.4071

VAR010      1.1278   -0.9742    0.9793   -0.1833    2.2268   -1.8747    3.6172    3.9768
```

```
RELIABILITY ANALYSIS                                          11/21/76     PAGE    4
DEFAULT MODEL USING METHOD 2 AND ALL STATISTICS
FILE   NONAME   (CREATION DATE = 11/21/76)

* * * * * * * * * R E L I A B I L I T Y   A N A L Y S I S   F O R   S C A L E   ( N O S P L I T  ) * * * * * * * * *
            CORRELATION MATRIX

            VAR003    VAR004    VAR005    VAR006    VAR007    VAR008    VAR009    VAR010

VAR003      1.00000

VAR004     -0.10794    1.00000

VAR005      0.27074   -0.00276    1.00000

VAR006      0.23388    0.06087    0.28988    1.00000

VAR007      0.16673    0.00051   -0.02584    0.12829    1.00000

VAR008     -0.26932    0.27372    0.04845    0.04008   -0.23816    1.00000

VAR009      0.26281   -0.31876    0.14726   -0.09007    0.05543   -0.56547    1.00000

VAR010      0.33343   -0.26710    0.20453   -0.02925    0.34203   -0.69184    0.71660    1.00000
```

```
     # OF CASES =    45.0

STATISTICS FOR          MEAN       VARIANCE      STD DEV    # VARIABLES
          SCALE        3.60000     63.10909      7.94412        8
    ITEM   MEANS       MEAN        MINIMUM       MAXIMUM      RANGE       MAX/MIN      VARIANCE

                       0.45000    -3.46667       2.82222      6.28889    -0.81410      6.79926
    ITEM  VARIANCES    MEAN        MINIMUM       MAXIMUM      RANGE       MAX/MIN      VARIANCE

                       5.59470     1.84646      10.65859      8.81212     5.77243     10.54634
 INTER-ITEM COVARIANCES MEAN       MINIMUM       MAXIMUM      RANGE       MAX/MIN      VARIANCE

                       0.32771    -1.94495       3.61717      5.56212    -1.85978      1.56217
 INTER-ITEM CORRELATIONS MEAN      MINIMUM       MAXIMUM      RANGE       MAX/MIN      VARIANCE

                       0.03460    -0.69184       0.71660      1.40844    -1.03578      0.08380
```

```
RELIABILITY ANALYSIS                                          11/21/76     PAGE    5
DEFAULT MODEL USING METHOD 2 AND ALL STATISTICS
FILE   NONAME   (CREATION DATE = 11/21/76)

* * * * * * * * * R E L I A B I L I T Y   A N A L Y S I S   F O R   S C A L E   ( N O S P L I T  ) * * * * * * * * *
ITEM-TOTAL STATISTICS         SCALE        SCALE      CORRECTED

                              MEAN         VARIANCE    ITEM-       SQUARED      ALPHA
                              IF ITEM      IF ITEM     TOTAL       MULTIPLE     IF ITEM
                              DELETED      DELETED     CORRELATION CORRELATION  DELETED

                VAR003        0.77778      51.08586    0.37724     0.20627      0.21022
                VAR004        7.06667      63.29091   -0.12120     0.11909      0.40330
                VAR005        0.91111      47.12828    0.30991     0.24340      0.20139
                VAR006        2.86667      44.48182    0.20857     0.16410      0.25195
                VAR007        4.02222      45.11313    0.16731     0.22846      0.28484
                VAR008        6.88889      70.23737   -0.39404     0.53820      0.45390
                VAR009        1.64444      52.77980    0.10664     0.57668      0.31895
                VAR010        1.02222      49.29495    0.35130     0.71283      0.20150
```

```
         ANALYSIS OF VARIANCE

SOURCE OF VARIATION            SS         DF     MEAN SQUARE       F        PROBABILITY

 BETWEEN PEOPLE             347.10000     44       7.88864

 WITHIN PEOPLE             3764.00000    315      11.94921
   BETWEEN MEASURES        2141.76667      7     305.96667      58.09136       0.0
   RESIDUAL                1622.23333    308       5.26699
     NONADDITIVITY           69.26457      1      69.26457      13.69263       0.00035
     BALANCE               1552.96877    307       5.05853
 TOTAL                    4111.10000    359      11.45153
 GRAND  MEAN =               0.45000
```

```
TUKEY  ESTIMATE OF POWER TO WHICH OBSERVATIONS MUST BE RAISED TO ACHIEVE ADDITIVITY =        0.9175851

HOTELLINGS T-SQUARED =        396.81644        F =        48.95787

DEGREES OF FREEDOM * * NUMERATOR =    7    DENOMINATOR=   38    PROBABILITY = 0.00000

     RELIABILITY COEFFICIENTS            8   ITEMS


     ALPHA =  0.33233        STANDARDIZED ITEM ALPHA =  0.22282
```

9.35 Split Model, Zero Variance, and Calculation Method 1

This example demonstrates the processing of variables with zero variance using method 1.

```
TASK NAME       HANDLING OF ZERO VAR USING METHOD 1
RELIABILITY     VARIABLES = VAR031,VAR003 TO VAR005,VAR032,
                VAR006 TO VAR008,VAR033,VAR034,VAR009,VAR010 /
                SCALE(NOSPLIT) = VAR031 TO VAR010 /
                SCALE(SPLIT) = VAR031 TO VAR010 / MODEL=SPLIT
OPTIONS         1 3
STATISTICS      1 4 9 10 11
```

Figure 9.35   Handling of Zero Variance—SPLIT Model and Method 1

```
RELIABILITY ANALYSIS                                          11/21/76      PAGE    7
HANDLING OF ZERO VAR USING METHOD 1
FILE   NONAME   (CREATION DATE = 11/21/76)

* * * * * * * * * R E L I A B I L I T Y   A N A L Y S I S   F O R   S C A L E   ( N O S P L I T  ) * * * * * *

                                    MEANS              STD DEV           CASES
          1.    VAR031            2.00000              0.0               45.0
          2.    VAR003            2.82222              1.69610           45.0
          3.    VAR004           -3.46667              1.82906           45.0
          4.    VAR005            2.68889              2.40097           45.0
          5.    VAR032            1.00000              0.0               45.0
          6.    VAR006            0.73333              3.14354           45.0
          7.    VAR007           -0.42222              3.26475           45.0
          8.    VAR008           -3.28889              1.35885           45.0
          9.    VAR033            3.00000              0.0               45.0
         10.    VAR034            4.00000              0.0               45.0
         11.    VAR009            1.95556              2.53122           45.0
         12.    VAR010            2.57778              1.99418           45.0

STATISTICS FOR          MEAN          VARIANCE        STD DEV    # VARIABLES
     SCALE           13.60000         63.10909        7.94412        12
```

ITEM-TOTAL STATISTICS	SCALE MEAN IF ITEM DELETED	SCALE VARIANCE IF ITEM DELETED	CORRECTED ITEM-TOTAL CORRELATION	ALPHA IF ITEM DELETED
VAR031	11.60000	63.10909	0.0	0.31987
VAR003	10.77778	51.08586	0.37724	0.19821
VAR004	17.06667	63.29091	-0.12120	0.38025
VAR005	10.91111	47.12828	0.30991	0.18988
VAR032	12.60000	63.10909	0.0	0.31987
VAR006	12.86667	44.48182	0.20857	0.23755
VAR007	14.02222	45.11313	0.16731	0.26856
VAR008	16.88889	70.23737	-0.39404	0.42796
VAR033	10.60000	63.10909	0.0	0.31987
VAR034	9.60000	63.10909	0.0	0.31987
VAR009	11.64444	52.77980	0.10664	0.30073
VAR010	11.02222	49.29495	0.35130	0.18999

```
RELIABILITY ANALYSIS                                          11/21/76      PAGE    8
HANDLING OF ZERO VAR USING METHOD 1
FILE   NONAME   (CREATION DATE = 11/21/76)

* * * * * * * * * R E L I A B I L I T Y   A N A L Y S I S   F O R   S C A L E   ( N O S P L I T  ) * * * * * *


                ANALYSIS OF VARIANCE
```

SOURCE OF VARIATION	SS	DF	MEAN SQUARE	F	PROBABILITY
BETWEEN PEOPLE	231.40000	44	5.25909		
WITHIN PEOPLE	4609.00000	495	9.31111		
BETWEEN MEASURES	2871.06667	11	261.00606	72.68802	0.0
RESIDUAL	1737.93333	484	3.59077		
NONADDITIVITY	7.18315	1	7.18315	2.00460	0.15341
BALANCE	1730.75019	483	3.58333		
TOTAL	4840.40000	539	8.98033		

```
GRAND MEAN =        1.13333

TUKEY ESTIMATE OF POWER TO WHICH OBSERVATIONS MUST BE RAISED TO ACHIEVE ADDITIVITY =        0.9134019



     RELIABILITY COEFFICIENTS

     N OF CASES =     45.0        N OF ITEMS = 12

     ALPHA =  0.31723
```

```
RELIABILITY ANALYSIS                                      11/21/76       PAGE    9
HANDLING OF ZERO VAR USING METHOD 1
FILE   NONAME   (CREATION DATE = 11/21/76)

* * * * * * * * *  R E L I A B I L I T Y   A N A L Y S I S   F O R   S C A L E   ( S P L I T      ) * * * * *

                                  MEANS              STD DEV            CASES

             1.    VAR031          2.00000            0.0               45.0
             2.    VAR003          2.82222            1.69610           45.0
             3.    VAR004         -3.46667            1.82906           45.0
             4.    VAR005          2.68889            2.40097           45.0
             5.    VAR032          1.00000            0.0               45.0
             6.    VAR006          0.73333            3.14354           45.0
             7.    VAR007         -0.42222            3.26475           45.0
             8.    VAR008         -3.28889            1.35885           45.0
             9.    VAR033          3.00000            0.0               45.0
            10.    VAR034          4.00000            0.0               45.0
            11.    VAR009          1.95556            2.53122           45.0
            12.    VAR010          2.57778            1.99418           45.0

STATISTICS FOR         MEAN         VARIANCE        STD DEV    # VARIABLES
            PART 1     5.77778      30.94949        5.56323         6
            PART 2     7.82222      25.74040        5.07350         6
            SCALE     13.60000      63.10909        7.94412        12

ITEM-TOTAL STATISTICS           SCALE         SCALE       CORRECTED
                                 MEAN        VARIANCE       ITEM-          ALPHA
                                IF ITEM      IF ITEM        TOTAL         IF ITEM
                                DELETED      DELETED      CORRELATION     DELETED

              VAR031           11.60000      63.10909       0.0           0.31987
              VAR003           10.77778      51.08586       0.37724       0.19821
              VAR004           17.06667      63.29091      -0.12120       0.38025
              VAR005           10.91111      47.12828       0.30991       0.18988
              VAR032           12.60000      63.10909       0.0           0.31987
              VAR006           12.86667      44.48182       0.20857       0.23755
              VAR007           14.02222      45.11313       0.16731       0.26856
              VAR008           16.88889      70.23737      -0.39404       0.42796
              VAR033           10.60000      63.10909       0.0           0.31987
              VAR034            9.60000      63.10909       0.0           0.31987
              VAR009           11.64444      52.77980       0.10664       0.30073
              VAR010           11.02222      49.29495       0.35130       0.18999


RELIABILITY ANALYSIS                                      11/21/76       PAGE   10
HANDLING OF ZERO VAR USING METHOD 1
FILE   NONAME   (CREATION DATE = 11/21/76)

* * * * * * * * *  R E L I A B I L I T Y   A N A L Y S I S   F O R   S C A L E   ( S P L I T      ) * * * * *


                    ANALYSIS OF VARIANCE

   SOURCE OF VARIATION              SS        DF      MEAN SQUARE         F          PROBABILITY

   BETWEEN PEOPLE               231.40000     44       5.25909
   WITHIN  PEOPLE              4609.00000    495       9.31111
     BETWEEN MEASURES          2871.06667     11     261.00606        72.68802       0.0
     RESIDUAL                  1737.93333    484       3.59077
       NONADDITIVITY              7.18315      1       7.18315         2.00460        0.15341
       BALANCE                 1730.75019    483       3.58333
   TOTAL                       4840.40000    539       8.98033

   GRAND MEAN =           1.13333

   TUKEY ESTIMATE OF POWER TO WHICH OBSERVATIONS MUST BE RAISED TO ACHIEVE ADDITIVITY =        0.9134019


        RELIABILITY COEFFICIENTS

        N OF CASES =      45.0          N OF ITEMS = 12

        CORRELATION BETWEEN FORMS =  0.11371         EQUAL-LENGTH SPEARMAN-BROWN =  0.20421

        UNEQUAL-LENGTH SPEARMAN-BROWN =  0.20421     GUTTMAN SPLIT-HALF =  0.20343

           6 ITEMS IN PART 1                            6 ITEMS IN PART 2

        ALPHA FOR PART 1 =   0.35209                 ALPHA FOR PART 2 =   0.13294
```

9.36 Repeated Measures Analysis of Variance

This example demonstrates the use of RELIABILITY to do a repeated measures analysis of variance.

```
   RUN NAME       REPEATED MEASURES USING RELIABILITY
   VARIABLES      DRUG1 TO DRUG4
   INPUT FORMAT   FIXED (4F3.0)
   INPUT MEDIUM   CARD
   N OF CASES     5
   TASK NAME      DATA FROM WINER, P. 268
   RELIABILITY    VARIABLES=DRUG1 TO DRUG4/ SCALE(REACTION)=DRUG1 TO DRUG4
   OPTIONS        1 3
   STATISTICS     1 10
   READ INPUT DATA
    30 28 16 34
    14 18 10 22
    24 20 18 30
    38 34 20 44
    26 28 14 30
   FINISH
```

Figure 9.36 **Repeated Measures ANOVA with RELIABILITY**

```
REPEATED MEASURES USING RELIABILITY                    11/21/76    PAGE    2
DATA FROM WINER, P. 268
FILE   NONAME   (CREATION DATE = 11/21/76)

* * * * * * * * * R E L I A B I L I T Y   A N A L Y S I S   F O R   S C A L E   ( R E A C T I O N ) * * * * * *

                              MEANS          STD DEV          CASES

            1.    DRUG1        26.40000       8.76356           5.0
            2.    DRUG2        25.60000       6.54217           5.0
            3.    DRUG3        15.60000       3.84708           5.0
            4.    DRUG4        32.00000       8.00000           5.0


            ANALYSIS OF VARIANCE

  SOURCE OF VARIATION           SS       DF    MEAN SQUARE      F       PROBABILITY

    BETWEEN PEOPLE          680.80000     4    170.20000
    WITHIN  PEOPLE          811.00000    15     54.06667
      BETWEEN MEASURES      698.20000     3    232.73333   24.75887     0.00003
      RESIDUAL              112.80000    12      9.40000
    TOTAL                  1491.80000    19     78.51579

    GRAND MEAN =        24.90000


        RELIABILITY COEFFICIENTS

        N OF CASES =     5.0          N OF ITEMS =  4

        ALPHA =  0.94477
```

9.37 Matrix Input and Various Models

The final example demonstrates using matrix input to RELIABILITY. The same scale is analyzed using different models. The INPUT parameter indicates that the triangular covariance matrix and means have a format of 8F10.4.

```
RUN NAME        REPRODUCE RELIABILITY EXAMPLES
VARIABLE LIST   VAR131 TO VAR133, VAR135 TO VAR138
N OF CASES      240
VAR LABELS      VAR131 ROLE PERFORMANCE INDICATOR A 1/
                VAR132 ROLE PERFORMANCE INDICATOR A 2/
                VAR133 ROLE PERFORMANCE INDICATOR A 3/
                VAR135 ROLE PERFORMANCE INDICATOR B 1/
                VAR136 ROLE PERFORMANCE INDICATOR B 2/
                VAR137 ROLE PERFORMANCE INDICATOR B 3/
                VAR138 ROLE PERFORMANCE INDICATOR B 4/
TASK NAME       DEMONSTRATE MATRIX INPUT FOR RELIABILITY
RELIABILITY     FORMATS = INPUT(1/1)/
                VARIABLES=VAR131 TO VAR138/
                SCALE(RPERF03) = VAR131 TO VAR138/
                MODEL = GUTTMAN/
                SCALE (RPERF04) = VAR131 TO VAR138/
                MODEL = PARALLEL/
                SCALE (RPERF05) = VAR131 TO VAR138/
                MODEL = STRICTPAR/
OPTIONS         3 4 6 7
READ MATRIX
67.33751 74.2      115.35    69.083333390.    76.916666766.5125
3257.3339
283.5    5111.58333
-179.5617 863.9046 2445.6678
-153.2504 1231.1465 973.9367  1962.5840
397.5941 1796.0460 643.4728  1053.0738 2566.9456
112.681   4069.9916 1228.0460 1620.2452 1729.2887 5785.0642
-110.5923 784.2276  412.9705  634.6816  576.3808  903.4613  731.8074
FINISH
```

Figure 9.37 **Matrix Input and Multiple Model Specifications**

```
REPRODUCE RELIABILITY EXAMPLES                         11/21/78    PAGE    5
DEMONSTRATE MATRIX INPUT FOR RELIABILITY
FILE   NONAME   (CREATION DATE = 11/21/76)

* * * * * * * * * R E L I A B I L I T Y   A N A L Y S I S   F O R   S C A L E   ( R P E R F 0 3   ) * * * * * *

    # OF CASES =     240.0


        RELIABILITY COEFFICIENTS            7  ITEMS

        LAMBDA 1 = 0.63323    LAMBDA 2 = 0.78333    LAMBDA 3 = 0.73876
        LAMBDA 4 = 0.84844    LAMBDA 5 = 0.79937    LAMBDA 6 = 0.79076
```

```
* * * * * * * * R E L I A B I L I T Y   A N A L Y S I S   F O R   S C A L E   ( R P E R F 0 4   ) * * * * * *

     # OF CASES =    240.0

   TEST FOR GOODNESS OF FIT OF MODEL        PARALLEL

   CHI SQUARE =      567.99557        DEGREES OF FREEDOM =      26
   LOG OF DETERMINANT OF UNCONSTRAINED MATRIX =     52.8963201
   LOG OF DETERMINANT OF CONSTRAINED MATRIX =       55.2929259
   PROBABILITY =  0.0

       PARAMETER ESTIMATES


   ESTIMATED COMMON VARIANCE =   3122.9980329
        ERROR VARIANCE =    2224.3673471
         TRUE VARIANCE =     898.6306857
   ESTIMATED COMMON INTERITEM CORRELATION =     0.2877462

   ESTIMATED RELIABILITY OF SCALE = 0.7387640
   UNBIASED ESTIMATE OF RELIABILITY = 0.7409501
REPRODUCE RELIABILITY EXAMPLES                                    11/21/76       PAGE    4


DEMONSTRATE MATRIX INPUT FOR RELIABILITY
FILE   NONAME   (CREATION DATE = 11/21/76)

* * * * * * * * R E L I A B I L I T Y   A N A L Y S I S   F O R   S C A L E   ( R P E R F 0 5   ) * * * * * *

      # OF CASES =    240.0

   TEST FOR GOODNESS OF FIT OF MODEL STRICTLYPARALLEL

   CHI SQUARE =      752.97822        DEGREES OF FREEDOM =      32
   LOG OF DETERMINANT OF UNCONSTRAINED MATRIX =     52.8963201
   LOG OF DETERMINANT OF CONSTRAINED MATRIX =       56.0734434
   PROBABILITY =  0.0

       PARAMETER ESTIMATES


   ESTIMATED COMMON MEAN=       79.91429
   ESTIMATED COMMON VARIANCE =   3387.8755955
        ERROR VARIANCE =    2524.1229729
         TRUE VARIANCE =     863.7526226
   ESTIMATED COMMON INTERITEM CORRELATION =     0.2522184
   ESTIMATED RELIABILITY OF SCALE = 0.7024714
   UNBIASED ESTIMATE OF RELIABILITY = 0.7091453
```

9.38 REFERENCES

Guttman, L. A Basis for Analyzing Test-Retest Reliability, *Psychometrika*, 10:4, pp. 255-282, December, 1945.

Joreskog, K. A General Method for Analysis of Covariance Structure, *Biometrika*, 57: pp. 239-251, 1970.

Kristof, W. The Statistical Theory of Stepped-up Reliability Coefficients When the Test Has Been Divided into Several Equivalent Parts, *Psychometrika*, 28: pp. 221-238, 1963.

—————. Statistical Inferences About Error Variance, *Psychometrika*, 28: pp. 129-153, 1963.

—————. Estimation of True Score and Error Variance under Various Equivalence Assumptions, *Psychometrika*, 34: pp. 489-507, 1969.

Mehrens, W. A. and R. L. Ebel (eds.) *Principles of Educational and Psychological Measurement*, Chicago: Rand McNally, 1967.

Novick, M. R. The Axioms and Principal Results of Classical Test Theory, *Journal of Mathematical Psychology*,3: pp. 1-18, 1966.

Novick, M. R. and C. Lewis Coefficient Alpha and the Reliability of Composite Measurements, *Psychometrika*, 32: pp. 1-13, 1967.

Wilks, S. S. Sample Criteria for Testing Equality of Means, Equality of Variances, and Equality of Covariances in a Normal Multivariate Distribution, *Annals of Mathematical Statistics,* 17: pp. 257-281, 1946.

Winer, B. J. *Statistical Principles in Experimental Design*, New York: McGraw-Hill, 1962.

RELIABILITY was written by Dr. David A. Specht, Monsanto Agricultural Products, with the assistance of Thomas A. Bubolz, Iowa State University. Support was provided by the Department of Sociology and Computer Center of Iowa State University. Dr. William J. Kennedy and the staff of the Statistical Programming and Numerical Analysis Section of the Iowa State University Statistical Laboratory provided valuable assistance.

Chapter 10

GET SCSS/SAVE SCSS:
Batch/Conversational Interface

As of Release 8, full communication between the SPSS Batch System and the SCSS Conversational System is established. All functions are provided in SPSS. That is, the communication is provided by allowing the SPSS Batch System to both write and read SCSS masterfiles. The commands are SAVE TRANSPOSE only in Release 7; SAVE SCSS and GET SCSS in Release 8. These functions are known as "transposition" since an SPSS system file is case-oriented, whereas an SCSS masterfile is variable- oriented. This and other differences are noted throughout this chapter.

10.1 SAVING AN SCSS MASTERFILE:
SAVE SCSS (SAVE TRANSPOSE)

SAVE SCSS is the Release 8 version of Release 7 SAVE TRANSPOSE. The following description of the command, its function, and operation applies to both. However, the JCL and core storage requirements are different and are described in separate sections.

SAVE SCSS is an SPSS Batch System (Release 8) command. Its function is to save the current SPSS Batch System file as an SCSS Conversational System masterfile for subsequent analysis with that system. From a mechanical point of view, SAVE SCSS transposes the data on a case-ordered SPSS system file to arrive at a variable-ordered masterfile to be accessed by SCSS.

The SAVE SCSS command has no specification field and is used very much like the SAVE FILE command in that it may appear only at the end of a run immediately prior to the FINISH command. While it is not possible to use either the SORT CASES or the REORDER VARS command on a run in which a transposed file is saved, it is possible to use the KEEP VARS or DELETE VARS and SUBFILE LIST or DELETE SUBFILES commands. The typical order of commands at the end of a run in which a masterfile is to be saved is as follows:

```
DELETE VARS    ALPHA BETA GAMMA
SAVE SCSS
FINISH
```

Note that, for a variety of technical reasons, it is not possible to have either a SAVE FILE or a SAVE ARCHIVE command in a run which includes a SAVE SCSS command. If you wish to save a file in both SPSS and SCSS formats, you must first do a SAVE FILE and then execute a second SPSS run including GET FILE (for the newly-created file) and SAVE SCSS. Although an archival file can not be transposed in its entirety, SAVE SCSS may be used with GET ARCHIVE. Only active variables will be saved in the SCSS masterfile.

SAVE SCSS need not be associated with a GET FILE command. An SCSS masterfile may be created with SPSS using raw data provided all the necessary SPSS data definition commands are supplied.

10.2 Limitations on Saving an SCSS Masterfile

While most of the information contained in an SPSS Batch System file can be converted to similar information in an SCSS Conversational System masterfile, there are some limitations:

- Since names in the SCSS Conversational System may contain only alphabetics and numerics, the name of the SPSS file may not constitute a valid masterfile name (the SPSS Batch System permits certain special characters in names). If the SPSS file name does not constitute a valid masterfile name, the name is changed to NONAME. Because the current version of SCSS identifies files by their data set names rather than by their internal names (as is the case in the SPSS Batch System), this name is of no consequence to the user.

- If the name of any variable does not constitute a valid SCSS system variable name, that variable is dropped from the SCSS masterfile. Names are considered invalid either because they contain special characters or because they are the same as SCSS reserved words. The only four known SCSS reserved words which are not reserved words in the SPSS Batch System are AGAINST, ON, SPSS, and SPSS0001.

- Since the handling of alphabetic values in SCSS is somewhat different from that in SPSS, any variable which has any values which are alphabetic or greater in absolute value than ten trillion are dropped.

- In the SCSS Conversational System, value labels may apply only to integer values. Thus any value labels applying to non-integer values are dropped when SAVE SCSS is executed.

There are a few peculiarities to the SAVE SCSS function which may not be obvious:

- The automatic variable CASWGT becomes the weighting variable for the SCSS Conversational System masterfile if it has any values other than 1.0. CASWGT is saved as a variable on the file even if it is a constant 1.0.

- Since the SPSS concept of subfiles does not exist in SCSS, an existing subfile structure is handled by changing SUBFILE to a discrete variable whose values range from 1 to the number of subfiles and whose value labels are the SPSS subfile names.

- The automatic variable SEQNUM is retained but has actual data associated with it as opposed to being generated every time the data are read as in SPSS.

- As implied earlier, the SPSS file name becomes the SCSS masterfile name. As with SPSS internal files, the SCSS internal file name does not have to be related to the actual external file name, although it is helpful if there is a relationship.

- Two new variables are added to the file. They are of no consequence to the user. However, they do have names which may not be used for other variables: SPSS and SPSS0001. Also, it is not advisable to attempt to analyze these variables in an SCSS session.

10.3 Output from SAVE SCSS

Several pieces of information are provided as the result of executing SAVE SCSS:

- Any occurrences of invalid names are reported with an explanation of what action was taken such as dropping the related entity or changing the name.

- A message is printed detailing the number of variables to be retained on the masterfile, the maximum number of value labels which can be kept for each variable (this is inversely related to the number of variables kept), and the size of the "initial strings". The initial strings are groups of cases for a given variable which are passed to the system SORT utility as a group. Longer initial strings will result in a quicker sort, but the size of the strings is inversely related to the number of variables kept.

- A report is printed for all the variables with valid names which are to be kept. For each variable, the following items are listed: name, label, type, bytes/case, valid cases, minimum, and maximum. The type may be discrete, continuous, or **DROPPED**. Discrete indicates that the variable has all integer values, continuous indicates at least some non-integer values, and **DROPPED** indicates at least some alphabetic or extreme values which caused the variable to be dropped from the masterfile. Bytes/case indicates the packing density of the variable's data on the masterfile. The density may be 1, 2, or 4 bytes per value depending on the nature of the values. Non-negative integer values of less than 255 (which includes most survey values) are packed 4 values per word or 1 byte per value. The valid cases column gives the number of unweighted non-missing cases for the variable. The minimum and maximum columns give the minimum and maximum values for the variable with missing values included.

- An alphabetic listing of the variables retained on the masterfile in a format similar to that used for LIST FILEINFO SORTVARS.

- A statement of the number of variables which were dropped due to invalid values.

10.4 JCL Required for SAVE SCSS
(IBM)

Transposition of an SPSS Batch System case-oriented file into an SCSS Conversational System variable-oriented masterfile is performed with the data resident on a direct access scratch file. The JCL considerations for SAVE SCSS related to this process are listed below. For systems other than IBM/OS, refer to the appropriate appendix in this manual or see your local SPSS coordinator.

REGION: SAVE SCSS uses all the memory allocated via the PARM operand on the EXEC statement, and the JOB statement REGION operand must be set accordingly. That is, SAVE SCSS uses the combined WORKSPACE and TRANSPACE. The amount of space required is roughly proportional to the square root of the number of variables to be transposed but is a step function which is difficult to express in a formula. The following table gives the number of variables which may be accessed with various PARM field values:

PARM	VARIABLES
10K	26
20K	106
40K	426
60K	1,024
80K	1,706

TIME: SAVE SCSS involves significant processing for each case for each variable on the file. For example, SAVE SCSS on a file of 64 variables and 1500 cases used 4.35 CPU seconds on an IBM 370/168.

FT04F001: The new SCSS masterfile which results from SAVE SCSS processing is defined by the FT04F001 DD statement just as a new SPSS system file would be in a run using SAVE FILE. Space requirements for the SAVE SCSS masterfile are similar in magnitude to those for the system file. Logically, the masterfile contains 164 byte records in 492 byte fixed-length blocks. Each variable requires at least two such records plus as many more as are required for its value labels and data values. In terms of 3330 tracks, an estimate of the required space might be

(NVARS*(NCASES/117+1))/20.

If it is known that a substantial number of the variables will require less than 4 bytes per value because the associated values are all small non-negative integers, the divisor of NCASES (117) may be increased to as high as 468 (all values stored as one byte per value). All masterfiles to be accessed from TSO must be catalogued. An example FT04F001 statement is

```
//FT04F001 DD DSN=A1508.STUDY1.MASTER,
//            DISP=(NEW,CATLG),UNIT=SYSDA,
//            VOL=SER=PUBV01,
//            SPACE=(TRK,(15,10),RLSE)
```

FT12F001: SAVE SCSS does not use the SORT utility, so SORT JCL is not required. Instead, the work file FT12F001 is required. The data set defined by the FT12F001 DD statement is used as a direct access scratch file during SAVE SCSS. Thus, the DD statement is required for all runs involving SAVE SCSS regardless of the number of subsequent passes of the data. The FT12F001 data set must be large enough to accommodate the "decompressed" transposed data in blocks of 1920 bytes each. Since the blocks are of fixed length, the data set must be somewhat larger than normally would be required for the FT02F001 file—perhaps 25% larger. An example of an FT12F001 DD statement is listed below.

```
//FT12F001 DD UNIT=SYSCR,SPACE=(TRK,(50,20))
```

10.5 JCL Required for Release 7 SAVE TRANSPOSE (IBM)

The JCL required for executing an SPSS Release 7 run which includes a SAVE TRANSPOSE command is identical to that for a run which includes SORT CASES and SAVE FILE. Unlike SAVE SCSS in Release 8, which does not use the SORT utility, Release 7 SAVE TRANSPOSE requires all the JCL described in *SPSS,* Second Edition, starting on page 598. However, Release 7 SAVE TRANSPOSE does not require the //FT12F001 DD card as documented for SAVE SCSS.

While Release 7 SAVE TRANSPOSE does not have any explicit work space requirements, it does invoke the system SORT utility, and the latter uses all of the SPSS work space and transformation space. Thus a total space of at least the default of 80,000 bytes is recommended to enhance performance.

The SCSS masterfile is identified by the FT04F001 DD statement. See the discussion for SAVE SCSS above.

Output from Release 7 SAVE TRANSPOSE also includes the somewhat terse report produced by the system SORT utility.

10.6   ACCESSING AN SCSS MASTERFILE: GET SCSS

The GET SCSS command permits the researcher to access an SCSS masterfile for processing with SPSS. As such, the command's function is similar to that of the GET FILE command, and the command must be placed at the beginning of the command sequence preceded only by run commands such as NUMBERED, RUN NAME, and EDIT. As with the GET FILE command, the GET SCSS command may be followed by commands requesting the reading of new variables or cases, for example ADD VARIABLES or ADD SUBFILES, and commands creating new variables via the transformation facility, e.g., COMPUTE, IF, COUNT.

The control field of the GET SCSS command contains the facility name GET SCSS, and the specification field contains the optional subfields VARIABLES= and MIS=.

```
GET SCSS        [VARIABLES=varlist        /][MIS=RECODE/]
                            $varlist                LEAVE
                            spssvar=scssvar         STOP
                            ALL
                            $ALL
```

10.7   The VARIABLES= Specification

The VARIABLES= specification is used to select or rename variables which are to be kept for processing. The list following VARIABLES= may contain one or more of the following elements:

VARIABLES=ALL

The keyword ALL is the VARIABLES= default; specifying VARIABLES=ALL has the same effect as omitting VARIABLES= from the GET SCSS command. All variables on the SCSS masterfile will be included in the SPSS system file in their recoded form.

VARIABLES=varlist

The simple variable list names the variables on the SCSS masterfile which are to be included in the SPSS system file. If desired, the TO convention may be used, and the implied order is that which exists on the SCSS masterfile. Examples of variable lists are

```
AGE
AGE, SEX, RACE
FRATMEM TO PROFMEM, EDUC, SES
```

VARIABLES=$varlist

If the variable name or variable list is prefaced with a dollar sign ($), listed variables are kept in their raw as opposed to recoded form. The SPSS variable names will not include the initial dollar sign. As with the simple variable list, the TO convention may be used. However, both variable names must be prefaced with a dollar sign and all variables implied are considered dollar sign variables. Examples of dollar variable lists are

```
$AGE
$AGE, $SEX, $RACE
$FRATMEM TO $PROFMEM, $EDUC, $SES
```

Simple and dollar variable lists may be mixed on the VARIABLES= specification.

VARIABLES=$ALL

This specification is similar to ALL except that all the variables on the SCSS masterfile will be saved on the SPSS system file in their raw form rather than in their recoded form. As with the dollar variable list, the SPSS variable names will not include the initial dollar signs.

spssvar=scssvar

The rename specification is made up of an SPSS variable name followed by an equals sign (=) and the name of a variable on the SCSS masterfile. The name following the equals sign may be prefixed by a dollar sign if the raw values are to be kept. The rename specification is useful for accessing a variable whose name is an SPSS reserved word, for accessing a variable in both its raw and recoded forms, or for cosmetic purposes. Examples of rename specifications are

```
SINTYPE = SIN
RAWAGE = $AGE
EDUC = V138
```

Note that, regardless of which VARIABLES= specification is used, a file which was weighted under SCSS will remain weighted under SPSS. Specifically, if the SCSS masterfile was weighted, the raw values of the weighting variable will become the values of CASWGT under SPSS. Whether or not the user also keeps the SCSS weighting variable does not affect this automatic assignment.

10.8 The MIS= Specification

When an SCSS masterfile is transposed into an SPSS system file, several types of problems may arise regarding the translation of missing values from one system to the other. It is possible, for example, to define more missing values for an SCSS variable than SPSS can handle; other problems may arise from the fact that missing values may be listed on variable masks (from which all information for the transposition process is read) in such a way as to make it impossible for SPSS to interpret the raw values from the information on the mask, when raw values are requested.

The MIS= specification determines the manner in which SCSS missing values which cannot be represented in SPSS are to be handled. It is possible to request that these values be left as is; that they be recoded to SPSS-valid missing values; or that if encountered, they force the run to stop. In all cases a report of the untranslatable values and the reasons why they can not be translated is printed at the end of the run. (See Section 10.9.)

There are three types of situations in which SCSS missing values may not be representable in SPSS.

* *Too many SCSS missing values:* An SCSS variable may have more missing value specifications than SPSS can handle. This is the case when an SCSS variable has more than three missing values, more than one missing value range, or a missing value range and more than one individual missing value.

* *Shuffled missing and valid SCSS values:* If the mask for an SCSS variable specifies a missing value range and a series of non-missing values within that range, it will not be possible to transpose the missing values directly into SPSS. This is due to the fact that in SPSS, it is not possible to specify a value as non-missing. Values in SPSS are marked as missing or not marked at all. Thus the values list on the SCSS variable mask which specifies values first in a range as missing, and subsequently enumerates a series of them as valid values, cannot be transposed by the GET SCSS facility. This situation may arise from such legitimate responses to the SCSS VALUES? prompt as:

```
VALUES?
0-9 (mis); 1,2,3,4,5,8,9
```

If the missing values had been enumerated in the mask, rather than specified as a range (e.g., as 0,6,7 (mis); 1,2,3,4,5,8,7) there would be no difficulty in transposing the variable.

* *Alphabetic range of SCSS missing values:* If the mask for an SCSS variable contains a range of alphabetic missing values, it will not be possible to retrieve the variable's values in their raw form from the information on the mask. This is due to the fact that the collating sequence used in SPSS and SCSS for alphabetic values are different. That is, the range 'AA' thru 'ZZ' will include different intermediate values in SPSS than it does in SCSS. Notice that this problem can only occur in the case of an attempt to access an alpha variable in its raw form, since SCSS requires that all alpha values be recoded to numeric values in the variable mask.

The MIS= specification provides three alternatives for the handling of non-translatable SCSS missing values. They are requested through use of MIS= keywords RECODE, LEAVE, and STOP.

MIS=RECODE

The keyword RECODE is the MIS= default; specifying MIS=RECODE has the same effect as omitting the MIS= specification from the GET SCSS command. RECODE specifies that, if a value is encountered which would be considered missing by SCSS but cannot be represented in SPSS, it is to be recoded to the first of that variable's missing values considered legitimate by SPSS. Note that, if the variable has a missing range, the output of this recoding process is the lower limit of that range.

MIS=LEAVE

Specification of this keyword results in the reporting of any values considered missing by SCSS but not by SPSS. However, the values are not recoded and therefore are not considered missing in the SPSS system file.

MIS=STOP

If this keyword is specified, the researcher is informed of any values considered missing by SCSS but not by SPSS. In addition, the values which would have resulted under the MIS=RECODE treatment are printed, and the run aborts after all the data have been read but before the relatively time-consuming transposition itself.

10.9 Output from GET SCSS

After the GET SCSS command has been analyzed, the system reports the maximum number of variables which could have been accessed with the given amount of memory, the number of variables requested (including CASWGT but not SEQNUM or SUBFILE), the file name (which should be the same as the SCSS internal file name), and the number of cases in the file.

Also included in the output is a report of SCSS variables with non-translatable missing values and warning messages indicating that variables with names invalid in SPSS have been dropped.

During the processing of the data from the SCSS masterfile, the system checks for problems in the handling of missing values and a report is printed. This report includes the names of all variables whose missing values present a problem to SPSS, the type of problem, the result value, and the first 50 problem values encountered. The problems are denoted in shorthand form as follows:

```
TOO MANY
```

This message is printed if the SCSS variable has more than three missing values, more than one missing value range, or a missing value range and more than one individual missing value.

```
OVERLAP
```

This message indicates the existence of a missing value range which includes non-missing values.

```
ALF RNGE
```

This message indicates the presence of values which are included in an alphabetic range of missing values under SCSS.

Under the column in the missing value report headed RESULT VALUE, are printed the values produced by the automatic recoding unless MIS=LEAVE was specified. If the result values are themselves missing, as they normally are, the values are followed by the letter M. The absence of the letter M indicates that the variable has no missing values and that problem values are recoded to the lower limit of a range which would have been missing under SCSS. Occurrences of the situation where recoding to a missing value is impossible will be quite rare and are accompanied by the following warning at the end of the report:

```
WARNING - SOME SCSS MISSING VALUES ARE NO LONGER MISSING
```

During the processing of the GET SCSS command, several conditions may be detected which result in warning messages rather than errors. These conditions are reported to the researcher, and the run continues. The specific warning messages are

```
VARIABLE 'xxxxxxxx' IS SCSS-SPECIFIC AND IS DROPPED.
```

This message indicates that the user either specifically or through use of the TO convention attempted to access a variable which has meaning only to the SCSS system, e.g., SPSS or SPSS0001. As indicated, the variable is simply not retained for processing.

```
'xxxxxxxx' IS A RESERVED WORD AND IS DROPPED
```

This message will be issued if the user attempts to access a variable (without renaming) which has a name considered a reserved word within SPSS. This circumstance is most likely to arise in the case of arithmetic function names such as SIN, COS, EXP, etc., which are considered reserved words within SPSS but not within SCSS. The message will also occur if the result name in a rename specification is an SPSS reserved word.

```
'xxxxxxxx' ALREADY EXISTS AND IS DROPPED
```

This message results from an attempt to access a variable by a name which has already been included. The situation is particularly likely to arise from an attempt to access a variable with the same name as an SPSS automatic variable, i.e., SEQNUM, SUBFILE, or CASWGT.

10.10 JCL Required for GET SCSS (IBM)

From a mechanical point of view, GET SCSS transposes the data on a variable-ordered SCSS masterfile to arrive at a temporary case-ordered data file which may be accessed by SPSS. The transposition is performed with the data resident on a direct access scratch file. The JCL considerations for GET SCSS are related to this process and are listed below.

REGION: GET SCSS uses all the memory allocated via the PARM operand on the EXEC statement and the JOB statement REGION operand must be set accordingly. That is, GET SCSS uses the combined WORKSPACE plus TRANSPACE. The amount of space required is roughly proportional to the square root of the number of variables to be transposed but is a step function which is difficult to express in a formula. The following table gives the number of variables which may be accessed with various PARM field values:

PARM	VARIABLES
10K	26
20K	106
40K	426
60K	1,024
80K	1,706

TIME: GET SCSS involves significant processing for each case for each variable on the file. For example, GET SCSS on a file containing 60 variables and 1500 cases required 3 CPU seconds on an IBM 370/168.

FT02F001: The data set defined by this DD statement is used as a direct access scratch file during GET SCSS. Thus, the DD statement is required for all runs involving GET SCSS regardless of the number of subsequent passes of the data. The FT02F001 data set must be large enough to accommodate the "decompressed" transposed data in blocks of 1920 bytes each. Since the blocks are of fixed length, the data set must be somewhat larger than normally would be required for the FT02F001 file—perhaps 25% larger. (Note: Normally this data set is used to store the case-ordered file between procedures. When so used, its block size is 2012, unless the DD statement provides a different block size). An example of an FT02F001 DD statement is listed below.

```
//FT02F001 DD UNIT=SYSCR,SPACE=(TRK,(50,20))
```

FT03F001: This DD statement defines the SCSS masterfile just as it would an SPSS system file. Since an SCSS masterfile accessed from TSO must be catalogued and on a direct access device, the DD statement need specify only the DSNAME and the DISP as follows:

```
//FT03F001 DD DSNAME=A1234.SCSSFIL,DISP=SHR
```

FT12F001: This DD statement defines a temporary data set for GET SCSS just as it does for GET ARCHIVE. The data set must be large enough to contain the case-ordered file and will normally reside on disk. An example is

```
//FT12F001 DD UNIT=SYSCR,SPACE=(TRK,(50,20))
```

GET SCSS and SAVE SCSS were designed, programmed, and documented by C. Hadlai Hull.

Chapter 11

Data Selection and Modification

The data selection and modification capabilities of SPSS have been extended to include exact-size and reproducible random samples, normal or uniform distributions of random numbers for generating test data, a date function, handling of constants in DO REPEAT, and a facility for handling files in which time lag is significant. These and other modifications are outlined in the following sections.

11.1 SAMPLE

A researcher blessed with an abundance of cases can frequently save processing time and cost by using a random sample of his data for certain analyses. SPSS provides the SAMPLE and *SAMPLE commands for drawing such samples.

SPSS now also provides the functions UNIFORM and NORMAL for generating random values from the named distributions. See Section 11.8.

11.2 Commands Executed in Sequence

SAMPLE and *SAMPLE commands are now executed in sequence. Previously, they would be executed first in a series of data selection statements, no matter where they occurred in the job.

11.3 Arguments Greater Than 1 Illegal

Arguments greater than 1 will no longer be accepted on SAMPLE or *SAMPLE commands. Previously, arguments greater than or equal to 1 were interpreted as percentages.

11.4 Exact-Size Random Samples

The SAMPLE and *SAMPLE commands now allow selection of random samples of exact size, if the exact size of the file is known. To specify a sample of n1 cases, use the command

```
SAMPLE        n1 FROM n2
```

where n2 is the number of cases from which the sample is to be taken. The n1 and n2 specifications must be positive integer constants (not variable names or expressions), and n2 must be specified correctly. To extract a 500-case random sample from a 10,000-case file, use:

```
SAMPLE        500 FROM 10000
```

The *SAMPLE facility can be used in the same way for temporary samples.

If one or more SELECT IF commands precede a SAMPLE command, the file size (n2) entered on the SAMPLE command should reflect the number of cases selected by them. SELECT IF's which follow the SAMPLE command have no effect on the correct value for n2.

If the n2 specified on the SAMPLE command is larger than the actual input file, the resulting sample will probably be too small, although it will still be a valid random sample. The expected sample size is n1/n2 times the true file size. The variance of the sample size in this situation is less than if SAMPLE had been specified with a single number representing n1/n2.

If the n2 specified on the SAMPLE command is smaller than the actual input file, a sample of n1 cases will be drawn from the first n2 cases. This is not a random sample of the whole file unless the file is in random order—in which case the first n1 cases in the file is just as good a sample and is cheaper to extract.

11.5 Previous SAMPLE Syntax Still Accepted

The SAMPLE syntax described in *SPSS,* Second Edition, p. 127 is still accepted and its results have not changed. Under this method, a single probability is specified; each case has that probability of entering the sample, independent of what happened to any other case.

Regardless of which method is used, the sampling is done without replacement, meaning that no case may enter the sample more than once.

11.6 REPRODUCIBLE RANDOM SAMPLES: THE SEED COMMAND

Ordinarily, neither samples nor random function values are reproducible: a given set of commands and given set of data will produce a different sample and different random function values for each run. The psuedo random number generator used by SPSS selects a seed based on the time of day at which the job starts.

The SEED command allows these random processes to be reproduced. The command has one of the following formats:

```
SEED        a large integer

SEED        PRINT
```

The first format provides the reproduction facility. If one runs a set of commands and data twice using a SEED command with the same integer, the same results will be produced. Any integer is acceptable. If 0 is specified, 1 will be used. If a small integer is used, the first few generated random numbers will be small.

The second format, using the keyword PRINT, causes the number in use for random number generation to be printed. This can be used to allow reproduction of a sample where the system has chosen the starting number.

The SEED command may be placed anywhere in the command sequence except between the OPTIONS and STATISTICS commands for a procedure, between the READ INPUT DATA or READ MATRIX command and data, and after a REORDER VARS, SORT CASES (Release 7), or SAVE FILE command.

Multiple SEED commands may be used. For example, assume several procedures are to be requested for a SAMPLE of the file. If temporary samples are used, the samples selected for each *SAMPLE command will be different. If a SEED command specifying the same value is used prior to each *SAMPLE command, the same sample will be selected for each procedure. The following set of commands illustrates this technique.

```
SEED            95765842
*SAMPLE         .05
FREQUENCIES     GENERAL = VARA TO VARD
SEED            95765842
*SAMPLE         .05
CROSSTABS       TABLES = VARA VARB BY VARC BY VARD
SEED            95765842
*SAMPLE         .05
FACTOR          VARIABLES = VARF TO VARX
```

To reproduce a sample in a later run, the user has two options. If the keyword PRINT is specified on the SEED command, the seed will be printed each time it is used. To reproduce the sample the user should specify this same value on the SEED command during the run. Alternatively, the user may specify the seed initially and use that same value in a later run.

The value specified on the SEED command is used only during the run. It is not saved on the system file.

11.7 SELECT IF

SELECT IF and *SELECT IF are now executed in sequence. If more than one SELECT IF or *SELECT IF command appear in a command sequence they are now connected by AND; that is, a case must satisfy the conditions specified on all SELECT IF and *SELECT IF commands to be selected. In all previous releases of SPSS all SELECT IF commands were connected by OR, so a case needed to satisfy only the conditions on one of the statements to be selected. For example, suppose the following commands appeared in an SPSS job:

```
SELECT IF       (V1 EQ 1)
SELECT IF       (V1 EQ 2)
```

Release 6 would select all cases having a 1 or 2 in V1; Releases 7, 8, and 9 will not select any cases, since no cases can have both a 1 and a 2 in V1.

All the SELECT IF commands are connected to all the *SELECT IF commands with AND in all releases.

11.8   RANDOM NUMBER FUNCTIONS: NORMAL AND UNIFORM

Two new functions are permitted on COMPUTE statements which will facilitate the generation of test data. The NORMAL function will generate a normally distributed variable with a mean of 0. The standard deviation must be requested as an argument to the function. For example, the following COMPUTE command will create a variable, RANDOM, which is a random sample from a population with mean 0 and standard deviation .5:

```
COMPUTE        RANDOM = NORMAL(.5)
```

The function UNIFORM will create a uniformly distributed variable. It has one argument, the upper limit. The lower limit will be 0. Neither the lower nor upper limit will be reached. For example, the following COMPUTE command will generate variable UNI:

```
COMPUTE        UNI = UNIFORM(100)
```

where $0 < UNI < 100$.

The UNIFORM function may be used to obtain a stratified sample. Assume a survey of 10,000 people has been taken. Initial inspection reveals that 80% of the sample is male, while the known universe (obtained from census counts) is 48% males. To obtain a sample which corresponds to the known universe, and which maximizes the size of the sample, 23.1% of the males and 100% of the females must be sampled. The following commands would select an approximately 23.1% sample of the males in the file:

```
COMPUTE        SAMPCT=1
IF             (SEX EQ 'M') SAMPCT =.231
SELECT IF      (UNIFORM(1) LE SAMPCT)
```

Given the above file, if a total sample of 2000 respondents is desired, the following commands would be required:

```
COMPUTE        SAMPCT=1
IF             (SEX EQ 'M') SAMPCT =.12
IF             (SEX EQ 'F') SAMPCT =.52
SELECT IF      (UNIFORM(1) LE SAMPCT)
```

In neither example will the exact sample size desired necessarily be obtained.

The NORMAL function may be used to create variables with known (approximate) correlations. The following commands would create two variables with a mean of 0 and a standard deviation of 1 which have a Pearson product moment correlation of .6:

```
COMPUTE        A = NORMAL(1)
COMPUTE        B = .6*A + NORMAL(.8)
```

Since an r of .6 explains .36 of the variance, the remaining variance is .64., or .8 squared. In the multivariate case, variances are additive provided that the independent variables are uncorrelated. Thus a variable could be created with a multiple R of .85 when regressed on two uncorrelated variables with the following set of COMPUTE statements:

```
COMPUTE        A = NORMAL(1)
COMPUTE        B = NORMAL(1)
COMPUTE        C = .6*A + .6*B + NORMAL(.62)
```

In this fashion an entire file of specified bivariate and multivariate relationships can be created.

11.9   DATA FUNCTION FOR COMPUTE, IF AND SELECT IF

In order to compute an interval of time between two calendar dates, the function YRMODA converts each date to a day number. Once the conversion from date to day number is made, the interval of time between two dates is given by subtracting the day number of the earlier date from that of the later date.

The YRMODA function counts days starting from the first day of the Gregorian calendar: day one is October 15, 1582. Succeeding days, through the year 47516, are numbered consecutively. Gregorian calendar rules are used in computations, meaning that every year whose number is divisible by 4 has an extra day, February 29, for a total of 366 days. The exception to this rule are years whose numbers are divisible by 100 but not by 400: such years are not leap years and have only 365 days.

According to these rules, the use of YRMODA on the COMPUTE, IF, or SELECT IF commands converts calendar dates to day numbers, returning the Gregorian calendar day number corresponding to the date given by year YR, month MO, and day DA. For example,

```
YRMODA(1582,10,15) = 1
YRMODA(1800,1,1) =79,337
YRMODA(1900,1,1) = 115,860
```

11.10   Validity of YRMODA Elements

The YRMODA year, month, and day elements are checked to see that they form a valid date in the Gregorian era which can be used in computing intervals. YRMODA(YR,MO,DA) is valid if

- YR is an integer between 0 and 99 or between 1582 and 47516. Years between 0 and 99 are assumed to be in the 20th century and the function adds 1900 to them. Dates before October 15, 1582 are considered invalid because of the differences between Julian and Gregorian calendar rules. (For example, the day before October 15, 1582 was October 5.) Years later than 47516 are not valid because the returned result would be too large to be accurately represented in a single precision floating-point word. This limit applies to IBM 360 and 370 machines; the limit on other machines may be different.
- MO is an integer between one and 13, inclusive.
- DA is an integer between zero and 31, inclusive.

Note that zero is a valid day. This makes it easy to use the last day of a month in computations. It is not necessary to specify whether the last day is the 28th, the 30th, or the 31st; the day may be indicated by a notation of the form

```
YRMODA(YR,(MO + 1),0)
```

Similarly, 13 is a valid month; this allows use of DA=0 to refer to the last day of December:

```
YRMODA(YR,13,0)=YRMODA(YR,12,31)
```

Further, the validity of MO=13 makes it possible to refer obliquely to the first month of the coming year:

```
YRMODA(YR,13,DA)=YRMODA(YR+1,1,DA)
```

The arguments to YRMODA can be constants, variable names, or arithmetic expressions; but if an argument is not a constant or variable name, it should be enclosed in parentheses. Since a comma and a space are equivalent in SPSS syntax, the program cannot distinguish

```
YRMODA(A,-B*D,C)
```

from

```
YRMODA(A-B*D,C)
```

and will complain (with error 232) that a wrong number of arguments has been used in either case. If the expression is written

```
YRMODA(A,(-B*D),C)
```

there will be no difficulty.

11.11   Treatment of Invalid YRMODA Elements

If a YRMODA entry is invalid, the result is the same as if the expression contained a division by zero. Treatment of invalid entries varies according to whether the function was used in a COMPUTE, IF, or SELECT IF statement.

COMPUTE. When an error in a YRMODA specification is encountered in a COMPUTE statement, the result variable is assigned a value according to the following rules:

- If an ASSIGN MISSING statement is in effect for the variable, the specified missing value is assigned.
- If a MISSING VALUE specification is in effect instead, the low end of any specified range of missing values, or, if no range was specified, the first missing value is assigned.
- If neither ASSIGN MISSING nor MISSING VALUES is in effect for the result variable, zero is assigned.

IF. If an error in a YRMODA specification occurs in the assignment part of an IF statement, the result variable is assigned a value according to the rules listed above for COMPUTE statement domain errors.

   If a YRMODA error occurs in the conditional part of an IF, the result variable is assigned a value according to the following rules:

- If an ASSIGN MISSING statement is in effect for the variable, the specified missing value is assigned.
- If no ASSIGN MISSING statement is in effect, the condition is considered false and no value is assigned to the result variable.

SELECT IF. If a YRMODA error is encountered in a SELECT IF statement, the case is not selected.

11.12 DOMAIN ERRORS IN COMPUTE, IF AND SELECT IF STATEMENTS

When a domain error is encountered in a transformation function specified on a COMPUTE, IF, or SELECT IF command, the case involved may be assigned a missing value according to the ASSIGN MISSING or MISSING VALUES specifications, or it may be assigned the value 0.

11.13 Possible Domain Errors on Data Transformation Commands

The "domain" of a function is the set of all numbers for which it is defined. When an attempt is made to perform a function on a number for which the function is not defined, a domain error results. The domain errors possible in SPSS COMPUTE, IF, and SELECT IF statements are

- Dividing by zero
- Taking the square root of a negative number
- Taking the natural or base-10 logarithm of zero or a negative number
- Raising a negative number to a non-integer power [It is permissible to raise a negative number to an integer power: $(-3)**4$ is executed. However, the transformation $(-3)**(1/3)$, for example, is not allowed.]
- Invalid arguments to YRMODA (see Section 11.10)

11.14 Domain Errors and the Assignment of Missing Values

COMPUTE. When a domain error is encountered in a COMPUTE statement, the result variable is assigned a value according to the following rules:

- If an ASSIGN MISSING statement is in effect for the variable, the specified missing value is assigned.
- If a MISSING VALUE specification is in effect instead, the low end of any specified range of missing values, or, if no range was specified, the first missing value is assigned.
- If neither ASSIGN MISSING nor MISSING VALUES is in effect for the result variable, zero is assigned.

IF. If a domain error occurs in the assignment part of an IF statement, the result variable is assigned a value according to the rules listed above for COMPUTE statement domain errors.

If a domain error occurs in the conditional part of an IF, the result variable is assigned a value according to the following rules:

- If an ASSIGN MISSING statement is in effect for the variable, the specified missing value is assigned.
- If no ASSIGN MISSING statement is in effect, the condition is considered false and no value is assigned to the result variable.

SELECT IF. If a domain error occurs in the evaluation of a SELECT IF expression, the case is not selected.

11.15 DO REPEAT

The DO REPEAT facility has been rewritten to handle and generate constants in the DO REPEAT statement, and several limitations have been removed.

11.16 Constants

Constants may appear in the substitution list for any stand-in variable just as variable names are used. For example,

```
DO REPEAT      VAR = V1 TO V4/
               MEAN = 63.81, 41.741, 12.98, 31.43
COMPUTE        VAR = VAR - MEAN
END REPEAT
```

can be used to adjust a series of variables so that they have zero means. The following data transformation statements would be generated:

```
COMPUTE        V1 = V1 - 63.81
COMPUTE        V2 = V2 - 41.741
COMPUTE        V3 = V3 - 12.98
COMPUTE        V4 = V4 - 31.43
```

Further, DO REPEAT can now generate consecutive integer constants using a form of the TO convention. For example, one can generate dummy variables for regression easily by using the following commands:

```
DO REPEAT      D = D2 TO D6/
               CODE = 2 TO 6
COMPUTE        D = 0
IF             (GROUP EQ 1) D = -1
IF             (GROUP EQ CODE) D = 1
END REPEAT
```

These statements will generate a series of variables (D2, D3, D4, D5, and D6) whose values are

-1 when GROUP has the value 1
1   when GROUP has the value (2 to 6) corresponding to the particular variable
0   otherwise

The statments generated are

```
COMPUTE        D2 = 0
IF             (GROUP EQ 1) D2 = -1
IF             (GROUP EQ 2) D2 = 1
COMPUTE        D3 = 0
IF             (GROUP EQ 1) D3 = -1
IF             (GROUP EQ 3) D3 = 1
                 .
                 .
                 .
IF             (GROUP EQ 6) D6 = 1
```

The rules and restrictions on generating constants this way are

- The syntax is m TO n, where n and m are integer constants. 1, 30 and -463875 are examples of such integer constants. 4.4 and 'B' are not integer constants. A decimal point may be used, but nothing other than zero may follow it.
- In 'm TO n', n must not be less than m. -6 TO 1 is valid; -1 TO -6, and 7 TO 1 are not. 6 TO 6 is valid (but pointless).
- The sequence m TO n implies n-m+1 values. Keep this in mind for insuring that substitution lists for all stand-in variables on a DO REPEAT command are the same length.

11.17 Limitations

The changes in limitations for DO REPEAT are

- The number of stand-in variables which may be defined is now limited only by the available workspace.
- The number of statements included between DO REPEAT and END REPEAT is now limited only by available workspace.
- The number of bytes of workspace required by DO REPEAT is calculated as follows:

WORKSPACE = 8 * (NM * (NV + 1) + NC + NELEM + NSUB)

NM = number of stand-in variables defined.

NV = length of each substitution list, including all variables and constants implied by TO.

NC = number of statements between DO REPEAT and END REPEAT.

NELEM = number of elements in the statements between DO REPEAT and END REPEAT. Each keyword, variable name, value, arithmetic, relational, or logical operator, parenthesis, slash or equals sign in these statements counts as one element. The common delimiters do not count as elements.

NSUB = the number of occurrences of stand-in variables in the statements between DO REPEAT and END REPEAT.

- The maximum number of elements in any single statement between DO REPEAT and END REPEAT is 250.

11.18 LAG FACILITY

In analyzing most (but not all) survey data, the element of time can be ignored. The researcher gathers data over a short period, and each case represents a different subject's opinions, status and state of being at the time he was questioned. There is no reason for the researcher to believe that one subject's responses are related to another subject's responses; the cases are treated as independent observations from the same population.

In many research fields, the opposite treatment is critical. An economist analyzes the state of an economy over time by repeatedly measuring the same variables for the same economy. His "cases" are not independent of each other: the consumer price index for 1975 may be related to the unemployment rate for 1973, or at least one cannot assume it is not, simply because they are measurements from different years.

There is no way SPSS can analyze such a relationship unless the values for these two variables (consumer price index and unemployment rate two years earlier) appear in the same cases. But the logical place to record the 1973 unemployment rate is with other 1973 economic indicators, including the 1973, not the 1975, consumer price index.

A variable composed of observations from earlier cases, such as the unemployment rate from two years ago, is called a lagged variable. SPSS provides the LAG command for creating such variables.

11.19 Format of the LAG Command

In its simplest form, the LAG command has the format

```
LAG             variable name 1 = variable name 2
```

For example

```
LAG             UNEMP1 = UNEMP
```

specifies that UNEMP1 is UNEMP lagged one case; that is, in each case in the file, UNEMP1 is to have the value UNEMP had for the previous case.

One could create a variable whose value was UNEMP lagged by two cases by specifying either

```
LAG             UNEMP1 = UNEMP
LAG             UNEMP2 = UNEMP1
        or
LAG             UNEMP1, UNEMP2 = UNEMP
```

The second method produces the same results as the first—UNEMP1 is UNEMP lagged by one case, and UNEMP2 is UNEMP lagged by two cases. The general form

```
            variable name
LAG               or          = variable name
            variable list
```

says that the first variable in the list is lagged one observation, the second is lagged two observations, and so on. The keyword TO can be used as it is used on the VARIABLE LIST command to specify a sequence of names:

```
LAG             GNP1 TO GNP10 = GNP
```

means that GNP1, GNP2, GNP3, . . . ,GNP10 are the names of variables which will contain GNP lagged one, two, three, . . . , and ten cases respectively. These names may be the names of new variables or existing variables.

On the LAG command, the keyword TO can be used only in the sense described above: to generate a series of names which start with the same sequence of characters and end with a number. If the VARIABLE LIST (or DATA LIST) command for a file defined the following sequence of variables

```
A, V1, B, C, V3, D
```

then

```
LAG             V1 TO V3 = A
```

would mean

```
LAG             V1 V2 V3 = A
```

and not

```
LAG             V1, B, C, V3 = A
```

It would place A lagged one case in the existing variable V1, create a new variable V2 for A lagged two cases, and use the existing variable V3 for A lagged three cases.

The lagging of more than one variable can be specified on a single LAG command by separating the lag specifications with a slash (/).

The complete general form of the LAG command is

```
            variable name
LAG               or          = variable name/
            variable list

            variable name
                  or          = variable name/
            variable list

            . . .
```

11.20 Missing Data

Lagging variables automatically creates missing values—all lagged variables are missing for the first case; any variable lagged two cases is missing for the first and second cases, and so on. Some value must be supplied for these missing observations.

SPSS supplies a value according to the following rules:

- If an ASSIGN MISSING command is in effect for a lagged variable, the value specified on it is used.
- If a MISSING VALUES command is in effect for the lagged variable, the value assigned will be either the low end value of a missing value range or, if no range was specified, the first value listed on the MISSING VALUES specification. For a discussion of missing value ranges, see MISSING VALUES in Chapter 19 of this manual.
- If neither ASSIGN MISSING nor MISSING VALUES is in effect, the value zero is supplied.

The value assigned to lagged variables in the first case in a subfile is determined entirely by the MISSING VALUES or ASSIGN MISSING specification for the lagged variable. It is not affected by the specification of missing values for the source variable.

Lagged variables can also have missing values because the source variable has missing values. In this case, the actual value of the source variable is passed to the lagged variable unless an ASSIGN MISSING command is used to specify the value to be assigned. In this case, the MISSING VALUE or ASSIGN MISSSING in effect for the source variable is used to identify the missing value, while the ASSIGN MISSING specifications in effect for the lagged variables are used to determine the value to be assigned.

Table 11.20 shows the values of GNP, GNP1, GNP2, and GNP3 for the first few cases of a hypothetical file and the commands used to generate them.

```
MISSING VALUES GNP(0)
LAG            GNP1 to GNP3 = GNP
ASSIGN MISSING GNP1 to GNP3 (-1)
```

Table 11.20

Case	GNP	GNP1	GNP2	GNP3
1	943	-1	-1	-1
2	980	943	-1	-1
3	1019	980	943	-1
4	0	1019	980	943
5	1034	-1	1019	980
6	1086	1034	-1	1019
7	1093	1086	1034	-1

11.21 Subfiles

If the SPSS file contains more than one subfile, lagging is started anew for each subfile. Values are never lagged across subfile boundaries.

11.22 Selection and Sampling

SPSS performs all transformations and all data selection and sampling in the order in which they are defined by the SPSS commands. This means that a lag is performed only on cases selected by any SELECT IF or SAMPLE commands which precede the LAG command in the run. Two examples follow to illustrate this relationship.

```
SELECT IF       (VAR1 NE 1)
LAG             B1 = B
ASSIGN MISSING B1(-1)
```

Original Data

Case	VAR1	B
1	3	9
2	6	18
3	1	46
4	2	40
5	4	31

Result File

Case	VAR1	B	B1
1	3	9	-1
2	6	18	9
4	2	40	18
5	4	31	40

```
     LAG          B1 = B
ASSIGN MISSING B1(-1)
SELECT IF      (VAR1 NE 1)
```

Original Data

Case	VAR1	B
1	3	9
2	6	18
3	1	46
4	2	40
5	4	31

Result File

Case	VAR1	B	B1
1	3	9	-1
2	6	18	9
4	2	40	46
5	4	31	40

The two result files have different values for B1 for the third case (case no. 4). The first example illustrates lagging selected data, while the second illustrates selecting lagged data.

11.23   Using LAG with Other Transformations

Like all the other data transformation commands in SPSS (RECODE, COMPUTE, IF and their starred versions), LAG commands are executed for each case in the sequence in which the transformation commands appear. This means that the results of a LAG statement can be affected by transformations which change the value of the source variable only if the commands for those transformations appear before the LAG command in the command sequence. Transformations which change the value of the source variable after the LAG command appears have no effect on the values of lagged variables in later cases.

All the values supplied by LAG for lagged variables come from the source variable, not from other lagged variables in the list, so transformations which change the value of one lagged variable in a list have no effect on the other lagged variables in the same list.

11.24   Temporary Lagging: The *LAG Command

As with other transformation statements, LAG has a temporary version, *LAG. The command and its effects are identical to LAG except that values supplied and variables created by it exist only for the next procedure.

11.25   Use with DO REPEAT

LAG and *LAG can be used between DO REPEAT and END REPEAT commands in Releases 8 and 9 but not in Release 7.

11.26   Using LAG for Data Checking

Since LAG allows for transformations across cases it can be used for ensuring that the sequence of cases is correct when sequence is important. A variable which contains the case identifier may be lagged one case. A new variable is then computed which subtracts the preceding observation (lagged case identifier variable) from the current observation (original case identifier variable). If the file is in ascending sequence, the result variable value should always be positive; and, if the sequence is consecutive, it should have the constant value 1.

11.27   TRANSPACE Requirements for LAG

A LAG command counts 1 toward the limit of recoded variables. Each lagged variable counts 1 toward the limit of recode values.

11.28   REQUIREMENTS AND LIMITATIONS

11.29   Reserved Keywords

NORMAL and UNIFORM are now reserved keywords which may not be used as variable names.

11.30   Space Requirements

Space requirements for transformations have been slightly changed. The method in which transformations are stored prior to computation does not lend itself to a straightforward calculation of TRANSPACE. Generally speaking, less space will be required than in Release 6. Space requirements are the same for all versions of SPSS. Previously SPSS, Version M required more space. A report of the amount of TRANSPACE required will follow every procedure if data transformations are used.

11.31 Limitations

- No more than 32767 recode values and lagged variables are permitted in one step.
- There is a limit of 20000 IF and COMPUTE commands.
- No more than 200 different constants may be referenced in COMPUTE and IF statements in SPSSG and SPSSH. This limit is 400 in SPSSM.

11.32 EQUAL SIGN MAY SUBSTITUTE FOR KEYWORD "EQ"

As of Release 8, "=" may be substituted for the keyword "EQ" in relational expressions. This substitution was one of the most common errors under previous releases; furthermore, the diagnostic message which the substitution generated was incorrect, naming "unbalanced parentheses" as the problem.

The data selection and modification enhancements discussed in this chapter were designed, programmed, and documented by Jonathan Fry.

Chapter 12

Raw Data Convenience Package

Several changes to the manner in which SPSS handles raw data entry have been made as of Release 8. These changes include the creation of an END INPUT DATA card and modifications in the use of the N OF CASES, READ INPUT DATA, and READ MATRIX cards. In addition, the handling of freefield input and the positioning of the N OF CASES and SUBFILE LIST cards have been altered. These changes are detailed below.

12.1 N OF CASES OPTIONAL WITH RAW DATA

The N OF CASES card is now optional with raw data input. If it is omitted, UNKNOWN is assumed. It need only be used under the following conditions:

• When the N is used to calculate tests of significance for procedures using matrix input which itself does not require group counts.

• When SPSS is restricted to reading the first n of cases of a larger file.

12.2 END INPUT DATA

It is now possible to specify N OF CASES UNKNOWN when reading raw data with INPUT MEDIUM CARD (that is, when the raw data are embedded within the SPSS control card series). The beginning of the raw data is indicated by the READ INPUT DATA card as in past versions; the end of the raw data is indicated by an END INPUT DATA card placed at the end of the raw data (and before the next SPSS control card).

The END INPUT DATA card should be used only when the input medium is specified as CARD and N OF CASES is specified as UNKNOWN. If the END INPUT DATA card is read as part of a raw input file with the input medium specified as something other than CARD, an error will result. If the input medium is CARD but N OF CASES is specified with a number instead of the keyword UNKNOWN, the END INPUT DATA card is unnecessary and will be ignored.

When each case requires more than one card, it is best to insert several END INPUT DATA cards after the data deck. Only the first card of each case is checked to see if it is END INPUT DATA; if the deck is missing a card, or has an extra card, a single END INPUT DATA card might be missed. If as many END INPUT DATA cards are inserted as there are cards in a case, one of them will be in the right place. The N OF CASES card need not be entered unless the the input medium is CARD and the END INPUT DATA card has not been entered, or unless only part of the input file is to be read.

12.3 READ INPUT DATA AND READ MATRIX

The READ INPUT DATA and READ MATRIX cards, previously required to signal the system to begin reading input materials, are now required only when the materials are included in the control deck (i.e., when the INPUT MEDIUM is CARD). If the data are in a separate file on tape or disk, the READ INPUT DATA or READ MATRIX cards may be omitted.

12.4 NEW DECK SETUP FOR RAW DATA ENTRY

The default for INPUT MEDIUM is CARD (this is not a change, but the fact is not in the SPSS manual). This fact, taken together with the changes described above, make a new, simpler, set of rules for setting up decks to read raw data.

If the raw data are on tape or disk, remember to include an appropriate INPUT MEDIUM card in the control deck before the first procedure. N OF CASES and READ INPUT DATA or READ MATRIX are not needed. A basic deck setup might look like this:

```
DATA LIST        ...
INPUT MEDIUM     DISK
FREQUENCIES      GENERAL=...
OPTIONS          ...
REGRESSION       ...
STATISTICS       ...
FINISH
```

If the data are on cards or included in the command file, the INPUT MEDIUM card may be omitted. The N OF CASES card should normally be omitted. Place the data deck, with READ INPUT DATA in front of it and END INPUT DATA behind it, after the first procedure card and its associated OPTIONS and STATISTICS cards. The example deck above, modified for card data, looks like this:

```
DATA LIST        ...
FREQUENCIES      GENERAL=...
OPTIONS          ...
READ INPUT DATA
data cards
END INPUT DATA
REGRESSION       ...
STATISTICS       ...
FINISH
```

12.5 FREEFIELD INPUT

When freefield input is used and the input medium is CARD and the NUMBERED option is in effect, columns 73-80 of the data cards are ignored. This means your data cards can be numbered just like your control cards. If the input medium is not CARD, or the NUMBERED card has not been used, columns 1-80 of each input data record are examined.

Freefield input can now be used with N OF CASES UNKNOWN. If the data cards are part of the control card deck, simply follow the last data card with an END INPUT DATA card. The N OF CASES UNKNOWN card can be omitted, since this specification is now the default.

12.6 N OF CASES AND SUBFILE LIST

In earlier releases, the occurrence of an N OF CASES card after subfiles had been defined (either by a SUBFILE LIST card or through GET FILE or GET ARCHIVE) caused an error message. This usage is now accepted in order to allow processing of small sets of data from large files to allow testing of control decks. SUBFILE LIST and N OF CASES cards may now appear at any point in the deck, and any number may appear. The only restrictions are that neither card may increase the number of cases declared to be in the file, and N OF CASES UNKNOWN is not allowed after an actual number of cases has been specified. The last N OF CASES or SUBFILE LIST card encountered is used for any procedure.

12.7 OSIRIS VARS

OSIRIS VARS no longer prints a dictionary of the variables extracted from the OSIRIS file. This information can be printed with LIST FILEINFO.

The Raw Data Convenience Package was designed, programmed, and documented by Jonathan Fry.

Chapter 13

Extended Input Format Facility

The SPSS extended input format facility provides format items beyond those included in standard FORTRAN formats. These additional format items permit reading files which contain binary, packed decimal, zoned decimal, or floating point data. The specific additional format items are described below. The extended input format facility is not available in DATA LIST or ADD DATA LIST.

13.1 "B" FORMAT ITEM

The B (for "binary") format item is used to read fields which contain fixed point binary (integer) data. These data might be generated by COBOL systems using COMPUTATIONAL data items, by PL/1 systems using FIXED BINARY data items, by assembler systems using fullword and halfword items, or by FORTRAN systems using INTEGER and INTEGER *2 items. The general format of binary data items is a binary number of 16 or 32 bits in length using twos complement notation for negative quantities. The complete form of the SPSS B format item is $nBw.d$ where "w" is the field width in bytes (not digits) and "d" is the number of decimal digits (not bytes or bits) to the right of the implied decimal point. There are only two valid values for w: 2 and 4 corresponding to halfword (16-bit) and fullword (32-bit) numbers. Examples, then, of valid B format items are

3B4.0   three fullword binary numbers with no implied decimal points.

B2.2   one halfword binary number with two digits after the implied decimal point.

13.2 "C" FORMAT ITEM

The C (for "commercial") format item is used to process data fields which contain packed decimal numbers. Such numbers are generated by COBOL systems using COMPUTATIONAL-3 data items, by PL/1 systems using FIXED DECIMAL data items, and by assembler systems using packed decimal data items. The general format of a packed decimal field is two four-bit digits in each byte of the field except the last. The last byte contains a single digit in its four leftmost bits and a four-bit sign in its rightmost bits. The number of digits in a field is, then, $2*w-1$ where "w" is the field width in bytes. The sign position may contain either a hexadecimal "C" or "F" to denote a positive field or a hexadecimal "D" to denote a negative field. If the sign position contains anything but a hexadecimal "C", "F", or "D", SPSS Error 1780 will be generated. The complete form of the SPSS C format item is $nCw.d$ where "w" is the field width in bytes (not digits) and "d" is the number of digits (not bytes) to the right of the implied decimal point. The value of d must not exceed the number of digits in the field (i.e. $2*w-1$). Examples of valid C format items are

C10.3   a single 10 byte (19 digit) packed decimal field with three digits to the right of the implied decimal point.

2C3.0   two packed decimal fields of 3 bytes (5 digits) each with no implied decimal point.

As of Release 8, a field to be read with a C format item may be entirely blank. If it is, the result is the same as if the field had been read with an F format item: the variable gets special value BLANK, which can be recoded but which acts as zero otherwise. See *SPSS*, Second Edition, p.92.

13.3 "R" FORMAT ITEM

The R (for "real") format item is used to read data fields which contain internal format floating point numbers. Such numbers may be generated by COBOL systems using COMPUTATIONAL-1 or COMPUTATIONAL-2 data items, by PL/1 systems using FLOATING DECIMAL data items, by FORTRAN systems using REAL or REAL*8 (DOUBLE PRECISION) data items, or by assembler systems using floating point data items. The general format of a floating point number is a single-bit sign (1 is negative), a seven-bit hexadecimal exponent with a bias of 64, and a 24- or 56-bit mantissa. Such numbers must be either four bytes (short precision) or eight bytes (long precision) in length. The complete form of the SPSS R format item is nRw where "w" is the field width in bytes (not digits, bits, etc.). Note that, since a floating point number defines its own decimal point location, the format item does not include a "d" subfield. Users should be aware that, while an R8 data item may have up to 56 significant bits, it will be truncated to a short precision number with a maximum of 24 significant bits (roughly 6 digits) prior to processing by SPSS. Examples of valid R format items are

R8   a single long precision (8-byte) floating point number.
5R4   five short precision (4-byte) floating point numbers.

13.4 "Z" FORMAT ITEM

The Z (for zoned) format item is used to read data fields which contain zoned decimal data. Such numbers may be generated by COBOL systems using DISPLAY data items, by PL/1 systems using PICTURE data items, or by assembler systems using zoned decimal data items. The general format of a zoned decimal number is one digit per byte. Each byte other than the last contains a hexadecimal "F" in the four leftmost bits and a four-bit digit in the rightmost bits. The final byte contains a sign in the leftmost 4 bits and a single digit in the rightmost 4 bits. Hexadecimal "F" and "C" are interpreted as positive signs while hexadecimal "D" is interpreted as a negative sign. Old computer hands will recognize that the zoned decimal field is nothing other than a formatted field in which the sign is an "overpunch" in the low-order byte. That is, the combination punch &,1 yields a plus one while the combination punch -,7 yields a minus seven. Looked at another way, this new format item permits the user to read fields as produced by the IBM 1401 without editing.

More specifically, the SPSS Z format item will produce precisely the same effect as an "F" format item except that the former will permit the coding of the sign as an overpunch in the rightmost position. The complete form of the SPSS Z format item is nZw.d where "w" is the field width in bytes and "d" is the number of digits to the right of the implied decimal point. While not strictly legitimate in the usual interpretation of zoned decimal fields, a decimal point which appears in the actual field will be accepted and will override the decimal point implied by the "d" subfield. The value of d must not exceed the field width. Examples of valid Z format items are

Z15.5   a single 15 byte zoned decimal field with 5 digits to the right of the implied decimal point.
8Z4.0   eight zoned decimal fields of four bytes each with no implied decimal points.

13.5 COMBINING FORMAT ITEMS

Although data containing mixed types are relatively rare, these format items may be intermixed on the format specification list. For example the following use was made of the extended facility: A dataset contained both actual and estimated data. Estimated data were distinguished by an overpunch in the last byte of each field. The analysis required that estimated data be analyzed separately in some instances. A flag variable was created for each actual variable in the file by reading the field using the Z specification and rereading the last byte using the A specification as follows:

```
Z4.0,T4,A1,Z6.2,T10,A1 . . .
```

The flag variables were then recoded, numerics to 1, zone punches to 0. SELECT IF statements were used when required to distinguish estimated from actual data.

The extended input format facilities were designed, programmed, and documented by C. Hadlai Hull.

Chapter 14

SORT CASES

SORT CASES has been completely rewritten as of Release 8. The specifications for this command described in Section 11.8 of *SPSS*, Second Edition, still apply, with the following changes:

• The SORT CASES command does not have to be at the end of the deck, just before SAVE FILE. It is no longer connected to SAVE FILE, and files can be sorted before any procedure.

• Alphanumeric variables will be sorted correctly.

• Up to 64 variables may be named as sort keys.

• SORT CASES can group cases and define subfiles automatically.

• The original sequence of cases can be preserved within sorted groups.

14.1 DECK PLACEMENT

In previous releases of SPSS, a SORT CASES command could be followed only by SAVE FILE and FINISH, plus optionally, REORDER VARS. SORT CASES and REORDER VARS actually only modified the SAVE FILE command, and the three commands had to be used together.

As of Release 8, SORT CASES is no longer part of the SAVE FILE group. The command can appear wherever a procedure command could appear, and the file will be sorted at that point in the run. It can be used more than once in a run.

SORT CASES is permanent; that is, any procedure run after the sort will use the sorted file; SAVE FILE will save the sorted file.

No temporary transformations (such as *RECODE or *COMPUTE) may be in effect when SORT CASES is run. If values to be used as sort keys must be built with data tranformations, the non-temporary transformation commands may be used. Temporary data transformations required for a procedure can follow SORT CASES.

14.2 ALPHANUMERIC VARIABLES

Alphanumeric values will be sorted correctly if the variables containing them are given a print format of A with the PRINT FORMATS command. On IBM machines, blanks fall first, followed by special characters, letters in alphabetical order, and digits in numeric order.

14.3 DEFINING NEW SUBFILES

SORT CASES can define new subfiles according to the values of variables on the file. Those variables should be specified first on the SORT CASES command, as described in Section 11.8 of *SPSS*, Second Edition. The list of sorting variables is then followed by /SUBFILES. For example, the following specification will set up subfiles based on race and sex:

```
SORT CASES    RACE SEX/ SUBFILES
```

SORT CASES will sort the file on RACE and SEX and define all the cases having any particular combination of values of those variables as a subfile. The first subfile will be named S1, the second will be named S2, and so on.

If SEX is coded 1 for males and 2 for females, and RACE is coded 1 for whites, 2 for blacks, and 3 for others, the subfiles can be assigned names as follows:

```
SORT CASES      RACE SEX/ SUBFILES = WHTMALE WHTFEM BLKMALE
                BLKFEM OTHMALE OTHFEM
```

If SUBFILES = is followed by a list of names, those names will be applied to the subfiles in the order given. The keyword TO can be used to generate names in the same way as it is used on the VARIABLE LIST and DATA LIST commands. GRP1 TO GRP4 means GRP1, GRP2, GRP3, GRP4.

If not enough names are supplied for all the subfiles, SORT CASES will use its own names for the ones left unnamed. In the example above, if there were actually eight combinations of values of RACE and SEX, the seventh and eighth subfiles would be named S7 and S8.

Cases can be ordered within each subfile. The sorting variables that are to be used to define subfiles are listed in parentheses after /SUBFILES. For example, the following specification should be used to sort a file of persons by place and census tract within subfiles defined by state code:

```
SORT CASES      STATE, PLACE, TRACT/ SUBFILES(STATE)
```

More than one variable may be listed, and the TO convention (first variable TO last variable) can be used.

The variables used to define the subfiles must appear first on the sorting list, before any variables used to order cases within subfiles. Therefore the list of variables in parentheses after SUBFILES must be an initial sublist of the list of sort key variables. In the example above, STATE or STATE and PLACE, or STATE, PLACE and TRACT could be used to define subfiles, but PLACE alone could not. SPSS will accept a single variable name in that spot as meaning all the variables up to and including the named variable on the list of sort keys. So the following two commands will have the same effect:

```
SORT CASES      STATE PLACE TRACT/ SUBFILES(STATE PLACE)
SORT CASES      STATE PLACE TRACT/ SUBFILES(PLACE)
```

If there are more than 100 different combinations of values of the variables used to define subfiles, the first 99 get a subfile each, and the rest are lumped into the 100th subfile. (In the M version, 200 subfiles can be defined, so the same thing happens if there are more than 200 different combinations.)

If the parenthesized list of grouping variables is omitted, all the variables named as sort keys will be used as grouping variables (except SEQNUM—see Preserving the Original Order below).

If the SUBFILES parameter is omitted, the sorted file will have one subfile, whose name is the same as the name of the file.

Whether or not new subfiles are defined, SORT CASES implies RUN SUBFILES ALL. That is, the effect of any previous RUN SUBFILES command is lost, and procedures after SORT CASES will act as if the file had no subfile structure. If each subfile, or group of subfiles, is to be processed separately, SORT CASES should be followed by an appropriate RUN SUBFILES command.

Since the G (Mini) version of SPSS does not allow subfiles, the SUBFILES parameter of SORT CASES is ignored in that version.

14.4 PRESERVING THE ORIGINAL ORDER

The original order of cases within the groupings produced by sorting will be preserved if SEQNUM (in ascending order) is added to the end of the list of sorting variables. The following specification will organize a file by state code but keep the original case order within each state:

```
SORT CASES      STATE SEQNUM/SUBFILES
```

SEQNUM will never be used to define subfiles. If it is named as a subfile definition variable, SORT CASES will give a syntax error. If SUBFILES is specified with no list of grouping variables, all sort variables except SEQNUM will be used as grouping variables.

14.5 SUMMARY

14.6 SORT CASES Syntax

```
SORT CASES      sort variable list [(A|D)]
                [sort variable list...]
                [/SUBFILES [(grouping variable list)]
                        [= subfile name list] ]
```

14.7 Limitations for SORT CASES

- No more than 64 variables may be named in the sort variable lists.
- No more than 8 variables may be used as grouping variables. If the grouping variable list is omitted, the first 8 sorting variables will be used as grouping variables if more than 8 variables are used for sorting.
- No more than 100 subfiles may be defined in the standard (H) version of SPSS, and no more than 200 subfiles may be defined in the maxi-version (M).
- The SPSS-generated variable SUBFILE cannot be used as a sort key. If no other variable identifies the subfiles, to reorder variables within subfiles while preserving the present subfile structure, one can make a copy of SUBFILE using a COMPUTE statement and sort on that variable first.

14.8 Job Control for SORT CASES.

- The JCL required for the OS versions has not changed, except that the FT04F001 DD card is not required by SORT CASES itself.
- The JCL required for the DOS versions has also not changed, except that no JCL for SVFILE is required by SORT CASES itself.

For system commands required by other computer systems, refer to the appropriate appendix in this manual or see your local SPSS Coordinator.

SORT CASES was designed and programmed by Jonathan Fry.

Chapter 15

DISCRIMINANT

SPSS DISCRIMINANT is an entirely new subprogram as of Release 8. All code from the previous release has been replaced. All specifications, options, and statistics listed in *SPSS,*, Second Edition, have been implemented. The temporary limitations on the subprogram (not listed in the manual but implemented in the program) have been removed. The various dimensions of the problem are now limited only by the available workspace. Changes in some details and several additions to the subprogram have also been made.

Procedure DISCRIMINANT calculations are now done almost entirely with double precision arithmetic. Options 13, 14, and 17-19 and Statistics 7 and 8 have been implemented as documented in *SPSS,* Second Edition. Options 15 and 16 (which request matrix output and input) have also been implemented, although their format and content differ somewhat from that documented in the manual. Statistic 10, which prints the structure matrix (correlations between the discriminating variables and the canonical discriminant functions) has also been added.

All DISCRIMINANT specifications listed in the manual have been implemented, with a few minor alterations. A new parameter, SELECT=, designed primarily to allow automatic computations of unbiased error rate estimates, has been added.

Stepwise output and inclusion methods have also been altered slightly. Backward stepwise inclusion is now available.

In general, the new DISCRIMINANT follows the documentation provided in *SPSS,* Second Edition. The major change concerns Options 15 and 16; the sections included in this document on Options 15 and 16 completely replace Section 23.6 in *SPSS,* Second Edition. All other changes or additions to the manual are listed below. With these exceptions, the manual can be considered current.

15.1 CHANGES IN COEFFICIENTS

Both the constants associated with classification functions and the canonical discriminant function coefficients printed by the present version of DISCRIMINANT are different from those printed by the previous version.

15.2 Classification Function Constants

Unlike the previous version, the present procedure adds the natural logs of the prior probabilities to the classification function constants so that this term need not be added to the function values when they are used to classify cases.

15.3 Discriminant Function Coefficients

The difference in the canonical discriminant function coefficients (which affects both standardized and unstandarized coefficients) is more complicated. The previous version calculated coefficients so that the total covariance matrix of the discriminant function values, when computed from the original sample, was an identity matrix (all the variances were one and all the covariances were zero). The present version's coefficients, when applied to the original sample, give function values whose pooled within-groups covariance matrix is an identity. Neither treatment is wrong, but the one used in the present version is more customary.

15.4 CHANGES IN STEPWISE OUTPUT AND INCLUSION RULES

A number of substantial changes appear in the step-by-step output from stepwise variable selection. Also, inclusion rules have been changed slightly.

15.5 Output of Criterion Statistics

There is no longer a column labeled CRITERION. Instead, the criterion statistic is named, and the actual value of the statistic is printed, rather than an intermediate result. The value printed is always the value the statistic would have if the variable listed with it were removed or included in the analysis, whichever is appropriate. For methods other than WILKS, this column will often be blank; the criterion statistics are expensive to compute, so the program usually avoids computing them when they are not needed to make the next step's decisions.

Further, for MAHAL and MAXMINF, which are the closest pair of groups criteria, the group codes of the two closest groups are also shown.

15.6 Even Inclusion Levels

The action specified by an even inclusion level has been changed somewhat. In previous versions, a variable named with an even inclusion level was included in the analysis if both its tolerance and its F-to-enter exceeded the specified levels. In the current version, F-to- enter is not examined; a variable named with an even inclusion level is entered if it passes the tolerance test.

15.7 Backward Stepwise Selection

Backward stepwise selection, which is particularly useful when most of the variables involved in the analysis contribute significantly to discrimination, can now be performed by procedure DISCRIMINANT. Any variable can now appear more than once in an ANALYSIS= list. If it appears at some even inclusion level and again at level 1, it will be eligible for removal when processing of level 1 begins. The following example illustrates backward stepwise variable selection for the variables V1 to V10:

```
DISCRIMINANT   GROUPS=G(1,5)/ VARIABLES=V1 TO V10/
               ANALYSIS=V1 TO V10(2)  V1 TO V10(1)/
```

In this example, V1 to V10 are included in the analysis when level 2 is processed; when processing for level 1 begins, they can only be removed. After the first step at level 1, of course, both inclusions and removals are possible. If you wish to prevent inclusions (which is not recommended), specify PIN=0.

15.8 Minimum Tolerance

A new statistic, which for want of a better name has been termed the "minimum tolerance", is printed in stepwise output. The minimum tolerance of a variable X is the smallest tolerance any variable in the analysis would have if X were included. Neither direct nor the stepwise methods will include a variable in the analysis whose minimum tolerance is less than the value specified in the TOLERANCE= parameter. (See Section 15.10.)

15.9 CHANGES IN DISCRIMINANT PARAMETERS

15.10 The TOLERANCE= Parameter

The TOLERANCE= parameter is unchanged, as is the default tolerance level of 0.001; but the use made of the specified tolerance level has changed and a new statistic, minimum tolerance, is listed in the stepwise output. The minimum tolerance test is used in both the direct and stepwise variable selection methods to give better protection against ill-conditioned matrices and multicollinear variable sets.

The tolerance of a variable in the analysis at any given step is the proportion of its within-groups variance not accounted for by other variables in the analysis; it is sometimes labeled "unique variance". The tolerance of a variable not in the analysis is the tolerance it would have if it were included. The minimum tolerance of variable X is the smallest tolerance any variable in the analysis would have if X were included.

Neither direct nor the stepwise methods will include a variable in the analysis whose minimum tolerance is less than the value specified in the TOLERANCE= parameter.

The minimum tolerance test is more fully described in James Frane's "Note on Checking Tolerance in Matrix Inversion and Regression" (1977, *Technometrics* 19, 513-514).

15.11 The MAXSTEPS= Parameter

The default value for the MAXSTEPS= parameter is now the number of variables named or implied at inclusion levels greater than one, plus twice the number named or implied at inclusion level 1. The previous MAXSTEPS= default value was twice the number of variables listed in the ANALYSIS= list.

The usual reason for specifying MAXSTEPS= is to prevent "inclusion loops", i.e., situations in which the same variable or set of variables is included and removed repeatedly with no other variables changing status. This precaution is probably not necessary in DISCRIMINANT; the procedure will detect loops involving only one variable and stop at the stage at which the criterion statistic has its optimum value (usually after including the variable the second time).

We know of no cases in which more than one variable has been involved in a loop; in fact, that may not be possible. If you can document a multiple-variable loop from any reliable stepwise regression or discriminant program, please let us know so the above uncertainty can be removed from this document.

15.12 The PIN=, POUT=, and VIN= Parameters

The parameters PIN= and POUT= (maximum significance of F to enter or remove a variable in stepwise analysis) and VIN= (minimum increase in Rao's V to enter under METHOD=RAO) have been implemented as documented in *SPSS, Second Edition.*

15.13 The SELECT= Parameter

A new feature of DISCRIMINANT as of Release 8 is the SELECT= parameter. SELECT= allows the sample to be split so that a portion of cases can be used to compute unbiased estimates of the misclassification rate. In order to use this feature, create a variable (possibly using the data transformation facilities) which has one value for all cases which are to be used in computing coefficients and only for those cases. Next, enter

```
SELECT=varname(value)
```

in the DISCRIMINANT command, where "varname" is the name of the selection variable and "value" is the value it assumes on cases to be used in computing coefficients.

SPSS uses only the cases which show the specified value on the selection variable to compute basic statistics (such as means and covariances) and to compute discriminant function coefficients. But when these coefficients are applied to cases to compute discriminant scores, plot scores, and classify cases, all the cases are used. Two classification results tables are printed (Option 5), one for the cases used to compute the coefficients and one for all other cases. The percentage of correct classifications is shown for each table.

The percentage of cases correctly classified will always be optimistic when the same cases are used both to compute the discriminant functions and in classification. Stepwise variable selection makes the situation much worse. To get an unbiased estimate of the error rate when a set of coefficients is applied to a different sample, randomly split the sample into two parts, one for computing coefficients and one for estimating the error rate. The following example shows how to do this assuming that 40% of the cases are to be used for computing coefficients and the other 60% are to be used for estimating the error rate:

```
COMPUTE         SET=TRUNC(UNIFORM(2.5))
DISCRIMINANT    GROUPS=GRPVAR(1,6)/
                VARIABLES=V1 TO V65/
                SELECT=SET(0)/
                ANALYSIS=..../
OPTIONS         5
```

In the COMPUTE statement, UNIFORM(2.5) generates uniformly distributed random numbers between 0 and 2.5. Of the numbers so generated, 40% can be expected to be between 0 and 1; TRUNC will give 0's for these numbers, and 1's and 2's for the others. Therefore, SET will be a random variable in which the expected probability of the value 0 is .40 (for any particular file, the proportion of zeros in SET will probably not be .40, but some number close to it). Note that a permanent COMPUTE is used here. If you use a selection variable that has been created with either the UNIFORM or NORMAL function; do *not* use a temporary transformation statement to create the variable. If the variable is created using a temporary transformation, when the file is reread for classification of the cases, the value of the variable changes and cases will be classified into different groups.

The SELECT= parameter specifies that only those cases for which SET has the value 0 are to be used to compute discriminant function coefficients, but all cases are to be classified.

Option 5 specifies that a classification results table and percentage of correct classifications are to be printed for each set of cases: those with a 0 in SET, and those with some other value. The percentage of correctly classified cases which did not have a 0 in SET is then an unbiased estimate of the percentage of this population that would be correctly classified if the same coefficients were used.

15.14   CHANGES TO DISCRIMINANT OPTIONS

15.15   Option 10: Print Territorial Map

The territorial map requested by Option 10 can now be printed even if the number of canonical discriminant functions exceeds two; if there are more than two functions, all their values except the first two are set to zero for plotting.

The map is no longer completely filled in; only the borders of regions of like classification are shown. This is done by plotting only the points not completely surrounded by points classified into the same group.

The + sign has been replaced as the symbol for the 37th group by the $ sign, so that the + sign can be used for registration marks.

15.16   Option 13: Varimax Rotation

Option 13 requests that the canonical discriminant functions be rotated to ease their interpretation. If Statistic 10 (structure matrix) is not requested, the matrix of standardized discriminant function coefficients is rotated; if Statistic 10 is requested, the structure matrix is rotated.

The rotation uses the VARIMAX criterion and Kaiser's normalization. The "communality" used for normalizing each variable is its within-groups squared multiple correlation (one minus its tolerance) if the coefficient matrix is rotated, or the sum of squared correlations with discriminant functions if the structure matrix is used.

The rotation matrix is always printed. Associated with each of its columns (corresponding to the rotated functions) is a number labeled % VARIANCE. This is the percentage of the sum of between- groups variances in all the functions rotated which is accounted for by each rotated function. If some functions were not rotated (because FUNCTIONS= was used to limit the number used), these percentages are not comparable to the percentages of variance printed in the table titled CANONICAL DISCRIMINANT FUNCTIONS.

Whenever rotation is performed, the matrix being interpreted (the structure matrix or the rotated coefficient matrix) is reordered to ease interpretation. Variables are grouped by the function with which each has the highest correlation (or coefficient), and, within each group, sorted by the magnitude of that highest correlation or coefficient. The largest number in each row (the one on which the row was grouped and sorted) is flagged with an asterisk.

When rotation is requested, the rotated functions are used for all further calculations.

15.17   Option 14: Individual Group Covariance Matrices

Option 14, requesting use of individual group covariance matrices for classification, is implemented as documented in *SPSS*, Second Edition. The Option requests that individual group covariance matrices be employed instead of the pooled within-groups covariance matrix in computing the probabilities of group membership during classification.

15.18   Option 15: Matrix Output

Procedure DISCRIMINANT Options 15 and 16 handle matrix output and input, respectively. If Option 15 is selected, subprogram DISCRIMINANT produces matrix-type output on the raw output data file. These matrix materials may be used as input for subsequent analyses using Option 16. (NOTE: The documentation of Options 15 and 16 in this manual replaces Section 23.6 of *SPSS*, Second Edition).

Option 15 produces records containing labeling information, weighted and unweighted counts, means, and covariance matrices for DISCRIMINANT groups. The matrix materials are written as 80-column records (so they can be punched on cards) with no sequence numbers. In this section, they will be described as if they were cards, even though they need not be.

The subprogram produces matrix materials for each group specified by the GROUPS= parameter. For each group, a card containing the group code, the unweighted and weighted counts, and the group label (the value label for the group code) is produced. Next, the group means for each of the variables listed after VARIABLES= are produced. Finally, either group covariance matrices or pooled within-groups covariance matrices are written, depending upon whether or not Statistic 7 or 8 or Option 14 has been requested.

If Statistic 7 or 8 or Option 14 is in effect, individual group covariances are required, and therefore group covariances are written when Option 15 is in effect and must be supplied when Option 16 is used. If neither Statistic 7 or 8 nor Option 14 is set (and therefore individual group covariances are not required) the group covariance matrices are replaced with a pooled within-groups covariance matrix.

When group covariance matrices are produced, they are written along with the other materials for each group, directly after the group means. When the pooled within-groups covariance matrices are required, they come last, after all other materials for each group. The matrix materials may be represented as follows:

For group covariance matrices (Statistic 7 or 8 or Option 14 is set):

    group 1   code, counts, labels
                 means
                 group covariance matrix

    group 2   code, counts, labels
                 means
                 group covariance matrix

                 .

                 .

                 .

For pooled within-groups covariance matrix (Statistics 7 and 8 and Option 14 are NOT set):

    group 1   code, counts, labels
                 means

    group 2   code, counts, labels
                 means

                 .

                 pooled within groups covariance matrix

(Note that the group standard deviations are not part of the materials supplied when pooled within groups covariance matrices are produced and cannot be inferred from them. For this reason Statistic 2, printing of standard deviations, is not available with matrix input unless group covariance matrices are required.)

When a group, as specified by the GROUPS= parameter, is empty, the means cards are not written. When group covariance matrices are being produced, no covariance matrices accompany empty groups, groups which contain only one case, or groups where the sum of the weights is not greater than one. Similarly, when pooled within-groups covariance matrices are produced, no matrices will be written if the total sum of case weights or the total number of cases is not greater than the number of groups. When matrix materials are used for input, no covariance matrix is expected when none would be written, given the same case counts.

The code, counts, and labels card produced for each group contains the group code in columns 1-10, the unweighted count in columns 11-20, the weighted count in columns 21-33 (with two decimal places), and the label in columns 35-54. All means and covariances are written five to the card, using 16 columns per number. Nine significant digits are always produced. Each set of means starts on a new card, as does each row of each covariance matrix. Covariance matrices are written in lower triangular form; that is, only the first element of the first row, the first two elements of the second row, the first three elements of the third row, and so on, are written. The redundant upper triangular elements of the matrix and the diagonal are omitted.

15.19 Option 16: Matrix Input

Procedure DISCRIMINANT Options 15 and 16 handle matrix output and input, respectively. Output produced from Option 15 may be used as input for subsequent analyses using Option 16. (NOTE: The documentation of Options 15 and 16 in this manual replaces Section 23.6 of *SPSS, Second Edition*).

Selection of Option 16 specifies that matrix materials are to be used as input for the analysis. These materials may be generated by SPSS through the use of Option 15. The minimum setup of a control deck for use with matrix input looks like this:

```
VARIABLE LIST   V1 TO V16, CLASS
DISCRIMINANT    GROUPS=CLASS(1,3)/
                VARIABLES=V1 TO V16/
                ANALYSIS= V1 TO V9(4) V10 TO V16(1)/
OPTIONS         16
STATISTICS      5
READ MATRIX
                .
                matrix materials
                .
FINISH
```

A VARIABLE LIST card is required to specify the number of variables and their names. The READ MATRIX card is always required with matrix input from cards. The other control cards which may be necessary are

- RUN SUBFILES: If the RUN SUBFILES card or GROUPS=SUBFILES specification were used in the run which produced the matrix materials, they must be used in runs which read the materials. The same subfile structure must be used in both runs. The number of cases specified for the various subfiles does not matter; the subprogram uses the counts on the code, counts, and labels card.
- If a RUN SUBFILES card is in effect when matrix materials are written, a complete set of materials is written for each subfile group. A run to use them all must contain a RUN SUBFILES card specifying the same number of subfile groups.
- INPUT MEDIUM: If the matrix materials are to be read from tape or disk, an INPUT MEDIUM statement must be supplied.
- LABELS: The SPSS labeling facilities, such as RUN NAME, TASK NAME, and VAR LABEL, have their usual effect. However, VALUE LABELS for the group variable will not be used; the labels on the code, counts, and label cards will be used instead.

15.20 Using Matrix and Data Input Together

DISCRIMINANT is the one procedure in SPSS which allows the use of both matrix input and data input in the same execution of the procedure. Since both kinds of input are allowed in the same run, one sample can be used to classify any number of later samples or to perform many analyses, aimed at improving the solution, on the same sample using all the plots and classification option without recomputing the basic statistics.

If Option 16 (matrix input) and any of Options 5-9 or 17-19 (which require either calculation of discriminant function scores or classification of cases or both) are specified, the program will require both matrix and data input. This section describes how to set up your SPSS control deck for such runs.

If both data and matrix materials are used, all the means, covariances, eigenvalues, and coefficients are calculated from the matrix materials, and variable selection and the territorial maps are based on them. The canonical discriminant function scores are computed from the coefficients calculated from the matrix materials applied to the values of the discriminating variables in the input data. Each case is classified on the basis of these discriminant function scores and on the group centroids computed from the matrix materials.

If the data are on a system file or archive file, the setup is very simple: use GET FILE or GET ARCHIVE first to make the data available; then run DISCRIMINANT using the setups described above for matrix input. The matrix materials may be in the control deck or on a file; use INPUT MEDIUM to specify which. The control deck's basic arrangement (for card input) is

```
GET FILE       ...
INPUT MEDIUM   CARD
DISCRIMINANT   ...
OPTIONS        16,...
READ MATRIX
               .
               matrix materials
               .
               other procedure control cards or
               temporary transformations
               .
```

If the data are not in system file form, three basic restrictions apply: First, SPSS allows only one input medium at a time. Second, the DISCRIMINANT procedure needs the matrix materials first, then the data. If both the matrix and the data originate from the control deck, the matrix materials must come first, followed by the data. Finally, either the data or the matrix materials must be on cards in the SPSS control deck.

If both the data and the matrix materials are on cards in the SPSS control deck, the deck setup is as follows:

```
               .
               data file description cards, such as
               DATA LIST, VAR LABELS, etc.
               .
INPUT MEDIUM   CARD
DISCRIMINANT   ...
OPTIONS        16, ...
READ MATRIX
               .
               matrix materials
               .
READ INPUT DATA
               .
               data cards
               .
END INPUT DATA
               .
               .
               .
```

Note that the data are available for use in other procedures after this execution of DISCRIMI-NANT. Transformations, selection, and all the other facilities of SPSS are available for use with it.

Because only one input medium is allowed at a time, special arrangements must be made when the matrix materials and data are on different media. Force SPSS to pass the data first, then change the input medium. Either a procedure or READ INPUT DATA can be used to do this. For example, if the data are on a disk file and the matrix materials on cards, the setup might be

```
                       .
               Data file description cards, transformations, etc.
                       .
   INPUT MEDIUM    DISK
   READ INPUT DATA
   INPUT MEDIUM    CARD
   DISCRIMINANT    ...
   OPTIONS         16, ...
   READ MATRIX
                       .
               matrix materials
                       .
                       .
                       .
```

If the data are on cards and the matrix materials are on a tape or disk file, the setup is

```
               Data descriptions, tranformations, etc.
   INPUT MEDIUM    CARD
   READ INPUT DATA
                       .
               data
                       .
   END INPUT DATA
   INPUT MEDIUM    DISK
   DISCRIMINANT
   OPTIONS         16, ...
                       .
                       .
                       .
```

Note that the READ MATRIX card is not needed unless the matrix materials are on cards.

If a RUN SUBFILES command specifying processing of more than one subfile group is in effect, it applies to both the matrix materials and the data. There must be a complete set of matrix materials for each subfile group. If matrix materials and data are on cards, all the sets of matrix materials must precede all the data.

If the matrix materials are read from an external file (not cards), they can be used in more than one execution of DISCRIMINANT; if they are on cards, a separate copy is required for each execution.

15.21   Options 17, 18, and 19: Output of Raw Data

Options 17, 18, and 19 produce output on the raw output file. All logical records so written are 80 columns long. Contrary to the statement in *SPSS,* Second Edition, there are no sequence numbers on these card-image records. The subfile name and case sequence number (within subfile) are always included as the first two items. They are followed by the actual and classified group numbers (if Option 19 is specified), the discriminant scores (if Option 17 is specified), and the group membership probabilities (if Option 18 is specified). Each field of each record is eight columns long, and each case begins on a new record. If the record for a case does not fit in 80 columns, the remainder is continued on subsequent records as needed.

OPTION 17   *Output discriminant scores.* The number of discriminant scores written for each case is equal to the number of functions specified in the FUNCTIONS= parameter or to the default number of functions, whichever is smaller. The default number of functions is the number of variables specified in the ANALYSIS= list or the number of groups less one, whichever is smaller. If fewer functions are actually generated (because, for example, FUNCTIONS= was used to extract only significant functions), the remaining fields on the output record will contain the missing value code −9999. If no function values are computed because a discriminating variable was missing and Option 2 was not specified, all the function values will be −9999.

OPTION 18   *Output membership probabilities for all groups.* The number of membership probabilities written is the number implied by the range specified in the GROUPS= parameter, even if some groups have no cases. The probability of membership in an empty group is always zero. If membership probabilities are not computed for a case because one or more discriminating variables are missing and Option 2 is not specified, all the probabilities take the missing value −9999.

OPTION 19   *Output actual group and classified group numbers.* The actual group code is truncated to an integer and written as is, whether or not it is missing or out of range. If a case cannot be classified because one or more discriminating variables is missing and Option 2 is not specified, the classified group code is −9999.

All fields on these records, except the first (the subfile name), should be read with a format of F8.0; those which are not integers contain decimal points, and the decimal points in discriminant function scores are not in a fixed location.

If more than one ANALYSIS= list is used, all of the output from the first list is written first, then all the output from the second list, and so on, even if more than one subfile group is being processed.

15.22 CHANGES AND ADDITIONS TO DISCRIMINANT STATISTICS

STATISTIC 7   *Test of equality of group covariance matrices.* Statistic 7 is correctly described in *SPSS*, Second Edition, with one exception. The manual states that if Option 14 (which requests use of individual group covariance matrices for classification) is in effect, the test is performed not only for covariance matrices based on discriminating variables, but also for matrices based on the discriminant functions.

In fact, the test of equality of the group covariance matrices based on the discriminant funtions is performed whenever those matrices must be computed (specifically, when Option 14 and any of Options 5-8, 10, or 17-19 are specified), whether or not Statistic 7 is requested. Thus, Statistic 7 requests only a test of the equality of the group covariance matrices based on the discriminating variables.

STATISTIC 8   *Group covariance matrices.* Statistic 8 is implemented in this release as documented in *SPSS*, Second Edition.

STATISTIC 10   *Structure matrix.* Statistic 10 causes the procedure to print the matrix of pooled within-groups correlations between the canonical discriminant functions and the discriminating variables (often called the structure matrix). Further, when Statistic 10 is specified, the program assumes that discriminant functions will be interpreted using the structure matrix rather than a matrix of coefficients.

Correlations are printed for each variable named or implied on the ANALYSIS= list, whether or not it was selected in variable selection; the only exception occurs if the variable has no within-groups variance. The matrix is ordered to ease interpretation; the variables are grouped according to the function with which they are most highly correlated. Within each such group, variables are sorted in descending order by the magnitude of that largest correlation. If there is more than one function, the largest correlation for each variable (the one used to group and sort) is flagged with an asterisk.

If Option 13 (varimax rotation) is also requested, the structure matrix, rather than the standardized discriminant function coefficient matrix, is rotated.

15.23 LIMITATIONS FOR SUBPROGRAM DISCRIMINANT

Release 7 temporary limitations on DISCRIMINANT (not listed in the manual but implemented in the program) have been removed. These limitations had specified a maximum of 100 groups, 100 variables, and 100 steps. The various dimensions of the problem are now limited only by the available workspace (see below).

15.24 WORKSPACE REQUIREMENTS

The formulas for calculating DISCRIMINANT's workspace requirements in *SPSS*, Second Edition no longer apply. The formulas for the new version are considerably more complicated than those for the old one, so they will not be published. However, some rough guidelines are given here to allow estimation.

When Option 8 is requested, the space for its scatterplots is often the largest portion of the workspace requirement. Each scatterplot requires 4116 bytes of workspace, and space for one such plot is required for each possible group (one for each integer in the range specified in GROUPS=), and one more for ungrouped cases (unless Option 9 is specified). Option 7 (the single plot of cases) requires one more. If only one discriminant function can occur (because there is only one variable or only two groups, or FUNCTIONS=1 was specified), only enough space for a histogram for each group is required at 648 bytes per group. In this case, no extra space is needed for Option 7.

Space for variable-by-variable matrices may exceed that for plots if the number of variables is large. Such matrices are always stored in triangular form by DISCRIMINANT, meaning the redundant upper triangle elements are omitted. Each matrix requires 4*NV*(NV+1) bytes of storage, where NV is the number of variables. Five such matrices are always required; if individual group covariance matrices are required, add one more for each group, less one. If Statistic 7 (test for equality of group covariance matrices) or Option 14 (classification using individual group covariance matrices) is specified, add two more. If neither Statistic 7 nor Option 14 is specified, but any of the stepping methods MAHAL, MAXMINF, or MINRESID has been requested, add one more.

These two space-eaters operate at different times, so only the larger applies. These estimates represent minimums, however, so allow plenty of extra space. If your problem is large and it would be inconvenient or expensive to underestimate the space on a full run, we suggest using the EDIT facility to have DISCRIMINANT calculate the space requirement for you.

Table 15.24 shows the space requirements in bytes for a variety of problem sizes. The first figure in each cell is almost a minimum for the given number of variables and groups. It is the number of bytes required when the classification results table is the only space-using option requested, and METHOD=WILKS. The second figure shows the bytes needed if all the space-using options except individual group covariance matrices are requested. The third figure is a maximum; Statistic 7 and Option 14 have been added to the specifications for the second figure so that individual covariance matrices are required.

Table 15.24

Number of Variables	Number of Groups 2	5	10	30
5	1,288	1,528	1,984	9,932
	2,256	29,796	51,560	142,200
	2,304	30,288	52,920	146,200
10	10,824	11,424	12,504	19,864
	12,984	30,460	53,400	149,344
	14,496	30,952	57,192	200,264
50	56,904	58,224	60,624	77,424
	68,304	69,624	71,824	160,480
	83,744	115,920	170,016	392,416
100	213,704	216,224	220,824	253,624
	256,504	259,024	263,224	280,024
	327,344	451,320	658,416	1,492,816

15.25 GENERAL WARNINGS

The criterion statistics for stepwise variable selection methods other than WILKS are expensive to compute. The extra time (above what would be required by WILKS) to compute a Rao's V is roughly proportional to the square of the number of variables presently in the analysis, and the time required for computing the minimum F or D squared, or the residual variance, is proportional to the cube of the same number of variables. Our advice is to use WILKS for stepwise variable selection unless there is a compelling reason to do otherwise or the number of variables is small.

The DISCRIMINANT procedure is well protected against the sorts of numerical difficulties that can occur when covariance matrices are computed by DISCRIMINANT from raw data. However, it is not so well protected from certain problems that can occur with matrix input. Specifically, if the pooled within-groups covariance matrix or some of the group covariance matrices are inconsistent (that is, they could not occur with real data; mathematically, they are not positive semidefinite), the behaviour of the program is not known. Such matrices could be the result of computing with pairwise deletion of missing data.

Note that these problems will not occur with the covariance matrices written by DISCRIMINANT in matrix output.

DISCRIMINANT was designed and programmed by Jonathan Fry.

Chapter 16

CROSSTABS

SPSS subprogram CROSSTABS now operates more quickly in general mode and has fewer restrictions in integer mode. It also offers three new options for raw data output and one new statistic, Pearson's product moment correlation.

16.1 SPEEDIER COMPUTATIONS IN GENERAL MODE

The singly-linked list algorithm for building CROSSTABS tables has been replaced, in general mode, by a hash table algorithm with pointers. In most cases this results in a substantial improvement in speed; even when it does not, the new algorithm is only slightly slower than the old.

Use of the new algorithm requires more workspace than the old. The workspace requirement, in bytes, is now given by the formula

WORKSPACE = NC * [10 + (4 * D)]

NC = the total number of cells in all tables requested
D = the number of dimensions of the table having the largest number of dimensions of those requested

For example, if twenty $2 \times 2 \times 2$ tables are requested,

WORKSPACE = 160 * [10 + (4 * 3)] = 3520

16.2 ALPHANUMERIC VALUES CORRECTLY ORDERED

CROSSTABS, general mode, now orders alphanumeric values alphabetically in the printed tables.

16.3 RAW OUTPUT FROM CROSSTABS

CROSSTABS now has two options for producing a raw output file suitable for use as an SPSS data file or as input to other programs, and a third option to eliminate printed output. The files produced contain a record for each cell of the table; each record contains the cell frequency, the values which identify the cell, and numbers to identify the table and subfile group from which the tables were built. The three new options are detailed below.

16.4 Options for Raw Data Output

OPTION 10 *Output of non-empty cells.* If Option 10 is in effect, CROSSTABS writes a record for each combination of values that occurs in the data, excluding combinations which include a missing value. If Option 1 (include missing data) is in effect, no values are considered missing, so no combinations are excluded from the output file. Option 10 overrides Option 11 if both are specified.

OPTION 11 *Output of all defined cells.* If Option 11 is in effect, CROSSTABS writes a record for each combination of values defined by the TABLES = portion of the control card. If neither Option 1 nor Option 7 (include missing data in tables but not in table percents or statistics) is in effect, no records are written for combinations involving one or more missing values. If Option 1 or Option 7 is in effect, all defined cells are written whether or not a missing value is involved. This option is available ONLY with the integer mode of CROSSTABS. If both Option 10 and Option 11 are specified, Option 11 is ignored.

OPTION 12 *Suppress printed output.* If Option 12 is in effect, CROSSTABS prints no tables and calculates no statistics but writes any output files requested by Option 10 or 11. If Option 12 is specified without either Option 10 or Option 11, no output at all will be produced.

16.5 The Output File

The CROSSTABS output file is written on the designated RAW OUTPUT UNIT (unit 9 is the default). Records are ordered on the following basis (minor order first):

the value of the row variable, within
the value of the column variable, within
the value of the first control variable, within
the value of the second control variable, within
  .
  .
  .
the value of the last control variable, within
the identity of the last control variable, within
the identity of the second last control variable, within
  .
  .
  .
the identity of the first control variable, within
the identity of the column variable, within
the identity of the row variable, within
each TABLES= list on the control card, within
subfile group.

This output order implies that

- Cells are written a column at a time.
- Tables are written in the same order as they are printed.
- While the value of the last control variable varies slowest, its identity varies fastest.

16.6 The Output Record

The output record from each cell contains the following information:

COLUMNS	CONTENTS
1–4	Subfile group number (numbered consecutively from 1.)
5–8	Table number (a table is defined by taking one variable from each of the variable lists connected with BY).
9–16	Cell frequency. The number of times this combination occurred in the data, or, if case weights are used, the sum of case weights for cases having this combination of values.
17–24	The value of the row variable (the one named before the first BY).
25–32	The value of the column variable (the one named after the first BY)
33–40	The value of the first control variable (the one named after the second BY).
41–48	The value of the second control variable (the one named after the third BY).
73–80	The value of the sixth control variable (the one named after the seventh BY).

The subfile group number, table number, and frequency are written as integers. If the integer mode of CROSSTABS is used, the values of variables are also written as integers. If the general mode is used, the values are written in accordance with the PRINT FORMAT specified for each variable. Alphanumeric values are written at the left end of any field in which they occur.

16.7 Using the Crosstabs Output File

If one ignores missing data considerations, the output file from CROSSTABS is a complete representation of the variables in each table over the file used, and is often much smaller than the original file. When used as a raw input file for SPSS, it allows the reproduction of the original table or any table which could be produced from the original file by dropping or rearranging variables in the TABLES= list. The basic setup for using the file as a representation of the original file is outlined below.

In the first run, write a file:

```
CROSSTABS       TABLES = A BY B BY C BY D BY E
OPTIONS         10
```

In the subsequent runs, use the cell frequency as a case weight:

```
DATA LIST       FIXED/ 1 FREQ 9-16
                A B C D E 17-56
INPUT MEDIUM    DISK
WEIGHT          FREQ

CROSSTABS       TABLES = C BY D BY E/
                A BY B BY D/
                .
                .
                .
FREQUENCIES     GENERAL = A TO E
```

Almost any statistical procedure which uses only the variables from one table can be run from the CROSSTABS output file as well as from the original file. The only exceptions occur when the order of cases is important, such as in the RUNS test in NPAR TESTS and in the Durbin-Watson statistic from REGRESSION.

If missing values are involved, a little more care must be used. Only combinations of nonmissing values get to the file, and a combination involving a missing value of D may involve no missing values of A, B, and C. In this case, use Option 1 when producing the file and redefine the missing values in the run which uses the CROSSTABS output file.

The CROSSTABS output file also can be used to combine tables in various ways. This usually comes up when one wants to change the unit of analysis. For example, a file of questionnaires in which the subjects were asked to rate five different airlines presents a problem if one wants to count ratings by airline and rating score. The unit of analysis is the questionnaire, not the rating, and MULT RESPONSE will not help, since it will associate each rating with all airlines listed on each case. To solve the problem, change the unit of analysis either by using WRITE CASES to generate new cases, or, more conveniently, by using CROSSTABS to generate new cases. The control decks might look like this:

```
CROSSTABS       TABLES= LINE1 BY RATING1/
                LINE2 BY RATING2/
                LINE3 BY RATING3/
                LINE4 BY RATING4/
                LINE5 BY RATING5/
OPTIONS         10 12
```

Second run:

```
DATA LIST       FIXED/ 1  FREQ 9-16
                          LINE RATING 17-32
INPUT MEDIUM    DISK
WEIGHT          FREQ

VAR LABELS      LINE AIRLINE CODE/
                RATING SATISFACTION RATING
VALUE LABELS    ...

CROSSTABS       TABLES = LINE BY RATING
```

The CROSSTABS output file can also be used as input to other programs such as ECTA (Everyman's Contingency Table Analysis Program, by Leo Goodman). Such programs generally require the entire table a row at a time, including empty cells. If such a program can accept a user-supplied format for the table input, the file produced by Option 11 will work. The input format required is (8X,F8.0) or, if I format is required, (8X,I8). Remember in this case that the SPSS file is organized to write a column at a time, rather than a row, so specify to SPSS the transpose of the table you wish to use in such a program. For example, if each row is to be defined by a value of SEX and each column by a value of PARTYID, then TABLES=SEX BY PARTYID gives the right table as printed by SPSS but the CROSSTABS output file will be in the wrong order for use by any program which wants the table a row at a time. In this case, use TABLES= PARTYID BY SEX.

16.8 STATISTIC 11 ADDED

In either integer or general mode, Pearson's product moment correlation may be requested with Statistic 11.

16.9 IMPROVEMENTS TO CROSSTABS, INTEGER MODE

Several improvements have been made to CROSSTABS, integer mode:

- The limit of 200 value labels no longer applies. More will be printed if enough workspace remains.
- The limit of 15 rows per subtable has been modified. The number of rows printed is contingent upon the pagesize specified. If NOEJECT is in force, the maximum number of rows printed is 200.
- The largest range which may be implied on the minimum-maximum specification on the VARIABLES= list is 32766.
- No more than 20 rows or columns of missing values may be printed under Option 7. See the optional specification for MISSING VALUES, Chapter 19.

Enhancements to CROSSTABS were designed and programmed by Jonathan Fry and Harvey Weinstein.

Chapter 17

ANOVA

Several significant improvements have been made to subprogram ANOVA, including a revised implementation of Option 9, regression approach, and a new statistic for producing a means and counts table.

17.1 REVISED AND NEW OPTIONS IN ANOVA

OPTION 9 *Regression approach.* The implementation of Option 9 has been changed so that it now generates dummy variables with values of -1, 0, and $+1$, as opposed to values of 0 and $+1$ as in previous releases. One of the more obvious results of this change is that Option 9 will, in the case of equal cell frequencies, give the same results as the default (classical) and Option 10 (hierarchical) approaches.

Two restrictions apply to the revised Option 9: The first is considerably more significant, as it applies to the data which may be analyzed using Option 9.

- The marginal frequencies for the lowest specified categories of all the independent variables must be non-zero. If this part of the restriction is violated, an appropriate message is printed identifying the first offending variable.

- Given an n-way frequency table for the independent variables, there must be no empty cells defined by the lowest specified category of any of the independent variables. This constraint does not apply to categories defined for an independent variable which do not occur in the data. If this constraint is violated, one or more levels of interaction effects will be suppressed, and an appropriate warning message will be issued. For instance, given two independent variables, each having categories of 1,2, and 4, the cell frequencies for the (1,1), (1,2), (1,4), (2,1), and (4,1) cells must be non-zero. Those for the (1,3), (2,3), (3,3), (4,3), (3,1), (3,2), and (3,4) cells are zero by definition, and those for the (2,2), (2,4), (4,2), and (4,4) cells may be zero, although the number of degrees of freedom will be reduced accordingly.

To comply with these restrictions, the user must specify precisely the lowest nonmissing category of each of the independent variables. Specifying a value range of (0,9) for a variable which actually has values of 1 through 9 will result in a non-fatal error and the production of no ANOVA table. Where conservation of memory is not a consideration, null categories within the specified range are handled correctly.

Second, the space requirements are marginally greater than those given in the manual (which still apply to the other approaches). To calculate a precise space requirement when Option 9 is specified, you must take the following additional steps:

- For each list on the ANOVA command, calculate the quantity $F = E-1$.
- For the entire ANOVA command, calculate the quantity SF = the sum of the individual values of F.
- Calculate the total WORKSPACE as $4 \times SM + SE + 36 \times MR + 8 \times MM + 4 \times SF$

For the sample calculation in the manual, the final term is $4 \times 15 = 60$ such that the total WORKSPACE is 2776 rather than 2716.

Statistic 1 (multiple classification analysis) will no longer be produced when Option 9 is specified.

OPTION 10 *Hierarchical approach.* While the manual stated without qualification that this option caused both main effects and covariates to be evaluated hierarchically, the program applied this technique to covariates only when Option 7 (include covariates with main effects) was specified. The covariate effects are now always evaluated hierarchically, regardless of the specification or absence of Options 7 and 8.

OPTION 11 *Print 80 columns only.* If Option 11 is specified, only 80 print columns will be used.

17.2 STATISTICS IN ANOVA

STATISTIC 2 The coefficients produced by Statistic 2 are unstandardized regression coefficients for the covariates. This has always been the case; the manual incorrectly stated that the coefficients are standardized.

STATISTIC 3 *Print means and counts table.* Statistic 3 requests printing of the means and counts of each dependent variable for each cell for each effect. This statistic is not available with Option 9.

   For each dependent variable, a separate table is printed for each effect, showing the means and cell counts for each combination of values of the the factor variables which define that effect, ignoring all other factors. If any of Options 4 through 6, which suppress higher order interactions, are specified, no cell means corresponding to suppressed interaction terms will be printed.

   The means printed are not adjusted for anything and are only for dependent variables, not covariates.

Chapter 18

ONEWAY

SPSS procedure ONEWAY now offers an option for using the harmonic mean of all groups (rather than of just the two groups being compared) in range tests; and, under certain conditions, multiple comparisons are automatically performed in Releases 8 and 9. Missing groups are now handled differently, and several calculations (notably that of polynomial contrasts) have been improved.

18.1 OPTION 10: USE HARMONIC MEAN FOR ALL GROUPS IN RANGE TESTS

The quantity compared to the difference between two means in any range test is

$$R\sqrt{\frac{MSW}{N}}$$

where
R = the appropriate critical range,
MSW = the mean square within groups,
and N = either the harmonic mean of the sizes of the two groups being compared, or, with Option 10, the harmonic mean of all group sizes.

The harmonic mean of any set of group sizes is given by

$$\frac{P}{\sum_i \frac{1}{N_i}}$$

where
P = the number of groups,
N_i = the size of group i,
and the sums are taken over the groups whose harmonic mean size is being calculated.

If all groups have the same size, both methods give the same results—the N used is the common group size.
    In releases prior to 8, ONEWAY finds homogeneous subsets by comparing the highest and lowest means in a subset and decides that the subset is homogeneous if the difference is not significant. If the default procedure is used to calculate the N for the comparisons, and the groups with the highest and lowest means are small, the program can conclude that the subset is homogeneous even though there are significant differences between other (larger) groups within the subset. With Option 10, this cannot occur because the same N is used for all comparisons. If the groups are all nearly the same size, the harmonic mean will be close to the average group size; if not, it will be considerably smaller than the average.

18.2 MULTIPLE COMPARISONS IN RANGE TESTS

Subprogram ONEWAY now performs multiple comparisons between all pairs of groups for LSD, LSDMOD, SCHEFFE, TUKEY, and TUKEYB range tests. If Option 10 (harmonic mean) is chosen, or if the group N's are equal, the previous multiple range tests are correct. If the harmonic mean is not used in the computation and if the groups have unequal N's, the five range tests listed above sometimes produced erroneous results by defining a homogenous subset in which a pair of significantly different groups was embedded. The new method avoids this danger by comparing all pairs of groups.
    The group means are sorted into ascending order. The comparisons are identical to the ONEWAY multiple range test algorithms previously in use. However, all non-redundant pairs are

tested independently instead of halting the computations when the bounds of a supposedly homogenous subset are discovered. All empty (N=0) groups are dropped from the computations.

The output is the lower triangle of the square matrix of groups. An asterisk flags significantly different pairs of groups; blanks imply no significant difference between the specified pairs.

18.3 MISSING GROUPS

When one or more of the groups specified in the GROUPS= phrase on the ONEWAY control card is not present in the data, ONEWAY now handles the situation differently. The number of degrees of freedom between groups is calculated from the number of non-empty groups, rather than the number of groups specified, and the degrees of freedom used in calculating critical ranges for multiple range tests is adjusted accordingly.

18.4 POLYNOMIAL CONTRASTS

The calculation of polynomial contrasts has been revised. The program now does the following:

• The sums of squares for each order polynomial are computed from weighted polynomial contrasts using the group code as the metric (labeled STEP in Release 7, WEIGHTED in Releases 8 and 9). These contrasts are orthogonal; hence the sum of squares for each order polynomial will be statistically independent.

• If sample sizes in each group are not equal, and empty groups do not occur in the range of non-empty groups, unweighted polynomial contrasts and sums of squares (labeled UNIQUE in Release 7, UNWEIGHTED in Releases 8 and 9) are also computed. These contrasts are orthogonal only when the sample sizes are equal.

• Deviation sums of squares are always calculated from the weighted sums of squares (Speed, 1976).

We are indebted to Professor F.M. Speed, of Mississippi State University, for the code.

When polynomial contrasts are requested, the WORKSPACE required to compute them is twice what it was in release 6. The new formula for calculating WORKSPACE in bytes for ONEWAY is

$$\text{WORKSPACE} = 4 \times NC \times (1 + 5 \times NV + 2 \times NP2 + NCO + NR)$$

NC = the number of categories specified by GROUPS=
NV = the number of dependent variables
NP2 = the specified highest degree for polynomial contrasts plus 2 if POLYNOMIAL= was specified; NP2 = 0 otherwise
NC0 = the number of CONTRAST= specifications
NR = the number of RANGE= specifications

18.5 RANGE TEST SPECIFICATION

The significance for the range test limits has been changed to 0 to 1. In previous releases significance levels were limited to .001 through .20. Any value greater than zero and less than one is now accepted; zero and one are not.

18.6 ANALYSIS OF VARIANCE TABLE

The computation of within groups sum of squares has been improved substantially. It is now much less sensitive to large values of the dependent variable or large numbers of cases, and will no longer print negative sums of squares because of truncation errors.

18.7 LINEAR CONTRASTS

The calculation of degrees of freedom for the separate variance estimate t statistic for linear contrasts has been corrected. The formula used is

$$df = \frac{\left(\displaystyle\sum_{i=1}^{k} \frac{C_i S_i^2}{W_i} \right)^2}{\left(\displaystyle\sum_{i=1}^{k} \frac{C_i^2 S_i^2}{W_i^2} \right)/(W_i - 1)}$$

18.8 MORE DEPENDENT VARIABLES ALLOWED

Although *SPSS,* Second Edition, states that a maximum of 20 dependent variables can be named in the ONEWAY command, the procedure actually permits up to 99 dependent variables (and one independent variable).

Chapter 19

Other Changes
and Improvements

Introduction of new algorithms and double-precision arithmetic has improved the performance or accuracy and changed the workspace requirements of a number of SPSS subprograms not discussed in earlier chapters. New options have been added to FREQUENCIES, GET AR-CHIVE, NONPAR CORR, and SCATTERGRAM, and a new statistic to CONDESCRIPTIVE. A usage data collection facility has been installed to supply information for further development of SPSS (and also information to the user about elapsed CPU time), and several program restrictions have been eased or removed. These and similar changes are detailed in this chapter.

19.1 AGGREGATE

19.2 New Formulas for Skewness and Kurtosis
Skewness and kurtosis are now calculated as Fisher's g statistics. See CONDESCRIPTIVE, Section 19.9, for appropriate formulas.

19.3 Double Precision for AGGSTATS
AGGREGATE now computes all AGGSTATS except MIN and MAX in double precision. The workspace requirements have increased correspondingly. The formula for workspace on page 215 of *SPSS*, Second Edition, is correct if the 6 at the end of the formula is replaced with 11. The full formula for AGGREGATE's workspace requirements is

WORKSPACE = 8 × (NGVAR + 2 + sum(NV(i) × (NS(i) + 11)))

NV(i) = the number of variables on the ith VARIABLES= list
NS(i) = the number of statistics on the ith AGGSTATS= list
NGVAR = the number of grouping variables

19.4 BREAKDOWN

19.5 Double Precision Used for Sums and Sums of Squares
The BREAKDOWN procedure now uses double precision arithmetic to accumulate sums of squares. This will give more accurate sums, means, variances, and standard deviations when the criterion variable has many significant digits. As a result of this improvement, the procedure now runs slightly slower and requires more core (see below).

19.6 More Core Storage Required
In general mode, BREAKDOWN requires the following amount of core storage space:

WORKSPACE = 4 × (NCELLS + 1) × (MAXDIMS + 6)

NCELLS = total number of cells in all of the tables requested in the TABLES= list, where a cell is defined as a unique combination of the values of the independent or control variables and of one dependent variable.

MAXDIMS = maximum number of dimensions in any of the requested tables, i.e., the maximum number of uses of the keyword BY in any of the tables lists.

In integer mode, BREAKDOWN requires the following amount of core storage space:

WORKSPACE = 20×NCELLS + 20×MAXLABS

NCELLS = total number of cells in all tables requested. The number of cells in a given table is calculated by multiplying together the permitted number of values for each of the independent variables as specified in the VARIABLES= list. NCELLS is simply the sum of the number of cells in each table.

MAXLABS = maximum number of value labels for any table. If the workspace is too small to accomodate all of the labels, the excess labels will not appear on the printed table.

19.7 Limit of 32766 Cells

The general mode of the BREAKDOWN procedure cannot process more than 32766 cells at a time. It never could, but this limit is now explicitly implemented. This means that workspace above that required for 32766 cells cannot be used except for labels. Table 19.7 shows the maximum amount of workspace that the procedure will use (allowing for 200 value labels, the upper limit) for various numbers of dimensions:

Table 19.7

Dimension	Maximum Workspace (in bytes)
1	921,476
2	1,052,544
3	1,183,612
4	1,314,680
5	1,445,748
6	1,576,816
7	1,707,884

19.8 CANCORR

Several corrections and improvements have been made to CANCORR:

- The number of canonical variates which may be produced is no longer limited to five.
- All canonical correlations are printed. Previously only significant correlations were printed.
- Degenerate correlations are now computed correctly. The subprogram requires at least two cases before it will compute a correlation.
- The formula for the computation of χ^2 has been corrected. The formula previously used was

$$\chi^2 = -(N - .5 - (NV1 + NV2)/2)\log\lambda$$

This has been corrected to

$$\chi^2 = -(N - 1 - (NV1 + NV2 + 1)/2)\log\lambda$$

where
N = the number of cases,
NV1 = the number of variables in one set,
and NV2 = the number of variables in the other set.

19.9 CONDESCRIPTIVE

An additional statistic is now available and new formulas have been implemented for skewness and kurtosis.

19.10   Statistic 12

The sum of a variable over all cases may be requested with Statistic 12.

19.11   New Formulas for Skewness and Kurtosis

Skewness and kurtosis are now calculated as Fisher's g statistics.* The first four moments are calculated using a provisional means algorithm:**

$$\text{Skewness} = \frac{WM^3}{(W-1)(W-2)S^3}$$

$$\text{Kurtosis} = \frac{W(W+1)M^4 - 3M^2\,M^2(W-1)}{(W-1)(W-2)(W-3)S^4}$$

n = number of cases

W = sum of the weights

$$M^r = \sum_{i=1}^{n} w_i(X_i - \overline{X})^r$$

S = standard deviation

*C. I. Bliss, *Statistics in Biology,* Vol. I (New York: McGraw-Hill, 1967), pp. 142-144.

**C. C. Spicer, Algorithm AS 52: Calculation of Power Sums of Deviations about the Mean, *Applied Statistics,* 21 (1972), pp. 226-227.

19.12   FACTOR

The accuracy of computation of standard deviations and correlations has been improved by the use of a provisional means algorithm, which frees more space for the storage of significant digits. As a consequence of the use of this algorithm, the procedure is a little slower when listwise deletion of missing cases is used and considerably slower when pairwise deletion is used.

19.13   FINISH

It is no longer necessary to supply a FINISH command in an SPSS run. If the command is not entered by the user, the program will insert it. In such cases, output from the run will note that the FINISH command was SPSS-supplied.

19.14   FREQUENCIES

19.15   New Formulas for Skewness and Kurtosis

The formulas used for the computation of skewness and kurtosis have been revised to conform to Fisher's g statistics. See Section 19.11 for the formulas used.

19.16   Rounding and Truncation Errors Detected

FREQUENCIES in general mode will now detect rounding or truncation errors due to large or non- integer weights and will provide a warning message.

19.17   Speedier Computation in General Mode

The singly-linked list algorithm for building frequency tables in general mode has been replaced by a hash table algorithm with pointers. In most cases this results in a substantial improvement in speed. One user ran FREQUENCIES GENERAL=ALL on a file with 120 variables and 51,000 cases on the University of Chicago's 370/168. Running Release 7.2, the run required 564.66 seconds of CPU time; with Release 8, it required 182.89 seconds.

Use of the new algorithm requires more workspace than use of the old. The workspace requirement is now given by the formula

WORKSPACE = 14 × NVALS

NVALS = the total number of values encountered, summed over all variables named or implied in the FREQUENCIES command. NVALS may not exceed 32767.

19.18   New Table-Ordering Options in General Mode

By default, procedure FREQUENCIES lists a variable's frequencies in ascending order of the variable's values. Frequencies for value 1 are listed first, then those for value 2, etc. With Release

8, three options have been added to the procedure to provide alternatives to this default treatment. All these options are available only in GENERAL mode.

OPTION 10   *Descending order of value.* Frequencies for the variable's highest value are printed first, frequencies for the lowest value are listed last.

OPTION 11   *Descending order of frequency.* Frequencies for the most frequently occurring value are printed first; frequencies for the least frequently occurring value are printed last.

OPTION 12   *Ascending order of frequency.* Frequencies for the least frequently occurring value are printed first; those for the most frequently occurring value are printed last.

19.19   Limitation in Integer Mode

The maximum of 32767 values over all variables which may be referenced by FREQUENCIES in general mode applies also to integer mode. This is true in all SPSS releases.

19.20   GET ARCHIVE

19.21   Option 1: Recover Bad Archive File

Releases 6 and 6.01 of SPSSH and 1 and 1.01 of SPSSM contained an error in SAVE ARCHIVE which occasionally made ARCHIVE files unreadable. Changes were made to GET ARCHIVE in Releases 6.02(H) and 1.02(M) so that these files could be read, and to SAVE ARCHIVE so that the problem would not occur. The change to SAVE ARCHIVE contained an error such that the new GET ARCHIVE code sometimes could not read new ARCHIVE files. SAVE ARCHIVE was corrected in Release 7.2 (H and M).

With Release 8, GET ARCHIVE has been changed so that it will always read files produced by releases 6.02 or 1.02 or later releases, and Option 1 has been added. If Option 1 is in effect, it will correctly process ARCHIVE files created with releases 6 and 6.01, 1 and 1.01, but may fail with newer files. To use this option, simply insert

```
OPTIONS          1
```

after the GET ARCHIVE or MERGE FILES command.

Note that all files named in the GET ARCHIVE or MERGE FILES command are processed the same way, so it may be necessary to get and resave an old file with Option 1 before merging it with newer files.

In Release 8, when a file name in the GET ARCHIVE or MERGE FILES command fails to match that on the corresponding file, a warning message is printed and the run proceeds. This was a fatal error in previous releases. If SAVE ARCHIVE is used, its file names must match those on the GET ARCHIVE or MERGE FILES command, regardless of the actual file names.

19.22   Change to the Documentation

The formula listed under GET ARCHIVE Limitation 7 (*SPSS*, Second Edition, p. 175) for calculation of the amount of core storage required by an archive file has been changed. The new formula is

$$TOTSPACE = [24 \times INPUTVARS] + [(NELEMENT + 2) \times 8] + 8000$$

TOTSPACE = WORKSPACE + TRANSPACE = total amount of core storage space allocated, in bytes
INPUTVARS = total number of variables on all input files
NELEMENT = number of elements (filenames, variable names, keywords, equal signs, or slashes) on the GET ARCHIVE command

For example, an archive file with 517 variables and 7 elements on the GET ARCHIVE command needs 20,472 bytes of space:

$$TOTSPACE = [24 \times 517] + [(6 + 2) \times 8] + 8000 = 20,472$$

19.23   LIST ERRORS

Neither *SPSS*, Second Edition, nor this update includes the error text for SPSS-generated errors since the text is provided at the normal end of job and error messages are updated frequently. Users who want a complete listing of error messages now have a facility to generate such a list directly from the program. The command LIST ERRORS will produce the listing. It has no specification field. The following sample run will list all errors:

```
LIST ERRORS
FINISH
```

The LIST ERRORS command may appear anywhere in the command sequence except

• Within the set of commands which call for a procedure and specify its options and statistics.
• After a REORDER VARS, SORT CASES (in Release 7), or SAVE FILE command.

The list of error messages currently requires about 1150 printed lines.

19.24   LIST FILEINFO

19.25   Check for Invalid Keywords

SPSS now checks for invalid keywords on the LIST FILEINFO command. A message is printed flagging the keyword, and processing continues.

19.26   Last 200 Value Labels Printed

The last 200 value labels per variable defined by the user are printed. Previously, the first 199 labels and the last label were printed. There is still a 200 value label per variable limitation on a saved system file.

19.27   MISSING VALUES

An optional specification of missing values has been implemented to conform to the OSIRIS convention for missing values. It is now possible to specify that any value between two given values is to be treated as missing, or that any value greater than or equal to (or less than or equal to) a given value is to be treated as missing, by using the keyword THRU in the value list of the MISSING VALUES command.

The MISSING VALUES command may have any of these formats:

```
MISSING VALUES varlist (value)
MISSING VALUES varlist (value 1, value 2)
MISSING VALUES varlist (value 1, value 2, value3)
MISSING VALUES varlist (value 1 THRU value 2)
MISSING VALUES varlist (value 1 THRU value 2, value 3)
MISSING VALUES varlist (value 1, value 2 THRU value 3)
MISSING VALUES varlist ( )
```

The last format is used to eliminate all previously defined missing value definitions.

The keywords HIGHEST and LOWEST can be used with THRU to designate values higher than the highest or lowest value taken by a variable. HIGHEST and LOWEST may be abbreviated with HI and LO, respectively. For example,

```
MISSING VALUES VARA, VARC (8 THRU 12)/
               VARB (8 THRU HIGHEST)/
               VARD (9, LOWEST THRU 0)/
               VARE (0, 8, 9)
```

This MISSING VALUES command specifies that any value between 8 and 12 (including 8 and 12) is missing for VARA and VARC. For VARB, any value of 8 or higher is missing. For VARD, 9 is a missing value, as are all negative numbers and zero. For VARE, the values 0, 8 and 9 are missing; no range of missing values is implied here, so 8.5, for example, would not be treated as missing for VARE.

No more than three values may be specified in the missing values list, including the upper and lower ends of a range; thus, a range and one other value may be specified as missing, but not a range and two other values. When a range is specified, the value before THRU must not exceed the value after it. The keywords HIGHEST and LOWEST may be used only with THRU. That is, (9, HIGHEST) is not a valid missing value specification.

Missing values specified on OSIRIS data files are now treated in SPSS as they are treated in OSIRIS; that is, the second specified missing value is one end of an indefinite range of missing values—the end closest to 0. Table 19.27 shows examples of OSIRIS missing value specifications and the equivalent SPSS missing values specification:

Table 19.27

OSIRIS		SPSS
Value 1	**Value 2**	
0	8	0, 8 THRU HIGHEST
9	−1	9, LOWEST THRU -11
9		9
	8	8 THRU HIGHEST

The OSIRIS VARS facility of SPSS will automatically translate OSIRIS missing values specifications in this manner.

NOTE: The CROSSTABS procedure in integer mode cannot process any row or column variable for which more than twenty distinct missing values appear.

WARNING: Earlier releases of SPSS will not correctly process system files or archive files which contain missing value ranges. Variables for which missing value ranges have been specified will be treated as if no missing values had been defined. If system files are going to be used with earlier releases of SPSS, missing values should be redefined to conform to earlier conventions (using Release 7 or 8) and saved prior to use with earlier releases. Files created by Release 7 or 8 which do not contain missing value range specifications can by processed normally by earlier releases.

19.28 NONPAR CORR

19.29 Improved Performance

The performance of the NONPAR CORR subprogram has been substantially improved by the introduction of an advanced sorting algorithm.* While the performance improvement is substantial for both Spearman and Kendall correlations, it is dramatic for Spearman correlations. For example, an SPSS run to compute a single Spearman correlation on 4080 cases required 20.95 seconds of processor time on an IBM 370/168 using Release 6. The same run using Release 7 required 1.71 seconds.

The improvement increases with increasing sample size, so a larger sample would show even greater proportional improvements. Conversely, runs on small samples will show less improvement.

19.30 Option 7

Option 7 provides for random sampling when there is not enough workspace to accomodate all the cases. When this option is in effect, NONPAR CORR will not quit when there is insufficient workspace for all the cases but rather will proceed with the analysis on the basis of a random sample of the cases as large as can be accommodated. If there is enough workspace for all the cases, they will all be used. If Option 2, listwise deletion of missing values, is in effect, the correlations for each correlation list will be based on a different random sample extracted from nonmissing cases only.

The sampling procedure used works as follows:

• Each time a case is encountered after the limit imposed by the size of the workspace has been reached, the program decides whether to include it in the sample or not at random. The probability that the new case will enter the sample is equal to the number of cases which can be held in the workspace divided by the number of cases so far encountered. If the program decides to accept a case, it then picks at random one of the cases previously stored in the workspace and drops it from the analysis, replacing it with the new case. Each case has the same probability of being in the sample.

• If case weighting is used, the NONPAR CORR subprogram may use a case more than once. For example, if the weight of a case is 2.3, the program will use that case twice and may choose at random, with a probability of .3, to use it a third time. If sampling is in effect, each of these two or three cases is a candidate for sampling.

19.31 More Cases Handled and Workspace Slightly Increased

Previous versions of NONPAR CORR would not correctly handle more than 32767 cases. This limitation has been removed at the cost of a slight increase in the workspace required. The two formulas on page 291 of *SPSS,* Second Edition, should read as follows:

• For the default missing data option (pairwise deletion):

WORKSPACE = 4 × NVAR × NCASE + 12 × NCASE

• When either Option 1 (inclusion of missing data) or Option 2 (listwise deletion) is used:

WORKSPACE = 4 × NVAR × NCASE + 4 × NCASE

*R. C. Singleton, An Efficient Algorithm for Sorting with Minimal Storage, *Communications of the ACM* Algorithm 347.

19.32 NUMBERED

The keyword YES is no longer required in the specification field on the NUMBERED command.

19.33 PAGESIZE

If the keyword NOEJECT is used, logical page numbers will be printed, permitting the use of the index options for FREQUENCIES and CROSSTABS. Previously NOEJECT suppressed pagination.

19.34 REGRESSION

Several modifications have been introduced to the REGRESSION Procedure:

• If the list of independent variables in a REGRESSION= specification does not end with an inclusion level, the variables for which no level was supplied are given the level 1 (included last and stepwise).
• The maximum number of variables which may be referenced on a VARIABLES= list is 200 for version M. The limit for version H remains 100.
• Unstandardized regression coefficents (labelled "B") are now printed to seven significant digits.

19.35 SAVE ARCHIVE

Archive file labels specified in the SAVE ARCHIVE command are not reproduced properly on output: numbers are reproduced as arbitrary special characters. This difficulty can be avoided if the archive filename and label are entered in a FILE NAME command at the beginning of the run and omitted from the SAVE ARCHIVE command. When the SAVE ARCHIVE command is entered without a new file name, the archive file will be saved with the name and label specified in the FILE NAME command.

19.36 SAVE FILE

The last 200 value labels declared per variable will now be saved. Previously the first 199 and last value label per variable were saved on the file.

19.37 SCATTERGRAM

Option 8, allowing the program to proceed if there were too many cases for the available workspace, has been changed to request random sampling. This is the same as Option 7 in NONPAR CORR as documented in Section 12 of this chapter.

19.38 SCRATCH FILE: FT02F001

In the past, SPSS always created a temporary file for storage of data during any run. Formerly, when it was clear that this scratch file would not be used in a run (because the data would be read only once), it could be dummied using the FT02 DD statement. Dummying an unnecessary scratch file saved the cost of the I/O operations necessary to write it, but not the CPU time.

With Release 8, SPSS's handling of the FT02 file has been modified so that if the file is unnecessary—i.e., if it is clear that the data are to be passed only once—it will not be written. The scratch file will be written, as always, if more than one procedure is being run or if subfiles are being processed out of order. It will be written even when only one procedure is being run if procedure options are in effect which require data to be read more than once—as may be the case with procedures CANCORR, CONDESCRIPTIVE, DISCRIMINANT, FACTOR, or REGRESSION. The only situation in which a scratch file might be written and not read is when raw data are input on cards. In this case, the scratch file will always be written.

19.39 T-TEST

Subprogram T-TEST has been modified to perform and store all computations in double precision. A new formula for computing WORKSPACE is in effect, replacing the formula listed under T-TEST Limitation 2 (*SPSS*, Second Edition, p. 274):

$$\text{WORKSPACE} = (56 \times \text{NP}) + (52 \times \text{NV}) + 4 \text{ [if NV is odd]}$$

$$\text{WORKSPACE} = (56 \times \text{NP}) + (52 \times \text{NV}) \quad \text{[if NV is even]}$$

NP = the number of pairs on the PAIRS= specification for paired t-tests
NV = the number of variables in the VARIABLES= list for group t-tests

For example, if there are 5 variables and 3 pairs in a T-TEST command, the WORKSPACE requirement in bytes will be calculated as

$$\text{WORKSPACE} = (56 \times 3) + (52 \times 5) + 4 = 432$$

19.40 WRITE CASES

19.41 Excessive Repetition Error

A repetition factor in the WRITE CASES format may not exceed 255. Previous releases wrote incorrect output when this limit was violated. This release will detect violations and generate error number 161.

19.42 Limit to Variable Lists

The variable list in SPSS Version H may not contain more than 250 symbols (variable names and occurrences of the word TO). In Version M, the limit is 500 symbols. This is not a new limit, but was omitted from *SPSS*, Second Edition.

Appendix A

Incompatibilities Between Releases 6, 7, 8, and 9

The following changes may cause problems with SPSS command files that ran correctly under Release 6 which is documented in *SPSS*, Second Edition.

A.1 MULTIPLE SELECT IFS

If two or more SELECT IF or *SELECT IF commands appear in a deck, they are connected by AND, so that a case must satisfy the requirements on all commands in order to be selected. In Release 6 and earlier, these commands were connected by OR, so that a case which satisfied the conditions on just one of the commands would be selected.

A.2 SAMPLE

Specifications larger than 1 are no longer accepted. Previously, such specifications were interpreted as percentages.

A.3 SORT CASES

The SORT CASES command cannot follow the REORDER VARS command.

A.4 WORKSPACE

The workspace requirements for many procedures have changed with introduction of new algorithms and double-precision arithmetic.

A.5 CORE MEMORY

Release 9 is substantially larger than previous releases and requires more core memory to run. Consult the appropriate appendix on Operating Systems in this manual for details.

Other changes documented in this update manual may cause slightly different output from that produced under Release 6 but should not cause jobs that ran correctly under Release 6 to misfunction.

Appendix B

SPSS Batch System Conversions

SPSS Inc. supports its software on IBM 360s, 370s, and 4300s (and software compatible counterparts, such as the Amdahl 470, CDC Omega, and NAS Computers) under OS, DOS, and CMS operating systems; on DECsystem-10s and DECSYSTEM-20S; on DEC VAX 11/780s and DEC PDP-11s; and on Burroughs Large Systems.

SPSS Inc. also licenses conversion sites to provide the SPSS Batch System to users of other computers and operating systems not currently supported by SPSS Inc. See below for a list of these machines.

While these conversions are generally comparable to the versions we distribute and support, certain features and procedures may have been added, modified, or removed from individual conversions. Several conversion sites have provided an appendix for their version of SPSS. These appendixes contain brief documentation on the differences in running SPSS on their machine and give examples of sample jobs where possible. Additional documentation on the various conversions of the SPSS Batch System is available from your SPSS Coordinator.

Other conversions are underway. Please contact SPSS Inc., Marketing Division, if you are interested in running SPSS on any machine not listed here.

BURROUGHS MEDIUM SYSTEMS
(B3700, B4700, B2800,
B3800, B4800)

CDC 3300

CDC CYBER & 6000 SERIES

DATA GENERAL ECLIPSE
& NOVA 3, 4, 840

FACOM M-SERIES
(OS IV/F4)

HARRIS /4, /7

HEWLETT-PACKARD 3000

HITAC M-SERIES

HONEYWELL 60/66/XX, 600,
6000, DPS
TOSBAC 5600 (ACOS)

HONEYWELL MULTICS

IBM 360, 370 (MTS)

ICL 2900 SERIES,
ICL 4-75 (EMAS, VME)

ICL 1900 & ICL 2900 (DME)
(Version H, Release 5 only)

ICL 1900 & ICL 2900 (DME)
(Version G, Release 6 only)

MODCOMP CLASSIC 7835/60/70
& UP

PERKIN-ELMER 7/32, 8/32, 3320

PRIME 400 & UP

SIEMENS (BS 1000)

SIEMENS (BS 2000)

UNIVAC 70/7, 90/60,
70, 80 (VMOS and VS9)

UNIVAC 90/25, 90/30,
90/40 (VMOS, VS9)

UNIVAC 1100

XEROX SIGMA SERIES

Appendix C

SPSS Batch System for Burroughs Large Systems

The SPSS Batch System for Burroughs Large Systems, Release 8.1, is maintained and distributed by SPSS, Inc. This appendix describes only those areas of operation requiring alternate documentation from that provided in *SPSS*, Second Edition and the body of this manual. Although the information presented generally applies to any Burroughs large system, users are advised to consult their local SPSS Coordinator for additional procedures or requirements necessary at their installation.

C.1 WORKFLOW CONTROL CARDS (WFL)

The following WFL statements are generally required to run SPSS, in addition to those needed to specify usercode, job initiation, resource limitations, and operations requests.

NOTE: The symbol <i> signifies an invalid character punch in column one of a card image, e.g., "?". Refer to Burroughs B7000/B6000 Work Flow Language Manual (Form No. 5001555) for a detailed description of syntax for the railroad diagrams used below.

C.2 RUN Statement

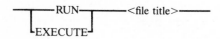

The RUN statement is used to initiate the SPSS code file. For example,

<i>RUN SPSS

C.3 File Equation Statement

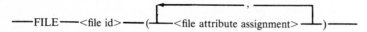

File equation is used to specify changes to the various file identifiers declared within SPSS. For example,

<i>FILE FILE8(KIND=DISK,TITLE=MY/DATA)

C.4 DATA Statement

The DATA statement is used to specify the SPSS control card deck which immediately follows as input. For example,

<i>DATA IOCR

C.5 BURROUGHS SPSS FILE SPECIFICATIONS

Table C.5 SPSS File Specifications

FILE ID	DEFAULT FILE ATTRIBUTES	FUNCTION
FILE1	(KIND=DISK,TITLE=IOSCR1, FLEXIBLE)	Scratch file for data
FILE2	(KIND=DISK,TITLE=IOSCR2, MAXRECSIZE=21,BLOCKSIZE=420, AREASIZE=560,AREAS=5,FLEXIBLE)	Scratch file for labels
FILE3	(KIND=TAPE,TITLE=SYSFILE, FILETYPE=7)	Input SPSS system file (GET FILE)
FILE3	(KIND=DISK,TITLE=SCSSFILE, FILETYPE=7)	Input SCSS masterfile (GET SCSS)
FILE4	(KIND=TAPE,TITLE=SYSFILE, FLEXIBLE,SAVEFACTOR=999)	Output system file (SAVE FILE/SAVE ARCHIVE)
FILE4	(KIND=DISK,TITLE=SCSSFILE, MAXRECSIZE=120,BLOCKSIZE=120, AREASIZE=30,BUFFERS=1, SAVEFACTOR=999,FLEXIBLE)	Output SCSS masterfile (SAVE SCSS)
FILE5	(KIND=READER,TITLE=IOCR, FILETYPE=7,MAXRECSIZE=14)	Input SPSS control card deck
FILE6	(KIND=PRINTER,TITLE=IOLP, MAXRECSIZE=22)	Printer output
FILE8	(KIND=TAPE,TITLE=IOBCD1, FILETYPE=7)	Raw input data file
FILE9	(KIND=PUNCH)	Raw output data file
FILE10	(KIND=DISK,TITLE=UDCFILE, FILETYPE=7,UPDATEFILE)	Usage data collection file
FILE11	(KIND=DISK,FLEXIBLE)	Work file for archive data
FILE12	(KIND=DISK,FLEXIBLE)	Work file for archive data
FILE15	(KIND=PUNCH)	Raw output data file
.	.	.
.	.	.
FILE20	(KIND=PUNCH)	Raw output data file
FILE21	(KIND=TAPE,FILETYPE=7)	First input system file (GET ARCHIVE/MERGE FILES)
FILE22	(KIND=TAPE,FILETYPE=7)	Second input system file
FILE23	(KIND=TAPE,FILETYPE=7)	Third input system file
FILE24	(KIND=TAPE,FILETYPE=7)	Fourth input system file
FILE25	(KIND=TAPE,FILETYPE=7)	Fifth input system file

C.6 Running SPSS from Timeshare (CANDE)

If SPSS is run from timeshare, the following changes are made in the default file specifications.

FILE4   (KIND=DISK)

FILE5   (KIND=REMOTE)   Unless the file is resident on disk

FILE6   (KIND=REMOTE)

FILE8   (KIND=DISK)   If the file is resident

In addition, record and block size attributes are dynamically assigned for files FILE1, FILE4, FILE11, and FILE12. Any raw output unit (FILE9, FILE15-FILE20) to which binary data is written also has dynamically assigned attributes.

C.7 SAMPLE JOBS

The following examples demonstrate SPSS deck set-up using Burroughs work flow language to label equate SPSS files to user files.

C.8 Raw Input Data File

In the simplest case, SPSS input consists of a deck of SPSS control cards and a deck of data cards. For example,

```
<i>RUN SPSS
<i>DATA IOCR
RUN NAME        SAMPLE PROGRAM 1
INPUT MEDIUM    CARD
N OF CASES      1000
DATA LIST       FIXED /1 VAR01 TO VAR05 1-15
<procedure card>
READ INPUT DATA
   1   2   5 87  3   5
   2   4   5 23  4   4
                .
FINISH
<i>END JOB
```

To input a raw data file from tape or disk, the user must label equate SPSS file FILE8. For example,

```
<i>RUN SPSS
<i>FILE FILE8(KIND=DISK,TITLE=MY/DATA,FILETYPE=7)
<i>DATA IOCR
RUN NAME        SAMPLE PROGRAM 2
INPUT MEDIUM    DISK
N OF CASES      1000
DATA LIST       FIXED /1 VAR01 TO VAR05 1-15
<procedure card>
FINISH
<i>END JOB
```

C.9 Output System File

To save an SPSS system file, the user must label equate SPSS file FILE4. For example,

```
<i>RUN SPSS
<i>FILE FILE4(KIND=TAPE,TITLE=VOTER/SYSTEM)
<i>DATA IOCR
RUN NAME        SAMPLE PROGRAM 3
FILE NAME       VOTERS
INPUT MEDIUM    CARD
N OF CASES      1000
DATA LIST       FIXED /1 VAR01 TO VAR05 1-15
<procedure card>
READ INPUT DATA
   1   2   5 87  3   5
   2   4   5 23  4   4
                .
SAVE FILE
FINISH
<i>END JOB
```

C.10 Input System File

To retrieve an SPSS system file, the user must label equate SPSS file FILE3. For example,

```
<i>RUN SPSS
<i>FILE FILE3(KIND=TAPE,TITLE=VOTER/SYSTEM)
<i>DATA IOCR
RUN NAME        SAMPLE PROGRAM 4
GET FILE        VOTERS
<procedure card>
FINISH
<i>END JOB
```

C.11 Raw Output Data Files

To output a raw data file to a unit other than the card punch, the user must label equate an SPSS raw output file (FILE9 [default], FILE15-FILE20). For example,

```
<i>RUN SPSS
<i>FILE FILE3(KIND=TAPE,TITLE=VOTER/SYSTEM)
<i>FILE FILE9(KIND=DISK,TITLE=NEWCASES,MAXRECSIZE=14,
            BLOCKSIZE=420,AREASIZE=1000,AREAS=1,
            FLEXIBLE)
<i>DATA IOCR
RUN NAME        SAMPLE PROGRAM 5
GET FILE        VOTERS
WRITE CASES     (3F3.0) VAR01 TO VAR03
FINISH
<i>END JOB
```

C.12 Input Archive/Merge Files

To retrieve multiple system or archive files, the user must label equate SPSS files FILE21 through FILE25, as needed, beginning with FILE21 as the first file input. For example,

```
<i>RUN SPSS
<i>FILE FILE21(KIND=TAPE,TITLE=FEMALES)
<i>FILE FILE22(KIND=TAPE,TITLE=MALES)
<i>DATA IOCR
RUN NAME        SAMPLE PROGRAM 6
GET ARCHIVE     FILE=FEMALES VARIABLES=ALL/
                FILE=MALES VARIABLES=ALL/
<procedure card>
FINISH
<i>END JOB
```

C.13 Output Archive Files

To save an archive file, the user must label equate SPSS file FILE4. For example,

```
<i>RUN SPSS
<i>FILE FILE21(KIND=TAPE,TITLE=DEMOCRATS)
<i>FILE FILE22(KIND=TAPE,TITLE=REPUBLICANS)
<i>FILE FILE23(KIND=TAPE,TITLE=INDEPENDENTS)
<i>FILE FILE4(KIND=TAPE,TITLE=VOTERS)
<i>DATA IOCR
RUN NAME        SAMPLE PROGRAM 7
MERGE FILES     FILE=DEMOS VARIABLES=ALL/
                FILE=REPUB VARIABLES=ALL/
                FILE=INDEP VARIABLES=ALL/
<procedure card>
SAVE ARCHIVE    VOTERS/
                FILE=DEMOS VARIABLES=ALL/
                FILE=REPUB VARIABLES=ALL/
                FILE=INDEP VARIABLES=ALL/
FINISH
<i>END JOB
```

C.14 SPACE ALLOCATION

Default space allocation (WORKSPACE = TRANSPACE) for Burroughs SPSS is 20,000 words.

WORKSPACE requirements tend to change with updates of SPSS. Rather than include WORKSPACE formulas here which may prove inaccurate with time, current formulas are always used by SPSS. Therefore, the most convenient means to insure adequate WORKSPACE and TRANSPACE is to rely on the EDIT facility to determine exact space requirements for an SPSS run, and then to employ the VALUE task attribute to override the default, if necessary. For example, the following WFL statement will increase total space allocation from 20,000 to 65,000 words:

```
<i>RUN SPSS;VALUE=65000
```

The relative amounts of WORKSPACE and TRANSPACE allotted are 7/8 and 1/8 of the total, respectively. The user may, of course, adjust this proportion with the use of the ALLOCATE card.

C.15 DIFFERENCES FROM IBM/SPSS

The following differences between the Burroughs version and the IBM 360/370 version of SPSS are currently supported. Users are advised to consult their local SPSS Coordinator for documentation on any additional differences which may exist.

C.16 RECODE/COUNT

The maximum number of variables which may be named or implied on the entire set of RECODE, *RECODE, COUNT, and *COUNT cards which are in effect for a given procedure is 500.

C.17 SEED

The SEED card changes the default seed from which the random number generator is initialized, producing different streams of random numbers. Use the SEED card with the SAMPLE card to get different cases in random samples.

C.18 Extended Input Format Facility

Burroughs SPSS relies on the Burroughs formatter to process formatted data. Since the Burroughs formatter does not provide for the format items B, C, R, and Z, these format items are not recognized.

C.19 Precision

Computations for all statistical procedures are done in single precision.

Sydney Springer, SPSS Inc.

Appendix D

CDC 6000 and CYBER Version of the SPSS Batch System

Much of the information in this appendix was taken directly from Appendix F of *SPSS*, Second Edition, and is intended to completely replace this earlier appendix.

The SPSS Batch System was converted to run on Control Data 6000 and CYBER computer systems by Vogelback Computing Center of Northwestern University. This version is referred to as SPSS-6000 and currently runs under the SCOPE, KRONOS, NOS, and NOS/BE operating systems. The information in this appendix describes Release 8.0 of SPSS-6000 that has been available since September, 1979. You should be aware that new releases are distributed approximately every 18-24 months, and the additional documentation describing the current release should be obtained from your local computing center.

This appendix is intended to guide users in the preparation of job decks for executing SPSS-6000. For the most part, an SPSS job for an IBM system can be run under SPSS-6000 by merely replacing the JCL with the appropriate system control cards. However, differences in operating systems, local procedures and other factors complicate the problem of describing system control cards and job deck setups. The examples given in the following sections are intended to illustrate the general format and placement of system control cards. Examples are presented for standard NOS and NOS/BE operating systems. Local modifications to SPSS or the operating system may require changes in the deck setups. You are advised to check system control cards and job deck setups in a local reference manual or with your local SPSS consultants.

There are a number of additional capabilities in SPSS-6000 and a few incompatibilities with the IBM implementation that are described in the local documentation. Among the additional features, there are six statistical procedures:

G3SLS	Two- and three-stage least squares
JFACTOR	Maximum likelihood factor analysis
NONLINEAR	Nonlinear regression analysis
PLOT	Calcomp plotting
SPECTRAL	Spectral analysis
TETRACHORIC	Tetrachoric correlation analysis

Three formats of printed output are available in SPSS-6000: standard batch output, abbreviated batch output, and online output. These optional output formats make SPSS-6000 very convenient to use from a terminal. Abbreviated output is particularly useful when you want to run SPSS from a terminal, examine the output, and then print it. See Section D.2 for additional information on requesting the format of the printed output.

D.1 SYSTEM CONTROL CARDS

System control cards are the functional equivalent of IBM JCL and are always grouped together as the first logical record of the job deck (often called the control card record). The system control cards for an SPSS-6000 job typically contain one or more job cards, an ATTACH card to assign the SPSS program to the job, the SPSS call card that causes SPSS to be loaded and executed, and any system control cards necessary for assigning data files to the job for processing and for properly

325

disposing of files after SPSS termination. The job cards are used to specify such information as job name, account number, passwords, priority, equipment requirements, and other job limits. Computer time and other limits must be estimated on the basis of the specific tasks being executed. The format of these cards is almost always specific to the local computing center, and you should check with the appropriate computer center personnel for the exact format of these cards.

One specification that is more or less standard across operating systems is the field length needed for an SPSS-6000 job (often called CM, central memory, or small core memory). SPSS requires approximately 50000 octal words to begin execution and will automatically adjust memory to the exact amount needed for each task. SPSS should be executed with an initial field length of at least 50000 with the capacity of increasing to a larger (perhaps significantly larger) value. See Section D.26 for more information about SPSS-6000 memory requirements.

D.2 SPSS Call Card

The SPSS call card causes the SPSS program to be loaded (brought into memory) and executed. Optional parameters are given in parentheses and specify operational modes and/or files to be used. The format is

   SPSS(p1,p2, ... ,pn)

The optional parameters *pi* can be listed in any order within the parentheses. Generally, a parameter can be specified in one of the following forms;

   pi = lfn (local file name)

or

   pi = value

where *pi* is one of the parameter keywords listed in Table D.2. and *lfn* is a 1 to 7 character alphanumeric file name, beginning with a letter. A file is always given an lfn (local file name) when it is assigned to or created by a job, and all programs in the job refer to it by this name. Throughout this appendix, local file name will often be abbreviated lfn.

All parameters have default values as noted in Table D.2. The defaults are those in effect at most computing centers. However, the defaults at your computing center may be different. The parameter defaults that are most likely to have been changed are the defaults for the PD, MF, and NR parameters; check with your local SPSS Coordinator for any differences.

SPSS accepts only one occurrence of any parameter.

Table D.2 SPSS Call Card Parameters

OPTION	DESCRIPTION
A=lfn	Alternate output is to be written on file lfn (matrices, residuals, Z scores, etc.).
A omitted	Alternate output is written on local file BCDOUT.
BL=kkk	Input data file is an L tape containing fixed-length records (see RL) with blocks of maximum size kkk. RL must be specified for both S and L tapes. BL must be specified for L tapes but is optional for S tapes (kkk less than 5120).
BL omitted	Input data is not on an L tape.
D=lfn	SPSS input data are to be read from file lfn. This parameter overrides the INPUT MEDIUM card if present.
D omitted	Data are to be read from local file INPUT.
ER=nnnn	Maximum number of allowable I/O errors (illegal characters in "F" format fields) is nnnn.
ER omitted	Maximum number of allowable I/O errors is 100.
G=lfn	SPSS system file will be read from lfn.
G omitted	SPSS system file will be read from local file GTFILE.
G1=lfn	Input ARCHIVE file 1 is lfn.
G1 omitted	Input ARCHIVE file 1 is GTARC1.
G2=lfn	Input ARCHIVE file 2 is lfn.
G2 omitted	Input ARCHIVE file 2 is GTARC2.
G3=lfn	Input ARCHIVE 3 is lfn.
G3 omitted	Input ARCHIVE file 3 is GTARC3.
G4=lfn	Input ARCHIVE file 4 is lfn.
G4 omitted	Input ARCHIVE file 4 ts GTARC4.
G5=lfn	Input ARCHIVE file 5 is lfn.

OPTION	DESCRIPTION
G5 omitted	Input ARCHIVE file 5 is GTARC5.
I=lfn	SPSS control cards comprise the next record on file lfn.
I omitted	SPSS control cards are on local file INPUT.
L=lfn	SPSS printed output is to be written on file lfn.
L omitted	Printed output is written on local file OUTPUT.
LO=ABRV	Specifies that abbreviated batch printed output format is to be used (80 character page width with page headings and carriage control).
LO=ONLINE	Specifies that online printed output format is to be used (80 character page width with no page headings or carriage control).
LO omitted	Specifies that standard batch printed output format is to be used (134 character page width with page headings and carriage control).
MF=value	Specifies the maximum field length that SPSS will attempt to use. Check with local computer center personnel for your installation's limits.
MF omitted	The maximum field length that SPSS will attempt to use is 200000 words (octal); procedures that need more than this maximum will be aborted. The default maximum field length is likely to vary from center to center; check with your local SPSS Coordinator.
NR	Data input files (either D= or G=) are not returned or unloaded by SPSS. They remain accessible in the job for later use. At many computing centers, NR is the default.
NR, U omitted	Data input files are returned after the data have been read. For disk storage files, there is no difference between "return" and "unload"—local files are removed from the job and the disk space is released. Permanent files are made available to other jobs. For tape files, "return" releases the magnetic tape reservation—the maximum number of magnetic tapes that can be used by the job is reduced by one. The U option (see below) for tape input files allows the tape to be released, without losing the drive reservation, so that another tape can be requested later in the job.
OS=lfn	File lfn contains an OSIRIS dictionary for use in conjunction with the OSIRIS VARS card. (A binary tape file or disk file can be used.) RL must also be specified.
OS omitted	The OSIRIS VARS feature is not being used.
PD=6 or 8	Specifies whether the printed output is to be formatted for 6 or 8 lines per inch printing.
PD omitted	Specifies that the printed output is to be formatted for 8 lines per inch printing. At a few computing centers, 6 lines per inch is the default; check with local consultants.
RL=nnn	Input data file is an S or L tape (written in coded mode) containing fixed-length records of length nnn characters. RL can also be used to read internal files with unit records (card images) longer than 150 characters. However, internal files contain end-of-line bytes that must be included in the length nnn, and you are strongly encouraged not to use such files without a thorough understanding of internal file formats.
RL omitted	Input data are not on an S or L tape.
S=lfn	SPSS system file will be written on file lfn, used with SAVE FILE or SAVE ARCHIVE.
S omitted	SPSS system file will be written on local file SVFILE.
U	Data input files are unloaded after the data have been read.
X=lfn	File lfn will be used to store the input data in binary form for second and subsequent SPSS procedure calls.
X=0	The scratch file with the binary data will not be written. This option can save computer time and disk space, but it can only be used on runs that execute one procedure and that do not have a subfile structure defined. Unless the data are on a file other than INPUT, SPSS can determine that only one procedure will be executed and will force this option. This option is currently not forced if the procedure is SAVE FILE; it must be explicitly requested. The binary data file cannot be suppressed with GET ARCHIVE or MERGE FILES or with SAVE FILE when the actual number of cases that will be saved on the file is unknown.
X omitted	Local file XXSPS2 will be used to store the binary data.

D.3 SPSS Error Processing

If SPSS detects an error while processing a job, the job will be abnormally terminated. This means that system control cards following the SPSS call card will not be executed unless the job provides for conditional execution of control cards in the event of an error.

D.4 BASIC SETUP WITH THE INPUT DATA ON CARDS

In the following sections, sample job deck setups are presented for standard NOS and NOS/BE operating systems. The SCOPE and KRONOS operating systems are obsolete and have been replaced by the NOS/BE and NOS operating systems, respectively. Therefore, if your computing center is using SCOPE, you should use the NOS/BE job decks as a guide; if your center is using KRONOS, follow the NOS job decks.

The most basic job deck setup for executing SPSS-6000 contains the system control cards, SPSS control cards and the data on punched cards. In these and the following examples, '7/8/9' is used to denote an end-of-record card that actually has 7, 8, and 9 multipunched in column 1; '6/7/8/9' is an end-of-information card that has 6, 7, 8, and 9 multipunched in column 1. Under the NOS operating system, end-of-record is often referred to as end-of-section (EOS), and end-of-information is called end-of-partition (EOP).

D.5 NOS Basic Job Deck with the Input Data on Cards

Under NOS, the SPSS program is typically saved under the user number LIBRARY. However, a different user number may be used at some computing centers; check with local SPSS consultants. In most cases, the default initial and maximum field lengths under NOS will be appropriate for executing SPSS-6000. If they are not, the CM parameter on the job card and the RFL control card can be used to define the maximum and initial field lengths, respectively.

```
Jobname,Tyyy, . . . .
USER,usernum,passwrd, . . . .
CHARGE, . . . .
ATTACH,SPSS/UN=LIBRARY.
SPSS.
7/8/9 End-of-Section
RUN NAME
  .
(SPSS control cards)
  .
READ INPUT DATA
  .
(data cards)
  .
FINISH
6/7/8/9 End-of-Partition
```

D.6 NOS/BE Basic Job Deck with the Input Data on Cards

Under NOS/BE, use the CM parameter on the job card to set the initial field length to approximately 50000.

```
Jobname,CM50000,Tyyy, . . . .
ACCOUNT, . . . .
ATTACH,SPSS,SPSS.
SPSS.
7/8/9 End-of-Record
RUN NAME
  .
(SPSS control cards)
  .
READ INPUT DATA
  .
(data cards)
  .
FINISH
6/7/8/9 End-of-Information
```

D.7 RUNNING SPSS DIRECTLY FROM A TERMINAL

SPSS control cards can be entered at a terminal using a text editing program, and SPSS can be executed directly from the terminal. When SPSS is used in this manner, the term "control cards" refers to the lines containing the SPSS commands. The SPSS control cards are saved in a permanent file, and normally the input data is stored in a separate permanent file. The SPSS call statement to execute SPSS directly from a terminal should include the I parameter to specify the local file name of the SPSS control card file, the D parameter to specify the input data file, and the L parameter to specify the local file name for the "printed" output file. The NR parameter that prevents the automatic return of the data file should also be included in the SPSS call statement.

The examples in Sections D.9 through D.13 show how to use a text editor to create SPSS commands, how to execute SPSS with the I, L, D, and NR parameters, and how to examine your output at the terminal and then print it. The examples are given separately for the NOS timesharing system and for INTERCOM, the timesharing system that runs under NOS/BE. The standard editor programs EDIT (for NOS) and EDITOR (for INTERCOM) are used. Many installations support and encourage the use of other text editor programs; check with local computer center personnel for the editing capabilities that are available at your computing center.

The four examples in Sections D.9 through D.13 assume that the permanent file MYDATA has already been created. All commands entered at the terminal are shown in lower case, and all prompts and responses from the computer are shown in upper case. The LO=ABRV parameter is included on the SPSS call statement in order to obtain output that is formatted for a line printer, but that is also narrow enough to be listed at the terminal.

D.8 Files Under the NOS Operating System

If you are running under NOS, there are two types of permanent files; direct access files and indirect access files. Direct access files are created by using the DEFINE command before the file actually exists; indirect access files are created by using the SAVE command after the file has been generated. These file distinctions are not made under NOS/BE, and if you are using SPSS under INTERCOM, you may skip to Section D.10. The basic difference between indirect and direct access files is the way that the files are retrieved. When an indirect access file is retrieved, a local copy of the file is made available to the job. If you make changes to an indirect access file, the changes are made to the local copy of the file rather than the permanent copy. The permanent copy is not changed until a REPLACE command is executed. On the other hand, when a direct access file is attached, a local copy of the file is not generated, and any changes must be made by purging the old file and defining a new one.

Another difference is the way in which NOS allocates space for direct and indirect access files. Disk storage space is allocated in groups of units called PRUs (Physical Record Units). When the DEFINE and SAVE commands are processed, a minimum number of PRUs are reserved, regardless of the actual size of the file. The minimum number of PRUs that will be allocated for either type of file is installation-dependent, but the minimum size of an indirect access file is always much smaller than the minimum size of a direct access file. At most installations, the smallest indirect access file is large enough to hold 300 to 600 characters of information. In comparison, the smallest direct access file will often hold over 30000 characters of information. Thus, indirect access files are appropriate for small files, and larger files should be stored as direct access files. If a file is large and is not being modified in the job, it is inefficient to save it as an indirect access file because copying such a file is completely unnecessary and requires a substantial amount of computer resources.

The NOS timesharing system also allows one indirect access file to be designated as a primary file. Any indirect access file can be declared a primary file, but there can be only one primary file at any given time. The purpose of the primary file is to simplify the commands that you must enter at a terminal in order to use the file. Many NOS commands assume that the requested action is to be performed on the primary file, unless another file is explicitly specified. The primary file is also rewound after the requested operation, eliminating the need for you to continually rewind the file. A primary file is usually defined only when running from a terminal, and the file chosen is usually the one that will be manipulated most often. For example, when using SPSS from a terminal, the file containing the SPSS commands is often defined as the primary file, since this file will usually be changed several times during the terminal session. Alternatively, you may want to designate the SPSS output file as the primary file because you will frequently be listing this file at the terminal.

D.9 Running SPSS from a Terminal under NOS

The following example shows how to run SPSS directly from a terminal under the NOS operating system. After logging into the system, the SPSS commands are collected into the local file CONCRD using the standard NOS edit program. Your installation may use a different editor program; check with local computer center consultants. The raw input data is stored in a permanent file MYDATA.

```
Login to the system.
/new,concrd                    Create an empty primary file CONCRD
/edit
 BEGIN TEXT EDITING.
? deftab:/;/                   Define semicolon as the tab character
? tab:/16/                     Set a tab stop at column 16
? add
 ENTER TEXT.                   Enter SPSS control cards into file CONCRD
? #run name;try nos timesharing
? data list;vl 1 . . . .
? n of cases;unknown
? frequencies;general=all
? finish#
 READY.
? list;*
RUN NAME        TRY NOS TIMESHARING
DATA LIST       Vl 1 . . . .
N OF CASES      UNKNOWN
FREQUENCIES     GENERAL=ALL
FINISH
 -END OF FILE-
? end
 END OF TEXT EDITING.
/save,concrd                   Save CONCRD as a permanent file
/attach,mydata.                Attach the data file MYDATA
/attach,spss/un=library.       Attach SPSS.  UN may not be needed
                               or may be different than LIBRARY
/spss,i=concrd,d=mydata,nr,l=out,lo=abrv.     Execute SPSS
 END SPSS
/rewind,out
$REWIND,OUT.
/list,f=out.                   List SPSS 'printed' output file at the terminal
        .
        .
        .
/route,out,dc=pr.              Send SPSS 'printed' output to a line printer
 ROUTE COMPLETE
```

D.10 Running SPSS from a Terminal under INTERCOM

Running SPSS directly from a terminal under the INTERCOM timesharing of the NOS/BE operating system is illustrated in the following example. The SPSS commands are entered into the local file CONCRD, and the input data is stored on file MYDATA. Check with your local computer center consultants for the editing program used at your installation.

```
Login to the system
COMMAND- editor
..create 10 10                 Enter SPSS control cards
    10=numbered
    20=run name        try intercom
    30=data list       vl 1 . . . .
    40=n of cases      unknown
    50=frequencies     general=all
    60=finish
    70==
..save,concrd                  Save the SPSS control cards in local file CONCRD
..end
COMMAND- store,concrd          Save CONCRD as a permanent file
ID= mine
AC= account
COMMAND- attach,mydata,mydata,id=mine.     Attach the data file MYDATA
 AT CY= 001 SN=SHARED
COMMAND- attach,spss,spss.     Attach SPSS
 AT CY= 005 SN=SHARED
COMMAND- connect,output        Equate the file OUTPUT to the terminal
COMMAND- rewind,concrd
COMMAND- spss,i=concrd,d=mydata,nr,l=out,lo=abrv.   Execute SPSS
 END SPSS
COMMAND- rewind,out
COMMAND- copy,out,output.      List SPSS 'printed' output at the terminal
        .
        .
        .
COMMAND- batch,out,print.      Send SPSS 'printed' output to a line printer
TYPE FILE ID-mine
IMINEIT BATCHED TO PRINT
```

D.11 RUNNING SPSS AS A SUBMITTED BATCH JOB

Running SPSS directly from a terminal is often referred to (somewhat erroneously) as an interactive job. When a card deck is submitted to the computer for processing, it is often called a batch job. SPSS batch jobs can also be created using a text editor and entered into the batch queue from a terminal. Such jobs are referred to as submitted batch jobs.

The basic difference between executing SPSS directly from the terminal and submitting a batch job which executes SPSS is that all system commands required for the SPSS job (e.g., any ATTACHs, DEFINEs, SAVEs or CATALOGs) must be included in the file with the SPSS control cards. This file is then submitted to the batch queue for execution. One practical reason for submitting a batch job is that control is returned to the terminal immediately; when SPSS is executed directly, control is not returned until SPSS has completed execution. The submitted batch method allows you to perform other tasks at the terminal or to logout. For this reason, if you are running a big SPSS job, the submitted batch technique is often preferred. In addition, a submitted batch job is the only way to obtain the dayfile (i.e., a complete record of the job) at many computing centers.

D.12 Submitting an SPSS Batch Job Under NOS

In the following example, the system commands and SPSS control cards for an SPSS job are entered into the local file BTCHJB. This file is then submitted for execution using the SUBMIT system command. The SPSS "printed" output is saved in file OUT. After the job has completed execution, the file OUT can be retrieved and listed at the terminal and/or printed on a line printer.

```
Login to the system.
/edit,btchjb                      Create the local file BTCHJB for the system commands
                                  and SPSS control cards
  BEGIN TEXT EDITING.
? deftab:/;/                      Define semicolon as the tab character
? tab:/16/                        Set a tab stop at column 16
? add
  ENTER TEXT.                     Enter system commands into BTCHJB
? #/job
? mmh,t30.
? user,usernum,passwrd.
? charge,account.
? attach,spss/un=library.
? attach,mydata.
? spss,d=data,l=out.
? noexit.
? replace,out.                    SPSS job will save the L file as a permanent file
? /eor                            Separates system commands from SPSS control cards
? run name;try submitted batch under nos
? data list; v1 1 . . . .
? n of cases;unknown
? frequencies;general=all
? finish#
  READY.
? list;*
/JOB
MMH,T30.
USER,usernum,passwrd.
CHARGE,account
ATTACH,SPSS/UN=LIBRARY.
ATTACH,MYDATA
SPSS,D=DATA,L=OUT.
NOEXIT.
REPLACE,OUT.
/EOR
RUN NAME        TRY SUBMITTED BATCH UNDER NOS
DATA LIST       V1 1 . . . .
N OF CASES      UNKNOWN
FREQUENCIES     GENERAL=ALL
FINISH
  -END OF FILE-
? end
$EDIT,BTCHJB.
/save,btchjb                      Save BTCHJB as a permanant file
/submit,btchjb.                   Submit the file BTCHJB as a batch job
  18.45.23.CIJQJVM                Job is assigned the name CIJQJVM
/enquire,jn=jvm                   Check status of all jobs with names ending in JVM
  CIJQJVM NOT FOUND.              Indicates job CIJQJVM is terminated
/get,out.                         Retrieve the 'printed' output file from the job
/list,f=out.                      List 'printed' file OUT at the terminal
    .
    .
    .
/route,out,dc=pr.                 Send the local copy of OUT to a line printer
  ROUTE COMPLETE
```

D.13 Submitting an SPSS Batch Job Under INTERCOM

The following example illustrates submitting a batch SPSS job from a terminal under the INTERCOM subsystem of NOS/BE. As in Section D.12, the system commands and SPSS control cards are entered into the file BTCHJB and this file is submitted as input for a batch job.

```
         Login to system.
         COMMAND- editor
         ..create 10 10                    Enter system commands and SPSS control cards
            10=mmh,cm52300,t20,ac=account.
            20=attach,mydata,mydata,id=mine.
            30=attach,spss,spss.
            40=spss,d=mydata.
            50=*eor                        Separates system commands and SPSS control cards
            60=numbered
            70=run name      try submitted batch under intercom
            80=data list     vl 1 . . . .
            90=n of cases    unknown
           100=frequencies   general=all
           110=finish
           120==
         ..save,btchjb                     Save entered lines in local file BTCHJB
         ..end
         COMMAND- store,btchjb             Save BTCHJB as a permanent file
         ID= mine
         AC= account
         COMMAND- batch,btchjb,input,here  Submit BTCHJB as a batch job
         MMHXBGB BATCHED TO INPUT          Job is assigned the name MMHXBGB
         COMMAND- files.                   Reports all remote output bles
         --REMOTE OUTPUT FILES--
           MMHXBFB
         COMMAND- batch,mmhxbgb,local      Retrieve MMHXBGB from the output queue
         COMMAND- connect,output.          Equate the output to the terminal
         COMMAND- copy,mmhxbgb,output.     List the 'printed' output at the terminal
            .
            .
            .
         COMMAND- batch,mmhxbgb,print.     Send 'printed' output to a line printer
         TYPE FILE ID- mine
         IMINEIT BATCHED TO PRINT
```

D.14   INPUT DATA ON TAPE OR DISK

Data cases can also be stored on magnetic tape or disk in coded (BCD) or binary format. If you use binary format (not a system file), consult local documentation for details on the type of file required by SPSS-6000 before generating the file.

In a job that reads data from a tape or disk, the key elements are

- The proper system control cards to assign the data file to the job prior to SPSS execution. Typically, REQUEST or LABEL cards are used to assign tape files. ATTACH cards are used to access permanent files (disk files).
- The use of the D parameter on the SPSS call card.
- The use of the RL and BL parameters on the SPSS call card for specifying information about S or L tape input, (for example, a blocked card-image tape created by a non-CDC system).

An input data file is read from its current position; that is, it is not rewound, and it is read until an end-of-file is encountered. Any end-of-records on the file are ignored. The file is not rewound after SPSS termination. It is therefore possible to use SKIPF or another utility program to position a data input file before SPSS execution. The examples given here will only cover the case in which the data are accessed directly from the file.

D.15   Basic Job Deck with Data on Tape or Disk

NOS/BE

```
Jobname,CM50000,Tyyy,NT1, . . . .
ACCOUNT, . . . .

LABEL,DATA, . . . .
ATTACH,SPSS,SPSS.
SPSS,D=DATA.
7/8/9 End-of-Record
RUN NAME
   . . . .
6/7/8/9 End-of-Information
```

NOS

```
Jobname,Tyyy, . . . .
USER,usernum,passwrd, . . . .
CHARGE, . . . .
LABEL,DATA, . . . .
ATTACH,SPSS/UN=LIBRARY.
SPSS,D=DATA.
7/8/9 End-of-Section
RUN NAME
   . . . .
6/7/8/9 End-of-Partition
```

This job will process data on a 9-track labeled magnetic tape. If the data is stored on a 7-track tape, use MT (rather then NT) on the job card to reserve a tape drive (this applies to NOS/BE sites only). Instead of LABEL, use REQUEST if the data is stored on an unlabeled tape or ATTACH if it is stored as a permanent file. If the data is stored on a permanent file, do not include the NT or MT parameter on the job card.

D.16   ALTERNATE OUTPUT FILES

A number of SPSS procedures generate an alternate output file that is normally not printed, but is intended for use by another program or a subsequent SPSS run. Examples of alternate output are the output from WRITE CASES and the output matrices that are optionally generated by PEARSON CORR, NONPAR CORR and other procedures. By default, alternate output is written to the disk file BCDOUT, although the lfn can be changed by using the A parameter on the SPSS call card. You have the option of printing or punching the alternate output or saving it on magnetic tape or disk through the use of the appropriate system control cards. BCDOUT is a local file which means that it will simply disappear at job termination, unless a system control card specifying otherwise is included in the job.

D.17   Basic Job Deck with Alternate Output Saved as a Disk File

NOS/BE	NOS
Jobname,CM50000,Tyyy, ...	Jobname,Tyyy, ...
ACCOUNT, ...	USER,usernum,passwrd, ...
REQUEST,BCDOUT,*PF.	CHARGE, ...
ATTACH,SPSS,SPSS.	ATTACH,SPSS/UN=LIBRARY.
SPSS.	SPSS.
CATALOG,BCDOUT,MYMATRIX, ...	SAVE,BCDOUT=MYMATRIX/PW= . . . .
7/8/9 End-of-Record	7/8/9 End-of-Section
RUN NAME	RUN NAME
. . . .	. . . .
REGRESSION	REGRESSION
OPTIONS 8	OPTIONS 8
READ INPUT DATA	READ INPUT DATA
. . . . data cases	. . . . data cases
FINISH	FINISH
6/7/8/9 End-of-Information	6/7/8/9 End-of-Partition

This job saves the correlation matrix produced by REGRESSION as the permanent file MYMATRIX. If the matrix were to be saved on a tape, a REQUEST or LABEL card would be used to assign BCDOUT to tape before executing SPSS; the SAVE card (under NOS) and the REQUEST,BCDOUT,*PF and CATALOG cards (under NOS/BE) would not be used. Under NOS the SAVE card saves BCDOUT as an indirect access file; if BCDOUT is a large file, it should be saved as a direct access file by using the DEFINE card prior to creating the file with SPSS.

D.18   Basic Job Deck with Punched Alternate Output

NOS/BE	NOS
Jobname,CM50000,Tyyy, ...	Jobname,Tyyy, ...
	USER,usernum,passwrd, ...
ACCOUNT, ...	CHARGE, ...
ATTACH,SPSS,SPSS.	ATTACH,SPSS/UN=LIBRARY.
SPSS,A=PUNCH.	SPSS,A=PUNCH.
7/8/9 End-of-Record	7/8/9 End-of-Section
. . . .	. . . .
6/7/8/9 End-of-Information	6/7/8/9 End-of-Partition

The file PUNCH has a special disposition code associated with it, and it is automatically punched at job termination. For this reason, a system control card for the alternate output file is not needed.

An alternative to the above setup is to allow the alternate output to be written on the default file BCDOUT and to use the ROUTE control card to cause BCDOUT to be punched. Under KRONOS and SCOPE, the DISPOSE card may be required instead of ROUTE; check with local computer center personnel.

NOS/BE	NOS
Jobname,CM50000,Tyyy, ...	Jobname,Tyyy, ...
ACCOUNT, ...	USER,usernum,passwrd, ...
REQUEST,BCDOUT,*Q.	CHARGE, ...
ATTACH,SPSS,SPSS.	ATTACH,SPSS/UN=LIBRARY.
SPSS.	SPSS.
ROUTE,BCDOUT,DC=PU.	ROUTE,BCDOUT,DC=PU.
7/8/9 End-of-Record	7/8/9 End-of-Section
. . . .	. . . .
6/7/8/9 End-of-Information	6/7/8/9 End-of-Partition

The advantage of this setup is that the ROUTE card will not be executed and the cards will not be punched if errors are detected during the SPSS run and the job is aborted. Under NOS/BE, the REQUEST,BCDOUT,*Q card may be necessary to explicitly assign BCDOUT to a mass storage device used only for printed and punched output files. This card may not be needed at your site, but it will cause no harm.

D.19 Basic Job Deck with Printed Alternate Output

It is sometimes desirable to print the contents of the BCDOUT file. This is easily accomplished with the COPYSBF control card. For example,

NOS/BE	NOS
Jobname,CM50000,Tyyy, ...	Jobname,Tyyy, ...
ACCOUNT, ...	USER,usernum,passwrd, ...
REQUEST,BCDOUT,*Q.	CHARGE, ...
ATTACH,SPSS,SPSS.	ATTACH,SPSS/UN=LIBRARY.
SPSS.	SPSS.
REWIND,BCDOUT.	REWIND,BCDOUT.
COPYSBF,BCDOUT,OUTPUT.	COPYSBF,BCDOUT,OUTPUT.
7/8/9 End-of-Record	7/8/9 End-of-Section
. . . .	. . . .
6/7/8/9 End-of-Information	6/7/8/9 End-of-Partition

D.20 INPUT AND OUTPUT OF SPSS SYSTEM FILES

SPSS system files are created by the procedure SAVE FILE. In some cases, the input to the run will be a raw data file (card, disk, or tape); in other cases, the input to the run will be an existing SPSS system file, in which case a new or updated file is generated that includes any modifications or data selections in effect. See Sections D.23 and D.24 for example job decks illustrating updating a system file.

The S parameter on the SPSS call card is used to specify on what file the SPSS system file is to be written; if not specified the lfn SVFILE is used.

An SPSS system file consists of a single binary file written without end-of-records. The file is not rewound by SPSS either before or after it is written. Since the file is written in internal binary format, its size in words can be approximated by

$$SIZE = (NCASES + 7) * (NVARS + 3)$$

where NCASES is the number of data cases on the file, and NVARS is the number of variables defined by the user. This formula does not account for the storage required for variable and value label information.

D.21 Basic Job Deck Which Saves a System File on Disk

This job will create an SPSS system file as a permanent file with the name MYFILE1.

NOS/BE	NOS
Jobname,CM50000,Tyyy, ...	Jobname,Tyyy, ...
ACCOUNT, ...	USER,usernum,passwrd, ...
ATTACH,SPSS,SPSS.	CHARGE, ...
REQUEST,SVFILE,*PF.	ATTACH,SPSS/UN=LIBRARY.
SPSS.	DEFINE,MYFILE1/PW=passwrd.
CATALOG,SVFILE,MYFILE1,ID=	SPSS,S=MYFILE1.
7/8/9 End-of-Record	7/8/9 End-of-Section
. . . .	. . . .
SAVE FILE	SAVE FILE
FINISH	FINISH
6/7/8/9 End-of-Information	6/7/8/9 End-of-Partition

Under NOS, DEFINE establishes MYFILE1 as a direct access permanent file. If MYFILE1 is small, it may be preferable to store it as an indirect access file by using the SAVE control card instead of DEFINE. For example, a very small system file (25 cases, 10 variables, no label information) is 9 PRUs and, because of the way that dirct access files are allocated, would result in very wasteful use of disk space if DEFINE were used. However, what is "small" varies from one computing center to the next; it is best to check with local computer center personnel about when it is better to use indirect access files. An example with the SAVE control card is shown in Section D.17. DEFINE tells the system that a file will be saved as a permanent file before the file is created, and SAVE can only be used to save an existing file as a permanent file. For this reason the DEFINE card is placed before the SPSS call card, and the SAVE card should be placed after the SPSS call card.

To write a system file on magnetic tape, a REQUEST or LABEL card is used and precedes the SPSS call card. The DEFINE card (under NOS) and the CATALOG and REQUEST,SVFILE,*PF cards (under NOS/BE) are not used. Under NOS/BE it may be necessary to specify on the job card that a tape drive will be needed with the NT or MT parameter.

D.22 Basic Job Deck Which Uses a System File on Disk

After an SPSS system file is created, it can be read by subsequent SPSS jobs using the lfn GTFILE or another lfn specified by the G parameter on the SPSS call card. As usual, permanent files are accessed by ATTACH, and tape files are accessed by LABEL or REQUEST (depending on whether the file is labeled or not). It is important to note that any modifications in the job are in effect for the run, but they do not affect the input system file. A new file can be written to preserve these modifications (see Sections D.23 and D.24).

This job uses the system file created in Section D.21 (permanent file MYFILE1)

NOS/BE

```
Jobname,CM50000,Tyyy, . . . .
ACCOUNT, . . . .

ATTACH,SPSS,SPSS.
ATTACH,GTFILE,MYFILE1,ID=. . . .
SPSS.
7/8/9 End-of-Record
RUN NAME
GET FILE

 . . . .
6/7/8/9 End-of-Information
```

NOS

```
Jobname,Tyyy, . . . .
USER, . . . .
CHARGE, . . . .
ATTACH,SPSS/UN=LIBRARY.
ATTACH,MYFILE1/PW=passwrd.
SPSS,G=MYFILE1.
7/8/9 End-of-Section
RUN NAME
GET FILE

 . . . .
6/7/8/9 End-of-Partition
```

D.23 Basic Job Deck Which Updates a System File, Disk to Disk

The permanent file MYFILE1 is read, and file MYFILE2 is written.

NOS/BE

```
Jobname,CM50000,Tyyy, . . . .
ACCOUNT, . . . .
ATTACH,GTFILE,MYFILE1,ID=. . . .
REQUEST,SVFILE,*PF.
ATTACH,SPSS,SPSS.
SPSS.
CATALOG,SVFILE,MYFILE2.
7/8/9 End-of-Record
RUN NAME
GET FILE

 . . . .
SAVE FILE
FINISH
6/7/8/9 End-of-Information
```

NOS

```
Jobname,Tyyy, . . . .
USER, . . . .
CHARGE, . . . .
ATTACH,MYFILE1/PW=passwrd.
DEFINE,MYFILE2/PW=passwrd.
ATTACH,SPSS/UN=LIBRARY.
SPSS,G=MYFILE1,S=MYFILE2.
7/8/9 End-of-Section
RUN NAME
GET FILE

 . . . .
SAVE FILE
FINISH
6/7/8/9 End-of-Partition
```

To update a system file stored on tape to a new tape file, use LABEL or REQUEST commands for both the old and new system files. These system commands replace the ATTACH, REQUEST, and CATALOG commands for NOS/BE and the ATTACH and DEFINE commands for NOS. See Section D.14 for further information on specifying tape files.

D.24 Basic Job Deck Which Merges a System File with an Alternate Output File

Often it is desirable to examine the relationship between one or more of the input variables and a variable that may be written to the alternate output file. Examples of such data would be residuals from REGRESSION, group statistics from AGGREGATE, and z-scores from CONDESCRIPTIVE. In order to analyze data from two different sources, SPSS can be executed twice in the same job. The first execution of SPSS generates the alternate output file and an SPSS system file, if one does not already exist. The second call to SPSS makes use of ADD VARIABLES to merge the variables in the system file with the data on the alternate output file. Please note that SPSS requires that the cases be in the same order on both files; therefore, if any data selection is in effect for one SPSS execution, the same data selection cards must be included in the other analysis.

This job is a regression analysis that also generates a bivariate plot of the residuals against the independent variable. In this job, both the system file and the alternate ouput file are local files which means that they disappear from the system at job termination. If the data files were large and expensive to create, it would be prudent to save them with a DEFINE card (under NOS) or a CATALOG card (under NOS/BE).

NOS/BE	NOS
Jobname,CM50000,Tyyy, ...	Jobname,Tyyy, ...
ACCOUNT, ...	USER,username,passwrd, ...
	CHARGE, ...
ATTACH,SPSS,SPSS.	ATTACH,SPSS/UN=LIBRARY.
SPSS.	SPSS.
REWIND,SVFILE,BCDOUT.	REWIND,SVFILE,BCDOUT.
SPSS,G=SVFILE,D=BCDOUT.	SPSS,G=SVFILE,D=BCDOUT.
7/8/9 End-of-Record	7/8/9 End-of-Section

```
    . . . .                                         . . . .
REGRESSION      VARIABLES=Y,X/          REGRESSION      VARIABLES=Y,X/
                REGRESSION=Y WITH X/                    REGRESSION=Y WITH X/
                RESIDUALS                               RESIDUALS
OPTIONS         8                       OPTIONS         8
READ INPUT DATA                         READ INPUT DATA
    . . . .                                 . . . .
SAVE FILE                               SAVE FILE
7/8/9 End-of-Record                     7/8/9 End-of-Section
RUN NAME                                RUN NAME
GET FILE                                GET FILE
ADD VARIABLES  RESID                    ADD VARIABLES  RESID
    . . . .                                 . . . .
SCATTERGRAM    X WITH RESID             SCATTERGRAM    X WITH RESID
FINISH                                  FINISH
6/7/8/9 End-of-Information              6/7/8/9 End-of-Partition
```

If a system file already existed and had been used as input to the first SPSS call, it would be necessary to include the NR parameter on the SPSS call card. This is because the system file would be needed for both SPSS calls, and the input file is automatically returned by SPSS without NR.

D.25   SCRATCH FILES

Besides the user-specified files mentioned in Section D.2, SPSS-6000 uses the following scratch files:

XXSPS1	Random-access label file
XXSPS2	
XXSPS3	Files used for temporary storage of matrices
XXSPS4	and/or data cases
XXSPS5	
XXSPS6	

If SORT CASES is requested, the files DATSTR, SAVE and a variable number of files with names of the form STRnn, where "nn" is a number from 1 to 99, may also be used. You should not use files with these names in SPSS jobs.

As the data cases are read for the first procedure, SPSS normally writes each case as modified by any non-starred transformations to XXSPS2. This file, rather than the original input file, is then read for subsequent procedures in the job. The size of XXSPS2 in PRUs can be calculated exactly using the formula,

$$NPRUS = ((NVARS +1)*NCASES)/64$$

where NVARS is the number of user-defined variables in the file, and NCASES is the number of cases being processed. Cases not selected for processing due to a SELECT IF, REJECT IF or SAMPLE are not included.

It is usually not necessary to be concerned with the size of XXSPS2. However, for very large files, the size becomes significant because the amount of disk storage that a job can use is limited, and your job will abort if the limit is exceeded (usually after considerable computer time has been used). Mass storage restrictions vary greatly across computing centers and, under NOS, may vary from one user to another. If you are in doubt about the limits that apply to you, compute the number of PRUs required for XXSPS2, and check with local computer center personnel before submitting a large SPSS job. If there is only one procedure in the run, XXSPS2 can often be suppressed. See the X parameter on the SPSS call card. If the job creates an uncompressed system file on disk and XXSPS2 cannot be suppressed, the number of PRUs written by the job will be more than twice the value of NPRUS.

D.26 MEMORY REQUIREMENTS FOR SPSS-6000

The field length (memory) needed to load and begin execution of SPSS varies from release to release, but a field length request of CM50000 should always be sufficient. Under NOS, the default field length should be adequate to begin execution of SPSS. Release 8.0 needs a field length of CM52300. Once loaded, SPSS-6000 handles memory management in a dynamic fashion; that is, it computes the amount of memory required and allocates it automatically. The WORKSPACE and TRANSPACE calculations given in *SPSS*, Second Edition and the body of this manual are not applicable to SPSS-6000. However, it is sometimes necessary to know how much CM will be needed for a job. In particular, before submitting a large job, it is prudent to determine if the job will run within the memory limits of the system.

The easiest and most accurate way to estimate memory requirements for an SPSS-6000 job is to use the EDIT facility. In addition to checking the syntax of SPSS control cards, an EDIT run also prints the CM needed and terminates with an error if the required CM exceeds the maximum CM available. In the standard version of SPSS-6000, the maximum CM available by default is 200000 octal words. Additional CM (up to a limit of 320000 octal words) is available by using the MF parameter on the SPSS call card. The actual CM limits in effect at your computing center may be different from these; check with local SPSS consultants.

The following procedures cannot determine the exact field length needed until the data has been read: MANOVA, NONPAR CORR, NPAR TESTS, PLOT, SCATTERGRAM, SURVIVAL, SPECTRAL, and the general versions of FREQUENCIES, CROSSTABS, and BREAKDOWN. Thus, EDIT cannot be used to ensure that sufficient CM is available to the job, although these procedures do report the maximum number of cases that can be processed in the available CM.

D.27 DIFFERENCES BETWEEN IBM SPSS AND SPSS-6000

The following features are not implemented in Release 8.0 of SPSS-6000 or work differently in the IBM implementation and SPSS-6000. These differences and additional capabilities are described in documentation available from your local SPSS Coordinator. Please note that the differences described here are subject to change in future releases of SPSS-6000. Many of the discrepancies between the IBM and CDC versions are expected to be eliminated in the next release of SPSS-6000.

ALLOCATE

The ALLOCATE control card is ignored by SPSS-6000. In general, SPSS-6000 will compute the exact amount of memory required and will allocate it automatically. Since the system handles memory management, it is never necessary to compute WORKSPACE or TRANSPACE. In rare cases, the REPORT, DISCRIMINANT, and MULT RESPONSE procedures may need additional field length that can be allocated using the SET CM control card (see the SPSS-6000 Update Manual).

Alphabetic Variables

The maximum field width of an alphabetic variable is A8 not A4. FREQUENCIES in GENERAL mode with OPTION 5 (condensed format) only displays the leftmost 4 characters of an alphabetic variable.

BLANK keyword

Blank data fields are normally treated as zeros by SPSS. However, when it is desirable to distinguish between blanks and zeros, a −0 can be specified on an SPSS control card and refers only to blank fields. The keyword BLANK (or BLANKS) may be used in place of −0 on any SPSS data definition or data transformation control card. BLANK (or BLANKS) is not recognized as −0 on a statistical procedure control card.

Compressed System Files

An SPSS system file (created by SAVE FILE or SAVE ARCHIVE) can require considerably more disk or tape storage than the corresponding BCD file. However, system files in which the data is stored in a packed format may be created; such files are known as compressed system files. See the local documentation for more information about compressed system files.

COUNT

The number of variables that can be named or implied on all RECODEs and COUNTs in SPSS-6000 is not limited to 400; the upper limit depends on the amount of memory that is available.

CROSSTABS

OPTION 7 is only available in integer mode, and it cannot be used with variables that have BLANK missing values.

Data Checking with REPORT. and STOP.

Very often it is desirable to be able to detect certain data conditions when running SPSS. For example, you may know from your CONDESCRIPTIVE output that a particular variable has illegal values in one or more cases. Another common situation is a file that contains multi-card cases, and you would like to be sure that each case has the proper number of cards and that they are in the proper order. The special variables REPORT. and STOP. provide a handy way of detecting these kinds of data exception conditions, reporting the offending cases, and optionally terminating execution when serious errors are found. See the local documentation for more information.

DISCRIMINANT

SPSS-6000 does not currently allow matrix input and raw data input in the same procedure. If matrix materials are read from a file on tape or disk, the file cannot be used for multiple DISCRIMINANT procedures. Both temporary and permanent transformations work properly with the SELECT= feature of DISCRIMINANT.

DO REPEAT

The number of stand-in variable names that can be defined is not determined by the available field length (workspace). It is limited by the restriction of 200 symbols (including variable names implied by the TO keyword) on the DO REPEAT statement. See the local documentation.

END INPUT DATA

The END INPUT DATA card is not currently implemented in SPSS-6000. If this card is used with N OF CASES UNKNOWN, it will be read as a data case, and SPSS-6000 may not inform you that a bad data case has been read (depending on the format used to read the data). An end-of-record (7/8/9) should be used with N OF CASES UNKNOWN to indicate the end of the data with card input. If your data is on a disk or tape file, an end-of-record is not needed.

Freefield Input

The NUMBERED option cannot be used in conjunction with freefield input. If it is, SPSS will not terminate with an error; rather, all 80 columns of each data card will be examined for freefield input, and the number in columns 73-80 will be treated as data.

FREQUENCIES

OPTIONS 10, 11 and 12 are available in both the general and integer version of FREQUENCIES.

GET ARCHIVE

OPTION 1 (recover bad archive file) has a different meaning in SPSS-6000; see the local documentation.

GET SCSS/SAVE SCSS

GET SCSS and SAVE SCSS are not implemented in Release 8.0 of SPSS-6000.

GUTTMAN

The GUTTMAN scaling procedure can handle a maximum of 12 scales with 50 items per scale. An alternate output format is used when there are more than 12 items per scale. See the local documentation.

INPUT FORMAT

The extended format facilities described in Chapter 13 of this manual are not available in SPSS-6000.

LAG

The LAG control card is not implemented in SPSS-6000. There is an equivalent function that can be used in conjunction with the COMPUTE statement. See the local documentation.

LIST CASES

READ INPUT DATA can be used without a statistical procedure in SPSS-6000. This means that a LIST CASES can be run without including a statistical procedure. When used alone, LIST CASES followed by a READ INPUT DATA card causes a separate pass of the data to be made.

MERGE FILES

The maximum number of active variables that can be merged from all of the input system files is 1000 in SPSS-6000.

NONPAR CORR

OPTION 7 (random sampling of cases) is not implemented in SPSS-6000.

NPAR TESTS

There is a maximum of 100 test specifications (rather than 200) on each NPAR TESTS card.

ONEWAY

The improvements to multiple comparisons in range tests have not been implemented in SPSS-6000.

RAW OUTPUT UNIT

The specification for RAW OUTPUT UNIT can be either a lfn or a unit number n—in which case the lfn of the alternate output file is TAPEn. OUTPUT is also a legitimate lfn.

READ MATRIX

The READ MATRIX card is always required with matrix input.

RECODE

The CONVERT specification can be used to convert numbers that were read under A format to floating point numbers. In SPSS-6000 leading blanks and non-numeric values are not converted as described in *SPSS*, Second Edition. Leading blanks are ignored, so that ' 9', ' 9', and '9' are all converted to 9. CONVERT will also convert a minus sign (−) to 11 and a plus sign (+) to 12 if either appears as the only character in the input field. If a + or − is converted and is not the only character in the field, the results are unpredictable. If an attempt is made to convert any other character, the value is set to −0 and a warning message is printed. The number of variables that can be named or implied on the RECODE card in SPSS-6000 is not limited to 400; the upper limit depends upon the amount of memory that is available.

REGRESSION

The SPSS-6000 version of REGRESSION has many features, OPTIONs, and STATISTICSs not described in *SPSS*, Second Edition. See the local documentation.

RELIABILITY

Two OPTION numbers are different in SPSS-6000. OPTIONS 15 and 16 in the IBM implementation are OPTIONS 17 and 18 in SPSS-6000. If the space saver solution (OPTION 14) is selected, the maximum number of variables in all VARIABLES= lists and SCALE= lists is 200, not 500. The maximum number in the combined SCALE= lists is 400, not 1000. All matrix input and output is in E format, rather than D format.

REPORT

The default width for alphanumeric variables in a STRING subcommand is 8 characters, not 4.

SAVE ARCHIVE

The SAVE ARCHIVE card can have the keyword COMPRESSED as the first specification to save a compressed system file.

The following restrictions on SAVE ARCHIVE do not apply to SPSS-6000.

- The order in which variables are saved on the output archive file depends on the order in which the files are named on the SAVE ARCHIVE card, not the order in which the files are named on the GET ARCHIVE card.
- DELETE VARS and KEEP VARS can be used to delete/keep existing variables (both latent and active) on the file created by SAVE ARCHIVE.

SAVE FILE

The maximum number of variables in an SPSS system file is 1000 in SPSS-6000, and the maximum number of VALUE LABELS that can be saved per variable depends on the number of variables being saved. It is usually larger than 200. The keyword COMPRESSED can be used as the first specification to save a compressed system file.

SCATTERGRAM

OPTION 8 has not been changed to random sampling of cases in SPSS-6000; it still works as described in *SPSS*, Second Edition.

SORT CASES

The capability to define a new subfile structure as part of the SORT CASES procedure is not implemented in SPSS-6000. A new subfile structure can always be defined by a SUBFILE LIST card following the SORT CASES card (if the exact number of cases in each subfile is known) or in subsequent runs. The maximum number of variables that can be used as sort keys in SPSS-6000 is 99, not 64.

Subfile Names

Subfile names can be up to 8 characters long, and the first four characters need not be unique.

SURVIVAL

The SURVIVAL procedures in Release 8.0 of SPSS-6000 and the IBM implementation are different; consult local documentation on SURVIVAL.

VALUE LABELS

The VALUE LABELS cards can appear in the job deck after the first statistical procedure card. This makes it possible to assign new labels to temporarily recoded variables. Value labels can only be redefined once per job for a given variable.

WRITE CASES

The maximum number of symbols on the WRITE CASES card is 1000, not 250 or 500. This does not include the format statement or variables implied by the TO convention.

YRMODA Function

The YRMODA function is not implemented in SPSS-6000; see the equivalent function JULIAN in the local documentation.

This was contributed by Mina Hohlen, Northwestern University.

Appendix E

The SPSS Batch System for DECsystem-10/20

The DECsystem-10/20 implementation of the SPSS Batch System is maintained and distributed by SPSS Inc. The following appendix supplements *SPSS*, Second Edition, and the body of this manual with discussions of those areas of the DECsystem-10/20 version requiring alternate documentation. Although this document generally applies to any DEC-10 or DEC-20 system, users are advised to consult local documentation for further information pertaining to their particular installation.

Credit and thanks are due to the following individuals for contributions to the development and documentation of the DECsystem-10/20 version of the SPSS Batch System:

Michael A. Matzek, University of Pittsburgh, for original contributions to the code and to previous versions of this document.

Dr. Griffith G. Smith, Jr., University of Pittsburgh, for contributions to the I/O subsystems and command line scanner.

Tim Hill, Wesleyan University, for OSIRIS file reading routine.

David A. Specht, Iowa State University, for extensions to the REGRESSION procedure.

E.1 RUNNING SPSS

Running the SPSS Batch System on a DECsystem-10/20 computer involves operations on some group of files that typically reside on disk but may reside on cards or magnetic tape. The specific nature, configuration, and utilization of these files is a function of both the particular application and the approach to using SPSS. It is assumed that the SPSS user has some familiarity with monitor commands available to batch and timesharing jobs, basic file editing facilities, and local procedures for accessing the system.

SPSS can be run in batch mode using control files on disk submitted from a terminal or on cards submitted from a card reader. SPSS can also be run in timesharing mode directly from a terminal. Users should be aware that running SPSS in batch mode is more economical and has less impact on system resources than SPSS from timesharing.

The command to run SPSS on the DECsystem-10 is

```
.R SPSS
```

The command to run SPSS on the DECSYSTEM-20 is

```
@SPSS
```

(NOTE: If running Version M, substitute SPSSM for SPSS.)

SPSS responds with an asterisk (*) prompting for a command line of the general form

```
*[destination=]source[,switches][;comment]
```

The source specification must identify an SPSS control card file which resides on disk (created with a timesharing editor or copied to disk from cards or magnetic tape). The destination of the SPSS output and any desired switches (see Section E.2) may optionally be specified. Continuation of the command line is possible by terminating each line with a hyphen (-). A semicolon (;) on the last continuation of the command line indicates a comment.

The complete syntax for command line source and destination file specifications is

```
dev:filename.ext[p,pn]<prot>
```

Embedded blanks will terminate the file specification. Subfile directories, DECSYSTEM-20 directory names, long file names, and generation numbers are not supported. For the source file specification, dev: defaults to DSK:; filename does not default; .ext defaults to .SPS; [p,pn] defaults to the user's own directory; and <prot> is inappropriate. For the destination file specification, dev: defaults to DSK:; filename defaults to the source file name; .ext defaults to .LST; [p,pn] defaults to the user's own directory; and <prot> defaults to the installation default.

E.2 SPSS Command Line Switches

Table E.2 defines SPSS command line switches. Switch names need contain only enough characters necessary to make the switch name unique. Refer to Section E.6 for the complete syntax for file specifications used with switches.

Table E.2   SPSS Command Line Switches

SWITCH	MEANING
/EDIT	Performs the same function as the SPSS control card EDIT
/HELP	Prints a listing of available switches on the job's log device
file spec/SCRATCH	Overrides DSK: as the default device for the scratch file used to hold observations between procedures. On the DECsystem-10 the size of the scratch file in blocks is (n of variables+3) * n of cases/128. On the DECSYSTEM-20 the size of the scratch file in pages is (n of variables+3) * n of cases/512.
/SPACE n[P] or n[K]	Overrides the default number of words allocated for SPACE (i.e., WORKSPACE + TRANSPACE). If P is specified, n is in units of 512 words. If K is specified, n is in units of 1024 words. If both P and K are absent, K is assumed when n is less than or equal to 255; individual words are assumed when n is greater than 255. (See Section E.3 for a discussion of default SPACE.) The minimum value allowed for SPACE is 1P.

E.3 Core Requirements

Core requirements for SPSS are presented in Table E.3. These amounts must be available if running from timeshare. If running virtual, the availability of this amount of physical core will avoid excessive page fault costs. Batch users should specify this amount with the /CORE:n switch on the $JOB card.

Table E.3   Core Requirements

Region	Version H			Version M		
	DEC-10 (KI/KL)	DEC-10 (KA)	DEC-20	DEC-10 (KI/KL)	DEC-10 (KA)	DEC-20
Sharable High Segment Code	15P	8K	15P	15P	8K	15P
Nonsharable Low Segment Code	53P	27K	53P	63P	32K	63P
I/O Buffers Plus Work Areas	6P	3K	6P	6P	3K	6P
Default SPACE (WORKSPACE + TRANSPACE)	6P	2K	40P	10P	5K	40P
Total Low Segment Core	65P	32K	99P	79P	40K	109P

Core requirements for I/O buffers and work areas vary with the number and type of I/O devices required by the program; 6P is usually sufficient.

The most convenient means to insure adequate SPACE is to rely on the EDIT facility to determine exact requirements for an SPSS run. However, it is possible to calculate WORKSPACE and TRANSPACE individually. WORKSPACE calculations are provided following the discussions of each procedure in *SPSS*, Second Edition (see Section E.35 for possible DEC exceptions to WORKSPACE calculations). Calculated results should be divided by 4 to convert from IBM bytes to DEC words. Refer to the discussion of the ALLOCATE card (Section E.7) for information concerning the calculation of TRANSPACE.

E.4   Examples

Batch Execution: SPSS control cards on disk submitted from a terminal to the Batch Controller

```
.SUBMIT MYJOB=TEST.CTL/PAGE:.../TIME:...
```

where TEST.CTL is a batch control file containing

```
.R SPSS
*TEST=TEST.SPS              ;output listing to TEST.LST
```

or

```
@SUBMIT TEST.CTL/JOBNAME:MYJOB/PAGE:.../TIME:...
```

where TEST.CTL is a batch control file containing

```
@SPSS
*TEST=TEST.SPS             ;output listing to TEST.LST
```

Batch Execution: SPSS control file on cards submitted from a card reader, using the SPRINT batch system

```
$JOB.../TIME:.../PAGE:...
$PASSWORD...
$TOPS10
.R SPSS
*LPT:=TEST.SPS/SPACE:4P    ;output directly to line printer
$EOJ
```

or

```
$JOB...TIME:.../PAGE:...
$PASSWORD...
$TOPS20
@SPSS
*LPT:=TEST.SPS/SPACE:20P    ;output directly to line printer
$EOJ
```

Timesharing Execution: SPSS control cards on disk submitted from a terminal in timesharing mode

```
.R SPSS
*TEST.SPS,NUL:/SCRATCH     ;output listing to TEST.LST
*<CTRL/C>
```

or

```
@SPSS
*TEST.SPS,NUL:/SCRATCH     ;output listing to TEST.LST
*<CTRL/C>
```

E.5   SPSS COMMANDS

E.6   Control Card Preparation

The standard format of the SPSS control card provides for a control field in card columns 1 through 15 and a specification field in card columns 16 through 80 (or 16 through 72 if the NUMBERED option is in effect).

The DECsystem-10/20 version of SPSS additionally allows a freefield format for SPSS control cards. The following conventions apply for freefield input.

- If column 1 contains other than a blank or tab, the control field is interpreted to be column 1 up to a tab, or column 1 up to two or more consecutive blanks, or columns 1 through 15. The remaining columns are interpreted as the specification field.

- If column 1 contains a blank or tab, the card is interpreted as a continuation card and all columns are part of the specification field.

- A specification field on any card contains a maximum of 65 characters, exclusive of leading blanks. A tab encountered in a specification field is replaced by a blank.
- If the NUMBERED option is in effect, columns 73 through 80 are always interpreted as sequence numbers or other identifying information.

When preparing SPSS control cards with a timesharing editor be sure to remove line numbers which may be prefixed by the editor. SPSS will not accept line-sequenced files as input.

If SPSS is executed interactively, control cards may be entered directly from a terminal by specifying TTY: as the source device. SPSS will prompt the user for each control card with a right angle bracket (>). After each prompt, the user may enter a control card in freefield format, terminating with a <CR>.

E.7 File Specification Cards

The syntax of SPSS control cards that specify files has been extended to provide for conventions of file specification common to DECsystem-10/20 operating systems.

The complete syntax for file specifications on SPSS control cards is

dev:filename.ext[p,pn]<prot>+vid2+...

where

dev:	is the device name or logical name of the storage device or file structure on which the file is or will be contained. It can be from one to six characters long and must terminate with a colon (:). The default device is DSK:.
filename	is the name of the file. It specifies the DEC directory file name and, if appropriate, also the internal name of the SPSS system file. The first one to six characters refer to the DEC directory file name. The first one to eight alphanumeric characters refer to the SPSS system file internal name. Any characters beyond the eighth are ignored.
.ext	is the file name extension indicating the type of file. It consists of zero to three aplhanumeric characters preceded by a period (.). Any characters beyond the third are ignored. Non-standard file extensions are acceptable, but the choice of extension should reflect the type of information in the file. Recommended extensions for SPSS files are .SPS for SPSS control card files; .DAT for raw data files; and .FIL for SPSS system files.
[p,pn]	is the directory name of the file. It consists of the project number and programmer number of the disk directory where the file is located. The default is the user's own directory. DECSYSTEM-20 users should use the TRANSLATE command to translate a <directory name> to its corresponding project-programmer number.
<prot>	is the access protection code of the file. The file protection digits provided specify user access to the file.
vid	is the visual identification of a magnetic tape volume. To use multi-volume magnetic tape files, the first magnetic tape volume should be mounted on some logical device using the system mount command. The file specification is then the logical device name terminated with a colon (:), followed by an internal SPSS file name, followed by a plus (+), and the vid of the second magnetic tape volume, etc.

Embedded blanks will terminate the file specification. Subfile directories, DECSYSTEM-20 directory names, long file names, and generation numbers are not supported.

E.8 FILE NAME

The FILE NAME card includes a file specification to identify an SPSS system file and an optionnal file label.

```
FILE NAME      file specification [file label]
```

The first one to six characters of the filename part form the directory file name. The first one to eight characters of the filename part become the internal name of the SPSS system file. Any characters following the first blank are part of the optional file label. The complete file specification is stored for possible use with a SAVE FILE request. If the FILE NAME card is absent, the file specification defaults to that encountered on a previous GET FILE card. If used in conjunction with a GET FILE card, the FILE NAME card renames an existing SPSS system file. If both FILE NAME and GET FILE are absent, the SPSS system file internal name and the DEC directory file name default to NONAME.

For example, the following FILE NAME card will name an SPSS system file with the internal SPSS file name, SYSFILE and file label, MY SPSS SYSTEM FILE and a DEC directory filename, SYSFIL.FIL.

```
FILE NAME      SYSFILE.FIL  MY SPSS SYSTEM FILE
```

The SPSS file name SYSFILE with corresponding label MY SPSS SYSTEM FILE will appear on output produced by SPSS. The DEC directory filename SYSFIL.FIL will be used for subsequent access of the file should it be permanently saved.

E.9 GET FILE
The GET FILE card includes a file specification to access a previously defined and saved SPSS system file.

```
GET FILE        file specification
```

If the first one to eight characters of the filename part differ from the internal SPSS file name saved when the file was created, a warning message is issued. The first one to six characters of the filename part identify the DEC directory file name. Dev: defaults to DSK:; .ext defaults to null; p,pn defaults to the user's own directory; prot is inappropriate. (Warning: After performing a GET FILE from a magnetic tape the position of the tape is indeterminate.)

For example, the following GET FILE card will access the SPSS system file from the previous example with the SPSS internal file name SYSFILE and DEC directory filename SYSFIL.FIL.

```
GET FILE        SYSFIL.FIL
```

E.10 GET SCSS
The GET SCSS card requires the additional syntax, FILE= followed by a file specification, to access an SCSS masterfile. The remainder of the GET SCSS syntax, following the FILE= specification is as documented in Chapter 10 of this manual.

```
GET SCSS        FILE=file specification/
                [VARIABLES=.../] [MIS=...]
```

The first one to eight characters of the filename part of the FILE= specification form the SPSS internal file name. The first one to six characters of the filename part are the DEC directory file name. Dev: defaults to DSK:; .ext defaults to null; p,pn defaults to the user's own directory; prot is inappropriate.

E.11 INPUT MEDIUM
The INPUT MEDIUM card recognizes a file specification or the keyword CARD.

```
INPUT MEDIUM    file specification
                CARD
```

The keywords DISK, TAPE and OTHER are treated as file names. Dev: defaults to DSK:; .ext does not default (the recommended extension is .DAT); p,pn defaults to the user's own directory; prot is inappropriate.

E.12 RAW OUTPUT UNIT
The RAW OUTPUT UNIT card recognizes a file specification or the keyword CARD, but does not recognize multiple volume tape syntax.

```
RAW OUTPUT UNIT file specification
                CARD
```

The keyword CARD writes a file with a device specification of CDP:, a filename corresponding to the source file name, and an extension of .CDP. When requesting card output, the user must include the /CARDS: switch on the $JOB card. If the RAW OUTPUT UNIT card is absent, the output file defaults to DSK:FOR20.DAT. When present, dev: defaults to DSK:; filename defaults to the source file name; .ext defaults to .DAT. If the file is to be printed and has no carriage control characters, the /FILE:ASCII switch should be used with the PRINT command.

E.13 SAVE FILE
The optional file specification on the SAVE FILE card directs the saved SPSS system file to a user-defined file.

```
SAVE FILE       [file specification [file label]]
```

The first one to eight characters of the filename part are saved as the internal SPSS file name. The user may include an optional file label to be saved with the system file. The first one to six characters of the filename part form the DEC directory file name. If absent, the file specification defaults to that provided on the FILE NAME card. If no FILE NAME card was present, the filename part defaults to NONAME. Dev: defaults to DSK:; .ext defaults to null; p,pn defaults to the user's own directory; prot defaults to the installation default. The scratch file device may not be NUL:. The recommended extension for SPSS system files is .FIL.

(NOTE: An SPSS system file is not ASCII and therefore cannot be printed, typed, or edited.)

E.14 SAVE SCSS
The SAVE SCSS card includes a standard DEC file specification, excluding multiple volume tape syntax.

```
SAVE SCSS      file specification
```

The use of the SAVE SCSS card is analogous to the SAVE FILE card. However, it cannot be used in conjunction with the SAVE FILE or REORDER VARS cards. The default file specification is DSK:FOR04.DAT.

E.15 DECsystem-10/20 Exceptions to Non-Procedural Control Cards

Only those control cards for which the DECsystem-10/20 implementation of SPSS differs in some way from the documentation in *SPSS, Second Edition* and the body of this manual are discussed here.

E.16 DATA LIST and ADD DATA LIST
The specification fields for the DATA LIST and ADD DATA LIST cards are identical.

```
DATA LIST       FIXED [(records per case)]/
    or          recnumber varlist start column [-endcolumn]
ADD DATA LIST   [(variable type)] [varlist...]/ [recnumber...]
                BINARY / 1 varlist 1
```

A print formats value for each variable is determined according to the variable type specification. If variable type is absent, the print formats value is zero. If variable type is present, the print formats value is that specified between parentheses. The BINARY format specification corresponds to the FORTRAN-10/20 definition of unformatted binary I/O. A file created using FORTRAN-10/20 unformatted I/O may be read with the BINARY specification. Each case must be contained on precisely one logical record and no variables may be skipped within the record. Trailing values can be ignored by naming fewer variables in the varlist specification than actually exist in the record.

E.17 ALLOCATE
The ALLOCATE card overrides the default number of words to be allocated for TRANSPACE. The default is the maximum of 384 words and one-eighth of the total SPACE. TRANSPACE calculations discussed on page 111 of *SPSS, Second Edition* should be multiplied by approximately 0.30 to determine the required number of words on a DECsystem-10/20.

E.18 ASSIGN BLANKS
The ASSIGN BLANKS card assigns the specified value to all blank fields encountered while reading numeric data. The general format for the ASSIGN BLANKS card is

```
ASSIGN BLANKS  value
```

The correct deck placement is before the first procedure request. If absent, blank data fields will be read as zeros.

E.19 INPUT FORMAT
The INPUT FORMAT card recognizes three types of format specifications; FIXED, FREEFIELD, or BINARY. The format list specification for BINARY files is not supported.

```
INPUT FORMAT   FIXED (format list)
               FREEFIELD
               BINARY
```

The format list of a FIXED format specification may include the characters A,E,F,G,O,T, and X as valid format items. The format specification Iw, if used, will be converted to Fw.0. The maximum field width for an A-type variable is 5. Characters are stored left-justified and blank-filled. If the field-width (w) exceeds five, the left-most characters will be ignored. Variables are automatically given a print formats value corresponding to specifications provided in the format list. Variables read with an Fw.d format will have a print formats value of (d). Variables read with an Aw format will have a print formats value of (A).

The FREEFIELD format specification corresponds to the FOROTS definition of list directed I/O. Each case must start on a new record. FREEFIELD may be used in conjunction with N OF CASES UNKNOWN. If input is from a terminal, a CRTL/Z or CRTL/C will provide the end-of-file.

The BINARY format specification corresponds to the FORTRAN-10/20 definition of unformatted binary I/O. A file created using FORTRAN-10/20 unformatted I/O may be read with the BINARY specification. The format list specification for BINARY files is not supported. Each case must be contained in one logical record and no variables may be skipped within the record. Trailing values can be ignored by naming fewer variables on the VARIABLE LIST card than actually exist in the record.

E.20 N OF CASES

The N OF CASES card specifies the number of cases in the file. It is optional with raw data input, except when more than one procedure is requested with data input from cards. If the number of cases is not known, the keyword ESTIMATED followed by a reasonable estimate of the number of cases will increase efficiency by allocating contiguous blocks of disk storage for scratch and system files. For example,

```
N OF CASES     ESTIMATED 1000
```

requests contiguous blocks of disk storage for 1000 cases. An exceeding quota message during execution indicates insufficient disk available for files, assuming no deletion of variables or cases.

E.21 PAGESIZE

The PAGESIZE card specifies the maximum number of lines per page for printed output. The default is NOEJECT.

E.22 OSIRIS VARS

An INPUT MEDIUM card must precede the OSIRIS VARS card when reading an IBM/370 OSIRIS tape. A .SET BLOCKSIZE (DEC-10) or @SET TAPE RECORD-LENGTH (DEC-20) monitor command must be issued in conjunction with the run. OSIRIS dictionary files have a blocksize of 1600 bytes (400 words). Data files may have larger record sizes. Use PIP to position the tape at the OSIRIS dictionary file. Tape-label files will be automatically skipped. The data file is assumed to follow the dictionary file but may be separated from it by tape-label files.

E.23 RECODE

The keyword BLANK is not recognized on the RECODE card (see ASSIGN BLANKS). When recoding alphanumeric values to numeric, an appropriate PRINT FORMATS should be provided.

E.24 SEED

The SEED card changes the default seed from which the random number generator is initialized, producing different streams of random numbers. If zero is specified, the normal starting for the random number generator will be in effect. The keyword PRINT is not recognized.

E.25 WRITE FILEINFO

The CHAR= specification on the WRITE FILEINFO card is not recognized since ASCII files are always generated.

E.26 DECsystem-10/20 Exceptions to Procedural Control Cards

Only those procedures for which the DECsystem-10/20 implementation *of SPSS differs in some way from the documentation in SPSS*, Second Edition and the body of this manual are discussed here.

E.27 AGGREGATE

The AGGREGATE procedure includes an additional available option. OPTION 20 causes the RMISS value to be assigned to the SUM function when all cases are missing from the group.

E.28 REGRESSION

Two additional options and one additional statistic are available for the procedure REGRESSION. OPTION 16 requests regression through the origin. It forces computation with the uncorrected sums of squares matrix rather than the correlation matrix. OPTION 17 forces the computation of STATISTIC 8 after every step regardless of how many variables are entered into the equation at that step. STATISTIC 8 requests the computation of a multiple partial correlation coefficient and a sequential analysis of variance which performs the hierarchical test described on page 339 of *SPSS*, Second Edition. If OPTION 17 is not in effect, computation occurs only after 2 or more variables are added to an equation during one step.

E.29 REPORT

DEC users should note the following about using the REPORT procedure:

- If alphanumeric variables used in strings are in A5 format, the (width) argument must be used to specify a character width of 5 (the default is 4).

- The)DATE argument for running heads and feet prints todays's date in the standard DEC format, dd- mmm-yy.
- Since NOEJECT is the default pagesize for the DEC version, a PAGESIZE card should be included specifying some appropriate pagesize for output.

E.30   SORT CASES

The SORT CASES procedure changes the sequence of cases in the file by sorting cases in ascending or descending order according to the values of the specified sort variables. The (A) specification requests an ascending sort (the default); the (D) specification requests a descending sort. SORT CASES may be requested before any procedure, but must be preceded by a GET FILE, GET SCSS, or READ INPUT DATA card. The scratch device must be DSK:.

```
SORT CASES      varlist  (A) or (D)
```

OPTION 20 requests the redefinition of subfiles according to the values of the first sort variable. New subfiles names are assigned in the following manner: If the first sort variable has a print formats of (A) subfile names will consist of the character 'S' plus the ASCII values of the variables with embedded blanks removed. For example, a sort variable SEX with values M, F, and blank will generate subfile names SM, SF, and S. If the first sort variable is numeric, subfile names will consist of the character 'S' followed by the values of the variable multiplied by 10.0 raised to the power of the variable's print format. In the case of negative values, the character 'M' will be the prefix. For example, a sort variable with a value of 9 and print format (0) will generate the name S0000009. The SUBFILE LIST card may be used to subsequently redefine subfile names. Space may be determined by the following calculation:

WORKSPACE = (number of sort variables + 1) * number of cases

E.31   T-TEST

The T-TEST procedure computes Student's t and probability levels for independent and paired samples. OPTION 20, used with the PAIRS= specification, pairs the first element of the first variable list with the first element of the second variable list, the second element of the first list with the second element of the second list, etc.

E.32   WRITE CASES

The WRITE CASES procedure outputs the specified SPSS variables to a raw output file in ASCII or FORTRAN-10/20 compatible binary format. The maximum field-width for F-type variables is 8 (e.g., F8.d).

E.33   DECsystem-10/20 Additional Procedure: TETRACHORIC

The TETRACHORIC procedure computes tetrachoric correlation coefficients between dichotomous variables assumed to be continuous and normally distributed. The computation of Tetrachoric r is based on the proportion of cases in each of the subcells of the 2×2 table generated from two dichotomous variables.

The general format of the TETRACHORIC card is

```
TETRACHORIC     VARIABLES=varlist(min,max)/
                CORRELATIONS=varlist [WITH varlist]/
                varlist [WITH varlist]/...
```

The VARIABLES= specification must include all variables for which tetrachoric correlations are requested, followed by the two values of each variable or list of variables. The CORRELATIONS = specification must include all variables for which correlation coefficients are requested. Use of the TO convention refers to the order of variables as specified in the VARIABLES= list. The keyword WITH requests that coefficients be computed for each variable named or implied preceding the WITH paired with each variable named or implied following the WITH. If the keyword WITH is not specified, all possible nonredundant correlations are computed from the variables named or implied in the CORRELATIONS= list. Only one CORRELATIONS= specification may be included on a TETRACHORIC card. However, multiple correlation lists, each terminated by a slash, may be requested.

STATISTIC 1   *Means, Standard Deviations, and Relative Frequencies.* Causes the mean, standard deviation, and relative frequency of each variable referenced in the correlation lists to be computed and printed.

OPTION 1   *Inclusion of missing data.* All cases will be included in the analysis regardless of any missing data values that have been declared.

OPTION 2 — *Listwise deletion of missing data.* A case will be omitted from the calculation of all coefficients requested in a single correlation list if the case has missing data for any variable in the list. The default is pairwise deletion of missing data (a case will be omitted from the computation of a given coefficient if the value of either of the two variables being correlated is missing).

OPTION 3 — *Two-tailed test of significance.* This option causes a two-tailed test of significance to be computed for each correlation rather than the default one-tailed test.

OPTION 4 — *Write correlation matrix on RAW OUTPUT UNIT.* This option causes a matrix of coefficients to be written on the RAW OUTPUT UNIT for all lists that are specified in matrix form (i.e., the keyword WITH must not be used). All matrices are output as card images with a format of 8F10.7. Each row of the matrix starts on a new card, and the row continues onto as many cards as required.

OPTION 5 — *Square matrix print format.*

OPTION 6 — *Write means and standard deviations on RAW OUTPUT UNIT.* This option may be used only when OPTION 4 has been requested. For each list following the CORRELATIONS= specification, the means for all variables appearing in the list are written, followed by the standard deviations for all variables in the list. Both means and standard deviations are written in 8F10.4 format.

OPTION 7 — *Print subcell proportions and subcell frequencies from which tetrachoric coefficients are computed.*

LIMITATION 1 — A maximum of 500 variables may be named in the VARIABLES= list. When the "var TO var" convention is used, each implied variable counts as 1 towards this total.

LIMITATION 2 — A maximum of 40 individual lists and 500 variable names may appear following the CORRELATIONS= keyword.

LIMITATION 3 — The maximum number of coefficients that can be requested on a single TETRACHORIC card (and its continuations) varies depending on whether STATISTIC 1 has been requested. The amount of WORKSPACE required for TETRACHORIC is

$$SPACE = (NCORE*4) + (MEANS*NVARS*3)$$

NCORE = the total number of correlations requested

MEANS = 1 if STATISTIC 1 has been selected, otherwise 0

NVARS = number of variables named or implied in the CORRELATIONS = list

Reference:

Guilford, J.P., and Benjamin Fruchter. *Fundamental Statistics in Psychology and Education.* Fifth Edition, McGraw-Hill Book Company, New York, 1973.

E.34 SPSS Control Cards Not Implemented for DECsystem-10/20

The following facilities are not implemented for the DECsystem-10/20 version of the SPSS Batch System:

```
END INPUT DATA
GET ARCHIVE
LIST ARCHINFO
LIST ERRORS
MERGE FILES
SAVE ARCHIVE
```

E.35 WORKSPACE CALCULATIONS

Included in this section are workspace calculations for statistical procedures which vary from the calculations provided in *SPSS,* Second Edition.

BREAKDOWN, in general mode, requires the following core storage space:

$$WORKSPACE = (NCELLS+1) * (MAXDIMS+7)$$

NCELLS =   total number of cells in all of the tables requested in the TABLES= list, where a cell is defined as a unique combination of the values of the independent or control variables.

MAXDIMS =   maximum number of dimensions in any of the requested tables, i.e., the maximum number of uses of the keyword BY in any of the TABLES= lists.

BREAKDOWN, in integer mode, requires the following core storage space:

WORKSPACE = 5*NCELLS + 5*MAXLABS

NCELLS =   total number of cells in all tables requested. The number of cells in a given table is calulated by multiplying together the permitted number of values for each of the independent variables as specified in the VARIABLES= list. NCELLS is simply the sum of the sum of the number of cells in each table.

MAXLABS =   maximum number of value labels for any table. If the workspace is too small to accomodate all the labels, the excess labels will not appear on the printed table.

CROSSBREAK, in integer mode, requires the following core storage space:

WORKSPACE = 5*NCELLS + 5*MAXLABS + 8*MAXVAL

NCELLS and MAXLABS are defined above, and

MAXVAL =   the maximum number of individual integer values of any variable in the CROSSBREAK= list.

Sydney Springer, SPSS Inc.

Appendix F

The SPSS Batch System for DEC VAX 11/780

The purpose of this appendix is to supplement *SPSS*, Second Edition, and the body of this manual with discussion and explanation of those areas of the DEC VAX version of SPSS Release 8.0 requiring additional or alternate documentation. For subsequent releases of the DEC VAX version of SPSS, this documentation will apply. However, additional features to facilitate the use of SPSS will be discussed in documentation available from your local SPSS Coordinator. Users are also advised to consult local documentation and computer center personnel for further detailed information regarding the DEC VAX computer and their particular installation of SPSS.

F.1 THE DEC VAX OPERATING SYSTEM

You communicate with the computer via the VAX/VMS operating system. This operating system allows users to share the computer and hardware devices such as disks, tapes, and printers. Conversation between you and the operating system consists of commands you type at the terminal or submit in a batch job and the messages that the system prints in response. The set of commands that the system recognizes constitutes the system command language called DCL (Digital Command Language).

Before running SPSS you should become familiar with the VAX login procedure, procedures for entering commands to the system, and the logout procedure. It is also useful to become familiar with a text editor, a program that lets you create and modify files. Using an editor you can create, modify, or save an SPSS command file or raw data file. The VAX/VMS default editor is called SOS. When you issue the VAX EDIT command, SOS identifies itself and you begin your editing session. When using SOS to create or alter an SPSS control file or raw data file, always end the session with the ET command. The ET command tells SOS to write the output file without line numbers and page marks. Page marks inserted by SOS will cause FORTRAN I/O conversion errors. Even though line numbers inserted by SOS are invisible to other programs such as SPSS, it is important to remove line numbers inserted by other editors; these may cause errors when running SPSS.

F.2 RUNNING SPSS

SPSS on the VAX can be run in batch mode either from a terminal or card reader. In either case, you can submit the SPSS commands directly from the terminal or card reader or refer to an SPSS command file on disk. SPSS can also be run in timesharing mode directly from a terminal. It is assumed that the SPSS user has some familiarity with DCL commands available to batch and timesharing jobs, basic file editing facilities, and local procedures for accessing the system. For more information, consult local VAX documentation and your computer center personnel.

The command to execute SPSS has the following format:

SPSS[/OUTPUT=filename] [control_filename] [workspace] [labelspace] where

/OUTPUT=filename	is an optional qualifier specifying the name of a file to receive the printed output of the SPSS run. If omitted, SYS$OUTPUT is assumed and the output will be printed at the terminal.
control_filename	is the name of the file that contains the SPSS commands and, optionally, raw data. If you specify TT:, SPSS prints the introductory message and waits for the commands at the terminal. If you are running SPSS from the terminal and do not specify the control filename, SPSS will prompt you for it. If you are running SPSS in a batch job and omit the control filename, SPSS assumes SYS$INPUT and expects to find the SPSS control file within the job submitted via batch.
workspace	is an optional parameter that specifies the amount of memory, in thousands of characters, to be allocated for use by the statistical procedures. If omitted, the SPSS default is 80 (80,000 characters), which should be sufficient for most runs. If additional space is required, SPSS will inform you at execution time.
labelspace	is an optional parameter that specifies the amount of memory, in thousands of characters, to be allocated for temporary storage of SPSS labels. The default is 30 (30,000 characters).

F.3 Timesharing Mode from a Terminal

To run SPSS in the timesharing mode from a terminal enter the execute command described in the above section. If the name of an SPSS control file is not specified, SPSS will prompt you for the control filename, as well as for the amount of workspace and labelspace. There is no default control filename; the default file type is DAT. Use the carriage return <cr> to accept the default amount of workspace and the default amount of labelspace.

If you specified an SPSS control filename on the SPSS execute command without specifying the amounts of workspace or labelspace, SPSS will assume that you want the default amounts.

If you specify TT: for the control filename, SPSS expects the commands to be entered at the terminal after the last prompt.

When you execute SPSS directly from your terminal, procedure execution will sometimes be delayed by one line. SPSS is not always able to detect that you have finished entering commands for a procedure until it encounters another procedure command or a FINISH command. For example,

```
GET FILE       GOVSTY        will be executed immediately
CROSSTABS      TABLES=A BY B will not be executed immediately
```

Example 1

```
$ SPSS <cr>
Please enter control filename: SAMPLE <cr>
Please enter bytes of workspace: 40 <cr>
Please enter bytes of labelspace: <cr>        User accepts default.
```

This example will run SPSS using the commands from the file SAMPLE.DAT, a workspace of 40,000 bytes, and default labelspace of 30,000 bytes. The output is printed at the terminal.

Example 2

```
$ SPSS/OUTPUT=RESULT.OUT  STUDYA.TST  40
```

Without prompting, SPSS will execute the commands in the file STUDYA.TST using a workspace of 40,000 bytes and the default labelspace. The output will be found in the file RESULT.OUT. Notice that the 40 indicates workspace; there is currently no way, except in the prompt mode, to specify labelspace without specifying workspace.

F.4 Batch Mode

SPSS can be run in batch mode using prepared control files on disk or cards.

F.5 Control Files on Disk

The format of the VAX BATCH command is

```
$ SUBMIT    filename
```

where filename is the name of a valid batch stream of commands. The default file type for filename is COM.

A valid batch stream for SPSS includes an SPSS execute command that either specifies the name of the SPSS control file or defaults to SYS$INPUT. Defaulting to SYS$INPUT implies that the SPSS commands follow the SPSS execute command. The output is found in the file filename.LOG unless otherwise specified with the /OUTPUT parameter on the SPSS execute command.

Example 1

```
$ SUBMIT SPSSJOB
```

where SPSSJOB.COM contains the single line

```
$ SPSS MYFILE
```

This job will run SPSS using the commands found in the file MYFILE.DAT with defaults for workspace and labelspace. The output will be found in the file SPSSJOB.LOG that is stored in the top-level directory, the initial directory when you logged in.

Example 2

```
$ SUBMIT SPSSJOB
```

where SPSSJOB.COM contains

```
$ SPSS
RUN NAME      TEST RUN
   .
   .
   .
  FINISH
$ EOJ
```

In this example SPSS will execute the commands specified explicitly in the file SPSSJOB.COM. The output will be found in the file SPSSJOB.LOG stored in the top-level directory.

F.6 Automatic Batch for SPSS

The implementation of SPSS on the DEC VAX contains a VAX procedure that will automatically submit an SPSS control file. It is an alternative to the VAX SUBMIT command explained above.

The format of this command is

```
$ SPSSBATCH   filename
```

where filename is the name of an SPSS control file.

Example

```
$ SPSSBATCH CASESTY
```

where CASESTY.DAT is an SPSS control file containing

```
RUN NAME      CASE STUDY ONE
   .
   .
   .
  FINISH
```

The output is found in the file CASESTY.LOG.

F.7 Batch Job Submitted from a Card Reader

SPSS can be run in the batch mode using control files on disk or cards and submitted from a card reader.

Example 1

```
$ JOB JOEUSER/NAME=SPSSTEST
$ PASSWORD SECRET
$ SPSS MYFILE 150
$ EOJ
```

SPSS will execute the commands found in the file MYFILE.DAT using a workspace of 150,000 bytes and the default labelspace.

Example 2

```
$ JOB JOEUSER/NAME=SPSSTEST
$ PASSWORD SECRET
$ SPSS
$ RUN NAME      TEST RUN
$  .
$  .
$ FINISH
$ EOJ
```

SPSS will execute the commands found on the cards within the batch stream. The default amounts of workspace and labelspace are used. To override default workspace and labelspace, specify the amounts on the SPSS execute command.

F.8 SPSS COMMAND PREPARATION

SPSS on the DEC VAX adheres to the standard format for SPSS commands (cards). The VAX SPSS will interpret the "TAB" character in statements as a skip to column 16. The input line must not exceed 80 columns. As mentioned before, when preparing an SPSS control file with an editor, be sure to remove line numbers which may be inserted by the editor. SPSS will not accept line-sequenced files as input.

When entering data from a terminal either directly or into a file, you may find it convenient to use either SPSS free field input, as described in *SPSS*, Second Edition (pp. 23-24), or a similar feature in VAX/FORTRAN. To use the VAX feature, specify an input field width larger than you need and separate the input data with commas. For example,

```
INPUT FORMAT   FIXED(8F10.0)
     .
     .
READ INPUT DATA
1,2,3.5,4,5,6.7,7,8
```

This type of free-format data may be intermixed with fixed-format data and may be quite useful when editing data read in from cards. For details on the use of this feature see the VAX FORTRAN manual.

F.9 Files

To access files that already exist, or to give names to files that you create with system commands, you must know how to identify files. A system or program usually identifies a file by its file specification. A file specification appearing on an SPSS command must be acceptable to the VAX VMS/RMS operating system. The syntax of a file specification acceptable to the VAX VMS/RMS operating system is as follows:

dev:[directory]filename.typ;version number

where

dev:	identifies the file's location; the physical device on which it is stored. When you log in to the system, the system assumes that all files you create or use are on a specific disk, your default disk. This default is provided for you by the system manager who sets up your account. Thus, if you do not specify a dev:, the system assumes your default device (SYS$DISK).
[directory]	is simply a catalog of the files on the disk that belong to a particular user. As with the default disk, the system also assumes that the files you refer to are cataloged in a default directory. The directory specification must be enclosed in brackets.
filename	is a 1- to 9-character string name for a file. The valid characters in file names are A-Z and 0-9.
typ	identifies the file type. It is a 1- to 3-character string and usually identifies the file in terms of its content. The default file type for SPSS on the VAX is DAT. The valid characters in file types are A-Z and 0-9.
version number	is a decimal number from 1 to 32767 that differentiates between versions of a file. When you update or modify a file and do not specify a version number for the output file the system saves the original version for backup and increments the version by 1. Version numbers must be preceded with a semicolon or period.

File specifications used in SPSS must be eight characters or less in total length. The following are valid VAX SPSS file specifications:

```
TEST.SPS
SPSSTEST    (uses the default file type of .DAT)
SD.TST;1    (uses version one of the file SD.TST)
SI1:SDY     (uses the file SDY.DAT on the device SI1:)
```

The following are *invalid* VAX SPSS file specifications:

```
SPSSTEST.SPS     (too many characters)
SI1:TEST55       (too many characters)
[SPSS]STUDY      (too many characters)
```

The limitation of eight characters for SPSS file specifications is sometimes inconvenient. However, the SPSS user can use the DCL ASSIGN command to associate a logical name to a file specification that is greater than eight characters.

The general format of the ASSIGN command is

```
$ ASSIGN   device_name:[directory]filename.typ      logical_name
```

For example,

```
$ ASSIGN  SI1:[SPSS.TST]CASESTUDY.SPS       CASESTY
```

will assign the file CASESTUDY.SPS in directory [SPSS.TST] on device SI1:, the logical name of CASESTY. The logical name CASESTY is then used on SPSS commands requiring a file name, such as GET FILE. Execute the DCL ASSIGN statement before running SPSS. For example,

```
$ ASSIGN [SOC.SPSS]SOCSDATA  SSDATA
$ SPSS  <cr>
Please enter control filename: TT:
Please enter bytes of workspace: <cr>
Please enter bytes of labelspace: <cr>
RUN NAME       STUDY OF SOCCDATA, 1980
GET FILE       SSDATA
 .
 .
 .
FINISH
```

For further information regarding the ASSIGN command, consult local VAX documentation or your computer center personnel.

All SPSS commands that name a file use either VAX/VMS file specifications that are eight characters or less or the logical name assigned by the DCL ASSIGN command.

F.10   Raw Data Output

Raw data output will be directed to logical unit 9, FOR009, unless otherwise directed with a RAW OUTPUT UNIT command. There are two exceptions:

• Output from a WRITE FILEINFO command will be written to a file called FILEINFO.DAT.

• Output from a WRITE CASES command will be written to a file called WCASES.DAT.

Again the DCL ASSIGN command is useful here to redirect or rename any of the raw output from an SPSS run. Use the ASSIGN command before creating the raw output file in SPSS. For example,

```
$ ASSIGN CORRMAT.DAT   FOR009
```

will create a raw output file named CORRMAT.DAT rather than FOR009.DAT, and

```
$ ASSIGN  DRA0:GOVINFO.DAT  FILEINFO
```

will create a raw output file named GOVINFO.DAT on disk DRA0: containing the WRITE FILEINFO output.

F.11   INPUT MEDIUM Command

The INPUT MEDIUM command serves the purpose of informing the SPSS system of the type of medium on which the raw data will be entered into the system. The syntax is the same as explained in *SPSS,* Second Edition.

F.12   Raw Data within the SPSS Commands.

Use the keyword CARD on the INPUT MEDIUM command when the raw data are within the SPSS commands. For example,

```
RUN NAME       EXAMPLE RUN
VARIABLE LIST...
INPUT FORMAT...
INPUT MEDIUM   CARD
 .
 .
READ INPUT DATA
(data entered here)
 .
 .
FINISH
```

F.13   Raw Data on Disk

When the data are separate from the SPSS commands, such as in a disk file, SPSS on the VAX expects to read the raw data from logical unit 8, FOR008, using FORTRAN formatted input-output routines. The raw data file, therefore, can have the name FOR008.DAT.

The DCL ASSIGN command, however, can be used before the SPSS run to redirect or rename the raw data file. For example, suppose the raw data are contained in a file called

RAWDATA.DAT and not within the SPSS command file. The following ASSIGN statement would be used:

```
$ ASSIGN  RAWDATA.DAT  FOR008
```

and the SPSS command file would be of the form

```
RUN NAME       STUDY A
 .
INPUT MEDIUM   DISK
 .
FINISH
```

F.14 Raw Data on Tape

When the raw data are in a file on a magnetic tape created on a VAX, use the MOUNT command to mount the magnetic tape and then proceed as if the data were in a disk file. See Section F.13.

When the raw data are in a file on a magnetic tape created on some computer other than a VAX, the system needs some additional information in order to process your data correctly. The tape must be a 9-track tape written using the ASCII character code. If it is written in some other character code, such as EBCDIC or BCD, it must be converted to ASCII before being processed by SPSS. See your computer center personnel for assistance.

To mount the tape you must also know the density, block size, and record size at which the tape was written. The density will usually be 800 bpi or 1600 bpi. The block size tells the number of characters in each block of data on the tape, and the record size tells the number of characters in each record within the block. The block size is usually an even multiple of the record size. All of this information is usually written on a label on the tape reel.

The final piece of necessary information is the number of the file on the tape in which your data resides. Many computers write labels in front of and/or after your data file on the tape. These labels appear to SPSS as if they were data files. Therefore, in order to know the number of your data file, you need to know if the tape has labels, and if there are both header and trailer labels, or only header labels. By counting the number of files (including labels) which occur on the tape before your data file, you can determine the number of your data file. This number should be specified in parentheses on the INPUT MEDIUM command (see example below). Before running SPSS, use the following commands to mount and assign a foreign tape:

```
$ MOUNT/FOREIGN/DENSITY=ddd/NOLABEL/BLOCK=nnn/RECORD=mmm MT:
$ ASSIGN MT: FOR008
```

where nnn and mmm are the block and record sizes of the tape and ddd is the density at which the tape was written.

The SPSS control file should contain the following command:

```
INPUT MEDIUM    TAPE(n)
```

where n is the number of the file on the tape in which your data resides. If n is omitted, the first file on the tape is assumed to contain your data.

Bonnie Labosky, Northfield Division of SPSS Inc.

Appendix G

Harris Version of the SPSS Batch System

This appendix describes how to use the SPSS Batch System as converted on the Harris computer. Differences in the implementation of SPSS and information on running an SPSS job and assigning data files is included. Users are also advised to consult local documentation and computer center personnel for further detailed information on the Harris computer and their particular installation of SPSS.

G.1 LIMITATIONS OF THE HARRIS VERSION OF SPSS

The intention of the Harris converter is to provide a full and complete version of SPSS which will handle data sets and statistical problems of realistic size and complexity. Conventions for describing data and files have been similarly preserved, and deviations of Harris SPSS from that described in *SPSS,* Second Edition, and the body of this manual are noted below.

G.2 Procedures

All procedures, with the exception of OSIRIS VARS, have been implemented.

G.3 Variable Names and Subfile Names

All variable names and subfile names must be six characters or less in length.

G.4 OUTPUT FILE Command

Raw data output which is to be sent to a file (the default) may be assigned a file name and account by the use of the OUTPUT FILE command. This command eliminates the need for external JCL. If the OUTPUT FILE command is used, the RAW OUTPUT UNIT command is unnecessary and should not be used except in the case of tape output.

G.5 File Names

File names associated with the INPUT MEDIUM command may be any valid Harris Vulcan file name. File names associated with GET FILE, SAVE FILE, GET ARCHIVE, SAVE ARCHIVE, OUTPUT FILE, or FILE NAME must be six characters or less in length. Use of these commands is described more fully in Sections G.15 through G.22.

G.6 Data Set Sizes

Harris SPSS is Level H of SPSS. The number of variables is limited to 500 and the number of subfiles is limited to 100.

G.7 Extended Input Records

Harris SPSS provides for the ability to automatically read raw data input records of up to 1200 bytes (columns) in length. This is done by using an appropriate format specification on the INPUT FORMAT command. No single part of the format specification may include a repeat factor or field specification greater than 255. The example below illustrates how this limitation may be

357

circumvented. To reach column 500, the following format might be used.

```
INPUT FORMAT   FIXED (250X, 249X, F1.0)
```

G.8   GET OLD Command

Due to changes in the SPSS system file, the command GET FILE will not retrieve a file created using SPSS Release 7.2. The command GET OLD has been added to SPSS to retrieve system files created under Release 7.2 of SPSS. The use and placement of this command is exactly the same as GET FILE.

G.9   MINIMUM HARDWARE AND SOFTWARE REQUIREMENTS

SPSS is distributed to users on a nine-track, 800 BPI tape, and all installations *must* be equipped to read this format. The Harris system must be run under the Vulcan operating system with at least release number 06A/2C. Since the Harris is a virtual machine, size of physical memory is not a limiting factor with respect to the SPSS program. However, SPSS was developed on a 64K word machine and it is not recommended that it be run on a smaller machine because of increased system overhead.

G.10   JOB CONTROL LANGUAGE FOR HARRIS SPSS

Harris SPSS should be run as a control point job, although it is possible to run it on-line if the appropriate logical file numbers are set by the user. However, to minimize the impact of SPSS on the system, the control point job procedure is recommended. Conventions for running SPSS as a control point job are described below. Discussion is in terms of disk files, but physical cards could be prepared in much the same fashion if the user prefers them.

G.11   Preparation of SPSS Command File

The Vulcan editor or QED should be used to assemble a file of SPSS commands. The syntax of these commands is fully discussed in *SPSS*, Second Edition, and the body of this manual. SPSS commands should begin in column 1 and specification information should begin in column 16. This set of commands would typically begin with a RUN NAME and end with a FINISH command.

G.12   Job Control Language

A $JOB card must be the first line of the control point job. It is followed by a line which causes SPSS to be executed. The last line in the file will be a $EOJ line. The structure of these commands appears below.

```
$JOB XXXX YYYYYYYY ZZZZZ TIME=AA,LINES=BBBB
8SPSS*SPSS8
RUN NAME        SIMPLE SPSS JOB
  .
  .
  .
FINISH
$EOJ
```

where

XXXX   is a four character job identification supplied by the user
YYYYYYYY is the user's qualifier
ZZZZ   is the user's secret word
AA   is the estimated running time in CPU seconds
BBBB   is the number of lines of output (9999 is recommended in most cases)

G.13   Submission of the Job

In the case of cards, the deck of SPSS commands and JCL as described above will be read at a card reader. In the case of a disk file of commands, the user would submit the job from a terminal by typing $IJ followed by one blank and the name of the file containing all of the SPSS commands and JCL.

G.14 Logical File Numbers

The following table provides reference information for users who are familiar with Harris data definition JCL. Data definition JCL is almost never needed with Harris SPSS, but should it be required, this table will enable an experienced programmer to lend assistance.

Table G.14   Harris SPSS LFNs

SPSS FUNCTION	LFN	MODE
All SPSS control cards	105	IN
Line Printer Output	106	OUT
System scratch (File W2)	111	IN/OUT
System scratch (File W3)	112	IN/OUT
Sort cases work (File U2)	96	IN/OUT
Sort cases work (File U3)	97	IN/OUT
Sort cases work (File U4)	98	IN/OUT
System File Input	103	IN
BCD Data Input	108	IN
RAW DATA Output (Default)	109	OUT
Error Message File	100	IN
System File Output	104	OUT
Labels Scratch File (File U1)	101	IN/OUT
Data Scratch File (W1)	102	IN/OUT

G.15   DESCRIBING DISK FILES USING A FILE IDENTIFIER

Harris SPSS provides for an optional command specification, a file identifier, which can be used to describe tape and disk files both to SPSS and to the Vulcan operating system. When file identifiers are used on the GET FILE, SAVE FILE, GET ARCHIVE, SAVE ARCHIVE, INPUT MEDIUM, or OUTPUT FILE commands, no additional JCL is required to define the relevant data sets and files. If a file identifier is not used on these commands, special data definition JCL cards must be appended to the beginning of the control point job to properly assign the input and output LFNs given in the table above.

G.16   Conventions

The same basic conventions are used for all operations using files as input and/or output media. The SPSS command keywords are used starting in column 1. These include GET FILE, SAVE FILE, GET ARCHIVE, SAVE ARCHIVE, INPUT MEDIUM and OUTPUT FILE. The use of these commands is discussed in *SPSS*, Second Edition. File identification information including file name and account qualifier (optional) is entered beginning in column 16.

G.17   File in the User's Account

To access a file in the user's own account, SPSS requires that only the file name appear starting in column 16. For example, to read a file of BCD data called DATA1 from one's own account, the syntax would be:

```
INPUT MEDIUM   DATA1
```

G.18   File in Another User's Account

If the file is in another user's account, the appropriate qualifier must precede the name of the file. Note that the file should be accessible by the user's account so the appropreate access flags should be set to enable reading of the file by Vulcan. The following example would read BCD data from a file called DATA1 in account 1801STAT.

```
INPUT MEDIUM   1801STAT*DATA1
```

G.19 File in 0SYST

Some installations may want to store certain widely used data sets in the master system account. These might include files used for instructional purposes by large numbers of classes and individuals. In the example that follows the file DATA1 will be read from the 0SYST (master system) account.

```
INPUT MEDIUM    *DATA1
```

G.20 ALTERNATE FORMS FOR THE RAW INPUT

Three additional options are provided for special input medium. These are obtained by using the keywords TAPE, DISK, or OTHER in place of a file specification on the INPUT MEDIUM card. Use of these keywords will cause raw data to be read from a device or file that has been RESOURCED or ASSIGNED prior to the execution of SPSS. To read raw data from a tape called A999, the following setup would be used.

```
$JOB XXXX YYYYYYYY ZZZZZ TIME=AA,LINES=BBBB
/OM PLS MOUNT TAPE A999, SLOT 1234,NO RING...DGW
$RS,108=A999,800BPI,3CPW,9TRK,WAIT
8SPSS*SPSS8
RUN NAME        JOB USING TAPE AS INPUT MEDIUM
         .
         .
         .
INPUT MEDIUM    TAPE
         .
         .
FINISH
$EOJ
```

To read raw data from a file called DATA1 in the user's own account by using an ASSIGN statement in Vulcan, the following setup would be used:

```
$JOB XXXX YYYYYYYY ZZZZZ TIME=AA,LINES=BB
$AS,108,DATA1
8SPSS*SPSS8
RUN NAME        JOB USING ALTERNATE FORM OF DISK FILE SPECIFICATION
         .
         .
INPUT MEDIUM    DISK
         .
         .
FINISH
$EOJ
```

G.21 OUTPUT FILES

SPSS operations such as SAVE FILE, SAVE ARCHIVE, and OUTPUT FILE create files for different purposes. Note that the command OUTPUT FILE replaces the standard SPSS command RAW OUTPUT UNIT. The user need not have GENERATED this area in Vulcan before running SPSS. SPSS will both create the disk area and write into it. Existing areas with the same name as specified on one of these commands will be overwritten, so the user should beware. An example of saving an SPSS system file called SYSFIL in the user's account would be

```
SAVE FILE       SYSFIL
```

The legal output units (LFNs in Harris terminology) which may be specified on the RAW OUTPUT UNIT card are 109 (the default) and 115 through 120. Use of any other numbers will produce an error message.

G.22 Tape Output

Raw output of intermediate statistics from several procedures to tape may be accomplished using a RAW OUTPUT UNIT card and specifying a Logical File Number (LFN) which has been previously resourced to a tape. (See Harris Vulcan user documentation for tape resourcing commands.)

SPSS system or archive files may be saved on tape by resourcing LFN 104 to a tape before running SPSS. The SAVE FILE or SAVE ARCHIVE card should then specify a file name only.

To retrieve an SPSS system file from tape, LFN 103 should be resourced to a tape before running SPSS. The GET FILE or GET ARCHIVE card should specify a file name only.

G.23 ESTIMATING AND SPECIFYING MEMORY REQUIREMENTS

SPSS uses memory to store the program itself, and any memory remaining after the desired SPSS routine has been loaded is relegated to workspace.

Different statistical procedures use different amounts of workspace for their calculations; the amount of workspace required is a complex function of such things as the number of variables involved, the numbers of levels of categorized variables, and the size and number of tables to be produced under one statistical procedure. It is difficult to estimate *a priori* how much workspace will be needed for a specific calculation. If there is insufficient workspace for a particular procedure, SPSS will print an error message indicating this fact, and the user then has two options: in subsequent runs, the amount of workspace can be increased by the use of the $MODE PS = XXX specification; or the statistical procedure can be broken up into smaller segments.

To increase the amount of available workspace the user must invoke the $MODE system option before the SPSS program is executed. The user requests the number of K words desired with the minimum and maximum being 100 and 255 respectively. The default and minimum is 100. The format and position of the $MODE command is illustrated in the following example.

```
$JOB XXXX YYYYYYY ZZZZZ TIME=AA,LINES=BBBB
$MODE PS=200
8SPSS*SPSS8
RUN NAME        JOB WITH LARGE WORKSPACE REQUEST
   .
   .
   .
FINISH
$EOJ
```

There is no clear guideline as to how much space is required because of the idiosyncratic nature of space requirements for each statistical procedure for each unique data set. If insufficient workspace is requested for a procedure or if too much workspace is requested (i.e., the memory capacity of the machine is exceeded), an error message explaining the problem will be printed for the user. Systems personnel familiar with the Vulcan operating system may be interested to know that Harris SPSS takes its workspace above the 64K boundary.

The most common cause of insufficient workspace is the request of too many tables on a particular procedure card, a situation remedied by breaking a large procedure into two or more smaller procedures. For example, if 100 variables are to be crosstabulated against two variables and there is insufficient workspace to complete the calculations, the procedure can be broken into two separate CROSSTABS procedures, each of which crosstabulates 50 variables against 2 variables.

Please note that workspace formulas for the IBM version of SPSS given in *SPSS*, Second Edition, are *not valid* for Harris SPSS and should not be used. However, the amount of workspace used is reported in doublewords during execution of Harris SPSS and is accurate.

This was contributed by David G. Whitmore, University of Vermont.

Appendix H

The SPSS Batch System for Honeywell Level 66 and Series 6000 GCOS Systems

This appendix provides basic information needed to use the SPSS Batch System on Honeywell 6000 and Series 60 Level 66 (including DPS) under the GCOS operating system. The Honeywell GCOS conversion of SPSS is supported and distributed by the University of Kansas Academic Computer Center. Additional documentation describing features of this conversion should be obtained from your local SPSS Coordinator, or from the convertor. It must be read to make use of Honeywell-specific features noted below.

H.1 GENERAL DIFFERENCES

A goal of the Honeywell conversion project is to produce an implementation of SPSS as much as possible like that described in *SPSS*, Second Edition, and the body of this manual. No statistical changes have been made except for adjustment of machine-specific tolerance values. However, a number of changes have been made to take advantage of features available under the GCOS operating system. These changes involve memory management and file handling.

H.2 Memory Allocation

The Honeywell (GCOS) conversion of SPSS has been modified to allow automatic memory expansion during execution. A maximum of 30K words of memory can normally be added as needed, but this limit may be set either higher or lower at your site. If the required amount of memory cannot be obtained, an SPSS error message will be printed informing you of the point in your job where more memory is needed and, if possible, information about the amount of memory needed.

Since adding core during execution incurs some overhead, you should estimate WORKSPACE and TRANSPACE requirements by using the formulas given in both *SPSS*, Second Edition, and the body of this manual. Divide the result by four to get the space requirement in words, rather than bytes referred to in the SPSS manual. By default, 300 words are reserved for TRANSPACE. This amount can be increased by using the SPSS ALLOCATE card.

All memory between that required for the SPSS procedure selected and that reserved for TRANSPACE is available for WORKSPACE. Procedures vary in size from 30K words for CONDESCRIPTIVE to 50K words for REPORT. The default amount of memory available to each SPSS run is 48K words. This amount may be modified as described in the resource limits paragraph of Section H.13. The procedures larger than the default memory size of 48K are RELIABILITY (49K) and REPORT (50K). The amount of WORKSPACE available to a procedure is printed on the SPSS output immediately after the procedure command. SPSS procedures REPORT, FREQUENCIES (general mode), and CROSSTABS (general mode) cannot add WORKSPACE. Sufficient memory for these procedures should be specified on your $ LIMITS JCL card. (See Section H.13.)

H.3 SORT CASES

The SORT CASES control card invokes the Honeywell Sort/Merge package. Prior to engaging the package, SPSS creates a 10-link random disk file for sort collation if no collation file is provided by the user's JCL. This random disk file is assigned to file code S1. Consult the Honeywell Sort/Merge manual for more information regarding collation files.

Sort variables will be treated as floating point real numbers unless the variable is declared as alpha with a PRINT FORMATS control card. Alpha variables will be sorted in the ASCII collating sequence. Note that lower case letters are not equivalent to upper case letters and will be sorted accordingly.

H.4 RAW OUTPUT UNIT

The RAW OUTPUT UNIT control card works as described in *SPSS,* Second Edition, with the following exceptions. Permissible unit values are 43 and 15 through 20 instead of 9 and 15 through 20. The default logical unit number for raw output is 43, not 9. The output unit number can be optionally followed by ,PRINT. This will cause the raw output to be written in a form acceptable for printing on the line printer through SYSOUT. In addition, a $ SYSOUT control card giving the logical unit number must be included in the JCL cards for the job. Only 43 should be used if raw output is to be punched, and 43 should *not* be followed by ,PRINT. If the data are to be saved on tape or disk, an appropriate JCL card must be used giving the logical unit number as the file code. Raw output written without such a JCL card will go to a scratch disk file.

H.5 INPUT MEDIUM

The INPUT MEDIUM control card accepts two optional keywords in addition to the standard ones and an input unit number specification, 43 or from 8 through 20. The unit number specification permits input from multiple raw data sources, as described in Sections H.10 and H.14 and in the University of Kansas documentation. The optional keywords are REWIND and BLANK=.

Normally the raw data file is not rewound prior to being read in order to allow input from a file other than the first on a multifile data tape. The REWIND keyword causes the raw data file to be rewound prior to being read by SPSS. If REWIND is specified when the INPUT MEDIUM is CARD, it is ignored.

Blanks read by SPSS under an F format are treated as zeros, but are distinguishable from true zeros. This allows SPSS procedures to process blanks as zeros (the standard FORTRAN treatment of blanks) while retaining the capability of recognizing the blanks using the keyword BLANK on COUNT and RECODE control cards. In order to assign blanks a special value without use of a RECODE control card, the keyword BLANK= may be used. The format required is BLANK= *value* which converts all blanks read to the specified value.

The general format of the INPUT MEDIUM control card is

```
INPUT MEDIUM   <medium> [(unit number)] [,REWIND] [,BLANK=value]
```

where items enclosed in square brackets are optional.

H.6 System File Usage

In the Honeywell version of SPSS, automatic tape positioning has been added to allow SPSS system and archive files to be easily saved on and retrieved from multifile tapes. Due to this change, the formats of the file processing control cards differ slightly from those in the original version. The general format of system and archive file commands in the Honeywell conversion for SPSS is

```
GET FILE        filename[(fc)] [/NOCATA[=n]]


SAVE FILE       [filename[,filelabel]/]
                [INITIALIZE or KEEP=n or
                NOCATA[=n]>] [(fc)]


GET ARCHIVE     FILE=infile1[(fc1)][NOCATA=n]
    or          VARIABLES= <var list  or  ALL>/
MERGE FILES     FILE=infile2 [(fc2)] [NOCATA=n]
                VARIABLES= ...


SAVE ARCHIVE    [filename[,filelabel] / ]
                FILE= infile1 VARIABLES= <var list or ALL> /
                FILE= ... [<INITIALIZE or KEEP=n or
                NOCATA[=n]>] [(fc)]
```

where [] indicates an optional item, <> indicates that any one of the enclosed options may be used, and "fc" indicates a file code. File codes for these commands should begin with the letter F, followed by another letter or number. The format of the MERGE FILES command is identical to the GET ARCHIVE command.

Files may be saved on tape either as standard GFRC labeled files or in a special format in which SPSS maintains a catalog listing of all file names on the tape. However, the two formats cannot be combined on a single tape. The SPSS catalog format allows the GET FILE command to access any file on a tape without requiring the user to indicate the position of the file.

The catalog is created when the INITIALIZE keyword is present on a SAVE FILE or SAVE ARCHIVE command. SPSS writes over any previous information on the tape when this keyword is used. Subsequent SAVE FILE commands which add new files to the tape do not require any special keyword. The SPSS file name of any file added must be unique so that positioning to the required file can be done based on the file name. The GET FILE command used to access a file from a cataloged tape does not require any special keywords.

It is possible to indicate that only a specified number of files at the beginning of an SPSS cataloged tape should be retained and any subsequent files deleted from the catalog and overwritten. This option is selected by the keyword KEEP=n, where the number n indicates the number of files currently on the tape which should be saved or kept. If n is greater than the number of files on the tape then all files will be saved just as if no special keyword had been used.

The NOCATA keyword is used to indicate that a save file tape has no SPSS catalog and is a standard GFRC labeled tape. The keyword is required on either GET FILE or SAVE FILE commands which use such a tape. The option may be given as either the keyword alone, in which case the file will be read from or written to the current postition of the tape; or as NOCATA=n, where the number n indicates that the tape should be rewound, then forward spaced over $n-1$ existing labeled files before reading or writing the SPSS system file. A file position number is required for archive file input. File names on such tapes do not need to be unique. Separate activities such as UTILITY activities can be used to position an uncataloged tape. Both SPSS files and non-SPSS files can be saved on the tape.

For system files on disk the control cards are exactly as shown in the McGraw-Hill manual.

In addition, the Honeywell Conversion supports the GET BMDP command which allows input of data files saved with the BMDP package. For additional information see the University of Kansas documentation.

H.7 Binary Output

AGGREGATE and WRITE CASES binary output write true binary records with one record per observation instead of 20 variables per record as stated in *SPSS*, Second Edition. Binary output should not be directed to the card punch.

H.8 Optional Control Cards

Certain control cards that are listed in the SPSS manual as required have been made optional for many situations in the Honeywell (GCOS) conversion of SPSS. These are as follows.

- If a JCL card defining file code 08 is present, SPSS will read raw data from that file instead of from cards included with the SPSS control cards. This change makes the INPUT MEDIUM control card optional.
- By default, raw data are read using FREEFIELD input format as described in *SPSS*, Second Edition. The default format is overridden by a DATA LIST or INPUT FORMAT control card.

H.9 REPORT Procedure

The default page width and maximum page width for the REPORT procedure is 131 columns instead of 132.

H.10 Multiple Input Data Files

The Honeywell conversion of SPSS has been modified to allow ADD VARIABLES, ADD DATA LIST, ADD CASES, and ADD SUBFILES to be used anywhere within an SPSS job. The most common use of this feature is to access data such as residuals or factor scores written by an SPSS procedure and use the data for processing by other procedures in the same SPSS job. See Section H.14 for an example illustrating this feature. For further information regarding the feature, refer to the University of Kansas documentation.

H.11 Raw Data File Formats

Raw data can be read from files with many formats, character sets, and record types. In addition to the standard Fortran "A" and "F" type formats, data fields can be zoned decimal, packed decimal, decimal precision binary, floating-point binary, or 16-, 32-, or 36-bit integer binary format, in any combination. The input character set can be ASCII, BCD, or EBCDIC. Data records can be any GFRC-compatible format that can be described using a $ FFILE JCL card.

This permits direct input to SPSS of many IBM-generated data files as well as a variety of Honeywell-written files. For specific information about using this facility see the University of Kansas documentation.

H.12 ASCII/BCD Considerations

The Honeywell conversion of SPSS uses the ASCII character set. This permits the use of upper and lower case letters in variable names and labels, as well as in data. All SPSS keywords and control field information must be specified in *upper* case. By default, SPSS printed output is translated to BCD. For information on obtaining ASCII output see the University of Kansas documentation.

H.13 JOB CONTROL LANGUAGE (JCL)

Job control language (JCL) statements, also called control cards, are used to describe to the computer system any job you want to run. They must be used to identify you as an authorized user, to specify the activity you wish to perform (for example, run SPSS), to define computer resource limits for the job, and to designate tape or disk files (if any) the job will use. A control card is identified by a dollar sign ($) in column one. The name of the card, beginning in column eight, specifies the purpose of the card. Beginning in column 16 are the operands which give specific information such as which user is running the job, what program is to be executed, what files are to be used, and so forth.

Honeywell Job Control Language (JCL) for a basic SPSS job with raw data input from cards looks like this.

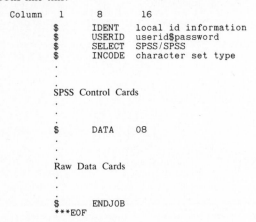

```
Column   1      8      16
         $      IDENT   local id information
         $      USERID  userid$password
         $      SELECT  SPSS/SPSS
         $      INCODE  character set type
         .
         .
         .
         SPSS  Control  Cards
         .
         .
         .
         $      DATA    08
         .
         .
         .
         Raw  Data  Cards
         .
         .
         .
         $      ENDJOB
         ***EOF
```

The purpose of each control card is as follows.

$ IDENT NNNN,NAME	This card is used to identify the user for accounting purposes. There are two fields of information separated by a comma and beginning in column 16. The first field is your project identifier. This is a code assigned by the installation manager. The second field is your last name or other information for identifying your printed output.
$ SELECT SPSS/SPSS	This card causes the system to bring in the SPSS program. It may be different at some installations. Check local documentation.
$ INCODE card code	If you submit your job via a time-sharing terminal the $INCODE card can be omitted; otherwise it is necessary to indicate the type of keypunch used to punch the SPSS commands. This is done by placing a $ INCODE card immediately before the first SPSS command. If you use an IBM 026 keypunch, the card code is IBMF. If you use an IBM 029 keyunch, the card code is IBMEL.
$ DATA 08	This card causes the operating system to assign a temporary disk file with file code 08 and to copy any data between this card and the next JCL card onto that file. The data copied are then available to SPSS.
$ ENDJOB	This card informs the system that this is the end of a computer run.
***EOF	This card informs the system that this is the end of a program deck.

All SPSS commands should be placed immediately before the $ DATA 08 card.

Additional JCL to reference files on tape or disk can be placed directly after the $ SELECT card. The default processor time, memory, and output limits can be overridden by placing a $ LIMITS JCL card after the $ SELECT card.

The predefined default limits for SPSS are 10 hundredths of an hour of processor time, 48K words memory, and 8K lines of output. The format of the $LIMITS card is

```
$        LIMITS  time,core,,output
```

If a limit is not to be changed, that field of the limits card may be omitted. The following card would increase the maximum number of lines of output to 10,240 lines while leaving the processor time set to 10 hundredths of an hour and memory set to 48K words.

```
$        LIMITS  ,,,10K
```

H.14 Multiple Input Data Example

This example uses the feature of multiple data input to access residuals created by the REGRESSION procedure for analysis with the SCATTERGRAM procedure. It uses SCATTER-GRAM to plot the residuals against each of the predictor variables.

```
Column   1       8        16
          $       IDENT    local id information
          $       USERID   userid$password
          $       SELECT   SPSS/SPSS
          $       PRMFL    08,R,S,catalog/filename
          RUN NAME         SCATTERPLOT REGRESSION RESIDUALS
          VARIABLE LIST    DEMO1 TO DEMO10
          INPUT FORMAT     FIXED(5F1.0,5F10.3)
          REGRESSION       VARIABLES=DEMO1,DEMO5 TO DEMO10/
                           REGRESSION=DEMO10 WITH DEMO1 TO DEMO9/
                           RESID
          STATISTICS       ALL
          OPTIONS          11
          INPUT MEDIUM     DISK(43),REWIND
          ADD VARIABLES    RESVAR
          SCATTERGRAM      RESVAR BY DEMO1, DEMO5 TO DEMO9
          $       ENDJOB
```

Note that if more than one input data file is used without a procedure between them, the INPUT MEDIUM control cards for each file must be separated by a READ INPUT DATA control card.

In this example, no INPUT FORMAT control card was necessary since the residuals could be read in free format. When an INPUT FORMAT is supplied, it must follow the ADD control card to which it applies.

H.15 File Codes

All Honeywell input and output is processed through designators called "file codes." Each type of input and output uses a unique code. The codes of most interest to SPSS users are

08	Default Raw Data Input
43	Default Raw Data Output
FR	Default System File Input
FW	Default System File Output
OT	"Printed Output"

To simplify the use of SPSS, default assignments have been made for commands and punched card data input, printed output, and raw data output. These assignments are the card reader, the printer, and a 120-llink scratch disk file, respectively. No additional system control cards are required if these are the only types of input and output to be done.

If any of the above assignments are to be changed or if other input or output files are used, one system control card is required per file. Usually the card will be one of the following.

```
$        TAPE
$        PRMFL
$        DATA
$        FILE
$        SYSOUT
```

These are described in the Honeywell Control Cards Reference Manual. The use of a $ DATA card to indicate the location of data on punched cards is recommended. The first item in column 16 of each of these cards is the file code.

This was contributed by Wes Hubert, University of Kansas.

Appendix I

Honeywell Multics Version of the SPSS Batch System

This appendix describes how to use the Honeywell Multics version of SPSS Batch System as converted by the Computing Center at the University of Southwestern Louisiana. Since Multics is designed primarily as an interactive timesharing system, all references to JCL cards in *SPSS, Second Edition,* and this manual can be ignored. Further, all references to cards of any kind (i.e. control cards, data cards) should be thought of as lines within a file (segment) created by an editor.

The current Multics version of SPSS can handle a maximum of 500 variables and does not include the OSIRIS interface facility.

There are two types of files referred to in this documentation: a control file and a data file. The control file contains all SPSS commands such as RUN NAME, N OF CASES, INPUT MEDIUM, VARIABLE LIST, REGRESSION, CROSSTABS, OPTIONS, etc.; the data file contains the data that SPSS is to act upon. The syntax and formats for the SPSS commands required in this control file are identical to those described in *SPSS,* Second Edition, and the body of this manual. The methods used within the Multics environment to perform the execution of SPSS using the control file and related data file in a timesharing or absentee session are the topics addressed by this appendix.

I.1 HOW TO EXECUTE SPSS ON MULTICS

The SPSS control file may be entered in upper case, lower case, or any combination desired; the resultant SPSS output will always be in upper case. Multics commands must always be in lower case.

Much of the information contained in this appendix may be obtained by using the Multics "help" facility; type "help spss" for on-line documentation.

The command to invoke SPSS on Multics is "spss." All file names given in the "spss" command may be either absolute or relative pathnames. The general syntax of this command is as follows:

spss control_file_name [data_file_name] [−arguments]

*Control*_file_name is the name given the control file containing the SPSS commands. This name may be any legal Multics segment name, but must contain a suffix of ".spss." If this suffix is not given in the above "spss" Multics command, it will be assumed. This name is required by the "spss" command.

*Data*_file_name need only be given if the data exists in ASCII form in a segment separate from the SPSS control file.

The available arguments are the following:

−list pathname	This pathname is the destination of the SPSS output. If this argument is not used, the default pathname will be "[wd]>control_file_name.list." Please note that [wd] is a Multics active function denoting the current working directory.

−data pathname	If a separate ASCII data file exists and is not given as the second pathname in the Multics "spss" command, this argument must be used to indicate the data file.
−save pathname	This argument is required if an SPSS SAVE FILE or a SAVE ARCHIVE command is given in the control file. The pathname is the destination of the requested SPSS system file.
−get pathname(s)	This argument is required if an SPSS GET FILE or a GET ARCHIVE command is used in the control file. The pathname specifies the SPSS system file to be read. If the SPSS GET ARCHIVE command is used, several pathnames may be listed.
−temp_dir dir_pathname	SPSS always requires several temporary work files during a run. If this argument is not used, these work files will automatically be created by SPSS in the user's process directory. If you want to place these files elsewhere, use this argument to specify the directory for the work files. This argument may be appropriate if the user's process directory quota is less than 512K words and a large data set is being used.
−tape	This argument informs SPSS that the data should be read from magnetic tape.

The following arguments are related to the SCSS Conversational System:

−savescss pathname	When an SPSS system file is to be used as input to an SCSS run, this argument is needed. It will generate the system file in a format suitable for SCSS use.
−getscss pathname	If a system file was created by an SCSS run and is to be used as input to SPSS, this argument will instruct SPSS to read in that SCSS system file.

I.2   FILE CONVENTIONS

SPSS uses four types of files: the raw data input file, the control file, the output (print) file, and the SPSS system file. The raw data input file contains the data described by the SPSS data definition commands. The control file contains the SPSS commands to run the SPSS job; the raw data can be included in this file rather than in a separate file. The output file contains the results of the requested statistical procedures; this file is usually displayed at a terminal or printed on a line printer. The SPSS system file is created by using the SPSS SAVE FILE or SAVE ARCHIVE command and is retrieved by using the GET FILE or GET ARCHIVE command. The specifications necessary to describe these files are discussed in the following sections.

I.3   Raw Data Input File

The SPSS INPUT MEDIUM command indicates the device on which the raw input data are stored. If the keyword used is DISK, SPSS assumes that the data are stored in a file separate from the SPSS control file. The name of this data file is specified in the second pathname in the "spss" command discussed in Section I.1 (or from the name given in the −data argument). For example, the following Multics "spss" command runs an SPSS job where the SPSS commands are stored in the file "simple_example.spss" and the name of the data file is "survey":

```
spss simple_example  survey
```

The SPSS control file "simple_example.spss" must contain all of the SPSS commands to describe the data, including an INPUT MEDIUM DISK command.

If the keyword used is either DISK or TAPE and the −tape argument is used in the "spss" command, SPSS will read the data from magnetic tape. The "io attach" Multics command must also be used to attach the I/O switch SPSS08 that is the SPSS tape usage switch.

If the keyword on the INPUT MEDIUM command is CARD, SPSS assumes the data are included in the control file immediately following the SPSS READ INPUT DATA command.

I.4 Output (Print) File

All of the "printed" output, tables and other statistical results, produced by the SPSS control file are stored in a separate file in the same directory from which SPSS was invoked (the working directory). This file is automatically created by SPSS and is named by the same name as the SPSS control file with a suffix of ."list" instead of ."spss."

The "spss" command in the section above will create an output file named "simple_example.list." This "list" file may be "printed," "dprinted," "deleted," etc. depending upon the user's need. However, the file is formatted for printing on a 132-character-width printer. For example, the output file can be printed on the line printer with the following Multics command:

```
dprint simple_example.list
```

It is possible to change the name of the output file that SPSS creates by using the −list argument on the Multics "spss" command (see Section I.1).

I.5 SPSS System Files

When using the SPSS commands that save or retrieve SPSS system files, such as SAVE FILE, GET FILE, GET ARCHIVE, and so forth, it is necessary to use the appropriate argument (−save, −get) on the "spss" command to ensure that the correct attachments are performed.

To save an SPSS system file, use the SAVE FILE command and the −save argument on the Multics "spss" command. The filename should be the same on both commands. For example, the following "spss" command creates an SPSS system file named "sample" using a control file named "create.spss" and a raw data file named "survey":

```
spss create survey −save sample
```

The SPSS control file "create.spss" must include a SAVE FILE SAMPLE command.

To retrieve an SPSS system file, use the GET FILE command and the −get argument on the "spss" command. The filename should be the same on both commands. For example, the following "spss" command retrieves the previously saved system file named "sample":

```
spss retrieve −get sample
```

The SPSS commands are stored in a file named "retrieve.spss" that must include a GET FILE SAMPLE command.

I.6 Special Output Files

When it is required that an external, ASCII file be written during an SPSS run, Multics SPSS automatically uses "file09" as the default file name. Examples of SPSS commands that produce "file09" output are WRITE CASES and the FACSCORE option in the FACTOR command.

The SPSS commands AGGREGATE and WRITE CASES BINARY will each produce a separate output file in binary format. The automatic pathname of this file is

[wd]>SPSSnn.binary.date.time

I.7 SPACE CONSIDERATIONS

The default WORKSPACE is 458,748 bytes with default TRANSPACE of 65,532 bytes. The current maximum WORKSPACE available is 512K bytes. As Multics is a virtual memory machine, and all SPSS object code is re-entrant, size is not a limiting factor.

I.8 A SPECIAL FEATURE FOR ABSENTEE USAGE

A special feature has been developed at the University of Southwestern Louisiana to simplify absentee usage of SPSS; this "batch-like" processing may be more suitable for lengthy computations or large data sets. Of course, the "spss" command can be entered through the regular Multics absentee procedures, but this new feature may be easier.

The "spss_abs" (or "spssa") command will automatically create and submit an absentee job consisting of the stated SPSS control file and related data file. The SPSS results are then automatically queued for printing on the line printer. The syntax of the "spssa" command is essentially the same as that of the regular "spss" command.

The absentee feature is always included with new Multics SPSS releases. To obtain more information on how this command is installed at a particular Multics site, type "help spssa" or contact the SPSS Coordinator at your installation.

This was contributed by Sally D. Haerer and Sam F. Bullard, University of SouthwesternLouisiana.

Appendix J

IBM/CMS Version of the SPSS Batch System

The IBM/CMS Version of the SPSS Batch System is maintained and distributed by SPSS, Inc. This appendix describes only those areas of operation requiring alternate documentation from that provided in *SPSS,* Second Edition, and the body of this manual.

J.1 CREATING AN SPSS CONTROL CARD FILE

Use CMS EDIT to create the SPSS control card file. This file should have a Filetype of SPSS and a logical record length of 80 (EDIT default). When you enter EDIT, use the EDIT subcommand TABSET 1 16 so that you can space over to column 16 with the TAB key (or with CNTL I on terminals without TAB keys).

J.2 INVOKING SPSS

SPSS is invoked by using the system command:

```
SPSS  filename  [( options]
```

where *filename* is a file of SPSS control cards. This file must have a Filetype of SPSS and is usually created using the CMS EDIT program. All minidisks attached to your virtual machine are searched starting at A for *filename* SPSS. You can specify more than one file of Filetype SPSS.
SPSS creates a new disk file containing the "printed" output that has the same filename as the SPSS control card file but a Filetype of LISTING.
If the default SPACE option value of 40K is used, the SPSS command requires a virtual machine size of 512K bytes.
Several options can be specified on the SPSS command. The available options and the defaults are listed in Table J.2.

Table J.2   Available Options

DIsk	(default) Output from SPSS is written to the disk file *filename* LISTING A.
PRint	Output from SPSS is written to your virtual printer.
ALLterm	All output is directed to your terminal. (NOTE: If your PROFILE EXEC contains the statement FILEDEF 6 TERM (PERM, the system will behave as though ALLTERM were selected.)
TErm	(default) Error messages are listed at the terminal as well as being written with the SPSS output.
NOTErm	Error messages are not listed at the terminal.
SPace nnnK	(default 40K) Total amount of WORKSPACE and TRANSPACE available to SPSS. If this is increased above 40K, you must increase the virtual machine size above 512K by a corresponding amount.
BCDIn fname	Raw data input to SPSS is to come from file *fname* SPSS. (This can also be accomplished by FILEDEF 8 ...)
BCDOut fname	Raw data output from SPSS should go to file *fname* SPSS A. (This can also be accomplished by FILEDEF 9 ...)

J.3 ADDITIONAL FILES USED BY SPSS

Some SPSS commands require the use of additional CMS commands to define input, output, or program library files. The CMS FILEDEF and GLOBAL commands are used to accomplish this. The appropriate command is entered before invoking SPSS. Table J.3 lists the SPSS commands and required prerequisite CMS commands.

Table J.3 SPSS Commands and Required CMS Commands

SPSS COMMAND	CMS COMMAND(S)
GET FILE	FILEDEF 3 DISK fname ftype fmode
SAVE FILE	FILEDEF 4 DISK fname ftype fmode

GET SCSS	First determine the number of records in the file by entering:
	    LISTFILE fname ftype fmode (ALLOC
	then enter:
	    FILEDEF 3 DISK fname ftype fmode (XTENT nrecs
	(This is necessary because GET SCSS reads using OS BDAM.)

SAVE SCSS	Same as for SAVE FILE.
GET ARCHIVE	FILEDEF FT03F001 DISK fname ftype fmode FILEDEF FT03F002 DISK fname ftype fmode ... FILEDEF FT03Fnnn DISK fname ftype fmode
SAVE ARCHIVE	FILEDEF 4 DISK fname ftype fmode
MERGE FILES	Same as for GET ARCHIVE.
RAW OUTPUT UNIT n	FILEDEF n DISK fname ftype fmode
MANOVA	If one or more interval-level variables is used as independent or covariate variables in procedure MANOVA, one additional scratch file is required. This file, having a DDNAME of SORTWK01, is dynamically allocated by SPSS; you need not do it yourself.
SORT CASES	SPSS uses an externally-provided OS-type sorting utility to perform the SORT CASES procedure. You should contact your local SPSS Coordinator concerning the availability of such a program. Assuming it resides in a publicly-available file called SORTLIB TXTLIB, you would make it available to SPSS by entering: GLOBAL TXTLIB SORTLIB The SORTWKnn files required by the sorting program are dynamically allocated; you need not provide them yourself.
SPSS Graphics	The SPSS Graphics procedures (PIECHART, BARCHART, and LINECHART) write an intermediate file that is processed in a subsequent step. A FILEDEF 13 command defines this file, which is written in card-image format. The size of the file will vary with the number, size, and complexity of the plots requested. To allocate this file: FILEDEF 13 DISK fname ftype fmode

J.4 SPSS DIFFERENCES

The IBM/CMS Version of SPSS contains no exceptions to SPSS as described in *SPSS*, Second Edition, and in the body of this manual.

The local procedure ANOVAR is no longer available in Release 9. It has been replaced by the new MANOVA procedure. Documentation for MANOVA can be found in Chapter 1 of this manual.

If an SPSS run ends in error, it returns a condition code of 8 to CMS.

The default workspace size is now 40960 (40K) bytes. If you request a different amount through the SPACE option on the SPSS command, your request will be rounded to the next larger multiple of 4096 (4K). For example, if you ask for 20000 bytes, you will get 20480 bytes, and if you ask for 30K bytes, you will get 32K, the next multiple of 4K up from 30K. This change is required because SORT CASES need not be at the end of your run. Whenever SORT CASES is used, SPSS gives up the workspace to the sort package, and it may not be able to get it back if its length is not a multiple of 4K.

The CMS BLIP feature, which did not operate while previous versions of SPSS were running, now works.

J.5 USAGE DATA COLLECTION

Releases 7, 8, and 9 of SPSS accumulate statistics on procedure use, size of file, and numbers of data transformations executed during a run. The information is written to a file on a public minidisk at the completion of the run. This file is dynamically allocated by SPSS.

Information acquired by the usage data collection facility is used in planning future enhancements to SPSS. A side benefit of this facility is the reporting of elapsed CPU time following every procedure in the SPSS output.

J.6 THE SPSS GRAPHICS POSTPROCESSOR

The postprocessor processes the intermediate file produced by the SPSS Graphics procedures in the SPSS Batch System.

Graphics terminals, such as the Hewlett-Packard 2647A, 2648A, and 7221 (attached to a normal CRT), and most Tektronix models, are plotted to as the logged-on terminal. Plotters, such as those made by Calcomp or Zeta, are plotted to either by allocating them with a FILEDEF command, or by writing a disk or tape file for later plotting. The postprocessor commands can be either entered directly at the terminal or read from a disk file.

J.7 Executing the Postprocessor

The SPSS Graphics postprocessor is invoked by the CMS command

    SPSSGP

The SPSSGP command will then ask you to enter the names of the CAGFILE and PRMFILE. These files are described below.

Enter the usual filename filetype filemode. If you omit filemode, it defaults to "A".

At this point you should enter the postprocessor commands, as described in Chapter 4 of this manual.

J.8 CMS Commands for Special Postprocessor Input and Output

If you are plotting on a Calcomp or Zeta plotter, you must first allocate the device (plotter or tape drive) via the command:

    FILEDEF 10 (specifications of the plotting device)

where the specifications on the FILEDEF command are installation-specific. Consult your local SPSS Coordinator. Then execute the SPSSGP command as above.

If you want the postprocessor commands to be read from a disk file, create it with CMS EDIT and allocate it with the command:

    FILEDEF 5 fname ftype fmode

Then execute the SPSSGP command as above.

J.9 Files Used by the Graphics Postprocessor

Files used by the SPSS Graphics procedures are:

CAGFILE The SPSS-produced intermediate file. This is the intermediate file written by the SPSS Graphics procedures PIECHART, BARCHART, and LINECHART. This file is read by the Graphics postprocessor. You specify its name, after entering the SPSSGP command, when prompted for it.

PRMFILE Each user must have a personal PRMFILE. It can contain several different types of information about your plots. If you use the SAVE subcommand of the SPSS Graphics procedures, it will also contain actual graphs for plotting with TELL-A-GRAF. Please consult local documentation on allocation and use of PRMFILE.

There are several other files that are automatically allocated by the SPSS Graphics procedures. All files are summarized in Table J.9, but one worth additional note is FT21F001. This is a file of special instructions for the postprocessor. It is shared by all users, and is placed on the system when SPSS Graphics is installed.

Table J.9 Summary of Postprocessor Files

FILE UNIT	IN/OUT	ATTRIBUTES'	FUNCTION
FT05F001	IN	* or RECFM=F	Postprocessor Commands
FT06F001	OUT	* or SYSOUT=A	Printed Output
FT10F001	OUT	Device Specific	Ofiine Plot File
FT13F001	IN	RECFM=FB,LRECL=80, BLKSIZE=800	Intermediate Plot File Produced by SPSS
FT21F001	IN	RECFM=F,LRECL=2000	Utility File (Read Only Shared File)
FT22F001	IN/OUT	RECFM=F,LRECL=2000	TELL-A-GRAF PRMFILE
FT23F001	IN/OUT	RECFM=F,LRECL=2000	Scratch File

Roger Deschner, SPSS Inc.

Appendix K

IBM/DOS Version of the SPSS Batch System

The facilities and features of the SPSS Batch System are described in detail in *SPSS*, Second Edition, and the body of this manual. This appendix describes the implementation of SPSS for the IBM/DOS operating system, the Job Control Language (JCL) needed to use it, and the differences between the system as described in the manuals above and as implemented. Because it is written for all IBM/DOS installations, it can describe the operation of the program only in general terms. Consult your computer center for information on the limitations of SPSS as installed there and for specific JCL instructions.

K.1 GENERAL INFORMATION

The IBM/DOS implementation of SPSS is virtually identical to SPSSH, Release 8.0, for IBM/OS systems. It provides no facilities not described in the standard documentation, but in adapting the OS version for IBM/DOS three facilities (OSIRIS VARS, SAVE SCSS, GET SCSS) have been eliminated and others have been changed or restricted. The only changes in SPSS control cards are

- Additional parameters may be required on the INPUT MEDIUM card.
- The specifications for the RAW OUTPUT UNIT card have been changed. It now accepts PRINTER, PUNCH, TAPE, and DISK but does not accept unit numbers.
- OSIRIS VARS, SAVE SCSS, and GET SCSS cards will not be recognized.

K.2 JOB CONTROL LANGUAGE FOR USING THE SPSSH/IBM/DOS SYSTEM

K.3 Basic JCL

If the input data is on cards and only printed output is required, the following JCL setup will suffice:

```
// JOB  ANYNAME
```

If the program is on a private library, then:

```
// DLBL    IJSYSCL,'library name'
// EXTENT  SYSCLB,vvvvvv,,,ssss,nnnn
ASSGN      SYSCLB,X'cuu'

// ASSGN   SYS007,X'cuu'       disk unit
// DLBL    IJSYS07,'UDC FILE'
// EXTENT  SYS007,vvvvvv,,,ssss,1
// ASSGN   SYS002,X'cuu'       disk unit
// DLBL    LABELS,'SPSS.LABELS',0
// EXTENT  SYS002,vvvvvv,,,ssss,nnnn
// ASSGN   SYS003,X'cuu'       disk or tape
```

If the scratch file for data is to be on disk, then:

```
//    DLBL    DATAWK,'SPSS.DATA',0
//    EXTENT  SYS003,vvvvvv,,,ssss,nnnn
```

Or, if this file is to be on tape, then:

```
//    TLBL    DATAWK,'SPSS.DATA'
//    EXEC    SPSS
      SPSS control cards and data
/*
/&
```

In the JCL above and in all JCL examples in this appendix, the following substitutions must be made.

for	substitute
cuu	the channel and unit number of the device
vvvvvv	the volume ID of a disk pack
ssss	the starting track number of an extent
nnnn	the number of tracks assigned

Your computer center may have made some or all of this JCL part of the partition standard label tracks, so that it may not have to be included in your deck. The computer center may also have a catalogued procedure for using SPSS.

K.4 Estimating Space Requirements

IJSYS07 is the SPSS usage data collection file. In it, the program counts the occurrences of various control cards, totals the time required to perform procedures and runs, and keeps statistics on the sizes of files. At your installation, the JCL required for it is always the same, since everyone uses the same file. It always requires exactly one track.

LABELS (SYS002) is a scratch file for label information and for information needed when the data must be read twice during one execution of a statistical procedure (such as in writing Z-scores, factor scores, and residuals). There is no fixed limit to the number of tracks required, but they can be estimated as follows.

- Each variable label will require one 40-byte block.
- The value labels for one variable will be written in blocks up to 800 bytes long. Each label requires 24 bytes.
- If GET ARCHIVE or MERGE FILES is used, all the labels for all the variables on all input files are stored on LABELS, as well as indices for all the labels. The indices require eight bytes for each variable and are written in 800 byte blocks.
- Each time a procedure is executed which must read the data file twice, it saves data on each subfile group in LABELS on the first pass of the data. This data may require as many as three 800 byte blocks per subfile group.

Experience indicates that space for one 800-byte block per variable is more than adequate; for 500 variables (the maximum unless GET ARCHIVE or MERGE FILES is used), one should assign 36 tracks on a 3330-type disk drive and an appropriately larger number for other types of disk drives with smaller tracks.

File DATAWK is used to record the data itself (variables and cases). It (an¹ all SPSS system files) is written in a blocked spanned format—that is, a tape or disk record may contain data from one or more cases and the data from a case may be split between two or more tape or disk records. The space required for it can be calculated fairly easily as follows.

- Each case requires four bytes for each variable plus eight bytes (four for the case weight and four for a record descriptor word). Temporary variables (those created by starred transformation cards) and cases rejected by SELECT IF cards require no space on this file.

- Each physical block will require eight bytes more— four for the block descriptor word and four for a segment descriptor word for the second segment of the case that was split across two physical records.

So, for example, if a file contains 100 variables and 600 cases, the cases will require $(100)(600)(4) + (600)(8) = 244800$ bytes of space. If the file is written in blocks of 1024 bytes (the size specified in the program as distributed), it will require $(244800)/(1024-8) = 240.95$ blocks, and space should be reserved for at least 241 blocks. On 3330 disk drives, this amounts to 22 tracks (since 11 blocks of 1024 bytes each will fit on a track). On 2314-type disk drives, this same file would need 41 tracks, since only six blocks will fit on a track.

The space for DATAWK must be allocated on its EXTENT card(s). Additional extents cannot be added by the operator during a run.

K.5 RAW INPUT FILES

The SPSS program can read data and matrices from cards, tape files, and disk files; the INPUT MEDIUM statement and job control statements specify the source for a particular file. Section 7.1 of *SPSS*, Second Edition and Chapter 12 of this manual, describes card order and deck setup for runs in which raw input data is used; it applies to the IBM/DOS version with no changes except in the INPUT MEDIUM card and in job control statements. This section describes what files the IBM/DOS version can and cannot read, the IBM/DOS version of the INPUT MEDIUM statement, and the job control statements required.

K.6 Card Files

When a matrix on cards is to be used for the analysis, the conventions and requirements specified in the manual for the procedure which is to use the matrix apply. The deck setup is similar to that for raw data, substituting the matrix for the data and a READ MATRIX card for the READ INPUT DATA card.

INPUT MEDIUM CARD really means "the data are part of the control deck," so if the control deck is on tape or disk, you still use INPUT MEDIUM CARD when the data and the control cards are in the same file.

K.7 Tape and Disk Files

The SPSS program can read raw data from tape files or from disk files on IBM 2311, 2314, 3330, 3340 and 3350 disk drives, or from disk drives similar to any of these. It can read fixed length blocked or unblocked records, variable length blocked or unblocked records, or unblocked undefined length records. There is an upper limit on the size of tape or disk blocks defined by your installation when the program was installed. The program can read only normal sequential files. It cannot read files with spanned records, files whose records occupy more than one disk track each, disk files with physical record keys (such as index-sequential files), or ASCII tape files.

The keywords TAPE and DISK on the INPUT MEDIUM card specify that the file to be read is on tape or disk, rather than on cards, but the keywords are interchangeable; DISK can be specified for a tape file and vice versa. The actual device type is that of the device assigned to SYS008. The program deblocks raw data files and matrices based on information supplied in the INPUT MEDIUM card. The device type on the INPUT MEDIUM statement can be followed by either one or two parameters in parentheses; the first is either the record length (for fixed length record files), the largest record length (for undefined length record files), or the keyword VARIABLE for variable length record files. The second parameter in parentheses is the size of the largest block in the file.

The program uses one IO area for all activity on the raw data file unless a block size is specified on the INPUT MEDIUM and that block size is not more than half the system maximum block size. In that case, it uses two IO areas for better performance.

The following sections describe the job control statements and INPUT MEDIUM statements used to read various types of tape and disk files.

K.8 Tape File Job Control

If the raw input data is on a tape, SYS008 must be assigned to a tape drive. The job control statement is

```
// ASSGN SYS008,X'cuu'     cuu is tape drive address
```

If your tape has standard labels, and your installation normally uses labeled tapes, add a TLBL card like

```
// TLBL RAWDATA,'file id'
```

'file id' in this statement is the name on the tape label. If your tape has standard labels and your installation normally uses unlabeled tapes, instruct the system to skip the labels by using

```
// MTC FSF,SYS008
```

instead of a TLBL statement.

If your tape has no labels and your installation normally uses unlabeled tapes, no special job control statement is needed; the ASSGN statement is enough. If, however, your installation normally uses standard labeled tapes, a label will be expected. Insert a TLBL card with no file- id, like

```
// TLBL RAWDATA
```

and notify the computer operator to reply 'IGNORE' to messages indicating the absence of a label.

K.9   Disk File Job Control
Disk files are always identified using job control statements like the following

```
// ASSGN SYS008,X'cuu'    cuu is disk drive address
// DLBL  RAWDATA,'file id'
// EXTENT SYS008,volume    volume is name of disk pack
```

K.10   Fixed Length Record Files
If all the records on your file have the same length, and the records do not contain length-giving information, it is said to be a "fixed length record" file. Files of this type are often blocked; that is, more than one record is written on the tape or disk at a time. This practice conserves both machine time and space on the medium. Such files are described to the SPSS program by INPUT MEDIUM cards like

```
INPUT MEDIUM    TAPE (178, 1780)
INPUT MEDIUM    DISK (63)
INPUT MEDIUM    TAPE
```

The first of these examples describes a tape file whose records are all 178 characters (bytes) long, written on tape 10 at a time (therefore, in blocks 1780 characters long). The first parameter in parentheses is the record size; the second is the block size. If the program has room, it will use two IO areas (areas in core into which tape or disk blocks may be read) for reading this file, which improves performance.

The second example describes a disk file whose records are all 63 characters long. The file may be blocked; if so, SPSS will deblock it properly, but, since the block size is not given, the program will never use two IO areas for reading it.

The third example describes a tape file whose records are 80 columns long; 80 character records are assumed if no record size is given. It too may be blocked and, if it is, it will be deblocked correctly. One IO area will be used.

In summary, fixed length record files are described by giving the record length in parentheses in the INPUT MEDIUM card. The block size may also be given as the second parameter. If it is given, the program will use it to decide whether to use one IO area or two.

K.11   Variable Length Record Files
IBM's operating systems for 360 and 370 machines provide a standard format for writing files whose records are not all of the same length; a record control word containing the record's length is appended to the front of each record, and a block control word, giving the block's length, is appended to the front of each block.

Files written using this format are called "variable length record" files, whether or not the records in the file actually differ in length. Describe such files to SPSS using INPUT MEDIUM cards like

```
INPUT MEDIUM    TAPE (VARIABLE)
INPUT MEDIUM    DISK (VARIABLE, 944)
```

The first example card describes a tape file with variable length record formatting. The file may or may not be blocked, and the blocks may be of any length up to the limit for your installation. Because no block size is given, only one IO area will be used.

The second example card describes a variable length record file on disk whose longest block is not longer than 944 characters. If the block size limit for this installation is 1888 characters or longer, two IO areas will be used; if not, only one will be used.

In summary, to process a variable length record file, specify the keyword VARIABLE in parentheses in the INPUT MEDIUM card. If the block size is also specified, the program will use it to decide whether or not to use two IO areas.

K.12   Undefined Length Record Files
If a file is not blocked, the SPSS program can read it even if its records vary in length but are not formatted using the standard variable-length record conventions. Such files are called "undefined length record" files. Describe such a file by supplying the length of the longest record on the INPUT MEDIUM card either once or twice. For example,

```
INPUT MEDIUM    DISK (156, 156)
INPUT MEDIUM    TAPE (91)
```

The first example card describes an undefined length record file whose records do no exceed 156 characters in length. As with the other record formats, the second parameter in parentheses determines whether one or two IO areas will be used. In this case, two will be used unless the system block size limit is less than 312 characters.

The second example card could be used to describe an undefined length record file whose blocks never exceed 91 characters. Only one IO area will be used, since no second parameter is given.

These cards could also describe fixed length record files. In fact, the processing is identical to that for fixed length records; when the program wants to read the second record from the file specified by the first example card, it reads another block if the first one was not more than 156 characters long. Otherwise, it assumes the second record starts at the 157th character of the first block. This procedure works for fixed length blocked files, and, if the record size was specified correctly, it also works for undefined length records.

K.13 OUTPUT SYSTEM FILES

Whenever the SPSS control deck specifies SAVE FILE, additional JCL cards must be used to specify where the saved system file is to be written. This JCL must precede // EXEC SPSS and looks like

```
// ASSGN    SYS016,X'cuu'
```

and either

```
// DLBL     SVFILE,'fileid'
// EXTENT   SYS016,vvvvvv,,,ssss,nnnn
```

(for disk files)

or

```
// TLBL     SVFILE,'fileid'
```

(for tape files)

where the following substitutions must be made.

for	substitute
cuu	the channel and unit code
fileid	the name to appear on the IBM/DOS file label (not necessarily the same as the one on the FILE NAME or SAVE FILE control card)
vvvvvv	the volume ID for a disk pack
ssss	the starting track number
nnnn	the number of tracks assigned

The space required for a system file on disk is calculated in much the same way as that required for the scratch data file (see Section K.4), except that additional space is needed for dictionary and label information. Experience indicates that an additional 10% over the space required for the data is usually enough.

As distributed, SPSS writes system files in blocks of 1024 bytes. This size may have been changed by your computer center.

As long as block sizes are compatible, system files written using this version of SPSS can be processed by this or any other version of SPSS distributed by SPSS Inc. for use on IBM 360 or 370 or compatible machines using either OS or IBM/DOS. They can also be processed by the special conversion programs available with some versions of the SPSS system set up for other manufacturers' machines. They cannot be processed by the earlier IBM/DOS versions distributed by Oberlin College, Waubonsee College, or American University, or by OS versions earlier than Release 5, or by versions of the SPSS system for other manufacturers' machines.

K.14 INPUT SYSTEM FILES

When the SPSS control deck specifies GET FILE, JCL cards must be included to identify the system file to be used. These JCL cards must precede the // EXEC SPSS card and look like

```
// ASSGN    SYS017,X'cuu'
```

and either

```
// DLBL     GTFILE,'fileid'
// EXTENT   SYS017,vvvvvv
```

(for disk files)

or

```
//  TLBL    GTFILE,'fileid'
```

(for tape files)

where the substitutions are the same as given in the previous section. This name is not necessarily the same as that which appears on the GET FILE card—that name must match the name specified in the SAVE FILE or FILE NAME card in the SPSS run which produced the system file.

When SPSS was installed at your computer center, the maximum block size for input system files was specified. There are 1024 bytes in the system file as SPSS is distributed but this block size may have been changed locally. Subject to this restriction, this version of the SPSS system (SPSSH/IBM/DOS, Release 8.0) will process system files created by itself or by earlier versions of SPSSH for IBM/DOS distributed by American University, or by any version of SPSS distributed by the National Opinion Research Center or SPSS Inc. for either the OS or IBM/DOS operating systems. It will not process system files written by the SPSSG version distributed by Oberlin College and later by Waubonsee College, or by SPSS versions running on computers other than the IBM 360, IBM 370, or compatible machines.

K.15 RAW OUTPUT FILES

Whenever the SPSS control deck includes a WRITE CASES or AGGREGATE control card or a procedure option which causes the system to write data other than a system file or printed matter (such as a correlation matrix or factor scores), the data is written on the unit specified by the last RAW OUTPUT UNIT control card encountered. This control card has the following format.

RAW OUTPUT UNIT   PUNCH or PRINTER or TAPE or DISK

If no RAW OUTPUT UNIT card appears in the run, data for this unit will be written to tape or disk, whichever is assigned to SYS006.

If this card specifies PUNCH, then the data is written to SYSPCH, which is normally a card punch.

If the card specifies PRINTER, the data is written on SYSLST, the same unit as the normal printed output (normally a printer). Please note, however, that your system will take the first character of each record written to SYSLST to be a printer line control character, and the SPSS program does not generally supply a character for line control for this data. This means that the first character will not be printed and may cause extra line skips and other printer misbehavior. If the output is coming from WRITE CASES, you can avoid such problems by starting your format with "1X,". Otherwise, check the description in the SPSS manual of the records produced by whatever option or procedure is in use to make sure that the first character of each record will be blank. If not, don't use the PRINTER option.

If the RAW OUTPUT UNIT card specifies TAPE or DISK, the tape or disk file to be used must be defined in JCL before the // EXEC SPSS card appears. The JCL needed looks like

```
//  ASSGN   SYS006,X'cuu'
```

and either

```
//  DLBL    IJSYS06,'fileid'
//  EXTENT  SYS006,vvvvvv,,,ssss,nnnn
```

(for a disk file)

or

```
//  TLBL    IJSYS06,'fileid'
```

(for tape files)

where the following substitutions must be made.

for	substitute
cuu	the channel and unit code
fileid	the name to appear on the IBM/DOS file label
vvvvvv	the volume ID for a disk pack
ssss	the starting track number
nnnn	the number of tracks assigned

This file is written by commands in the FORTRAN language, so the way FORTRAN is implemented under IBM/DOS puts restrictions on it. If the file is written to tape, each record will be as short as possible, but never shorter than 18 bytes, and no blocking will be done. If the file is written to disk, all records will be 260 bytes long and any unused portion of each record will be blank. In either case, records longer than 260 bytes cannot be written.

If you read one of these files with SPSS, whether on tape or on disk, use

```
INPUT MEDIUM    TAPE(260,260)
```

This does not mean that the records will actually be 260 bytes long, only that they will not be longer. Except for WRITE CASES output, there will never be more than 80 bytes of data on a record.

K.16   OSIRIS INPUT FILES

The OSIRIS VARS feature of SPSS is not implemented in this version.

K.17   MERGING FILES

The SPSS control cards GET ARCHIVE and MERGE FILES can be used to access variables from two or more SPSS system files which have corresponding cases. The JCL required for the first system file is as described in Section K.14. The JCL required for each system file after the first is similar except for the file name and logical unit number. These are shown in Table K.17.

Table K.17   Files used for GET ARCHIVE and MERGE FILES

SYSTEM FILE NUMBER	LOGICAL UNIT NUMBER	FILE NAME
1	SYS017	GTFILE
2	SYS018	GTFILE2
3	SYS019	GTFILE3
4	SYS020	GTFILE4
5	SYS021	GTFILE5

In order to limit main storage requirements, the system is distributed with the third, fourth, and fifth input files disabled. This means that no more than two input files can be processed in one run, although more than two can be merged together by using several runs (where each run merges in one more file). Check with your local computer center for information on the maximum number of input files available.

When GET ARCHIVE or MERGE FILES is used, two additional work files are required. These are defined using JCL similar to that used for the work data file described in Section K.4 except that these files require TLBL or DLBL cards for the names ARCHWK1 and ARCHWK2, and ASSGN and EXTENT cards for SYS004 and SYS005.

File ARCHWK1, on SYS004, is used to hold the data for active variables. If assigned to a disk unit, it will require an amount of space which can be calculated as described in Section K.4 , using only the number of active variables.

File ARCHWK2, on SYS005, is used to hold the data for all the variables on all the system files accessed. If it is assigned to a disk unit, the space it requires may be calculated in the same way as the space for DATAWK, but for all the variables rather than for only those active in this run. If the run does not include a SAVE ARCHIVE card, you can assign SYS005 to IGN and omit other JCL for this file. This means that write commands for this file will be ignored.

If ARCHWK1 or ARCHWK2 is on disk, enough space for it must be provided in its EXTENT card(s). It cannot be extended by the operator at run time.

When SAVE ARCHIVE is used to create a new archive file, its JCL requirements are identical to those for a saved system file (see Section K.13).

K.18   THE SORT CASES FEATURE

The SORT CASES card calls on the utility sort package to sort the data. This package requires a disk work area which must be provided through JCL commands like

```
// ASSGN  SYS001,X'cuu'
// DLBL   SORTWK1,'SORT AREA',0
// EXTENT SYS001,vvvvvv,,,ssss,nnnn
```

where

cuu   is the channel and device code

vvvvvv   is the volume ID of the disk pack

ssss   is the starting track number of the area to be used

nnnn   is the number of tracks in the area

Your computer center can provide information on estimating the space required for sorting.

K.19 FILE SUMMARY TABLE

Table K.19 shows all the files used by SPSSH/IBM/DOS, their symbolic unit names, and the SPSS control cards associated with them.

Table K.19   Summary of Files Used by SPSS

SYMBOLIC UNIT NAME	FILE NAME	SPSS CONTROL CARD	DESCRIPTION
SYSIPT	SYSIPT	none	control card file
SYSLST	IJSYSLS	none	printed output
SYSPCH	IJSYSPH	RAW OUTPUT UNIT	punched card
SYS001	SORTWK1	SORT CASES	sort work area
SYS002	LABELS	none	work file for labels
SYS003	DATAWK	none	work file for data
SYS004	ARCHWK1	GET ARCHIVE MERGE FILES	work file for data from active variables
SYS005	ARCHWK2	GET ARCHIVE MERGE FILES	work file for all input data
SYS006	IJSYS06	WRITE CASES AGGREGATE OPTIONS	raw output (data, matrices, etc.)
SYS007	IJSYS07	none	usage data collection file
SYS008	RAWDATA	INPUT MEDIUM	raw data input
SYS016	SVFILE	SAVE FILE SAVE ARCHIVE	output system file
SYS017	GTFILE	GET FILE GET ARCHIVE MERGE FILES	(first) input system file
SYS018	GTFILE2	GET ARCHIVE	2nd through 5th
SYS019	GTFILE3	MERGE FILES	input system files
SYS020	GTFILE4		
SYS021	GTFILE5		

Jonathan Fry, SPSS Inc.

Appendix L

Changes to Job Control Language For IBM OS Installations

This appendix updates Appendix E in *SPSS,* Second Edition. With few exceptions, the job control language documented there still works with SPSS Releases 7, 8, and 9. However, additional files are now required for certain facilties in SPSS and the amount of region required has been increased.

L.1 RAW OUTPUT UNIT

The default DCB characteristics for the standard raw output unit (FT09F001) are changed to RECFM=U, BLKSIZE=80. Previously, the default block size was 800.

L.2 CONDITION CODE 8

SPSS now terminates with a condition code of 8 if any numbered error (except 1780) occurs during its operation. If no errors occurred, its condition code is zero. Error 1780 occurs when a data field read under a numeric format contains an invalid character. Whenever the condition code is 8, the message STOP 8 is sent to the system console. This message has no meaning other than that some numbered error occurred.

L.3 WORKSPACE NOW COMES IN 4K CHUNKS

The default workspace size is now 81920 (80K) bytes, rather than 80000. If you request a different amount through the PARM parameter on your EXEC statement, your request will be rounded to the next larger multiple of 4096 (4K). For example, if you ask for 20000 bytes, you will get 20480 bytes, and if you ask for 30K bytes, you will get 32K, the next multiple of 4K up from 30K.

This change is required because SORT CASES need not be at the end of your run. Whenever SORT CASES is used, SPSS gives up the workspace to the sort package, and it may not be able to get it back if its length is not a multiple of 4K.

L.4 ADDITIONAL REGION REQUIRED

Release 9 of SPSS requires an additional 32K of core memory above that required to run Releases 7 or 8 of SPSS. Assuming the default SPACE of 80K and modest buffer space for various files, the maxi- version (Version M) of SPSS now requires a region of 276K and the standard version (Version H), a region of 252K.

L.5 ADDITIONAL FILES

The Batch/Conversational Interface, SPSS Graphics, and MANOVA procedure require additional files for intermediate processing of data.

L.6   JCL Required For GET and SAVE SCSS

The input masterfile accessed by GET SCSS is defined by the FT03F001 DD statement. This file must be on a direct access device such as a disk. The output masterfile saved by SAVE SCSS is defined by the FT04F001 DD statement. Usually the file is written to a direct access device and catalogued for use with TSO. Since FT03F001 is also used to define an existing system file and FT04F001 is used for a saved system file, the catalogued procedure at your installation probably makes provision for these two logical units. Additional information concerning appropriate parameters for the GET SCSS and SAVE SCSS commands is provided in Chapter 10 of this document.

One additional scratch file is required when either a GET SCSS or SAVE SCSS command is included in the command file. An FT12F001 DD statement defines the temporary file in which the detransposed case-ordered file is stored during GET SCSS processing. It will normally reside on disk. The same logical unit is used as a direct access file during SAVE SCSS processing. When used with SAVE SCSS, it must be allocated to disk and should be 25 percent larger than the scratch work file (FT02F001).

Note that FT12F001 is also used for archive processing and may already be included in any catalogued procedure used at your installation.

L.7   JCL Required for MANOVA

If one or more interval-level variables is used as independent or covariate variables in procedure MANOVA, one additional scratch file is required. A SORTWK01 DD statement defines this temporary file. Enough space to store all the cases for all the interval-level variables being used in a given MANOVA command is required for this file. The SORTWK01 file is also used for SORT CASES processing. However, when used with MANOVA, it does not require contiguous disk space.

L.8   JCL Required for SPSS Graphics

The SPSS Graphics procedures (PIECHART, BARCHART, and LINECHART) write an intermediate file that is processed in a subsequent step. An FT13F001 DD statement defines this intermediate file which is written in card image format. The size of the file varies with the number of plots generated, the number of points and lines within the plots, and the types of options specified. An example of an FT13F001 DD statement is

```
//FT13F001  DD   DSN=$3YC080.SSKS.IPFILE,DISP=(NEW,CATLG),
//               UNIT=SYSDA,DCB=(RECFM=FB,LRECL=80,BLKSIZE=800),
//               SPACE=(80,(500,100),RLSE)
```

L.9   USAGE DATA COLLECTION

Releases 7, 8, and 9 of SPSS accumulate statistics on procedure use, size of file, and numbers of data transformations executed during a run. The information is written to a file on a direct access device at the completion of the run. Any run must now include an additional DD card as part of the job control language (JCL) to define this file. If a catalogued procedure has been installed in your installation's procedure libary, you will not need to provide the FT10F001 card defining the file. If you are not using a catalogued procedure you must get the name of the dataset to be referenced on the FT10F001 card from your local SPSS Coordinator. Failure to include a correct FT10F001 card will result in an SPSS error.

Information acquired by the usage data collection facility is used in planning future enhancements to SPSS. A side benefit of this facility is the reporting of elapsed CPU time following every procedure in the SPSS output.

L.10   THE SPSS GRAPHICS POSTPROCESSOR

The postprocessor processes the intermediate file produced by the SPSS Graphics procedures in the SPSS Batch System. It can be run interactively, with its commands entered at the terminal, or in batch mode, with its commands coming from a file or the input stream.

In interactive mode, the postprocessor runs under TSO in 512K with the plotting terminal or device connected directly, as the logged-on terminal. Interactive mode is used with graphics terminals such as Hewlett-Packard 2647A, 2648A, and 7221 (attached to a normal CRT), or most Tektronix models. The postprocessor reads the intermediate file, and plots directly on the plotting device. In interactive mode the postprocessor commands described in Chapter 4 of this manual are normally entered directly at the terminal.

In batch mode, running as an OS Batch job step, the postprocessor reads the intermediate file produced by SPSS and writes the plots out to a batch-accessible device, such as a plotter connected through HASP, or a tape to be transported to an offline plotting device. Batch mode is normally used for plotting on CALCOMP and ZETA devices. In batch mode the postprocessor commands would normally be entered in the batch job stream in OS.

L.11 Running the Postprocessor in Interactive Mode

Typically, your SPSS Coordinator will have installed a file of system commands, called a CLIST, which allocates all necessary files for the postprocessor by simply prompting you for the file names. In TSO the SPSS Graphics postprocessor might be invoked by the command:

```
SPSSGP
```

The SPSSGP command may differ at your installation. The postprocessor then asks you to enter the names of the CAGFILE and PRMFILE, which are described below.

Enter the name according to normal TSO naming conventions. If the file name is not saved under your account, or if you are unfamiliar with TSO dataset naming conventions, enter the fully qualified name and enclose it in apostrophes (').

L.12 Running the Postprocessor in Batch Mode

Typically, your SPSS Coordinator will have installed a catalogued procedure for the postprocessor run in batch mode. To use it, submit the following batch job step:

```
// EXEC SPSSGP,CAGFILE='cagfile',
//       PRMFILE='prmfile'
//PLOTTER DD (specifications of plotting device)
//SYSIN DD *
(postprocessor commands)
```

The dataset names of the CAGFILE and PRMFILE are entered fully qualified, and enclosed in apostrophes ('). The specifications on the PLOTTER DD card are installation-specific; consult your local SPSS Coordinator.

The postprocessor step can be run in the same job as the SPSS step that runs PIECHART, BARCHART, or LINECHART. However, it is probably not a good idea to use a temporary dataset (&&name) for the CAGFILE in such a two-step job. If the SPSS step should work and the postprocessor step fail, you could then rerun just the postprocessor step from the saved CAGFILE, thus saving the expense of rerunning the SPSS step.

L.13 Files Used in the Above Procedures

Files used by the SPSS Graphics procedures are:

CAGFILE   The SPSS-produced intermediate file. This is the intermediate file written by the SPSS Graphics procedures PIECHART, BARCHART, and LINECHART. This file is read by the SPSS Graphics postprocessor. You specify its name either as a parameter (OS Batch) or when prompted for it (TSO).

PRMFILE   Every execution must access a PRMFILE that can be personal or shared among several users. It can contain several different types of information about your plots. If you use the SAVE subcommand of the SPSS Graphics procedures, it will also contain actual graphs for plotting with TELL-A-GRAF. Please consult local documentation on allocation and use of PRMFILE.

There are several other files that are automatically allocated by the SPSS Graphics procedures. All files are summarized in Table L.13, but one worth additional note is FT21F001. This is a file of special instructions for the postprocessor. It is shared by all users, and is placed on the system when SPSS Graphics is installed.

Table L.13 Summary of Postprocessor Files

FILE UNIT	IN/OUT	ATTRIBUTES	FUNCTION
FT05F001	IN	* or RECFM=F	Post-processor Commands
FT06F001	OUT	* or SYSOUT=A	Printed Output
FT10F001	OUT	Device Specific	Ofiine Plot File
FT13F001	IN	RECFM=FB,LRECL=80, BLKSIZE=800	Intermediate Plot File Produced by SPSS
FT21F001	IN	RECFM=F,LRECL=2000	Utility File (Read Only Shared File)
FT22F001	IN/OUT	RECFM=F,LRECL=2000	TELL-A-GRAF PRMFILE
FT23F001	IN/OUT	RECFM=F,LRECL=2000	Scratch File

ViAnn Beadle, SPSS Inc.

Appendix M

Prime Version of the SPSS Batch System

This appendix describes how to use the SPSS Batch System and the extended features unique to the Prime version. Additional information on the Prime implementation can be found in *PDR 3173—User's Guide, Statistical Package for the Social Sciences (SPSS),* a manual available from Prime, Inc.

M.1   INTRODUCTION

SPSS runs on Prime 400 and higher computers under the PRIMOS operating system by Prime Computer, Inc., Framingham, Massachusetts. Prime supports SPSSM, the 1000-variable maxiversion. Prime's goal, to support SPSS exactly as described in the McGraw-Hill manuals, has been achieved with only one exception. The exception deals with the explicit use of FORTRAN logical units on the RAW OUTPUT UNIT card. This exception is described in detail at the end of this appendix. Otherwise, any SPSS control deck which runs on the IBM version will run correctly on the Prime version provided that the IBM JCL is replaced with the appropriate commands on the user terminal both before and after the SPSS run.

Because of the time-shared nature of the PRIMOS operating system, several optional extensions to control cards which either directly or indirectly reference files have been implemented. These extensions allow the user to avoid any JCL-type setup for an SPSS run. Also, there is a convenient way to use SPSS in an interactive mode. Note, however, that this is not a conversational version of SPSS. It is the batch version which has been adapted to communicate with the user terminal for all input and output (except system files). However, none of the line printer output is reformatted for user terminals. Since Prime does not support the SCSS Conversational System, the facility for creating SCSS system files has not been implemented.

M.2   MEMORY REQUIREMENTS

Prime SPSS allocates SPACE (i.e., TRANSPACE + WORKSPACE) in one-segment (128K byte) chunks. Default SPACE is one segment, except when SORT CASES are requested. To accommodate SORT CASES when SPACE is one segment, a second segment is allocated automatically. Maximum SPACE is 10 segments (1.28 Mega-byte). The default TRANSPACE to WORKSPACE ratio is 1:7. This ratio can be changed with the SPSS ALLOCATE control card.

M.3   FILES AND TREE NAMES

Because of the ease of use and flexibility of the Prime file system, no direct card reader, line printer, or magnetic tape support has been implemented. Instead, Prime utilities transfer files to and from these media. Once the files are on disk, the entire body of Prime's software, in particular the text editor, can be used to modify them.

For Prime SPSS to recognize file names embedded within SPSS control cards, the disk file tree names must be enclosed within square brackets as in the following example:

INPUT MEDIUM   [<PACKID>UFD1>SUBUFD11>FILE]

The control card syntax descriptions in this appendix use square brackets to indicate an optional parameter. For simplicity, the notation tree-name indicates a tree name enclosed within the required square brackets. Parameters listed in all uppercase letters are to be supplied exactly as shown. Those in lower case should be replaced by an appropriate value or text string. If more than one parameter is possible, the options are shown enclosed within braces ({ }), separated by vertical bars (|).

M.4 SPSS STARTUP

SPSS is invoked by typing a command of the form

SPSS [−INPUT input,] [−LISTING listing,] [−SIZE size,] [options]

where names preceded by a minus sign are called keywords and the combination of a keyword and its value (−KEYWORD value) is called a parameter.

M.5 Keywords

Keywords are defined as names, preceded by minus signs (−), which identify a following value. The keywords which SPSS recognizes are −INPUT, −LISTING, −SIZE, −PAGESIZE, −PRINTBACK, −MAXERROR, and −EDIT. These keywords may be abbreviated to −I, −L, −S, −P, −PR, −M, and −E respectively. However, the values which follow the keywords may not be abbreviated. Note that since the keywords identify what follows, parameters may be specified in any order.

M.6 File Names (−INPUT, −LISTING)

The −INPUT and −LISTING keywords identify the primary (CARD image) input file and the primary (LINE PRINTER/SPOOL) listing file. These keywords may be omitted, but if they are, the input and listing file names must be specified in the order shown above.

M.7 Batch Mode

In batch mode, SPSS operates from an input file prepared before the run, and directs line printer output to a file which can be printed after the run. Note that file names may be PRIMOS tree names, but unlike the tree names on SPSS control cards, these initial names are not enclosed within square brackets. Also, if embedded blanks must be included in the name, the entire name should be enclosed within apostrophes. If no file names are supplied, the user must first open the input file and listing file with the PRIMOS INPUT and LISTING commands. If an input file is supplied but the listing file is omitted, the listing file name will be the input file name suffixed by the characters ".LIST." The input and listing files are opened on PRIMOS file units 1 and 2 (FORTRAN logical units 5 and 6). Any files which are not explicitly opened by SPSS will be neither truncated nor closed by SPSS at the conclusion of the run.

Two special listing file names are recognized for batch mode. If the name NOLIST is specified, the SPSS listing file is suppressed. If the name SPOOL is specified, the listing file will be automatically spooled to the system line printer using the input file name for the listing banner. In this case, no listing file will appear, even temporarily, in the user's UFD.

M.8 Interactive Mode

In interactive mode, SPSS operates from control card strings entered at the user terminal. If the special name TTY is used for the input file, SPSS treats the user terminal as the primary input stream for all SPSS commands and input data that would be specified as CARD on the INPUT MEDIUM control card. SPSS prompts for terminal input with the character $. In addition, the backslash character (¢) can be used as a logical tab to column 16 on both the first line of an SPSS command and on all subsequent continuation lines. Note that the backslash character tabs to column 16 even if typing has proceeded beyond that point, and so can be used to retype the specification portion of a command. Also, the control-C character can be used to signal end-of-file (for the N OF CASES UNKNOWN facility).

If TTY is specified as an input file, but no file is specified for the listing file, line-printer output goes to a file named TTY.LIST.

If the name TTY is specified for the listing file, all line printer output is directed to the user terminal, regardless of the input file specified. To avoid losing output when printing on a CRT terminal, the page size is automatically set to 11 lines to allow for wrap-around of output lines longer than 80 characters. This default can be explicitly overridden either with the −PAGESIZE startup parameter or with a PAGESIZE control card. At the end of each terminal page, SPSS pauses and displays this message; (TYPE <CR> TO CONTINUE, −Q TO QUIT). Typing a Q will cleanly abort the run, closing all files.

M.9 WORKSPACE CONFIGURATION (–SIZE)

The default allocation for SPACE (WORKSPACE + TRANSPACE) is one segment (128K bytes). If this is not sufficient for a run, the allocation may be increased by specifying the –SIZE keyword where size is interpreted as the decimal number of segments to be used. The minimum size is 1 segment and the maximum size is 10 segments (655,360 words, or 1280K bytes).

M.10 OTHER OPTIONS (–EDIT, –PAGESIZE, –PRINTBACK, –MAXERROR)

Other options can be specified when SPSS is invoked. These include EDIT mode, PAGESIZE, the various PRINT BACK modes, and the maximum number of errors permitted before the run is aborted. The options are specified as follows:

```
–EDIT
–PAGESIZE  {NOEJECT | #}                       (DEFAULT =54)
–PRINTBACK {NO | FORMAT | CONTROL | YES}       (DEFAULT =YES)
–MAXERROR #                                    (DEFAULT =40)
```

If an option is specified in this way, the effect is the same as if the corresponding SPSS control card were included in the input file. The only difference is that the options are in effect immediately, rather than after the particular control card is processed. This is particularly true of the PAGESIZE option since even with the PAGESIZE control card present, the first page is always the default of 54 lines long.

M.11 MODIFIED SPSS CONTROL CARD SYNTAX

Eight SPSS control cards have expanded capability on the Prime version of SPSS. The following SPSS control cards either directly or indirectly reference files:

RAW OUTPUT UNIT
INPUT MEDIUM
GET FILE
SAVE FILE
GET ARCHIVE
MERGE FILES
SAVE ARCHIVE
OSIRIS VARS

In general, the command syntax has been expanded to include optional, embedded tree names where appropriate. See Section M.3 for a description of the expanded syntax.

M.12 PRIME SPSS FILE USAGE

The following table shows the FORTRAN logical units and corresponding file units used by Prime SPSS.

Table M.12   Files Used by Prime SPSS

FORTRAN#	FILE#	SPSS Name	Usage
1	TTY	IOCR/IOLP	Interactive I/O
2-4	—	—	Not used
5	1	IOCR	Primary Input (Card Reader)
6	2	IOLP	Primary Output (Line Printer)
7	3	DICTIN	OSIRIS Dictionary

FORTRAN#	FILE#	SPSS Name	Usage
8	4	IOBCD1	Alternate Input
9	5	IOBCD2	RAW OUTPUT UNIT 9 or tree-name
10	6	—	Not used— reserved for command file
11	7	ISR11	Archive Work File
12	8	ISR12	Archive Work File
13	9	IOSRC1	Scratch File #1 (Data)
14	10	IOSRC2	Scratch File #2 (Dictionary)
15	11	IOFIL2	SAVE FILE/ARCHIVE - RAW OUTPUT UNIT
16	12	IOFILE(1)	GET/MERGE FILE/ARCHIVE - RAW OUTPUT UNIT
17	13	IOFILE(2)	GET/MERGE FILE/ARCHIVE - RAW OUTPUT UNIT
18	14	IOFILE(3)	GET/MERGE FILE/ARCHIVE - RAW OUTPUT UNIT
19	15	IOFILE(4)	GET/MERGE FILE/ARCHIVE - RAW OUTPUT UNIT
20	16	IOFILE(5)	GET/MERGE FILE/ARCHIVE - RAW OUTPUT UNIT
21	17	SPOOLER	−LISTING SPOOL temporary file unit

M.13   Unit Conflicts: Exception to IBM Compatibility

Since only 17 units are available in PRIMOS to SPSS, units 11 through 16 (FORTRAN logical units 15 through 20) are used both for system files and RAW OUTPUT. As a result, certain specification combinations which work for the IBM version of SPSS do not work for Prime SPSS. In particular, if the RAW OUTPUT UNIT card is used with unit numbers 15 through 20 (comparable to Prime units 11 through 16), possible conflicts can arise with system file unit usage. For example, if RAW OUTPUT UNIT 15 is used in the same run as SAVE FILE, both cards assume a different file to be previously open for writing on the same unit. Since this is impossible, an error will be generated rather than saving the system file in the raw output file which makes it impossible to access. However, if a tree name is specified on the SAVE FILE card, the previously open raw output file will first be closed (but not truncated). In a similar way, conflicts can arise with RAW OUTPUT UNITs 16 through 20 and GET/MERGE FILE/ARCHIVE. In this case, the system input files are left open on the appropriate units for reading and the raw output would be appended (had the files been open for read/write) to the end of the system file, making it inaccessible. Instead, an error will be generated. However, if a tree name is specified on the RAW OUTPUT UNIT card, FORTRAN logical unit 9 will be used and the system input files will not be affected.

In general, if Prime SPSS users always specify tree names on the control cards, unit conflicts will never arise.

This was contributed by Robert Crowling and Steven Paris, Prime Computer, Inc.

Appendix N

Univac 1100 Series Version of the SPSS Batch System

This appendix describes how to run the SPSS Batch System on the Univac 1100 Series computers.

N.1 CALLING SPSS

Call SPSS with the statement

```
@SPSS
```

followed by the SPSS control cards. (The name of the SPSS processor may be different at your installation. Consult local documentation or your SPSS Coordinator.)

A simple SPSS run can be set up as described in the SPSS manuals, with the addition of the @RUN, @SPSS, and @FIN cards. For example,

```
@RUN    (accounting information)
@SPSS
RUN NAME        REGRESSIONS
VARIABLE LIST   A,B,C,D
INPUT FORMAT    FREEFIELD
INPUT MEDIUM    CARD
N OF CASES      200
REGRESSION      VARIABLES=A TO D/
                REGRESSION=A WITH B TO D(2)
READ INPUT DATA
   .
   .
(data cards)
   .
   .
FINISH
@FIN
```

N.2 FILE HANDLING

(NOTE: The University of Wisconsin is investigating alternative file handling conventions. Look for changes in later documentation.)

If your input is on cards and you do not require any file or card output, you do not need to read this section.

This section describes the Sperry Univac Operating System cards needed to

• read and write SPSS SAVE FILES and SAVE ARCHIVE files
• punch raw data, matrices etc., on cards
• read or write raw data, matrices, etc. from/to SDF disk or tape files.

SDF files are Sperry Univac System Data Format files which are read and written by other Sperry Univac processors such as @DATA, @FOR, @FTN, etc. See your local handbook or the *Sperry Univac Programmer's Reference Manual* for more information. SDF files are the only files which can be read or written by SPSS other than SPSS SAVE FILE, SAVE ARCHIVE, and BINARY files. BCD or EBCDIC tape or disk files must be reformatted to SDF files by some utility program before they can be read by SPSS.

Table N.2 shows a summary of all files used by SPSS and their associated unit numbers.

Table N.2 Summary of Files Used

UNIT	FUNCTION
1	Punch output
3	Input for GET FILE/First input for GET ARCHIVE
4	Output for SAVE FILE/SAVE ARCHIVE
7	Default file for output for WRITE CASES or statistical procedures using options to output to tape or disk
8	Input for raw-input-data tape and disk files
9-12	Additional input files for GET ARCHIVE
15-20	Alternate Output for WRITE CASES or statistical procedures using output option to tape or disk; specify unit on RAW OUTPUT UNIT card
SPS$SC	Working data file during execution

N.3 GET FILE

If you use a GET FILE command, SPSS expects to read data from file (tape or disk) unit number 3.

If your file is not named "3," you need to use a @USE card. (Consult your local systems handbook or *Sperry Univac Programmer's Reference Manual* for more information on the use of the @ASG and @USE cards.) For example, if your file is named MY*SPSSDATA, you should set up your runstream as follows:

```
@RUN    (accounting information)
@ASG,A MY*SPSSDATA.
@USE 3,MY*SPSSDATA.
@SPSS
  .
  .
  .
GET FILE        (name)
  .
  .
FINISH
@FIN
```

(See Section N.21 about reading Release 6 SAVE files.)

N.4 GET ARCHIVE

If you use a GET ARCHIVE command, SPSS expects to read data from one to five files (tape or disk), unit numbers 3 and 9 through 12.

Follow the same procedure as above. For example,

```
@USE 3,MY*FIRSTFILE.
@USE 9,MY*SECONDFILE.
@USE 10,MY*THIRDFILE.
```

(See Section N.22 about reading Release 6 ARCHIVE files.)

N.5 SAVE FILE or SAVE ARCHIVE

If you use a SAVE FILE or a SAVE ARCHIVE command, SPSS expects to write on file (tape or disk) unit number 4.

Follow the same procedure as above. For example,

```
@USE 4,MY*SPSSDATA
```

All files output to tape are marked with hardware end-of-file marks, but the tape is not automatically rewound at the end of the SPSS run.

N.6 Raw Input Files

If you specify TAPE or DISK on the INPUT MEDIUM card, SPSS expects to read from a file (tape or disk) unit number 8. Maximum record length is determined from the input format statement. Any record size up to 8188 ASCII characters or 12,282 Fieldata characters is acceptable. SDF segmented records cannot, however, be processed.

N.7 Raw Output Files

N.8 Writing SDF Tape or Disk Files

If you use a WRITE CASES command or a statistical procedure option which outputs matrices, residuals, etc., SPSS will write the output on an SDF (tape or disk file) unit number:

- 7, if no RAW OUTPUT UNIT card is present, or
- on the specified unit, from the allowable range of 15 through 20, on the RAW OUTPUT UNIT card.

All files output to tape are marked with hardware end-of-file marks but the tape is not automatically rewound at the end of the SPSS run.

Some processors cannot read SPSS Release 8 output files because such files are written in ASCII characters rather than Fieldata.

N.9 Punching Output on Cards

If you prefer to punch the output on cards, you need to specify unit number 1 on the SPSS RAW OUTPUT UNIT control card.

```
@RUN    (accounting information)
@SPSS
  .
  .
  .
RAW OUTPUT UNIT1
WRITE CASES      (format,list)
  .
  .
  .
FINISH
@FIN
```

(NOTE: WRITE CASES BINARY is operational only if the data are output to a tape or disk file rather than to punched cards.)

N.10 Scratch Data File

The scratch data file is not assigned to unit 2. It is assigned to SPS$SC with a limit of 99,999 tracks.

The following formula approximates the size of the scratch data file needed:

$$(NVARS + 2) \times NCASES/1792$$

where

NVARS   is the number of variables after the permanent transformations have been applied.
NCASES   is the number of cases.
1792   is the number of words per track.

N.11 SPACE ALLOCATION AND COMPUTATION

N.12 Requesting SPACE

SPACE, the total amount of working memory available to your run, is equal to the amount of required WORKSPACE (memory needed to store matrices, tables, etc.) plus the amount of TRANSPACE (memory needed to store information for COMPUTEs, IFs, and other transformations).

Your SPSS run is automatically allocated 9000 words of SPACE. This is usually enough to handle a medium-size problem. (This allocation may have been changed at your installation. Consult local documentation or your SPSS Coordinator for the local allocation.) If you need more or less SPACE insert the following control card immediately after the @SPSS processor call statement.

```
ALLOCATE        SPACE = m
```

where m is the total amount of SPACE requested. For example, to request 15,000 words of SPACE your runstream would begin as follows:

```
@RUN (accounting information)
@SPSS
ALLOCATE        SPACE=15000
```

An ALLOCATE card with a SPACE command must, if it appears at all, be the first control card following the @SPSS processor call statement.

N.13   Requesting TRANSPACE

By default your SPSS run is allocated TRANSPACE equal to one-eighth the amount of total SPACE (one- eighth of the 9000 word default amount or one-eighth the amount of space allocated in a SPACE= command). If you need more or less than the one-eighth allocation, specify

```
ALLOCATE        TRANSPACE = m
```

where m is the number of words needed. For example, if you need 3000 words of TRANSPACE out of the default 9000 words of SPACE, specify

```
ALLOCATE        TRANSPACE = 3000
```

An ALLOCATE card without a SPACE specification can be placed anywhere in the SPSS control deck before the transformation cards.

Both SPACE and TRANSPACE allocations can be specified on the same card. For example, if you need 15,000 words of SPACE of which 3000 should be TRANSPACE, specify

```
ALLOCATE        SPACE=15000/TRANSPACE=3000
```

If such a card appears it must be the first control card following the @SPSS processor call statement.

N.14   Computing SPACE

The formula for computing WORKSPACE and TRANSPACE do not apply to Release 7 and above. The Sperry Univac 1100 Series versions of Release 7 and above make their computations in words rather than bytes. (There are four bytes per word.) Note also: The SPACE requirements are not always consistent with Sperry Univac 1100 SPSS Release 6 either.

In general you can calculate SPACE requirements by using the formula in the SPSS manuals and dividing the results by 4. There are, however, some exceptions. An EDIT run will help you determine the necessary SPACE and TRANSPACE allocations.

N.15   OTHER DIFFERENCES AND NOTES

N.16   INPUT FORMAT

The maximum character length for an A format specification is now 4, instead of 6. (Release 7.0 and subsequent releases use ASCII rather than Fieldata character codes.)

The BINARY keyword used without a format specification on the INPUT FORMAT card causes BINARY coded variables to be read from a single record (for example, 30 variables are read with format 30A4). However, both WRITE CASES   BINARY and AGGREGATE output files with no more than 20 variables per record. For example, they write 30 variables with format 20A4/10A4. Therefore if more than 20 variables are output, multiple records per observation are written. When these files are read back in with INPUT FORMAT   BINARY, their multiple records must be identified with a format specification. For example, if 25 variables are written by the AGGREGATE procedure the correct INPUT FORMAT statement is

```
INPUT FORMAT   BINARY(20V/5V)
```

N.17   INPUT MEDIUM

The keyword OTHER is not allowed. Also, BCD and EBCDIC tapes cannot be read directly in this release.

N.18   PAGESIZE

The PAGESIZE control card works as described in other SPSS documents except that top and bottom margins are modified to accommodate the number of lines requested and the default is set at 50 lines per page. (Consult local documentation or your SPSS Coordinator about page and margin definitions at your installation.)

N.19   RAW OUTPUT UNIT

As noted above, the default output unit is 7, not 9, as described in other SPSS documentation, and RAW OUTPUT UNIT 1 specifies punched card output.

N.20 Multiple Reel Tape I/O

Currently multiple reel tape I/O is not operational. If you need to read or write multiple tapes, see your SPSS Coordinator.

N.21 Reading Release 6 SAVE Files

Files written with the SAVE FILE command by previous Sperry Univac 1100 Series SPSS Releases 6.0 through 6.04 can be read by Release 7 and above. However, if you saved any alphanumeric (A format) variables without specifying that variable as "A" on a PRINT FORMATS control card, you need to use the special Sperry Univac SPSS "R6 ALPHA LIST" control card to specify which variables in your file are alphanumeric. This card must immediately follow the GET FILE card. For example,

```
@RUN  (accounting information)
@ASG,AX 3.
@SPSS
     .
     .
     .
GET FILE       MYFILE
R6 ALPHA LIST  SEX,RACE,ITEM1 TO ITEM5
     .
     .
FINISH
@FIN
```

Note, however, that files written by Release 7 and above cannot be read directly by previous releases. (The incompatabilities are due to the fact that Release 7 and above use the ASCII character set, and previous releases use the Fieldata character set.)

N.22 Reading Release 6 ARCHIVE Files

Files written by the SAVE ARCHIVE command in Release 6, cannot be read directly by Release 7 and above. However, a special Sperry Univac SPSS control card R6 CONVERT is available to translate Release 6 ARCHIVE files so that they can be read.

The input Release 6 ARCHIVE file and output converted Release 8 ARCHIVE file must be different files assigned to the run on file (tape or disk) unit numbers 3 and 4, respectively. The minimum SPACE assigned to the run must be two times the number of variables in the file. (The default SPACE allocation of 9000 words handles a file of up to 4500 variables.) The R6 CONVERT card must include the SPSS file name which was given to the file when it was written by Release 6. The R6 ALPHA LIST control card (see Section N.21) may be used to specify variables as alphanumeric (A format). For example,

```
@RUN  (accounting information)
@ASG,A MY*R6FILE.
@USE 3,MY*R6FILE.
@ASG,A MY*R7FILE.
@USE 4,MY*R7FILE.
@SPSS
ALLOCATE       SPACE=10000
R6 CONVERT     file name
R6 ALPHA LIST  variable list
FINISH
@FIN
```

No additional procedures are possible in this job because the file information is not saved for use within an R6 CONVERT run.

N.23 Reading and Writing Binary Data

Data output by a WRITE CASES BINARY procedure in Release 6 cannot be read by Release 7 and above. Also, data output by a WRITE CASES BINARY statement in Release 7 and above can be read only if they were output to a disk or tape file, not punched cards.

N.24 ADDITIONAL FEATURES

The University of Wisconsin Academic Computing Center has developed an easy method of linking user- written Fortran routines to SPSS. These routines can read and transform data records in nonstandard data sets, transform data after it is read in or after SPSS has performed permanent transformations, or process SPSS system files. For details contact MACC, 1210 W. Dayton St., Madison, WI 53706.

This was contributed by John Soper, University of Wisconsin, Madison.

Index

N (keyword), NEW REGRESSION, 102, 104, 105
N OF CASES
  convenience package, 285, 286
  NEW REGRESSION, 104
  RELIABILITY, 257
  REPORT, 194, 199
NAME (keyword)
  BARCHART, 141, 143
  LINECHART, 152
NCENTER (keyword), BOX-JENKINS, 91
NCOMP (keyword), MANOVA, 39, 66
NCONSTANT (keyword), BOX-JENKINS, 86, 91
NEGSUM (keyword), MANOVA, 67
nested designs, MANOVA, 22-24, 31
NEW REGRESSION, 94-121
  subcommand specifications, 99-113
NO (keyword)
  BARCHART, 139, 140
  LINECHART, 150-151
  PIECHART, 128
NO PREVIEW, Graphics postprocessor, 161
NOBALANCED (keyword), MANOVA, 64
NOCONSTANT (keyword), MANOVA, 65, 78
NOEJECT (keyword)
  CROSSTABS, 304
  PAGESIZE, 316
  REPORT, 199
NOLASTRES (keyword), MANOVA, 64
NOLIST (keyword), REPORT, 171
nonadditivity, see additivity, Tukey's Test
NONAME, SAVE SCSS, 268
NONE (keyword)
  BARCHART, 145-146
  LINECHART, 156
  NEW REGRESSION, 102, 105
  PIECHART, 131
  REPORT, 192
nonorthogonal designs, see unequal cells frequencies
NONPAR CORR, 315-316
  NPAR TESTS, 238
  OPTIONS, 315
nonparametric tests, see NPAR TESTS
nonseasonal differencing, see differencing
NOORIGIN (keyword), NEW REGRESSION, 109
NOPRINT (keyword), MANOVA, 2, 65-68
NORMAL (keyword)
  data modification, 277
  DISCRIMINANT, 294
  MANOVA, 57, 68-69
  NEW REGRESSION, 106
  NPAR TESTS, 224
  reserved keyword, 283
NORMPROB (keyword), NEW REGRESSION, 110
NOROTATE (keyword), MANOVA, 39, 66
NOTITLE (keyword), REPORT, 178
NOTOTAL (keyword), REPORT, 171
NPAR TESTS, 220-239
  CROSSTABS, 303
  limitations, 239
  OPTIONS and STATISTICS, 238-239
  RELIABILITY, 250, 254
  summary table, 220
NTEST (keyword), BOX-JENKINS, 91
NUMBERED, 314
  freefield input, 286
  GET SCSS, 271
  PIECHART, 128

OBSERVATIONS (keyword), MANOVA, 64
OMEANS (keyword), MANOVA, 67-68, 78
ON (SCSS reserved word), 269
One-Sample Chi-Square Test, NPAR TESTS, 220, 221, 222-223, 238

One-Sample Runs Test, see Runs Test
ONEWAY, 307-309
  MANOVA, 66
  options, 307
OPTIONS
  ANOVA, 305-306
  CROSSTABS, 301-302
  DISCRIMINANT, 295-298
  FREQUENCIES, 312-313
  GET ARCHIVE, 313
  MANOVA, 78-79
  MULT RESPONSE, 246
  NONPAR CORR, 315
  NPAR TESTS, 238
  ONEWAY, 307
  REGRESSION, 120
  RELIABILITY, 257-261
  SURVIVAL, 214, 215, 216-219
ORDER (keyword)
  BARCHART, 144-145, 147
  LINECHART, 153-155, 157
  PIECHART, 129-131, 132
ORIGIN (keyword)
  BOX-JENKINS, 92
  NEW REGRESSION, 106, 109
ORTHONORM (keyword), MANOVA, 60-61, 63, 67
OSIRIS VARS, 286
  MISSING VALUES, 314-315
OTHER (keyword), RELIABILITY, 257
outliers, MANOVA, 56
OUTLIERS (keyword), NEW REGRESSION, 110, 111
OUTPUT (keyword), RELIABILITY, 258
OUTS (keyword), NEW REGRESSION, 107
OVERALL (keyword), MANOVA, 66

P (keyword), BOX-JENKINS, 90-91, 92
PACF (keyword), BOX-JENKINS, 93
packed decimal point, format items, 287
PAGE (keyword), REPORT, 178, 189-190, 193, 194
PAGESIZE, 316
  NEW REGRESSION, 110
  REPORT, 167, 171, 199
PAIRED (keyword), MULT RESPONSE, 245
PAIRS (keyword), T-TEST, 317
PAIRWISE (keyword), NEW REGRESSION, 103
pairwise deletion
  DISCRIMINANT, 300
  FACTOR, 312
  NEW REGRESSION, 103
  NONPAR CORR, 315-316
  RELIABILITY, 259
PARALLEL (keyword), RELIABILITY, 250, 254, 255, 257
parallel model, RELIABILITY, 249, 250, 254, 256
parameter estimation
  BOX-JENKINS, 86-88, 90-92
  DISCRIMINANT, 293-294
  MANOVA, 4, 36, 41-42, 43, 64-65, 67
  RELIABILITY, 250
PARAMETERS (keyword), MANOVA, 67
PARM
  GET SCSS, 273
  SAVE SCSS, 269-270
partially balanced incomplete blocks, MANOVA, 19-20
PARTITION (keyword), MANOVA, 3, 6-7, 28-29, 31, 32, 49, 71-72, 77
patterns
  BARCHART, 144
  LINECHART, 154, 155
  PIECHART, 130
PBIB designs, see partially balanced incomplete blocks
PCON (keyword), BOX-JENKINS, 92

PCTBTN, PCTGT, PCTLT (keywords), REPORT, 181, 184, 193
PEARSON CORR, NEW REGRESSION, 104
Pearson correlation
  CROSSTABS, 303
  data modification, 277
PERCENT (keyword)
  BARCHART, 135
  LINECHART, 148
  PIECHART, 128
PERIOD (keyword), BOX-JENKINS, 90
perturbation increments, BOX-JENKINS, 92
PIECHART, 123-124, 126-134, 163
  operation, 126-134
  patterns, 130
  special plotting, 133-134
  syntax summary, 163
PIEWISE (keyword), PIECHART, 131
Pillai's criterion, MANOVA, 33-34, 43
PIN (keyword)
  DISCRIMINANT, 293, 294
  NEW REGRESSION, 100, 106, 107
PLOT (keyword)
  BARCHART, 135-139, 147-148
  BOX-JENKINS, 93
  LINECHART, 148-150, 157-158
  MANOVA, 2, 55, 68-69
  NEW REGRESSION, 111
  PIECHART, 126-127, 132-133
plots, MANOVA, 55-59
PLOTS (keyword), SURVIVAL, 211-213, 216, 217
PLOTWISE (keyword)
  BARCHART, 145-146
  LINECHART, 156
  PIECHART, 131
plus sign, MANOVA, 77
PMEANS (keyword), MANOVA, 58, 68, 69, 70, 78
POBS (keyword), MANOVA, 47, 58-59, 68, 69, 70
POINTS (keyword), LINECHART, 153
POISSON (keyword), NPAR TESTS, 224
POLYNOMIAL (keyword)
  MANOVA, 61-62, 74
  ONEWAY, 308
postprocessor, SPSS Graphics, 161-163
  multiple plots per page, 133-134
POUT (keyword)
  DISCRIMINANT, 294
  NEW REGRESSION, 100, 106, 107
power transformations, BOX-JENKINS, 80, 90
POWER (keyword), BOX-JENKINS, 90
PP, PQ (keywords), BOX-JENKINS, 92
PRED (keyword), NEW REGRESSION, 109, 111, 112
PREVIEW, Graphics postprocessor, 161
PREVIOUS (keyword), NEW REGRESSION, 99
PRIMARY DEVICE?, Graphics postprocessor, 161
principal components analysis, MANOVA, 38-39
PRINCOMPS (keyword), MANOVA, 66
PRINT (keyword)
  BOX-JENKINS, 93
  MANOVA, 2, 3, 5, 37, 38, 45-46, 65-68
  SEED, 276
PRINT FORMATS
  CROSSTABS, 302
  REPORT, 199
  SORT CASES, 289
probability density function, SURVIVAL, 206, 207, 211
product moment correlation, see Pearson's correlation
PROPORTION (keyword), LINECHART, 149
PSP, PSQ (keywords), BOX-JENKINS, 92
PUNCH (keyword), MANOVA, 2, 69-70